Instructor's Manual

to accompany

STRATEGIC MARKETING MANAGEMENT CASES

Sixth Edition

David W. Cravens
Texas Christian University

Charles W. Lamb, Jr.
Texas Christian University

Victoria A. Crittenden
Boston College

Boston   Burr Ridge, IL   Dubuque, IA   Madison, WI   New York   San Francisco   St. Louis
Bangkok   Bogotá   Caracas   Lisbon   London   Madrid
Mexico City   Milan   New Delhi   Seoul   Singapore   Sydney   Taipei   Toronto

Irwin/McGraw-Hill
A Division of The McGraw-Hill Companies

Instructor's Manual to accompany
STRATEGIC MARKETING MANAGEMENT CASES

Copyright ©1999 by The McGraw-Hill Companies, Inc. All rights reserved.
Previous edition(s) 1983, 1986, 1990, 1993, 1996 by Irwin.
Printed in the United States of America.
The contents of, or parts thereof, may be reproduced for use with
STRATEGIC MARKETING MANAGEMENT CASES
David W. Cravens, Charles W. Lamb, Jr., and Victoria A. Crittenden
provided such reproductions bear copyright notice and may not be reproduced in
any form for any other purpose without permission of the publisher.

2 3 4 5 6 7 8 9 0 QSR/QSR 9 3 2 1 0 9 8

ISBN 0-256-26127-X

http://www.mhhe.com

PREFACE

The sixth edition of *Strategic Marketing Management Cases* focuses on the changing role of marketing as we enter the 21st century. This edition has been substantially revised to reflect marketing management priorities in the decade ahead. At the center of these changes is the substantial adoption of market-driven, customer-oriented strategies by many organizations. Importantly, there is mounting evidence from business practice and academic research that market-oriented companies perform better than those that are not market oriented.

Two-thirds of the cases in this edition are new or revised. Over forty of the forty-five situations described in the cases in this edition took place in the 1990s; some as recently as 1998. Additionally, around 25 percent of the cases feature women protagonists, reflecting the workplace of the 1990s.

Eleven video cases are included in this edition, responding to the high interest generated by the videos included in the last edition. To receive complimentary copies of these videos, please call Irwin/McGraw-Hill Faculty Service at (800) 338-3987. A video to accompany a twelfth case, "Battered Women Fighting Back!" is available in many college and university libraries.

Over half of all cases in this edition include some form of quantitative data, most frequently financial information. The *Instructor's Manual* includes data files that contain numerical exhibits from cases in this edition. Data files are available on Excel spreadsheet format.

Over 135 transparency masters and PowerPoint slides are also included in the *Instructor's Manual* to assist in the development of lectures regarding the case method and to introduce the various sections of the book

Many instructors prefer that students focus their case analyses on the time frame and situation described in the case. However, more recent information may be useful as a follow-up to the class discussion of the case. The *Instructor's Manual* lists Web sites for 25 of the organizations featured in cases in this edition.

Situations described in this edition do not fall neatly into individual marketing mix categories. Rather than organize the book around the 4-Ps (Product, Place, Price, Promotion), we have chosen section classifications that more realistically reflect the types of decisions frequently encountered by marketing managers in the late 1990s. The *Instructor's Manual* continues to provide detailed and comprehensive analyses and supporting materials for each case. Several teaching notes include epilogues describing actions taken by the organization and/or how it has fared since the case was prepared.

To meet the teaching/learning preference of instructors who wish to use the case analysis process described in detail in the Appendix, a substantial portion of the teaching notes follow this format. The discussion questions are not listed at the end of the cases so that instructors can assign questions in advance or raise them during case discussions.

This manual is the result of the efforts of many people in addition to ourselves. Several of the case authors provided teaching notes for their cases, and we appreciate the use of their notes. Special thanks to Fran Eller at TCU and Elizabeth Shanley at Boston College for typing the manuscript and for their assistance in other aspects of the project, and to David Angus of Boston College who worked diligently on various aspects of this project. We appreciate the support and encouragement of our deans, H. Kirk Downey and John J. Neuhauser, and our colleagues in the Marketing Departments at TCU and Boston College.

Finally, we would like to acknowledge the support and suggestions that we have received from adopters of the previous five editions of this book. Many of the features of this edition were implemented in response to advice and counsel from colleagues around the world.

David W. Cravens
Charles W. Lamb, Jr.
Victoria Crittenden

CONTENTS

Introduction 1
SECTION I   CASE TOPIC GRID AND CASE WEB SITE INDEX 7
SECTION II   SAMPLE SYLLABI 11
SECTION III   SAMPLE CASES AND ANALYSES 27
SECTION IV   QUANTITATIVE EXERCISES 59
SECTION V   TEACHING NOTES 67

Part 1: Market-Driven Strategy 69
    Case 1-1   Enterprise Rent-A-Car: Selling the Dream (Video) 71
    Case 1-2   Coca-Cola (Japan) Company (Video) 84
    Case 1-3   Battered Women Fighting Back! (Video) 93
    Case 1-4   Wind Technology 99
    Case 1-5   The Metropolitan Museum of Art 103
    Case 1-6   California Valley Wine Company 107

Part 2: Market Orientation and Organizational Learning 111
    Case 2-1   Navistar International Transportation Corporation (Video) 113
    Case 2-2   Floral Farms 120
    Case 2-3   Quality Plastics International S.A. De C.V. 127
    Case 2-4   Food Lion, Inc. 143
    Case 2-5   Banco Nacional de Comercio Exterior, S.N.C. (BANCOMEXT) 148
    Case 2-6   Optical Fiber Corporation 157

Part 3: Growth Strategies 163
    Case 3-1   Golden Valley Microwave Foods, Inc. (Video). 165
    Case 3-2   Blockbuster Entertainment Corporation 172
    Case 3-3   Systemsoft Corporation 179
    Case 3-4   Angostura Bitters, Inc. 190
    Case 3-5   The Bacova Guild, Ltd. (A) 199
    Case 3-6   The Faith Mountain Company 205

Part 4: Target Market Strategies 215
    Case 4-1   Amtech Corporation (Video) 217
    Case 4-2   Düring AG (Fottle) 225
    Case 4-3   Murphy Brewery Ireland 233
    Case 4-4   Shorin-Ryu Karate Academy 241
    Case 4-5   Lojack Corporation (Video) 251
    Case 4-6   Algonquin Power and Light Company 259

Part 5: Marketing Relationships 269
    Case 5-1   ABB Traction Inc. (Video) 271
    Case 5-2   Ambrosia Corporation San August 279
    Case 5-3   Electro-Products Limited 290
    Case 5-4   Southern Home Developers 296
    Case 5-5   Konark Television India 303
    Case 5-6   Powrtron Corporation 311
    Case 5-7   Taurus Hungarian Rubber Works 317

Part 6: Marketing Program Development 333
    Case 6-1   Dunkin' Donuts Bagel Blitz (Video) 335
    Case 6-2   Rollerblade, Inc. (Video) 343
    Case 6-3   L'oreàl Nederland BV 351
    Case 6-4   Apache Power, Inc 358
    Case 6-5   Capital (A) Magazine 376
    Case 6-6   National Breweries 402
    Case 6-7   Chemical Additives Corporation Specialty Products Group 408

Part 7: Organizing, Implementing, And Assessing Performance 417
    Case 7-1   Cutco (Video) 419
    Case 7-2   Yoplait USA (Video) 437
    Case 7-3   Cima Mountaineering, Inc. 445
    Case 7-4   Longevity Healthcare Systems, Inc. 461
    Case 7-5   The La-Z-Boy Chair Company 469
    Case 7-6   Bear Creek Golf Range 480
    Case 7-7   Wentworth Industrial Cleaning Supplies 492

SECTION VI   TRANSPARENCY MASTERS 499

Index of Cases 638

INTRODUCTION

The *Instructor's Manual* to accompany the sixth edition of *Strategic Marketing Management Cases* was prepared to aid instructors in the preparation and teaching of the case material. This introduction highlights several features of the manual.

Overview of Companies

There is a brief paragraph about each of the cases at the end of the introductory material in each major part of *Strategic Marketing Management Cases*. In this *Instructor's Manual* we provide an overview, in grid form, of various application areas for each of the cases. This can be particularly helpful for instructors who want to make certain that material from various areas of marketing is covered in the class or for those who want to customize the cases to fit needs aside from the major part heading in the book. As with most cases, the focus of many of the cases in the book can be different than the major part heading should the instructor wish to concentrate on another/additional marketing issue in the case.

The application areas covered in the grid are: size of company, consumer/industrial/service/non-profit, business strategy, situation analysis, target market strategy, marketing program positioning strategy, product strategy, distribution strategy, price strategy, promotion strategy, evaluating marketing performance, and marketing research. Additionally, there are columns in the grid which denote the format of the teaching note, whether the company is a non-U.S.A. company, the international content of the case, and whether the case protagonist is a female.

We have added a new exhibit following the application areas grid that identifies Web sites for 25 of the cases included in this edition.

Accompanying Data Files

This edition of the *Instructor's Manual* to accompany *Strategic Marketing Management Cases* includes spreadsheet templates of quantitative exhibits for all cases containing this information. The data are available in Excel for Windows. Our goal in preparing these templates was to reduce the amount of time students have to spend entering data for analysis. As previous users of the book and survey respondents requested, the templates do not provide answers, they only display data. A novice-level of understanding of Excel is needed to manipulate data matrices.

While almost all of the cases in this edition have some variety of financial, competitive, and demographic data, users have asked for additional variety in the types of data included in strategy cases. For those users interested in utilizing some primary market research data in the case analysis process, the following cases might be of particular interest: The Metropolitan Museum of Art, Bacova Guild Ltd., Shorin-Ryu Karate Academy, and L'Oreal Nederland B.V. As well, the Floral Farms and Powrtron Corporation cases include both marketing and production data.

Course Planning Examples

Three examples of course outlines are included in the *Instructor's Manual*. These provide varying approaches to designing the marketing course. The outlines can be modified easily to fit an individual instructor's course needs or used as is. Two of the examples fit with the major part headings of the book. One example is for a graduate-level advanced marketing strategy course. The other example is for the undergraduate, capstone marketing management course. The third example is for instructors who want to use the cases with the more traditional, introductory marketing management course.

The group case presentation framework presented in the undergraduate marketing management course syllabus mirrors the format for many case competitions which some of our students have been involved in. The format has been tested extensively, both at the graduate and undergraduate levels, over the past couple of years and has received excellent reviews from both instructors and students. This format can easily be adapted to the graduate marketing strategy syllabus. However, it has been less successful in the beginning graduate marketing course (probably since the students are both new to the marketing material and the case method).

Additionally, we provide two examples of evaluation forms for case presentations for those instructors who have students present cases in class.

Sample Cases and Analyses

For some students, the class in which *Strategic Marketing Management Cases* is being used may be the student's first case-based course. If so, the instructor will find it advantageous to spend a class session analyzing a case with the students. We have provided two cases that can be used for that purpose. Additionally, we have provided the note, "Case Preparation for the Beginner: A Nudge Toward an Open Door," that can be photocopied and distributed to students if the instructor feels that students need more information on case analysis.

The two cases provided, "Port-Marine" and "Pyramid Pizza," vary in the analysis that accompanies each. For a beginning case class, Pyramid Pizza can be used to walk students through a situational analysis, as well as help students identify the critical success factors for the company. The case allows students to brainstorm recommendations and learn that creativity in thinking through options is needed in analyzing cases. The case is very short and can be photocopied and distributed to the students with the accompanying preparation questions. Pyramid Pizza is an excellent example for the students to see how much analysis can be done on a very short case. The case is also a good one to use in showing how "cold-calling" works in a classroom setting. The instructor can open the class by asking a student to identify the company's internal strengths and weaknesses. The class then moves through the process of looking at the company and what has made it successful to date. From there, the instructor should force students to make specific recommendations as to the company's future. The material in the *Instructor's Manual* consists of the case, case questions, and sample responses to the questions.

The Port-Marine case is a broader case situation and provides financial data for students. The Port-Marine case is heavier on content than Pyramid Pizza. The case analysis shows the students the importance of understanding the firm's financial structure in making marketing strategy decisions. The case is an excellent example to use when describing the mechanics of case analysis. The material in the *Instructor's Manual* consists of the case, a student's analysis of the case, and comments on the student's analysis. The material can be distributed sequentially. The case is short and can be photocopied for distribution prior to the class discussion. After a short, in-class discussion of the case scenario, the instructor can distribute the accompanying student analysis of the case. The instructor can provide a few minutes for the class to read over the student's analysis. Then, a discussion of the approach taken by the student as well as the analysis itself, can ensue. At the end of the class discussion, the instructor can distribute the "comments" on the student analysis.

Both of the cases work well for those students needing a review of the case method approach to learning. Students who have never done case analysis will benefit from using both Pyramid Pizza and Port-Marine. Students needing a refresher class will probably not need the Pyramid Pizza case, but will need the Port-Marine case. Experienced students may not find it necessary to use either case. The instructor can move directly into the cases in the text.

Quantitative Exercises

We have found that even our advanced marketing students need a quantitative refresher at the beginning of the course. In addition to the financial information in the Appendix of the book, we have included two brief financial exercises (Snapamatic Camera Company A & B), along with answers, in the *Instructor's Manual*. The exercises can be photocopied and distributed to students either as an in-class exercise or for the student's individual review should such a review be deemed useful.

Teaching Notes

We have made a major effort to develop useful and complete teaching notes for each case. Detailed analyses are provided for all cases, especially those that include quantitative data. While it is not possible to anticipate all uses of the cases, each note contains sufficient discussion and analysis so that the instructor can develop specific areas beyond those discussed in the note.

A survey of marketing casebook users revealed that most instructors use one of two teaching/learning approaches in the case process. Many prefer to have students analyze cases using the process described in Appendix B of the book. This six-step process includes analyzing the situation, defining the problem or decision to be addressed, identifying alternatives, specifying decision criteria, analyses, and recommendations. To meet the needs of these instructors, we have structured a substantial number of the teaching notes in this *Instructor's Manual* to coincide with the six-step case analysis process.

Other survey respondents expressed a preference for a discussion question and answer approach to case learning. To meet the teaching/learning approach preferred by these instructors, we have organized many of the teaching notes in terms of discussion questions and answers. The questions are not included at the end of the cases in the book. They appear only in the *Instructor's Manual*, along with possible answers. We have found that some instructors will include the discussion questions in the syllabus.

As an additional feature, several of the cases present the analysis in the question and answer format with the individual steps of the six-step process noted alongside the answer to the question.

Most of the teaching notes contain seven to eight sections:

1. *Synopsis:* This is a brief overview of the case situation.

2. *Video Summary (where appropriate):* This describes the content of the accompanying video.

3. *Teaching/Learning Objectives:* These are both the pedagogical objectives and key learning issues for which the case can be used. We have found it useful to end class with a review of the objectives of the particular case discussion. This provides closure for the students and helps them see where everything discussed during the particular case class fits in the broader business sense. While optimally, we would like to think that students leave a class thinking about what they learned from the discussion, we have found that this does not generally happen. Having a transparency of the teaching/learning objectives facilitates this learning process.

4. *Discussion Questions:* These are questions which can be provided to the student to guide the case preparation or questions which can be used in the classroom.

5. *Analysis:* As discussed previously, the analysis will generally follow either the six-step process or the question and answer format.

6. *Teaching the Case:* The cases have all been used in student discussions. Where appropriate, we suggest various ways to start the class discussion as well as provide some hindsight as to issues that might arise. If the case is a video case, we also suggest when the video should be used in the class.

7. *Epilogue:* Students tend to want to know "what happened." Thus, an epilogue is provided for many of the cases. Please be sure to remind the students that "what happened" is not "the answer." Rather, the epilogue provides information since the date of the case. No one knows for certain if what the company did, or is doing, is right or wrong. The Web site index in this *Manual* is also useful for identifying current information about many organizations featured in the 6th edition of *Strategic Marketing Management Cases.*

8. *Exhibits:* Several of the notes have information summarized in exhibit format. It may be appropriate, in many instances, to use exhibits as overhead transparencies to emphasize or summarize a point.

Presentation Material

Over 135 transparency masters have been included in this manual to assist instructors in introducing the major sections of the book and explaining the case analysis process. These can be found in the last section of this *Instructor's Manual.*

The same material is also available on PowerPoint for instructors who have access to computers in the classroom. The PowerPoint version is included on diskette with this *Instructor's Manual.* Additional material can easily be added to the PowerPoint presentation if the instructor chooses to do so.

In addition to the information regarding each of the seven parts of the book, we have included case analysis instructional material. This instructional material has been used successfully in the first few days of the course to help students who are not familiar with the case analysis process. In such situations, we recommend having a general class discussion about cases—why they are used and what the classroom process will be like (using the instructional material found in this manual). Then in the subsequent classes, the Pyramid Pizza and/or Port-Marine case can be used. (The case instructional material has been used successfully, as well, in MBA orientation programs and Executive Education orientation programs.)

Video Cases

We have expanded the video cases to a total of twelve. The Table of Contents shows each video case. To receive complimentary copies of the video package, please contact Irwin/McGraw-Hill, Faculty Service at 1-800-338-3987/

Organization of the Manual

Section I.	Case Topic Grid and Case Web Site Index
Section II.	Sample Syllabi
Section III.	Sample Cases And Analyses
Section IV.	Quantitative Exercises
Section V.	Teaching Notes
Section VI.	Transparency Masters

SECTION I

CASE TOPIC GRID

AND

CASE WEB SITE INDEX

Case		Teaching Note Format Question & Answer (Q); Six-Step Process (P); Both (B)	Product/Service	International I = Company C = Content	Female Protagonist	Data C = Competition; F = Financial; M = Marketing; P = Production
Part 1:						
1-1	Enterprise Rental Co.	Q	automobile rentals			C
1-2	Coca-Cola (Japan) Company	B	canned tea	I/C		F
1-3	Battered Women Fighting Back!	Q	education		yes	
1-4	Wind Technology	Q	power supplier	I	yes	C,M
1-5	The Metropolitan Museum of Art	Q	art			F,M
1-6	California Valley Wine Company	Q	wine			M
Part 2:						
2-1	Navistar International	Q	trucks	C		
2-2	Floral Farms	Q	fresh-cut flowers	I/C	yes	M,P
2-3	Quality Plastics International	B	plastic molding	I/C		C,F
2-4	Food Lion, Inc.	P	retail grocery products			M
2-5	Bancomext	Q	financial/promotional	I/C	yes	
2-6	Optical Fiber Corp.	Q	fiber optics			F,M
Part 3:						
3-1	Golden Valley Microwave Foods, Inc.	B	microwave foods	C		
3-2	Blockbuster Entertainment	Q	video cassettes			F,M
3-3	SystemSoft	B	software			F
3-4	Angostura Bitters, Inc.	B	food/drink	I/C		
3-5	Bacova Guild Ltd.	Q	signs			F,M
3-6	The Faith Mountain Company	Q	mail order and retail store		yes	F,M
Part 4:						
4-1	Amtech Corporation	Q	electronic identification devices	C		F,M
4-2	During AG (Fottle)	B	plastic bottle	I/C		M,C
4-3	Murphy's Brewery Ireland, Ltd.	Q	beer	I/C		M,C
4-4	Shorin-Ryu Karate Academy	Q	martial arts			F,M,C
4-5	LoJack Corporation	Q	automobile security	C		F,M,C
4-6	Algonquin Power and Light Company	P	gas and electric public utility			C
Part 5:						
5-1	ABB Traction, Inc.	B	trains	I/C		
5-2	Ambrosia Corporation-San August	Q	ice cream	I/C	yes	C,P
5-3	Electro-Products Limited	P	small electronic appliances	I/C		M
5-4	Southern Home Developers	B	home construction			M
5-5	Konark Television India	Q	television sets	I/C		
5-6	Powrtron Corporation	Q	electronic circuitry	C	yes	M,P,F
5-7	Taurus Hungarian Rubber Works	Q	tires and rubber products	I/C		M,F
Part 6:						
6-1	The Dunkin' Donuts/Bagel Blitz	Q	bagels	I		
6-2	Rollerblade, Inc.	B	in-line skates	C	yes	M
6-3	L'Oreal Nederland B.V.	Q	cosmetics	I/C	yes	M
6-4	Apache Power, Inc.	Q	engines		yes	F,M
6-5	Capital	Q	magazines	I/C		M,C
6-6	National Breweries	B	beer	I/C		C,F,M
6-7	Chemical Additives	Q	specialty chemicals			F,M,C
Part 7:						
7-1	Cutco	B	cutlery	I/C		M
7-2	Yoplait USA	Q	yogurt			
7-3	Cima Mountaineering Inc.	P	boots	C	yes	C,F,M
7-4	Longevity Healthcare Systems, Inc.	Q	health care		yes	M,F
7-5	La-Z-boy Chair Company	Q	furniture			M,F,C,P
7-6	Bear Creek Golf Range	Q	golf facility			F,M,C
7-7	Wentworth Industrial Cleaning	B	cleaning supplies		yes	M

Case:	Size: Small (S); Medium (M); Large (L)	Consumer (C) Industrial (I) Service (S) Nonprofit (N)	Business Strategy	Target Market Strategy	Marketing Program Positioning Strategy	Product Strategy	Distribution Strategy	Price Strategy	Promotion Strategy	Evaluating Marketing Performance
Part 1:										
1-1	L	C/S	x	x	x	x	x		x	
1-2	L	C	x		x	x	x			
1-3	S	N/S	x	x	x	x	x		x	x
1-4	M	I	x	x		x			x	
1-5	M	C/N	x		x					x
1-6	M	C	x	x		x				
Part 2:										
2-1	L	I	x	x			x			x
2-2	M	C/I	x			x				x
2-3	S	I	x							x
2-4	M	C	x	x	x					
2-5	L	S	x	x					x	x
2-6	L	I	x			x			x	
Part 3:										
3-1	S	C		x		x	x			
3-2	M	C	x			x				
3-3	L	I	x			x				
3-4	M	C	x		x	x				
3-5	S	C			x	x	x	x	x	x
3-6	M	C	x	x	x					
Part 4:										
4-1	M	C/I	x			x				
4-2	M	I		x	x	x	x		x	
4-3	L	C		x	x	x	x	x	x	
4-4	S	S	x	x					x	
4-5	M	C	x	x	x	x	x	x		
4-6	M	C/I/S/N	x	x	x	x				
Part 5:										
5-1	L	I	x			x				
5-2	L	C	x		x	x	x			
5-3	M	C		x	x	x	x			
5-4	S	C/I	x	x		x				
5-5	M	C				x	x			
5-6	S	I	x	x		x				x
5-7	M	I/C	x			x				x
Part 6:										
6-1	L	C	x		x	x	x			x
6-2	M	C		x	x	x	x		x	
6-3	L	C			x	x	x	x	x	
6-4	S	I			x	x	x	x	x	
6-5	L	C/I	x	x	x	x	x	x	x	
6-6	M	C	x		x	x	x			
6-7	M	I		x	x	x		x		
Part 7:										
7-1	L	C/S	x	x						x
7-2	L	C		x	x	x	x	x	x	x
7-3	M	C		x	x	x	x	x	x	
7-4	M	S	x	x		x		x	x	
7-5	L	C	x		x	x				x
7-6	S	S	x	x	x					x
7-7	L	I	x				x	x	x	x

Index of Case Web Sites

ABB Traction, Inc. [Video]	www.abb.com
Amtech Corporation [Video]	www.amtech.com
Angostura Bitters, Inc.	www.angostura.com/
Bacova Guild Ltd.	www.burlington-ind.com/bacova.html
Banco Nacional de Comercio Exterior, S.N.C.	www.bancomext.com.mx
Blockbuster Entertainment Corporation	www. blockbuster.com
Coca-Cola (Japan) Company [Video]	www.cocacola.co.jp/
Cutco [Video]	www.cutco.com
Dunkin Donuts [Video]	www.franchise1.com/comp/dunkin1/html
Enterprise Rental Co. [Video]	www. pickenterprise.com
Electro-Products Limited	www.connectworld.net/electro
The Faith Mountain Company	www.faithmountain.com/
Food Lion, Inc.	www.foodlion.com
Golden Valley Microwave Foods, Inc. [Video]	www.gvmf.com

La-Z-Boy Chair Company

    edgar.stern.nyu.edu/ptest/auto/extracts/La_Z_Boy_Chair_CO/10_K/LA_Z_BOY_Chair_CO.extr.10-K.2.html

LoJack Corporation [Video]	www. lojack. com
L'Oreal Nederland B.V.	www.loreal.com
The Metropolitan Museum of Art	www.metmuseum.org
National Breweries	www.mbendi.co.za/orgs/cang.htm
Navistar International Transportation Corporation [Video]	www.navistar.com
Rollerblade, Inc. [Video]	www.rollerblade.com
Shorin-Ryu Karate Academy	www.ultranet.com/~st-james/
Systemsoft	www.systemsoft.com
Wind Technology	www.nrel.gov/wind
Yoplait USA [Video]	www.yoplait.fr

SECTION II

SAMPLE SYLLABI

Undergraduate Marketing Management (capstone course)

Course Objectives

Traditionally, each functional area performs specialized portions of the organization's tasks. For example, marketing resolves questions concerning what products to sell, what price to charge, how to distribute, and the necessary promotional activities. Marketing functional-level operations issues have comprised the major portion of marketing electives (as well as the Principles course). The major objective of this marketing capstone course is to give the student a solid foundation for applying the concepts and theories learned in other marketing courses. As such, the course provides the student with a necessary mix of: (I) critical analysis, (II) application, and (III) communication.

Class Format

This is a 99.9 percent case class. Case studies provide one of the major vehicles for **applying** marketing concepts and theories. Case analysis requires **critical evaluation** (including interpretation) of both facts and logic to allow effective case discussions. Cases also require that the student be prepared and **actively involved** (communication) in class discussions. Cases allow us to learn, from written scenarios, about company situations and predicaments. These scenarios and predicaments are very well defined and focused by the case writer and/or by any preparation questions provided for the case. The concepts and theories were introduced first in your basic marketing course and expanded on in various marketing electives. The class consists of general case discussions of assigned cases (preparation questions are provided for these types of classes), group written analysis and presentation of cases (no preparation questions provided), and an individual case analysis.

Regarding the **group analysis**, groups will consist of five students (groups will self-form, with possibly some assistance from the professor) with group formation and case assignment completed on September 10. The written analysis is a two-page memo prepared for the decision maker in the case. The memo is to be single-spaced (double-space between paragraphs), one inch margins, 12-point Times New Roman font, with the opening in memo form (TO: FROM: DATE: RE:). One page of exhibits is allowed. The group is also required to turn in copies of all visuals used in the presentation. Groups will make a 30-minute presentation of their case analysis on the assigned day. The presentation is expected to utilize state-of-the-art visuals (e.g., PowerPoint). Immediately after the presentation, the non-presenting groups will be allowed 10 minutes to prepare a critique of the presentation. Two groups will then be randomly selected to present a five minute critique of the presentation (blank transparency masters will be provided). The remainder of the class will be used for Q&A. (No external information [e.g., people, secondary research] is to be accessed when preparing the case, nor can outside observers view your group case presentation prior to the assigned class.)

The **individual case write-up** will consist of answers to specified case questions. Each person will submit a typed, double-spaced, one inch margin, 12-point Times New Roman font paper--maximum length five pages (plus unlimited exhibits). Since this is an individual case, there is not to be any communication with anyone or any attempt to access external information during the preparation of the case. Offenses against this mandate will be taken seriously and handled via proper academic integrity channels.

Class **participation** is an important element of case discussions. Learning depends heavily upon thorough and lively participation. The primary emphasis should be on quality participation, not quantity. The quality of participation, as reflected in careful reading of cases and assigned material, thoughtful reflection, and clear and concise comments, is extremely important. However, one cannot make quality contributions without some quantity. It is particularly important that your comments fit into and build on previous comments. This requires that we all listen carefully to each other. Class participation will be judged on the basis of quality and consistency of effort on a daily basis. Attendance is <u>not</u> participation. I do grade rather rigorously on class participation. Additionally, there is no way to make up "missed" participation opportunities!

Required Material

Cravens, David W., Charles W. Lamb, Jr., and Victoria L. Crittenden (1999), *Strategic Marketing Management Cases* (6th ed.), Burr Ridge, IL: Irwin/McGraw-Hill.

Grading

Group Analysis/Presentation	35%
Individual Case Analysis	40%
Participation	25%

Classes	Topic	Assignment
Week 1	Introduction to Course Case Analysis	Appendix B *Pyramid Pizza* (handout) Appendix A *(exercises as outside assignment)* Port-Marine *(handout)*
Week 2	Market-Driven Strategy *(group formation and case assignment)* Service Provider	Part 1 Introductory Material Enterprise Rental Co.
Week 3	International Market Entry Not-For-Profit Marketing	Coca-Cola (Japan) Company Battered Women Fighting Back!
Week 4	Marketing Dilemmas Market Orientation and Organizational Learning Industrial Products	California Valley Wine Company Part 2 Introductory Material Navistar International
Week 5	Marketing/Production Interactions Growth Strategies Entrepreneurial/Consumer Prod.	Floral Farms *(Group 1 Presentation)* Part 3 Introductory Material Golden Valley Microwave Foods, Inc.
Week 6	Mature Products Retail	Angostura Bitters, Inc. *(Group 2 Presentation)* The Faith Mountain Company *(Group 3 Presentation)*
Week 7	Target Market Strategies Hi-Tech One-Product Offering	Part 4 Introductory Material Amtech Corporation LoJack Corporation
Week 8	Education Marketing Relationships Customer Partnership	Shorin-Ryu Karate Academy *(Group 4 Presentation)* Part 5 Introductory Material ABB Traction Inc.
Week 9	Partner Selection Internal Partners	Ambrosia Corporation, San August Powrtron Corporation *(Group 5 Presentation)*
Week 10	Distribution Partnership Marketing Program Development Guerrilla Marketing	Konark Television India *(Group 6 Presentation)* Part 6 Introductory Material Rollerblade, Inc.
Week 11	New Product Offering Industrial Growth	Dunkin' Donuts Apache Power, Inc. *(Group 7 Presentation)*

Classes	Topic	Assignment
Week 12	Organizing, Implementing, & Assessing Performance Large Company Direct Marketing	Part 7 Introductory Material Yoplait USA Cutco
Week 13	Small Company Service Provider	Bear Creek Golf Range *(Group 9 Presentation)* Longevity Healthcare Systems *(Group 10 Presentation)*
Week 14	Wrap-up Individual Case Analysis Due	

Graduate Marketing Strategy

About the Course

Traditionally, each functional area performs specialized portions of the organization's tasks. For example, marketing resolves questions concerning what products to sell, what price to charge, how to distribute, and the necessary promotional activities. Marketing functional-level operations issues comprised the major portion of your Marketing Management course. This strategy course expands on the knowledge gained in marketing management and your marketing elective courses. The topics discussed in the Marketing Strategy course are: market-driven strategy, market orientation and organizational learning, growth strategies, target market strategies, marketing relationships, program development, and organizing, implementing, and assessing performance. The major objective of the course is to assist the student in developing the knowledge and skills necessary to actually formulate and implement marketing strategies.

Required Material

Cravens, David W., Charles W. Lamb, Jr., and Victoria L. Crittenden (1999), *Strategic Marketing Management Cases* (6th ed.), Burr Ridge, IL: Irwin/McGraw-Hill.

Grading

Individual Written Case I	25%
Individual Written Case II	25%
Individual Paper	25%
Participation	25%

Individual Written Case I and II

The first individual case write-up will be the analysis of SystemSoft Corporation. The case questions, which you will answer, will be distributed a week before the write-up is due. The second case you will analyze is Cima Mountaineering Inc.

Individual Paper

The project in this class consists of an individual current topics paper. I am very open to various types of papers. You must obtain permission from me for your paper topic. The paper should be related to at least one of the major topics of the class. We will discuss this project in detail in class.

The final paper should be about 10 pages long, although reasonable deviation from this length in either direction is fine. If you expect major deviation in either direction, you must obtain the professor's permission in advance. Exhibits such as charts, graphs, and diagrams are not covered in the page limit. [All papers must be typed, double-spaced.]

Participation

Class participation is an important element of case discussions. Learning depends heavily upon thorough and lively participation. The primary emphasis should be on quality participation, not quantity. The quality of participation, as reflected in careful reading of cases and assigned material, thoughtful reflection, and clear and concise comments, is extremely important. However, one cannot make quality contributions without some quantity. It is particularly important that your comments fit into and build on previous comments. This requires that we all listen carefully to each other.

Class participation will be judged on the basis of *quality and consistency of effort* on a daily basis. Attendance is not participation. I do grade rather rigorously on class participation. Additionally, there is no way to make up "missed" participation opportunities! For those of you who have not had one of my classes previously, please feel free to stop by and discuss this with me further.

Week		Subject/Case	Text
1		Course Introduction	
	Topic:	Market-Driven Strategy	Introductory Material, Part 1
	Case:	Enterprise Rental Co.	
2	Topic:	Market-Driven Strategy	
	Case:	Coca-Cola (Japan) Company	
	Case:	Wind Technology	
3	Topic:	Market Orientation and Organizational Learning	Introductory Material, Part 2
	Case:	Navistar International	
4	Topic:	Market Orientation and Organizational Learning *cont.*	
	Case:	Floral Farms	
	Case:	Banco Nacional de Comercio Exterior, S.N.C.	
5	Topic:	Growth Strategies	Introductory Material, Part 3
	Case:	Golden Valley Microwave Foods, Inc.	
6	Topic:	Growth Strategies *cont.*	
	Case:	Bacova Guild Ltd.	
	Case:	The Faith Mountain Company	
7	Topic:	Target Market Strategies	Introductory Material, Part 4
	Case:	LoJack Corporation	
		INDIVIDUAL WRITTEN CASE 1 DUE – SystemSoft	
8	Topic:	Target Market Strategies *cont.*	
	Case:	Murphy's Brewery Ireland, Ltd.	
	Case:	During AG (Fottle)	
9	Topic:	Marketing Relationships	Introductory Material, Part 5
	Case:	ABB Traction Inc.	
10	Topic:	Marketing Relationships *cont.*	
	Case:	Ambrosia Corporation, San August	
	Case:	Southern Home Developers	
11	Topic:	Marketing Program Development	Introductory Material, Part 6
	Case:	Dunkin' Donuts	
12	Topic:	Marketing Program Development *cont.*	
	Case:	L'Oreal Nederland B.V.	
	Case:	Capital	

Week	Subject/Case		Text
13	Topic:	Organizing, Implementing, & Assessing Performance	Introductory Material, Part 7
	Case:	Cutco	
14	Topic:	Organizing, Implementing, & Assessing Performance	
	Case:	Longevity Healthcare Systems	
	Case:	Wentworth Industrial Cleaning	
15		INDIVIDUAL WRITTEN CASE II DUE – Cima Mountaineering Inc. INDIVIDUAL PAPERS DUE	

Graduate Marketing Management (first marketing course)

Course Objective

The major objective of this marketing course is to give the student a solid foundation for applying the concepts and theories of marketing. More specifically, by end of the semester you will have: (i) become acquainted with the role of marketing in society, (ii) developed an understanding of the role of marketing in the business firm, and (iii) developed an ability to make marketing strategy decisions. This should result in the capability to prepare a good marketing plan. As the beginning course in the marketing area, the material covered is very broad. We discuss all facets of marketing from the perspective of consumer, industrial, service, and not-for-profit firms.

Teaching Vehicles

The course provides the student with a necessary mix of: (i) critical analysis, (ii) application, and (iii) communication. Much of the learning is expected to occur by participation. My plans are to have a discussion (e.g., lecture, video, open discussion) of the assigned marketing topic and then to discuss the assigned case relating to that topic. Additionally, your experiences in various firms and industries can be a source of interesting and informative discussions (when they relate to the topic being covered).

Case studies provide one of the major vehicles for **applying** marketing concepts and theories. Case analysis requires **critical evaluation** (including interpretation) of both facts and logic to allow effective case discussions. Cases also require that the student be prepared and **actively involved** (communication) in class discussions. Cases allow us to learn, from written scenarios, about company situations and predicaments. These scenarios and predicaments are very well defined and focused by the case writer and/or by any preparation questions provided for the case.

Required Material

Cravens, David W., Charles W. Lamb, Jr., and Victoria L. Crittenden (1999), *Strategic Marketing Management Cases* (6th ed.), Burr Ridge, IL: Irwin/McGraw-Hill.

[Marketing Management text optional]

Grading

Individual Written Case I	25%
Individual Written Case II	25%
Group Project	30%
Participation	20%

Individual Written Case I and II

These will be take-home individual case analyses. The integrative case assignments will consist of 4 to 5 questions that you must answer. Each person will submit typed, double-spaced, one inch margin, 12-point Times New Roman font papers—maximum length five pages (plus unlimited exhibits). Since these are individual cases, there is not to be any communication with anyone or any attempt to access external information during the preparation of the cases. Offenses against this mandate will be taken seriously and handled via proper academic integrity channels.

Group Project

Each group of students will prepare a marketing plan for a new product (conceptualized by the group!). The marketing plan is due the last week of the class. Each group will make a short, convincing presentation with the focus being, "Why Should We Want This Product/Service?" We'll discuss the project throughout the semester. However, it is imperative to begin the project immediately since there will have to be some industry research conducted (as well as a lot of other work!).

Participation

Class participation is an important element of case discussions. Learning depends heavily upon thorough and lively participation. The primary emphasis should be on quality participation, not quantity. The quality of participation, as reflected in careful reading of cases and assigned material, thoughtful reflection, and clear and concise comments, is extremely important. However, one cannot make quality contributions without some quantity. It is particularly important that your comments fit into and build on previous comments. This requires that we all listen carefully to each other.

Class participation will be judged on the basis of *quality and consistency of effort* on a daily basis. Attendance is **not** participation. Each student can ascertain the adequacy of her/his participation by occasional discussion with the instructor. However, careful self-monitoring using the following criteria for effective classroom participation may be useful:

- Do comments generate discussion, or do they tend to be ignored by others?
- Do others appear confused when the participant makes a point?
- Are others left with a "so-what" feeling, or does the discussant reach a conclusion that is clearly understood and appreciated?
- Do comments develop on evidence from the assignment, or do they just relate what everyone already knows?
- Are participants able to clarify important aspects of previous comments and relate them to the problems and topics under discussion?
- Do comments distinguish among different kinds of data—facts, opinions, beliefs, theories—in their construction?

You are expected to be prepared (actively involved) for every class. Since I frequently call on individuals even when their hands are not raised, you should let me know before the start of class if some emergency has made it impossible for you to be prepared adequately for that class. Naturally, there are students who do not feel comfortable participating verbally in the classroom. We should all try to make the classroom atmosphere as congenial as possible to assist all of our colleagues in the participation process. Students are encouraged to meet regularly outside of class to discuss assignments (except individual ones) before the scheduled class activity. Missed classes could affect (severely) your performance in the class. There is **no way** to make up "missed" participation opportunities.

Week		Subject/Case	Text
1		Course Introduction Introduction to Case Analysis Pyramid Pizza *(handout)*	Appendix A Appendix B Port-Marine *(handout)*
2	Topic: Case:	Marketing Mix Overview National Breweries	
3	Topic: Case:	Marketing Dilemmas California Valley Wine Company	
4	Topic: Case:	Not-For-Profit Marketing Battered Women Fighting Back!	
5	Topic: Case:	Market Segmentation Amtech Corporation	
6	Topic: Case:	Communication Capital	
7	Topic: Case:	INDIVIDUAL WRITTEN CASE I due at beginning of class Pricing Apache Power, Inc.	
8	Topic: Case:	Distribution Konark Television India	
9	Topic: Case:	Product Policy Coca-Cola (Japan) Company	
10	Topic: Case:	Marketing Research L'Oreal Nederland B.V.	
11	Topic: Case:	Strategy Formulation Golden Valley Microwave Foods, Inc.	
12	Topic: Case:	Planning, Organizing, Budgeting Yoplait USA	
13	Topic: Case:	Performance Assessment Bear Creek Golf Range	

Week	Subject/Case	Text
14	Group Presentations *(maximum 10 minutes per group!)* INDIVIDUAL WRITTEN CASE II due	

Sample 1: Evaluation Forms For Case Presentations

Case _____ Presenters _____
Date _____   _____
                                          _____

Please rate today's presentation on the following scale:

	not at all				very much
Content					
1. Did the situation audit provide an overview of the case?	1	2	3	4	5
2. Did the situation audit lead to the problem statement?	1	2	3	4	
3. Was the problem statement clear?	1	2	3	4	5
4. Was the set of alternatives comprehensive and mutually exclusive?	1	2	3	4	5
5. Did the alternatives address the problem?	1	2	3	4	5
6. Was the set of decision criteria comprehensive?	1	2	3	4	5
7. Did the group use the same set of decision criteria to assess each alternative?	1	2	3	4	5
8. Was the analysis thorough and clear?	1	2	3	4	5
9. Did the group present appropriate financial analysis to support key points?	1	2	3	4	5
10. Was the analysis persuasive?	1	2	3	4	5
11. Was the alternative selected reasonable?	1	2	3	4	5
12. Did the group present a reasonable implementation plan?	1	2	3	4	5
Style					
1. Did the group project a professional appearance?	1	2	3	4	5
2. Did the group involve you in their presentation?	1	2	3	4	5
3. Were overheads and other visuals used to support key points	1	2	3	4	5
4. Were overheads understandable?	1	2	3	4	5
5. Did the group handle questions appropriately?	1	2	3	4	5
6. Were transitions between group members smooth?	1	2	3	4	5

1. What was the strongest part of the presentation?

2. What would have made their presentation

Sample 2: Evaluation Forms For Case

Both oral and written:	*Poor*	*Satisfactory*	*Good*	*Excellent*
Quality of organization	____	____	____	____
Clarity of explanations	____	____	____	____
Logic of the analysis	____	____	____	____
Thoroughness of the analysis	____	____	____	____
Justification for the recommendations	____	____	____	____
Practicality of the recommendations	____	____	____	____
Quality of illustrations, exhibits. etc.	____	____	____	____
Oral presentation:				
Handling of questions from the audience	____	____	____	____
Adequate answers	____	____	____	____
Courtesy	____	____	____	____
How well did the team hold the interest of the audience?	____	____	____	____
Written analysis:	____	____	____	____
Grammar	____	____	____	____
Spelling	____	____	____	____
Neatness	____	____	____	____

Remarks:

Grade:

SECTION III

SAMPLE CASES AND ANALYSES

CASE PREPARATION FOR THE BEGINNER: A NUDGE TOWARD AN OPEN DOOR[*]

A business case is a narrative that describes a situation that has taken place. Sometimes the case describes a managerial situation requiring a decision. Other times, it may portray what appears as a business success or a managerial mistake. A student frequently studies theories as though they exist in isolation, while all other activities are held constant or in abeyance. This constancy and isolation do not exist in real situations. The purpose of a case is to transcend the process of learning from the classroom to real-life experiences. Case study is meant to actively involve the reader in the processes of learning, developing, and decision making. According to Crittenden (1988):

> Business cases are written to develop the reader's skills, approaches, and philosophy of management. The case approach fosters the development of "doing" skills by forcing the reader to take an active role in considering key managerial factors, weighing the significance of these factors, and making an action-oriented decision. Furthermore, when offered a variety of industries and organizational settings over time (e.g., during a semester or quarter), the reader learns to recognize and understand similarities and differences.[**]

The objective of case analysis is to develop and present a plan of action to improve the organizational situation. Problem solving relies on developing a solid analysis from imperfect information subject to varying degrees of uncertainty. Generally, the most powerful and interesting cases are those that permit multiple interpretations of the same information to lead to different but equally plausible solutions. This is because the emphasis is on the process of decision making rather than its product. Students decide what's the 'right answer" to a case during their deliberations, debate, and discussions.

Preparing the Case

Most cases offer a complex web of interrelationships that may appear overwhelming. It is important to sort through the available information and understand what is going on, what is fact, and what is opinion. When reading the case in this context, assume statements made in the case by the case writer as true. However, if a statement is made by one of the characters in the case, treat it as though there is a question mark hovering over it. Assume the time period as that indicated in the case.

The important elements in evaluating student performance on case analyses consist of (a) the care with which facts and background knowledge are used, (b) demonstration of the ability to state problems and issues clearly, (c) the use of appropriate analytical techniques and theory, (d) evidence of sound logic and argument, (e) consistency between analysis and recommendations, and (f) the ability to formulate reasonable and feasible recommendations for action. As beginning case students, you are not expected to do all these things well immediately. However, the following guidelines should help in preparing cases.

---

[*] This note was prepared by Associate Professor William F. Crittenden of Northeastern University. Permission to duplicate sections or entirety of this note is granted assuming appropriate acknowledgment. Original copyright July 1990. Revised January 1998.
[**] Crittenden, William F. "Business Case Writing in the Nonprofit Setting." Proceedings of the Fifth Annual NACRA Symposium on Case Development and Research. Anaheim, California. August 6, 1988: 77-88.

Determine What is Going On

First, read the case rapidly to determine the general nature of the company and its setting. Next, examine the case more carefully. Jot down, in list form, the significant facts of the case. Classify, sort, and combine this information. If provided, case questions can help this categorizing process. However, it is not sufficient to be able to state the central issues without substantiation by facts, data, and clearly stated rationale.

Analyze

Assess the information available. Simply stating facts is not analysis. One must identify problems and/or opportunities indicating a need for management action. Frequently, the most difficult aspect of diagnosing a case is to determine what the problems are. Furthermore, there generally are some problems and/or opportunities that are major and some that are minor. Identify and rank based on urgency and importance. To successfully manage a large number of issues, it may be necessary to combine problems dealing with similar subjects.

Be sure to consider the information provided in any tables and exhibits. It is common practice to put the quantitative details of the case in exhibits and appendices. Unfortunately, exhibits and appendices are seldom read with the same level of discernment as the text portion of the case. Do not make this mistake[1]

Determine What is Missing and What is Relevant in the Case

Items that are possibly important may be missing in a case because it is missing in the firm. Such an omission should be not only noted but also considered in terms of its overall importance. In addition, you must be able to sort out irrelevant information and make sound assumptions when certain facts are not available. A decision must be made even though it appears that more data would be desirable.

Develop Alternatives

Consider a number of feasible alternative actions or programs. Do not be satisfied with the first answer that comes to your mind. Your fourth or fifth solution, or a combination of solutions, may provide the best answer. Explore the consequences of solutions you have developed, including the value of the possible outcomes and the risks that are involved. Seek basic objectives and broad strategies which will provide guides to the solutions of the problems.

Evaluate the Alternatives

Determine what action recommendations are acceptable to top management. Review the alternative sets of goals, strategies, and problem solutions. Evaluate by listing and weighing the advantages and disadvantages of each alternative. Carefully articulate and apply theory and principles to the situation. This step is important in integrating theory and practice.

Make a Decision

Recommendations are central to a case analysis. On the basis of your evaluations, prepare a set of specific recommendations for action. Avoid generalities— take a stand. Clearly indicate the key actions which are crucial to the plan's success or failure. Always be prepared to support the reasons for your position. It is normal for anyone beset with trying problems to recommend calling in outside help (consultants, researchers, etc.). Do not make this recommendation. <u>You</u> are the outside help!

Case Discussion

A business case is examined in a community of students. Each student has invested several hours sifting through the information, assessing the problems, and thinking of solutions. Each has probably uncovered some evidence others have overlooked. Each has likely interpreted identical information in a slightly different manner [this is the value of a diverse community of students]. Each is ready to offer an assessment of the situation and a set of recommendations for management. If a student is not prepared to discuss their view, then the process of learning for the entire community of student is impaired.

Once discussion has begun, each student must continually rethink the validity of the individual analysis as the group debate unfolds. Listening to other students and remaining open-minded is critical to the education process. Learning often comes from defending one's view or abandoning it as the group moves in some direction not supported by the individual's analysis. It is important to note you cannot realistically expect to be right all the time. Learning comes partly from making mistakes. If your classmates or professor reveal an error in your logic or analysis, accept it. Trying to defend an error-filled position is the mark of a poor manager.

Some Final Thoughts

During a case course, you may find it hard to keep a finger on the pulse of how much you are learning from the cases. This contrasts with lecture and/or problem courses where experience has given you an intuitive feeling for how well you are acquiring substantive knowledge of theoretical concepts, problem-solving techniques, and institutional practices. But in a case course, where analytical ability and the skill of making sound judgments are less apparent, you may lack a sense of solid accomplishment, at least at first. Admittedly. additions to one's managerial skills and powers of diagnosis are not as noticeable or as tangible as a loose-leaf binder full of lecture notes. But this does not mean they are any less real or that you are making any less progress in learning how to be a manager.

In the process of hunting around for solutions, very likely you will find that a considerable knowledge about types of organizations, the nature of various businesses, the range of management practices, and so and has rubbed off. Moreover, you will be gaining a better grasp of how to evaluate risk and cope with the uncertainties of enterprise. Likewise, you will develop a sharper appreciation of both the common and the unique aspects of managerial encounters. Such is the essence of management and learning through the case method is no less an achievement just because there is a dearth of finely calibrated measuring devices and authoritative crutches on which to lean. If throughout the course you can remain open to the diverse views found in your community of students, while developing your own skills of critical reasoning and decision making, your learning will climb to heights accessible to only a select few.

PYRAMID PIZZA

Nestled between Pyramid mountain and the Conasauga River, the Pyramid Pub was not providing much of a living for Michael and Joseph Gramz back in 1968. The Gramz brothers were licensed to sell only beer in their tavern, and it took a lot of 25 cent brews to support two families, even in a town of 3,000 people 80 miles northwest of Atlanta. What they needed, both agreed, was something special to serve with their beer, other than the standard fare of peanuts, chips and an occasional ham sandwich. The new offering had to be something that would appeal to their regular customers, many of whom were students at a nearby church-related school or year round employees at the numerous carpet mills in the area.

After an accident put Joe's leg in a cast, he began experimenting with recipes for pizza, the dish that he and Mike had agreed would be most likely to draw patrons. With each attempt, Joe passed out free slices at the bar and solicited suggestions for making a better product. Joe was determined to make the tastiest pizza anyone had eaten since - if industry lore is to be believed - the Persian soldiers of Darius the Great first spread dough on their shields and baked it with cheese and dates over their campfires. Joe's experiments led the brothers to found Pyramid Pizza which distributes frozen Pizza in a fifteen state area ranging from the Atlantic ocean to Arkansas and as far north as Cincinnati. The company has a US$9.2 million factory and warehouse, 151 freezer trucks, and 250 employees.

The Gramz brothers began rolling out the dough at just the right time. Pizza has been one of the fastest growing segments of the food industry for years, expanding 10-12 percent annually in real terms. There are over 52,000 pizza restaurants in the U.S., with Pizza Hut, Domino's, and Little Caesar dominating the fresh pizza market. People living in the North Central states are the most avid pizza fans, eating pizza about 35 times a year. Today, sales of both fresh and frozen pizza amount to an estimated US$14 billion a year, with the frozen variety accounting for over US$1.8 billion per year. Pizza is one of the most sought items in the frozen foods segment at supermarkets, accounting for over 13 percent of supermarket frozen foods sales. Pizza's popularity has not gone unnoticed by the big food processors. Kraft, Pillsbury, and others have either acquired companies that supply supermarkets with frozen pizza or started their own operations from scratch. But the battle for market leadership, waged with costly advertising, discounting, and promotions, has kept profit margins low. Furthermore, recent growth in the frozen pizza market has not kept pace with the overall pizza market.

Backhaul to Pyramid

The Gramz brothers expect US$3.5 million in pretax earnings this year, on sales of almost US$100 million. While making 63 million pizzas a year, Mike and Joe have bypassed the supermarket chains and concentrated on selling to taverns, which are sparse in the "Bible Belt" and to small grocery stores and independent convenience stores which are abundant in the rural areas of the 15 state region which Pyramid serves. Pyramid Pizza does no advertising. Additionally, Mike and Joe have kept promotional costs down, relying on the likelihood that anyone who has enjoyed a Pyramid Pizza at a favorite bar will be a ready customer when seeing the product displayed at a neighborhood mom-and-pop store. Pyramid saves on freight charges by having its delivery trucks backhaul pizza ingredients to the factory.

Unlike most food processors, Pyramid distributes its products store by store. Its system requires great amounts of labor and capital, and distribution costs are high. Pyramid drivers double as salespeople on

---

*This case was prepared by William F. Crittenden, Northeastern University. Permission to duplicate is granted assuming appropriate acknowledgment. January 1998.

commission, filling a store's freezer, rotating stock, and removing old or damaged merchandise. They are instructed to make sure that freezer cabinets are always full and that their pizzas get eye level display space on frozen food shelves. This takes personal attention by each driver.

Growth

The management team is headed by Mike (58), the president of Pyramid, who was once a lumberjack in the great timberlands of southern Georgia. He is a serious, private man who likes to work around his farm on weekends, Joe (54), secretary-treasurer, is much more outgoing. He often visits to neighboring taverns to have a few beers with employees. On the rare occasion when the brothers disagree on a business matter, the split vote usually turns out as a mandate for Mike's point of view. Joe's wife, Nancy, is the company's vice-president. Mike's wife, Marie, handles public relations. Three of the brothers' five children also work in the company.

A few years after Joe perfected his pizza recipe, the brothers decided to branch out. With the help of their wives, they prepared an extra 100 pizzas a week, froze them, and carried them in a cooler to other taverns. "It was all cold selling," says Mike. "We'd walk into a tavern and ask the owner to cook up a free Pyramid Pizza for customers. Then we relied on the tavern's customers, after tasting a sample, to sell the owner on them." The idea took off! In the early 1970s the Gramz' got a US$10,000 loan to buy a freezer truck that could carry 2,000 pizzas. Business boomed and before long they purchased a second truck. In 1980, the brothers purchased 10 acres of land and built a modern facility which has been expanding ever since.

Implementation or "Gettin' Some Management"

During the years of tremendous growth, the Gramz' gradually lost their grip on some company operations. They were accustomed to running everything themselves, and even as problems developed, they were reluctant to delegate authority. Most problems occurred in the distribution of pizzas. As Joe recalls, "We just put them on trucks and kissed them off." There was no statistical reporting system to indicate exactly where they were going or what variety was selling best. New sales people received little training. The Gramz' also contracted with independent distributors without adequately investigating their financial conditions. Each of these distributors went out of business for one reason or another during, and immediately after, the most recent economic downturn.

With complaints mounting about poor service, Mike visited some of the grocers and tavern keepers himself. "I've never been sworn at so much in my life," he says. "It got so bad I just identified myself as a guy sent out by the main office. We knew that Pyramid Pizzas were priced competitively, offering reasonable mark-up for the retailer. But, that wasn't enough. It appeared obvious there was inadequate management, no guidance. Our company name was being injured. I felt we'd better get some additional management to straighten us out."

It was no easy task recruiting good managers to live and work in rural northwest Georgia. But the Gramz' were able to find a couple of young executives who had grown up in the area and wanted to return. One of those who joined was Dan Coker (33), a marketing executive, who had worked as a good-ol' boy bartender at the Pyramid Pub while attending college. After college, Dan had worked for Proctor & Gamble in one of their marketing divisions. Coker was responsible for having a state of the art computer system installed which replaced Pyramid's previous antiquated billing system. Dan also implemented a product distribution scanning and tracking system. Preliminary data suggested sales were divided about 60-40 between taverns and grocery/convenience stores.

Next Steps

While Mike and Joe were pleased with recent changes and were genuinely proud of what they had accomplished with their family owned business, they knew Pyramid Pizza's position was hardly secure. With the frozen pizza market becoming more competitive, Mike and Joe pondered if further changes were needed.

PYRAMID PIZZA [NOTES TO ACCOMPANY CASE]*

This mini-case was written for use in one of the beginning classes of a strategy course. Or, the case works well in an introductory, principles class. The intent of the mini-case is to initiate students into the art and science of "pulling" information out of a particular scenario and then structuring this information in a general strategic analysis.

The length of the case is somewhat deceiving. There is a tendency to skim over the material since students often think that there is an association between length of reading and amount of important content. It is interesting to hear student comments once they work through a SWOT analysis, determine the company's strategy (including the firm's competitive landscape), and make some general recommendations to the company's management team. They are generally surprised at what they have been able to do with a two-page case.

The case discussion keeps the students attention—all students know about the product! Since all students are intimately familiar with the product, it is good to let students voice their opinions about frozen pizza before getting into the real "meat" of the case—what they like/don't like about frozen pizza, when they eat it. why they eat it, etc. The professor can keep track of these opinions by structuring them into the consumer buying process for frozen pizza. Structuring student comments into a familiar process offers students an early glimpse of how a case class really works—students make comments, the professor keeps track of these comments in a logical flow/framework, students begin to want their comments written on the board, students realize that repeating what someone else has already said is obvious, and the professor helps shift gears if students don't do so themselves.

There are three general preparation cases for the class discussion. If the case is distributed prior to the class session, the questions can also be distributed in advance. However, the case is short enough (with a familiar product) that students can read the case at the beginning of the class session. (It only takes a few minutes to read through the case). Then, the professor can discuss the three general questions with the students while helping the students work through the issues. The preparation questions are:

1. What are Pyramid Pizza's strengths and weaknesses? Are there any external opportunities and threats?
2. What is Pyramid Pizza's strategy? How do they compete?
3. What recommendations do you have for Pyramid's management team?

A sample analysis of the case. along the lines of the three discussion questions, follows.

1. What are Pyramid Pizza's strengths and weaknesses'? Are there any external opportunities and threats?

Strengths.

- competitively priced product, with reasonable margins for retailers
- computerized billing
- a few young, new executives (e.g.. Coker)

---

* This note was prepared by William F. Crittenden, Associate Professor of Management, Northeastern University, to accompany the "Pyramid Pizza" mini-case. Revised 1998.

- 15 state distribution network
- approximately $100 million in sales (average $1.59 per pizza)—by implication, the product must be good!
- approximately 5.5% share of frozen pizza market
- $3.5 million in pretax earnings (3.5% of pretax return on sales)
- substantial assets:
    a. $9.2 million factory (oldest part approximately 18 years old): at least 63 million capacity, thus capable of making around 252,000(pizzas per day (assumes 250 work days a year)
    b. 151 freezer trucks
- low promotional expenditures

Weaknesses

- no oversight of distribution and routing
    Note to instructor: You may want to stop and talk about this weakness for a few minutes. Some sample questions to ask students include:
    a. *Is distribution a problem?*
    b. *What roles do Pyramid drivers take?*
    c. *Are the drivers overextended?*
    d. *Are the drivers adequately prepared?*
- no training of new drivers/salespeople
- historically, some weak independent distributors
- pursuit of growth overrides use of control systems
- historic lack of delegation
- unclear objectives

    growth—"expanding ever since"

    good service—Mike went out to investigate

    profits—clearly making enough money to support two families
- reliance on one product
- limited market focus

The instructor may want to stop here and pose the following question:

Why didn't the Gramz brothers hire outside management as they were growing—before they began to run into problems?

Opportunities

- growth market (1(1-12% annual growth)—the number of pizza restaurants in the U.S. now rivals (and may even exceed) the number of hamburger restaurants: pizza in its multiple forms (e.g.. frozen. packaged kits, fresh deli) ranks in the top 10 sales category for supermarkets and in the top 4 of convenience food service sales
- $14 billion market

- frozen pizza market is large—frozen pizza is ranked as one of the top 10 snack foods in the U.S.

Threats

- growth in frozen pizza market (6-7%) is not keeping pace with overall pizza market
- *big* food processors have entered the pizza market
- competitors have very deep pockets
- marketing expenditures (i.e.. advertising, promotions, discounting) leads to lower profit margins and could force small players out of the frozen pizza market
- unstable shelf life (e.g., spoilage) could hinder expansion for small player in market

This may be the first time many students have conducted a SWOT analysis. It is good to keep track of the strengths. weaknesses, opportunities, and threats on the board in bullet form to get students in the practice of doing this type of analysis.

2. **What is Pyramid Pizza's strategy? How do they compete?**

Pyramid's strategy has the following characteristics:

- Costly, personal attention while distributing store-to-store
- Delivery personnel double as salespeople (on commission)
- Focus on taverns (60%) and small grocery stores (40%)—bypassing supermarket chains and thus avoiding head-to-head competition with large food processors
- Focus on frozen pizza
- Provide "quality" product
- Keep promotion costs low (unlike larger competitors)
- Save on incoming freight charges through backhauling

Overall Pyramid's strategy provides a good tasting product in an exclusive niche:

1. The strategy is not easily *replicable.*
2. When properly implemented, the strategy *adds significant value* for customers (taverns & grocery stores).
3. Pyramid has the resources to effectively *exploit* this strategy.

Questions the professor could ask at this junction are:

Why is the market Pyramid goes after not overrun by large competitors?

Does Pyramid's strategy fit the external environment?

Most students ultimately conclude that the strategy is a good one but is poorly implemented.

3. **What recommendations do you have for Pyramid's management team?**

Typical suggestions include:

- Use wholesalers
    * negates differentiation strategy?

- Sell to large chains
  * attract attention of large competitors?
- Separate duties of drivers and salespeople
  * cost?
  * is it premature to split without more information? is there a real conflict in the jobs?
- Hire better management
  * requirements? cost?
  * who knows more about this business than the Ganz family members?
- Stabilization strategy—concentrate resources on present business, focus upon improving performance of some functional areas. (After period of prolonged fast growth. a company may become inefficient or unmanageable.)
- Geographic expansion
  * where? (Most students want to be in the North Central states (heaviest pizza consumption) or the heavily populated Northeast and or California
- Improve information systems
  * what information would be useful to the company?

  Regarding what information would be useful:
  * Location of customers-plot for efficient coverage, is extra driving required to cover a specific retailer or are all retailers easy stops?
  * Sales to retailer—$, units, variety1
  * Profits from each retailer
  * frequency of old or damaged merchandise at each retailer
  * frequency of stops at each retailer do some retailers need more frequent coverage to keep freezer cabinets full?

  How should Pyramid collect this information?
  * Record keeping by drivers/salespeople (technology is now available that simplifies this process, but would require training)

A discussion around these questions provides an interesting and provocative class discussion. To fulfill the objective of providing students with an overview of a case discussion class, it is good to wrap up the class with a summary of class objectives. These might include:

Structure

- Provide an overview of what will be expected in forthcoming classes
- Show students the amount of information they can derive from cases
- Present a widely-used strategic tool—S WOT analysis

Content

- Growth options for a small, entrepreneurial firm
- Move from entrepreneurial management to professional management
- Market segmentation issues
- Distributor relationships
- Marketing program development
- Organizational issues related to functional concerns and specialties
- Assessment and change management

PORT MARINE*

Port-Marine is a sailboat manufacturing company which was formed three years ago in Portland, Maine. Revenue from sales in the first full year of operation totaled $225,000. This was increased to an estimated $1,240,000 in the present year. This dramatic growth is considered to be the result of its excellent products and extensive sales promotion.

The initial product line consists of three different types of fiberglass sailboats. The P/M-17 is a small day cruiser with berths for two adults and two children and a sail area of 130 square feet: it weighs one-half ton and has an overall length of a little over 17 feet. The manufacturer's price is $3,000.

The P/M-34 is a relatively large motor sailer that sleeps seven people in three separate compartments. The main saloon contains an adjustable dining table, a complete galley, and a navigator's compartment. The main saloon is separated from the forecabin by a folding door. The aft cabin, which is entered by a separate companionway, contains a double berth, wardrobe, washbasin, and lockers. The toilet and shower are situated between the forecabin and the main saloon. The boat has a sail area of 530 square feet, weighs about five tons, and has an overall length of 33 feet 8 inches. The most significant feature of this craft, however, is that it is equipped with a full-sized diesel engine (36 or 47 horsepower). The manufacturer's price is $40,000.

The P/M-36 was designed for a different purpose. While the P/M-17 and P/M-34 are oriented toward a family approach to sailing by combining the features of safety and comfortable accommodations with reasonable sailing ability, the P/M-36 is first and foremost a sailing craft. It does have two berths, a small galley, and toilet facilities, but the emphasis is on sailing and racing rather than comfort. The boat has a sail area of 420 square feet, weighs a little less than four tons and has an overall length of 35 feet 10 inches. The boat is also equipped with a small (7 horsepower) diesel engine for emergency power situations. The manufacturer's price for the P/M-36 is $20,000. The hulls of all three boats are constructed of GRP (glass reinforced plastic), and the quality of the woodwork and other finishing items is quite good.

Most of the marketing effort to date has been performed by the president of the company. During the first year of operation, a sales manager was hired; however, he resigned to take a similar position with a larger, more established boat manufacturer. Rather than trust the marketing to another new person at this critical time in the development of the company, the president assumed this responsibility himself.

In his opinion the first priority was to establish an effective channel of distribution for the sailboats. From information obtained from friends and contacts in the industry, he compiled a list of potential pleasure boat dealers along the East Coast. He then visited these dealers in order to evaluate their showrooms, service and marina facilities, and marketing capabilities. His next step was to persuade some of the most likely candidates to handle the products of Port-Marine. For two reasons, he was quite successful in this effort. He invited each of the interested dealers to Portland to visit the factory and to evaluate the sailboats firsthand; secondly, he offered to sell them a P/M-17 on consignment. That is, the dealers could return these boats to Port-Marine if they were unable to sell them to customers. Because of the stronger position of the dealers in the market, virtually all of the subsequent sailboats sold to the dealers were sold only after the dealers had firm orders from their customers. Thus, the dealers did not have to provide any capital to finance these sales. In addition, Port-Marine was assuming all of the marketing risk.

---

* From James H. Sood. *Situations in Marketing* (Plano, Texas: Business Publications. Inc.). pp. 76-80.

In order to improve the relatively weak position of the company in this channel of distribution, the president decided to try to develop another channel. His idea was to advertise and sell directly to the final customers and thus eliminate the dealers in these transactions. His intention in this maneuver was to achieve a sufficient amount of sales in this manner and thereby use this success as a means of improving the company's bargaining position with its dealers. He selected a number of the leading newspapers in the major cities in the East and placed large four-column ads in these papers, describing the sailboats and instructing interested buyers to contact the company directly. Although this was a relatively new approach in the sailboat industry, it achieved a fair amount of success in terms of boats sold. Approximately 25 percent of the orders received in this current year were received directly from the final customer. The negative aspects of this approach are the very large advertising expenditures and the fact that the company is not staffed to operate this way. In addition, a number of the dealers have voiced very strong objections, since they feel that any of their customers can now purchase directly from Port-Marine and save the dealer's commission.

Port-Marine is also about to announce the introduction of a new sailboat. Whereas the present products were designed completely by relatively unknown (to the customers) people in the company, the hull of the new sailboat has been designed by an internationally known boat designer. The cost of these design services for the company was a $10,000 initial fee plus a $1,200 royalty fee for each boat produced. The new sailboat is called the P/M-29 and has an interior quite similar to that of the P/M-34. This is not unexpected, since the same Port-Marine people designed the interior and decks of both sailboats. The new boat is a motor sailer that sleeps six people in three separate compartments, is 28 feet 9 inches long, weighs four tons, has a joined cabin space and a separate aft cabin, a small galley, toilet and shower facilities, and a 12-horsepower diesel engine. Because of a new construction technique that greatly reduces the amount of fiberglass required, the company is able to offer the boat at $20,000. The initial interest in the P/M-29 is exceedingly high, and the company is now concerned that the sales of this product might have an adverse effect on the sales of the P/M-34.

The company is in the process of preparing its production and marketing plan for the coming year in order to arrange for the financing of this plan. The president has indicated strongly that he is committed to continuing the rapid growth of the company, as shown by his proposed plan in Exhibit 1. The present balance sheet and analysis of costs are shown in Exhibits 2 and 3, respectively.

There are three current ideas concerning the pricing of motor sailers. The predominant theory is that, most generally, price is a function of the overall length of the boat; however, a number of sailing people believe that the overall weight of the craft is a more accurate basis. The third group consists of those people who argue that neither of these ideas holds water and that the price is a function of the special features and equipment. Exhibit 4 illustrates the present market prices for new motor sailers as a function of overall length.

Exhibit 1 Marketing Results And Plans

	First year			Present year			Proposed plan		
	Number	Average price	Revenue	Number	Average price	Revenue	Number	Average price*	Revenue
P/M-17	20	$ 2,500	$ 50,000	120	$ 3,000	$ 360,000	240	$ 3,300	$ 792,000
P/M-29	—	—	—	—	—	—	40	20,000	800,000
P/M-34	4	35,000	140,000	20	40,000	800,000	30	44,000	1,320,000
P/M-36	2	17,500	35,000	4	20,000	80,000	4	22,000	88,000
Total revenue			$225,000			$1,240,000			$3,000,000

*Estimated prices to cover anticipated increases in cost

Exhibit 2 Port-Marine Present Balance Sheet

Assets		Liabilities	
Cash	$ 20,000	Current liabilities	$ 620,000
Accounts receivable	380,000	Short-term debt	450,000
Inventory	200,000	Long-term debt	950,000
Raw materials		Net worth	
Parts and equipment	200,000	Common stock (privately held)	200,000
Partial and completed sailboats	300,000	Retained earnings	(120,000)
Fixed assets	1,000,000	Total liabilities and net worth	$2,100,000
Total assets	$2,100,000		

Exhibit 3   Variable-Cost Analysis

The variable production costs for labor, materials, and parts and equipment have been averaging 65 percent of the manufacturer's selling price for all boat types.

Fixed-Cost Analysis

	Present year	Estimated next year
Production costs:		
Building expenses	$38,000	$45,000
Management salaries	30,000	62,000
Other overhead items	2,000	18,000
Total production costs	70,000	125,000
Product design costs:		
Salaries	30,000	40,000
Prototypes	65,000	70,000
Testing	25,000	30,000
Consultants	10,000	50,000
Total production design costs	130,000	190,000
Administration costs:		
Salaries	25,000	37,000
Insurance	15,000	30,000
Office expenses	5,000	8,000
Total administration costs	45,000	75,000
Marketing costs:		
Salaries	35,000	65,000
Advertising	130,000	175,000
Boat shows	45,000	60,000
Sales promotion	31,000	30,000
Travel expenses	23,000	30,000
Total marketing costs	264,000	360,000
Total fixed costs	$509,000	$750,000

Exhibit 4 Price of Sailing Cruisers as a Function of Length

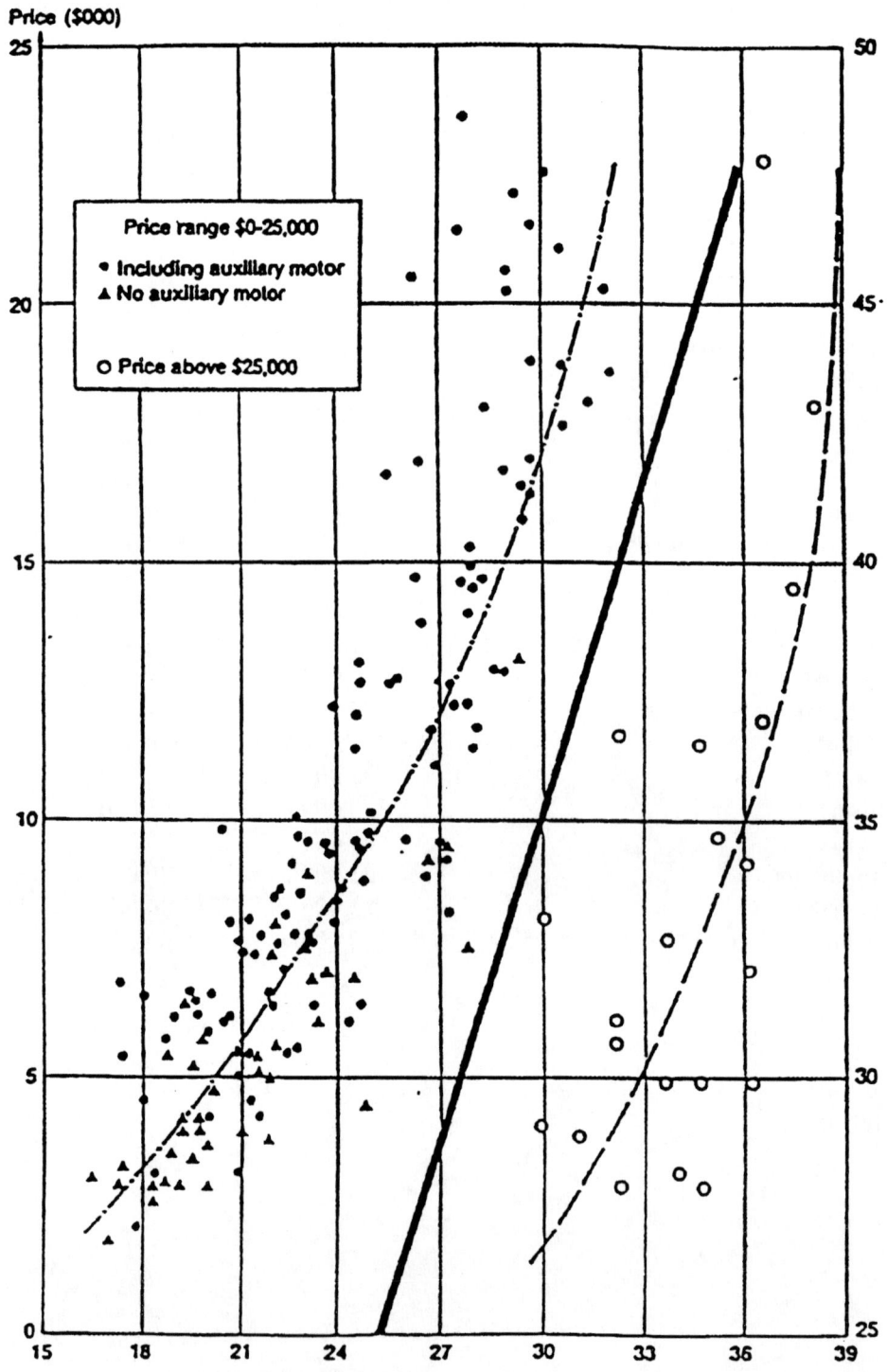

Student Analysis of the Port-Marine Case

Step 1: Situation Audit

Corporate scope and objectives

Port-Marine is a small, relatively new manufacturer of three types of fiberglass sailboats with current sales totaling $1,340,000. These sailboats appeal to two market targets: consumers that purchase sailboats for family outings or pleasure trips and consumers that purchase sailboats for competitive racing purposes. The only apparent corporate objective is to continue Port-Marine's rapid growth as outlined by the president's proposed sales forecast. Port-Marine is presently preparing a production and marketing plan to arrange the necessary financing for this growth. However, its weak financial status and its poor marketing strategy make this goal unrealistic.

Financial structure

Liquidity. According to liquidity ratios. Port-Marine may not be able to meet maturing obligations. A look at a current ratio of 1.03 (1,100.000/620.000 + 450.000) shows that the firm is barely able to meet short-term debt. A quick ratio of 0.64 (400,000/620,000) shows that without inventory, which is the least liquid item, Port-Marine could not even meet short-term debt. These ratios reveal that Port-Marine is insolvent and in order to even continue current operations must acquire additional funds. Obviously, long-term obligations cannot be met.

Port-Marines financial structure will not attract future investors. A glance at the balance sheet shows a negative balance of $120,000 in retained earnings, currently $700,000 of assets is committed to inventory and $380,000 is tied up in accounts receivable. The inventory and accounts receivable turnover ratios, 1.77 and 3.26, respectively, are too low and reflect an inefficient use of company assets.

Further analysis shows that in order to finance inventory and accounts receivable, Port-Marine has acquired much debt. Total debt to total assets (2,020,000/2,100,000) shows that 96 percent of the firm's financing has been supplied by creditors. Thus creditors would be reluctant to lend Port-Marine more money. Port-Marine's management has subjected the firm to bankruptcy by allowing the company to become so highly leveraged.

Sales and costs. About 94 percent of present sales can be attributed to the sale of the pleasure sailboats, the P/M-17 and the P/M-34. The P/M-36 only represents 7 percent of sales. The first-year sales forecast of the introduction of the P/M-29 represents 27 percent of projected total sales. This prediction is not based on any market research.

Advertising is an important cost, representing 49 percent of total marketing costs and, in turn, 25 percent of total fixed costs consultant costs in the present year can be directly linked to the design of the P/M-29 in the present-year data.

Net profit (loss). Although Port-Marine has reported a significant growth in sales, the firm has not reported a net profit but rather a $75,000 loss in the current year. as shown in Exhibit 1. The forecasted sales figure of $3 million will allow for a net profit after taxes of $180,000. The return on sales is 6 percent (180,000/3,000,000).

Exhibit 1   Present-Year Income Statement

Sales revenue	$1,240,000
Less: Cost of goods sold (65 percent of sales)	806,000
Equals: Gross profit margin	434,000
Less: Fixed costs	509,000
Equals: Net profit before taxes	(75,000)

Marketing strategy

Competition, target markets, and objectives. Port-Marine does not use or have pertinent data concerning its competition or target market. It seems that the main advantages of Port-Marines competitors are that they have established distribution channels through dealers and successful pricing policies. (See Marketing program" and "Pricing strategy"). The target market is undefined. There are not identifiable marketing objectives. This lack of data and objectives has resulted in a weak marketing program.

Marketing program. Port-Marine products have two distinct advantages—high quality and a new construction technique. This technique has reduced expenses in the manufacturing of the P/M-29. Can this new technique be used in the construction of other P/M-sailboats? The sales of the P/M-34s will decrease due to the introduction of the new P/M-29. Both are pleasure boats with nearly the same amenities, but the P/M-29 has a $24,000 price advantage and the notoriety of a well-known boat designer who consulted on its construction. Cannibalism within the product mix is inevitable unless a pricing or promotional strategy is devised to mute this effect.

Two channels of distribution are evident: One channel is through dealers on consignment, and the other is directly to the consumer induced by advertising. Dealers resent Port-Marine's attempts to by-pass dealer distribution. Since both of these methods cannot exist simultaneously, which is more effective?

The prices of Port-Marine's products are not competitive. Case Exhibit 4 shows that the price of P/M-17 seems to be in line with the industry average price based on length, yet P/M-29 and P/M-36 are well below the average industry price and P/M-34 is quite high. (See Exhibit 2). Port-Marine's pricing policy is a weak variable in its marketing program.

Exhibit 2   Pricing Audit

	Port-Marine	Industry
P/M-17	$3,300	$2,500— 3,500
P/M-29	20,000	27,000—30,000
P/M-34	44,000	31,000—34,000
P/M-36	22,000	35,000

According to Exhibit 4 In Port-Marine case.

Assumptions and opinions

Assumptions. It is assumed that the underlying marketing objective of the firm is to produce a quality product that the target market desires at competitive prices. It has also been assumed that the president has a limited background in marketing.

Opinions. The president believes he does not need and cannot trust a new marketing person in his firm at this critical time. His first priority is to establish an effective channel of distribution.

Summary of opportunities and problems

While Port-Marine's strengths lie in its quality products and its new cost-saving construction technique, weaknesses in its financial and marketing strategies may force the company into bankruptcy. The firm's hope lies in its restructuring of these faults. Other problems arise due to the lack of a sales force and the lack of control over rising costs.

Step 2: Problem/decision statement

How can Port-Marine survive?

Step 3: Alternatives

1. Port-Marina can maintain current strategies and attempt to reach the forecast sales figure.
2. Port-Marine can review its financial structure and redesign its marketing strategies.

Step 4: Critical Issues

1. Corporate objectives
2. Financial status/obligations
3. Profitability
4. Competition
5. Target market
6. Product strategy
7. Distribution channels
8. Pricing policy
9. Promotional strategy
10. Marketing organization
11. Costs of implementing alternatives

Step 5: Analysis

Alternatives 1

Sales forecast. The proposed sales forecast supplies Port-Marine with a net profit of $180,000, as shown in Exhibit 3. However, this forecast seems to be the result of a need to increase sales to cover expenses and to report a profit rather than a reflection of market potential, competitor strength, or realistic opportunities for the introduction of a new product.

Exhibit 3   Proposed Income Statement

Sales revenue	$3,000,000
Less: Cost of goods sold (65 percent of sales)	1,950,000
Equals: Gross profit margin	1,050,000
Less: Fixed costs (estimated)	750,00
Equals: Net profit before taxes	300,000
Less: Taxes (assume 40 percent corporate)	120,000
Equals: Net profit	$180,000

Break-even analysis. The break-even analysis in Exhibit 4 shows that Port-Marine must sell 169 P/M-17s, 29 P/M-29s, 22 P/M-34s, and 3 P/M-36s for each product to break even. This plan would require Port-Marine to double its current sales of P/M-17s and sell 40 of the new P/M-29s. This task seems impossible. In addition, if the introduction of the P/M-29 has a cannibalistic effect on P/M-34 sales, Port-Marine would lose the contribution margin of its most profitable boat. For example, if P/M-34 sales fell from the projected 30 to 10, the income statement might be:

Revenues	$2,120,000
Variables costs (65 percent of sales)	(1,378,000)
Fixed costs	(750,000)
Profit (loss)	(8,000)

Due to Port-Marine's financial situation, it could not withstand this loss. Therefore, this alternative is eliminated. Port-Marine must review its financial structure and redesign its marketing strategies.

Alternative 2

Financial structure. In view of Port-Marine's financial structure, as discussed in the situation audit, Port-Marine is near bankruptcy. The firm must develop an immediate plan to raise additional capital to meet short-term debt and therefore continue the firm's existence. The firm can obtain these funds from external sources or by factoring assets.

Exhibit 4 **Break-Even Analysis: Port-Marine Proposed Plan**

Product	Total revenue	Percent x Total fixed costs*	Specific product line allocated fixed costs
P/M-17	$ 792,000	26% x $750.000	$195,000
P/M-29	800,000	27% x 750.000	202,500
P/M-34	1,320,000	44% x 750.000	330,000
P/M-36	88,000	3% x 750.000	22,500
	$3,000,000	100%	$750,000

$$\text{BEP (units)} = \frac{\text{Allocated fixed costs}}{\text{Sales price - Variable costs (65\%)}}$$

$$\text{BEP (P/M-17)} = \frac{195,000}{3,300 - 2,145} = \frac{195,000}{1,155} = 169$$

$$\text{BEP (P/M-29)} = \frac{202,500}{20,000 - 13,000} = \frac{202,500}{7,000} = 29$$

$$\text{BEP (P/M-34)} = \frac{330,000}{44,000 - 28,600} = \frac{330,000}{15,400} = 22$$

$$\text{BEP (P/M-36)} = \frac{22,500}{22,000 - 14,300} = \frac{22,500}{7,700} = 3$$

*Assume allocation of fixed costs based on the amount of sales each product represents.

Port-Marine's balance sheet will not attract external investors in the form of loans or the sale of stock. The potential profitability of the P/M-29 could be used to induce some investors; however, 96 percent of the firm's debt is already supported by creditors.

Port-Marine could collect its accounts receivable and reduce its inventory. A maximum of $380,000 in accounts receivable might be collected. These funds would provide Port-Marine with capital to meet some of its short-term debt and compensate for the negative retained earnings. Inventories totaling $700,000 should be reduced, especially unfinished sailboats, which represent 43 percent of inventory. Data are not available to determine the amount of inventory that represents sailboats on consignment to dealers.

Estimated fixed costs are to rise by $236,000 next year. Variable costs already represent 65 percent of the selling price. Port-Marine could attempt to reduce fixed costs by analyzing each entry to see if the expenditure is necessary. If the new construction technique used on the P/M-29 could be applied to Port-Marine's other products, these variable costs could be reduced.

Product line strategy. Port-Marine needs to consider if it should continue including the P/M-36 in its product line. This product only represents 3 percent of total sales in the proposed forecast and is not contributing as much as it should to cover fixed costs because of its lower turnover rate. This boat is also the only product geared toward racing. This boat is also the only product geared toward racing. If the firm eliminated this product, Port-Marine could limit its scope of operations and only appeal to the pleasure boat consumer. This would simplify Port-Marine's target market to those who buy sailboats primarily for pleasure purposes. However, the market potential of the racing segment is unknown.

With the introduction of the new P/M-29, cannibalism of the sales of the P/M-34 will occur. However, since Port-Marine is a new, small firm, this new product may establish some credibility for the firm because of the well-known designer consulting on its construction. Pricing and promotional strategies can be developed to make a notable distinction between the P/M-29 and the P/M-34 and their respective target markets.

Distribution. Port-Marine can distribute its products through dealers or sell the products directly to the end—consumers themselves. The question is, which one is more profitable or compatible with Port-Marine?

Dealers are willing to accept these boats on consignment, and Port-Marine can choose dealers that reach the desired target market. However, in this situation Port-Marine is taking all the marketing risk by allowing dealers to sell on consignment.

Past sales produced from direct sales to the consumer represent 25 percent of total revenue. The proposed advertising expenditure totals $175,000. Further analysis shows that last year this method lost $21,500, as shown below:

Sales revenue (25 percent of sales)	$ 310,000
Less: Cost of goods sold (65 percent of sales)	201,500
Equals: Gross profit margin	108,500
Less: Advertising cost	130,000
Equals: Net profit/loss	(21,500)

Port-Marine's organization is not set up to handle direct distribution, and dealers object to this method because they obviously lose potential sales. If this channel were dropped, fixed marketing costs would be reduced tremendously.

Promotional strategy. If Port-Marine follows its proposed plan, advertising expenditures will increase to $175,000. This advertising may make the general audience aware of Port-Marine and its products. Apparently, it is not reaching its target market, or advertising sales would have been profitable last year. Port-Marine truly cannot afford this expenditure. Eliminating direct consumer sales can reduce advertising expenditures by approximately $100,000. Further, promotion tactics should be used to build or strengthen a dealer network, and advertising should be coordinated with dealers.

A main advertising message distinguishing the P/M-29 and P/M-34 should be developed to help deter cannibalism. One of the products could be considered the deluxe model, the designer boat, or the high-priced luxury P/M-34.

Marketing organization. Port-Marine's president can continue operating as the marketing head, or he can hire a marketing manager to assume these duties. Port-Marine's poor marketing strategies are the result of poor management. A professional marketing manager would realize the need to establish corporate and marketing objectives and to perform a marketing opportunity analysis (MOA) to gather data concerning the target market, competitors, and potential of the sailboat market. Hiring a marketing manager would introduce additional costs.

Pricing strategy. Currently there is not an identifiable pricing strategy that Port-Marine utilizes. The present system, however, has resulted in losses. Port-Marine can develop a pricing strategy that infers high quality products by pricing toward the upper end of industry averages. Another alternative strategy is to set lower prices compared to its competitors to enter or penetrate the market successfully. Since Port-Marine's products are of a high-quality nature and the consumer may not accept drastic changes in established high prices (assuming P/M-36 is dropped), the latter strategy would be applicable. Port-Marine should then also consider closing the gap between the new P/M-17 and P/M-34 to prevent cannibalism.

The proposed price for the P/M-17 reflects the high-price/high-quality strategy, since $3,300 is near the upper range of the average. The price could even be higher.

The P/M-29's proposed price, based on the whims of Port-Marine, leaves a gap of $24,000 between the price of P/M-29 and P/M-34. Fortunately this product has not been introduced, and the proposed price could easily be changed. The proposed $44,000 for the P/M-34 is still above the industry average. If P/M-29's price was based on the same price per foot as the P/M-34, the price would be approximately $34,150 ($1,188 x 28.75 feet).

Step 6: Recommendations

In order to stay afloat, Port-Marine must take specific actions and change its strategy before it becomes bankrupt. Immediate steps are necessary to be able to meet short-term debt.

Since Port-Marine cannot attract new investors, it should collect accounts receivable, reduce inventory, eliminate extraneous costs, and try to apply the new construction techniques to all of its products. In the long run, the firm can attract investors by pledging inventory and issuing subordinated long-term debt, and raise additional equity through the profit potential of the P/M-29. In addition, the firm may be able to permanently reduce accounts receivable by developing alternative sources of customer financing through dealer or local institutions.

A marketing manager should be hired despite the additional cost. A MOA is necessary in Order to establish viable marketing strategies. These benefits will outweigh the costs in the long run.

Port-Marine should drop the P/M-36 because of the small portion of revenues and contribution margin it represents. This enables the firm to concentrate on pleasure sailboats at least until its operations become stabilized. Port-Marine can always re-enter the racing market if research shows a potential market. It is also recommended that, in the future, Port-Marine incorporate consumer needs into the design of its products and the choice of products added to the product line.

Distribution through dealers is clearly the viable alternative. A Port-Marine sales force is recommended to approach dealers and maintain contact. Initially, one or two salespersons should be concentrated on the East Coast to keep costs low. Elimination of the advertising expenditures would reduce fixed costs. Promotional efforts should be concentrated on building an effective dealer network, since Port-Marine's competitors have established dealers.

A pricing strategy reflecting the cost and characteristics of Port-Marine's products should be developed. This recommended strategy infers high quality through high prices and reduces the gap between P/M-29 and P/M-34.

P/M-17. $3,600. At this price, P/M-17 falls at the upper end of the industry average. Inflation and the inevitable increase in industry average prices have been taken into consideration.

P/M-29. $34,500. This represents roughly the same price per foot as the P/M-34, reduces the gap, and provides Port-Marine with a desirable profit margin it needs to survive.

P/M-34. $40,000. This is a price freeze. The industry average range is still way below this figure. Exhibit 5 is a proposed sales forecast and income statement incorporating the above recommendations. This proposal reflects a return on sales of approximately 21 percent and should be viewed as a maximum outcome.

Exhibit 5   Sales Forecast

Unit	Number	Average price	Revenue
P/M-17	170	$ 3,600	$ 612,000
P/M-29	30	34,500	1,035,000
P/M-34	30	40,000	1,200,000
			$2,847,000

Proposed Income Statement

Sales revenue	$2,847,000
Less:	
variable cost (55 percent of sales)	1,565,850
P/M-29 royalty fees	36,000
Equals: Net contribution margin	1,245,150
Less: Fixed costs	650,000
Equals: Net profit before taxes	$ 595,150

Reflects a reduction in construction or materials.
$75,000-$100,000 of advertising expenditures.

In conclusion, Port-Marine must first implement the proposed financial steps and at the same time begin to restructure its marketing strategies. If this is accomplished, Port-Marine will survive.

Comments on the Preceding Student Analysis

Overall, the student case analyst did a reasonably good job of utilizing the case information. If you worked through the case yourself, you have probably already concluded that its length is deceptive. Although market and industry data are not given, sufficient information is provided to conclude that Port-Marine is in serious trouble. In order to reach this conclusion, however, one must analyze the data provided in the exhibits. As is often the case, the financial condition of the firm is crucial to the analysis. The following comments follow the six-step approach to case analysis suggested in Appendix B and employed by the student analyst.

Step 1: Situation Audit

The situation audit is generally adequate. It is diagnostic rather than descriptive, and it identifies the critical financial situation facing Port-Marine. Information regarding Port-Marine's presumed mission and objectives is assessed, as are company strengths and weaknesses. since the case contained little environmental, product-market, or competitor information, there was not much opportunity to address these issues. Assumptions and opinions are clearly and appropriately identified.

Several specific comments regarding the situation audit are in order. The statement that Port-Marine's products appeal to two market targets illustrates an incomplete understanding of the product-markets. While it is true that the smaller sailboats appeal to the leisure/recreation market and the P/M-36 appeals to the serious sailor, the substantial differences in the sizes and prices of the P/M-17, P/M-29, and P/M-34 indicate that each of these products probably appeals to a different age, income, and lifestyle segment. For Port-Marine to succeed, proper identification of these product-markets is essential. The need for market information was clearly identified by the analyst.

The student analysis shows that the available financial data were carefully evaluated. Liquidity ratios were reported, and the calculations were shown. This is a good idea. Other relevant ratios were calculated and discussed. Some others might have also been calculated, such as inventory to working capital, current debt to inventory, current debt to net worth, fixed assets to net worth, and working capital turnover. These would have reinforced the assessment of serious financial problems and identified particular areas where problems are most evident. Another possibility would have been to compare selected ratios to industry averages. For many types of businesses, this information is available in a number of publications in most libraries.[1] One important omission is the cost of debt service. Case Exhibit 2 indicates that Port-Marine's long-term debt is $950,000. At a very conservative 10 percent interest rate. Port-Marine's annual interest requirement is $95,000. This is a significant obligation that the student case analyst failed to consider.

The situation audit also reveals the minor contribution that the P/M-36 makes to overall sales and the relationships between advertising, total marketing, and total fixed costs. The importance of this information is revealed later in the analysis.

Several problem areas are accurately revealed, including the company's failure to define target markets, the lack of product and pricing objectives, poorly conceived promotion, channel coordination problems, the apparent lack of information about competitor or industry trends, and the company's failure to explicitly define its mission and objectives. These problems are somewhat offset by the high quality of Port-Marine's products and by a new construction technique that could play a major role in Port-Marine's future.

---

[1] For example, Value Line Investment Survey, published each week by Arnold Bernhard & Co., provides financial analyses of several industries and companies.

The conclusion that the two channels of distribution now used by Port-Marine cannot exist simultaneously is probably correct in the present situation. To support this conclusion, the analyst should carefully evaluate the pros and cons associated with the dual distribution strategy. Multiple channels can be effective, but Port-Marine's management probably has its hands full with one channel for now. Considering that 75 percent of sales are coming from dealers, this seems to be the best channel alternative.

Step 2: Problem/Decision Statement

Case analysts should not find it difficult to identify the problems lacing Port-Marine. The difficulty lies in synthesizing these problem areas. The question, "How can Port-Marine survive?" illustrates the case analyst's recognition that the company faces imminent disaster if major changes are not made soon. This is the central issue in the case and the major question that must be addressed. A few summary paragraphs identifying the main parameters of this issue might have been helpful.

Step 3: Alternatives

As we noted in Appendix B, a "no change" alternative is rarely a viable solution. Obviously it is not appropriate for Port-Marine. The case analyst apparently felt that it was necessary to consider this option because the company s proposed plan, if successful, would produce a net profit of $180,000. Evaluation of the proposed plan reveals that this outcome is not likely.

The second alternative suggests broad yet unspecific changes. This often leads to an incomplete evaluation of possible strategies to resolve a major problem/decision facing the firm. One possibility for overcoming this limitation would have been to divide the problem into its major components and consider alternatives to address each subproblem. For example, the situation audit revealed that the company needs to address or take action in each of the following areas:

- _____ Mission and objectives determination.
- _____ Market target definition and analysis.
- _____ Liquidity.
- _____ Organization.
- _____ Marketing program.

Although these areas are all addressed in the evaluation of Alternative 2, a more thorough assessment would have considered potential options to solve each sub-problem independently.

Step 4: Critical Issues

Two alternatives were analyzed. The first, the company's proposed plan, was critically evaluated and rejected. This is an appropriate conclusion. Alternative 1 could have been more thoroughly evaluated in terms of the identified critical issues; however, this would have only reinforced the conclusion that this alternative is not viable.

You may have noticed that the second sentence under the break-even analysis heading is incorrect. Exhibit 4 shows that Port-Marine would have to increase sales of the P/M-17 by 41 percent (not 100 percent) and sell 29 (not 40) of the new P/M-29s to break even. This is a simple yet noteworthy error. Supporting details are important in case analysis. Check your calculations.

The analysis of Alternative 2 illustrates the potential problem that was pointed out in the alternative identification section. The analyst is proposing solutions without exploring options. If the various subproblem areas had been Individually explored, other possible strategies (such as selling through manufacturer's representatives and alternatives to selling on consignment) might have been revealed. The end result, of course, would have been a more specific, complete set of recommendations.

Overall, the critical issues are addressed in the evaluation of Alternative 2. These include raising short-term capital, making product line decisions, minimizing the effects of P/M-29 sales on P/M-34 sales, revising the distribution structure, making promotional changes, and adding a marketing manager to analyze Port-Marine's present situation and opportunities.

Step 6: Recommendations

The recommendations section also addresses the critical issues and proposes appropriate specific actions. Issues that need to be resolved but are not addressed in the recommendations section include:

- Developing specific company and marketing objectives.
- Developing policies to guide future marketing program decisions
- Incorporating P/M-29 production techniques into the P/M-34, if possible, to reduce costs.
- Developing a selective distribution strategy through a strong dealer network.
- Getting out of the consignment business.

The recommendations section might also have included additional pro forma financial statements and budgets to support the recommendations. For example, refer back to the student's income statement following Exhibit 4 that shows the effect of a decrease in P/M-34 sales from 30 to 10.units. In addition to calculating the pro forma income statement, the student could easily have calculated new break-even and ratio analyses, using any of the personal computer spreadsheet software programs.

To illustrate, the computations shown at the end of this comment are based upon the assumption that P/M-34 sales fall from the projected 30 to 10. Revenue would fall from $3 million to $2.12 million, and a net loss of $151,000 would be incurred. Some of the figures in the income statement are different than those in the student's income statement for two reasons. First, she did not include in her income statement a $1,200 royalty fee for each P/M-29 sold. Interestingly, she did include the royalty fee in Exhibit 5. It is not clear which approach is most appropriate. It is, however, important to be consistent. Adding the $1,200 per boat royalty fee to the estimated variable cost is the mast conservative approach and therefore probably the most appropriate. The second difference between our income statement and the student's is that she did not include any interest expense for debt service.

The recalculated break-even analysis indicates that substantially more P/M-17s will need to be sold than had been originally planned. The recalculated ratios are not dramatically different than those calculated by the student. They do, however, present a more accurate description of the situation, given the assumption of a sales decrease for the P/M-34.

In sum, this student's case analysis represents a good start. Attention to several of the areas discussed above could significantly strengthen the analysis. It is much easier to critique a case analysis than to prepare one. Most of the comments on the analysis dealt with ways in which it could be strengthened by going into more detail. Undoubtedly, additional comments about the analysis might be made. The purpose, however, is not to provide an exhaustive set of comments but rather to highlight the key strengths and weaknesses of the analysis in order to provide you with an example and some guidelines to follow.

	Present Year			Proposed Plan		
Model	Number	Average Price	Revenue	Number	Average Price	Revenue
P/M-17	120	3,000	360,000	240	3,300	792,000
P/M-29				40	20,000	800,000
P/M-34	20	40,000	800,000	10	44,000	440,000
P/M-336	4	20,000	80,000	4	22,000	88,000
			1,240,000			2,120,000

Income Statements

	Present Year	Proposed Plan
Sales Revenue*	1,240,000	2,12,0000
Less: COGS**	806,000	1,426,000
Equals: Gross Profit Margin	434,000	694,000
Less: Fixed Costs	509,000	7,500,000
Equals: Profit B.Tax & INT	-75,000	-56,000
Less: Interest Expense**	95,000	95,000
Equals: Net Profit B. Tax	-170,000	-151,000
Less: Taxes (40%)	0	0
Equals: Net Profit	-170,000	-151,000

* 65% of sales and including148,000 in P/M-29 Royalty fees for COGS
**Estimate—assumes a 10% debt service annually not including principle

Break Even Analysis

$$\frac{\text{Allocated Fixed Costs (\% x TFC)}}{\text{Sales Price} - \text{Variable Costs (65\%)}} \quad \text{Break-Even Point (Units)}$$

P/M-17	$\frac{280,188.7}{1,115}$	=243
P/M-29	$\frac{28,3018.9}{7,000}$	= 40
P/M-34	$\frac{155,660.4}{15,400}$	= 10
P/M-36	$\frac{31,132}{7,700}$	= 4

Ratio Analysis

Current Ratio	$\frac{1,100,000}{1,070,000}$	= 1.028037
Quick Ratio	$\frac{400,000}{620,000}$	= .6451613
Debt to Total Assets	$\frac{2,020,000}{2,100,000}$	= .9619048

Inventory to Net VC	$\dfrac{700{,}000}{30{,}000}$	= 23.3333
Gross Profit Margin	$\dfrac{694{,}000}{2{,}120{,}000}$	= .2313333
Return on Total Assets	$\dfrac{-151{,}000}{2{,}100{,}000}$	= -.071905
Long Term Debt to Equity	$\dfrac{950{,}000}{80{,}000}$	= 11.875
Total Debt to Equity	$\dfrac{2{,}020{,}000}{80{,}000}$	= 25.25

SECTION IV

QUANTITATIVE EXERCISES

FINANCIAL ANALYSIS EXERCISES

Exercise A-1   Snapamatic Camera Company (A)

This exercise presents a situation requiring several basic financial calculations. It is a useful means of identifying where to review financial analysis methods.

Snapamatic Camera Company has introduced a new line of low-priced cameras called "Click Quick," and the information for that product line is given below.

a. Retail selling price $25 per unit
b. Retailer's cost $20 per unit
c. Wholesaler's cost $15 per unit
d. Manufacturer's variable selling expense as % of age of selling price 10%
e. Fixed selling and advertising expense $800,000
f. Annual sales for Snapamatic 150,000 units
g. Estimated market size for low-priced cameras 800,000 units
h. Variable manufacturing cost $2.50 per unit
i. Fixed manufacturing cost $100,000

Discussion Questions

1. What is the variable cost per unit of Click Quick for Snapamatic Camera Company?
2. What is Snapamatic's contribution margin per unit?
3. Calculate the break-even volume in units and in dollars.
4. Estimate the market share that Click Quick has to command in order to (a) break even and/or (b) attain a before-tax target profit of $600,000.

Exercise A-2   Snapamatic Camera Company (B)

The management of Snapamatic Camera Co. is considering introduction of a new product called "Click-O-Matic," which is to be marketed in addition to Click Quick. This is intended for a higher-priced (meant for the more avid and sophisticated photographer) segment of the market. The following information has been compiled for managerial decision making:

Retailer's margin	20%
Jobber's margin	15%
Wholesaler's margin	$5 per unit
Variable selling expense as % age of sales	10%
Retailer's selling price	$60
Incremental fixed selling expense	$300,000
Promotion and advertising for Click-O-Matic	$500,000
New equipment required	$500,000
	(to be depreciated over 10 years)
Direct factory labor	$4 per unit
Raw materials	$5 per unit
Factory and administrative overhead	$3 per unit
	(at a 50,000 unit volume level)

Discussion Questions

1. What is the contribution margin per unit for the Click-O-Matic line?

2. Calculate the break-even sales in dollars and in units.

3. How much sales volume in dollars should Snapamatic Camera Company attain on Click-O-Matic to get 20 percent return on the equipment?

4. Customers initially may be very sensitive to the higher price of $60, so it is considered worthwhile to perform an analysis using a unit price of $55 per unit and raise the retail margin to 25 percent. What is the break-even volume in units?

Solution to Exercise A-1

1. Variable manufacturing cost per unit $ = $2.50
   Variable selling expense per unit (15 x 0.1) = $1.50
   Total variable cost of "Click Quick" per unit = $4.00
2. Contribution Margin of "Click Quick":

$$\frac{\text{Manufacturer's selling price} - \text{manufacturer's total variable cost}}{\text{Manufacturer's Selling Price}} = \frac{\$15 - \$4}{\$15} = 73.33\%$$

The per unit contribution is $15-4 or $11.

3. $$\text{Break even sales in units} = \frac{\text{Fixed expenses}}{\text{Contribution per unit}} = \frac{\$800,000 + \$100,00}{\$15 - \$4}$$
   $$= 81,818 \text{ units}$$

$$\text{Break even sales in dollars} = \frac{\text{Fixed expenses}}{\text{Contribution margin}} = \frac{\$800,000 + \$100,000}{73.33\%}$$
$$= \$1,227,329$$

4. Estimated market share for "Click Quick" to break even:

$$\frac{\text{Break even sales in units}}{\text{Estimated market size for low - price camera}} = \frac{81,818}{800,000} = 10.23\%$$

Number of units to be sold to attain a before tax target profile of $600,000:

$15 x = $4x + $900,000 + $600,000

$11 x = $1,500,000

$$x = \frac{1,500,000}{\$11} = 136,364 \text{ units}$$

Estimated market share for "Click Quick" to attain a before tax target profit of $600,000:

$$\frac{136,634}{800,000} = 17.05\%$$

Solution to Exercise A-2

1. | | | |
    |---|---|---|
    | Unit selling price | | $60 |
    | Less retailers margin @ 20% | = | 12 |
    | | = | $48 |
    | Less jobber's margin @ 15% | | 7.2 |
    | | = | 40.8 |
    | Less wholesaler's margin | | 5.0 |
    | Manufacturer's selling price | = | $35.8 |
    | Total variable expenses per unit | = | (10% of $35.8) + $4 + $5 |
    | | = | $12.58 |
    | Contribution per unit | = | $35.80 - $12.58 = $23.22 |
    | Contribution margin percentage | = | 64.86% |

2. The break even volume in units $= \dfrac{\text{Fixed expenses}}{\text{Contribution per unit}}$

    $$= \dfrac{\$300{,}000 + \$500{,}000 + \$50{,}000}{\$23.22}$$

    $$= \dfrac{\$850{,}000}{\$23.22} = 36{,}606 \text{ units}$$

    The break even volume in dollars $= \dfrac{\$850{,}000}{64.86\%} = \$1{,}310{,}515$

3. Let the number of units to be sold in order to attain 20% return on equipment be x, then x can be determined by solving:

$$35.8x = 12.58x + 850{,}000 + (20\% \times 500{,}000)$$

$$23.22x = 850{,}000 + 100{,}000$$

$$x = \frac{950{,}000}{23.22} = 40{,}913 \text{ units}$$

4.

Revised selling price	=	$55
Less retailers margin	=	13.75
		$41.25
Less jobber's margin		6.20
		35.05
Less wholesaler's margin		5.00
Manufacturers selling price		$30.05

Total variable expenses per unit = $3.01 + $4 + $5 = $12.01

The break even volume in units = $\dfrac{\$850{,}000}{\$30.05 - \$12.01} = \dfrac{850{,}000}{18.04} = 47{,}118$ units

SECTION V

TEACHING NOTES

Part 1

Market-Driven Strategy

CASE 1-1
ENTERPRISE RENT-A-CAR: SELLING THE DREAM[*]

Case Objectives and Use

This case illustrates Enterprise Rent-A-Car's pursuit of a focused strategy that uses the operational excellence value discipline. Enterprise's successful implementation of this strategy has resulted in its becoming the largest rent-a-car company in the U.S. in terms of number of rental cars and number of office locations. The case allows students to apply marketing concepts to develop recruitment programs that will "sell" Enterprise to college graduates who are looking for employment. One of Enterprise's major challenges in continuing its growth is recruiting a steady supply of quality employees. The case also allows the discussion and development of marketing strategies to continue the firm's rapid growth.

The case is based on field research. Enterprise officials cooperated in the development of the case. Because Enterprise is privately owned, the case does not include specific company financial data. Officials at *Auto Rental News,* an industry trade publication, also provided data for the case.

Synopsis

This case presents an overview of a simple yet very effective strategy that has catapulted Enterprise Rent-A-Car into position as the largest rent-a-car company in the United States in terms of number of cars and locations. As of early 1997, when the case is set, Enterprise had $3.1 billion in revenue, $5 billion in assets, 330,000 vehicles, more than 3,000 locations, and more than 30,000 full-time and part-time employees.

The company's founder, Jack Taylor, began leasing cars in 1957 while working with a car dealer in St. Louis, Missouri. When his customers lost the use of their cars due to accidents or the need for repairs. Jack saw the opportunity to rent them replacement vehicles. Thus, he founded Enterprise Rent-A-Car in 1962, focusing on the "home-city" rental replacement market and leaving competitors such as Hertz and Avis to slug it out in the airport market.

As it grew, Enterprise crafted a simple strategy based on a simple philosophy. Jack Taylor believed that by taking care of the customer first and then his employees, profits would take care of themselves. Taylor focused on doing "whatever it took" to satisfy customers. He hired primarily college graduates and promoted them rapidly, putting them in charge of branch offices that they ran basically as independent businesses.

Managers earned most of their compensation based on the profitability of the branch or branches for which they were responsible. This combination of customer orientation, local-market focus, profit-based incentive, and educated employees, proved to be a powerful formula for success in the local market. Enterprise also kept its costs low by staying away from expensive airport locations and by keeping its cars a little longer than the airport-based companies.

---

[*] Copyright © 1997. Lew Brown, Gary Armstrong, and Philip Kotler. All rights reserved. Teaching manual is for use by instructors using the "Enterprise Rent-A-Car: Selling the Dream" case prepared by the authors, and reproduction for any other purpose is prohibited. The teaching manual represents the authors' analysis: and the inclusion of the analysis. conclusions, and possible recommendations in the manual should not be taken as their being certified by Enterprise Rent-A-Car.

Enterprise grew slowly until the 1970s, when courts ruled that insurance companies had to offer coverage to allow their customers to replace their cars following accidents. This change jump-started Enterprise's growth. The company established relationships with insurance companies and their agents and with local auto dealers and repair shops. These referral agents became Enterprise's key sources of business.

By early 1997, Enterprise was riding a string of 11 years of growth at a compound annual rate of 25 percent and had overtaken the more well-known rent-a-car companies that still primarily compete in the airport market.

This rapid growth raises two general issues. First, to grow this rapidly, Enterprise must develop a steady supply of college graduates. The case indicates that Enterprise must hire more than 5,000 college grads in 1997 alone. Yet, because of the company's low-key nature, many college grads do not know about Enterprise, or they have the general feeling that the rent-a-car industry does not offer attractive careers that require a college education. Enterprise must compete with other large companies for these candidates in a strong economy where unemployment is low. How can it improve its image and attract the interest of college graduates?

Second, due to its rapid growth, Enterprise controls more than 50 percent of the home-city market and has achieved nationwide coverage in the U.S. What options are open to the company to continue to fuel its growth and to allow it to continue to provide the opportunity for rapid advancement that its employees want?

Teaching Objectives

The teaching objectives of this case are:

1. To allow students to analyze a focused, operationally excellent strategy in the area of service marketing.
2. To allow students to apply marketing concepts to the challenge of enhancing the firm's recruitment efforts.
3. To allow students to develop marketing strategy recommendations as to how Enterprise can continue its rapid growth.

Discussion Questions

1. Outline Enterprise's marketing strategy. Why has this strategy been successful?
2. How do the nature and characteristics of a service affect Enterprise's strategy?
3. What opportunities and threats does Enterprise face?
4. How can Enterprise use marketing concepts to improve its recruitment program? What specific recommendations would you make to Enterprise to improve its recruitment program?
5. What marketing recommendations would you make to Enterprise to guide its growth?

Discussion

1. Outline Enterprise's marketing strategy. Why has this strategy been successful?

Students should begin by identifying Enterprise's basic competitive strategy as being a **focus concentrated targeting or niche strategy**. Rather than competing for the entire $14.6 billion rent-a-car market,

Enterprise has focused on the home-city market that accounts for about half of the total market. Students may also suggest that Enterprise focused on one sub-segment of the home-city market—the replacement market. Further, Enterprise has pursued a **value discipline** of **operational excellence.** This value discipline requires that the company provide superior value by leading the industry in price and convenience. A company pursuing this strategy must control costs and develop a lean, efficient value delivery system that serves customers who want reliable, good-quality products and services delivered cheaply and easily. Some students will also suggest that there are elements of **customer intimacy**. Enterprise has precisely segmented its markets and tailored its product offering to match exactly the targeted customer's needs. It has also empowered its employees to respond quickly to customers' needs. One reason for Enterprise's decentralized structure is to allow its branch offices to tailor their offerings to fit the needs of each market area. Generally, however, companies that use the customer-intimate strategy pursue a premium-pricing strategy and are less focused on the cost control.

Students may suggest that Enterprise has pursued an overall cost leadership strategy due to the case's reference to the fact that its prices may be significantly lower than those of the airport-based companies. However, students should see that the lower prices are the result of its focus on the home-city market and the economics of that market. Although Enterprise has lower prices than airport-based companies, it is not using those prices to attract the traveling customers that the airport-based companies serve.

Target Market: Enterprise targets customers in the home-city market. These are customers who primarily rent cars for use in their local area as opposed to using the cars for travel/vacation purposes. The case notes that there are three sub-segments of this market. In addition to the replacement market, which involves renting a car while the customer is having his/her car repaired due to an accident or mechanical problem, there are the "leisure/discretionary" and corporate markets. Exhibit 2 indicates that about 78 percent of Enterprise's business is from the replacement market. Footnote 3 in that exhibit states that *Auto Rental News* estimates that about 7 percent of Enterprise's business comes from airport travelers. (Although Enterprise does not target such travelers, some do reserve cars through Enterprise, with an Enterprise shuttle picking them up at the airport.) The sum of the replacement and airport segments account for 85 percent of Enterprise's business. The footnote also indicates that the remainder of its business is split equally between the leisure and corporate markets, giving us an estimate of 7.5 percent of the company's revenues from each of these two segments.

In the replacement market, there are two groups of customers. First, there are the insurance companies and their agents. If the end customer, the car owner, has an accident and has replacement coverage in his/her policy, it is the insurance company that pays Enterprise for the replacement rental. The insurance company is interested in its customer having a hassle-free experience when he/she rents a replacement vehicle. If the customer is not satisfied, he/she may allow that dissatisfaction to spill over to the insurance company itself, blaming the company for using/recommending Enterprise. This negative experience may cause the customer to be dissatisfied with the insurance company. The case also indicates that Enterprise employees check with the repair shops and keep the insurance agents informed as to the vehicle's repair status. Students should see that this is a valuable service for the agent, and that Enterprise must make the agents/adjusters happy so that they will continue to recommend Enterprise to the policyholders. Some replacement customers, of course, will not have insurance coverage for the replacement rental and will be paying for the rental themselves as in a typical customer relationship.

Product: Enterprise's **core product** is personal transportation. It provides this product at a time when the customer has lost use of his/her vehicle or needs an additional vehicle for some reason. The **actual product** is the rental vehicle. Due to limitations on what the insurance company will pay, customers may not be able to rent the car they would rent if they had their choice. Thus, Enterprise may not have to offer as wide a variety of cars or cars that are quite as new or fancy as an airport-based company. The customer will expect that the car is clean and in good condition. Enterprise **augments** its product by offering to pick up the customer. Often, the customer may be stranded at the scene of an accident or at a repair shop. Picking up the customer makes Enterprise's service more convenient and keeps the customer from having to worry about how to get to a rent-a-car location. Enterprise's practice of keeping insurance agents informed also augments the value of its service.

Students who analyze the case more closely will realize that Enterprise must also dispose of its used cars once they are no longer suitable for rental. Thus, one if its products is its own cars.

Because this is a service business, the employees are also part of the product. In the case Dan suggests (page 5, column I) that a typical branch manager may manage a branch with four to six employees and 100-150 cars. We can assume that there is one full-time employee for every 25 cars.

Price: Exhibit 2 indicates that the industry average replacement daily rental rate is $23 and that the average rental period is 12 days. On average, the companies earn about 7 percent additional revenue through added insurance coverage and other rental items. Given that Enterprise has over 50 percent market share, we can assume that the $23 rate is a good estimate of Enterprise's average rental rate. If so, and if, as the case suggests, Enterprise's rates are about 30 percent lower than airport-based rates, one can estimate that airport rates will average around $32 per day.

Students should note that the insurance coverage provided by a policy may be at a relatively low daily rate, such as $16 per day. Enterprise rents cars at this rate, but these are the smaller compact and subcompact cars. Individuals renting a car may be used to having a larger car and be willing to pay a higher rate in order to have a larger car. Thus, even though the insurance company may be paying, Enterprise can increase its revenue by encouraging customers to "trade up" to a car with a higher daily rate.

The students who realized the importance of selling Enterprise's used cars will also realize the importance of getting good prices for those cars and, if possible, making a profit on the sale of the used cars. This means that used car supply and demand will be important factors for Enterprise to watch.

Place: The case indicates that Enterprise has over 3,000 locations. Enterprise is pursuing a strategy of **selective distribution**, with an emphasis on the intensive end of the intensive-exclusive continuum. It must locate its offices in an area that is large enough to support the office, so it must be selective. But given that an area is large enough, Enterprise appears to be targeting each such area. This should suggest to students that, at least within the U.S., Enterprise may be approaching saturation in terms of the number of locations. Certainly, there is room for growth, but given the size of the market and the existence of competition, there is a limit to the number of new locations Enterprise can establish in order to spur growth. This fact has implications for growth strategy, as discussed in question 5.

The place variable in the marketing mix has been a key to the company's strategy. First, it has targeted the home market, locating its branches in normal business areas within a community. Such locations are often more convenient than airport locations for the non-traveler who wants to rent a car. Second, the locations should normally be less expensive than airport locations, helping Enterprise keep its costs, and therefore its rates, lower.

Promotion: <u>Advertising</u>. The case indicates that, until 1989, Enterprise did no advertising. Students may be familiar with the "wrapped car" commercials and the theme, "Pick Enterprise. We'll pick you up," which has been the basic theme since 1989. Although Enterprise's awareness has increased substantially from 20 percent, where it was in 1989, the case points out that only about a third of consumers surveyed were aware of the company's nearby locations or its pick-up policy.

If we examine Exhibit 1, we can estimate that Enterprise had about 225,000 cars in 1994. Exhibit 2 estimates that Enterprise spent $22 million in measured advertising that year. This works out to about $98 per car per year. or about $8 per car per month. If we assume that Hertz, which Exhibit 2 indicates had 250,000 cars in 1996, might have had about the same size fleet as Enterprise in 1994, we see that its $47 million in spending was about $200 per car, about double Enterprise's spending. Students will note that Alamo spent $31 million even though it had about half as many cars as either Enterprise or Hertz (130,000 cars in 1996).

Students may suggest that the lower level of per-car spending is the reason so many people are still unaware of Enterprise or of its locations or services. The instructor may wish to point out, however, that advertising is less important when the primary referral source is the insurance agent or repair shop employee. Enterprise has historically depended on personal selling and word-of-mouth promotion because, as the case notes. few of its customers get up in the morning planning to have an accident and rent a replacement car that day. The *Advertising Age* data in Exhibit 2 focuses on measured advertising. It does not count the value of all the pizzas and donuts that Enterprise's employees deliver to their referral customers!

The local branches can also spend money on local media, such as yellow pages and newspaper/radio advertising.

Personal Selling. Students should see that Enterprise's branch employees are its field sales force as well as its operational employees. By having each employee call on referral agents, Enterprise fields a huge personal sales force. These employees can establish personal relationships with the referral agents. Thus, the employee's personality is an important consideration in making hiring decisions. Not only must the employees be able to use a computer and deal with customers at the office, they must also be comfortable in a one-on-one selling situation in someone else's office.

Sales Promotion. Although the rent-a-car business is known for its price promotions, there is little mention of this in the case. The only sales promotion mentioned is Enterprise's weekend promotion rates. Apparently, Enterprise has not felt the need for promotions, given its already lower prices and the nature of its target markets.

Publicity/Public Relations. There is also no mention of this activity in the case. Students will speculate, however, that for a company in the local market business, it will be important to use these tools to establish awareness and community involvement.

A key point in this discussion is that Enterprise's strategy has been successful because each of the pieces fits together and because all of the pieces fit the target market. Each decision makes sense in terms of the targeted home-city market and the focused, operationally excellent strategy used to attract these targeted consumers.

Further, Enterprise has developed its strategy to support **internal marketing**, a key in any service business. Because Enterprise allows its employees to "run their own businesses" and because it pays its managers based on branch profitability, the employees have the incentive to work as a team to provide customer satisfaction. Jack and Andy Taylor have clearly established customer satisfaction as the company's main goal. The decentralized structure with incentivized employees creates a culture to support that goal.

Enterprise also understands interactive marketing—the fact that perceived service quality depends on the quality of the buyer-seller interaction during the service encounter. Obviously, the customer will judge Enterprise's value based on the quality of the car he/she rents. However, the interpersonal aspects of the exchange will be equally important. Given Enterprise's target market, many of its customers may be upset and unhappy during the rental process. The company's employees must have good interpersonal skills in order to deal with these customers. Enterprise believes that employees with a college education will be better at this and more capable of dealing with a high-stress work environment that often requires the employee to make quick decisions. The "role-playing" situation in the case provides such an example.

Despite the company's obvious success, students will point out that it is weak in the third type of marketing in service firms—**external marketing**. As noted, the company did not begin national advertising until 1989. Andy Taylor realizes that the company "still has a way to go" in building customer awareness. College students who are in the job market are not familiar with Enterprise. Many students will want to go to work for a well-known company. Moreover, as the case notes, working at a rent-a-car company does not seem to be a high-status job to many college students.

Enterprise has been successful because its strategy fits with the target market, because of the strength of its internal and interactive marketing, and because of top management's commitment to quality. Enterprise has used its people and its system to differentiate itself through **service delivery**.

2. How do the nature and characteristics of a service affect Enterprise's strategy?

Marketing texts note that one can characterize services based on four factors: intangibility, inseparability, variability, and perishability.

Services are by their nature exchanges of ownership. Although one can rent the car from Enterprise, the actual basis of the exchange is the process of renting and using the car, not the car itself. Buyers will look for signals of service quality, drawing conclusions from the place where the company offers the service, the people who offer it, the price, and how the company communicates the offer. Each of these **intangible** aspects of the service will shape how the customer perceives the service. Enterprise has clearly focused on the people who deliver the service, believing that these people could differentiate its service.

Enterprise realizes that services are **inseparable** from the people who provide the service. Therefore, it has chosen to hire college graduates, realizing that it should get well-educated employees who, besides being able to understand income statements and balance sheets and to set and achieve goals, will also be able to understand and deal with customers who may be upset as the result of losing the use of their car unexpectedly. The provider-customer interaction is a central feature of services marketing.

A service's third characteristic is **variability**. Although hiring college graduates may provide Enterprise with good employees who can deal with uncertain situations, treating each of the 3,000 or so branch offices as independent businesses creates a problem in handling variability. McDonald's controls the quality of its hamburgers and fries by carefully controlling the quality of the meat and potatoes its stores use and by carefully shaping its training so that a Big Mac in Los Angeles tastes the same as one cooked in New York City. Yet, Enterprise prides itself in allowing each of its offices to shape its marketing to react to the needs of the local market. Although this allows Enterprise to "micro-market," it raises the problem of having a "standard" offering. Some students will argue, however, that McDonald's serves travelers who are moving from market to market, while Enterprise does not target travelers, making inter-market variability less important. Other students will suggest that Enterprise may have fewer problems with variability than other rent-a-car firms that use a franchise method, where franchisees run the offices. These franchisees are not company employees and may be more difficult to control.

Finally, services are **perishable.** Enterprise has this problem in that the demand for its rentals is highest during the week. The case indicates that the company has developed special promotional prices in order to encourage customers to rent its cars during the weekend. Students should see that Enterprise is a high-fixed-cost operation. In such an operation, volume is important. It is better for Enterprise to rent a car on the weekend at a rate above variable cost than to have it sit idle during that weekend and produce no contribution to overhead and profit. Students who have analyzed the case more closely will also realize that Enterprise has little control over demand. A sudden winter storm can cause a flurry of accidents and a rapid increase in demand for replacement cars. As the case notes, Enterprise max' be able to rush more cars to the branch office to meet demand, but it is difficult for it to add employees rapidly. Thus, in peak demand situations, employees could be under increased stress. The peak demand problem contributes to employee stress and service variability in service businesses.

3. What opportunities and threats does Enterprise face?

Although the case indicates that Enterprise has over 50 percent of the home-city market. it also indicates in Exhibit 2 that the other players in the market are much smaller. Thus, Enterprise has opportunities to continue to grow in the local market by acquiring or overwhelming smaller competitors. The exhibit also indicates that only about seven percent of Enterprise's revenues come from the airport/traveler market. It could enter this market, but this segment is highly competitive and would require a significant change in strategy.

The leisure/discretionary and business markets represent more realistic expansion opportunities for Enterprise. Together, they represent only 15 percent of Enterprise's business. The case does not indicate how much of the 73 percent of the total market accounted for by leisure and business rentals is attributable to the home-city market. As the case suggests, however, more businesses are seeing the advantages of renting versus owning, and more people are seeing the benefits of leisure/discretionary rentals.

Some students will suggest that Enterprise's distribution system also would work for trucks or for other types of equipment rental. The case does not discuss the home-city truck-rental business, but students should be familiar with Ryder, U-Haul, and other companies that already operate in the local truck-rental business. There are also established equipment rental companies, including Hertz.

As for threats, careful analysis will suggest that the main reason for Enterprise's success has been its narrow, carefully controlled focus. Anything that threatens this focus can be a threat if Enterprise is not careful.

Enterprise is also subject to threats from forces outside of its control. For example, oil shocks, such as those that occurred in the 1970s and 1980s, could reduce the supply of oil and cause people to have to drastically reduce their dependence on the car. Less driving would mean fewer accidents and fewer business/discretionary rentals.

Further, Enterprise must have a steady supply of capital to purchase cars. Sudden interest rate spikes could make borrowing money unaffordable. Students who analyze the case more closely will see that Enterprise has over $5 billion in assets to support $3 billion in sales. This asset turnover ratio of about .6 means that Enterprise needs about $1.66 in assets to support every dollar in sales. Continuing to grow the company at 25 percent per year will require significant borrowing.

Tied to purchasing cars is the need to dispose of cars that have reached the end of their useful rental lives. Students may see that Enterprise must sell many cars each year. It would hope to make a profit or at least break even selling these cars. Thus, an oversupply of used cars that depress used-car prices would be of concern to Enterprise.

A final threat, one that ties to a central issue in the case, is that there may not be a sufficient labor supply to fuel Enterprise's growth. It has built its strategy on having a supply of well-educated, highly motivated employees. As it gets larger, it needs more and more employees. In a robust economy, as existed in early 1997, college graduates have more choices. They can hold out for jobs that offer higher pay. This could cause Enterprise to have to increase its salaries, raising its costs. Students may also suggest that not everyone wants to work at a rent-a-car company and that employees must "fit" with the culture that Enterprise has developed. As the company continues to grow, it could reach the limit of the supply of potential employees who fit its culture.

4. How can Enterprise use marketing concepts to improve its recruiting program? What specific recommendations would you make to Enterprise to improve its recruitment program?

Everything flows from the target market. As the case's title suggests, Enterprise is selling a dream. Many college graduates have the dream of being financially successful and running their own businesses. Enterprise must sell them on the idea that it can allow them to realize that dream. Students will suggest that "college graduates" is still a very broad target market. Can Enterprise narrow the target market, improving its focus just as it has had a narrow focus on the home-city market?

First, students will note that Enterprise's branches will be recruiting from colleges in their areas. So, a first step would be to list all of the colleges in the recruiting area and to analyze the characteristics of typical graduates from those colleges. One might speculate, for example, that Enterprise may have a difficult time recruiting from prestigious universities that typically train their graduates to enter graduate school in areas like medicine or law to pursue specialized degrees in areas like engineering or the applied sciences. We might guess that Enterprise will have better results focusing on liberal arts graduates who may be unsure of what kind of career to pursue when they graduate, or on undergraduate business majors who may be interested in running their own businesses while working for a large firm.

The regional managers like Dan Miller will also want to keep track of the colleges that have produced successful Enterprise employees. One would expect that positive word-of-mouth would be an important factor in improving Enterprise's image and reputation on a campus and increasing the likelihood that students would be interested in talking to Enterprise.

So, recruiters would want to identify those colleges in their geographic areas where they are more likely to find the types of candidates they want and where they are more likely to be successful in recruiting those candidates. Students will also suggest that Enterprise may want to study the personality profiles of successful managers. Exhibit 3 reports that successful managers were active in clubs and organizations, and were active in athletics. Further, Enterprise may find that these managers have common personality traits. Tests like the Myers-Briggs profile may provide information on common characteristics of managers that can be useful to Enterprise in the recruiting process.

Thus, the first approach students should take is to help Enterprise narrow the target market, focusing its recruiting efforts on those campuses and on those candidates where it has a higher likelihood of success.

Once students have narrowed the target market, they should turn their attention to the marketing mix. Enterprise's product is a job or career. The case describes the job, and Exhibit 3, numbers 1 and 2, suggests the benefits Enterprise offers. It offers graduates an opportunity to start in a job where they will learn how to run a business; where promotion can be rapid because of the company's rapid growth and the fact that promotion is from within; where they work in a friendly, team environment; and where they have great earning potential.

As for **price**, students should see that there is a "price" that graduates must pay if they work for Enterprise. That price is the physical and mental energy that Enterprise demands from its employees. The employees must work long hours, often in stressful situations, and be willing and able to perform a wide variety of tasks—from washing cars to dealing with insurance companies. These long hours may contrast with those worked by some of their friends, who may take more normal 9-to-S jobs and make as much or even more money in the short term. Thus, there may be a "psychological price" that employees must pay. Job candidates and employees must be able to overcome the perception that working for a rent-a-car company is not a glamorous job that requires a college education.

As for **place**, Enterprise operates in the home-city market. This, and its 3,000 locations, means that employees have the opportunity to work in their communities if they want to. Because Enterprise does not force employees to relocate, this also means that an employee can continue to work in one area. If an employee does want to work in other geographical areas, he/she will have the opportunity to do that while advancing within the company. At this time in the discussion, students should see that the significant challenge Enterprise faces is in the area of **promotion**. How can Enterprise improve its communication to the targeted students in order to overcome their potential objections and get them to "buy" the dream?

The case indicates that Enterprise has been performing all the "normal" recruiting activities, such as attending career days, advertising in the campus newspapers, and participating in the college Placement Office's activities and programs. These, however, are normal activities, and Enterprise may be at a disadvantage because students do not know about Enterprise and may have negative feelings about working in the rent-a-car business.

Students may recommend that Enterprise increase its measured advertising spending to a level comparable on a per-car basis to the other leading rent-a-car companies. As we saw in analyzing Exhibit 2 above. Hertz appears to be spending at least two times more per car on advertising ($200 vs. $98) and Alamo is spending about $238 per car per year ($31 million divided by 130,000). Students should point out that Enterprise will have to consider the effect of any increased spending on its cost structure.

Students can recommend a two-pronged advertising attack. First, Enterprise must continue to increase consumers' awareness of the company and its services. Despite the recent advertising, Andy Taylor indicates that only about one-third of the people surveyed were aware that Enterprise would pick up its customers or that it had nearby offices. Students can suggest that Enterprise continue its "wrapped car" ads, which stress convenience. They can also recommend that Enterprise develop some **"corporate"** advertising that communicates that Enterprise is the largest rent-a-car company in terms of number of vehicles and locations and that it serves the customer's local market. Such **image** advertising is important to continue to build awareness and to establish an image as a successful, well-known company. Students may suggest that Enterprise assess its image on a number of key dimensions, determine what image it would like to have on those dimensions, and then measure progress in changing the image as a way of measuring the advertising's effectiveness.

Enterprise should direct the second prong in the advertising campaign towards improving its communications with college students. Based on Exhibit 3, students can suggest that Enterprise develop a series of ads designed to run in college newspapers and on college radio stations. The ads should focus on the themes suggested in Exhibit 3. They should point out that Enterprise is a $3 billion company growing at 25 percent per year that offers students the opportunity to run their own business, advance rapidly based on their performance, have fun working, and earn attractive compensation. However, the ads must be up-front with the facts that the price of such an opportunity is hard work involving long hours and stress. The ads can present these "negative" facts as a challenge. After all, Enterprise wants to attract students who are willing to face these challenges and pursue the dream. It is of no value to attract applicants by listing all the benefits and avoiding the requirements to realize those benefits. So, students can argue that straight-forward, hard-hitting ads can get graduates' attention and help pre-select those who will be better candidates. Students may also propose that Enterprise use its own employees' stories as a focus for these ads. Just as the case highlights Dan Miller's and Dean Pittman's rapid promotions, ads could tell such stories, stressing both the hard work and the rewards.

Tied in with this national advertising attack, Enterprise should launch local public relations and advertising programs. Exhibit 3, number 3, outlines the backgrounds of successful managers. They are often involved in extracurricular activities, athletics, and clubs. This should suggest that local Enterprise operations design advertising and public relations activities targeted for these kinds of activities. For example, Enterprise could become a sponsor of athletic teams at targeted colleges. Donating money to support a baseball team, for example, and getting a billboard mounted on an outfield fence would increase exposure to both the athletes and fans. Enterprise could also sponsor clubs, like marketing or human resources clubs, that operate as a part of business schools at the targeted colleges. Enterprise branches could offer to send speakers to these clubs and support their programs in other ways.

Students who analyze the case more closely will also note that Exhibit 3, number 5, suggests that Enterprise also has some internal promotion problems. The Exhibit notes that employees leave Enterprise due to long hours, stress, and low pay. Part of this turnover may result from attracting employees who do not fit with Enterprise's culture. This is why it is so important to educate the potential employee about the true nature of the job prior to the hiring decision. However, the information also suggests that Enterprise cannot stop "selling the dream" once an employee comes on board. Students will suggest that it develop an internal program to spotlight successful employees. It must keep the dream alive in employees' minds to help them see the rewards of the hard work.

Because the students who study this case are themselves in, or soon will be in, the recruiting process, they are in a unique position to design promotions that would appeal to students like themselves. They should be able to develop some creative promotions that would catch college students' attention and communicate Enterprise's message.

5. What marketing recommendations would you make to Enterprise to guide its growth?

As the case ends, Andy Taylor raises the general question of how Enterprise can continue to grow without losing its focus. In some sense, this is a good problem to have, and it is one that all successful, rapidly growing organizations face.

Enterprise is clearly focused on the local, home-city market. Exhibit 2 indicates how strong a position it holds in this market. If 27 percent of the $14.62 billion rent-a-car market falls in the replacement market, as part III suggests, then the replacement market is $3.947 billion. If we take Enterprise's estimated U.S. revenue of $2.61 billion and multiply that by the estimate that 78 percent of that revenue is in the replacement market, we get an estimate of $2.036 billion in replacement revenue. Dividing this amount by the total market estimate ($3.947) yields a market share estimate of 51.6 percent. Students will notice that if Enterprise grows another 25 percent in 1997, it will have to add $509 million in replacement revenue

($2.036 billion times .25). This amount is larger than the revenue of any other home-city competitor. If it bought the Ford *and* Chrysler replacement operations, it would pick up $490 million in revenue. This should point out for students what a challenge it is to grow continuously at a 25 percent rate!

One way to attack this question is to use the **growth strategies matrix**.

Market Penetration: Some students will suggest that Enterprise will have to increase the number of days it rents each car or its revenue per car. That is, it will have to increase each car's productivity. Dividing total revenue listed for each company in Exhibit 3 by the number of cars listed for each company yields a rough revenue-per-car estimate. Note that this revenue would include the revenue from the sale of cars as well as the rental revenue. This calculation shows that Enterprise earned $8,286 of revenue per car. Two other companies earned more, U-Save at $8,518 and Advantage at $8,444. Super Star earned $8,190. Ford and Chrysler systems earned the least at $5,937, and Snappy earned $6,452. This analysis suggests that Enterprise is doing a pretty good job, at least relative to other players in the industry. Because rental and sales revenue is mixed here, we can't estimate what percentage of the time vehicles are rented, but we would estimate that Enterprise's utilization rate is at least in line with the industry.

In the replacement market, it may be hard for Enterprise or others to increase the average rental period (12 days in the exhibit), because the insurance companies want that period to be short and will keep pressure on body shops and others to get the cars fixed and back to the owners. Thus, to grow, the companies must find more people who will rent from them—implying that they must take share from other companies to the extent they want to grow faster than the rate of growth in the number of accidents.

It may also be difficult to increase revenue by raising prices. Insurance companies will keep pressure on suppliers to keep prices low. If insurance companies want to negotiate national contracts with replacement car suppliers, they have considerable bargaining power. It would also be difficult for Enterprise to raise prices in markets where Hertz and other major competitors operate.

The increased advertising program recommended above should help Enterprise increase sales to current markets. However, students should see that it will be difficult for Enterprise to realize its growth goals through market penetration.

Market Development: Exhibit 2 indicates that about 15 percent of Enterprise's revenue is from the business and leisure markets, with this revenue split evenly between the two. Although the business and leisure markets represent 73 percent of the total rental market (Exhibit 2), we do not know the breakdown between the airport and home-city markets. We would expect that the majority of these markets would be in the travel sector. But both represent opportunities for Enterprise. The case indicates that the company has been developing the small business and discretionary' markets.

Students should see that the average rental period in these two markets will probably be significantly less than the average 12-day rental period in the replacement market. This means more transactions per day of rental. Although Enterprise's information system can certainly handle this increased workload, the additional transactions may add significantly to the workload of branch personnel. The question will be whether or not the differing transaction patterns will work within Enterprise's established procedures. One advantage of discretionary rentals is that they are usually for a fixed period of time, like a day or a week. Thus, these rentals make it easier to forecast the availability of cars for future rentals. With replacement rentals, the repair may take longer than expected or there may be unforeseen delays. Therefore, there is uncertainty as to when the customer will return the car.

The increased advertising recommended above can help to develop the discretionary market as more people learn about Enterprise's nearby locations and its interest in discretionary rentals. Students will recommend that these types of rentals should become the focus of some advertising, both local and national. Branch personnel will probably have to continue to develop the local business market through personal sales calls. Students who have analyzed the case more carefully will see that targeting the discretionary market means that Enterprise needs to have office locations that are visible and easily accessible. This may require locations that cost more than Enterprise's traditional out-of-the-way locations.

Some students will suggest that Enterprise enter the airport/traveler market. Such a move does not fit with Enterprise's cost structure or the nature of its work. In such settings, its employees are stuck behind the counter. Further, because of the entrenched competition, attacking this market would be expensive, and Enterprise would have no competitive advantage.

Finally, students should identify entering international markets as a significant growth opportunity. The case mentions that Enterprise has an "international" headquarters in St. Louis, but does not present information about the company's international operations. Enterprise operates in Canada and England and is developing operations in Europe. Students will recommend that it pursue these markets as a primary area for growth. Although laws, legal systems, and business environments will be different in these markets, anywhere there are cars, there are accidents. Enterprise has a well-developed business system that should be exportable.

Product Development: The next matrix cell provides for offering new products to current markets. A possibility that the teaching notes mentioned earlier is for Enterprise to offer trucks for rental. Although this fits with its local market focus, other major players are already in this market. To enter would require a major capital investment and a head-to-head battle. It is not clear that Enterprise would have any competitive advantage in this market. The same is true for the equipment rental market. In addition, the equipment rental business requires maintenance of an expensive inventory and employees who are familiar with complicated equipment.

Diversification: At the time of the case, there was much turmoil in the automotive sales market. Car Max, AutoNation, and others were applying the superstore concept to used-car sales, while Wayne Huizenga was pursuing a vertical integration strategy that included purchasing new car dealers to go with superstore used-car lots and rent-a-car companies. These options are open to Enterprise. but it is difficult to see it pursuing such moves given its focused, conservative culture.

Of course, many options are available in the area of unrelated diversification, targeting new markets with new products in businesses unrelated to the rent-a-car business.

Students can make many possible recommendations, but it seems most likely that Enterprise will continue to pursue penetration of the replacement market while broadening its efforts in the home-city business and discretionary markets and pursuing opportunities in international markets.

Teaching Suggestions

This is an excellent case for field research by student groups. Groups can study the entire automobile sales market to analyze events in that market. They can also visit local companies that focus on the replacement market in order to study how these companies work and their relative strengths and weaknesses.

Enterprise Rent-A-Car has also indicated that it will cooperate with instructors by having representatives visit classes and participate in the class discussion. Instructors who want to have an Enterprise employee visit their class can call 1-888-WWW-ERAC and ask for the General Manager or Regional Vice President.

To begin the class discussion, instructors may wish to survey the class to see if anyone has had experience with Enterprise or knows someone who works for the company.

Epilogue

One step the company has taken is to develop a new print advertising campaign to target college students. Samples of the ads are included with this teaching manual. The ads address characteristics of the type of people the company is seeking with the idea that people with those characteristics will then want to talk with Enterprise. The ads are designed to imply a fun, innovative atmosphere. Enterprise will run the ads in targeted colleges' newspapers and include them in other printed material. The ads also advertise Enterprise's website, where it can also offer additional information of interest to job seekers.

CASE 1-2
COCA-COLA (JAPAN) COMPANY*

Synopsis:

The Coca-Cola (Japan) Company (CCJC) had become the industry leader in the beverage market in Japan in improving quality standards and introducing new products. Their strategy in forming strategic alliances with powerful Japanese corporations resulted in soaring sales and dominance in the market. CCJC's success was also attributed to its direct marketing approach and the company's distribution system of independent local franchisees.

The soft drink industry was highly competitive, but CCJC also had to compete with other beverages. Japan was becoming more health conscious, and consumers were interested in nutritious food and beverage products. In addition to soft drinks, CCJC produced juice drinks, ready-to-drink coffee, water, and an isotonic drink.

Arthur Grotz had to decide whether he should recommend that Coca-Cola launch a ready-to-drink tea in Japan. Tea was considered a traditional Japanese beverage, and there were many competitors in the tea market. CCJC had been successful with its other product lines, but there was the risk that canned tea might be a passing fad.

Video summary:

The video begins with a little background on when Coca-Cola entered the Japanese market and how it became Japan's soft drink of choice. The video discusses the company's "multi-local" partner strategy, its adoption of local business and social practices, and the tailoring of its products to meet Japan's needs. The company's advertising strategy is also discussed and several different commercials are shown throughout the video. While not about the canned tea market specifically, the video provides the student with a clear image of Coca-Cola's marketing strategy in Japan. The video is around nine and a half minutes long and can be used either at the beginning or end of class.

Teaching/learning objectives:

As one of the first cases in the Cravens, Lamb, Crittenden book, the case can be used to highlight many different marketing issues which, as marketers, we must address in today's business environment.

Specifically, the case:

- focuses upon a large successful American company and its international marketing pursuits,
- shows the importance of distribution in expanding into international markets,
- highlights the long-term impact one marketing decision can have on a brand manager's career, and
- shows the importance of the implementation plan in making a "go" decision.

---

* This teaching note was prepared by Victoria L. Crittenden, Laura Gow, Stephanie Hillstrom, and David Angus, Boston College, as an aid to instructors using the case, "Coca-Cola (Japan) Company." Revised 1998.

Discussion Questions:

1. Why has Coca-Cola (Japan) been successful in the Japanese market?
2. Is the marketing approach of CCJC different from the marketing approach of Coca-Cola in the United States? How?
3. How is the Japanese beverage market segmented?
4. What is the market potential for a tea product in Japan?
5. Should Coca-Cola enter the tea market in Japan? Why/why not?

Analysis:

The decision in the case is whether or not Coca-Cola (Japan) Company should launch a ready-to-drink canned tea. The company already offers a variety of drink products in the Japanese beverage marketplace. Arthur Grotz, brand manager, must make a go (introduce)/no go (do not introduce) recommendation to his boss. Thus, the problem/decision statement is the central focus of the case. As well, there really is not a need for brainstorming various alternatives for Grotz. He might need alternative new product ideas later on in his career at CCJC, but this case focuses specifically on the tea market entry decision. However, the instructor should push students hard on which type of the tea they recommend (e.g., oolong, green, black) that CCJC introduce (assuming a go recommendation is made).

1. Why has Coca-Cola (Japan) been successful in the Japanese market?

This question is consistent with the situation audit step in case analysis. The expectation should be that students would conduct a SWOT analysis of CCJC since there is enough information provided in the case to at least touch upon strengths, weaknesses, opportunities and threats. A sample SWOT analysis is provided in Exhibit TN–1.

While some students may attempt ratio analysis here, case information highlights the financial strength of Coca-Cola both domestically and abroad (case Exhibits 1, 5, and 6 as well as percent of profit information at the end of the CCJC section).

Questions 2 and 3 aid the student in analyzing the go/no go decision situation faced by Arthur Grotz. Question 4 helps in getting a handle on an important criterion used in making the decision.

2. Is the marketing approach of CCJC different from the marketing approach of Coca-Cola in the United States? How?

Coca-Cola, as a worldwide giant, was successful at "transporting" its U.S. leadership qualities to the Japanese market. The company used the same direct marketing approach and distribution system in Japan that helped make the company successful in the U.S. Another similarity between Coca-Cola (U.S.) and Coca-Cola (Japan) was the company's ability to almost become part of each country's "lifestyle." Students will, no doubt, remember Coca-Cola's "New Coke" entry in the U.S. They will recall the consumer's overwhelming concern regarding the product's place in U.S. culture and tradition. It seems that CCJC worked hard to penetrate the Japanese lifestyle and culture as well.

Probably the one major difference in the company's international approach to doing business has been the notion of partnerships with local companies. Strategic alliances (e.g., Mitsui, Mitsubishi, and Kikkoman) were critical to CCJC developing an understanding of the Japan marketplace and to the acceptance of CCJC by Japanese consumers. Another difference might be the way products are sold in Japan via the vending machine. CCJC probably placed more effort in vending machine sales (e.g., machine location and service) than Coca-Cola in the U.S.

Understanding these similarities and differences should help the student have a better understanding of Coca-Cola both in the U.S. and in Japan.

3. How is the Japanese beverage market segmented?

Market segmentation is occasionally confused with product segmentation. There may be a tendency for some students to suggest the product segments found in the Japanese Beverage Market section of the case: colas, other carbonated drinks, juices, teas, coffees, waters, and sports drinks. When (assuming it does) this "segmentation" approach is identified, it is important to write the segments on the board—a little separate from other approaches. Once you feel that the class has done a good job of identifying various approaches, it is important to talk about the difference between market segmentation and product segmentation. In essence, these various product categories are in response to the needs of the market segments. (The same holds true if students identify product types of tea such as oolong, black, and green.)

The case is not clear on the various market segmentation approaches in Japan. However, our knowledge about markets would suggest that there would probably be segmentation according the four major categories of variables: demographic, geographic, psychographic, and behavioralistic.

Regarding demographic, age and ethnicity might be two means of segmenting the market. For example, younger or newer tea drinkers may have a preference for a different kind of tea than older tea drinkers. Or, common heredity or cultural tradition may lead to differences among the Japanese population.

People in different parts of the country may prefer certain types of tea as well (geographic segmentation). We can safely assume some geographic segmentation with the 17 regions in the Japanese market. Additionally, the notation that 75 percent of the Japanese population are urban dwellers suggest some reason for segmentation.

Psychographic segmentation is definitely evident in the Japanese market. Lifestyle is apparent in the Japanese consumer's concern with health issues.

Behavioralistic segmentation is apparent in the brand loyalty evidenced through market share and growth statistics. It is also evidenced in the tea market through the benefit expectations of consumers regarding the possible medicinal benefit of tea made from the bark of the tochu tree.

4. What is the market potential for a tea product in Japan?

Students can calculate market potential through various approaches. Unfortunately, the approaches do not converge on the same final numbers. However, students need to know that this is not uncommon in marketing and their job is to be able to justify why each of the various calculations makes sense.

Some students may calculate market potential using vending machine information. There are 2,000,000 vending machines selling canned drinks. Assuming 10,000 cans were sold per vending machine and 50 percent of beverage sales were through vending machines, the Japanese beverage market is equal to around 40,000,000,000 cans (2,000,000 x 10,000 x 2). The tea market is estimated to be nine percent of the market or 3,600,000,000 cans (40,000,000,000 x .09). Potential could be approximated at 360,000,000,000 yen (3,600,000,000 x 100 yen) or US$2.5 billion. Total tea market could be broken down according to oolong, black, and green teas since market share for each is given.

Some students may simply say that the Japanese beverage market is worth US$18,000,000,000 and that tea is nine percent of that market which would be equal to around US$1.6 billion (US$18,000,000,000 x .09 = US$1,620,000,000).

Some might take the above calculation and attempt to forecast CCJC's potential share of this market. While CCJC is not in the tea market, we do know that the company has around 10 percent of the non-cola, non-carbonated market. Assuming the same market share for tea, a prediction of US$162,000,000 can be made (US$1,620,000,000 x .10 = US$162,000,000).

Some students may attempt to calculate the market size in terms of number of tea drinkers. Assuming age and urban are important segmentation variables, market potential might be:

123,000,000 (country population) x .66 (2:1 ratio of adults to children and assuming children do not drink tea) = 81,000,000 adults [using 123,000,000 rather than 81,000,000 would tend to overstate the number of tea drinkers in Japan]

81,000,000 adults x .75 (urban dwellers) = 61,000,000 adult/urban consumers

61,000,000 x .09 (tea market) = 5,490,000 tea drinkers

5,490,000 x .57 = 3,129,000 oolong tea drinkers

5,490,000 x .31 = 1,702,000 black tea drinkers

5,490,000 x .12 = 659,000 green tea drinkers

The case states that Suntory held about 50 percent of the oolong tea market. Even assuming that Ito En Ltd. held 50 percent of the green tea market and Kirin held 50 percent of the black tea market, there would still be 2,745,000 tea drinkers for CCJC to focus upon. However, one would have to wonder about the loyalty of tea drinkers to particular brands and if there would be switchers among such consumers. If so, there are over 5,000,000 tea consumers available.

Regardless of the approach, market potential must be one of the major criteria used in making a decision as to whether or not CCJC should introduce a ready-to-drink tea in Japan.

5. **Should Coca-Cola enter the tea market in Japan? Why/why not?**

Students should be asked the pros and cons of entering the tea market. Responses to questions 2–4 are important issues that should arise in the pros/cons analysis. Exhibit TN–2 provides an example of a pro/con listing. Students should also be asked about important criteria used in making the go/no go decision. These might include market potential, profitability, company objectives regarding international expansion and market leadership, and impact on Grotz' future. Market potential tends to stand out in this case as a major issue.

Students recommending a tea entry should also recommend whether CCJC introduce an oolong, a green, a black tea, or a Western-style tea. Students supporting a no go recommendation should be pushed hard on the "why not" component of the question as well as have some ideas as to what CCJC should be doing.

Teaching the Case:

The case is an easy one for class discussion probably because the students are so familiar with the company and its products. Whether the opening approach is a "What do you recommend?" or the more traditional situation assessment, the instructor has to be careful to balance the discussion of Coca-Cola, the giant international company, and Coca-Cola (Japan). Making certain that Question 2 of the discussion questions is addressed early on helps provide this necessary balance.

Since the analysis of various alternatives is not the main focus in the case, one may find it too easy to skip over issues. However, the importance of this decision to the decision maker's future suggests that a thorough and thoughtful analysis must be conducted and brought out in the classroom. As well, the case provides the opportunity to show the importance of an implementation plan as part of the recommendation. Students should be pushed hard here.

The video is about Coca-Cola (Japan) in general and can be used at the beginning of class to provide students with visuals regarding the company's Japanese business. Or, the video can be used at the end of the case discussion to help provide closure on the case discussion. Either way tends to work well.

Students tend to get confused when playing around with the numbers. The $18 billion figure refers to *retail* sales. However, other dollar amounts relate to CCJC numbers—not the retail dollar amount. Gross sales in Japan refer to sales of the soda in stores and vending machines. However, Japan's profits include the concentrate price that is about four times higher than in the U.S. and currency fluctuations. The end result is that Coke earns around 20% of its total worldwide profits on only 6-7% of its volume. So, the numbers are not real straightforward. The professor might want to warn students in advance so they don't get caught up doing calculations and ignoring the real issue in the case.

Epilogue:

In March 1988, CCJC launched two new tea products—"Saryu Sai Sai," an oolong tea in a PET 1500 container and "Kocha Kaden," an English tea with milk in a 250 milliliter can. These products have been very successful and have captured 16 percent of the market in just five years.

The decision was based on several factors. First, since the 15th and 16th centuries, there have been changes in consumer perception about tea. Before, tea preparation was considered a ceremonial event of which boiled tea leaves were a major part. Now, with a global economy and technological advances, many aspects of cultural life have been redefined. This was illustrated in expanded consumer perception of appropriate drinking occasions, hence Japan's acceptance of canned tea. Second, ready-to-drink tea was an emerging trend that complimented the health focus of the Japanese consumers. Teas, known for their medicinal qualities, provided a nutritional, yet great tasting, alternative to colas and waters offered in most vending machines. Third, it offered a quick alternative for busy people who don't have the time to boil tea leaves in water. Additionally, the decision to diversify into the tea market fit in with the Coca-Cola Company's strategic mission to create value by "developing new products to fulfill changing consumer desires, always seeking to make what we can sell, instead of merely trying to sell what we make."[1] With CCJC's powerful distribution system, trademark, and local partners, it was able to act quickly to meet changes in consumer demand.

By 1996, the Japanese retail beverage market was worth US$26 billion. Tea and coffee sales in Japan were experiencing strong growth in 1996, while carbonated drink sales were flat. Coca-Cola Japan expanded its distribution to include Canada Dry Ginger ale Perilla. The ale is made specifically for the Pacific market by adding a red-leaf plant—Perilla. The drink is light pink and is considered an exotic drink. Also, CCJC declared war on generic sodas by offering lower-priced soft drinks.

---

[1] Source: Coca-Cola Company Annual Report, 1993.

Exhibit TN–1 SWOT Analysis

Strengths

- strategic alliances with Mitsui, Mitsubishi, Kikkoman
- direct sales distribution system removed layers of expense and inefficiency, generated activity in the local economy vis-a-vis the competition
- industry leader in established quality standards
- industry leader in new product development
- understanding of business implications of Japanese culture
- established Japanese-style distribution system of independent local franchises
- economies of scale and scope which facilitate CCJC's ability to provide Japanese bottlers with syrups and concentrates, distribution channels, and a promotional program at a lower cost than bottlers could do
- command of cola market
- dominance of soft drink market since 1965
- profitability
- public image (helping citrus farmers, forming strategic alliances with Japanese companies)
- increasing revenues (1986-1987)

Weaknesses

- late entry to tea market
- behind the technology curve in production of quality canned teas
- long decision process as to whether to enter market
- increasing COGS (1986-1987)
- increasing SG&A (1986-1987)
- decreasing income (1986-1987)
- touting electrolyte replacement drinks as health drinks could draw criticism

Opportunities

- strong Yen versus dollar
- growing Japanese economy
- increasing standard of living in Japan, leading to increased consumption and desire for higher-margin products
- new niche market developing—"health conscious consumers" demanding healthier products, possibly willing to pay more for healthier products
- new products in the non-cola carbonated drink market

Threats

- government regulations
- trade restrictions
- increasing health consciousness of Japanese consumer, leading to decreased consumption of soft drinks
- increased competition from companies entering "health conscious" segment of the market
- competitive environment (other soft drinks and beverages)
- Japanese citizens "guarding purse strings" despite healthy economy
- cannibalization of flagship product
- pressure on capacity of bottlers may hurt quality, image of Coca-Cola's existing product line

Exhibit TN–2   Pros/Cons of Entering The Ready-to-Drink Tea Market

Pros

- new product development
- recent boom in consumer spending with increasing higher standard of living
- increasing health consciousness of Japanese consumer, leading to decreased consumption of soft drinks, which appeared to be gaining momentum into the 1980s
- respond to increasing competition from the "proliferation of nutritious food and beverage products"
- past success in the ready-to-drink caffeinated beverage market with *Georgia*, a ready-to-drink coffee
- past success with new product introduction overall
- very limited presence in the non-carbonated drink market (10%) relative to the cola (90%) and non-cola (60%) carbonated drink market—there is room for growth
- understanding of business implications of Japanese culture
- network of Japanese-owned bottlers, if used to produce and distribute the new tea product, would help to allay concerns that a large American corporation was desecrating a Japanese tradition—the tea would be produced and distributed by Japanese bottlers.
- increasing revenues (1986-1987)
- profitability
- deep pockets—worst case scenario (attempt and failure in the ready-to-drink tea market would not ruin Coca-Cola Japan as long as relationships with bottlers remained strong)
- economies of scale, scope which facilitate CCJC's ability to provide Japanese bottlers with syrups and concentrates, distribution channels, and a promotional program at a lower cost than bottlers
- strong Yen versus dollar—may be able to underprice
- growing Japanese economy
- increasing standard of living in Japan, leading to increased consumption and desire for higher-margin products
- new niche market developing—"health conscious consumers" demanding healthier products, possibly willing to pay more for healthier products
- new products in the non-cola carbonated drink market
- increased competition from companies entering "health conscious" segment of the market
- competitive environment (other soft drinks and beverages)

Cons

- late entry to tea market
- behind the technology curve in production of quality canned teas
- If Coca-Cola is going to act, they must act now. Even if they do, they may have to incur losses on the product for several years. Success in ready-to-drink coffee market, in which there was less competition, was attained only after five years of consideration and several years in the market.
- the ready-to-drink tea market could be a fad—any losses up front may not be recovered

- increasing COGS (1986-1987)
- increasing SG&A (1986-1987)
- decreasing income (1986-1987)
- Japanese citizens "guarding purse strings" despite healthy economy
- may incur government regulations because of strong traditions behind tea consumption
- diversification may negatively impact bottlers if their capacity is exceeded
- pressure on capacity of bottlers may hurt quality, image of Coca-Cola's existing product line
- It may be difficult for Coca-Cola's network of independent bottlers to be equipped with the new technology used by Ito En. Assuming that the technology is not proprietary, the availability of plant space, personnel, and capital could preclude adoption of the technology by the entire bottler network. Without the new technology, quality would suffer vis-a-vis Ito En. With the new technology, distribution might suffer.
- cannibalization of flagship product

CASE 1-3
BATTERED WOMEN FIGHTING BACK!*

Synopsis:

The leading cause of injury to women in the United States was domestic violence. Domestic violence was a crime which usually involved the assault of a woman by a man who was her spouse or boyfriend. There were many shocking statistics that proved domestic violence to be a serious issue. Certain events in the 1990s challenged some of the prior negative conceptions and assumptions about this issue.

Many charitable organizations were available to victims of domestic violence through funding by various communities and corporations. Massachusetts alone had many resources available to women, and there were several resources on the national level.

Stacey Kabat was the woman behind Battered Women Fighting Back!, a Boston based education and advocacy group. The program's main focus was to create educational programs designed to end domestic violence in society and to promote human rights for everyone. Although this program received local and national recognition, Stacey wanted to obtain funding for resources and educational programs across the United States, and maybe even the world. She had to figure out a way to get information to the people who needed it most. Stacey also wanted to market BWFB!'s idea that domestic violence was not just a women's issue, but a human rights violation.

Video Available:

"Defending Our Lives" by Cambridge Documentary Film Company tells the disturbing true stories of severely abused women who fought back. This Oscar winning documentary focuses on four imprisoned women who killed their abusers. These women tell about the abuse they suffered and their current situation because of it. The video itself brings to light the severity of the social problem of domestic violence in American society while giving a scary glimpse into the lives people who have lived it. The video runs approximately 30 minutes.

"Defending Our Lives" by Cambridge Documentary Film Company is available in most university libraries. If your university does not have the film, it can be purchased for $150 or rented for $45 from: Cambridge Documentary Film Company, PO Box 390385, Cambridge, MA. 02139. The phone number is (617) 484-3993.

Teaching/Learning Objectives:

BWFB! is a case about a nonprofit organization. As such students get a good, broad picture (when combined with for-profit cases) of the breadth of marketing. As an early discussion in the class, the case allows the student to get a better understanding of the:

---

* This teaching note was prepared by Victoria L. Crittenden, Stephanie Hillstrom, and David Angus, Boston College, as an aid to instructors using the case, "Battered Women Fighting Back!." Revised 1998.

- nature of nonprofit organizations and the issues such groups must confront,
- need for good marketing even when the bottom-line is not profit,
- notion of what/who a customer is,
- interplay between culture of the people who work in a company and the need for good business decisions,
- tangible and intangible nature of an organization's products, and
- the need for a good marketing plan regardless of organization classification.

Discussion Questions:

1. What is BWFB! as an organization? How is it doing?
2. What does "market" mean in terms of BWFB!? What/Who is the target market?
3. Does BWFB! face a competitive environment? How would you describe the organization's external environment? What is "unique" about BWFB!?
4. What is BWFB!'s product?
5. Put together a marketing program which addresses the marketing challenges identified by Stacey Kabat at the end of the case.

Analysis:

1. What is BWFB! as an organization? How is it doing?

Battered Women Fighting Back! is both a service organization and a nonprofit organization. While the organization is not affiliated with a national organization (i.e., there is not a national BWFB! group which oversees the Boston group), BWFB! is loosely affiliated with other local battered women groups in that referrals to BWFB! are made. As well, BWFB! can draw on the research and support provided by national, nonprofit battered women groups.

Students need to understand the difference between Battered Women Fighting Back! and many other battered women groups. BWFB! is an education and advocacy group which disseminates educational programs. The organization does not provide housing for battered women or counseling services. The case describes some other types of organizations which serve battered women. For example, *Brookline Women's Shelter* and *RESPOND* were shelters. *Community Services for Women* and *Services Against Family Violence* were largely counseling facilities. BWFB! sought to heighten community awareness of domestic violence, particularly amongst victims of abuse. BWFB! wanted victims to recognize that they were being victimized and that help was available.

BWFB! relies on donations/contributions for funding its operations. This is very similar to other nonprofits (e.g., religious organizations, youth groups, animal rights groups). This is very much unlike a business organization.

A class would be remiss in not discussing the heritage of Battered Women Fighting Back!. The history of the organization and its leader, Stacey Kabat, provide valuable information in achieving a better understanding of the organization. In addition to Stacey Kabat who had a personal interest in domestic violence (the daughter and granddaughter of battered women), the founders, themselves, were victims (and prisoners). As is typical in nonprofit organizations, the administrator(s) and workers (often volunteers) work for the "cause" or "belief" rather than being selected based on talent (e.g., workers in a business are hired due to expertise in certain areas). So, there is reason to believe that BWFB! is being run both strategically (Stacey Kabat) and operationally (three full-time, three part-time, and volunteers) by people who have a strong interest in domestic violence rather than by people trained/educated in making business-type decisions. One has to wonder if dedication can supplant business training.

Regarding how BWFB! is doing, the local and national recognition is phenomenal. The organization must be well-run given the ranking by *Financial World* in 1993, and one of the organization's tangible products won an Oscar. However, it is difficult to say whether the organization should be receiving more funds that its $150,000 budget shows. If so, then BWFB! is not doing as well as it should. Also, there may be some concern regarding the organization's goals and strategy. Does the group have any specific goals and objectives? What strategies are in place?

A situation analysis, such as a SWOT analysis (see exhibit TN-1 for an example), will aid students in evaluating BWFB! and how it is doing.

2. What does "market" mean in terms of BWFB!? What/Who is the target market?

This is crucial to the marketing challenges faced by Stacey Kabat and BWFB!. There are essentially two markets.

Stacey Kabat would probably say that her most important market is the victims of domestic violence (i.e., abused women). She wants to get her product (education) to these "consumers."

However, there are many who would say that Stacey's most important market is a subset of the general public—donors and potential donors. These are the people who provide the funding so that Stacey and BWFB! has educational information to provide users of this service organization. Without funding and support (time, spokesperson), the organization does not have anything to offer the women who need help.

This is a common scenario in nonprofit organizations, and one which causes marketing to be extremely useful as well as tricky. BWFB! essentially has two broad markets. Victims of abuse are targets for BWFB!—a target market which BWFB! would like to see shrink. Donors are another market. Stacey Kabat needs to determine who this target market is—anyone who can give money and/or time? celebrities? college administrators? social workers? the wealthy?

Students may tend to overlook the fact that BWFB! needs places to disseminate its materials. Thus, high schools, universities, churches, physician's offices, and libraries are also part of the group's "market." These seem to be the BWFB!'s retailers or channels of distribution.

There may be another market which BWFB! needs to serve—abusers themselves. Abusers might also benefit from information about domestic abuse. Should BWFB! be targeting them? Should monies be allocated to this market? Or, is the money better spent (i.e., achieving the organization's objectives) on victims and/or those who can give?

The discussion surrounding BWFB!'s market should be very interesting. It is a unique way to look at markets and target groups. Be careful—it can also become confusing to students.

3. **Does BWFB! face a competitive environment? How would you describe the organization's external environment? What is "unique" about BWFB!?**

BWFB! definitely faces a competitive environment! Someone with money has to first decide whether to buy items with the money or donate the money to a charitable group. Time-wise, a person must choose amongst employment, volunteering, or recreational activities.

Regarding donations, BWFB! faces competition from any receiver of donated funds (550,000 such organizations in 1993, a 50% increase from 1985 and a 71% increase from 1980). For example, a donor has to decide how to allocate his/her dollars and time. Should the money/time go to a church? a health-related association (cancer, heart, diabetes)? an animal rights group? a youth sports group? should the money/time be split amongst a number of groups?

Then, naturally BWFB! competes with other domestic violence organizations for money and volunteers (over 30 just in the Boston area).

From the recipient's point of view, the victim can choose amongst several domestic violence organizations. It is doubtful, however, that a battered women's organization would say that it is competing for users of its services.

4. **What is BWFB!'s product?**

BWFB! created and disseminated educational programs designed to eradicate domestic violence and promote human rights for everyone. So, its product is an intangible one of education. The education, however, came about through the group's program, "Peace in the World Begins at Home." This program consisted of two tangible items: the Oscar-winning documentary and a booklet.

5. **Put together a marketing program which addresses the marketing challenges identified by Stacey Kabat at the end of the case.**

The following issues must be addressed in a marketing program for BWFB!:

> What are the objectives ? (e.g., decrease domestic violence, frame domestic violence as a human rights violation, obtain funding, take the program international)
>
> Who/what is the target market(s)?
>
> What is the product? (Is the "Peace in the World Begins at Home" program enough? Is this program what BWFB! is really marketing to its donors?)
>
> How should BWFB!'s product(s) be distributed?
>
> Is price a component of the marketing program at BWFB!?
>
> How can/should marketing communication be used most effectively? (e.g., Would fear appeals work?)
>
> How will Stacey Kabat know if BWFB! is a success?

Teaching the case:

The case tends to generate a high level of excitement if the class is allowed to first discuss BWFB! in general, domestic violence in general, and nonprofit organizations in general. Therefore, it is not an easy case for an opening of "What would you do?" Due to the nature of the organization (battered women), the issue may be particularly emotional for some in the class. Therefore, be very careful about cold-calling students. An instructor might unintentionally call upon someone who has been a victim or relative of a victim and place the person in an uncomfortable situation. Also, since the issue relates to women, it might be too easy to focus upon female students for discussion. Or, the reverse might be true in that the focus might be upon male students to avoid the chance of making a female uncomfortable. However, there has to be a balance of both male and female perspectives.

The video has been used successfully in the classroom. Since it is a very emotionally-involved video, users have found it works best to show the video to the class prior to the case discussion. This allows the students to see the real horror of domestic violence, yet not bring this horror into the case discussion in quite the same way. Rather, the lapse in time between seeing the video and then discussing the case lets the student bring back into focus the marketing issues Stacey Kabat wants to address. Doing both the video and case in the same class has tended to bring too many emotions into the case discussion. If it is necessary due to class timing to do both during the same session, be sure to provide a break between the video and discussion.

Epilogue:

BWFB! is very much involved, currently, in the issues the case addresses. However, two items are occurring at this time. One, the nonprofit is in the process of trying to add several well-known celebrities to its board. Also, the organization is changing its focus so that it is not limited to battered women. For example, abused children have become a part of its educational concern. The organization has thus changed its name to "Peace at Home."

The issue of battered women continues to receive considerable attention. A focus of concern at the beginning of 1995 was the problem battered women were having in obtaining life, health, disability, property, and homeowners insurance. Protective legislation has been proposed at the national level to prohibit denying coverage or raising premiums for victims of domestic violence.[1]

The women featured in the *Defending Our Lives* video have had a lot happen to them since the release of the video. All the of inmates except Patricia Hennessy have been released. Many of the women have used their fame from the documentary to promote awareness of domestic violence. Two of the women have had trouble adjusting to life after this whole ordeal. Shannon Booker is back in prison for stealing a wallet which violated her parole. Patricia Allen committed assault with a deadly weapon and has since returned to prison. The remaining women have moved on with their lives and have avoided legal trouble.

---

[1] Judith Gaines, "Battered Women Finding Fewer Insurers," *The Boston Sunday Globe*, March 12, 1995, p. 1+.

Exhibit TN-1   SWOT Analysis

Strengths

- empathic leader who is a survivor of domestic violence
- connections with prominent and influential individuals in Hollywood, etc.
- committed staff
- accolades of *Financial World* magazine helpful in securing limited funding resources

Weaknesses

- funding
- business and marketing experience

Opportunities

- capitalize on fame—"spotlight" from Academy Award, *Financial World* endorsement, Reebok Human Rights Award4
- capitalize on timing—much political attention and press on issue of domestic violence
- the Violence Against Women Act (1994) which has allocated $1.8 billion over five years for police, prosecutors, shelters, communication efforts, and prevention programs
- $20 million in pro bono advertising provided by the Advertising Council
- much corporate attention being paid to those suffering from domestic violence, including on-sight workshops, phone hotlines, pledge money, art/education projects, shelters, and on-sight groups
- consolidation/coordination with agencies providing similar services
- lobby to obtain funding as a part of any health care reform which might evolve

Threats

- 550,000 501(c)(3) charities vying for the same fundraising dollars
- other agencies and services fighting domestic violence in the same areas as BWFB!
- denial by abusers and abused undermines efforts to fight domestic violence
- denial by abusers and abused undermines efforts to communicate atmosphere of urgency and increase fundraising
- backlash by ultraconservatives encouraging a "it's none of my business" attitude
- economy

CASE 1-4
WIND TECHNOLOGY*

Overview

Wind Technology was experiencing severe cash flow problems due to the slow development of its wind profiling market and was threatened by a possible cutoff of funds from the company's parent firm. Kevin Cage and Anne Ladwig developed a swivel strategy which calls for marketing a sub-component, the high voltage power supply (HVPS) which had been developed for the company's major product, a wind profiling system. The case is structured in such a way that students must evaluate the advantages and disadvantages of marketing the HVPS, with particular emphasis placed on selecting a target market, positioning the company and its HVPS, and developing a promotion strategy for the HVPS.

Teaching Objectives

Students should learn how to weigh equally risky decisions. This case illustrates the riskiness of the fast paced high-technology market where a firm's success is highly correlated with the organization's ability to anticipate the timing and nature of customers' future needs. Furthermore, the use of marketing sub-components as a survival strategy is creative.

Students should also learn that decisions about target market selection typically include trading off some desirable characteristics for others. The case is a realistic display of the complexities which arc commonplace in the industrial market, especially with respect to segment definition and the importance of synergy in product/markets.

Finally, students will be challenged to select a promotions mix in light of serious financial constraints.

Decisions

1. **Should Wind Technology compete in the HVPS market?**

A ½% market share objective corresponds to a $1.185M sale, goal (based on the estimated "attainable" market potential of $237M). After subtracting out production costs (70%), a gross margin of $355,500 could be realized if the objective is attained. After accounting for promotion costs (estimated at 10% of sales, or $118,500), the decision of whether or not roughly $237,000 in profit is a sufficient incentive for Wind Technology to pursue the market is a judgment call. We are not told what sort of revenue they are currently earning from their primary product line, the wind profiling system, nor what their immediate financial liabilities are. We are only told that there is a critical need to have some sort of a cash flow infusion. You might approach the judgment call of whether or not a profit of $237,000 is sufficient to offset the risk of entering a new mark t by asking students to list the relative advantages and disadvantages of entering the HVPS market.

---

* Teaching notes by case authors Ken Manning and Jakki Mohr

Advantages

1. Potential of $237,000 profit in first year.
2. Ability to tide company over until the wind profiling market develops.
3. If they pursue the customized option, no production costs will be incurred until the product is ordered. Given this fact, the only out-of-pocket expenses will be for promotion. Assuming they spend roughly $237,000 on promotion (roughly 10% of sales), many students will see the risk as minimal. (However, what is "minimal" will depend on the company's current cash flow situation, of which we are not apprised.)
4. The HVPS is already developed; Wind Technology merely needs a buyer/a market.

Disadvantages

1. Unfamiliar with the marketplace.
2. Start-up time involved in any new market, trying to gain awareness and trial behavior.
3. If the objective of ½% market share is not reached, may be wasting resources that the company cannot afford to waste.
4. They may want to concentrate their efforts where their strengths lie—not in the HVPS market.
5. Attempting to sell a product that already exists does not follow the marketing concept; in fact, it follows a reverse logic. (However, because the HVPS can be customized, this may not be the blatant violation of the marketing concept that it first appears.)
6. Given that no competitor appears to exceed a 3% market share, the product appears to be a commodity.

Given Wind Technology's need for a cash infusion and the time available ("slack") to the company in the short term (i.e., until the wind profiling market develops), it appears that the opportunity afforded by the HVPS situation is worth pursuing. Table 2 provides a more specific quantitative analysis.

2. Which segments should the company target? How should the company and its product be positioned?

One way for Wind Technology to overcome the disadvantages cited previously would be to select a market segment with which the company is familiar and in which customers are familiar with the company. While the growth rate in the target segment, the dollar potential, and amount of competition within each segment are also important considerations, to the extent that wind Technology already has a base level of customer contacts and name awareness the downside of entering the HVPS market can be minimized. Thus, because of the high degree of synergy with the radar systems target (the wind profiling system is a type of radar), Wind Technology should pursue this segment. Thus, they would need to capture 4.17% of the radar market [$1.185M/$28.44M]. The $28.44M is 12% of the total "attainable" HVPS market, $237M.

Students may suggest focusing on other segments, based on growth rates or the levels of customization and system integration. A solid argument can be made that the level of customization and system integration should be the primary basis for segmenting the market and selecting a target. Wind Technology cannot expect to successfully market its power supply as a standardized product. The main reasons for this are that HVPS users have a broad range of needs, and market trends indicate increasing levels of product customization being demanded in the future. It would be to Wind Technology's advantage to use its vast engineering talent and high-technology expertise *to* market a customized and/or system integrated HVPS. However, the product cannot be highly customized or integrated because the development of the product would likely require too large a portion of the firm's resources.

Positioning: Wind Technology's differential advantage rests upon its ability to provide technical expertise and superior product support. Given the importance of product quality and reliability to purchasers of HVPS products, Wind Technology should emphasize (1) its product's reliability and quality (rather than price), and (2) its interest in developing close, long-term, mutually beneficial relationships with customers.

3. What promotion strategy should be pursued?

Collateral materials are a must for business-to-business marketing. These materials, such as company/product brochures, aid in moving the customer along to an eventual sale. In creating the collateral material, the designer should seek to develop the desired positioning strategy.

The *public relations* option (i.e., sending out product announcements) is also a must for Wind Technology. Some of the inquiries generated by the product announcements may not match the description of the desired target customer, but as each contact is screened, valuable market information may be gathered.

These contacts should be mailed a packet of collateral material. Those contacts that meet the description of the desired target customer (i.e., is in the radar target market) should also be followed up with a *telemarketing* call. Thus, Wind Technology should also hire an *inside salesperson.*

The firm should also undertake a *direct mail campaign.* Students may try to estimate the size of a mailing and the number of mailings to use. Focusing on the radar segment again, assuming a price of $6,500 per unit, the radar market has a potential of 4,375 units ($28.44M/$6,500). Assuming each customer site buys 3 units, about 1,458 (4,375/3) possible customers exist. Thus, a mailing of 1,500 may be sufficient for the market. Usually, more than one mailing is recommended, i.e., 2-3 mailings. Follow-ups to inquiries may include telemarketing.

Because the target segment selecting for the HVPS overlaps significantly with Wind Technology's target for their wind profiling systems, it may not be necessary to hire new field salespeople. When contacts with the wind profiling customers are made, the personnel can also provide information on the HVPS. The charge to the HVPS will be 10% of direct selling costs (estimated in the case to be $105,000), or $10,500. Not, however, that if a large number of potential HVPS customers emerge, the substantial increase in customer contacts could strain the capacity of existing personnel. In any case, the hiring of field salespeople is not immediately necessary, given the overlap in the HVPS radar target market with Wind Technology's existing customer base.

Trade shows should be visited in order to gather market information, but not used to exhibit the power supply due to cost (unless a radar-specific show is available). During the initial phase, these shows will be valuable tools for gathering customer and competitor information.

These tools above are the minimal promotional activities necessary to introduce the product, yet they do not expose the company to a high level of risk (investment). Table 1 summarizes these expenses. Increased publicity efforts might take the form of loaning HVPS to a university or research center.

Many students will suggest advertising in trade journals. However, the only journal that matches the radar target is the *Weatherwise* publication, and this includes hobbyist readers Given the wasted coverage and low impact, a direct mail campaign would make more sense.

Table 1   Suggested Promotion Budget—Year 1

Collateral Materials	$27,5000
Public Relations	500
Direct Mail:	
List	5,000
Mailing #1	7,500
Mailing #2	7,500
Inside Sales	50,000
Direct Selling Costs	10,500
Trade Show Travel Expenses	10,000
TOTAL	$118,500

Table 2   Pro forma HVPS Income—Years 1-3

	Year 1	Year 2	Year 3
Sales	$1,185,000	$1,323,645*	$1,478,511*
Production	829,500	926,551	1,034,958
Gross Margin	$355,500	$397,094	$443,553
Promotion	118,500	132,364	147,851
Pre-Tax Profit	$237,000	$264,730	$295,702

*Growth in sales is 11.7%

CASE 1-5
THE METROPOLITAN MUSEUM OF ART*

Synopsis

The Metropolitan Museum of Art was established on April 13, 1870. The state of New York granted a charter to a group forming the corporation to operate the Museum. The City of New York owns the building which houses the Museum. The Metropolitan Museum is located on the east side of Central Park and the Cloisters, a branch museum, is located in Fort Tryon Park on the northern tip of Manhattan Island. The collections of the museum and the Cloisters include ancient and modern art from Egypt, Greece, Rome, the Near and Far East, pre-Columbian cultures, the United States, and European medieval art.

Activities at the museum include guided tours, lectures, gallery talks, concerts, educational programs, inter-museum loans, and permanent, temporary, and traveling exhibitions.

The Metropolitan ended the 1990-91 fiscal year with an operating deficit of $1.9 million, from a $2.6 million deficit in 1989-1990. The deficit can be largely attributed to a nine percent increase in expenditures. The absence of large-scale ticketed exhibitions or "blockbusters" also curtailed admissions revenue.

The museum is a non-profit, tax exempt [501 (c) (3)] organization which is supported by external and internal revenue sources. External sources include revenue from endowments, gifts, and governmental appropriations and grants. Internal sources include earnings from merchandising operations, auditorium rental, parking garage fees, restaurants, admissions, memberships, royalties and fees. Operating expenses stem from costs associated with curatorial departments, providing educational programs and libraries, providing public information, development activities, stocking merchandise inventories, and other administrative costs.

Because of declines in governmental support, recent changes in the tax code resulting in a decline in charitable giving, and rising levels of expenditures, the museum management must become more self sufficient by generating additional revenue. Revenue increases must come from both internal sources as well as from external corporate donors.

Teaching/Learning Objectives

1. To acquaint students with problems faced by non-profit organizations, especially in tough economic times.

2. To discuss and determine possible solutions to generate additional museum revenue from internal sources.

3. To discuss the market potential for museum retail sales and the competition from for-profit retailers.

4. To acquaint students with the difficulties faced in long-term planning when the allocation of funds from federal, state, and local governments is questionable.

---

* This teaching note was prepared by Marilyn M. Helms, Paula J. Haynes, and Tammy L. Swenson, The University of Tennessee at Chattanooga. Used by permission.

Answers to Discussion Questions

1. **What are the strengths of the Met?**

    a. Reputation

    b. Variety of collections

    c. City support and appropriations of funds to the museum

    d. Library of art

    e. Variety of educational activities offered

    f. Dual management style

    g. Changing exhibits

    h. Retail shops featuring items in the museum's collections

    i. Top tourist attraction in New York City

2. **What are the weaknesses of the Museum?**

    a. Financial Stability

    b. Competition from other area museums

    c. Competition from other area tourist attractions

    d. Tax law changes toward donations restricting revenues

    e. Pressures from non-tax-exempt shops and retailers

    f. Increased postal rates affecting costs of mail order operations

3. **What is the primary strategic issue in this case?**

The primary strategic issue for the museum is growth. The museum must develop creative and effective ways to sustain financial stability and growth in the changing environment.

4. **What should the museum do to prevent future deficits?**

It is evident the increasing costs of operation must be covered by revenue in order to provide the public continued access to the gallery and its offerings. The museum ended the 1990-91 fiscal year with an operating deficit of $1.9 million, from a $2.6 million deficit in 1989-90. Therefore, in order to prevent future deficits large-scale ticketed exhibitions or "blockbusters" must continue to be offered, cost controls must be put in place, and some auxiliary operations should be decreased, and possibly eliminated. Thus a combination strategy of growth in attractions and stability in cost control should be pursued.

5. **How could the retail operation be changed to increase the profit margin?**

The Met could examine the alternative of expanding its retail operations to other parts of the United States and abroad. In addition, placing items on consignment in other retail establishments to avoid lease costs for space, storage costs, and labor and overhead expenses could increase the profit margin and lower operating costs. Mail order offerings could be expanded and special promotions considered. However, increased emphasis on mail order operations must take into account increased postal rates and the threat of a broadened application of sales tax to mail order items. Mail order customers must be targeted effectively to minimize the number of non-ordering households receiving catalogs.

6. Should the museum try to lobby to protect its competitive position? Should supporters lobby to repeal the part of the 1986 Tax Reform Act as it relates to charitable donations?

Competitive position lobbying activities could backfire and draw undue attention to the Met's situation. However, lobbying against the Tax Reform Act would be in the museum's best interest. Part of the reason for the current financial situation is the limitations on tax deductions of art work donations imposed by TRA86.

Financial Ratio Analysis

	1991	1990	1989	1988	1987
Liquidity Ratios:					
Current Ratio	5.63	5.53	5.31	4.75	5.83
Quick Ratio	5.47	5.34	5.17	4.62	5.70
Activities Ratios:					
Inventory Ratio	0.786	0.650	0.698	0.828	0.914
Total Asset Utilization	0.023	0.022	0.019	0.023	0.020
Profitability Ratios:					
Profit Margin on Sales	(0.138)	(0.202)	0.322	0.096	0.408
Return on Investment	(0.003)	(0.004)	0.006	0.002	0.008
(No tax for non-profit organizations)					
Debt/Asset Ratio:	0.178	0.181	0.188	0.211	0.171

Strategic Alternatives

1. Continue large scale ticketed exhibitions.

    The museum should continue large-scale ticketed exhibitions. During the past ten years, each time these special events were offered, additional revenue was earned which helped to support *all* museum activities. For the year ended June 30, 1990, however, there were no large-scale ticketed events at the museum and total revenues from admissions dropped by 27 percent.

2. Increased use of a point-of-sale (POS) system in the retail operations.

    Increasing the use of a point-of-sale system in the retail operations may give the museum sufficient data to track the demand as well as inventory for products. This data could then be used to increase efficiency of the overall operations by automatically determining when orders and deliveries from suppliers need to be made. POS operations can also be used to gather data from all ten off-site stores on a timely basis.

3. Increase admission by at least $1 for each category.

    Depending on customer's price elasticity an admission increase of $1 for each category might not increase total revenue. In a slow economic environment, customers might choose other forms of cultural entertainment. A better option would be to concentrate on donations and reducing operating expenses in order to increase margins.

4. Train additional volunteers to act as tour guides to increase the volunteer pool.

As women continue to enter the workforce, it will become more and more difficult for non-profit organizations to find volunteers to work during the day. Because the museum depends on approximately 800 volunteers to lead tours of school children and other groups, part-time workers, retired people, or college students may become the primary source of volunteer support. Additionally, some type of self-guided tours might be used for school children with teachers receiving self-guided tour information prior to visiting the Museum.

5. Implement an organization wide cost reduction program to reduce core expenses

This is always a good solution, and particularly for non-profit organizations whose budgets are even more constrained. Though not-for-profit organizations face different competitive pressures than for-prof it companies, cost efficiencies are equally important to maintaining a viable market position.

6. Begin another nationwide public fund raising campaign.

The Met ran its first formal public fund raising campaign from 1982 to 1987 to raise $150 million. Even though the Museum met its goal, a deficit occurred during the 1989-90 and 1990-91 fiscal years. To offset future deficits other fund raising techniques have been employed (i.e., endowed chairs, corporate sponsorships, memberships, government grants, gifts, and admissions). However, these methods alone have not raised sufficient funds. Therefore, another nationwide campaign may be the only fund raising technique that will secure sufficient funds for the museum. Increases in the contribution required for each membership category may also increase revenue.

7. Expand retail operation to other parts of the United States and abroad.

Franchising is an option. Increasing the number of retail stores could add to revenue as well as to generate tourism interest for the museum. With the increasing postal rates, retail stores could be more competitive with mail order. Franchising could provide the means to achieve expansion without requiring substantial capital investment by the museum.

8. Place items on consignment in other retail establishments to avoid lease costs for space and storage as well as labor and overhead.

This alternative may risk losing control over the sales function as well as damaging the museum's reputation depending on the retail establishment and locations selected.

Epilogue

In the Wednesday, March 4, 1991 *Walll Street Journal* (p. A1) a proposed bill in the House of Representatives would create a procedure to value property before a donor gives it to charity. Backers of the tax bill, including the Met, say their goal is to keep costly audit disputes from arising years after donors take big deductions for gifts of major artwork. It would allow a process for donors and the Internal Revenue Service (IRS) to agree in advance on appraisal of artwork and collectibles valued at over $50,000. While donors may inflate their charitable deduction estates, they tend to undervalue their taxable bequests of art. The IRS has an Art Advisory Panel of outside experts to review these works of art.

CASE 1-6
CALIFORNIA VALLEY WINE COMPANY*

Synopsis

California Valley Wine Company (CVWC) has experienced diminishing sales and declining profitability in recent years (see case Exhibit 1). Maxwell Jones, new products/special project manager for CVWC must recommend a new product strategy to the vice president of marketing tomorrow, to the New Product Evaluation Committee by the end of the week, and to the Social Responsibility Committee sometime later.

After considering several possible products, Maxwell narrowed his alternatives to either a wine cooler or an inexpensive, so-called, dessert wine product. His recommendation, if accepted, is expected to shape the future of CVWC.

Both of the possible recommendations Jones is considering present serious potential problems. The wine cellar option entails entering a very competitive market and one in which demand appears to be flattening. The fortified wine option is problematic because the primary target market of inexpensive fortified wines is destitute alcoholics.

Case analysts will be challenged to evaluate the strengths and weaknesses of the two options and prepare a recommendation. Some may propose a third option such as not introducing either product.

Teaching/Learning Objectives

This case is intended to raise ethical issues in a marketing decision-making situation.

The case can be used to accomplish the following teaching/learning objectives:

1. To recognize the fundamental ethical issues involved in the marketing of alcoholic beverages.
2. To illustrate ethical concerns regarding the new product development process.
3. To demonstrate the difficulty of making ethical choices in a tough competitive and corporate environment.
4. To raise students' awareness of ethical issues regarding product, price, distribution, and promotion decisions.

Answers to Discussion Questions

1. What are the fundamental ethical issues in this case?

A fundamental ethical issue in this case is whether the manufacturing and marketing of the products is inherently unethical. The health problems associated with the product and its misuse or overuse are discussed in the case and widely known. The MADO/SADO groups bring this point out clearly. There are potential product liability questions with all kinds of alcoholic beverages.

---

* This teaching note is based upon a teaching note prepared by the author of the case, Professor Patrick F. Murphy, Notre Dame University. Used by permission.

Even if the students decide that it is proper to market alcoholic beverages and wine in particular, the question of responsibility to certain groups in our society is an issue here. For example, should all wine bottles contain a warning that in effect says that fetal alcohol syndrome is related to excessive consumption of wine and other alcoholic beverages? The case does bring out the point that Max is considering that the product should be used in moderation. What responsibility does CVWC have to consumers and the general public to promote responsible consumption of its product?

This issue should be discussed early in the class, but it should not be the focal point of discussion. The company probably does not have the option to go into another line of business and Max has the responsibility for developing a wine product in this case. Therefore, even though students may have concerns about the fundamental nature of alcoholic beverages, a decision has to be reached within the context of the products that they currently offer. The issues of product liability and responsibility are ones that the instructor should try to emphasize in this part of the case.

A second fundamental ethical issue is the production of dessert/fortified wine products. These products, as they are currently used in the *Wall Street Journal* article, have little socially redeeming value. They appear to be consumed by alcoholics and indigents. Therefore, the current target market is one that is definitely an underprivileged one.

Some students will correctly point out that the product inherently is not bad. That is, fortified wines have been used and consumed by the general public without any severe side effects. It is a question of whether the market needs or demands this kind of product. The past history discussed in the case could be emphasized in that fortified wines have a legitimate history within the wine industry. Some students will reject outright that the production of fortified wines is an option at all. The instructor should try to move them beyond this initial negative view of the product and force them to evaluate it from a marketing context. The target market, product, price, channel of distribution, and promotion should be examined. This moves us into the ethical questions pertaining to marketing in the case.

Students will probably not raise ethical issues with respect to the wine cooler option. The one situation that may come up with this option is the fact that wine coolers are pitched towards underage drinkers in certain instances. Max must be careful not to have this occur. The other issue that could surface in the discussion of wine coolers is that the potential for excessive consumption or overuse of wine coolers appears to be potentially relevant. Students may argue that wine coolers in their age group are consumed much the same as beer and the problems with moderation and consumption are definitely relevant. This may be a stimulating and interesting discussion-provoking technique for the instructor to use concerning the wine cooler option.

The major focus of the discussion will likely be on the dessert/fortified wine option. The target market of this product will likely draw some emotional discussion. The *Wall Street Journal* article gives a rather graphic description of the current target market. Also, the wine industry will likely come under some criticism by students for their current practice of disguising the manufacturer of these types of wine. If the dessert wine option is proposed by some of the students, they will likely argue that the company should stay away from the street drunks target market and go to the table wine consumer.

2. Identify and discuss product-related ethical issues raised in the case.

There are several important product issues that relate to the fortified wine option. The brand name, packaging and labeling all are relevant to this alternative. The brand name of "Warm Nights" gives the connotation the product would be pitched toward street people. Students will likely reject this option. A name that is descriptive, but yet overcomes the clutter of many existing wine brand names is a real challenge here. If the student tries to avoid the current target market for this product, they will likely suggest that the fortified wine not be bottled in the pint or breast pocket type bottle shape. By packaging the product in a larger container, they could discourage consumption by the street people market.

As mentioned above, the "doing business as" practice of the wine industry should likely be discussed as an ethical issue. Is it justifiable for Gallo and Canandaigua to protect their image by not putting their company name on the bottle? If not, what are the ramifications of requiring them to identify themselves on the product? This is a difficult question and one that students should be encouraged to think about and evaluate. Is it justifiable for large wineries to market these products if they know who actually consumes them?

3. **Identify and discuss pricing-related ethical issues raised in the case.**

The pricing of the fortified wine option could have a lot to do with the positioning of it. If the company decided to go after more of an upper income socio-economic group, they would likely prestige price this product. Even though this does not appear to be an expensive wine to manufacture, the company may want to avoid odd pricing and other low-price mechanisms to discourage the street people market from buying the product. If students do defend the practice of marketing the fortified wine to the broader market, they may argue that the product should be somewhat lower in price to gain a large market share. If students do take this position, the instructor should press them as to what ethical rationale they are using for making this judgment.

4. **Identify and discuss distribution-related ethical issues raised in the case.**

The question of where to distribute the fortified wine is likely to come up in the discussion. Mainstream retail stores like the Liquor Barn do not carry the existing fortified wine products. Could this relatively small manufacturer get retailers to carry a new wine product? If they want to go after a more upscale target market, it would be essential to get the product into more mainstream outlets. Are there other kinds of concerns that should be considered by CVWC in setting up distribution outlet possibilities for this product?

5. **identify and discuss promotion- and advertising-related issues raised in the case.**

How could the fortified wine product be promoted? Currently, it appears that the wine companies do not promote it in any way to the street drunks market. The students could be encouraged when they are reading and preparing the case to come up with promotion and advertising plans or messages for both of the product options here. This would cause them to focus on both strategic and ethical issues in coming up with messages to describe their product. It would be difficult for CVWC to compete with Bartles and James and Matilda Bay and other major wine coolers currently on the market. It appears that CVWC could not compete in the national television market effectively. Therefore, they would likely rely more on print media or regional media in promoting their product.

How could the fortified wine be positioned so that it appeals to a broad target market? Companies should be careful not to deceive the potential market into thinking that this product is different than it really is. Students should be encouraged to be creative and will likely come up with some good options for promoting either the wine cellars or the fortified wine alternative. The question of whether the company should include a warning or disclaimer such as "enjoy in moderation" or other health kinds of messages could be incorporated into a discussion of promotion here. Is it the responsibility of CVWC to advise the consumer on what would seem to be common sense?

Other questions that might follow these discussion questions or be used to direct a more traditional case analysis are as follows:

1. What is the major decision facing Maxwell Jones?
2. What alternatives should be considered?
3. What are the main criteria, including company objectives and ethical considerations, that should be used to evaluate alternatives?
4. Evaluate each alternative in terms of each criteria.
5. Advise Maxwell Jones.
6. Propose a plan to implement your recommendation.

A final set of question might focus on identifying the questions that might be raised by the vice-president of marketing, the New Product Evaluation Committee and the Social Responsibility Committee.

Answering these questions will be significantly more challenging than raising them.

Concluding Comments

One interesting way to involve the whole class in this case is to role play. Key roles include Maxwell Jones, the vice-president of marketing, the New Product Evaluation Committee and the Social Responsibility Committee. Students assigned to each role should be given at least a couple of days to prepare. The class begins with Jones making a presentation to the vice president. After about 15 minutes he then makes his presentation to the New Product Committee (a second person can assume Jones' role here). After about 15 minutes a third meeting between Jones (possibly a third person in the role) and the Social Responsibility committee can begin. This exercise will surely lead to an interesting and heated discussion among students.

Part 2

Market Orientation and Organizational Learning

CASE 2-1
NAVISTAR INTERNATIONAL TRANSPORTATION CORPORATION*

Synopsis:

Navistar was a manufacturer and marketer of medium and heavy trucks. There were six other competitors in the medium and heavy truck categories. Many of these manufacturers focused on ways to address the transportation industry's concerns, and at the same time introduced engineering advances to keep costs down. Truck manufacturers in the United States were also entering markets in Mexico, South America, and Chile.

Although Navistar was the largest truck manufacturer in the United States, Gary E. Dewel knew that Navistar had to focus on customer oriented actions to compete in the industry. Navistar struggled in the early 1980s, but new management in the early 1990s focused on reducing costs and increasing customer service in hopes of gaining a competitive advantage. The company had to come up with a way to combine these two strategies.

Video Summary:

The first half of the video provides detail about the company's micromarketing strategy and how Navistar found out its customer's needs and applied this knowledge to its technology. The video explains how Navistar's micromarketing program was structured to fit a dealer in Milwaukee. Also mentioned is what the company did to profile their product against the competition's product.

The second half of the video discusses what Navistar was doing to bring costs down, profits up, and increased customer satisfaction. The importance of meeting time requirements and the difficulties in doing so are also discussed. The Truck Order Processing System (TOPS), Electronic Data Interchange (EDI), and the Just In Time approach (JIT) are mentioned. Also stated are the future goals which will help Navistar maintain a competitive advantage in the marketplace.

The video is fairly long, with the first half about 12 and half minutes and the second half almost 11 and a half minutes. The detail and discussion provided by the speakers make the video well worth the class time used to view it.

Teaching/Learning Objectives:

The major objective of this case is to focus students' attention on the difficulty of formulating and implementing a customer focus/market orientation strategy. Specifically, the case:

- addresses the internal and external components of a market orientation,
- highlights the often contradictory issues that must be resolved in formulating and implementing marketing strategy,

---

* This teaching note was prepared by Victoria L. Crittenden, Stephanie Hillstrom, and David Angus, Boston College, as an aid to instructors using the case, "Navistar International transportation Corporation." Revised 1998.

- allows the analysis of a huge company stifled by too much corporate bureaucracy, and
- draws attention to the market potential in Mexico, Central, and South American markets

Discussion Questions:

1. How competitive is the truck market? Assess Navistar's situation in this marketplace.
2. What is meant by a "customer focus" at Navistar? Why does Dewel think customer focus and cost cutting are contradictory?
3. What role should South America and Mexico play in Navistar's long-term customer focused, reduced cost strategy?
4. How can Navistar implement a market orientation? Formulate a customer oriented, cost cutting strategy for Navistar. What is the role of technology in this strategy? Who are the players involved in the implementation of the strategy?

Analysis:

1. How competitive is the truck market? Assess Navistar's situation in this marketplace.

There were seven leading competitors in the medium and heavy-duty truck categories (Classes 7 and 8). These seven companies, along with numerous other truck manufacturers, were vying for a marketplace which had expected growth rates of around two percent. For individual classes however, Class 7 showed signs of growth while Class 8 was a declining market. Each of the seven competitors was attempting to address pressing concerns in the transportation marketplace. Thus, competition in such a slow/no growth market was intense.

The international marketplace (e.g., Chile, Mexico) appeared lucrative for truck manufacturers. These markets, however, had competitors in addition to the seven leading contenders in the U.S. market (i.e., international manufacturers).

Exhibit TN-1 presents a sample SWOT analysis for Navistar.

2. What is meant by a "customer focus" at Navistar? Why does Dewel think customer focus and cost cutting are contradictory?

This is a great opportunity to have a general discussion regarding a "customer" or "market orientation" (if the class has not had one already). The market orientation material in the text provides a springboard for the discussion. Shapiro's *Harvard Business Review* piece, "What the Hell is 'Market Oriented?'" is also a good piece for the instructor to read before the class discussion.

An interesting approach that has been used with this case is to ask each student (at the start of class before any discussion of a market orientation) to write down, in 25 words or less, what it means to be customer or market oriented. Then ask several of the students to read their definitions. After a student has read his/her definition ask if Navistar's definition would be the same. A good touch which reinforces the notion of a market orientation is to collect the individual definitions, type each individual definition (this should not take too much time or space since each student has been asked to write fewer than 25 words), and distribute the many definitions at the beginning of the next class. This approach emphasizes the importance/central theme of a market orientation in marketing strategy. The instructor should keep a copy of these definitions handy, as it is interesting to refer to various definitions throughout the course of the semester or quarter.

In general at Navistar, a customer focus refers to a better understanding of the company's current and potential external customers and the simultaneous, individual response to each customer's demands. Many reasons exist for this push toward a customer focus. The driving force (according to the case) is the notion that a customer focus will provide a competitive advantage. Some students may suggest that a customer focus will not be a competitive advantage but rather a necessity since many of Navistar's competitors already seem to have a customer focus in place. For example, Ford's rapid scheduling system for special orders and its 24-hour emergency road service are examples of implementing a customer focus. Freightliner, Mack, and Volvo GM were also attempting to respond to customer needs (e.g., driver shortage/turnover) in truck design and offerings.

The need to customize had become essential in the trucking industry. Statistics showed that more and more buyers were requesting "built to order" fleets (94% of fleets operating over 100 Class 8 trucks requested built to order trucks.) This level of customization would be difficult for Navistar without strong relationships with individual customers.

Consistent with the reasons of competitive advantage and customization were issues surrounding the business recession in the early 1990s which resulted in slow growth and the company's objective that half of its revenue come from new business by 1997.

Dewel's concern that customer focus and cost cutting are contradictory gets to the implementation issues surrounding a customer focus. A customer orientation raises both internal and external concerns. Naturally, one's first inclination is that cost cutting (an internal issue) will lead to fewer people or services which in turn will lead to less satisfaction by the customer (an external issue). It is hard for a student, as it was for Dewel, to visualize that the two can go hand in hand.

3. **What role should South America and Mexico play in Navistar's long-term customer focused, reduced cost strategy?**

Given that the U.S. truck market is experiencing "sluggish" growth, South America and Mexico (as well as other international markets) are of prime importance to Navistar. The potential in South America and Mexico is tremendous (South America: 4,000 heavy-duty trucks and 2,500 medium trucks in 1992; Mexico 33,000 medium and heavy-duty trucks by 1992). Some students will state that any strategy formulated by Navistar management would need to be implementable in these markets. Others, however, may suggest that a combined customer-focus, cost-cutting strategy will not be important at this stage of market development in South America and Mexico. This would lead to different strategies for local and international markets. Students suggesting a different international strategy should be questioned regarding the possible international strategies of Navistar's competitors. Additionally, there may be students who suggest that Navistar should stay out of market development until it cleans up its current operations.

The pros and cons of one strategy for the U.S., South America, and Mexico, multiple strategies for the U.S., South America, and Mexico, and not entering South America and Mexico should be presented and evaluated. [If, by chance, no one suggests not entering South America and Mexico, the instructor should ask if Navistar is in a position to pursue a strategy of market development when it appears to have several issues which need to be resolved on the home front.]

4. **How can Navistar implement a market orientation? Formulate a customer oriented, cost cutting strategy for Navistar. What is the role of technology in this strategy? Who are the players involved in the implementation of the strategy?**

After a general discussion of the situation Navistar faces, what it means for the company to be market oriented, and the notion of market development, divide the class into several groups. The charge for each group is to formulate a customer-oriented, cost cutting strategy for Navistar. The instructor should emphasize the importance of being specific about what Navistar should do.

The questions about technology and various players hint to the students about the significance of these two issues in the formulation of the strategy. Depending upon time, it is interesting to hear from each group. However, there may not be time to hear from all.

Teaching the Case:

The case highlights many issues faced by businesses in today's environment (customer focus, cross-functional integration, partnering with distributors, international markets, slow growth markets). Thus, it is an easy case to teach as it generates a strong interest amongst students.

Probably the most critical issue in teaching this case is timing. The various items that make class interesting and fun (i.e., defining market orientation, group formulation of a strategy, and the video) also take a considerable amount of time. The instructor must be careful to allocate time for each component, consistent with the overall time set aside for the case.

The video should be shown at the end of the case discussion as it shows what Navistar did both internally and externally to implement a customer-focused, cost cutting strategy.

Epilogue:

To bring costs down, profits up, and increased customer satisfaction, Navistar developed Material Requirement Planning (MRP). This planning system compressed the order cycle time and improved customer order slack credibility. Navistar understood customer needs better and, as a result, pulled ahead in the marketplace.

The company revamped its ordering, scheduling, moving of material, and manufacturing of products. It also teamed workers up and broke functional barriers, which changed the orientation of personnel and the management of the flow of materials. The Truck Order Processing System (TOPS) was developed, which used Electronic Data Interchange (EDI). This method enabled Navistar to use the Just In Time approach (JIT), which was expected to reduce delivery time.

In 1996, Navistar's share price dropped to $9, which was $.50 above its lowest point ever. The CEO believed that the stock was severely undervalued. He urged his 30 top executives to use their own money to purchase shares of Navistar to show they supported the company. Nobody took his suggestion because they feared the stock price would drop even further. The CEO didn't give up and he purchased as much he could using cash and his 401(k) account. In 1997, the stock price rose to $25, a 172% return. Although 1997 showed a 10% growth in tractor trailer rigs, this high growth trend is not expected to continue. There was still the concern that buyers might not want to buy a new truck every year. This is one of the reasons why Navistar is looking internationally.

Navistar has moved into Mexico and Brazil. Currently, Navistar services Mexican customers through a number of technological and supply agreements with Dina Camiones. However, this agreement expires in 1998. Navistar plans to make additional expansions into the Mexican market by building a manufacturing facility in the town of Escobedo, located near Monterey, Nuevo. In addition to the manufacturing plant, Navistar currently runs a parts distribution center located near Mexico City, 23 location dealer network, and a contract manufacturing arrangement, all of which were established in 1996. Navistar believes that the demand for the trucks will increase as the Mexican economy recovers. To better serve its South American customers, Navistar has entered an agreement with a Brazilian equipment manufacturer Agrale, S.A. to build trucks. By manufacturing in Brazil, Navistar will be able to enter additional markets because of the Mercosul trade agreement.

Exhibit TN–1   SWOT Analysis

Strengths

- U.S. made vs. Volvo-Ford
- Speed to market, e.g., U-Haul prototype developed in five months
- strategic alliances/partnerships with Dana Corporation, Good Year, and Caterpillar
- financing/leasing offered ("one-stop shopping")
- refocused on what it does best (trucks, not construction equipment), allowing partnership with Cat to take place
- use of EDI leading to cost savings
- glider kits offered as a less costly way to maintain fleet, retain customers at less expense to the customer

Weaknesses

- late entry into foreign markets
- possible conflict between finance and sales (as warranty length is increased, replacement cycle is lengthened)
- as of late 1980s--bloated bureaucracy, payroll
- channels of communication and promotion clogged/cluttered (e.g., magazines and publications being showered upon fleet managers)

Opportunities

- foreign markets in Chile, Mexico, and other South American countries
- Kamaz owners in Chile may be looking for replacement parts or equipment assuming lower quality in Russian -made product
- strategic alliances with foreign producers in Chile and Mexico
- partnerships with unions rather than traditional conflictual relationships
- provide more affordable financing, leasing and insurance to cost-conscious trucking companies
- use EDI to further partnering with suppliers and buyers by offering education to those not yet using it
- growth opportunities in light duty (Classes 3 and 4) and medium-duty (Classes 6 and 7) markets
- built-to-order trucks in all classes, not just heavy (Class 8) trucks
- single-vocation, job specific trucks in all classes
- marketing through less clogged channels and to the end-user (i.e., the driver), not just the fleet manager
- increased demand for heavy trucks in the 1990s as replacement occurs
- helping fleet owners hold down costs through education and support programs
- working with fleet owners to decrease turnover
- use of CAD in product development like Ford uses to further accelerate time-to-market

Threats

- large number of late-model used class 6 and 7 trucks
- current depressed market for Class 8 trucks
- increased competition as all producers become customer focused, concentrate on increased fuel efficiency and driver comfort/satisfaction
- Ford spending three times Navistar on heavy-duty trucks to upgrade every piece of equipment by 1995
- recession, leading to increased fleet expenses, decreased freight traffic, and low rates of growth in oil prices
- union discord

CASE 2-2
FLORAL FARMS*

Synopsis

The case opens as Vice President/Sales Manager, John August, and Marketing Manager, Leslie Stair, of Floral Farms (producer/distributor of fresh-cut flowers) are discussing the heated exchange that had taken place earlier in the day. The Miami (Florida) based marketing group and the Colombian based production group of this agricultural firm had reached a deadlock on what products to grow and market for the coming fiscal year. In addition to being upset over the interactions during the planning meeting, August and Stair were also disgruntled over what appeared to be just "talk" regarding the firm's need to have a market orientation.

Teaching/Learning Objectives

The case provides an excellent opportunity to discuss the concept of a market orientation in conjunction with the interactions that must transpire, internally, to facilitate the implementation of such an orientation. Specifically, the case:

- allows students to experience the day-to-day implementation of a market orientation,
- provides excellent insight into the internal conflict that occurs between marketing and production and how such conflict is exacerbated when functions are located in different countries,
- goes outside the typical manufacturing realm and has students study an agricultural/commodity-driven firm, and
- provides interesting insight into how commodity products are bought and sold.

Discussion Questions

1. What can you learn from a situational analysis of Floral Farms?
2. What is the precise nature of the problem at Floral Farms?
3. What does the term "market orientation" mean at this company?
4. What markets comprise the company's target market?
5. Are there any internal/external relationships that are particularly relevant for this firm? Diagram these relationships.
6. Why was the January Planning Meeting such a "big deal?"
7. What avenues are open to August and Stair?
8. What do you recommend?

---

*This teaching note was prepared by Victoria L. Crittenden, Boston College, and William F. Crittenden, Northeastern University, as an aid to instructors using the case, "Floral Farms."

Analysis

1. **What can you learn from a situational analysis of Floral Farms?**

When one looks at the SWOT analysis in Exhibit TN-1, we see that the company is in a very strong external position, with many internal strengths. The fact that more Americans are spending money on fresh-cut flowers provides much promise to Floral Farms. However, combining this with the firm's weaknesses regarding inflexible production, lack of internal communication, and physical separation paves the way for some potential problems. Now is the time for Floral Farms to "fix" these internal weaknesses—before they begin to weaken the firm by, for example, decreased delivery times, lower quality product, or dampened employee morale.

2. **What is the precise nature of the problem at Floral Farms?**

The problem boils down to a lack of coordination between marketing and production. Floral Farms wants to become more market oriented. However, a key component of a market orientation is interfunctional coordination. While the company has made some attempts to build a strong cross-functional team (marketing visiting the production sites, cross-functional planning meetings), there is strong divisiveness—particularly, it appears, on the production side of the picture. (One might even wonder if production has bought into the notion of a market orientation or is just paying lip-service to the company owner.)

3. **What does the term "market orientation" mean at this company?**

While student explanations will differ slightly, a market orientation at Floral Farms involves profitably providing the customer with the desired product(s) at the desired time.

4. **What markets comprise the company's target market?**

The major form of segmentation at Floral Farms is the distribution format. Distributors can be segmented into wholesalers in different cities, supermarket retail chains, end users, and importers. Interestingly, this was the extent of segmentation at Floral Farms. However, we do know that end-users can be differentiated based on country (geographic segmentation). Customers around the world buy fresh-cut flowers—some (e.g., Europeans) more than others. Fresh-cut flowers accounted for around 75% of flower purchases in the U.S. Floral Farms executives seemed to understand the buying locations (i.e., supermarkets, discount stores, department stores, corner push-carts, electronic kiosks, catalogues, florist) of the end user better than they understood the actual end-user's buying process. Based on the case information, Floral Farms knows very little about its target market—beyond who they are in terms of distribution.

5. **Are there any internal/external relationships that are particularly relevant for this firm? Diagram these relationships.**

There are three major sets of internal relationships at Flora Farms:

Leslie Stair	←→	John August
Carla Williams	←→	Manuel Ortiz
Carlos Diaz	←→	Manuel Ortiz

From an organizational structure perspective, we see:

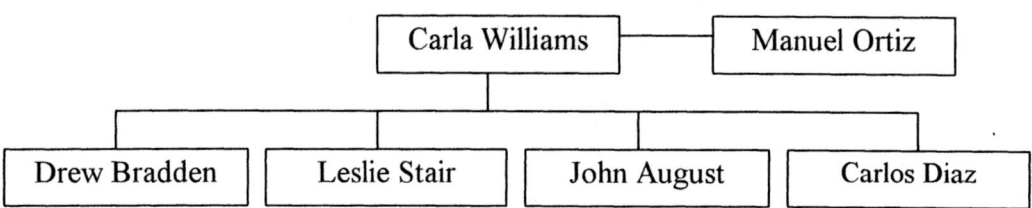

The nature and direction of the relationships are particularly relevant given the lack of internal communication within Floral Farms. The major players at the management level appear to be Stair, August, and Diaz. Drew Bradden appears to be pretty much out of the daily product activity of the firm. It would seem that his main concern is the financial aspect, with no interest in the actual product which makes the finance function necessary. Additionally, Bradden does not seem to have been conferred with regarding the land purchases Diaz was considering. So, one has to wonder about how much weight he actually carries when it comes to more strategic issues of managing the firm.

Marketing people appear to be talking only with each other (Stair and August). They profess to having made attempts to include production in their communication. However, Diaz seems to have very little interest in being a part of their team—one might look at the situation from Diaz' point of view and wonder why he would want to interact with Stair and August (or even Williams) when he can communicate directly with the company president. Unfortunately, Williams does not help the communication situation very much. While she has daily responsibility/control, there does not appear to be a lot of hands-on management with respect to marketing or production. Carla's personal relationship with Manuel and his family may put her in a position that does not lend itself to addressing the direct line of communications between Diaz and Ortiz. However, this direct line could lead to insubordination. But, Williams may not be concerned about that if her main concern is the Williams-Ortiz connection.

The bottom line is that the marketing group appears to be left out in the cold when it comes to relationships within Floral Farms. Both the company president and production v.p. have direct lines to the owner. Marketing does not seem to have much of a direct line anywhere internally.

Interestingly, the major external relationship appears to be between Stair/August and the company's distributors. At the present time, there do not appear to be any issues affecting this external relationship. It is rather interesting how, internally, marketing is "out-of-the-loop," but externally, they are the connection with the customer! This is very consistent with the traditional concept of marketing being the only function that interacts with the customer (i.e., marketing owns the customer). As we see in the business community of today, this is not a viable option long-term. Thus, Floral Farms will need to do something to address this somewhat solely internal (production) focus and somewhat solely external (marketing) focus.

6. **Why was the January Planning Meeting such a "big deal?"**

Four major issues surround the planning meeting.

One, August and Stair were really excited about the prospects for the coming year. The market for fresh-cut flowers was picking up, and the marketing group expected an increase in sales for all product lines.

Two, August and Stair thought they had done a good job in making their demand projections. Although demand forecasts in most industries are not easy, demand forecasts in the fresh-cut flower market are made even more difficult since price is an exogenous variable (i.e., the nature of the bidding process of such a commodity meant that the "going" rate for products was *told* to sales people rather than the firm setting the product's price). Floral Farms marketing thought it had done a great job of incorporating the price variable into their demand expectations.

Three, this was the first planning meeting since the idea to have site visits. In addition to having all parties plan together for the first time, August and Stair thought that they had a better understanding of the company's internal needs due to their visit to the company's Colombian farms.

Four, marketing saw this as a chance to orient production and other management personnel to the marketing-side of the business. This would be a chance to show what marketing was all about.

All-in-all, marketing saw this as the first opportunity to do market planning with their new knowledge base combined with other managers in the company.

7. **What avenues are open to August and Stair?**

August and Stair mention a couple of options at the end of the case. One, they could go back to Colombia to do more site visits and possibly become better informed as to the production process. Another option was to wait for Diaz to contact them. (There was some hint that August and Stair saw Diaz as not being open to the consultant's suggestion regarding better communication.) There are concerns with both of these options. One was there more to gain by looking at the growing fields again? And, would such a trip mean that August and Stair were admitting that their sales forecasts were wrong due to their lack of understanding of the production side of the business? However, given Diaz' nonchalant attitude toward marketing and his closeness to Ortiz, how long would August and Stair have to wait for a call from Diaz? There's a chance that he would head back to Colombia and continue doing things "his way." He could even place the blame on August and Stair since they did not contact him to open communications. So, it appears to be a lose-lose situation for August and Stair.

Students should be forced to come up with additional options (alternatives). Assuming students are familiar with the suggested mechanisms for forging cross-functional relationships, alternatives will tend to follow the thinking of: changes in organizational design, improved communications, changes in the reward system, and use of information technology.

The consultant working with Floral Farms management had suggested the need for an improved communications process. The company had begun the on-site visits as the initial step in improving communications. The Miami-based marketing group had visited Colombia and now the Colombian growers were in Miami. This was all in an attempt to foster cross-functional interaction. However, as we see from the case, this was not enough. Students will most likely pick up on the ineffective communication flows (see question 5 above) within Floral Farms. A typical response will be to hold seminars or workshops that focus upon improving communications. This should help improve communications between the two groups. Marketing seems to know much more about production now than vice-versa.

Changes in the firm's organizational design should be discussed. Floral Farms is structured along the traditional functional breakdowns. In conjunction with the functional division of labor, the decision-making process follows a linear flow rather than a simultaneous process. This resulted in marketing's development of a plan that was unacceptable to production (the concept of silos and "throwing ideas over the wall"). However, the physical separation of marketing and production may make it virtually impossible to organize the company differently. It would be virtually impossible to move production to the U.S. (the year-around growing process must take place in the South American climate), and one would not recommend moving marketing to South America since the vast majority of business takes place in the U.S. Interchanging jobs in this company would prove to be somewhat difficult. It is tough to imagine a marketing person from the States being able to actually grow beautiful, healthy flowers.

The development of a joint reward system might influence, significantly, the effectiveness of functional integration. Yearly bonuses would be tied to the company's overall profitability. This might meet some resistance from company owners, however, in that it is doubtful that the owners want their privately-held company's profitability made known in such a way.

The use of information systems is another method for improving cross-functional communications. Diaz seemed to ignore marketing's projections, which could have been due to the nature of marketing data. The qualitative aspect of marketing data often causes production managers to make light of marketing projections. This is not surprising; one only has to look at Exhibit 2 to see the hard, factual component of production's data. Diaz can very precisely relay production time and output information. An information system that allowed marketing and production to sit in the same room and conduct "what-if" analyses might be a real eye-opener for both parties. Even with marketing's solid presentation of sales projections, no one knows if Diaz is wrong in keeping his production plan the way it is currently. There is no framework for showing either party what the final outcome will be.

8. What do you recommend?

Students will probably put together a combination of many of the above factors.

Additionally, there should be discussion as to whether the additional land in Ecuador and/or Peru should be purchased. Even if it is purchased, it will take some time to bring it "on-line." Thus, marketing would not receive final product in the time frame they are shooting for. A major issue to be considered with the new farms would be the product(s) grown on these farms. With a seven-hour ground transportation requirement in Ecuador, certain flowers might not be viable. The Peruvian farm land would probably be looked upon favorably by the marketing group since a couple of the flowers slated to be grown there are ones with fairly large expected sales increases (Gypsophila at 97% increase and Statice at 166% increase) over the previous season. Production hoped to try some new variations of roses, another product with an expected increase in demand (46% over previous season). While the other three flower types do not see as large expected increases, at least there are expected gains. (Marketing will, undoubtedly, be relieved that lilies are not planned for the Peruvian farm land.) While bringing additional capacity on-line will take time, there seems to be great long-term potential if marketing and production can "get their act together".

In the short-term, however, an immediate decision must be made by August and Stair. Should they wait for Diaz to call them? Should they contact Diaz? Or, what should they do?

Teaching the Case

Following the order of the discussion questions tends to work best with this case. The case does not work well with a "What would you do?" opening. The students tend to learn best from the case when they are led through the market orientation theme, types of internal/external relationships needed for a market orientation, barriers to strong internal relationships, and methods for improving relationships. This type of discussion is particularly important for understanding the components of a market orientation. The case is rich for discussion, so the instructor has to be cognizant of time elements in the class. One might want to consider allocating equal (and larger amounts of) time to discussion surrounding questions 1, 2, 5, 6, & 7. Questions 3 and 4 tend to fall easily out of the discussion. The final recommendation flows easily from the discussion of question 7. However, don't forget to find out who is going to make the first move!

Epilogue

The consultant actually facilitated the first move. Having been at the planning meeting, she was very upset by the actions of both Ortiz and Diaz. As an external person, contracted by Ortiz and Williams, the consultant spoke to both of them directly. The consultant suggested a way to improve on the initial communication steps taken by marketing (particularly) and production. Floral Farms management agreed to commission the development of a decision support system in order to conduct on-the-spot "what-if" analyses. The decision support system that was finally developed included production and marketing data. Output of the model included quantity (by product, by week, by market type), revenue (by product, by week, by market type), costs (by product, by week), and contribution (by product, by week, by capacity unit [hectare of land]). The decision variable was a planting decision of how much capacity to allocate to the product type on a per week basis and included differing growing periods for each product.

Testing of the model was not flowing smoothly, as production had sent its input data in Spanish and it was having to be translated by a professional translator.

Exhibit TN–1   SWOT Analysis

Strengths

- Experienced owners/operators
- Diverse product line
- Reputation for quality
- Dedicated employees
- Large, well-respected farms
- Annual planning meeting
- On-site visits to foster shared knowledge
- Multiple production locations
- Year-round growing capability
- On-time delivery

Weaknesses

- Inflexible production; fixed supply
- Lack of internal communication
- Separation of two key functional areas (production & marketing)
- No advertising
- Inability of manage retail stores effectively
- Lack of name recognition
- Expected constrained capacity

Opportunities

- Annual retail sales of US$25 billion; opportunity for growth
- Americans more money on fresh-cut flowers
- New distribution channels
- New cooling procedures for extended shelf life; thus, shipment capabilities to more distant locations
- International sales opportunities
- Land availability in year-round growth climate

Threats

- Reliance (95%) on U.S. marketplace
- Decreased profitability of imported product
- More government regulations
- Transportation complications could hinder production expansion possibilities

CASE 2-3
QUALITY PLASTICS INTERNATIONAL S.A. de C.V.*

Synopsis:

Quality Plastics International S.A. de C.V. had grown significantly in its seven years of existence. The company credited this growth to quality products, existence as an independent company, excellent labor management relations, and personal and corporate integrity. The company had started as a component manufacturer and then entered the market for finished products.

The process of developing the company had led to problems. Machines for plastics manufacturing had been discounted, and Sergio Trevino de Elizondo, the founder of QPI, took advantage of this and purchased additional new machinery. This resulted in worker training and maintenance difficulties.

There was also a high level of competition in the plastic injection molding and extrusion businesses worldwide. QPI was very customer-oriented, they had hoped that it would help them in North American markets. QPI had gained many customers because of this focus, but problems with the record keeping of the company resulted from the large amount of customers.

QPI was gaining new customers in Canada and the United States. Because of the North American Free Trade Agreement and QPI's focus on customer satisfaction, the company had more opportunities than ever before. Trevino, however, had to figure out a way to solve the internal problems of the company that had resulted from his efforts to promote growth.

Teaching/Learning Objectives:

This case provides an excellent opportunity to discuss the notion of a customer orientation and what it entails. Specifically, the case:

1. introduces the notion of a customer orientation and highlights the internal company issues that must be addressed in implementing such an orientation
2. focuses upon the market orientation issue in an international context
3. allows for the determination of a comprehensive marketing strategy
4. provides the opportunity to develop an implementation plan complete with performance assessment measures

Discussion Questions:

1. Assess the issues for this industry and Quality Plastics International in particular. What threats and opportunities exist?
2. Identify the different organizational groups that QPI must interact with.
3. What are QPI's objectives?

---

* This teaching note was prepared by Steve Domeman, Devin Kelly, Kristina Lumsden, Sharie Poulin, and William Crittenden, Northeastern University, as an aid to instructors using the case, "Quality Plastics International S.A. de C.V."

4. Identify issues facing QPI.
5. What demands are placed on QPI by its customers? Can QPI give the customers what they want?
6. What does it mean to be customer-oriented at QPI?
7. Analyze QPI's performance to date.
8. What can you determine regarding QPI's potential markets?
9. What alternatives are available to Trevino and QPI?
10. What recommendations would you make to Trevino and his management team?

Analysis:

[Step 1. Situation Audit]

1. Assess the issues for this industry and Quality Plastics International in particular. What threats and opportunities exist?

We have divided this analysis into two components: internal and external. A sample internal analysis is included in Exhibit TN–1 and a sample external analysis is summarized in Exhibit TN–2. (NOTE: There are several regional strengths related to Nuevo Leon which we have included in the internal analysis.)

Exhibits TN–3 through TN–5 provide example calculations that are helpful in understanding QPI. Exhibits TN–6 through TN–9 show ratio analysis for instructors interested in this level of detail.

2. Identify the different organizational groups that QPI must interact with.

- Customers (both OEMs and distributors)
- Suppliers (both raw materials and equipment)
- Employees
- Owners (Trevino = 65%, management = 15%, Texas investment firm = 20%)
- Community
- Government
- Management

3. What are QPI's objectives?

In addition to basic survival/profitability, QPI seems to have two major objectives: (i) to be a customer-oriented company and (ii) growth. The strategy to achieve these objectives has been to be a *local*, reliable, low cost alternative selling to OEMs.

4. Identify issues facing QPI.

QPI is facing several key issues which can either help or hinder the achievement of its objectives. Regarding *growth*, two questions arise. One, does past success equal ability to compete globally? Two, can QPI remain low cost and high service while growing? In reference to *profit*, we see a slowing of profit as a percent of sales. The *mission* of the company may have to be redefined, specifically regarding plastics extrusion/molding and industrial versus consumer goods. The company faces issues surrounding *diversification* and *experience in South and Central America*. An additional issue facing QPI is a *human resource* issue regarding the apparent stress in manufacturing and accounting.

[Step 2: Problem/Decision Statement]

The situation audit, through the use of the first four questions, should aid the student in stating what he/she finds the problem/decision facing QPI to be. Questions 5 - 8 help in focusing upon the company's problem.

5. What demands are placed on QPI by its customers? Can QPI give the customers what they want?

QPI appears to have a very demanding customer base. These demands have strong implications for manufacturing. Demands include:

a. good prices

b. guaranteed prices for year

c. reliable delivery

d. continuity of relationship

e. multi-sourcing

f. response to seasonality

g. quotes under time pressure

h. customization

All of these demands make forecasting very difficulty. QPI has been able to meet most of its customers demands, but there is concern about meeting these demands with the growth objectives of Trevino. For example, good prices often means low prices. Reliable delivery may have problems regarding border crossings. Continuity of relationship often means a long selling time. Response to seasonality can cause problems regarding equipment and raw material inventory. Also, there are potential conflicts regarding QPI's response to seasonality, customization, and reliable delivery.

6. What does it mean to be customer-oriented at QPI?

A customer-orientation at QPI could mean:

a. manufacturing based on market needs

b. providing the desired product/service at lowest appropriate price

c. customizing products/services

d. responding to changing needs of customers

e. being proactive

f. providing top service to specific market segments

g. managing tradeoffs with customer desires

h. responding to customer's order of priority

i. forging a strong link between customer needs and company operations

The instructor should also push students to think about the problems that occur with each of the above (and others identified by students).

7. Analyze QPI's performance to date.

There have been both "good" and "bad" performance issues at QPI:

Good:

    a. growth in sales outpacing 7-9% forecasts

    b. profitable

    c. solid export sales/growth

    d. assuming 71.5% of sales in injection, QPI is modestly larger than average injection firm

Poor:

    a. growth in profit lagging growth in sales during last three years

    b. 0.0002 market share worldwide [8.3 million/(165 billion + 203 billion)]

[Note: It is interesting to ask students how meaningful market share is in this instance.]

    c. assuming 28.5% of sales in extrusion, they are substantially smaller than average extrusion firm

    d. cash position is going down

    e. cost of goods sold is going up

    f. selling expenses are going up

    g. decline in operating income during the last two years

These performance issues help identify future concerns of QPI:

    a. becoming too diversified on product and customer dimensions

    b. equipment maintenance

    c. employee training

    d. record keeping

    e. financing

8. What can you determine regarding QPI's potential markets?

Injection Molding:

  203 billion peso

  40,000 competitors

  [average = 51 million pesos]

  Extrusion:

165 billion peso

15,000 competitors

[average = 11 million pesos]

Total market = 368 billion peso

[Step 3: Identification of Alternatives]

9. **What alternatives are available to Trevino and QPI?**

Possible alternatives are almost endless in this situation and include:

Alternative 1:	Focus on injection molding
Alternative 2:	Focus on extrusion
Alternative 3:	Develop in-house R&D capabilities
Alternative 4:	Focus on consumer products
Alternative 5:	Focus on components
Alternative 6:	Continue expansion into U.S. and Canada
Alternative 7:	Tighten accounts receivable
Alternative 8:	Modify policy guidelines
Alternative 9:	Strategic Alliance
Alternative 10:	Sell company

[Step 4: Criteria, Step 5: Analysis, Step 6: Recommendation]

10. **What recommendations would you make to Trevino and his management team?**

Answering this question will require that the student conduct a thorough and thoughtful analysis of his/her alternatives. Criteria for evaluation might include growing market, general political climate, consistent with goal of growth, new industries, meets production capabilities, meets management capabilities, as well as the traditional criterion of potential sales volume, variable costs, contribution margins, market share, business strengths, and profitability.

The student should be pushed for the pros and cons of each of the various alternatives. Exhibits TN–10 through TN–18 provide the proposed implementation and possible performance measures for a recommendation which focuses upon expansion into new industries within QPI's current markets. The recommendation includes selling additional equity and controlled expansion supported by the necessary expenditures.

Teaching the Case:

The case allows for early discussion of the notion of a market orientation. Additionally, enough information is provided to allow for thorough analysis which can lead to a somewhat detailed recommendation plan.

While the order of the questions follows a scientific approach to case analysis, we suggest an alternative approach to class discussion. We recommend starting the class with a discussion of customer orientation in the context of QPI (Question 6). The ensuring discussion should bring up issues identified in Questions 5 and 7. After the market orientation issue and its implications for QPI have been discussed, it is somewhat easy to move to Questions 1 and take the class through a discussion, analysis, and recommendation flow.

We recommend pushing the students for a plan of action (implementation plan) for QPI. As an early case, this shows the importance of the "how" component of marketing. Asking for specifics regarding the performance assessment measures reinforces the need to know if what marketing is doing are the right things as well as is marketing doing them correctly.

As a note, the case is more difficult to teach when the opening focuses upon the recommendation to Trevino and his management group. Working backward in this particular case makes it difficult to highlight the customer orientation and surrounding internal stress issues.

Epilogue:

The weakened Peso enhanced the price of the product on the international market, especially relative to Canada and the United States. However, investment in Mexico has been drying up and bank financing has been constrained.

QPI's growth is constrained from a cash flow standpoint. There is a continual requirement for investment in equipment and accounts receivable. Yet, investment dollars have not been readily available.

[Instructor's note: It is interesting to draw attention to the fact that issues surrounding a market orientation seem to be pushed aside when times are tough financially.]

Exhibit TN-1   QPI Internal Analysis

Strengths:

- customer oriented
- low costs
- cheap labor
- strong domestic sales force
- flexibility
- no union
- skilled workforce (Nuevo Leon)
- close to U.S.A. (Nuevo Leon)
- solid infrastructure (Nuevo Leon)
- dynamic industrial activity (Nuevo Leon)

Weaknesses:

- customer controls molds
- no R&D
- plastic waste
- lack of experience in international markets
- limited management experience to grow the company
- accounts receivable collection period is growing

Exhibit TN-2 QPI External Analysis

Opportunities:

- NAFTA
- plastics: 7-9% growth
- new applications
- biodegradable
- cheap supplies/raw materials
- plastics consumption:
    - electronics
    - construction
    - health care
    - transportation & automobiles
    - food processing
- economy emerging out of a slump

Threats:

- increased competition
- unionization
- low market barriers to entry
- recycling
- government
- currency devaluation
- machine changeover
- varying customer needs
- cyclical/seasonal demand

Social:

- low cost of labor
- 30% female (meets social needs)
- 35% of workforce is unionized
- worker safety

Technical:

- new recycling technologies
- ease of entry concerns with new equipment/automation
- second-hand machines
- use of biodegradable materials may obsolete current equipment

Economic:

- low industrial growth (yet Mexican plastic expected to increase 7-9%)
- increasing long term interest rates
- worldwide excess capacity

Environmental:

- plastic and other manufacturing wastes
- worker health concerns

Political:

- NAFTA, GATT, LAFTA (increased competition)
- government manufactured dominated industry
- new president

Exhibit TN–3 QPI Operating Results (Mexican New Peso, Figures in Thousands)

	Sales	% Change Prior Year	Net Profit	% Change Prior Year
1993	8,304	.28	298	.21
1992	6,475	.48	246	.27
1991	4,385	.28	193	.25
1990	3,426	.25	154	.4
1989	2,741	.75	110	.90
1988	1,570	.91	58	n/a
1987	821		<15>	

Current exchange rate 3.21 Pesos per US $

Exhibit TN–4 QPI's Income Statement Information (Constant Mexican New Pesos, Figures in Thousands)

	1993		1992		1991		1990	
Net Sales	8304	1.000	6475	1.000	4385	1.00	3426	1.000
Cost of Goods Sold	6228	0.750	4662	0.720	2937	0.670	2261	0.660
Gross Profit	2076	0.250	1813	0.280	1448	0.330	1165	0.340
Selling Expenses	1254	0.151	965	0.149	548	0.125	428	0.125
Administrative Expenses	392	0.047	383	0.059	242	0.055	232	0.068
Operating Income	430	0.052	465	0.072	658	0.150	505	0.147
Foreign Exchange Gain (loss)	28	0.003	-87	-0.013	-361	-0.082	-268	-0.078
Income After Foreign Exchange	458	0.055	378	0.058	297	0.068	237	0.069
Taxes	160	0.019	132	0.020	104	0.024	83	0.024
Net Profit	298	0.036	246	0.038	193	0.044	154	0.045

Source: Quality Plastics International S.A. de C.V. annual report

Exhibit TN–5 Key Accounts in Canada & USA (U.S. Dollars, Figures in Thousands)

	1993 Sales	1993 Sales in Pesos	% Total Sales
Bombardier	102	327.42	0.03943
Carrier Air Systems	253	812.13	0.0978
Fisher Price	71	227.91	0.02745
Ideal Toy	525	1685.25	0.20294
Little Tykes	26	83.46	0.01005
Sears	32	102.72	0.01237

[Instructor's Note: Although sales to Ideal exceed 20 percent of revenues, QPI's *policy* is in terms of production capacity. This is one of those "gotcha" issues that will occasionally trip up a few students.]

Exhibit TN–6   Liquidity Ratios

	1993	**1992**	**1991**	**1990**
Current	2223/915 = 2.4	1928/837 = 2.3	2028/688 = 2.9	1890/613 = 3.1
Quick	1148/915 = 1.3	893/837 = 1.1	1137/688 = 1.7	1026/613 = 1.7
Inventory to Net Working Capital	1075/1308 = .82	1035/1091 = .95	891/1340 = .66	864/1277 = .68
Cash	261/915 = .29	385/837 = .46	734/688 = 1.1	684/613 = 1.1

Exhibit TN–7   Profitability Ratios

	1993	**1992**	**1991**	**1990**
Net Profit Margin	298/8304 = .036	246/6475 = .038	193/4395 = .044	154/3436 = .045
Gross Profit Margin	2076/8304 = .25	1813/6475 = .28	1448/4385 = .33	1165/3426 = .34
ROI	298/3302 = .09	246/2946 = .08	193/2972 = .06	154/2834 = .05
ROE	298/905 = .33	246/708 = .35	193/544 = .35	

Exhibit TN–8   Activity Ratios

	1993	**1992**	**1991**	**1990**
Inventory Turnover	8304/1075 = 7.7	6475/1035 = 6.3	4385/891 = 4.9	3426/864 = 4.0
Net Working Capital Turnover	8304/1308 = 6.3	6475/1091 = 5.9	4385/1340 = 3.3	3426/1277 = 2.7
Asset Turnover	8304/3302 = 2.5	6475/2946 = 2.2	4385/2972 = 1.5	3426/2834 = 1.2
Fixed Asset Turnover	8304/1079 = 7.7	6475/1018 = 6.4	4385/944 = 4.6	3426/944 = 3.6
Average Collection Period	887/22.8 = 39	508/17.7 = 29	403/12.0 = 34	342/9.4 = 36
Accounts Receivable Turnover	8304/887 = 9.4	6475/508 = 12.7	4385/403 = 10.9	3426/342 = 10

Exhibit TN–9   Leverage Ratios

	1993	**1992**	**1991**	**1990**
Debt/Asset	2293/3302 = .69	2146/2946 = .73	2356/2972 = .79	2362/2834 = .83
Debt/Equity	2293/1009 = 2.3	2146/800 = 2.7	2356/616 = 3.8	2362/472 = 5.0
Long Term Debt/Equity	1378/1009 = 1.4	1309/800 = 1.6	1668/616 = 2.7	1749/472 = 3.7
Current Debt/Equity	915/1009 = .91	837/800 = 1.0	688/616 = 1.1	613/472 = 1.3

Exhibit TN–10 QPI's Proposed Objective:

The objective is to increase QPI operating income from the current 430,000 pesos to 960,000 pesos by 1997.

Requirement:

To accomplish this will require an additional one million pesos in investment funds.

Exhibit TN–11 Proposed Marketing Strategy: Fund and Sustain Continued Growth

1. Sell additional equity
2. Expand into new industries in current markets
3. Make the necessary capital expenditures in the form of equipment, personnel training, advertising, and distribution

Exhibit TN-12

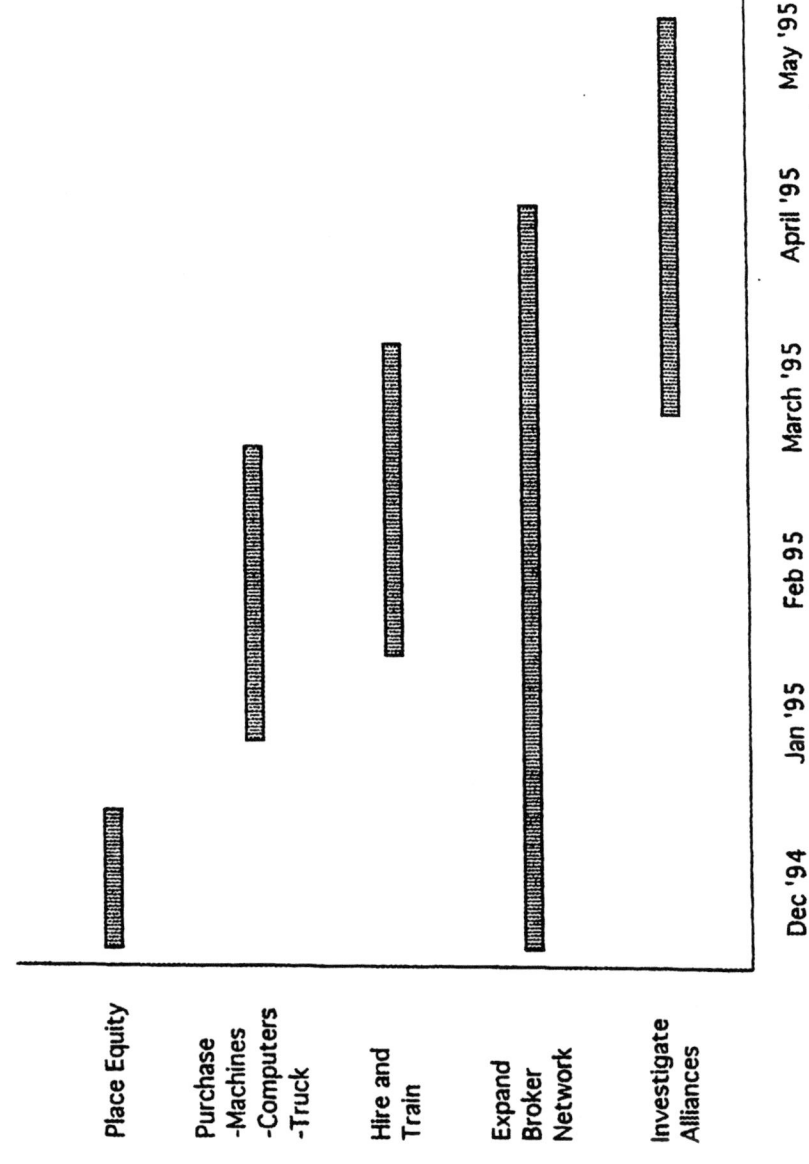

Exhibit TN–13

QPI OWNERSHIP

PROPOSED

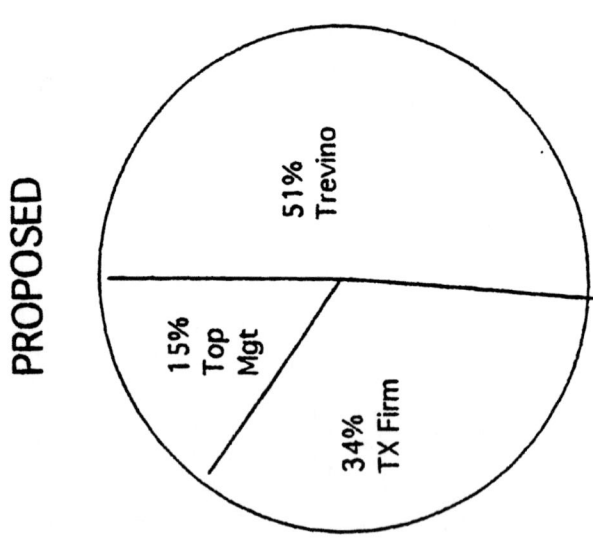

NOW

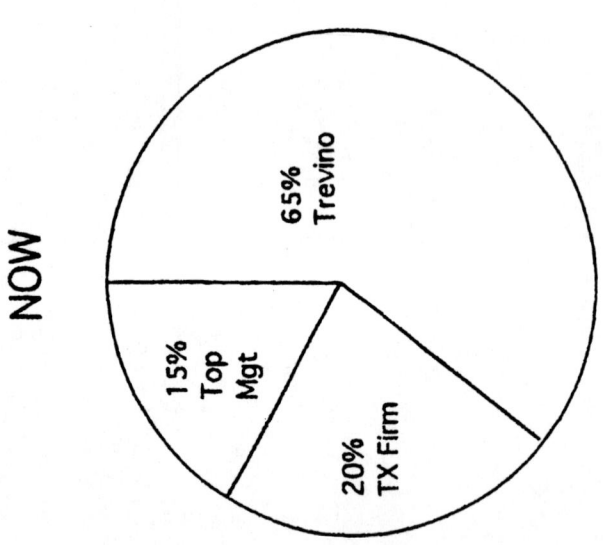

Exhibit TN–14 Current and Projected Sales

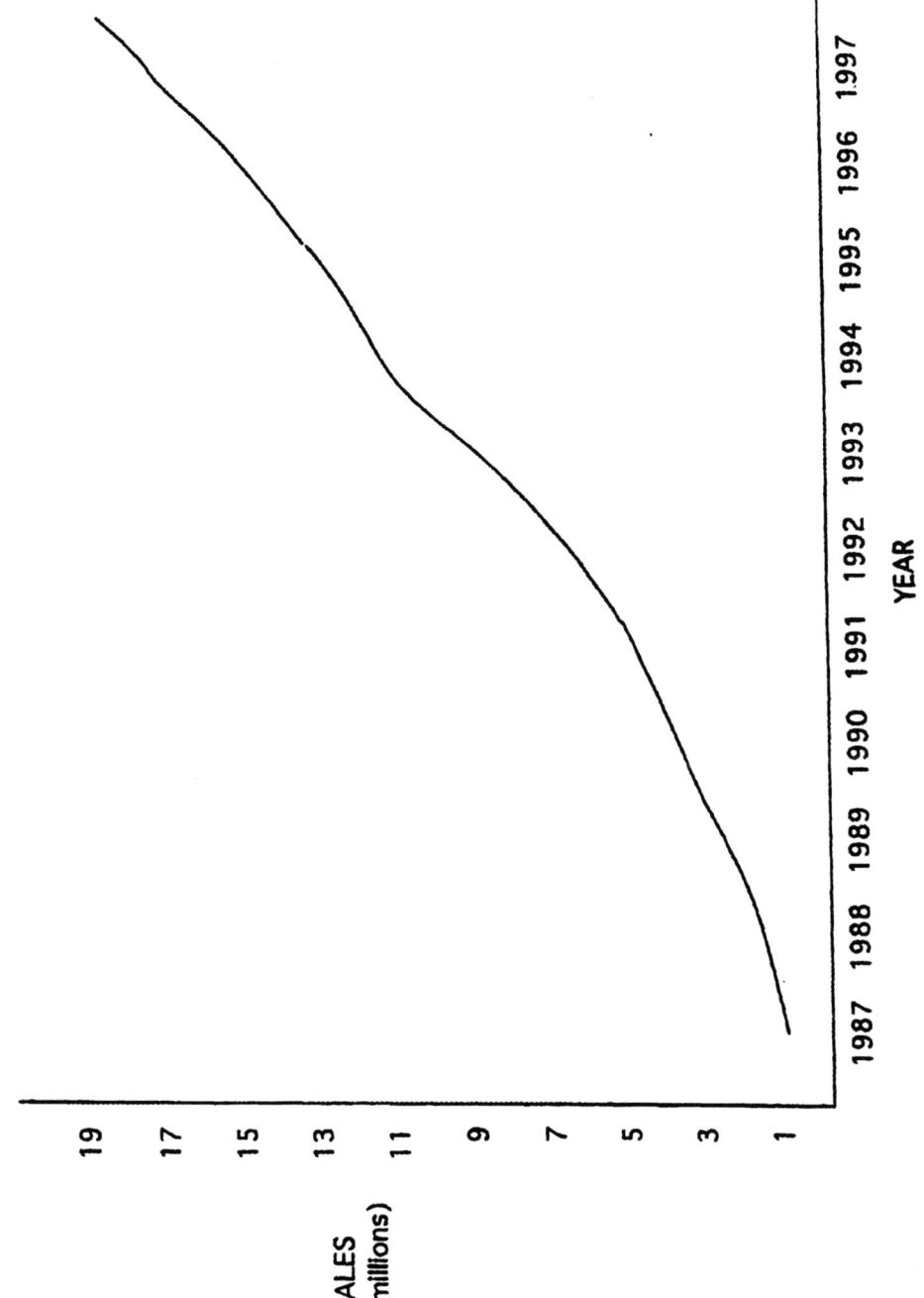

Exhibit TN–15   Expenditures

	Dollars	Pesos
2 extruders @ $52,000	104,000	333,840
4 injectors @ $24,250	97,000	311,370
2 computers	5,000	16,050
6 workers/direct labor 15,000 pesos	28,038	90,000
2 administrators ($6,000)	12,000	38,520
1 truck	7,500	24,075
inventory/supplies	25,000	80,250
training	10,000	32,100
advertising	30,000	96,300
other	30,000	96,300
Total	350,000	1,118,800

Exhibit TN–16   Projected Income Statement (in Pesos)

	Year 1	Year 2	Year 3
Sales	11,600,000	15,370,000	19,200,000
COGS	9,300,000	11,900,000	14,400,000
Gross Profit	2,300,000	3,470,000	4,800,000
Selling Expenses	1,500,000	2,168,000	2,880,000
Administrative Expenses	460,000	676,000	960,000
Operating Income	340,000	626,000	960,000

Exhibit TN–17   Projections

	1995	1996	1997
Profit Margin	2.1%	2.9%	3.5%
Asset Turnover	2.9x	3.0x	3.0x
Return on Assets	6%	8.7%	10.5%

Exhibit TN–18

Company Valuation

Current =	Projected	Proposed =
$2.5 million	3 year	$6 million

Trevino

Current 65% =	Projected	Proposed 51% =
$1.625 million	3 year	$3.06 million

CASE 2-4
FOOD LION, INC.

Synopsis

Food Lion is a successful regional retail grocery chain with stores located in the Southeast. The firm's stores are concentrated in North Carolina and Virginia. It operates in eight states. The company was founded in 1957 by former Winn Dixie retail grocery employees. Food Lion had grown to become the 10th largest chain with annual sales exceeding $3.8 billion (1988). Management pursues a strategy of steady growth coupled with tight control of operations. Financial performance in recent years has been strong in a very competitive industry. A grocery chain in Belgium controls 51% of the Food Lion stock.

Management is faced with several challenges concerning the future strategy of the firm. The past pursuit of discount pricing and cost control have proved to be important in appealing to a segment of supermarket customers. Management must develop a strategy for sustaining Food Lion's competitive advantage as the chain moves toward the 1990s.

Teaching/Learning Objectives

The case provides students an opportunity to analyze a company's business and marketing strategies during the growth stage of the firm's life cycle. Food Lion illustrates how selective targeting and positioning by a relatively small regional chain are used successfully. The case can be used to examine several important analysis and strategy topics including:

1. The influence of industry/market trends on strategy.
2. Choice of business growth strategies in a highly competitive industry.
3. Market analysis and segmentation.
4. Competitor analysis.
5. Developing and sustaining competitive advantage in a mature industry.
6. Development of market targeting and positioning strategies.

Situation Audit

Food Lion has been performing well in a very competitive retail consumer products market. The situation analysis indicates several company advantages and no major problems. However, important changes are occurring within the industry that are likely to impact Food Lion in the future.

Market Analysis and Trends

Food Lion's Sunbelt location displays favorable population growth to the year 2000 and beyond. Georgia and Florida will be the fastest growing states in the region. Demographic changes are likely to affect supermarket patronage. The population is growing older, single person households are expanding, and consumers are increasingly trying to reduce shopping and food preparation time. The cost of foods continues to be an important factor in food purchasing. Food Lion's low price advantage has been an important factor in the success of the chain. Case Exhibit 2 shows sales trends for several types of retailers. Food stores as a percent of total U.S. retail sales, declined 1.7% from 1983 to 1987.

Competition

Food Lion is currently concerned with regional competition, although if management decides to expand geographically new competition may be relevant. The major competitors in the southeast are American Stores, Kroger, Super Value, Winn-Dixie, Publix, and Brano's. Kroger is the largest of the southeastern supermarket chains. Food Lion's net profit margins are the highest of the group (2.9% of sales). It has a very high margin in an industry where margins usually are less than 2%.

Market Targeting

Food Lion is following a selective market segmentation targeting strategy. The chain appeals to budget conscious shoppers. The retailer is likely to attract medium to lower income shoppers. The product offering consists of the basic items. It does not have seafood counters and flower shops, although it does operate a bakery department.

Marketing Program Positioning

Food Lion has an interesting positioning strategy. Stores provide basic supermarket format. They are not intended to be expensive in appearance. Prices are discounted and locations are carefully selected to access targeted grocery shoppers. Stores are designed to keep operating costs as low as possible. Stores have been concentrated in selected metro-areas. Advertising and sales promotion efforts feature Food Lion's actions toward cost reduction and social responsibility. Management has developed several cost-saving innovations that enable the firm to charge lower prices.

Financial Performance

Food Lion is financially strong. Net profit margins have remained between 2.3 and 3.2% for a decade. These are high margins in the industry. The national industry average was 1% in 1987. The other selected financial ratios shown in Exhibit VII are also generally favorable. Food Lion's return on equity is high for the industry and long term debt is low.

Problem/Decision Statment

Food Lion must examine its overall strategy to determine if its business focus should be altered in view of market and industry trends. Should management expand into new geographical areas and/or alter targeting and positioning strategies?

Alternatives

A. Adopt a modified store format

B. Continue using conventional store formats and targeting and positioning strategies, but expand geographically.

C. Combination of A and B.

Criteria for Analysis/Evaluation

1. Mission/objectives impact
2. Market analysis/trends
3. Segments

4. Industry/competitor analysis
5. Competitive advantage
6. Targeting/positioning
7. Financial considerations

Analysis

A. Adopt a Modified Store Format

Mission/objectives Impact. Adopting a modified format would change Food Lion, moving the chain toward larger supermarket stores, offering seafood, cheese, and other specialty departments. Store size would need to be increased and targeting/positioning would be affected.

Market Analysis/Trends. The general trends are toward larger stores with specialty departments and non-food items. Several large chains have moved into the general merchandise area. A&P tried unsuccessfully to compete with these superstores in the 1970s, but did not have the size and location of stores necessary to compete against Kroger and others that adopted this format.

Segments. Food Lion's success in the Southeast suggests that there are buyers that seek the attributes offered by Food Lion (e.g. low prices, clean stores, adequate items, stocked, convenient locations, and good service). There appear to be differentiated needs among consumers in the total market. The key issue is identifying the segments and deciding which one(s) to target. Food Lion has identified a niche in the market and successfully appeals to the buyers' needs/wants. There is no indication that this segment will not grow at least as fast as the total market. Moreover, management understands this segment and knows how to meet its needs.

If Food Lion changes its format it will likely appeal to a different (and perhaps more) segments. Expanding outside the present segment will place the retailer head on with competitors like Kroger. This change will also require management to expand its knowledge about buyers in other segments of the market. An important issue is determining the size and growth trends in the conventional format segment. With competitors moving toward super-store and combination formats, a format change by Food Lion may move the firm into a highly competitive sector of the market. If there are enough buyers that want the conventional format, Food Lion may be better off trying to dominate this segment in metro-areas where distribution centers are profitable. Food Lion's growth record to date suggests that this segment offers opportunity, although further evaluation of market segment opportunity is needed to substantiate this premise.

Industry/Competitor Analysis. Food Lion's commitment to its format and operating style is widely acknowledged throughout the industry. The firm seems to be very good at servicing the needs of its targeted buyers. Competition comes from several sources including: (1) competition for consumers budgets, (2) fast-food retailers (take-outs), (3) discount retailers and drug stores, (4) direct competitors like Bruno's, and (5) wholesale clubs (e.g. Sam's, Price stores). Case Exhibit V provides a detailed analysis of competitive supermarket chains. Exhibit TN-1 compares the various store formats.

Analysis of Competitive Advantage. Food Lion has several competitive advantages in the conventional format segment of the market. The company is a classic example of the use of selective targeting coupled with a low cost, low price strategy. Food Lion's low prices, efficient operations, no frills, and favorable brand image are key advantages over other super-store and conventional food chains. Management understands the market and has developed a successful strategy for competing in a mature industry.

Deciding how to compete in the future is an important issue. Should Food Lion continue to build market position using the conventional store format or instead adopt the superstore format. There are clear indications of a general industry trend toward larger stores. However, there appears to be a viable segment of buyers that seek low prices with less items than offered by superstores coupled with convenient locations. Food Lion does not appear to have any unique skills or resources for developing competitive advantage using the superstore or combination format. However, management must carefully evaluate the future trends for the segment and even if Food Lion's format is not changed, allowing for possible future changes may be appropriate (e.g., using store designs that can be modified.)

Targeting/Positioning Strategies. If management should decide to change Food Lion's format, it will require expanding into other segments of the market and changing the conventional format positioning strategy. This change will involve altering several aspects of strategy (e.g. expanding the range of items offered). Management's experience in the industry should facilitate the change. Nevertheless, altering targeting and positioning strategies will require design and implementation of a revised store format strategy.

Financial Considerations. Food Lion has been able to finance expansion primarily from internal operations. The firm's performance in the conventional store segment is impressive. Management has developed a planning and operating format that works very well. the financial attractiveness of format change is not clear. Expanding to a superstore format will require more resources per unit. However, the company should be able to handle these requirements if the decision is made to change Food Lion's format strategy. Additional market and financial analyses are needed to more fully explore the impact of format changes.

B. Expand Geographically Using the Conventional Store Format.

Since the above discussion also applies to this alternative for many of the evaluative criteria, the analysis considers the issue of geographical expansion as a way to continue Food Lion's growth. Two important questions concerning expansion are: (1) where to expand and (2) how to expand. The southeast is a logical region for Food Lion to continue its expansion. However, there are several factors that seem to be important in expansion. Food Lion's efficient distribution system requires distribution centers that can access ret\ail stores at distances no more than 200 miles away. Two centers are planned for Tennessee and Jacksonville. Market areas must be identified that will support one or more distribution centers. Thus, expansion should be driven by a cluster of stores within a circle with a 200 mile radius. Potential market areas must be identified that offer strong market potential and favorable competitive characteristics.

Management must identify and evaluate expansion targets. Favorable characteristics include population centers that can support a distribution center. There is no apparent reason why these expansion targets have to be contiguous. Computer information capabilities enable networking throughout the U.S. Purchasing can be either centralized or by distribution center. The important consideration is that geographical proximity of one center to another does not appear to be necessary. For example, Food Lion could target the Dallas/Fort Worth metroplex, without having to serve the geographical areas between DFW and Food Lion's current markets. The key issue is whether the market potential in an area will allow Food Lion to apply its "ink blot" formula.

Recommendations

There are clearly important changes taking place in the industry. However, whether Food Lion should change its store format is less clear. There are no market size and growth data in the case. Nevertheless, company growth has apparently been successful in the southeast. Management's expansion plans in Florida and Tennessee suggest that market opportunities are available. There does not appear to be an immediate requirement to changing store format. And management does not appear to favor changing format. In fact, movement of several larger competitors toward the superstore format may create more favorable opportunities for Food Lion's conventional store format. However, management should continue to carefully evaluate market trends and segment opportunities. Performance of the existing base of stores will give some indication of the potential for this segment of the market.

Management should identify and evaluate market target areas and establish priorities to guide expansion. The rate of geographical expansion should be gauged by the availability of people and financial resources. Competitor monitoring should also continue to evaluate trends (and threats). If indications develop of the decline of the conventional store format, then management must consider alternative format strategies.

Epilogue

In 1991 Food Lion pursued its expansion strategy in the Dallas/Fort Worth metroplex using its "ink blot" formula. The company continued its impressive sales and income growth since 1987. It was one of the fastest-growing grocery chains in the U.S. Sales in 1992 were estimated at $8 billion, over double 1988 sales *(Value Line)*. The chain had 800 stores in mid-1991.

The DFW strategy followed the established store formula and construction of a 735,000 square foot distribution center to supply 42 planned stores. Eventually, the company may open as many as 80 stores. The attack on the $7 billion metroplex grocery market followed the basic strategy: offer low prices, convenient store locations, 15,000 items, and 33,000 square feet of space. The management plans larger stores than in the southeast and all will have bakeries. Tom Smith spearheaded the advertising campaign which was several months ahead of store openings. Apparently management evaluated the market and competitive situation to be favorable for Food Lion's store concept and marketing approach.

Additional Information Sources

Richard W. Anderson, "That Roar You Hear is Food Lion," *Business Week*, August 24, 1987, pp. 65-66.

Stephen Bennett, "What's in Store for the Core," *Progressive Grocer*, November 1989, pp. 54-58.

Claire Poole, "Stalking Bigger Game," *Forbes*, April 1, 1991, pp. 73-74.

CASE 2-5
BANCO NACIONAL DE COMERCIO EXTERIOR, S.N.C. (BANCOMEXT)[*]

Synopsis:

BANCOMEXT, the Mexican Bank for Foreign Trade, was in charge of extending federal government credits, guarantees, and promotional service in support of Mexico's foreign trade. The North American Free Trade Agreement (NAFTA) allowed Mexican firms to expand in the United States and Canada, but this also meant that American and Canadian firms would be competing in the Mexican marketplace. The main goal of BANCOMEXT was to support Mexican companies to increase their productivity and competitiveness.

NAFTA presented many opportunities for BANCOMEXT, but the small and medium-sized companies that the institution placed emphasis on did not share the bank's market oriented strategy. Ms. Maria Rosa Gonzalez had to either attempt to create a market oriented culture in the companies that BANCOMEXT worked with or find an alternative to the selective orientation strategy.

Teaching/Learning Objectives:

This case combines many different issues into one scenario. One, the often vague notion of a market orientation is focused upon. Two, BANCOMEXT is an international company. Three, the bank is a service organization. Four, NAFTA issues are highlighted.

Specifically, the case allows for:

- an understanding of the complications associated with a market orientation,
- a different view of a service organization (i.e., a bank offering promotional services),
- a discussion of the role of government in a company's approach to doing business, and
- attention to the international component of doing business.

Discussion Questions:

1. What is a selective orientation?
2. Why is the export market so important to BANCOMEXT?
3. Is it unusual for a bank to take on such a large promotional role?
4. Assess the strengths and weakness of BANCOMEXT. Identify the organization's opportunities and threats.
5. How does BANCOMEXT differ from its competitors?

---

[*] This teaching note was prepared by Victoria L. Crittenden and Stephanie Hillstrom, Boston College, and William F. Crittenden, Northeastern University, as an aid to instructors using the case, "Banco Nacional de Comercio Exterior, S.N.C."

6. Is an alternative to the selective orientation strategy more appropriate? What are the alternatives and which one would you suggest?
7. Is BANCOMEXT market oriented? Why/Why not?

Analysis:

1. What is a selective orientation?

This is not an easy question to answer. While the second paragraph of the case basically repeats the way Maria Rosa Gonzalez defines a selective orientation, it is not very easy for the case analyst to state, specifically, the bank's notion of a selective orientation. [By the way, the case writer asked this question several times and got the same response from both Maria Rosa Gonzalez and one of the bank's regional directors.]

After asking the question and getting a few responses from students, it is useful to "back up" a bit with the case. Here are a few suggestions for clarifying a confusing business situation for the class, before moving on in the discussion.

First, what is BANCOMEXT? The bank, in general, is defined in the first paragraph of the case. It is both a financial service institution and a promotional service institution (described later in the written case). The case focuses upon the promotional side of the bank. However, one cannot forget about the financial service component since it is likely that promotional service customers are also financial service customers.

Second, what is the Promotional Services component of BANCOMEXT? The case describes this group in detail. Basically, the bank attempts to introduce Mexican companies in the international market. This is achieved through: agreements with promotional groups in other countries, direct promotion by BANCOMEXT, and training programs/counseling for the bank's promotional service customers so that these customers can become more knowledgeable about doing business in other parts of the world.

After a general discussion/clarification of BANCOMEXT, the class is probably ready to move back to the question of a selective orientation. Basically, the bank promotional services group is interested in working with Mexican small/medium-sized businesses that produce goods/services which are in particular product categories and which satisfy the needs of certain target markets. The promotional services group has identified market niches which it feels have strong potential (e.g., telecommunications). The promotional services group after identifying these niches wants to work with Mexican companies who provide goods/services for these niches. So, if someone who produces Mexican arts and crafts wants promotional help from BANCOMEXT, a market for Mexican arts and crafts would have to have been identified by BANCOMEXT as a market with strong potential. If not, in theory, the bank would not provide promotion services to this Mexican producer.

Once companies which satisfy needs in particular market niches are identified, the plan is for the promotional services arm of BANCOMEXT to work with these companies so that each company produces goods/services which are wanted/needed by the customers in the identified/targeted market segments. That is, a "production orientation" by the Mexican small/medium-sized producers is not acceptable.

So, the bank wants to be market-oriented by providing goods/services demanded by the consumer. Implementing a market orientation occurred through carefully identifying viable market segments (niches) and then identifying Mexican companies who could provide goods/services to these segments.

2. Why is the export market so important to BANCOMEXT?

It is important to note that BANCOMEXT is The Mexican Bank for Foreign Trade. As such, it is the Mexican government's financial institution and is the bank for foreign trade (the bank was created by the Mexican government for the promotion of foreign trade). Thus, BANCOMEXT has the charter of dealing with the foreign market in terms of exports. The export market is *the* market for BANCOMEXT.

Mexico had, historically, relied on oil exports for growth. However, the early 1980s found this market to not be viable and forced Mexico to pursue alternative markets for sustainable growth. At the heart of this was foreign trade. Foreign trade was a foundation for Mexico's economic recovery, growth, and modernization in the 1980s. Many foreign trade policies (programs, NAFTA, zero rate for VAT) were enacted by the Mexican government with the effect to be the strengthening of exports.

Thus, the export market was a key component of the bank's mission.

3. Is it unusual for a bank to take on such a large promotional role?

It is not easy to picture a bank here in the U.S.A. taking such an active role in what appears to be a marketing issue. Typically, banks are thought of as financial advisors, not advisors on the best way to promote a company's product/service.

However, officials at BANCOMEXT were wise to create a promotional arm of the bank given that the bank's success is driven by the success of Mexican businesses in the export market. Bank officials must have realized that financial advice would not be enough to make Mexican firms successful when faced with international competition.

4. Assess the strengths and weakness of BANCOMEXT. Identify the organization's opportunities and threats.

Exhibit TN–1 provides a sample SWOT analysis.

5. How does BANCOMEXT differ from its competitors?

There is not really any information provided about the bank's competition. One can see by looking at the English translation for the names of competitive banks that none of the competitors focused extensively on foreign trade. The competition, as with BANCOMEXT, was created with specific purposes in mind such as housing, agricultural development, interior commerce. Naturally, however, these issues overlap with the same Mexican companies that BANCOMEXT targets for its foreign trade issues. And, there is nothing to prevent a Mexican company from conducting its foreign trade affairs (i.e., financial needs) with a bank other than BANCOMEXT.

The distinct difference between BANCOMEXT and its competitors is the bank's focus (and thus level of expertise) on foreign affairs. It is unlikely that any of the competitors have a separate division for promotional services. Due to the bank's focus, BANCOMEXT also could assist its clients with affairs in its international offices (not available from the competition).

6. **Is an alternative to the selective orientation strategy more appropriate? What are the alternatives and which one would you suggest?**

Expect the responses here to be mixed. Some students may find the selective orientation too confusing to be of much use. Others, who have worked their way through the idea, may find it as a viable alternative.

Students who have bought into, and understand the notion of, a market orientation will think that the selective orientation is the only possible route for Mexican firms to be successful in a global marketplace. As Maria and the promotional services group have found, however, it is highly unlikely that small and medium sized Mexican firms will have a market orientation initially. So, implementation of the selective orientation will involve a lot of education and training on the part of the small and medium sized business managers.

An alternative might be to determine where Mexican companies are the strongest (e.g., agriculture, arts & crafts) and focus specifically upon promoting these particular industries. This would be playing upon the current strengths of Mexico and the goal would then be to get these products into the international marketplace.

Another possibility might be to establish partnerships between national and international firms in particular product areas. The Mexican company would basically be the production component and the international company could focus getting the products into the international market. However, this would not move Mexico into the international market as a strong player. Such a weak role is probably not what the Mexican government had in mind with its economic recovery.

From a little different perspective, some students may feel that BANCOMEXT needs to focus upon particular markets (countries) rather than attempting to cover the globe initially. Exhibit 7 shows export projects in markets such as Benelux, United Kingdom, Japan, United States, Germany, Spain, and Sweden. One idea might be to focus upon a few countries and work exclusively in those markets before broadening the scope.

As this is really the decision point for the case, it is important to push for several alternatives along with the pros and cons of each. After listing the pros and cons, the instructor needs to return to at least one or two of the alternatives (particularly the selective orientation alternative) and discuss an implementation plan for each. The instructor needs to begin early in the course to let the students know that implementation is critical to success. The "how" will move the students from "what sounds good" to what might work.

7. **Is BANCOMEXT market oriented? Why/Why not?**

This is a good way to end the class. The focus has really been upon the promotional services division of the bank. However, theoretically, a true market orientation would encompass the entire organization. There may be some doubt as to whether this is true at BANCOMEXT.

While some students may not agree that the bank is market oriented, most students tend to respond "yes" to this question. BANCOMEXT is committed to a customer focus (via its selective orientation), it attempts to coordinate and communicate its marketing (via the CSCE), and, naturally, it wants to make money on the transactions via Mexican firms being successful in foreign trade (if Mexican firms are successful, BANCOMEXT makes money on its financial transaction and the Mexican government makes money).

We do not know, however, if this concern toward the market place extends into the financial services side of the bank. If it does not, then there may be strong doubt as to whether the bank is market oriented or whether the promotional services group is market oriented. While so much emphasis seems to be on the promotional side, a quick look at the organization chart shows that the financial side outweighs the promotional side by at least 3 to 1.

One might think, though, that the bank's emphasis upon promotional services shows a high level of market orientation. Concerning how well the theme permeates throughout the entire organization might be questionable.

Teaching the Case:

The case is not straightforward to teach. A clear plan should be in place before entering the classroom. While the class may deviate from the plan, careful attention must be given to moving back to the planned approach. The order of the questions is one approach, used successfully, to teach the case. This allows for targeted, yet general, discussion of the issues and moves easily into whether a selective orientation is the right alternative.

As a warning, the nature of the topic, market orientation, makes the case too easy to discuss in circles.

Epilogue:

The promotional services group continues to follow a selective orientation strategy. The implementation of the strategy focuses upon educating/training the owners/managers of Mexican small and medium-sized businesses. The education occurs in all aspects of business. Educators travel to both the CSCE and other locations in Mexico to conduct seminars on various topics. In some instances the Mexican managers are brought to the United States to attend short educational programs.

The mind set of the managers continues to be an issue for the group. Mexican managers are not used to thinking about the customer in quite the way a market orientation suggests. Also, for many of the owners/managers of these small to medium-sized companies, tools and techniques which we find so routine (e.g., market research) are new to them.

Additionally, members of the promotional services group attend executive training programs. This keeps group members abreast of leading edge business topics in the international market place. Additionally, it is probably reinforcing to know that the Executive Director of the regional office in Monterrey attended a four-week marketing program in Boston in 1991. Bank officials must be driven to understand marketing issues better through its funding for such a long program (both in costs and time). While the bank has continued to send one person to the program each summer, the person now being sent is part of the promotional services group. So, there may be some mixed signals here.

Issues were arising, in 1994 and 1995, regarding the Mexican economy as a whole, which would have an effect on BANCOMEXT.

The Mexican economy was having serious troubles, resulting in the Clinton Administration's proposal of $40 billion in loan guarantees to rescue the economy. Congress wanted Mexico to pay stiff premiums and begin stringent economic reforms before any U.S. taxpayer money was exposed. The Mexicans would have to pay a fee of around 10 percent of guaranteed loans they drew on and pledge oil revenues for collateral. Mexico would also have to make large cuts in government spending and sell off state-owned industries.

President Ernesto Zedillo was hurting his ability to manage Mexico's troubled economy. By bringing a member of the opposition into his Cabinet and ordering a complete remake of the corrupt justice system, he might have been causing future protest over social inequality, U.S. interference, and job losses. Zedillo's advisors planned to maintain strict fiscal and monetary discipline and hold the line on inflation. They wanted to move quickly on privatization to raise money and encourage investment in the Mexican economy, because most of the credibility that Mexico had built up over the previous six years was lost.

A one and a half percent decline in gross national product and an inflation of 25 percent or more was predicted, and the government wanted a seven percent wage ceiling. Mexico's economic failure could be a major strain on the North American Free Trade Agreement. In addition, the country's banking system was likely to suffer further losses from the economic slowdown.

Exhibit TN–1   SWOT Analysis

Strengths

- large supply of low-wage workers
- network of international offices able to identify market opportunities and develop relationships for stable, long-term trade with the host countries
- access to information on export markets and opportunities, as well as the knowledge of how to penetrate those markets
- extensive communications technology to facilitate "free of charge" marketing and information services
- deep pockets and accessibility of other resources (national and international data banks; export guides; product classification systems; and domestic/import/export directories) as a governmental agency
- in position to speed the internationalization of Mexican companies by determining both the product demands of foreign markets and the production capabilities and needs of Mexican companies
- relationships with foreign banks and trade offices
- diverse product offerings as a financial intermediary
- diverse promotional services offered: agreements with promotional institutions in foreign markets (e.g., The China External Trade Development Council of Taiwan and The Belgian Foreign Trade Institute); export development projects; investment projects; and advisory, information, counseling, and training services through the CSCE
- goal and resources to educate the Mexican business person in modern business techniques through consultations and training courses covering all functional areas.
- market orientation, e.g., the introduction of new credit services and modification of existing products to meet changing requirements of Mexican companies

Weaknesses

- overlap with other government agencies (e.g., COMPEX worked on the development of export projects; SIMPEX identified and promoted trade and investment projects that had both Mexican and foreign company interests; the State Export Promotions Programs addressed deregulation, administrative issues, and coordination; BANCOMEXT worked on identification of market niches with the greatest potential, the promotion of exportable goods and services with the highest value-added. All four agencies are involved in the promotion of Mexican export. Not only is this costly, but there is also the potential for much infighting and competition.)
- operational costs of Mexican offices three times the cost of all international operations
- lack of focus, i.e., promotional **and** financing services
- government-owned/controlled companies (public utilities, petroleum, and certain manufacturing industries) not attractive to foreign investors
- less well-developed Mexican network than its development bank competitors
- lack of communication across functional areas (See Exhibit 5)

Opportunities

- Foreign Trade Law (1993) and related foreign trade policy provided for:
  * promotion of non-oil exports
  * attempted to regulate/control unfair practices
  * foreign exchange control
  * customs simplification
  * external restrictions
  * transportation
  * transit revision
  * phytosanitary restrictions
  * registration of brands
- electronically network offices within Mexico to bring down operational costs
- government/government economic modernization and revitalization policies of 1985 and 1986
- long-term commitment of government
- globalization
- membership in trade agreements (GATT, NAFTA, Andean Development Corporation and Permanent Committee of the Conference on Asian and Pacific Economic Cooperation)
- new and diverse trade and investment opportunities
- export to Asian markets
- expanding exports to US and Canada, Europe, and Latin America
- attract industries from higher-wage countries
- collaboration, alliances with other government agencies and banks to eliminate duplicative efforts, allow each participant to focus on comparative advantages, e.g., BANCOMEXT concentrates on promotional, informational, and training activities, while the myriad of specialized development banks listed on page 6 concentrate on providing general and industry-specific financing and export credit for Mexican companies.
- growing economy, new law (1993) designed to establish clear rules and procedures to promote
- opportunity to increase foreign investment in commerce, entertainment, and services
- opportunity to increase foreign investment from Great Britain, Germany, France, Japan, and Switzerland
- export of agricultural products, electrical and electronic equipment, automotive products, non-metallic minerals, plastic and rubber products, and steel, metallic products, machinery and equipment, and textile and leather products were all experiencing export growth

Threats

- concomitant decline in import growth (from 24 percent in 1992 to 5 percent in 1993) might lead to a backlash against Mexican imports in export markets, e.g., "Buy American," "Made in U.S.A."
- membership in trade agreements (GATT, NAFTA, Andean Development Corporation and Permanent Committee of the Conference on Asian and Pacific Economic Cooperation) will increase competition from U.S., Canadian, and other imports as access is increased, tariffs are cut, trade and investment barriers are eliminated
- pressure from environmental groups in the U.S. and elsewhere concerned about the lack of international environmental regulations contained in NAFTA may lead to boycotts or other consumer actions
- high volume/low cost products of competitor banks
- non-payment in foreign trade, leading to increased outlays for export guarantees
- expropriation of projects in less stable, undemocratic countries
- default by Mexican companies in debt to BANCOMEXT
- in 1993, a rapid increase in credit issued, both in total dollars granted (47 percent increase) and the number of companies served (115 percent increase)
- non-market-oriented culture of Mexico's small and medium-sized companies
- inflation

CASE 2-6
OPTICAL FIBER CORPORATION (OFC)*

Synopsis

Optical Fiber Corporation illustrates the marketing issues that confront a rapidly growing company in a high technology industry. The case study presents an opportunity to formulate corporate marketing strategy for a business with several attractive marketing opportunities that is facing the threat of additional competition. Students will learn about a new technology and be challenged to conceptualize a marketing strategy to competitively position OFC in the fiber optics market for the next several years.

OFC is a comprehensive marketing case emphasizing marketing opportunity analysis and strategic marketing at the corporate level. The strategic issues center on diversifying a product mix and customer base, cost reduction to discourage competitive entry, product development, and vertical integration by internal development or acquisition. A combination of opportunities must be selected to develop a strategy in the context of limited financial and marketing resources.

Teaching Objectives

1. To introduce students to a relatively new technology that will significantly impact their lives and the practice of marketing in the next century.

2. To introduce and teach strategy formulation at the corporate level for a rapidly expanding business with exceptional marketing opportunities.

3. To illustrate the importance of selecting a marketing strategy that is consistent with available financial and marketing resources.

Discussion Questions

1. What is the current financial position of OFC?

Students should be instructed to review the income statement in Table 1 and the balance sheet in Table 2 with the intent of assessing the financial strength of OFC. A summary of the key financial ratios is presented in this Instructor's Note—Exhibit 1 (on the following page).

A review of the liquidity, asset management, and profitability ratios indicates that OFC is in reasonably strong financial condition. The company has good liquidity and a strong cash position. Comparative ratios for asset management and profitability are not available because the industry has so few firms, but generally the ratios are very favorable. OFC has a good profit margin on sales and is earning a reasonable return on assets for a manufacturing company. Instructors should note that OFC is generating $8.0 million in cash flow from operations, but it has $2.31 million of long-term debt on its balance sheet and a $3.00 million license fee payable in 1993. Overall, the business has no obvious financial problems and seems capable of financing the marketing opportunities presented in the case with cash or external financing.

---

* Prepared by Lawrence M. Lamont, Professor of Management, Washington and Lee University, 1993.

Instructor's Note—Exhibit I   OFC Financial Ratios, 1992

Liquidity
   Current Ratio $31,022,000/$12,493,000 = 2.48
   Quick Ratio   ($31,022,000 - 6,656,000)/$12,493,000 = 1.95
Asset Management Ratios
   Inventory Turnover $30,475,000/$6,656,000 = 4.58
   Total Asset Utilization $48,764,000/$56,476,000 = 0.86
Profitability Ratios
   Profit Margin on Sales $10,231,000/$48,764,000 = 21.0%
   Return on Total Assets $10,231,000/$56,476,000 = 18.1%
Cash Flow From Operations $8.0 million
License Fee Payable in 1993 $3.0 million
LT Debt to Equity Ratio $2,310,000/$43,983,000 = 5.3%

2. What is the nature of competition in the optical fiber industry?

Competition in the industry is unique and worthwhile discussing with students. Historically, the number of participants was limited by patents covering the fundamental optical fiber technology, the need for substantial capital investment, the availability of specialized equipment, and access to personnel with the requisite technical expertise. Also, during the early 1980's, there was a surplus of capacity for producing optical fiber. The imbalance of supply and demand significantly intensified competition which caused price erosion and high expectations from customers for product performance. In recent years it appears that growth in demand has eliminated excess supply and prices have stabilized.

OFC's main competitors are its licensors to whom it pays royalties and who have substantially greater resources and operating experience. OFC competes for sales based on its ability to fill orders promptly at competitive prices, product performance and customer service. Although it is not mentioned in the case, the two licensors are Corning, Inc. (formerly Coming Glass) and AT&T Technologies, Inc., (formerly Western Electric Company, Inc. a subsidiary of AT&T). Thus, OFC is in the unique position of competing with its licensors. Students will be even more surprised to learn the OFC's largest customers are also AT&T and Siecor Corporation, a company owned by Corning, Inc. Both AT&T and Siecor account for more than 10 percent of OFC sales.

It is likely that the market will have new entrants in the next few years as the patents covering optical fiber technology continue to expire. Additionally, both licensors have retained the right to license additional firms to produce optical fiber and cable if they wish to do so. The obvious conclusion is that the market will become increasingly competitive and OFC must take immediate steps to fortify its position in existing markets before it pursues new marketing opportunities.

3. What are the strategic weaknesses that OFC must address in the process of formulating a corporate marketing strategy?

The case identifies two weaknesses that must be addressed as OFC prepares its corporate marketing strategy. First, the company should attempt to reduce its dependence on products sold under the patent licenses. OFC pays 9.0 percent royalties on licensed products with the agreement now in force. By diversifying its product mix to include products not covered by the agreement OFC can increase profits and reduce its dependence on the licensors who are also competitors.

Second, OFC needs to diversify it customer base. Presently 70 percent of its sales come from three customers, two of which are licensors and competitors. OFC is vulnerable to the loss of a major customer. A significant effort needs to be made to expand the customer base by developing new customers.

4. How would you assess the present marketing capability of OFC?

Marketing at OFC would not be considered a strategic strength. The company is driven by technology and managed by former engineers. The present capability is probably adequate for marketing an industrial component which optical fiber is for a cable manufacturer. Product quality and performance, customer service, and competitive pricing are crucial elements of the marketing strategy and OFC seems able to provide these benefits to its customers. Even though OFC seems adequately staffed with salespeople, a strategic marketing capability will need to be developed. As the company plans its future corporate marketing strategy additional investment in marketing will be necessary as well as an organization structure capable of implementing and supporting the strategy.

5. What strategy should OFC pursue to protect its core business and competitive advantage?

The threat of expiring patents and impending competition makes the need to protect the existing multimode fiber business for data communications the highest priority. OFC should seek a cost advantage by emphasizing R&D to reduce manufacturing costs for multimode fiber and to incorporate the latest technology to improve the quality and performance of its products. Continued emphasis must be placed on competitive pricing and manufacturing technology as barriers to discourage competitive entry into the industry. The annual R&D expenditure is an important pan of the strategy to maintain a competitive advantage. If this aspect of the strategy is performed effectively it should enable OFC to expand its customer base and reduce its vulnerability to the loss of a large customer.

In preparing the case study, students will often overlook the importance of R&D to preserve and enhance the competitive advantage in the existing multimode fiber business. Instructor's should emphasize that no strategy is complete without cost reduction and product improvement as the cornerstone of the corporate marketing strategy. A significant portion of the annual R&D expenses shown in case Table I should be used for this purpose.

6. Of the marketing opportunities presented in the case study, which seem to make the most sense for OFC? Why?

As mentioned, R&D for cost reduction and product improvement must be at the heart of any strategy. Extending the product line of specialty optical fibers is a natural development of an existing capability. Specialty optical fibers have higher profit margins because royalties are not paid, the fibers are coated which adds to their value, and the niche markets are not as attractive for competitive entry.

OFC should make the annual commitment of $400,000 to fund the necessary R&D to deepen the product line of specialty fibers. Additionally, the company should hire a sales manager, a product manager, and a marketing assistant at an annual expense of $325,000 to establish the line. Because the specialty products require a different marketing strategy than the existing multimode products, a separate marketing team needs to be established to ensure that the new products receive proper attention. Students should be encouraged to design an organization arrangement for the specialty fibers group.

Initially, manufacturers' representatives should be used to represent the product line to prospective customers. The representatives efforts would be coordinated by the sales manager who would also select the organizations and the geographic locations where sales representation would be established. Eventually, OFC would want to replace them with its own employees.

The implementation of the cost reduction and product improvement program (discussed in question 5) combined with the additional development of the specialty optical fibers would be an acceptable low risk corporate marketing strategy that would enable OFC to continue its growth in sales and improve profitability. A summary of the financial implications of such a strategy is shown in this Instructor's Note - Exhibit 2.

Instructor's Note—Exhibit 2   Financial Implications of Marketing Opportunities

Project	Capital Expenditure	Annual Expense
1. Cost Reduction and Product Improvement		$1,170,336*
2. Product Development of Specialty Optical Fibers		$400,000
Marketing Support		$325,000
3. Product Development of Singlemode Fibers	$4,000,000	$2,500,000
Vertical Integration into cable manufacture Internal		
Development	$5,000,000	$500,000
Acquisition	$10,000,000	
4. License Fee Payable	$15,000,000	$3,000,000

*Cost Reduction and Product Improvement estimated at 2 percent of annual sales. Annual sales assumed to increase by 20 percent in 1993.

7. Should OFC develop and market singlemode fibers?

Yes, OFC needs to immediately pursue the development of a product line of singlemode optical fibers to capitalize on the marketing opportunities in the telecommunications and CATV industries. Even though OFC would not be a primary source of fiber for the cable companies serving these markets, the growth projected and the size of the markets should enable OFC to gain entry as a secondary supplier and develop a profitable business. It is not likely to be as profitable as the specialty fiber business, but it will diversify the product mix and the customer base.

The marketing capability that exists to market the multimode fibers will probably be adequate since the strategies are quite similar. As the business develops, OFC will find it necessary to expand its personal selling capability so that it can continue to provide outstanding service to its new customers. The financial implications to develop and market singlemode fibers are also shown in the Instructor's Note - Exhibit 2.

8. Does forward integration into the optical cable business make sense for OFC? If yes, what market entry strategy should be pursued?

Students invariably argue for forward integration and usually prefer internal development instead of the purchase of a cable company. The reasoning seems to be that no reasonable marketing opportunity should be overlooked if the company has the requisite financial resources. However, it doesn't make sense in this instance.

The large number of domestic and foreign competitors producing cable is a significant problem. They are well entrenched in the market and some, such as Siecor, are divisions of much larger companies that also make optical fibers. Eventually, it would place OFC in the position of competing with its best customers for sales to cable users.

Second, the cable business requires a much different manufacturing capability. Optical fibers are cabled in a myriad of different ways to meet the very specialized needs and requirements of users. Technology and technical skills, while very important in producing optical fibers are less important in producing optical cable. However, design and fabrication skills along with the engineering to combine a variety of raw materials and components into a finished cable are of importance. Even though two OFC founders have previous experience in the cable business, it would be incorrect to conclude that OFC has the fabrication and manufacturing skills to successfully enter the industry.

Finally, OFC must resist the temptation to pursue every marketing opportunity that seems attractive. Other than the expertise to manufacture the optical fibers that are used for cable manufacturing, OFC has no other apparent competitive advantages that would suggest a successful entry into cable manufacturing. If the company speeds its resources among too many projects, it simply increases its vulnerability to competitive challenge in the core business of producing and marketing optical fibers.

A more reasonable approach would be for OFC to enter into a partnership or strategic alliance with one or more cable manufacturers that would enable it to sell into the telecommunications and CATV markets. Students will generally not be aware of this option, so instructors should plan to explore it during the case discussion.

Part 3

Growth Strategies

CASE 3-1
GOLDEN VALLEY MICROWAVE FOODS, INC.[*]

Synopsis:

Golden Valley Microwave Foods, Inc. (GVMF) strived to link technology, quality, convenience, and price into products that consumers would buy regularly. The company was extremely successful with its Act II microwave popcorn but was not as successful with its microwave breakfast items. GVMF was also test marketing microwave french fries. In 1991 ConAgra, the second largest food processor in the US, acquired GVMF.

The snack food market was very large with many competitors, and the microwave food market had its ups and downs. But as a division of ConAgra, GVMF did not face the same risks as it had when it was started. Jim Watkins had to decide on a solid growth strategy to remain as a profitable division of the corporation.

Video Summary:

Jim Watkins, founder of Golden Valley Microwave Foods, Inc., talks about his company's focus. He discusses how technology was used to design better microwave products, and talks about the kinds of products he wants to market and the international markets he wants to enter. The problem of distributing microwave foods and the intricate packaging technique used for the french fries are mentioned. The video runs 11 minutes, 18 seconds.

Teaching/Learning Objectives:

The case holds student interest due, in part, to the popularity of the product. Issues regarding entrepreneurship, international expansion, as well as growth arise in the case.

Specifically, the case:

- highlights the correlation between growth strategies and the marketing program,
- illustrates the strategic demands of expanding the product mix and/or developing new markets,
- provides the opportunity to show the importance of various elements of the marketing mix, such as distribution, in moving into new markets (e.g., international),
- allows practice in segmenting markets for the purpose of identifying a growth strategy, and provides an opportunity to study a relatively small, entrepreneurial
- firm and the issues/challenges encountered by the firm after it has been acquired by a large corporation.

Discussion Questions:

1. How can GVMF's market be segmented?
2. What is the market size for Golden Valley's product offerings?

---

[*] This teaching note was prepared by Victoria L. Crittenden, Stephanie Hillstrom, and David Angus, Boston College, as an aid to instructors using the case, "Golden Valley Microwave Foods." Revised 1998.

3. What are the strengths and weaknesses of GVMF? Are there any opportunities or threats?
4. What is Jim Watkins trying to do with Golden Valley Microwave Foods?
5. What are the growth possibilities for GVMF?
6. Where should Watkins focus his attention? Why?

Analysis:

The first three questions encompass the situation audit step in the suggested approach to case analysis.

1. How can GVMF's market be segmented?

Segmentation occurs in each of the four major classification categories: (i) geographic, (ii) demographic, (iii) psychographic, and (iv) behavioralistic. The major geographic segmentation occurs if Golden Valley takes its microwave foods internationally. Taste preferences vary by country as evidenced with the taste differences found in popcorn (buttery, sugary, cheesy, spicy). Simultaneous with geographic differences internationally, we see demographic segmentation noted particularly in Great Britain where age segments the popcorn market. A number of demographic segmentation variables are surely found in the microwave foods market such as age, family size, and income. Psychographic variables are likely evidenced in the lifestyle and/or health conscious trends related to the snack foods market. GVMF's market can be segmented behavioralistically in terms of user/non-user of microwave foods (numbers could be derived broadly from penetration rates related to microwave ovens) and buying conditions regarding the location of purchase (e.g., grocery store, vending machine).

Students may also identify regular, flavored, low-fat, low-sodium, and low calorie as a forms of segmentation. While this is true, be sure to note that this is product segmentation rather than market segmentation. These product offerings are meeting the needs of particular market segments.

2. What is the market size for Golden Valley's product offerings?

Very broadly, market size for microwave food items is the number of households which own microwave ovens. This would be around 68,000,000 U.S. households using footnote two as a reference point (acknowledging that this is an old number). [If one percent equals 800,000 homes, then 85 percent equals 68,000,000 homes.] Translating this into dollars is possible using the average yearly household expenditure for microwave foods of $15. Thus, market size for Golden Valley's microwave food products could be around $1,020,000,000. [68,000,000 times $15 equals $1,020,000,000.] This is substantially more than GVMF's $140 million in revenues in the early 1990s. Yet, it does show that GVMF represents almost 14 percent of the microwave foods marketed currently.

The above calculations do not take into account international figures. Microwave penetration figures showed that there was a lot of room for growth in both Japan and the United Kingdom (microwave ovens were the fastest-growing home appliance in Western Europe). There is a chance that as more and more consumers become accustomed to microwaves that the purchase of microwave-only foods will grow as well.

In looking at the snack food market, we see a large market of $10 billion to $15 billion. Per capita consumption of snacks in the U.S. was around 20 pounds or 5 billion pounds in total. So, the snack food market is a large potential market. However, there are a number of major players in the marketplace such as Frito-Lay and Keebler. Any entry in this market would probably have to be of a "healthy" nature.

There are many numbers for students to play around with in this case. Some forms of number crunching will get the students somewhere, others will not. However, the instructor should encourage students to talk about the types of quantitative analyses attempted with this question.

Some structuring of the data is:

Microwave Ovens:

- 1980s penetration was 40 percent
- 800,000 homes equaled 1 percent
- 1993 penetration was 85 percent

Microwave Oven Foods:

- $15 average yearly household expenditure

Golden Valley Microwave Foods:

- $140 million equals company revenues
- 90 percent was popcorn
- 10 percent was Morning Line

Snack Foods Market:

- $10 billion to $15 billion in dollar size
- 1991 = 5 billion pounds
- U.S. per capita = 20 pounds

Popcorn:

- 14 percent of 5 billion pound snack food market
- U.S. per capita = 50 quarts in 1990s
  13 billion quarts total
- U.S. expenses for popcorn = $1 billion
  $600 million = microwave popcorn
- historically, 25% annual growth rates
- possibility of mature market ahead for microwave popcorn
  GVMF predicted growth rate of 15%

Fast Food:

- $55 billion market

- 75% in home consumption and growing

It is expected that many of these numbers will be referred to when deciding where Watkins should focus his attention.

3. **What are the strengths and weaknesses of GVMF? Are there any opportunities or threats?**

Exhibit TN-1 provides an example SWOT analysis.

4. **What is Jim Watkins trying to do with Golden Valley Microwave Foods?**

This is Step 2 in the case approach, the problem/decision statement.

Jim Watkins needs to determine the long-term growth strategy for GVMF. It is interesting to open the class with this question. There is a tendency to start crunching numbers and loose sight of what the decision actually is. The students will still have to discuss the type of analyses described above, yet tend to keep in mind the case and the issue at hand.

5. **What are the growth possibilities for GVMF?**

This question is consistent with Steps 3, 4, and 5 in the suggested approach to case analysis.

There may be some confusion surrounding the identification of GVMF's current market. Some students may identify the current market as owners of microwave ovens in the U.S. Others may separate the market into "big" microwaves and "small" microwaves. Numerous other approaches exist, based largely on the responses to question 1. The following provides some suggestions using the current market base as U.S. households with microwave ovens. The instructor should be careful to clarify the various definitions so that there will not be confusion. While the options remain the same in a broad context, the various definitions lead to major differences in suggestions.

Basically, GVMF has three major options. **One, GVMF could attempt greater penetration with their current products in their current markets.** The numbers in question 2 suggest that there is an opportunity here. Golden Valley holds only around 14 percent of the market. Additionally, GVMF's popcorn revenues were $126 million. Yet, the microwave popcorn market was estimated to be $600 million. (The data is unclear as to whether this $600 million is for the U.S. only or for U.S. and international. It seems to be for the U.S. only.) Thus, there seems to be a lot of opportunity with this strategy. Implementation of this strategy would probably require changes in both distribution and pricing.

Two, **GVMF could develop new products for its current market.** Consistent with the above analysis, there is still potential in the U.S. microwave foods marketplace. Additionally, U.S. households are spending a mere $15 yearly for microwave foods. This is no where near expectations for microwave foods. If GVMF could develop new products, using its packaging technology and a more aggressive communications approach (e.g., the company may have to overcome the "not healthy" image of its foods in order to be successful), there is a strong chance this per household average could increase. Healthy snack foods are the fastest growing segment in the snack category. By developing healthy microwave snack foods, GVMF could gain a portion of this $248 million segment.

Three, **GVMF could develop new markets for its current products.** Microwave oven penetration is fairly low in foreign countries, but with predictions of rapid growth. GVMF could take its current products international and grow in this manner. While not really changing the base product, small local market changes (e.g., popcorn tastes) would probably have to be made as would the mode of distribution.

A useful approach to keeping track of various options is to list the pros and cons of each on the board. Upon completing this discussion, the instruction could ask the class to vote on which option he/she would recommend.

6. **Where should Watkins focus his attention? Why?**

This is Step 6, Recommendations, in the case analysis approach presented in the text.

Naturally, decisions will vary among students. If the instructor has kept good mental track based of the discussion surrounding question 5, it is good to call on at least of couple of students who have made different recommendations. Students should be pushed hard regarding the implementation of their suggested strategy. What will be the company's objectives? How will the marketing mix be changed (if at all)? Basically, what is the plan of action and how long will it take?

Teaching the Case:

The nature of the products makes this an easy case for students to discuss. There is a chance that all of the class will have tried microwave popcorn at some point. As well, many may have tried various other microwave foods and will want to express their personal opinions of these foods. It is good to allow some of this and the discussion can easily fall under the SWOT analysis section of the board. So, it will not appear that you are just wasting class time. However, be careful not to let too much of this go on and, where possible, relate personal opinions to facts/issues in the case.

As mentioned earlier, opening the class with the decision/problem statement tends to keep the class focused on the case. However, be sure to spend a considerable amount of up-front class time on the market segmentation and size issues. As well, push hard for specifics regarding the implementation plan for recommendations.

Watching the video at the beginning of the class discussion allows for a better understanding of the french fry technology.

Epilogue:

Sales of Golden Valley Microwave Foods' microwave french fries turned out to be disappointing. The most successful product for Golden Valley continued to be its microwave popcorn. James Watkins has since been promoted to president and chief operating officer of ConAgra Diversified Products Companies.

EXHIBIT TN-1 SWOT Analysis

Strengths

- innovative, patented packaging which facilitates <u>complete</u> popping
- leader with enthusiasm and a strong belief in his products
- successful product offering has made a name for the company
- part of Con Agra, the 2nd largest food processor in the United States
- large financial backing that comes with being a division of a major corporation
- ConAgra's experience, already own Orville Redenbacker
- Distribution system already in place

Weaknesses

- new product development lagging
- lack of customer focus in new product development, e.g., french fries not healthy like consumers want and are usually consumed in restaurants
- packaging (except for popcorn), which is the key to maintaining taste from shelf to table
- channels of distribution, i.e., supermarkets and grocery stores, clogged, highly competitive
- lack of marketing and business "clout" in this highly competitive arena
- efforts at communication, "education" of new markets unclear or almost non-existent
- loss of direct control because Golden Valley is now a division of ConAgra
- bureaucracy that comes with large organizations
- 90 percent of revenues from one product
- quality of non-popcorn products

Opportunities

- New Product Development
  * snack food market (more use oven to warm up leftovers than cook entire meals, estimated to be $10 to 15 billion).
  * healthy products
  * gourmet products
  * products for "low wattage" ovens for areas of potential growth in microwave food consumption. e.g., workplace, cafeterias, dorms
  * popcorn-related products, since popcorn consumption still growing at 15–25%, 60% of $1 billion popcorn market in microwavable popcorn
  * develop food tailored to the nutritional needs of the mature market (92% oven ownership), some of whom may be more house bound and less able to prepare healthy meals due to physical limitations
- license popcorn bag technology
- global markets for popcorn—but local R & D, appeal to local tastes, e.g., jalapeño-flavored popcorn in Mexico

- global markets (Japan, UK, Europe) for other products
- unique partnership with packaging supplier—offer a percentage of profits over and above price paid for packaging to encourage development of technological breakthrough in microwave packaging which maintains food quality, is safe and non-combustible, environmentally sound, and clearly labeled
- microwaves in 32 million US households

Threats

- take out food better tasting and accessible to consumer after work or on the way home
- increasing health-consciousness of the American public
- up and down market for microwavable products
- high tech packaging required—competitively priced product needed

CASE 3-2
BLOCKBUSTER ENTERTAINMENT CORPORATION*

Synopsis:

On May 19, 1991, Wayne Huizenga, Chairman and CEO of Blockbuster Entertainment Corporation, met with his top executives to consider some early signs that the video rental market might be approaching maturity. Although Huizenga saw no reason to panic, he did believe that this was an appropriate time for his executive team to review market conditions and to formulate market strategies for the '90's. Huizenga was not convinced that the industry had yet reached maturity but he knew that maturity was, in fact, a future reality and he wanted his staff to plan its strategies with this contingency in mind. At the conclusion of the meeting, Huizenga gave his Vice President of Marketing, Tom Gruber, the specific assignment to pull together information on Blockbuster's current situation and to identify and evaluate various growth strategies for the future.

Blockbuster has been an amazing success story. In the five year period from 1985 to 1990, it had grown from one company owned video rental store to almost 1500 owned and franchised stores. Blockbuster's revenues had grown from $10 million in 1985 to $1.1 billion in 1990. The video rental industry, fueled by the dramatic growth in home VCR's, was experiencing similar growth—from $3.6 billion in 1985 to $10.6 billion in 1990. Blockbuster was the clear leader in the field, with three times as much sales revenue as its next eight competitors combined. Blockbuster's success was built around the Video Superstore concept that provides customers with an unusually large selection of videos in a pleasant, family oriented and spacious shopping atmosphere—10,000 square feet with 10,000 tapes. The company's growth was achieved through three procedures: new company stores, new franchise outlets and buy-outs. Its basic operating strategy was to expand nationwide through the construction of company-owned stores in mid-sized and large cities and the franchising of stores in smaller towns.

In approaching his assignment, Tom Gruber began by framing the central question: "What major directions and what strategies should Blockbuster pursue in order to sustain its record of growth and success through the 1990's?" In addressing this question, Gruber used the traditional Product/Market Expansion Grid (Market Penetration, Product Development, Market Development and Diversification) to help him organize and identify the various alternatives. Having identified a number of possibilities for the executive committee to consider, he reminded himself that the question had to be tackled at two different levels: First it was important to devise a realistic marketing strategy to position the company to operate effectively in a mature market situation characterized by slower growth and more aggressive competition. At another level, he recognized the importance of planning a long range strategy for the company, including serious evaluation of different business opportunities and directions. In short, his assignment was the initial step in the formulation of Blockbuster's major business strategies for the years ahead.

---

*This teaching note was prepared by Raymond Keyes, Boston College, as an aid to instructors using the case, "Blockbuster Entertainment Corporation."

Teaching/Learning Objectives:

The case was written to illustrate the challenge of strategy formulation for a successful company facing maturing market conditions. The case was designed to accomplish the following objectives:

- To illustrate how a successful marketing strategy can propel a company into leadership in a dramatic growth industry.
- To provide industry and company information for students to interpret in relation to possible maturing of a market.
- To introduce students to the product/market expansion grid as a framework for identifying and organizing the various growth options.
- To emphasize the importance of short term strategy formulation for a company that is trying to maintain its position in a maturing market situation characterized by slower growth and more aggressive competition.
- To show the importance of planning a long range strategy for the company including serious evaluation of different business opportunities and directions.
- To encourage students to develop creative ideas and directions for strategy formulation.

Discussion Questions:

1. What is the industry situation? What has made Blockbuster so successful in this market?
2. What evidence is there that the Video Rental market is approaching maturity? What are the implications of market maturity to Blockbuster?
3. How can Blockbuster continue to grow in a maturing market? How can they capture a larger market share? What growth options do they have?
4. How can the product/market expansion grid be used to help in identifying opportunities for short term and long term growth?
5. Should Blockbuster continue to concentrate on the video rental business or should it consider other business directions? What other business options represent a good strategic fit for Blockbuster?

Analysis:

Industry Situation *(Question 1)*

Industry Size and Growth:

The consumer market for prerecorded videocassettes (comprised of the rental and purchase of feature length and other films) is experiencing continuing growth but there are signs that the growth is leveling off. Exhibit 5 shows that the industry has grown from $3.6 billion in 1985 to $10.6 billion in 1990 and to a projected $14.5 billion in 1993. Annual growth in dollars is down from $1.4 billion in 1986 to an estimated $1.2 billion in 1993. If students calculate the annual percentage of growth, they can see that the growth rate is down from 39% in 1986 to 14% in 1990 and an estimated 9% in 1993. Therefore, while the industry continues to enjoy significant growth, it is growing at a decreasing rate.

Exhibit 5   Industry Revenues (In Billions)

Year	Rental	Increase $	Increase %	Sales	Increase $	Increase %	Total	Increase $	Increase %
1985	$ 2.9			$ 0.7			$ 3.6		
1986	$ 4.2	$ 1.3	45%	$ 0.9	$ .2	29%	$ 5.1	$ 1.4	39%
1987	$ 5.2	$ 1.0	24%	$ 1.1	$ .2	22%	$ 6.3	$ 1.2	24%
1988	$ 6.4	$ 1.2	23%	$ 1.5	$ .4	36%	$ 7.9	$ 1.6	25%
1989	$ 7.1	$ 0.7	11%	$ 2.2	$ .7	47%	$ 9.3	$ 1.4	18%
1990	$ 7.7	$ 0.6	9%	$ 2.9	$ .7	39%	$10.6	$ 1.3	14%
1991(E)	$ 8.4	$ 0.7	9%	$ 3.7	$ .8	28%	$12.1	$ 1.5	14%
1992(E)	$ 8.9	$ 0.5	6%	$ 4.4	$ .7	19%	$13.3	$ 1.2	10%
1993(E)	$ 9.4	$ 0.5	6%	$ 5.1	$ .7	16%	$14.5	$ 1.2	9%

Comparison of industry rental versus sale figures shows that the rental growth rate dropped off from 45% in 1986 to 6% in 1993 while the tape sales growth rate decreased less rapidly, from 29% in 1986 to 16% in 1993. It is significant to note that the dollar increase in tape sales of $700 M in 1990 exceeds that of rental income at $600 M and continues higher in the following three year forecasts. The increasing strength in the tape sales market provides a good clue for students to consider as it relates to Blockbuster's future growth options.

A further indication of the growth in tape sales may be obtained by calculating the percentage of tape sale to total market revenues (Exhibit 5):

1985	.7/3.6	=	19.0%	1989	2.2/ 9.3	=	23.7
1986	.9/5.1	=	17.6%	1990	2.9/10.6	=	27.4%
1987	1.1/6.3	=	17.5%	1991E	3.7/12.1	=	30.6%
1988	1.5/7.9	=	18.9%	1992E	4.4/13.3	=	33.1%
				1993E	5.1/14.5	=	35.2%

Blockbuster Sales and Growth:

In five years, Blockbuster has grown from zero to $690 million in company revenues and $1.1 billion system wide revenues (including franchises). It has grown from 2 outlets in 1985 to almost 1500 outlets in 1990 (769 company owned and 698 franchise outlets = 1467 total). During this period, they purchased five video chains adding 533 retail stores. Exhibits 1, 2, and 3 provide data on their growth in units and revenues during the five year period. As with the industry figures, students should refer to Exhibit 3 and calculate the Blockbuster's growth increases in dollars and percentages. Here again, it is evident that the company has had significant growth but this growth is beginning to level off.

Exhibit 3   Blockbuster Revenues (In Millions)

Year	Rental	Increase $	Increase %	Sales	Increase $	Increase %	Total*	Increase $	Increase %
1986	$ 3			$ 4			$ 7		
1987	$ 19	$ 16	533%	$ 22	$ 18	450%	$ 41	$ 34	485%
1988	$ 87	$ 68	358%	$ 41	$ 23	105%	$128	$ 85	207%
1989	$283	$196	288%	$101	$ 60	146%	$384	$ 256	200%
1990	$468	$185	94%	$129	$ 28	28%	$597	$ 213	55%

* This total does not include income from royalties/other

While it is realistic to expect that the percentage figure would decline, it is significant to note that the rental income figure has leveled off at approximately $190 M and the tape sales income has only increased $29 M. The declining rate of growth in the tape sales portion of the business is in sharp contrast to the industry experience (see above). As mentioned previously, students may identify this tape sales area as one in which Blockbuster could direct more attention.

Blockbuster's dominant position in the market is dramatized by the following share of market calculations:

Share of Market (In Millions)

Year	Company Sales* ÷ from Ex. 3	Industry Sales from Ex 5	= Market Share
1986	$ 25	5,100	.5%
1987	98	6,300	1.6%
1988	283	7,900	3.6%
1989	663	9,300	7.1%
1990	1,133	10,600	10.7%

* This is system sales, including franchises

When asked to explain what has made Blockbuster successful *(Question 1)*, students should point out that they have done an excellent job of identifying the needs of its family oriented target market (selection, convenience and rental rates) and in responding with their Superstore concept. Blockbuster's growth strategy calls for them to (1) open new stores, (2) acquire stores in key growth areas, (3) enhance store revenues and (4) expand internationally. Exhibit 1 shows how effective they have been in opening new stores and franchise outlets. Exhibit 2 identifies the major purchases that they have made of major video chains. 533 stores have been added via the purchase of five major chains over a three year period. Exhibit 6 shows, however, that there are not many large chains left to be acquired. The majority of stores (26,000 out of 29,000 or 90%) are "mom and pop" stores, under 3,000 square feet and approximately 3,000 tapes. Here is another area that students might consider as a possible avenue for increasing market share. Is there some sort of role that Blockbuster can play in supporting these smaller retail outlets with inventory and systems support. The case points out that the grouping of convenience stores, drug stores, supermarkets, and mass merchandisers (220—500 video titles) are placing more emphasis on sales rather than rentals. Is there room for Blockbuster to act as an advisor/supplier to these outlets and, in so doing, for Blockbuster to strengthen the sales portion of their business?

The case also points out the recent efforts that Blockbuster is making in its efforts to expand internationally. It has begun to establish itself in the United Kingdom (127 Superstores) and Canada (51 Superstores), it has letters of intent for development of Superstores in Mexico, Australia, Spain and Japan. The international market is clearly a significant area for future growth.

In considering Blockbuster's success to date, students may identify many areas covered in the case description—their Superstore concept, their effective store management systems, their strong franchising program, their creative pricing approach, their aggressive advertising and promotion programs, etc. A discussion of these successful strategies can give the students a genuine appreciation for the effectiveness of a comprehensive marketing strategy— involving a clear understanding of target market needs and a creative marketing mix response.

Market Maturity: *(Question #2)*

As discussed previously, there are clear signs that the dramatic growth rate for both the industry and for Blockbuster is beginning to slow down. Although there is still significant growth taking place, the industry increases are flattening and declining in both dollar revenues and percentage increases.

It is apparent that some of the players in the market are forecasting market maturity as is exemplified by the Cox Enterprise's decision to sell all of its 82 Blockbuster franchises. Other industry analysts are predicting a slow down and an increase in competition.

Much of the growth in the video rental business in recent years has been fueled by the dramatic household penetration of VCR's. Exhibit 4 shows that this penetration has reached 72% in 1990 and is forecasted to reach 91% in 1995. While this continuing growth in household VCR's has provided a built in impetus for the growth of prerecorded videocassettes, this will not continue to be so as new VCR's home installations approach the saturation point. Therefore, students should recognize that future growth will depend on getting <u>more usage</u> from existing VCR owners versus <u>more users</u> from new VCR owners. Students should be encouraged to consider ways that Blockbuster can develop programs and incentives to promote increased use by existing customers. Here again, a review of the marketing mix elements may uncover new ideas or tactics for encouraging more usage. Students might be encouraged here to volunteer their own ideas concerning ways that Blockbuster might use its product, price and promotion elements to develop additional business.

Another sign of impending market maturity comes in the form of increased competition, both direct and indirect. Direct competition can be anticipated simply because no growth industry can go for long without attracting competition. RKO Warner is an example in point. Exhibit 6 shows RKO Warner with 40 store versus Blockbuster's 1620. However, whereas Blockbuster is averaging sales of $698,000 per store ($1,130 M÷1630 stores), RKO Warner is averaging $1,075,000 per store ($43 M÷40 stores). It appears that RKO Warner has developed a very successful format that could represent a competitive challenge. In addition to competing directly with other videocassette dealers, Blockbuster competes for the consumers' entertainment dollar. This broadens the competitive picture to include movies, sports, network T.V., cable T.V. and other leisure time activities. Pay-per-view T.V. looms significantly on the horizon as a major threat with advances in video and communications technology. Students might like to talk about the threat of pay-per-view T.V. How long will it be before pay-per-view T.V. becomes a technological and economic reality and what must Blockbuster do to anticipate and meet this challenge?

Overall, it is safe to say that Blockbuster will be competing in a more mature market situation in the years ahead and students should be reminded that a mature market is characterized by product/service modifications, increased competition, more aggressive pricing, increased expenditures for advertising and promotion and increased pressure on margins and profitability.

Strategy Formulation: *(Questions 3, 4 and 5)*

Confronted with the prospect of market maturity in the foreseeable future, students should consider the implications of these conditions in relation to Blockbuster's short term and long term strategy formulation.

First, students should be encouraged to discuss the implications to Blockbuster if they do not react to the impending changes in the market. This can lead to a good discussion of the perils of the three C's that all too often characterize an industry leader: Complacency, Conservatism and Conceit. Students should recognize that Blockbuster cannot sit still in this fast moving environment nor can they assume that their successful strategies will continue to be successful in the ever changing marketplace. When students conclude that Blockbuster must continue to a pursue an aggressive market strategy, they should be asked how the company can shape this strategy to capture a larger market share. The previous sections have identified three possible areas for consideration: (1) video sales, (2) "mom and pop" support, (3) international markets. Students should be asked to contribute ideas concerning other possible avenues that Blockbuster might consider.

At an appropriate point in the discussion, it is helpful to bring in the product/market expansion grid as a useful tool for organizing the growth options and for pointing up some logical directions. This section of the case analysis can be quite energizing for the students as they brainstorm about the various marketing opportunities. This discussion can be exciting but it may also be somewhat disorganized. The instructor may wish to remind the students to identify their individual contributions with one or another of the boxes in the product/market expansion grid. Or the instructor may prefer to begin with the four options (market penetration, product development, market development and diversification) and ask the students to identify various opportunities within each of the boxes. The instructor may also refer to the product/market opportunities identified by Tom Gruber and ask the students to evaluate them in terms of their strategic implications.

It may be helpful in this discussion to differentiate between short term and long term strategies. Blockbuster's immediate challenges are centered around strategies that will help them to maintain their growth and momentum in their existing prerecorded video sales and rental business. There are some genuinely interesting things that they might to do to enhance their position in their current business. On a broader scale, however, students should be asked separately to consider possible new business directions which Blockbuster should consider in its long range strategy formulation. Here, it is useful to point to the importance of the uncontrollable variables in the external environment, most especially, technological change. Students should be asked to consider various growth options and to explain why in each case, the option might represent a good "strategic fit" for the company. In either a class discussion of the strategies or in a written case, the instructor should not be looking for any particular strategies but rather for strategies that students can articulate in terms of their appropriateness relative to Blockbuster's specific strengths and competencies. This is a good way to get students to give serious thought to the whole concept of "strategic fit."

Teaching the Case:

The case is an enjoyable one to teach. Students easily identify with Blockbuster and its strategy formulation issues. At the outset, in the discussion of the industry and company situations, it is effective to point out the importance of sound marketing strategy as it is exemplified in the Blockbuster experience. It is good for students to see that marketing strategy plays such an important role in the performance of a successful company. All too often, we use cases which emphasize marketing deficiencies and mistakes. It is good to have a case situation where the company has performed well and where the main question focuses not on what must be done to save the company but rather what should be done to maintain the company as a leader in its field.

The initial question positions students to analyze the quantitative information in the case. The actual quantitative techniques are not particularly sophisticated but they do encourage students to push the numbers and interpret them. In this case, the numbers do support the concern that the industry and the company are facing the prospect of market maturity in the not too distant future. While this is not a catastrophe, it is the signal for Blockbuster to go to the drawing board to consider ways that it might formulate strategies to respond to the changing market conditions.

The final part of the case involves student identification and consideration of various short and long term strategies. The product/market expansion grid provides a useful tool to help them organize and categorize their thinking. Finally, as they venture their ideas for strategic directions, the students are asked to defend them in relation to the company's strengths and competencies—or "strategic fit." Overall, the case is a good, upbeat situation which provides an effective platform to explore issues and opportunities related to marketing strategy formulation.

Epilogue:

Blockbuster has done so many things that it is hard to keep track of them. To summarize:

- 1992—acquired music retailers Sound Warehouse and Music Plus (500 music stores)
- 1992—entered a joint venture with London-based Virgin Retail Group to develop music megastores domestically and abroad (17 locations in Europe, Australia, and the U.S. with plans to build 50 more megastores by 1995, including 10 in the U.S.)
- 1993—acquired 35 percent of Republic Pictures
- 1993—acquired a majority interest in Spelling Entertainment Group, a producer and distributor of both theatrical and television entertainment (70% ownership)
- 1993—entered into an agreement with IBM to develop disk-on-demand, a technology that will create CDs on-site at music stores
- 1993—acquired an interest in Discovery Zone, an operator of indoor children's playgrounds
- 1993—exploring possibilities of mini-amusement parks with virtual-reality "rides" in which computer simulators produce effects
- 1993—formed partnerships with Pace Entertainment of Houston, Texas, and Sony Music Entertainment to build outdoor amphitheaters
- 1994—opened Blockbuster Golf and Games in Sunrise, Florida, (other family oriented, high tech video arcades in planning stages)
- 1994—merged with Viacom and the merged company was successful in its effort ($9.75 billion) to buy Paramount Communications Inc. (after a lively bidding war against QVC Network Inc.); the resulting multimedia complex will include Blockbuster's 3,600 video stores, 500 music stores plus Viacom's cable operations (MTV and Showtime) and Paramount's famous studio and movie library, Simon and Schuster and Prentice-Hall publishing divisions, Pocketbooks, Madison Square Garden, and the New York Knicks and Rangers
- Future Plans—Sports/Entertainment Complex in South Florida (25,000 acre complex in the planning stages, will include baseball stadium, hockey arena, theme park with water rides and Blockbuster Village which will be an outdoor arcade with shopping, movie theaters, and entertainment)

Clearly, Wayne Huizenga and company have looked into the future and decided that the way to remain competitive in the rapidly changing entertainment world against such giants as Time Warner and Disney is to a be part of a giant entertainment complex themselves.

CASE 3-3
SYSTEMSOFT CORPORATION*

Synopsis

SystemSoft developed system-level software that allowed the operating system of a PC to interface with the hardware. The company had been highly successful in its core product lines of BIOS, PC Card, and power management software. Systemsoft operated in a highly competitive environment in which technological innovation was a key driver to success. William O'Connell, Senior Vice President, Strategic Accounts and Business Development, had to decide whether to proceed in developing a new call avoidance product category. Call avoidance software had a significant market potential and there was no comprehensive problem resolution software on the market.

Teaching/Learning Objectives

SystemSoft is a high tech company and, thus, operates in a highly competitive, rapidly growing marketplace. In addition to allowing students to focus upon a company in a high tech industry, the case illustrates:

- the risks associated with moving beyond a company's core product lines,
- new product development in a rapidly changing marketplace, where technological obsolescence occurs quickly,
- organizational changes that accompany product line changes, and
- relationship marketing's vast role in new market entry.

DISCUSSION QUESTIONS

1. Describe SystemSoft's core products.
2. What markets does SystemSoft operate in?
3. Who are SystemSoft's competitors and how does it fare in relation to these competitors?
4. Conduct a SWOT analysis for SystemSoft.
5. What decision confronts SystemSoft?
6. What options are available to O'Connell? What issues should he consider when making a growth decision?
7. What is your recommendation? How should this recommendation be implemented?

---

* This teaching note was prepared by Victoria L. Crittenden, Boston College, and William F. Crittenden, Northeastern University, as an aid to instructors using the case, "System Soft Corporation."

Analysis

[Case Analysis Process: Step 1 = Questions 1-4; Step 2 = Question 5; Steps 3-5 = Question 6; Step 6 = Question 7.]

Describe SystemSoft's core products.

SystemSoft's products are not noticeable to the end-user, although anyone with a portable computer could be the owner of a SystemSoft product. The following shows the three major product categories with particular SystemSoft products shown in parenthesis.

BIOS (Plug and Play specification)—software that enabled PC hardware components to interact with the operating system software. For example, even though many computers are IBM compatible, they have a wide variety of options (e.g., system memory, controllers, peripherals). System-level software such as BIOS enables the vast array of hardware options to run the same operating system.

PC Cards (CardSoft, CardWizard PRO, and CardLite)—about the size of a credit card and was inserted into the PC similar to a floppy disk, allowed user to configure operating system hardware. For example, user might receive a message that the Modem card was "unknown." The CardWizard allowed the user to easily make changes to operating system which would allow the system to recognize the previously "unknown" card. The CardWizard made all of the necessary changes to resolve conflict and enable the card (with the user only having to click on the "Wizard" button). This product is a part of the PCMCIA (Personal Computer Memory Card International Association) technology and computers include at least one PCMCIA slot.

Power management software (Smart Battery Software System)—reduced power consumption when system components not in use. For example, as computers become more powerful they also consume more power. This results in shorter battery life. With software such as Smart Battery, power is reduced or turned off to elements immediately after their function is performed.

2. **What markets does SystemSoft operate in?**

SystemSoft operates in three major markets with their product offerings:

- Mobile Computer Market—e.g., notebooks, personal digital assistants
- Personal Computer Market—e.g., desktop computers, notebooks, PC card readers, network connectivity
- Home Market—e.g., home computers, notebooks

3. **Who are SystemSoft's competitors and how does it fare in relation to these competitors?**

Phoenix Technologies—competed in all three of SystemSoft's product categories. Phoenix was the leader in the notebook BIOS and power management markets.

American Megatrends—major competitor in the BIOS segment. American Megatrends was second in the notebook BIOS and power management markets.

Award—major PC Card competitor.

SystemSoft was the dominant player in the PC Card market with 64% market share and supplying 14 of the 15 notebook vendors. The company had approximately 20% share of BIOS and power management in the notebook market, but the company's share of the desktop BIOS and power management was small. Overall, SystemSoft appeared to rank third behind Phoenix Technologies and American Megratrends in the BIOS and power management markets and first in the PC Card market.

4. Conduct a SWOT analysis for SystemSoft.

A sample SWOT analysis is presented in Exhibit TN–1.

5. What decision confronts SystemSoft?

The strategic decision facing SystemSoft is: *How should it maintain its high level of growth in the future?* Students may identify the decision as being whether or not SystemSoft should enter the call avoidance market or stick with its core product line. However, these are the options for SystemSoft to consider when addressing the bigger growth issue.

6. What options are available to O'Connell? What issues should he consider when making a growth decision?

The three major growth options for O'Connell to consider are: market penetration, product development, and market development.

Market Penetration: When examining the three core product lines at SystemSoft, we see that the company is dominant in one category and third in the other two (question 3). Therefore, a strategy of market penetration would focus upon SystemSoft becoming a dominant player in the BIOS and power management markets. The company does very little advertising and promotion which suggests that there are opportunities to grow the current business via some strong marketing communications programs.

Product Development: SystemSoft operates in a highly competitive environment. Technological innovation was a key driver of success in this market. This leads one to believe that product development is a major route for SystemSoft to pursue. Identifying product-markets that lack strong presence is critical in a rapid-growth, technological environment. SystemSoft is considering just such an option with a new call avoidance product category. Research had suggested a significant market potential, with no comprehensive problem resolution software in the market. As a dominant, well-established player in its current markets, SystemSoft should not experience problems introducing a new product into its established markets.

Market Development: SystemSoft could focus upon moving its core technologies into new markets. SystemSoft's current market focus is in the computer marketplace. However, the power management products are important in the mobile communications market (e.g., pagers, cellular phones). This is a growing marketplace and might hold potential for SystemSoft.

Several criteria for alternative evaluation emerge in the analysis of this case. Examples include: company mission, technological leadership, fit with current customer base, fit with current distributor base, competitor activity, competitive advantage, relationship opportunities, market size, growth opportunities, current human resources, current financial resources, and long-term financial payback. Each of the alternatives is evaluated relative to these major criteria in Exhibit TN–2. Financial ratios are provided in Exhibit TN–3.

The exhibit provides a sample of how students could rank each of the alternatives on the specified criteria. Rankings will vary based on the student rationale for each. Basically, students need to provide justification for each of their rankings. There are no right/wrong rankings. This type of analysis can taken a step further and have weights provided to each of the criteria as shown in Appendix B of the case book. This process would result in a final score (relative weight * score) which would suggest the most appropriate alternative given the criteria used in the analysis. If using the weighting process, students will probably cluster the criteria into major groups (e.g., company resources, market, competition).

7. What is your recommendation? How should this recommendation be implemented?

The student's recommendation should flow from the analysis thus far. For example, the recommendation resulting from this current analysis would be to pursue the product development route with the introduction of the call avoidance software. This is a unique opportunity in that it allows SystemSoft to enter a large market with virtually no competition.

Implementation of such an option would include: product development, acquisition of technical expertise, identification of key relationships, changes in organizational structure (e.g., salespeople), and buy-in by stockholders due to rising software capitalization costs. Students should develop a timeline which shows the necessary actions (such as these) that must take place. Many of the actions will need to occur simultaneously. This allows students to understand the overlapping processes involved in managing a large organization (make sure students do not just place actions in a linear framework). Additionally, students should identify the person(s) in charge of implementing the tactical issues related to the selected option and resulting timeline.

Teaching the Case

Most of our students are not familiar with the types of products that SystemSoft produces. Thus, it is important to discuss SystemSoft's products before moving into recommendations and implementation. Since students are familiar with the products from which demand for SystemSoft's products is derived, a good way to begin class is to focus upon the products that students might own/use that have SystemSoft's component products. Then, it is fairly easy to "back into" the company's product lines. The case does not work well with a "what do you recommend" opening. (An exception to this might be in a High-Tech MBA program.) The issue—growth—is fairly straightforward in the case, but the product is not. The case works well when following the case analysis process as outlined above.

Epilogue

The call avoidance product was launched in June 1996 under the name, "SystemWizard." (Product data sheets are included with this note.) SystemSoft had commitments for the sale of 8 million units when the product was launched. Customers included: US Robotics, AST, Micron, and Packard Bell. The company experienced record revenues and earnings in the third quarter of 1996.

The company divided the sales force by product so that certain sales representatives were dedicated to the SystemSoft product. In November of 1996 at Comdex, SystemSoft announced partnerships with several independent software vendors, independent hardware vendors, and support-knowledge providers to expand the problem-solving capability of the SystemWizard. In December of 1996, SystemSoft replaced its third-party Asian representatives with company-owned offices and sales employees.

SystemSoft acquired Radish Communications in December 1996. VoiceView, by Radish, complemented the SystemWizard. VoiceView exploited patented modem protocol firmware technology that Radish had developed and licensed to companies representing more than 90 percent of the worldwide modem market. VoiceView enabled end-users to connect to an OEM support center or MIS help group and talk with a support representative who, during the same phone call over a single phone line, could view the end-user's system, diagnose any problems, and send necessary solutions to the computer while maintaining the voice conversation.

In November 1996, Phoenix Technologies announced that it had signed a license agreement to distribute CyberMedia's First Aid product through the OEM channel. AST also agreed to license the software, and SystemSoft's shares fell. The CyberMedia products had strong technical features and were very similar to SystemWizard, making it more and more difficult to differentiate the products.

EXHIBIT TN–1 SWOT Analysis

Strengths

- world's leading supplier of PC Card software
- reputation
- technologically innovative
- market share
- ability to influence market place
- dominance in mobile computing
- prominent customers
- strong direct sales force
- alliances/support from companies such as Digital and Intel
- financial status

Weaknesses

- lack of experience in advertising and promotion
- heavy reliance on relationships
- call avoidance software not "necessary" product
- not enough human resources to support product line expansion (e.g., engineers, sales)
- negligible share of desktop computer market

Opportunities

- market for traditional products such as BIOS, PC Card, and power management is strong
- few competitors in the call avoidance market
- demand for mobile computing is expanding
- market is ripe for relationships that build on competencies of several companies
- PC industry expected to spend nearly $4 billion on help-desk support in 1996
- key competitor in call avoidance market lacks ability to be total provider
- growth in cellular phone marketplace will result in increased need for PCMCIA support

Threats

- potential for rapid obsolescence
- competitive activity is high
- pressure from stockholders to reduce capitalization costs
- barriers to entry in software market not as high as in other technology industries

EXHIBIT TN–2 Alternative Evaluation

	Market Penetration	Product Development	Market Development
Company Mission	1	3	2
Technological Leadership	2	3	1
Fit with Current Customer Base	3	2	1
Fit with Current Distributor Base	3	1	2
Competitor Activity	1	3	2
Competitive Advantage	1	3	2
Relationship Opportunities	1	3	2
Market Size	1	3	2
Growth Opportunities	1	3	2
Current Human Resources	3	1	2
Current Financial Resources	3	1	2
Long-term Financial Payback	1	3	2

Ranking:

3 = best opportunity
2 = o.k. opportunity
1 = weakest opportunity

EXHIBIT TN–3 Financial Ratios

	1995	*1994*	*1993*
Profitability			
Net Profit Margin	0.13	0.03	-0.41
ROA	0.10	0.03	-0.68
ROE	0.12	-0.03	0.36
Liquidity			
Current	5.99	2.17	1.04
Leverage			
Debt to Assets	0.16	2.06	2.91
Debt to Equity	0.19	-1.95	-1.52
Times-interest-earned	188.15	10.82	-63.12
Activity			
Asset turnover	.72	1.24	1.65

Comprehensive, Automatic, Problem-Resolution Software
Increases Customer Satisfaction and Lowers Technical Support Costs

SystemWizard™ Client

A Breakthrough in Preventing Support Calls

SystemWizard Client is the front-end portion of SystemSoft's breakthrough solution for automatically resolving software problems with PCs and peripherals. Residing on a Windows 95 or Windows NT-equipped computer (notebook or desktop), SystemWizard Client quickly solves approximately 20 percent of the problems that spur technical support calls. SystemWizard could save your organization millions of dollars each year, depending upon your call volumes.

With its own expert system and local knowledge base(s) SystemWizard Client uses information from the computer itself to solve the most common problems on the spot. Thanks to SystemSoft's intimate knowledge of system-level software, users can click on a few simple questions (e.g. yes/no/don't know), and be back up and running usually within a few minutes.

With SystemWizard Client, PC OEMs and independent software and hardware manufacturers can provide their customers with an independent way to resolve problems at any time without needing to call for technical support. That increases customer satisfaction and lowers your support costs.

Solves Numerous Common Problems

SystemWizard Client is the perfect solution for diagnosing problems, identifying the underlying reasons, and implementing the proper solution automatically. It can resolve common problems associated with:

- Multimedia configurations
- Printers and drivers
- Modems and communication software
- Video display
- Peripherals such as printers and mice
- Network connections
- SCSI devices
- PC Card set up
- Configurations and resource conflicts
- Power management
- Application software
- Operating systems
- Internet connection difficulties
- Manufacturer-specific issues
- Much more

The user can launch SystemWizard Client at any time and click on a simple graphical user interface to begin the diagnosis. Or, SystemWizard will start automatically in the event of a Windows error or General Protection Fault. The graphical interface mirrors the layout of the user's desktop, tower, or notebook computer.

SystemWizard Client

SystemWizard Client gathers and analyzes key information that already resides on the PC from the Plug-and-Play BIOS, Windows Registry, Desktop Management Interface (DMI) files, configuration files, manufacturers utilities, and more.

Using an expert-system diagnosis engine, SystemWizard evaluates the various sources of information to assess probabilities of suspected faults. After assessing this information, SystemWizard Client may, if necessary, pose a brief series of simple "yes/no/don't know" questions that narrow down the focus to a specific cause. Unlike text-based alternative products, SystemWizard's "gather-and-focus" methodology enables it to quickly narrow down the problem to a particular category. Even if the user doesn't know where the trouble lies, SystemWizard will get to the root of the problem quickly and easily.

Using the answers provided and the system information gathered, SystemWizard Client searches its local "core" Knowledge Base on the PC for a solution. This core Knowledge Base consists of:

- A collection of "generic" problem-resolution cases associated with Windows 95, add-on peripherals, and software applications that are commonly found on most computers.
- Detailed knowledge about applications and peripherals that have been installed on the PC since shipment.
- System-specific knowledge that SystemSoft or the manufacturer can customize for a specific product.

Once it finds the solution, SystemWizard lets users choose between an AutoCorrect button, which implements the solution without any user intervention, or a Correct button that steps the user through the changes that will fix the problem. There's also a BackUp button that will undo the last correction.

An Optional Second Level of Problem Resolution

SystemWizard Client can solve your problems on a "stand-alone" basis for fast, "on-the-spot" troubleshooting and repair. It also helps form a more comprehensive end-to-end solution for solving a broader, more recent set of problems as well.

If SystemWizard Client can't solve the problem through its local Knowledge Base, it can automatically connect you through the Internet, asynchronous dial-up, or LAN – with remote SystemWizard Servers that contain larger, more up-to-date problem-resolution sets.

Feature	Benefit
Automatic Problem Resolution.	Increases customer satisfaction and reduce technical support costs.
Graphical Interface.	Intuitive, non-technical, and easy-to-use.
AutoCorrect provides one-button correction of problems.	Immediate resolution of 20 percent of common support issues.
Preview ability.	Enables users to preview or even print out the solution prior to execution.
Expert system diagnosis engine.	Identifies problem, even if user can't, sometimes requiring a few simple "yes/no/don't know" questions.
Local Knowledge Base(s).	Comprehensive Knowledge Bases provide additional, up-to-date soltuions available 24-hours a day through automatic connection.
Connects to remote SystemWizard Knowledge Bases.	Extended automatic solution transparently solves additional problems.
Resides on notebook or desktop.	Solves problems on all types of systems.

SystemSoft®

Corporate Headquarters
2 Vision Drive, Natick, MA 01760-2059
Phone: 508/651-0088, Fax: 508/651-8188
Email: wizard@systemsoft.com
Web: http://www.systemsoft.com

Branch Offices: Santa Clara, California, Phone: 408/988-6756, Fax: 408/988-6758 • Oxnard, California, Phone: 805/486-6686, Fax: 805/486-3343 • Taipei, Taiwan, Phone: +886-2-545-5370, Fax: +886-2-5452960 • Tokyo, Japan, Phone: +81-45-547-0021, Fax: +81-45-547-2086

International Representatives: Hong Kong (Arcon Electronics Ltd.), Phone: +852-24238873, Fax: +852-24872429, • Taipei, Taiwan (Regulus Technologies, Ltd.), Phone: +886-2-7697921 Fax: +886-2-7697922

© 1996, SystemSoft Corporation. All rights reserved. Printed in the U.S.A. SystemWizard and CardWizard are trademarks of SystemSoft Corporation. All other brand, product, and company names are trademarks, registered trademarks, or service marks of their respective holders.

A Network of Knowledge Bases to Provide Timely Solutions,
New Drivers, Latest Software Patches, and More

SYSTEMWIZARD™ SERVER

AN EXTENDED LEVEL OF AUTOMATED, ON-DEMAND SUPPORT

SystemWizard Server is the server-based software portion of SystemSoft's breakthrough solution for automatically resolving software problems with PCs and peripherals. It contains a superset of SystemWizard Knowledge Bases that seamlessly work in tandem with SystemWizard Client to provide a comprehensive, end-to-end solution for automatic problem resolution that increases customer satisfaction and decreases technical support costs.

Acting as the secondary level of support through LAN, Internet, or asynchronous dial-up connections, SystemWizard Server extends the SystemWizard family by providing access to a broader collection of computer problem-resolution sets than that shipped with SystemWizard Client. The result: fast, timely solutions to more technical support problems.

SystemWizard Server is designed for PC OEMs, independent software and hardware vendors, and in-house MIS or third-party technical support organizations that wish to create custom Knowledge Bases that encompass greater detail about their own product support issues. For example, a software maker may want to create a Knowledge Base on its own SystemWizard Server that has latest patches for a new release. SystemWizard Clients can then connect to the latest problem-resolution information in that specific SystemWizard Server. Or MIS Help Desks can maintain a SystemWizard Server for 24-hour problem resolution by employees all over the world.

COMPREHENSIVE END-TO-END SOLUTION

SystemWizard Server enters the problem-solving picture when the user's SystemWizard Client does not have the solution in its local Knowledge Base(s). In cases like this, the Client automatically connects to SystemWizard Server — through the Internet, asynchronous dial-up, or LAN — which takes control of the troubleshooting session. SystemWizard Client hands off all diagnosis information to SystemWizard Server, which scans its larger set of Knowledge Bases for a solution. To the end user, the session looks just like it did before the connection.

SystemWizard Servers can encompass numerous Knowledge Bases that contain more comprehensive databases of solutions with more up-to-date entries and less common problems not found on SystemWizard Client's "core" Knowledge Base. If the proper solution calls for software patches, DLLs, drivers, or upgrades, SystemWizard Server has all necessary enabling software to download and install the solution as well.

In addition, SystemWizard Server can even update the local core Knowledge Base on the SystemWizard Client enabling the user to solve more problems locally, without dialing into SystemWizard Server.

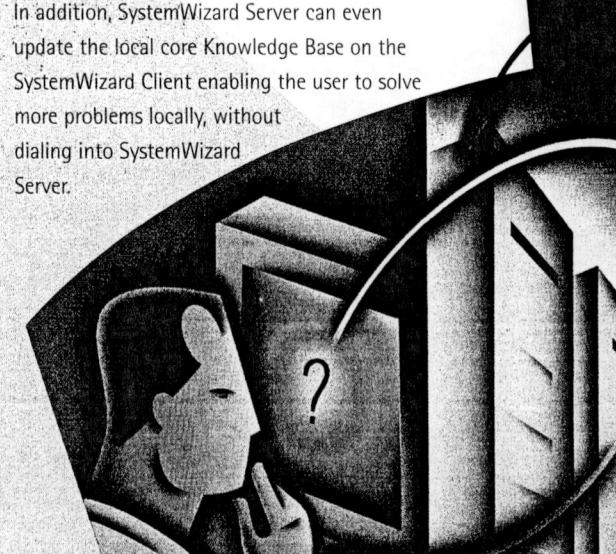

SYSTEMWIZARD SERVER

If SystemWizard Server can't solve the problem, it turns the case over to the technical support representative. SystemWizard speeds the "person-to-person call" by eliminating possible causes and providing the representative with a full briefing of the incident before he even speaks to the user. Since support engineers often spend 80 percent of their time collecting information (and as little as 20 percent actually solving the problem), SystemWizard can save technical support dollars, even if it doesn't yet have the solution.

Once the support engineer solves the problem, he can enter the problem-solution set in the Knowledge Base on SystemWizard Server using the SystemWizard Builder. That means the problem is solved by a support engineer once and the solution is replicated out to users through SystemWizard Server. It's solved "once and for all."

SystemWizard Server will also be integrated with leading Help Desk management programs. When a user calls help desk and provides a case number, the rep can then access SystemWizard's diagnosis information right from within the Help Desk software environment.

Given the dynamic nature of computer technical support, the industry requires a comprehensive solution that enables manufacturers and users to stay up-to-date with new problem-resolutions for the latest products and versions.

Feature	Benefit
Comprehensive end-to-end solution for computer support.	Increases customer satisfaction with product, and reduces product returns.
Reduces need to call for support questions.	Reduces technical support costs.
Integrated with SystemWizard Client.	Familiar SystemWizard Client interface transparently connects to SystemWizard Server, extending the problem-solving session whenever needed.
Larger collection of Knowledge Bases for more timely problem resolution.	Manufacturers can publish recent, less-common problem solutions to solve an additional 10 percent of support problems.
Connect through LAN, Internet, or dial-up.	Dynamic network of Knowledge Bases means your users can reach help 24 hours a day.
Automatically retrieves and installs fixes, patches, and solutions as needed.	Save numerous tedious steps and potentially, hours of work.
Update SystemWizard Client.	SystemWizard Server can download updates to local Knowledge Base(s) on the PC for even faster resolutions in the future.
Add new problem-solution sets through SystemWizard Builder.	Solve new problems "once and for all" by publishing them on SystemWizard Server.

SYSTEMSOFT®
Corporate Headquarters
2 Vision Drive, Natick, MA 01760-2059
Phone: 508/651-0088, Fax: 508/651-8188
Email: wizard@systemsoft.com
Web: http://www.systemsoft.com

Branch Offices: Santa Clara, California, Phone: 408/988-6756, Fax: 408/988-6758 • Oxnard, California, Phone: 805/486-6686, Fax: 805/486-3343 • Taipei, Taiwan, Phone: +886-2-545-5370, Fax: +886-2-5452960 • Tokyo, Japan, Phone: +81-45-547-0021, Fax: +81-45-547-2086

International Representatives: Hong Kong (Arcon Electronics Ltd.), Phone: +852-24238873, Fax: +852-24872429, • Taipei, Taiwan (Regulus Technologies, Ltd.), Phone: +886-2-7697921 Fax: +886-2-7697922

© 1996, SystemSoft Corporation. All rights reserved. Printed in the U.S.A. SystemWizard and CardWizard are trademarks of SystemSoft Corporation. All other brand, product, and company names are trademarks, registered trademarks, or service marks of their respective holders.

CASE 3-4
ANGOSTURA BITTERS, INC.*

Synopsis:

Angostura Bitters, Inc. was a small company located on the islands of Trinidad and Tobago. This company was known around the world for its aromatic bitters, a liquid blend of herbs and spices which was generally alcoholic, and was often used in mixed drinks, sauces, and dressings.

The U.S. market was the largest market for Angostura bitters, although the sales of bitters in the United States had declined, as did the sales of spirits in general. Americans had become more health-conscious and had cut back on alcohol consumption. Although the sales in the U.S. spirits market had decreased, rum's share of the market had increased, due to the fact that rum was used in more mixed drinks than any other spirits.

Angostura had tried, unsuccessfully, to introduce bottled rums into the U.S. market. Carl Ambrose, the Brand Manger for Angostura Bitter, Ltd., was debating whether to launch a new bottled rum under the Angostura name (as opposed to a different brand name), develop new sauce products, or create more uses for bitters.

Teaching/Learning Objectives:

The case focuses upon an international company attempting to grow. Specifically, the case is well suited to illustrate:

- various growth strategies in mature markets,
- targeting and positioning strategies in mature markets,
- the individual strategic evaluation that must take place when a company operates in various product market areas, and
- the importance of a detailed implementation plan in the complete development of a growth strategy.

Discussion Questions:

1. What does the future look like for the bitters, sauces, and spirits markets?
2. Does Angostura Bitters, Inc. face any competition?
3. Conduct a strengths, weaknesses, opportunities, and threats analysis for Angostura Bitters, Inc.
4. What growth options are available? What are the advantages and disadvantages of each option?
5. What growth option should Ambrose recommend for Angostura Bitters, Inc.?
6. Develop the recommended growth strategy.

---

* This teaching note was prepared by Victoria L. Crittenden and Stephanie Hillstrom, Boston College, and William F. Crittenden, Northeastern University, as an aid to instructors using the case, "Angostra Bitters, Inc."

Analysis:

Carl Ambrose needs to determine the optimal growth opportunities for Angostura Bitters, Inc. The company participates in three markets. Ambrose has to recommend what the company should pursue in all three markets. *[Step 2 in the case analysis process.]*

[Questions 1, 2, and 3 comprise Step 1 in the case analysis process.]

1. **What does the future look like for the bitters, sauces, and spirits markets?**

Since the markets for each are different, it is a good idea to separate the discussion based upon the three markets. Issues such as market growth and market size in the U.S. and worldwide are important.

Bitters:

Bitters is a product with an extremely long shelf life. As such, repeat purchases are few and far between. Bitters also seems to be a product known better amongst members of the "older" generation than the younger crowd. This is related to the alcoholic consumption habits of the younger age group (i.e., possibly more of a tendency to drink beer or wine than so-called hard liquor which is where bitters would be used).

U.S. sales of Angostura Bitters peaked in 1980 (80,000 cases). By 1990, U.S. sales were 50,000 cases. The decline was attributed to consumer moderation in alcohol consumption. Thus, bitters appears to be in a derived demand situation. Assuming nothing is done to promote bitters for uses other than an alcohol mixer, then the future is very dependent upon the future of alcoholic products.

Sauces:

Sauces and dressings were a multi-million dollar ($4,331 million) business in the U.S. and accounted for 1.6 percent of U.S. supermarket sales. There were at least 10 kinds of sauces, with soy, teriyaki, and worcestershire being the dominant three (and also the three where Angostura had product offerings). Supermarket sales of soy and teriyaki sauce had increased from 1989 to 1990 (4% growth), with the reduced salt segment seeing the largest percentage increase (28% growth). Angostura expected an annual growth rate of 20 percent in the sauce marketplace.

Spirits:

The world spirits market was somewhat mixed regarding sales growth. As a whole, the market experienced a six percent decline. Yet, sales of the top 100 brands grew by four percent. Premium-priced brands were experiencing the best growth. Additionally, consumption was expected to increase in some countries (i.e., Greece, Spain, and Japan) and decrease in others (i.e., United States).

Regarding the U.S. market, 1991 was the worst year since Prohibition with a decline of 5.6 percent. Sales were expected to decline even more through the middle 1990s.

Within the rum product offering, the market had experienced growth from the middle 1970s to the 1990s. Rum was used in more mixed drinks than any other spirits. Angostura rums which held a huge share in Trinidad and Tabago, were not successful, to date, in the U.S.

Thus, bitters was in a very mature market, the sauce market was still growing, and the spirits market was declining in some areas and growing in others.

2. **Does Angostura Bitters, Inc. face any competition?**

Yes. Angostura faces competition in all three of its markets. Rivalry exists in the U.S. and worldwide. Students need to think about who the competitors are, how big they are, and the competitors' strengths. Additionally, substitute products can be identified.

Regarding **bitters**, the company name is almost synonymous with bitters and, thus, is the market leader. Direct competition comes from regional companies. However, the company does experience competition from other types of spirits' mixer products, from substitute food flavoring products (e.g., vanilla extract), and from medicinal products.

In the **sauce** category, the company faces stiff competition. Kraft and Beatrice Foods' La Choy are the two major players in the U.S. market, with numerous other sauce and dressing manufacturers in the U.S. and around the world.

The **spirits** market is dominated by four companies (Int'l. Distillers & Vintners owned by Grand Metropolitan, United Distillers owned by Guinness, Seagram, and the Hiram Walker Group owned by Allied-Lyons). The rum market is basically controlled by Bacardi, with the market leader brand and a budget brand (ranked 44th). Other rum producers are Smirnoff (second largest) and Seagram.

Thus, Angostura faces little competition in its bitters market and very stiff competition in the sauces and spirits markets.

3. **Conduct a strengths, weaknesses, opportunities, and threats analysis for Angostura Bitters, Inc.**

Exhibit TN-1 provides a sample SWOT analysis.

4. **What growth options are available? What are the advantages and disadvantages of each option?**

[Steps 3 and 5 in the case analysis process.]

This case is great for using the BCG framework of analysis. If a discussion of this framework has not taken place already, building the students' responses into such an approach is a useful way to teach the case and introduce the BCG framework. The product-market grid is not a very useful tool here since Angostura is already attempting these four strategies (i.e., market penetration, product development, market development, diversification).

Angostura has three major product categories in which it can maneuver. It can attempt growth in any or all three categories. No matter which market(s) Ambrose determines to have future opportunities, all three marketplaces have to be dealt with internally. Decisions such as build, hold, harvest, or divest have to be made.

One approach the instructor can take is again a separation of the three product categories. Within each category, analysis could flow around the four alternatives of build, hold, harvest, and divest. A board plan might look something like Exhibit TN-2. The exhibit also provides examples of some of the pros and cons students might identify for each option.

5. **What growth option should Ambrose recommend for Angostura Bitters, Inc.?**

[Steps 4 and 6 of the case analysis process.]

Regarding growth, students may elect to attempt growth in all three product offerings or only one or two of the offerings. Push students to identify the criteria used in making the decision. Growth potential, market share, sales volume, niche sales, business strength, niche attractiveness, customer loyalty, and profitability are all criteria which could be used.

If students decide to focus on only one or two product offerings, be sure to find out what should be done with the other (s).

6. **Develop the recommended growth strategy.**

[Step 6 of the case analysis process.]

Students should be able to suggest the specifics of an implementation plan for the recommended growth strategy. When and where are very important issues which should be addressed.

For example, if the recommendation is to pursue growth in rum, where becomes very important. Should the company attempt growth in the U.S. or elsewhere (e.g., Hungary, Germany, Poland, Czechoslovakia, or Canada where per person consumption is highest)? The resulting marketing plan would probably be different for the U.S. than for countries where consumption is high.

If the recommendation is to pursue growth in sauces, one would expect the student to identify the type of sauces (e.g., regular or reduced salt, in addition to soy, teriyaki, worcestershire). The promotional plan is very important in the implementation of this growth strategy. [As a side note, sauces receive moderate ad and display support in grocery stores. This compares to heavy ad and display support for items such as carbonated beverages, cookies, crackers, juices, and pasta. Cereals receive both light ad support and light display support. Coffee receives moderate ad support and light display support, while prepared food receives heavy ad support and light display support.[1]]

Whatever the recommendation, the student should be able to state clearly who should do what, when, and where. The more specific the suggested marketing plan, the better. Budgets should include both time allocation (if more than one product/market is being pursued) and money. Students can also be pushed regarding how performance will be assessed for the recommended growth strategy.

Teaching the Case:

The case is interesting to teach since the class is actually discussing three markets simultaneously. However, this can also be confusing so the instructor has to help keep comments tied to specific markets/products.

The discussion begins easily with a statement of the decision Ambrose faces. Once the decision is identified, it is easy to move into the analysis and then to the recommendations. Starting with the "What do you recommend to Ambrose?" poses problems in getting to the analysis of each of the markets. This is not to say that the class cannot start with this approach, only that it is more a difficult approach to use.

Epilogue:

In 1991, the U.S. liquor industry experienced one of its worst years since the Prohibition, and the U.S. market was the single largest market for Angostura bitters. The overall decline in sales was due to price and tax increases, the recession, and a continued trend in moderate drinking. Consumers were looking for value, and researchers predicted that lower priced alcoholic beverages would sell more than premium

---

[1] *Progressive Grocer*, November 1991, p. 68.

brands. Bacardi rum was the top selling liquor brand overall, but its sales decreased by 10 percent. Only one of the top ten liquor brands had sales growth in 1991.

Angostura bitters were also used in sauces, and in 1991, retailers showed moderate support in promoting sauces through ads and displays. Moderate support means that a minimum of one-half of the categories in the product group received ad or display support from at least 50 percent of supermarkets in the United States at least once during the 52 weeks through the first quarter of 1991.

Angostura Bitters, Inc. was still attempting to determine the best growth route for the company. They were beginning to focus more attention on the rum business, with a dedicated division working to increase sales of rum. The bitters product was expected to continue its no/declining growth trend.

EXHIBIT TN-1   SWOT Analysis

Strengths

- brand name recognition
- product recognized for its versatility (i.e., a stomachic, a pick-me-up, and an ingredient in mixed drinks) and appeal to both the health conscious and consumers of spirits
- free access to U.S. market vis-a-vis the "Big Four" producers based in Great Britain
- secret recipe known by only a few

Weaknesses

- bitters packaging may be too large?
- versatility of bitters not known (people buy for a single recipe then forget about bottle)
- product awareness low in younger (18 to 24 years old) consumers
- only 3 in 10 equated Angostura with bitters

regarding alcoholic beverages:

- lack of extensive distribution network outside of U.S. vis-a-vis large global producers (top four controlled 35 percent of global market, owned 40 of the top 100 brands)
- rum a seasonal spirit (summer, Christmas)

Opportunities

- growth opportunities
    * new products
    * new markets (with globalized economy)
- new packaging for bitters
- better communication of uses for bitters, i.e., recipe development, free and more accessible distribution of cookbook in grocery and/or liquor stores
- be part of trend, a driver in changes in tastes

regarding alcoholic beverages

- increased consumption in Hungary, the former East Germany, Poland, Czechoslovakia, Canada, Greece, Spain, and Japan
- no impediments (tariffs and trade barriers) to U.S. market following CARICOM and the Caribbean Basin Initiative
- while overall spirit consumption is on decline, rum still has potential because it is most used as a mixer
- new rum drink recipes
- new "regional" recipes, e.g., "Boston Tea Party" to encourage spirit consumption in areas of use where consumption is low
- consumers interested in new drinks, e.g., Bacardi Breezers and other fun, convenient, already-mixed drinks

- consumers interested in premium-priced alcoholic beverages (consumers were "drinking better", which could make up for losses in decreased consumption)
- sales of rum on the incline despite decline of spirit sales overall
- form joint venture with Bacardi, which controlled the global rum market, to become bulk supplier for the rum giant
- increasing affluence and alcohol consumption in places such as Greece, Thailand, and Brazil
- form joint venture as supplier of rum to one of the big three spirits producers, not just smaller Puerto Rican producers, to help them catch Bacardi (e.g., Seagram's, which is only 0.1 percent behind in the US market), and to get their rum into growing markets otherwise difficult to penetrate (especially without an established global distribution network)
- look into markets where the spirits industry enjoys a higher status, e.g., Great Britain
- new rum drinks for "off-season," i.e., early fall, late winter, and spring

regarding non-alcoholic products

- in increasingly health-conscious markets, e.g., the US, market healthful uses of Angostura bitters (as in 1990 ad campaign)
- to enter regional markets, develop strategic alliances with local companies, e.g., Tennent's in Great Britain
- sales of sauces and dressings growing, while sales of spirits on decline overall

Threats

- negative publicity for increased distribution in markets with growing consumption of alcoholic beverages
- increased sugar prices
- increased taxes
- economic downturn leads consumers to cheaper rums and spirits
- increasing health consciousness
- further declining status of spirits industry in U.S. (the U.S. accounts for nearly 50 percent of all world liquor imports so even a small decline could mean a large loss for producers and distilleries)
- innovative, fun, convenient products (i.e., Bacardi Breezers, Seagram's Gin and Juice, and Jack Daniel's bourbon and lemonade) on shelves or hitting them soon—little time for Angostura to think about the next move

EXHIBIT TN-2

Bitters

	Pros:	*Cons:*
Build	• strong reputation • company has knowledge about the product • no major competitors	• the amount of cash it would take to build the share • doubtful that this product will ever become a "star" again
Hold	• can maintain market share without altering cash input • cash cow • slow/no growth market	• market already experiencing drop • derived demand
Harvest	• could provide short-term cash to invest in other opportunities	• uncertain as to what could be done to harvest the product
Divest	• use cash and other resources in sauces and/or rum • consumption of bitters is dropping • "bitters" is not recognized by younger consumers	• this is what Angostura is known for

Sauces

	Pros:	*Cons:*
Build	• growing market • may be firm's "?" product with "star" potential	• stiff competition • cash requirements
Hold	• would not require cash input	• minor player in market already, this strategy might lead to automatic dissolution • market is growing
Harvest	• [so underdeveloped that there are no benefits]	• Angostura business position is not established enough for such a strategy
Divest	• would not require cash input, use cash elsewhere	• not sure there is a buyer for such an undeveloped Angostura product offering

EXHIBIT 2 (cont.)

Rum

	Pros:	*Cons:*
Build	• company has distilling capacity • 95% of T&T market • relationship with Puerto Rican rum manufacturers • market for rum still growing • facility in New Jersey already	• <u>stiff</u> competition • cash requirements • had experienced problems in U.S. market already
Hold	• no cash input • already 95% of T&T market, not much more to gain • slow growth marketplace	• could lose T&T share if global competitor entered T&T market
Harvest	• [really no benefits here since market position is that of providing unbranded rum to other manufacturers (e.g., Bacardi)]	• not established enough for such a strategy
Divest	• use resources elsewhere • declining spirits market • stiff competition • name has no meaning globally • consumers drinking less	• large share of T&T market • backbone of export business • new markets are opening up

CASE 3-5
THE BACOVA GUILD, LTD. (A)[*]

Synopsis

John Walters, Director of Marketing for the Hardware Division of the Bacova Guild, Ltd., faces important decisions on a new consumer product. SignMaster™ is a decorative house sign introduced by The Bacova Guild in August, 1990. The product received a favorable review from the trade, but sales have been disappointing. Management is reviewing the sales results and the marketing strategy for SignMaster™ with the intent of making improvements. The firm has retained an independent marketing research organization to conduct survey research and a market test to identify the reasons for the weak consumer response.

The Bacova Guild is a comprehensive marketing case emphasizing pricing and promotion strategy. It provides students with the opportunity to review an introductory marketing strategy and use the research results to conceptualize a new strategy for the product. The case also provides background information on the firm's approach to product development and raises the issue of how it might be altered to improve the new product development process.

Teaching Objectives

1. To evaluate the approach to product development used by The Bacova Guild and suggest improvements.

2. To evaluate an introductory marketing strategy for a new product.

3. To allow students to analyze information from survey research, a test market and market introduction to formulate a marketing strategy for a product that is not meeting expectations.

Discussion Questions

1. Discuss the product development of SignMaster™.

In recent years, the Hardware Division product markets have matured and competition has imitated the highly successful Bacova mailboxes. Pricing has become more aggressive and profit margins for many Bacova products have declined.

To replace the lost sales and profits, the Hardware Division has pursued new product development. Postmaster™ and SignMaster™ represent the two most recent efforts described in the case.

Generally, Bacova's approach has been to generate a promising new product idea, develop a prototype, conduct limited market research within the trade, and in the absence of negative trade reaction, proceed to market introduction. Adjustments in marketing strategy were then made based on early sales experience and trial and error. Eventually, an acceptable marketing strategy would result.

Bacova has had success with this approach, but it can easily be improved to avoid the problems experienced with SignMaster™. One improvement would be to restructure the product development process

---

[*] Prepared by Lawrence M. Lamont, Professor of Administration, Timothy J. Halloran, and Thomas D. Lovell, Class of 1991, Washington and Lee University.

to generate more new product ideas initially and then screen them carefully prior to prototype development. Consumer input into the early part of the process is missing and it should be used to supplement management's judgment and guide the process. Bacovs needs to use consumer research to (1) help select new product ideas, (2) provide direction for concept and prototype development, and (3) along with the trade, participate in the market testing of new products prior to market introduction.

By not adequately testing SignMaster™ prior to market introduction, Bacova was unable to determine whether a need existed for the product and characteristics of the target market. Eventually, the firm had to go back and conduct the necessary consumer research to improve the marketing strategy. In this instance it would have been more efficient to conduct the consumer research prior to product development rather than later. Trade confidence in Bacova's new product efforts can be easily lost if it continues to bring products to market that require continuous trial and error to determine the marketing strategy.

2. **What are the important findings from the consumer research and their implications for consumer behavior?**

The survey research results indicate the potential target markets for SignMaster™ include young homeowners, owners of vacation and recreation homes and older retired coupes. The purchasers would be primarily female living in suburban locations and small communities. For most consumers SignMaster™ was perceived as a new product and it is likely to be a one-time purchase. Two buying decisions are necessary for SignMaster™. First, the consumer must select the preferred shape and design and then purchase the house numbers. The purchase is likely to be planned with a careful examination of the product before a sale is made. More than one visit to the retail outlet may be required before the consumer decides on the most appropriate shape and design.

Hardware stores appear to be a good retail location for SignMaster™, although home center stores and mass merchandisers were also mentioned by survey respondents. Based on an examination of the product, consumers expected to find advertising for SignMaster™ in three types of media: magazines, mail order catalogs and direct mail fliers.

SignMaster™ packaging was a problem for some consumers. The package design made it difficult to examine the product to determine its thickness and texture. Others believed that the package color would not have the necessary appeal to be successful in a self-service environment.

The mounting tape used to install SignMaster™ on an exterior surface seems to be a problem. After removing the house sign from the package, consumers questioned the adhesive ability of the tape and suggested that an alternate mounting technique be provided. Others mentioned that the installation instructions enclosed in the package were complicated and required too many steps to apply the numbers to the sign.

At market introduction, SignMaster™ was available in three shapes and nine decorative designs. The research indicated that only a few combinations were popular with consumers. The decoy, country house and classic border were the preferred designs, while the tavern and oval were the popular shapes.

An important finding was that women tended to price SignMaster™ higher than men. The median retail price mentioned by women was $10.99, while men mentioned a price of $7.99. A similar pattern was found for the house numbers.

3. What do the market test results suggest about retail pricing and the nature of demand for SignMaster™?

The market test was conducted in voluntary wholesale and retail cooperative hardware stores. The test results confirm the survey research and strongly suggest $9.95 as the most acceptable price to consumers. Based on a review of the research, students should recommend a $9.95 retail price for the house sign and $0.69 per students should recommend a $9.95 retail price for the house sign and $0.69 per number. Using demand-backward pricing along with the margin, allowance, commission and cost information provided in the case, the Bacova selling price can be determined for the house sign and numbers. A summary is provided in Exhibit 1 of this Instructors Note.

Instructor's Note—Exhibit 1   Financial Implications of a SignMaster™

	House Sign	(3) House Numbers	Total
Retail Sales Price	$ 9.95	$ 2.07	$12.02
Markup, 40%	3.98	.83	4.81
Bacova Selling Price	5.97	1.24	7.21
Advertising Allowance	11.15		1.15
Sales Commission, 5%	.30	.06	.36
Net to Bacova	4.52	1.18	5.70
Product Costs	3.15	.33	3.48
Unit Profit	1.37	.85	2.22
Return on Sales, %	22.9	68.6	30.08

The test market results also suggest that the demand for SignMaster™ will be seasonal with sales concentrated during the summer months when consumers are spending time outside their residences. Introductory advertising for SignMaster™ in newspaper supplements should plan to feature the product during spring and early summer.

Instructors can also use the market test results to emphasize the importance of research design in conducting a test market. The choice of a factorial design in conducting a test market where prices are rotated between test periods and stores provides credibility for the test results. Even though the market test was modest in scope, it illustrates the value of following survey research with a market test to refine a pricing decision.

4. Evaluate the introductory marketing strategy for Sign Master™

Assuming a market exists for the product and given the results of the research, the marketing strategy was not effective. The new product was introduced without a clear understanding of the market and consumer buying behavior. Additionally, the initial sales results were disappointing because management underestimated the time necessary for consumers to learn about the product and determine if it was a desirable addition to their residence.

The introductory distribution plan for SignMaster™ included a discount department store and a building supply store. The research found that hardware stores were the preferred retail outlets, followed by home center stores and mass merchandisers. The firm did not introduce the product in the channels where consumers expected to find the product.

Consumer promotion was inadequate for the product. SignMaster™ was a product that most consumers had never seen before. It represented a new approach to identifying a residence and required separate purchases of the house sign and numbers because they were sold separately. Additionally, the product was available in a variety of shapes and designs which required additional time and thought to make a purchase decision. Without consumer education through advertising and point-of-purchase promotion, it is unlikely that the product would sell very quickly in a self-service environment.

The product packaging was a problem for some consumers because if concealed the product, seemed complicated to install, and lacked impact at the point-of-purchase.

SignMaster™ retail prices were too high. The introductory retail prices for the house sign ranged from $13.50 to $15.95. Research indicates that a $9.95 price would be appropriate for consumers. Bacova's representatives were motivated by their commission arrangement to sell the product at a high price. After the retailers added their markup, the product was priced outside the range considered reasonable for most consumers.

5. What should Bacova do with SignMaster™?

Although the initial sales of SignMaster™ are disappointing, it is likely that the introductory marketing strategy is a major part of the problem. It is too early to conclude that a market does not exist for the product.

An appropriate course of action for John Walters and his marketing group would be to revise the marketing strategy and continue selective commercialization of the product. The most important indicator of consumer acceptance for the product will come when the retail trade begins to reorder to replenish inventory. At this point, many of the sales are simply filling the distribution channels.

While the market research was helpful in identifying prospective target markets for the product the geographic location of the market and the characteristics of consumers purchasing SignMaster™ are still not well known. As the product begins to sell, market research should continue to determine where the product is being purchased and who the buyers are. Without a more complete profile of the market, it will be difficult to make significant improvements in marketing strategy. However, some obvious improvements can be made.

SignMaster™ packaging must be changed to improve the visual impact at point-of-purchase and allow inspection of the product. Package colors are light gray and white and they do not stand out against the light background of the peg board displays used in retail outlets. Recessing the house sign in the corrugated package makes it difficult to determine the thickness and texture of the product. This could be corrected by displaying a sign at point-of-purchase or changing the package to enable a visual inspection.

The instructions included in the package to align and mount the house numbers on the house sign are complicated. Approximately 13 separate steps are required. Although the step-by-step procedure results in a satisfactory application, the instructions and mounting process need to be simplified for consumers. It is important to note that consumers purchasing products in a self-service environment generally expect to open the package and complete the installation in a short time. SignMaster™ probably requires a bit more time and patience than most consumers are willing to give.

The adhesive mounting tape is a problem because consumers don't believe it will permanently attach the house sign to a residence, especially where the surfaces are rough and uneven. The difficulty with the mounting tape is imagined because the tape is quite satisfactory. However, Bacova needs to consider including some information and alternative mounting approaches on the outside of the package.

Some of the decorative designs originally available with the house sign have proven to be of little interest to consumers. Unpopular designs should be eliminated and new designs created to simplify inventory management and enhance the retail sales of SignMaster™.

Trade acceptance of the product generally has not been a problem, but consumer acceptance has been slow because the product presents a new approach to meeting a need. Promotion will be necessary to reflect the more complex consumer behavior and to help consumers understand what the product is and what it does. Magazine advertising, suggested by the research, is not appropriate for economic reasons, but advertising allowances to the trade to feature the product in newspaper supplements would be helpful. Bacova should offer an off-invoice program of about $1.15 a unit to retailers for approved promotion of SignMaster™.

SignMaster™ should be sold where the consumer expects to find it. Distribution through hardware stores is a top priority with secondary distribution in home center stores and mass merchandisers. Within the retail outlet, the product must be displayed where females shop because they are the most likely purchasers of the product.

A pricing strategy designed to bring the product to consumers at a retail price of $9.95 for the house sign and $0.69 for the number should be implemented. If hardware stores, for example, take a markup of 40 percent on the house sign, then the Bacova selling price would be approximately $5.97. A $1.15 off-invoice advertising allowance would drop the net price to $4.82. Sales commissions would further reduce the net to Bacova to 4.52. Exhibit 1 describes the financial implications for a consumer purchase of one SignMaster™ house sign and three numbers. Students should be encouraged to apply the pricing concepts to arrive at the appropriate Bacova selling price and the return on sales.

The use of a point-of-purchase display as sales promotion in the market test appeared to be helpful in securing shelf positioning to create consumer awareness. If Bacova wishes to use the display along with advertising allowances as part of an introductory marketing strategy and preserve the $9.95 retail price for the house sign and $0.69 per number, the cost of the display will probably have to be covered by the profit margin. Assuming the display were sold with 12 signs (three each of the four most popular designs) and 100 house numbers, the financial implications of the offer would be as illustrated in Exhibit 2 of the Instructor's Note (on the following page).

Some students will question the reason for including 100 house numbers with 12 house signs in the display. The test market results indicated that some consumers purchased the house numbers for other uses without purchasing the house sign. As Exhibit 2 of the Instructors Note illustrates, the house numbers are very profitable for Bacova as well.

Again, students should be instructed to consider the profit implications with and without the point-of-purchase display.

Instructor's Note-Exhibit 2   Financial Implications of a SignMaster™ Point-of-Purchase Display

	(12) House Signs	(100) House Number	Total
Retail Sales	$119.40	569.00	$188.40
Markup, 40%	47.76	27.60	75.36
Bacova Sales	71.64	41.40	113.04
Advertising Allowance	13.80		13.80
Display	7.52		7.52
Sales Commission	3.58	2.07	5.65
Net to Bacova	46.74	39.33	86.07
Product Costs	37.80	10.90	48.70
Profit	8.94	28.43	37.37
Return on Sales, %	12.5	68.7	33.1

For illustrative purposes. Assumes sales of all signs and numbers in the display. Retail markup of 40%, $1.15 advertising allowance, $7.52 display costs, and a 5% sales commission for manufacturer's representatives.

Epilogue

The Hardware division has moved quickly to improve SignMaster™ marketing strategy and increase the market penetration of the product. The packaging has been redesigned to show the dimensions of the product, improve its visual appeal, and emphasize that the product is a house sign. It is likely that additional improvements will be made as the current inventory of the product is depleted. For example, the firm expects to include 30 house numbers (3 of each digit) in the SignMaster™ package during the 1002 selling season to simplify the consumer purchasing process. The additional costs will be offset by moving from corrugated to fiberboard packaging and redesigning the numbers so their cost can be reduced.

The trade continues to respond favorable to the product Introductory sales have been made to 112 Servistar hardware stores, 80 Hechinger's home center stores, 65 Home Club stores in California home center chain) and one Grossman's home center store in Massachusetts. Management has also arranged an introductory sales test with 4060 Wal Mart stores to test the product in a mass merchandising environment Consumer acceptance of the product is unknown since only a few reorders have been received for the product.

Trade sales of the SignMaster™ house sign and numbers totaled approximately $138,378 in 1991 The most popular decorative designs were the Country House, Cardinal Chickadee Floral, Classic Border and the Duck Decoy. Despite the disappointing sales, the unit profit on SignMaster™ is very attractive. During 1991, the profit margin on sales exceeded most all of the other products in the Hardware Division.

Demand for SignMaster™ appears to be quite seasonal. Peak sales months will probably be mid-April through mid-October when consumers are working outside on their homes and lawns and thinking about exterior home improvements.

CASE 3-6
THE FAITH MOUNTAIN COMPANY*

Synopsis

Faith Mountain Company is a budding entrepreneurial enterprise that is positioning itself as an innovative mail-order catalog firm and retail store merchandiser. As of late 1991, the company's business consisted of developing, manufacturing, and marketing high-quality gift items, apparel, and home accessories through its mail-order catalog and its retail store in Sperryville, Virginia. Fiscal year 1991 sales were about $5 million and the company posted its first-ever annual profit of $161,000.

As the December 1991 holiday season brought sales that promised another record year, Cheri and Martin Woodard—the founders, majority owners, and senior executives of the company—contemplated Faith Mountain's future direction and strategy. The Woodards had recently established some lofty goals for the company: $25 million in revenues by 1995, with $10 million coming from the current catalog, $10 million from a new catalog that might be developed in-house or acquired, and $5 million from retail operations. The case sets forth some of the Woodards' thinking about how the goals could be achieved, but a detailed strategic plan has yet to be developed.

The case offers rich detail about the company's start-up period, the Woodards' management style and business philosophy, and how the young company is managed on a day-to-day basis. Overall, the current situation at Faith Mountain is very good. Current operating problems are minor in comparison to company performance.

The case calls on students to do three things: (1) assess the company's current situation; (2) evaluate the Woodards' goals—are they achievable? reasonable?; (3) provide specific recommendations to the Woodards to answer the question: What should they do next? One of those recommendations must be to develop a comprehensive plan, and with the information provided in the case, students should be able to outline a preliminary long-range strategy.

Teaching/Learning Objectives

The case authors do a fine job of "storytelling" and drawing out the character and personalities of Cheri and Martin Woodard. This permits you to really delve into the ambitions and aspirations of the founders and show students how these factors shape a company's character, culture, ways of doing things, and long-term strategic direction. The case provides you with a golden opportunity to illustrate

1. How entrepreneurs arrive at strategic visions and business missions, set objectives, and move incrementally toward developing a full-blown strategy.

2. How a company's policies, operating practices, and culture begin to take shape as a new business grows and as the thinking and judgment of the founding entrepreneurs starts to mature.

3. The role of senior executives in shaping the character and personality of the company.

---

* Based upon a teaching note that appeared in Arthur A. Thompson, Jr. and A. J. Strickland III, Instructor's Manual to Accompany *Strategic Management Concepts and Cases*, 7/e, Richard D. Irwin, Inc., 1993, pp. 169-179. Portions of this teaching note, particularly the analysis section, were developed by the case authors.

4. Why the future success of a company depends so heavily on the strategy-making and strategy-implementing skills of top management.

Answers to Discussion Questions

1. What impresses you about Faith Mountain Company? Are you surprised at the success Faith Mountain has had, given the backgrounds and business experiences of the founders? What kinds of people are the Woodards? What accounts for their success at Faith Mountain?

Thoughtful students will come up with several things that are impressive about Faith Mountain and the way the Woodards have brought the business along:

- From a small proprietorship selling herbs and antiques, Faith Mountain has blossomed into a $5 million mail-order catalog and retail operation with plans for growing to $25 million in sales over the next five years—this is pretty impressive.
- Cheri Woodard seems to have excellent business instincts. Cheri is the real entrepreneur; Martin is more of a manager-administrator. Together, they make a good managenal team.
- Cheri Woodard has infused the company with a unique quality and distinctive image that grows out of its Blue Ridge Mountain location, the nature of its product line, the fact that the Woodards live the lifestyle of the customers Faith Mountain is trying to cultivate, and the company's name. All this contributes to the company's customer appeal.
- Cheri Woodard has excellent people management skills.
- The company is well-managed; current operating problems are quite minor.

There's ample reason to conclude that Faith Mountain is a company with a promising future. The Woodards are interesting people. Cheri is creative, energetic, civic-minded, and concerned about treating employees well. She is attentive to the people side of the business and takes all human resource matters seriously. Martin handles catalog production, merchandise selection finance, and administration. They complement each other well.

Several factors account for the company's success so far:

- The company's appealing product line of traditional, nostalgic, whimsical, and romantic gifts, apparel, and home accessories.
- Cheri's entrepreneurial skills in defining Faith Mountain's market and building a clientele of customers.
- The company's location in the Blue Ridge Mountains.
- The Woodards have exhibited good management skills and sought good advice when they were unsure how to proceed.

We would give the Woodards an A for their efforts in building Faith Mountain's business to the $5 million level.

2. Have Cheri and Martin Woodard done a good job of long range direction-setting? Do they have a strategic vision of what kind of company they want Faith Mountain to become? Have they set long range objectives?

The answers to all three questions are yes. There's not much room to debate whether the Woodards have charted a course for Faith Mountain. They want to company to have $25 million in sales by 1995-$10 million from the current catalog, $5 million from retail store sales, and $10 million from a newly developed or acquired catalog. In addition to the revenue targets, the Woodard's strategic vision for Faith Mountain included seven other targets:

- Grow as quickly as possible, yet maintain profitability.
- Grow at a rate that does not hurt product quality and customer service.
- Aggressively develop new products and exclusive vendor relationships.
- Stay close to customers through surveys, the store, and personal contact.
- Provide the best quality and value in unique and unusual products.
- Be the best company to do business with.
- Provide a work environment that allows employees personal and professional growth, to insure the highest levels of motivation and knowledge among employees, and therefore the highest level of quality in all aspects of the company.

These are sufficiently straightforward and specific to provide meaningful long-term direction. At the same time, though, specific catalog sales projections have been developed (case Exhibit 10) and there are pro-forma financial projections (case Exhibit 11). In addition, the Woodards want to have sufficient free time to have a life outside the business. All this constitutes a reasonably explicit strategic vision and long-term direction setting. The Woodards are doing some strategic thinking about what kind of company they want Faith Mountain to become.

This is not to say, however, that they have crafted a comprehensive and detailed strategy designed to make their vision a reality. Clearly, they have not gotten this far. But they have established a long-term mission and strategic vision and they do have long range strategic and financial objectives.

3. **What is Faith Mountain's current strategy?**

The company's strategy has several key elements that students need to recognize:

- A focus on the needs of women between the ages of 30 and 50 who are homeowners with family incomes of $40,000—$60,000.
- Finding and developing quality merchandise to feature in the catalog before competitors discover the same products.
- Using Faith Mountain herb and floral arrangements designed by Cheri Woodard as the company's distinctive signature products.
- Pursuing two distribution channels simultaneously—mail-order catalogs and retail store sales
- Emphasizing "lifestyle theme of traditional, cozy, and family-oriented life."
- Seeking exclusive marketing rights for products
- Beginning to move more aggressively to private labeling
- Offering only merchandise of the highest quality relative to price, thus providing "best value" products
- Manufacturing about 20% of the merchandise sold
- The use of incentive plans for both warehouse and customer service employees to reward error-free performance

- An emphasis on superior customer service (a toll-free order line, sending UPS to the customer's home to pick up items customers were dissatisfied with, guaranteed low prices, optional Federal Express delivery, extremely quick shipping)
- Using the retail store to attract buyers who preferred not to buy from the company by mail
- Using the retail store to promote the companies image as a good, hardworking, honest family business

The case makes it clear that Faith Mountain's strategy has *evolved* over the years and *is still evolving*. You should stress that this is a normal condition for any business as it grows and develops, as market conditions change, and as new opportunities open up.

4. **What are the chief approaches the Woodards have used to implementing Faith Mountain's strategy? The most important strategy-implementing features include:**

- An emphasis on progressive human resource management practices
  * an employee handbook describing personnel policies and practices
  * use of incentives
  * an emphasis on proper motivation
  * careful selection of employees
  * providing a work environment that offers employees personal and professional growth
- Living the lifestyle of the firm's customers
- Stressing doing a quality job in all aspects of company operations
- Initiating ways to provide superior customer service
- Developing an organization/staff of employees capable of carrying out the strategy successfully
- Making sure the company has adequate administrative support systems (taking and filling orders, design and production of catalogs, aggressive merchandise selection practices, customer service)
- Staying close to customers through surveys, the retail store, and personal contacts.

5. **Does the company have a bright future? Are there market opportunities it can exploit? Can it compete successfully in the mail-order business? Is the mail-order catalog business a good industry to be in?**

The case provides ample data for assessing the attractiveness of the mail-order catalog business, sizing up Faith Mountain's closest competitors, and getting a good feel for the company's growth opportunities in mail-order sales. It is worth 5-10 minutes of class time exploring this area and introducing the class to the concept of industry and competitive analysis. Several points can be made about industry and competitive conditions:

- Mail-order sales are growing a bit faster than retail and department store sales generally.
- Demographics and consumer lifestyles are favorable for continued growth in consumer purchases via mail-order.
- Entry barriers into the catalog industry are low; the prospects for growth are attracting many new entrants, thus boosting competition.
- The industry is fragmented; there are some 16,000+ vendors in 28 segments; each segment has several hundred competitors (see case Exhibit 8).

- Excluding books, magazines, newspapers, and computer products, there are some 9,520 mail-order businesses accounting for $30.9 billion in sales, equal to an average of $3.25 million per business (see case Exhibit 8).

Conclusions: While competition among rival mail-order catalog firms is likely to be vigorous, there are opportunities for a creative, well-managed firm like Faith Mountain to grow and to succeed. The keys to success are a distinctive product line that is presented in a distinctive manner—i.e. a good differentiation strategy. From Faith Mountain's standpoint, this is a good industry to be in and there's no strong reason why Faith Mountain should be intimidated by competitors.

After a brief discussion of the industry environment, you can ask about specific market opportunities that Faith Mountain has. Students ought to be able to compile a list of market opportunities that includes the following:

- *Mail order sales growth:* currently 3.2% of all retail sales; $44.5 billion in '90 sales to mail order specialty merchandisers; despite concerns of some experts quoted in case, it's hard to argue that catalog sales have peaked.
- *Favorable and growing target market.* demographic, societal trends portend growth in Faith Mountain's target market-more women having families, growing older, gaining disposable income, using credit cards; traditional retailer squeezed in recession cut back on service, encouraging more people to shop by mail; credit card companies also pushing consumers to try catalogs
- *Increased possibility of private labeling:* more experience with offshore manufacturers may bring more opportunity to build Faith Mountain franchise, earn more margins
- *Untapped market segment:* explore products for males
- *Increasing funds from operations:* Using the sales forecast per Exhibit 11 and assuming low capital expenditures and no dividends, enough cash is generated to pay off the short-term bank loans and have excess cash in the $200,000 range by 1995.
- If Faith Mountain pays a 15% dividend payout and has capital expenditures of $350,000, the bank debt is still reduced to $124,000 in 1995.
- The projected growth in sales in Exhibit 11 is modest. If Faith Mountain were to continue growing at its current rate, sales would reach $18.7 million in 1995, with before-tax income of $1.1 million. Higher sales will require greater funding needs but at this point Faith Mountain should have greater borrowing capacity.
- *Interest rates low:* is it time to borrow for expansion?
- *Two specific options for growth identified by Woodards*: retail store expansion acquisition/development of new catalog

6. What strengths and weaknesses does Faith Mountain have?

Strengths

- *Owners' involvement, dedication, knowledge of the business and key connections* in the industry based on 14 years' experience
- *Customer list* size, growth—now at 251,771 names; apparently strong franchise in the mail-order industry
- *Merchandising* has built broad product line, nurtured consistent "lifestyle" image for company, established reputation for quality, built good relationships with craftspeople, vendors

- *Manufacturing* of herb wreaths, other products allows better margins on top-sellers in catalogs, customization of product
- *Retail store* is profitable, cements company identity in the Blue Ridge Mountains, synergy and support for mail-order sales, and outlet for catalog overstocks
- *Customer service* policies and operations place customer first; staff is empowered to do what it takes to satisfy customer; attention to this by President, supporting efforts of merchandising staff apparently succeed in retaining repeat purchasers
- *Plant and equipment* sufficient to support growth; phone, computer/software systems sound bases for growth
- *Bank relations* apparently good, recent extension of line of credit
- *Strong sales growth, profitability* even in the face of economic recession
- *Employee satisfaction/commitment* very high, low turnover, high dedication and support
- *Strong board of directors*, particularly the mail order experts Don Press and Joan Litle
- *Good relations with local community*

Weaknesses

- *Owners' involvement* may be too high, both in terms of personal burnout risk and in terms of low delegation and trust to other FM employees
- *Difficult recruitment* of new managerial employees location, pay, work expectations
- *Financial health, history, performance*
- Current ratio 1.35, Quick ratio— .74— both weaker than desired rules of-thumb
- Total debt to total assets, .76—at this leverage, company must be careful
- Cash flow difficulties due to seasonality of sales—with vendors' current tight credit policy, payables critical to monitor
- Sovran loan covenants are restrictive
- The company is using short-term debt to finance long-term projects—not advisable
- Venture capitalists exerting pressures for dividend payout
- Equity sales seem questionable; sold "only" 1150 of 1500 shares offered in 1990. Who will buy now? What would be the effect on ownership control?

7. What do you see as Faith Mountain's biggest problem? as the Woodard's biggest challenge?

These two questions go to the heart of the case and are a valuable stage-setting prerequisite for developing a pragmatic set of action recommendations. The class may have some trouble with the answers because Faith Mountain has no glaring operating problems and is performing well.

A good argument can be made that Faith Mountain's biggest problem concerns *how to achieve the $25 million in revenues by 1995.* While the Woodards have set forth a vision and a direction and established long-range performance targets, they lack a long-range strategy and a detailed game plan to make it happen." What's missing right now is "how." Faith Mountain needs a growth strategy expanding sales fivefold in five years will require more than just growing the present business. Acquisition or development of another catalog is an OK idea, but what kind. What should the criteria for another catalog be and when should the new operation be launched (it will have to be soon to generate $10 million in sales by 1995). It is time for the Woodards to develop a 5-year strategic plan. The Woodard's biggest challenge will be making the transition from an entrepreneurial family business to a professionally managed company. It is one thing for Cheri and Martin Woodard to be the chief strategists and chief strategy-implementers for a $5 million family business. But Faith Mountain cannot realistically expect to grow into a $25 million company with only a 2-person senior executive team. Cheri will not be able to personally hire every new employee needed; many of the tasks she performs now will have to be delegated. Martin will not be able to personally handle catalog production and mailing, merchandise selection, and financial planning in a $25 million company. Do Cheri and Martin really want to become professional managers? Do they want the added burdens and responsibilities of running a $25 million company? Do they have the skills to head up a $25 million company? How will they be able to preserve Faith Mountain's essential character and homespun qualities? Much will have to change in the way the Woodards manage.

Neither Faith Mountain's lack of a detailed growth strategy nor the Woodard's need to adapt their management style and develop professional management skills constitute insurmountable obstacles. But they do have to be recognized and dealt with soon.

8. What is your evaluation of Faith Mountain's strategic alternatives and what recommendations would you make to the Woodards?

There is plenty of meat in this case for a lengthy discussion of alternatives and recommendations. At the very least, you will need to spend 15-20 minutes covering alternatives and recommendations; ideally, you could spend 30-40 minutes on this part of the case. It really depends on how much emphasis you want to put on developing action recommendations at this juncture in the course. Also, it depends on the pace you elect to set in covering the previously mentioned teaching points. The following presentation and analysis of alternatives and recommendations represents the work of the case authors.

Evaluation of The Proposed Growth Strategies for Faith Mountain

a. Option 1: *Expansion of Retail Operations*

    (1) *Arguments for*

        (a) Additional stores will expand market for Faith Mountain products, introduce company to new customers.

        (b) Other catalog companies have done this successfully (Williams-Sonoma, The Sharper Image)

        (c) Catalog and retail stores sales have synergy—surge in Sperryville store sales with each catalog mailing; two divisions will build on each other's growth

        (d) Real estate is cheap now, costs of expansion are low

    (2) *Arguments against*

        (a) Possible damage to image of company—can down-home, small-town country image of Faith Mountain be preserved, replicated in multiple outlets?

        (b) Location—where to put stores? Strip malls? Big malls? Old houses? In what towns?

        (c) High costs of search, and of building, rebuilding outlets

        (d) Recession—risky time to enter the retail business

        (e) Managerial control over far-flung operations—Sperryville store now two miles from company offices, owners—how many could they manage, and where?

        (f) Just established first budget for Sperryville store—don't yet know enough about how to manage stores profitably

- (g) Personnel to run it—who? Strain on Cheri?
- (h) Profitability seems low compared to investment—mail order easier
- (i) Goal of $5 million implies 12 stores doing $400,000 each in '95, while Sperryville is shooting for $300,000 in 1 992—too ambitious?
- (j) Alternate stores might actually decrease sales in Sperryville store

b. Option 2: *Another Catalog—Acquisition or Developed In-House?*
  (1) Arguments for Acquisition
    (a) Better utilization of assets, knowledge; balance FM cyclicality
    (b) Low start-up costs, facilities in place
    (c) Ideal product is seeds: small, easy to warehouse, connection to herbs
    (d) Acquisition may be possible through debt capacity of *acquired* firm
  (2) *Arguments against Acquisition*
    (a) Cost—how much? Where would funding come from?
    (b) Management would have to remain in place—not possible for Woodards to take on an entirely new operation without help
    (c) At present there are no known candidates; who will search?
    (d) Location—nearby best
    (e) What products? Connection to FM lifestyle, image? From market data, promising growth in drugs, vitamins—is that Faith Mountain? Sportswear?
  (3) *Arguments against In-House Development*
    (a) Who will lead, carry out, manage? Constraints on Woodards' time.
    (b) Cost of expansion—Company facilities/support systems?

9. **Can the Faith Mountain catalog achieve the stated goal of $10 million in sales by 1995?**
  (1) *Yes*
    (a) Market growth/target segment growth
    (b) Recession: Sales increase now implies *even greater growth when* recession ends? It can be argued that $10 million goal is in fact *too conservative.*
    (c) Support systems, technology will support this growth with relatively low investment.
  (2) *Strategies for Increasing Current Catalog Sales*
    (a) Building the House List: students may suggest tell-a-friend promotions, advertisements, coupons; proposals and additional list rentals must address Martin Woodard's rule of thumb of 3:1 return on promotional costs.
    (b) Going for new markets: Males? First-time home buyer/homemaker?
    (c) Product Mix: More private label? More sportswear? Sell seeds, garden supplies in spring catalog; growth in drugs, vitamins sales by mail order; men's apparel?
    (d) Pricing: given guarantee of quality, unique merchandise, can our prices go higher? Guaranteed lowest prices is part of our current strategy—should it be?
  (3) *Barriers to Achieving $10 million Sales Target with Current Catalog*
    (a) *Need for additional staff:* Woodards are aware they are working at or near capacity. Additional managerial support staff will be needed soon. There are at least three potential new positions to add, but role and responsibilities are unclear for each:

- *Manager, Personnel:* although *only one* personnel problem is related in the case, it is clear that Cheri believes better human resources practices might have avoided it. A manager with this full-time responsibility might be appropriate, but Cheri likes to do this work herself.
- *Director, Operations:* there is no evidence of any real problem here now, but Cheri's direct supervisory responsibility for telephone operators troubles students. Should one customer service supervisor be named manager? Would that destroy currently effective team approach? Would this position also manage warehouse and manufacturing?
- *Manager, Finance:* for all but long-term financing, bank relations, would free Martin from supervisory responsibility, focusing him on catalog; is that the right allocation of his time?

In addition, *all* proposals for new staff, including the above managers and any additional buyers or added telephone staff to permit *in-house* 24-hour operation, must address the following key constraints:

- Cost of new staff?
- Timing of adding positions?
- Hire from within? Source for new managers?
- Will Woodards accept this advice?

(b) Willingness of Cheri and Martin Woodard to delegate authority, accept changing role. Both recognize their limitations in the case; Cheri knows she doesn't have the time to do all the human resources training, etc., in the future; Martin knows his weaknesses, tries to avoid people responsibility.

Yet there is no explicit recognition of trouble with delegating: is it a problem or isn't it? The case evidence is not convincing. Their involvement with all major decisions is not necessarily ill-advised. The merchandise selection process attracts student concern, but if merchandise is key to success, why should they change this successful formula?

Similarly, one problem with one employee of thirty-nine, over many years of experience, does not imply a character issue about "control" which many students seem to find is the case. In fact, Cheri's honest recognition of discomfort at the first hiring decision she did not personally approve may be the best evidence of her awareness of the need to change: she delegated, it felt funny but she's not saying it was the wrong thing to do, or that she will never do it again.

(c) *Support systems upgrades necessary:* computer system update due in '92, system overall good through 1995; phone system will need update in 1993; warehouse sufficient to support growth through 1995. Plans must acknowledge, estimate costs of these upgrades.

(4) Requirements for a Preliminary Strategic Plan for Faith Mountain Company

The first requirement is to acknowledge that the Woodards must determine for themselves what they want. Students may detect evidence in the case that Martin and Cheri have different views of the future of Faith Mountain and of their own lives. Some see Martin as less emotionally committed to the content, the higher purposes of the business, and more to its success, while Cheri seems more interested in "making a difference." If true, these differences may have significant implications for the future of the company.

For example, though we expect students to evaluate the growth alternatives, it is equally valid to suggest that the Woodards plan to sell out. Cash flows currently value the firm at between $1.5 and $2.4 million. Why not sell, live the good life, start again? Along with a strategic plan, then, it is clear that the Woodards need to examine their own life plan, their goals and dreams, and factor them into the plans for the business.

Students' plans for Faith Mountain should include the following basic elements:

1. An overview, defining mission and parts
2. Specific set of objectives against which performance can be measured
3. Growth strategy
4. Marketing plan
5. Personnel recruitment
6. Operations plan
7. Materials purchasing plan
8. Plan to raise capital

Part 4

Target Market Strategies

CASE 4-1
AMTECH CORPORATION[*]

Synopsis:

Amtech Corporation was a leader in IVHS (Intelligent Vehicle Highway Systems) and AEI (Automatic Equipment Identification), which included the electronic toll and traffic management systems market and the transportation market. The AEI system was used by railroads, trucking companies, intermodal shippers, and the security access market. The IVHS system was used wherever there were toll roads.

Amtech was the only company producing equipment in the AEI market that met the standards of the Association of American Railroads, but there were many competitors in the IVHS market. The large companies and strong alliances put pressure on Amtech to develop the best technology.

G. Russell Mortenson, Amtech's president, thought that Amtech should focus on the transportation segment of the market because of the money potential. He needed to decide whether to continue in both the AEI and IVHS markets, and then decide which segments in one or both of the markets Amtech should target.

Video Summary:

The video begins with humorous scenes of the "old" way people paid tolls and how companies kept track of their trucks. It then goes on to describe the technology of Amtech, the markets that Amtech served, and the use of Amtech's technology in these markets. The IVHS system is described in some detail. The video also mentions the possible international markets that Amtech wants to enter. After the main part of the video, there is a short sample of an ad for the "PikePass" (Oklahoma's system). The video is about seven minutes long, plus a few seconds for the PikePass ad.

Teaching/Learning Objectives:

The evaluation of a company, such as Amtech, allows students to visit a high-tech firm which serves both the business-to-business market and the consumer market. The case provides the opportunity to:

- demonstrate the need to change from an entrepreneurial focus once a product begins to move through the product life cycle, yet maintain the entrepreneurial spirit in the development of new products and product uses,
- illustrate the need for effective resource allocation strategies in a high growth industry, and
- evaluate market options to identify the appropriate market target.

Discussion Questions:

1. Describe Amtech's marketing strategy, to date, and identify the strategic decisions Amtech is facing. What internal and external issues does the company face?
2. Compare the AEI and IVHS markets.

---

[*] This teaching note was prepared by Victoria L. Crittenden, Stephanie Hillstrom, and David Angus, Boston College, as an aid to instructors using the case, "Amtech Corporation." Revised 1998.

3. Who are Amtech's customers?

4. What are Amtech's growth possibilities in each of the two markets? What are the elements of success in each market?

5. What are the pressures on Mortenson?

6. What should be Amtech's target market? What issues does your target market selection pose for Amtech?

Analysis:

1. Describe Amtech's marketing strategy, to date, and identify the strategic decisions Amtech is facing.

Although Amtech has been described as "shooting from the hip" and going by instincts when making decisions, its marketing strategy regarding the firm's target market has been well defined and planned. Amtech's target market has been transporters of shipping containers, such as ships, trucks, and railroads. The product is relatively new and the industry is dynamic.

Competition and substitute products, however, have begun to pose major threats to the company. Thus, several strategic decisions need to be made:

- organizational objectives to become a major player,
- amount of available resources, including cash, capacity, and human,
- how to respond to changing needs of customers
- how to differentiate its product
- how to increase market share
- the number of competitors and the stage of the product life cycle
- strategic advantages and limitations

A SWOT analysis is provided in Exhibit TN–1.

2. Compare the AEI and IVHS markets.

While the two markets are described in the case, students need to succinctly define the differences/similarities in the markets. One approach is outlined in the table on the following page.

While the two markets are separate, there appears to be overlap which dims the line between the two. For example, truck fleets (AEI market) are beginning to use the system to participate in the Oklahoma Turnpike automatic toll system (IVHS market). Also, the security access market is part of the AEI marketplace, yet the system appears to be very similar to the IVHS toll road system in that some automobiles can go unstopped through the gate while autos without the special equipment must stop.

	AEI	IVHS
Product Use	traditionally, inventory management	improve traffic flow (road-based)
Products	tags reader sites	tags scanners
Customer	railroads truck fleets intermodal shipping	toll authorities auto drivers
Competitors	none approved for rail satellite-based networks	Mark IV Industries Hughes AT/Comm Inc. AT&T Rockwell Intl. (in addition, there were many companies in other areas of IVHS)
Complementary Products	gauges portable readers improved tag programmers	traffic management systems highway telecommunications

3. Who are Amtech's customers?

As noted above, Amtech's current customers are railroads, truck fleets, intermodal shippers, and the security access market in the AEI market. The current customer in the IVHS market is the toll authority. Regarding the IVHS market, Amtech had installed bases in the North Dallas Tollway, the Oklahoma Turnpike system, and toll roads in parts of Louisiana (U.S.), Georgia (U.S.), Mexico, France, Spain, and the United Kingdom.

4. What are Amtech's growth possibilities in each of the two markets? What are the elements of success in each market?

Amtech has only begun to penetrate both the AEI and IVHS markets. However, neither market appears to be one to offer much repeat business. Naturally, repeat business can come in the tagging of new containers, but one would doubt that the installed bases would require replacement equipment too often. Rather, growth comes from the number of new bases such as the expected growth in the reader site network for railroads in North America (expected to increase to 3,000 to 5,000 sites) or the number of toll roads switching to electronic service and/or the building of new toll roads. Growth can also occur through the penetration of the fleet, intermodal, and security access markets for AEI. These markets offer vast opportunity for use of Amtech's current product.

In the AEI market, market penetration and market development seem to offer strong growth opportunities at this point in time. Given the competitive activity in the IVHS market, product development seems to be the area of opportunity, along with continued market penetration into those toll areas which have not automated. These growth strategies also offer their own elements of success. Both market penetration and market development require that Amtech build strong *relationships* with potential customers (both transportation associations and individual companies). As with the railroad, setting Amtech as standard is very important. *Speed* is another important element for Amtech. With the large potential AEI market, there is undoubtedly another company attempting to enter the market. Amtech must move quickly to begin relationships with customers. The somewhat competitive IVHS market means that Amtech must use the elements of the *marketing mix* to its advantage. Price may become an important competitive factor. *Technology* is also another element of success in this market. The market appears open to new, technologically sophisticated products. Amtech would be unwise to focus solely on its toll tags should it decide to remain in this market. *Relationship* development is important to further penetrate the toll authority market as well as identify trends in new products.

5. **What are the pressures on Mortenson?**

Amtech has been known for its participation in the IVHS market. However, the company's revenue stream has shifted to the AEI marketplace. Mortenson must decide if the company can continue to do business in both markets or if a focus on only one of the markets is advisable. Amtech was a relatively small company, competing against competitors with extensive corporate resources. A move into concentrating solely on the AEI market would steer Amtech away from some of the big IVHS players. However, such a move might only be temporary given the potential of the AEI market. And, Amtech had been able to use its technology in the product shifts made since the company's origination. Leaving the IVHS might signal that Amtech had reached the "end of the line" in its technological capabilities.

Many eyes were upon Amtech and any move the company made was surely to be reported in the financial press. This could send stock prices up or down.

The organizational structure of the company is probably of concern to Mortenson. As the company has moved from its entrepreneurial state, changes have had to be made to its use of people and money. Mortenson is probably wondering what type of organizational structure is appropriate for taking the company into the year 2000.

As a small company that has had major changes in its financial operations (see Exhibit 1 in case), Mortenson knows that a larger company could be interested in owning Amtech. Good or bad, this pressure is also upon Mortenson's shoulders.

6. **What should be Amtech's target market? What issues does your target market selection pose for Amtech?**

Students' responses here will vary from only the AEI market, only the IVHS market, or both the AEI and IVHS markets for reasons identified in earlier questions. Students should be questioned regarding many issues related to the selected target market. An interesting approach is to compare these issues, given different target markets. An example framework for discussion might be:

	AEI	**IVHS**	**Both**
Company Objectives			
Marketing Mix			
Organizational Structure			
Strategic Partnerships			
Competitors			
Market Research			
Positioning Strategies			
International Issues			
Performance Assessment Measures			

Teaching the Case:

Students may find the case somewhat confusing because of the nature of the product. Therefore, it is good to start the class with a general discussion of the technology. The descriptions and diagrams in the case are helpful in describing what the technologies do. Another helpful tool here is to show the video at the beginning of the class. After the general discussion of the video, the class moves easily into comparing the AEI and IVHS markets and Amtech's marketing strategy to date.

Because of the nature of the product, the class has not worked well when the opening focuses upon the selection of the target market. Too many students seem to get "left behind" too early in the class.

Even with the complicated nature of the product, students tend to enjoy discussing the company. It is a small, entrepreneurial venture that has been very successful. It competes with the likes of AT&T and Hughes, and it has become the standard in the AEI railroad market. As all students have driven/ridden on toll roads at some point, they will be familiar with that aspect of the product and the ease that an automated toll tag would place on both the driver and the toll authority.

If there is time and it has not already come up in class, it is fun to brainstorm new uses (both in terms of markets and products) for both the AEI and IVHS technologies.

Epilogue:

Amtech decided to completely "overhaul" its organization. The company transformed itself from a pioneering radio frequency identification company to a broader provider of systems and solutions utilizing wireless data technologies. While the IVHS and AEI markets/technologies were at the heart of the transformation, the company felt that it would need to have a much broader mission to grow and prosper in the future. The overhaul resulted in the company reorganizing into three market-oriented groups: Electronic Security, Interactive Data, and Transportation Systems. The Electronic Security Group is a world leader in the electronic security and access control market. The Interactive Data Group focuses on real-time reporting and management for logistics, manufacturing, and transportation operations. The Transportation Systems Group specializes in wireless identification, tracking and monitoring for fleet, rail, and intermodal management. In addition to these areas, this group also concentrates on parking access control and airport applications. Thus, the target market selection process led the company to realize that the long-term decision was much more encompassing than it had thought initially.

In February of 1998, Amtech Corporation announced that David P. Cook would become the new Chairman, President, and CEO of the company. Mr. Cook was one of the founders of the company, as well as a former CEO of Blockbuster Entertainment Corporation. Mr. Mortenson remained with Amtech as an outside director of the company.

A few highlights regarding Amtech's business:

In July of 1997, Amtech Corporation was awarded a $3.5 million contract to design, install, and integrate an electronic toll and traffic management system for the city of San Antonio Texas. This system will extend the capabilities of the TransGuide system, the advanced traffic management system already in place.

In October of 1996, Dick Simon Trucking, the 15th largest refrigerated truck fleet in the U.S., chose Amtech to provide wireless, hands-free technology. The AEI system will be used in the entire fleet. Dick

Simon Trucking will use the technology for gate access, maintenance identification, and for fueling operations.

In September of 1996, Amtech Systems Corporation won the contracts to provide wireless identification for Houston Hobby and Houston Intercontinental Airports. These airports are the 14th and 15th to purchase this type of technology from Amtech.

Exhibit TN-1 SWOT Analysis

Strengths

- deep pockets
- faith of prominent venture capitalists
- joint ventures, leading to a global presence in Europe with Mitsubishi
- versatile technology, useful in both the traffic management and transportation markets
- wide-spread benefits (transportation companies and their customers, commuters, cargo insurers, governments, the public, and those concerned about the environment and wasted natural resources all would benefit)
- customers enthusiastic about product, apparently willing to forgive errors, as when ground radar system led to misdirected cars for the Santa Fe Railroad

Weaknesses

- customer base concentrated—56 percent of business with four customers, giving each of the four much leverage
- trouble keeping up with demand

Opportunities

- opportunity to create and market new, complementary products, such as tags which could interface with EDI, other communications technologies, and portable readers
- joint risk-sharing with insurers of transportation companies, governments
- develop technologies compatible with other emerging communications technologies, e.g., cellular communications
- develop specialized AEI technologies for specific industries
- use of GPS to eliminate the need for transceivers
- large growth in export sales
- sell tags compatible with both a standardized IVHS technology and industry-specific AEI technologies to capture segments from both markets
- make the technology more attractive to potential customers by pushing for state, national, and international government benefits for those using IVHS and AEI (e.g., border inspection bypass)

IVHS

- lobbying for public (from state and federal department of transportation) and industry (e.g., the auto industry and other potential beneficiary/ customers) funds to share costs of developing IVHS technology, costs of which are estimated at $450 billion from 1992 to 2011
- joint cooperative research with competitors, other governments since all stand to gain if costs can be shared, none stand to gain if costs cannot be shared
- gain the support of environmental lobbying groups
- develop specialized security devices for walled communities, industry, and other limited-access needs

- as federal dollars to states for road construction and repair shrink, states will probably turn to use of tolls to fund highway infrastructure
- push for adoption of a standardized IVHS technology by state and federal governments, touting its first-mover experience in the technology—with expected yearly revenues of $5 billion to $10 billion by 2000, IVHS is potentially lucrative if the costs of R&D can be shared

AEI

- the European railroad market, which is five times larger than US rail market
- work with American Trucking Association to sanction AEI as a mandated reporting method since $0.77 of every goods transportation dollar is spent on trucking
- work with maritime shippers to sanction AEI as a mandated reporting method to facilitate the adoption of AEI as a standard in intermodal transport
- encourage use of higher-priced, more versatile tags ($35 to $60 range)

Threats

- current and emerging competition, e.g., the development of GPS technology by Geostar and Qualcomm
- competitors were large
- as ex-defense contractors, competition might benefit from sympathies of government and other customers
- several key competitors are strong Fortune 500 companies

CASE 4-2
DÜRING AG (FOTTLE)*

Synopsis

Walter Düring, a Swiss entrepreneur and CEO of Düring AG, a small engineering "ideas" company is examining the possibility of launching its latest liquid packaging invention, the foldable bottle or Fottle®, into the French market for milk packaging. The bottle provides ecological as well as cost advantages in terms of using less garbage space, being composed of a single recyclable material, and using less plastic than traditional plastic bottles. The milk market in France, although it is currently dominated by carton brick packaging, is on the lookout for alternative innovative packaging ideas. Düring AG, a small nimble company, obsessed with the idea of remaining small, must develop a marketing plan for entering the French milk packaging market. It must decide not just which segments of the market to target and how, but also how its offering will be defined. The options are: (1) bottle molds can be licensed directly to dairy manufacturers to be used on their existing bottling machinery; (2) the packaging innovation can be provided as a turnkey solution, including machinery and raw materials; or (3) the design could be licensed to engineering companies which provide packaging machinery to dairy producers. These options for defining the offering need to be considered in relation to the selected market segment and the stated strategic objective of remaining small and nimble.

Teaching/Learning Objectives

The Fottle case is intended for use in a marketing or entrepreneurship module of an MBA or Executive course. It addresses the issue of a small entrepreneurial firm taking an innovative product idea to market. Related issues of defining the product offering and segmentation/positioning of the market are addressed.

The case allows the following issues to be discussed:

Immediate Issues

How can a small entrepreneurial company gain access to a potentially world-wide market?

How can an innovative product idea be defined as a market offering so as to maximize market penetration?

How can the dual goals of capturing a world-wide market and remaining small and nimble be balanced?

Which segments of the French market should the company target so as to maximize market penetration?

Basic Issues

Analysis of the attractiveness of different market segments

Consideration of different positioning options for the same product

Balancing of long term strategic objectives (remaining small) with the necessity to maximize return on a limited-life (patented) innovative product idea.

---

*This teaching note was written by Niraj Dawar, Assistant Professor at INSEAD, as an aid to instructors in the classroom use of the case. Copyright © 1996 INSEAD, Fontainebleau, France.

Key Points

- A product needs to be defined for the market—the form in which a product is put on the market depends on:
  * Segmentation of the market
  * Customer requirements
  * Company competencies
  * Benefits required by different segments
- Packaging is an integral part of product positioning. The benefits offered by packaging may provide a means of:
  * Appealing to untapped segments
  * Differentiating the product vis-à-vis competitors
  * Differentiating the product vis-à-vis other products in the line
- The additional rent generated by producing a lower cost alternative to existing packaging systems will be divided through the value chain depending on the value-added: turnkey (high value added) versus licensing (low value added)

Teaching Suggestions

Students may be given the following set of discussion questions to guide their analysis of the case:

- How would you characterize the French market for milk packaging? Which segments can you identify and what are their characteristics?
- Which of the segments identified appear attractive for the Fottle, and why?
- Develop a product definition and mechanism for selling the Fottle to the chosen segment(s).

Suggested Analysis

The French Milk Market

In 1993, the milk market through mass retailing in France was worth approximately FF12 billion (3 billion litres). The market had been stable in terms of volume for the past ten years with a slight decline in the last year. It is predicted that repositioning by milk producers (as a healthy adult beverage), consumer trends to high value drinks and improvement in the French economy will lead to moderate future growth in the market. The market is structured as presented in TN--Exhibit I (on next page).

Large producers are attempting to differentiate through product, positioning and packaging innovation. Medium and small producers are generally producing private labels and discount brands and are subject to cost pressures. Part of the cost pressure derives from the capacity utilization of their packaging machinery which is obtained on lease from TetraPak. They are also subject to pricing pressures from their contracts with retailers.

TN Exhibit I   Value Chain for French Milk Market

Suppliers	*Producers*	*Distributors*	
• machinery • packaging materials • milk	SMALL MEDIUM ――――― LARGE	HARD DISCOUNTERS ――――― RETAIL CHAINS	C U S T O M E R S

Segmentation

The market can be segmented by product (UHT, pasteurized and sterilized, flavored, specialty; see case, Table 1); by brand category (national brands, private labels and discount brands or *premier prix*); or by size (large, medium, small). Case Exhibits 6a and 8 can be used to arrive at a segmentation as shown in TN-Exhibit II. Two national brands (Candia and Lactel) dominate the market with 42% market share by value and 32% by volume (of milk sold through mass distribution; see case Exhibit 6a); private labels represent 22% in value; and "premier prix" a further 31%. The market is very competitive and this has led to price pressure on milk producers. The players differentiate themselves mainly through price, but increasingly through branding, packaging and retail channels. As mentioned in the case, for Candia's brands, Viva and Grand Vivre, packaging plays an increasingly important role in the positioning of brands and the communication of their image. Further, packaging offers the opportunity of communicating potentially relevant issues for the future, for example, the environment.

TN-Exhibit II outlines a segmentation analysis of the market based on the criteria of size of milk producer and types of brands (on next page).

The three large producers Cedilac (Candia brand), Besnier (Lactel brand), and Gervais-Nactalia control the market in all three types of brands. They are also most innovative in adopting new packaging. However, because of cost and price pressures, the medium and small producers are on the look out for alternative packaging suppliers. If Düring were to target large producers, the selling proposition would have to be based on innovation, differentiation, and environmental and convenience appeal to the final customer. For medium and small producers, the appeal would have to be strongly price oriented. Large producers have engineering departments and may require less hand-holding. Medium and small producers require turnkey solutions and perhaps financing (leasing) arrangements, given their strapped financial situation.

TN-Exhibit II Segmentation Analysis of French Milk Producers

Producer Size

Brand Type	Large	Medium	Small
National Brands	29% volume share. 60:40 split of carton and plastic. High-Value added. Focused on differentiation and innovation, including through packaging	2.6% of total market by volume. Small, fragmented. Producers produce for other national brands.	Negligible(<1% of total market by volume).
Private Labels + Small Retailing*	16% volume share. Growing market. Assumed 60:40 split of carton and plastic. Growing trend of plastic.	7.7% volume share. Growing market. 80:20 split of cartons and plastic. Cost sensitive.	12.5% volume share. Growing market. 90:10 split of cartons and plastic. Cost sensitive
Discount Brands *Premiers Prix*	27% volume share. Characterized by price competition, low differentiation. Used by large producers for capacity filling.	3% volume share. Small, fragmented. Producers use this for capacity filling	2.5% volume share. Fragmented and fierce competitive market. Mainly price competitive. 90:10 split of carton and plastic. Highly cost sensitive.

*small retailing assumed to be 50% of column 6 in case Exhibit 8.

The French Milk Packaging Market

The milk packaging market earns revenues of approximately FF1.8 billion[1] per annum. This is split between machinery sales, maintenance and sales of packaging materials.

The French market is made up of two product segments: cartons (where the same suppliers provide both equipment and carton board) and plastic bottles (where equipment, bottles, and bottle closures may be supplied by different suppliers). While both segments involve one-way, disposable packaging, the carton segment generates sales of approximately FF 1,427 million (2.46 billion litres) and is quite distinct from the plastic bottling segment which generates FF 432 million (540 million litres) (see Table I in the case for percentages) and is subject to different technology and cost constraints.

The market for cartons is dominated by TetraPak, which has built a strong position based on selling a turnkey solution to the milk producers. TetraPak's use of its quasi-monopolistic power with the milk producers, together with consumer preference for less messy, re-sealable packages and a drive by the national brands for product differentiation has allowed plastic bottling to gain a position in the milk market. Six years after their introduction, plastic bottles now have an 18% share by volume of the total milk market, despite costing the retailer about 30% more than cartons (see Table I and case Exhibit 7).

---

[1] Calculated from cost structure of industry.

TN-Exhibit III   **Comparison of Attractiveness of Large vs. Medium Small Milk Producers**

	Large Producers	*Medium/Small Producers*
Pros	<ul><li>High penetration of plastic</li><li>Fit with Düring's selling marketing skills in detergents</li><li>In-house engineering skills</li><li>Looking for innovations</li><li>Large market, few firms</li></ul>	<ul><li>Fottle appealing due to:<ul><li>low cost</li><li>alternative source of supply</li></ul></li><li>Large number of firms</li></ul>
Cons	<ul><li>Few firms: make or break</li><li>May require exclusivity in contracts</li></ul>	<ul><li>Fragmented market: small gains from any one contract leads to high cost of servicing</li><li>Current penetration of TetraPak—severe competition</li><li>May require financial assistance to install new line</li><li>No in-house engineering: may require high levels of hand-holding</li></ul>

Product Positioning Options Analysis

At present, Düring is considering the following options for defining the Fottle product offering:

Option 1: Offer a turnkey solution with the Form-Fill-Seal process. Machinery and engineering know-how to be supplied by a partner who would need to be identified.

Option 2: License Fottle molds directly to dairy producers.

Option 3: License Fottle to engineering firms that provide bottling machinery.

TN-Exhibit IV lists the key advantages and disadvantages of the three options (on next page).

TN-Exhibit IV   Key Advantages and Disadvantages of the Three Options

	Key Advantages	*Key Disadvantages*
Option 1: Turnkey Solution	• Manufacturing efficiency (integrated system: low inventory, no pre-cleaning of bottle) • Competitive pricing versus both carton and plastic • Ability to control access to selected sub-segment • First turnkey plastic solution—competes well with both TetraPak and other plastic bottling solutions • High profit potential from long term contracts; creating barriers to entry for future	• High investment required: poten involvement in packaging engineering, marketing, sales, a maintenance • High initial costs for milk produ may create switching hesitation • Potentially competing with bott technology firms—unknown ma for Düring • Lack of experience (different structure from detergents busin • Negotiations, power- and profit sharing with packaging enginee
Option 2: Licensing to Producer	• Ability to control access to selected segments of the market • Meets objective of remaining a small "ideas" company • Low investment required on the part of Düring • Similar to detergents business • Low switching costs for milk producers with existing plastic bottling lines	• May require offering exclusivit milk producers • Linked to existing plastics • Producers may require complet solution
Option 3: Licensing to Engineering Firm	Low cost, low risk strategy Meets objective of remaining a small "ideas" company Requires no marketing expertise	Loss of control over pricing, positic marketing push Loss of control over the developmer an integrated Fottle system Power- and profit-sharing with an engineering firm

The current packaging systems available to milk producers in France are:

- the carton Form-Fill-Seal (F-F-S) system where conditioned milk and carton boards are fed into a machine which forms the carton, fills it with milk and then seals the package; and
- the plastic bottle fill-seal system where a bottle, produced off-site, is filled and sealed on the milk producers' machinery.

The variety of products (shapes and sizes) available with the Fottle and a new distinctive packaging design make the Fottle a potentially desirable product for those companies seeking to differentiate themselves. This, together with the environmental advantages of the Fottle (which may increase the export opportunities for French milk producers) and the cost savings offered by the Fottle over current packaging systems suggests that there is an opportunity for Düring to profitably exploit the Fottle concept in the French milk market.

In the case of Fottle Form molds and licensing, only producers currently using bottling technology can be reached. This is, however, the growing technology in the milk market. The key advantages of each product format are set out below:

- Fottle molds facilitate easy market entry with low switching costs for producers currently using plastic bottle technology;
- The Fottle Form mold allows access to the low cost, in-line system without requiring a complete new machine purchase.
- For the Fottle mold, working with a large milk producer should capture significant value for Düring. The disadvantage being that Düring will be restricted to large producers; and
- Licensing to a packaging company appears attractive due to low involvement and investment and a strong bargaining position with respect to the packager (as Düring holds the key to an attractive market). However, the licensing option needs to be weighed against the loss of control in the positioning of the product and the licensee's control over the marketing push and resources that will go behind the Fottle.
- The Fottle F-F-S system creates high switching costs (once the product has been adopted) and fully exploits the Fottle F-F-S technology by making it available to the entire milk market. It also requires the highest capital investment for the milk producer.

However, the F-F-S system requires engineering capabilities in packaging machinery that Düring currently does not have.

Strategic Issues

The long-term development of the Fottle product has to be considered in terms of building market positions which emphasize its differentiation possibilities. This implies that milk producers who differentiate themselves on quality form an ideal target.

The major benefit to the milk producer is the cost efficiency of the Fottle F-F-S system which will allow them to increase margins at the same time as reducing cost to the retailer. The advantage of the Fottle F-F-S system over the Fottle molds is that it allows access to the carton segment of the market, where cost savings may not be such a large selling point. Admittedly, the Fottle F-F-S system may lead to faster market penetration, but entering the carton segment as a first move is also liable to produce a strong competitive reaction from TetraPak, a much larger firm than Düring with very powerful resources.

From the market analysis it appears that the national brands, with their strong desire for product differentiation, would place most value on the Fottle system, particularly if they had exclusive rights to this type of packaging. This, together with some of the disadvantages associated with the other options, indicates that an agreement with one of the three large milk producers to supply a Fottle form system (perhaps using outside engineering expertise) to complement existing fill-seal equipment will enable Düring to maximize the benefits of the Fottle concept in this market.

To gain an assessment of the revenue potential of Fottle, consider its cost advantage over plastic bottles (liter size). At 0.80 FF the plastic bottle costs 0.30 more than Fottle, giving it a 0.30 FF saving potential to the milk producer. Suppose Düring considers a royalty of 0.05 FF, 0.10, or 0.15, and decides to target Gervais-Nactalia (annual sales of 81 million liters). Assume that Fottle can attract 10 or 20 percent of G-N's business. The following are the estimated revenuee to Fottle:

	.05*	0.10	0.15
10%	405,000	810,000	1,215,000
20%	810,000	1,620,000	2,430,000

* .10 x 0.05 x 81 mil = 405,000 FF

TetraPak too may have an interest in obtaining the Fottle concept because of the competitive advantage it could obtain. Using its wide distribution network and engineering expertise, TetraPak could potentially create a dominant position in plastic packaging. From a strategic perspective, it would also allow them to control the rate of substitution of cartons to plastic. From the point of view of Düring, dealing with TetraPak may not be ideal since TetraPak has a vested interest in carton packaging. It may make economic sense for TetraPak to buy and suppress the Fottle product, and therefore one would have to design a TetraPak licensing agreement with this in mind. This would imply the use of a high fixed cost, low variable cost licensing agreement which would mean TetraPak's marginal costs for Fottle production were reasonably low. TetraPak can be considered to be a less attractive "customer" for the Fottle product than either of the large national brands because of the likely difficulty in reaching an agreement and the fact that Düring may lose control of the Fottle.

Epilogue

Düring AG entered into negotiations with a packaging engineering firm to propose a turnkey F-F-S Fottle system to milk producers. At the same time (January 1995), one of the largest brands of mineral water, Evian, launched the crushable bottle (as opposed to Foldable), backed with a large advertising and PR campaign. While the success of this introduction raised awareness about the need for environmentally friendly packaging, it also usurped the Fottle's unique selling proposition. As this teaching note is being written, Düuring AG is marketing its turnkey solution to large producers of national brands in France.

CASE 4-3
MURPHY BREWERY IRELAND*

Synopsis

This case examines the marketing of Murphy's Irish Stout at the time of the merger between Guinness and Grand Metropolitan. Murphy Brewery is owned by Heineken International and has expanded its scope beyond Ireland in recent years. However, the brand is a distant second internationally to Guinness in the stout category. Furthermore, the company has launched a new brand—Murphy's Irish Amber.

This case discusses the Murphy's situation in Ireland, the UK and Europe as well as the United States. One of the issues to be examined is whether the company should have similar positioning worldwide.

The case concludes with a series of questions that are posed in a hypothetical management meeting at Murphy Brewery Ireland. The individuals in the case are the actual managers employed by the brewery.

Teaching/Learning Objectives

Key Issues

Marketing Strategy Questions—This case is intended to challenge students to address the marketing strategy questions facing Murphy's. For example, what target market should the company focus upon? Is its product line broad enough? Is the pricing strategy accurate? How can the channels of distribution be deepened for the brand? How should the brand be positioned and promoted?

Divisional versus Corporate Objectives—How extensively is Heineken willing to promote Murphy's brand worldwide? Should Heineken concentrate its efforts only on the more "affluent" segments throughout the world given the high status and price of the brand? How should Heineken address the impending production shortage at Murphy Brewery located in Cork?

Ethical Issues—Can Murphy's promote these brands as "authentically" Irish if they are not manufactured in Ireland? What responsibilities does Heineken and other breweries have for promoting responsible consumption especially if they are targeting young adults?

Teaching Objectives

1. To examine the entire marketing program of an Irish brand.
2. To discuss the interplay between overall corporate objectives and subsidiary objectives of marketing penetration and profit maximization.
3. To analyze international marketing problems facing a particular firm.
4. To raise potential ethical issues faced by one marketer.

---

* Teaching note by case authors, Professor Patrick Murphy, University of Notre Dame and Don O'Sullivan, University College, Cork, Ireland.

Target Audience

The case is intended for upper division undergraduate students. It does not contain enough numbers for most MBA classes. The case could potentially be used as a comprehensive case at the end of a Principles or Introductory Marketing course, but it probably represents a better possibility for a Marketing Strategy or Marketing Problems case at the advanced undergraduate level. Students with more knowledge of positioning, strategy formulation, brand equity and other more sophisticated marketing tools would be able to analyze this case more fully. If the case were used at the MBA level, the authors would recommend some supplementary information on the beer market in a particular country or region of the world. These data are available on a country by country basis and can be relatively easily identified. In addition, the *International Drinks Bulletin* is a good source of data. In the United States, *Jobson's Wine Handbook* is another excellent source of data on the beer industry.

Discussion Questions and Analysis

The case concludes with a number of questions that the Murphy's executives are considering. One approach to analyzing the case is to begin with these questions. They will be discussed here as well as additional approaches to analyzing the case.

How important is a strong showing in the Irish domestic market to Murphy's? Must they make a strong showing there to be successful world wide?

This is an important question and one about which Murphy's management feels strongly. They believe that the company must have a better than its current 5% share of the Irish market to establish a strong basis for the international market Historically, Murphy's has been a regional brand in Ireland with a penetration primarily in the Cork/Munster region in the country. With Heineken's support, the company has expanded dramatically in recent years. However, the data in the case show that it is still not performing well in its own country. The company is spending substantial amounts of money on advertising and promotion there to create brand awareness, but significantly less than Guinness.

A logical argument could be made that Heineken should invest more in the American and other large world markets and not be that concerned about a market of less than four million people on the island of Ireland. There is a downside to this approach in that it is an Irish brand and, as Patrick Conway mentioned in the case, its "backbone" could be threatened. However, most global consumers are not that aware of a brand's showing in its own country. While this point is somewhat debatable, a strong argument could be made that more of a worldwide investment should be made rather than so much in Ireland.

The writers learned that Heineken have relocated the export and international marketing managers from Cork to its headquarters in Amsterdam. This move signals that the company is planning to place more emphasis on the Murphy's brands in the future.

Instructor's Note: Students should be challenged to defend their viewpoint on this question. Possibly, a debate might be conducted with students taking opposing sides on this question.

Should Murphy's employ a global rather than a local marketing strategy worldwide?

Probably, the best positioning for Murphy's is as an Irish company (see Exhibit 9 in the case). The consistency of the message and image appears important to the company. (The company is pursuing a slightly different approach in the United Kingdom however, because it is somewhat of a unique market and Murphy's has a strong brand identity there already.) If the company is going to be successful internationally, a consistent theme and message is essential to the brand. Heineken's success with its flagship brand and its green bottle is a good example of how consistency has already worked for the company. It is a strategy that Murphy's would do well to emulate. Students should pick up on this point and apply it to Murphy's. The draughtflow bottle is a tangible example of the company attempting a consistent brand image.

The UK campaign appears to be successful and should be maintained as long as it is working. However, this differing approach should not undermine a consistent message for other markets. The carryover between UK and continental European markets is not that strong. The U.S. market can be viewed as much different but should probably have a consistent message throughout North America.

Instructor's Note: The most successful global brands appear to e those that have consistent positioning (e.g. Coke, McDonald's, Sony, etc.).

Is Murphy's destined to be a "niche" product forever? Will these brands ever reach the place where they command a substantial market share?

The data in the case indicate that Murphy's is clearly a low market share product. There is probably is not a substantial percentage of drinkers outside of Ireland and the UK who have developed a strong taste for stout It is a distinct product and one which many consumers find too heavy. Heineken can be successful in "growing" the brand in the U.S. as well as another markets in Europe as they are doing now. The Murphy's Irish Amber appears to be a potentially successful product and could make inroads in the premium red ale category. This will require substantial investment in distribution and promotion by Heineken.

An issue to be discussed is Heineken's corporate commitment to Murphy's. The parent company likely possesses the resources to assist Murphy's in becoming a "world brand" over time. However, how much they are willing to invest in Murphy's is unclear at this time. One point that students should understand is that as a "private" company, Heineken does not have the stock market pressures of GMG and other publicly traded firms. Therefore, they can plan for the long term and make investments in Murphy's that may not pay immediate returns to them.

The answers to these questions are that these brands have a long way to go to attain substantial market share. However, as Guinness has shown over the years, there is a viable niche segment for the stout in many countries beyond Ireland. Their current campaign in the U.S. (see Exhibit 7) should help Murphy's in growing the brand category. The Irish amber appears to be positioned well for future growth, but will also need promotional investment by Heineken to gain inroads into the ale market. Therefore, the growth opportunities for the Murphy's Irish Stout and Murphy's Irish Amber brands are promising, but depend upon Heineken's corporate objectives.

Instructor's Note: This question is also one that lends itself to debate. Some students are likely to be pessimistic regarding Murphy's possibilities given the dominance of Guinness. Others, however, will see potential for the brands given their unique Irish identity and strength of the parent company.

Should the company continue to make the two brands only at the Cork brewery for the lucrative U.S. market or should they consider making the product in that country? It worked for automobiles, why not beer?

This appears to be a fundamental "ethical" question facing Murphy's at this time. The company has positioned these brands as authentic Irish products and uses "Irish" in the brand name. Also, as the labels in Exhibit 3 show, the Irish heritage is strongly promoted on the product itself. If the product was made/brewed in the U.S. or other markets, there is a potential for deception of consumers. A decision to brew the product in the United States and not change the brand label, would likely present an ethical violation using the Kantian principles of duty or intentions. That is, it would be the intention of Murphy's to sell the product as being authentically Irish when it is not.

A question that can be debated with the students is whether after a number of years and the brand experiences some success then the name could be changed to Murphy's Stout and Murphy's Amber. If Irish was not in the name and the labels were changed, there would be much less likelihood for consumers to be deceived into thinking the products were just made in Ireland. The Japanese automobile industry has been successful in making its cars in the United States and still selling it under the Japanese name plate. Some students may not seeing anything wrong with this. While the point is one that is debatable, one of the issues relating to ethics is that the answers are not black and white. The Murphy and Heineken management seems to understand this and are reluctant to change their manufacturing strategy at the present point in time. However, the capacity limitations of the Cork brewery may force a decision soon..

Some students will mention that Guinness is brewed throughout the world in many locations and if it is OK for them, why not Murphy's? However, Murphy's have made much of stating that their products are authentically Irish and have much potentially to lose with such a decision.

Another potential ethical issue that could be discussed in Europe and Ireland is whether Heineken should have a responsibility to expand its Irish base of operations. Ireland has experienced strong economic growth in recent years but is still a relatively "poor" country compared to the rest of Europe and certainly North America. Does Heineken have a ethical responsibility to Murphy's to expand operations there rather than take the easier route and make the product in the United States? Will the U.S. and other markets support these high prices that the Irish manufacturing and cost of bottle and distribution in Europe demand for the company? These are additional ethical issues that can be discussed.

Instructor's Note: If these do not surface as "ethical issues", the instructor should guide the students in examining them in this context. Furthermore, the larger ethical question for all beer marketers is targeting underage consumers. This issue could be added to those above in discussing the ethical aspects of the case. The position of the authors is that Murphy's should take the "high road" and not target underage drinkers.

Will Murphy's ever to able to achieve the status of other products that are famous for the Irish heritage such as Guinness, Bailey's Irish Creme, Jameson Irish Whiskey, Waterford Crystal and Belleek China?

While this question is hypothetical, it does represent a major marketing challenge for Heineken and Murphy's. This should be both company's long term marketing objective. If the brand gained greater penetration in Europe, North American, and Asia and Heineken decided to put its substantial financial muscle behind the brand, it has the potential to be seen as the same league as these other world brands from the country of Ireland. Students could be asked to develop strategies to raise the profile of the brand.

Instructor's Note: As much or as little class time can be devoted to this question as the instructor wants. It is somewhat of a fishing expedition by the writers to challenge students to think about the long term and having high aspirations for a brand.

Additional Analyses

An examination of the classic marketing questions can also occur during the discussion of this case. They are as follows:

What market segment should serve as a target for Murphy's Irish Stout and Irish Amber?

Although the case does not explicitly examine segmentation and targeting, it should be the focus of part of the classroom discussion. The major target for MIS should be on "young" consumers who are above the minimum drinking age. The reasoning for this strategy is twofold. First, Guinness in Ireland and many other countries has the "older" consumers "locked up" and they are not likely to change brands. Second, the brand loyalty of young consumers are still being formed and Murphy's may be able to gain lifelong drinkers if they can convince them to buy Murphy's instead of Guinness.

Students analyzing the case probably fall into this segment and their own experiences can be brought to bear on this discussion. They would likely have good ideas on how to target their own age group. In the U.S. this group is sometimes described as Generation X with differing attitudes and values from their parents and even older siblings.

Murphy's Irish Amber probably should seek and older and more sophisticated drinker. The high price (especially for the packaged product) means that it is likely out of the acceptable range for many younger consumers. It can be positioned as a more mature product but one that appeals to the taste of the discerning red ale consumer.

What product and brand issues should Murphy's alter?

The quality and taste of MIS and MIA appear to be sound and acceptable to the market. So, product formulation is not an issue faced for these brands.

Some students might argue that Murphy's should "fill out" its product line by offering a lager. This is not an acceptable strategy in that Heineken already has a world famous lager that is extremely successful. Any new entry would tend to "cannibalize" the market for its flagship brand. Furthermore, the market is very cluttered or glutted with lager brands and a new one would have great difficulty competing in this market.

The brand equity in the Murphy's name is one that the firm can build upon. This is a recognizable name and the brewery has a long and impressive tradition that can be further exploited.

One product "problem" is the bottle size in the U.S. While it would be quite expensive to change the size, a twelve ounce bottle should probably be used in that market. The bars/pubs sell beer in this size glass and it is more that Murphy's can expect to force them to buy new size glasses to serve one product. Furthermore, the size of 16.9 ounces is even larger than a pint. This is probably a problem in European markets as well.

What should be Murphy's pricing strategy for its brands?

The premium pricing strategy should be maintained. The "price-quality" relationship is held strongly by many beer drinkers. Murphy's does not want to be a mass market product (except in Ireland) an the high price signals high quality to its consumers. They should continue to stress their quality image through their pricing strategy.

One additional pricing issue that Murphy's should continue to pursue is their policy of offering the trade a slightly lower price than Guinness. This incentive is one that is a good idea and may help gain market penetration especially in new markets without strong levels of established brand loyalty to the competing brand.

What should be the distribution policy and strategy for Murphy's?

The strategy in the U.S. of beginning with the large cities and major population or tourist areas is a sound one. They need to get greater penetration in virtually all markets so that they have an opportunity to grow their brands.

The case does not address the on-premises v. off-premises distribution objective of Murphy's. The company has told the authors that they use off-premises distribution primarily as a way to build awareness and loyalty to the brands for consumption on-premise. The margins, especially in supermarkets, are razor thin and the company realizes they will never compete with the high volume local brands. Therefore, their preference is to stress the relatively high margin on-premises trade.

Some students may bring up the pull v. push distribution strategy. At this point, it appears Murphy's need some of both. They are not in the position to engage in extensive mass media advertising. However, they cannot rely exclusively on a push strategy and ignore the end consumer. They must devise a system where they can employ both strategies simultaneously at an acceptable level. Students might be encouraged to discuss exactly where in their market Murphy's should try for greater market penetration.

What promotional strategy should Murphy's utilize for their brands?

The advertising strategy of Murphy's in markets other than Ireland is not specified in the case. Students should take note of the decision not to use the broadcast media in the U.S. The decision not to use TV seem to be a sound one given the fact that both brands are low market share products. This a significant limitation, but offers an opportunity to discuss the merits of magazines v. newspapers. Magazines aimed at the youth market may be a good vehicle because the use of color can help Murphy's communicate the image desired for MIS. Advertising for MIA should also utilize magazines but ones aimed at a more affluent and mature market.

The point should be made that the company should consider an international ad campaign with a single message to position the product and raise its profile. It is essential for pulling the product through the channels of distribution.

Students could be given the assignment for this case of investigating beer ads in their country and attempt to position Murphy's from the information shown in the case relative to the others. Several signals for possible messages are contained in Exhibit 9.

Guinness' successful current TV ad campaign in the U.S. (Exhibit 7) should help Murphy's and allow them to build on the knowledge of Americans for the brand category. Students may want to discuss the merits of the current UK campaign that positions Murphy's as being less bitter than Guinness.

Two other possible promotional strategies can be raised. One is for Murphy's to develop their own website. Heineken has one, but has no information about Murphy's on it. Murphy's may consider some type of competition such as a "pub tour" of Ireland aimed at Americans. This would be modeled on the Guinness "win a pub" competition but would be much less costly and Murphy's could possibly work with the Irish Tourist Board in the pub tour or other tourism ideas. The home page and website would raise the profile of the brand with their "young" target market. At the time of this case in 1997, Murphy's did not have a presence on the world wide web. This would seem necessary for a company with international aspirations.

A second promotional possibility is for Murphy's to expand their sponsorship of golf tournaments. They currently sponsor the Irish Open and English Open (not to be confused with the British Open) tournaments. Both in the Asian and American markets, golf is a popular sport. especially with the more affluent communities. Golf is a good "match" between the product image and the intended market. Furthermore, the "Tiger Woods phenomenon" likely means that golf will have greater exposure and interest in the U.S. for the foreseeable future. Murphy's may consider sponsorship of smaller PGA events in the U.S. and tournaments in Asia as a vehicle to reach a good market for the Murphy's Irish Amber beer particularly. In fact, a golf theme that ties into several of the positive characteristics of Ireland (Exhibit 9) might be considered for a worldwide positioning of the brand.

Teaching Suggestions

The exhibits contain valuable information that should facilitate discussion and analysis of the case. Exhibit 1 shows Murphy's growth since its takeover by Heineken. The recent growth is particularly impressive and likely signals a more aggressive posture by Heineken toward the brands. MIS consumption in Ireland is relatively flat and even the recent ad campaign has not led to significant sales improvement. The export market for Murphy's products has "exploded" in the mid 1990s.

Exhibit 2 is intended to convey useful information about the stout product. For students who are unfamiliar with the product category, this should prove helpful. The exhibit contains useful data that "proves" that Murphy's is less bitter than Guinness.

Exhibit 3 should be studied closely by student to understand the branding and labeling strategy for the two brands. The date that Murphy's was established—1856 is included on the front panel as well as the Murphy's family crest below the date. The back panel contains the historical perspective on the MIS product and the product quality emphasis. The U.S. government mandated warning is shown on both labels from the U.S.. Furthermore, the warning to not drink directly from the bottle is an example of the company taking an ethical posture.

Exhibit 4 shows that Heineken is a major worldwide player in the beer market. Its percentage of 89% is the highest of all brewers. Its size is only sixty percent of AB.

Exhibit 5 depicts the GMG brands. The size of Guinness compared with Murphy's is much larger. The fact that with the merger GMG has Bailey's Irish Creme in its stable of brands is significant.

Exhibit 6 shows the most popular imported brands in the U.S.. The Murphy's size of the market can be calculated from the two sets of numbers by multiplying the gallons from Ireland in 94, 95 and 96 by 2.25 and subtracting the Guinness numbers from them.

Exhibit 7 is a good for discussion with the class. The *Wall Street Journal* article captures the current strategy of Guinness and its recent success in the U.S.. Students can be encouraged to search Out similar business press articles from their country.

Exhibit 8 shows the size of the world beer market. It should be noted that the specialty category is growing faster than the others which is good news for Murphy's.

Exhibit 9 depicts information about the country and Irish people. Students might be asked whether they agree with these characterizations and to come up with other descriptors that might be used by Murphy's to capture its Irishness.

Additional Readings

Hays Dawson, "Brand Brewing," *Beverage World*. October 1995, pp. 50-60.

G. Kelly, Q. Travis, and Ray Goldberg, "Guinness PLC", Harvard Business School Case, 9-595-021.

CASE 4-4
SHORIN-RYU KARATE ACADEMY*

Synopsis

At the time of the case, Shorin-Ryu Karate Academy (SKA) had been in operation 17 years. The academy started in Sensei James True's garage and later moved to its current state-of-the-art training facility in Waltham, Massachusetts (USA).

Sensei Jim's success with the academy (as well as his own personal desires) led him to explore various avenues of growth. Initially, and from a current market perspective, Sensei Jim wanted to increase the number of students attending classes at the Waltham facility. Questions that arose with this goal were the level of satisfaction with student instructors (which would likely increase if the student population increased) and the effectiveness of the academy's advertising approaches. Ultimately, Sensei Jim needed to know "who" would comprise this growth opportunity and "how" he could reach them. Sensei Jim also had visions of taking his product/service into new markets by opening a second location. Intertwined with both growth options was Sensei's desire to better manage his business.

Sensei Jim had enlisted the help of an MBA student consulting group to help him explore his options. The information gathered by the student team is presented in the case.

Teaching/Learning Objectives

The Shorin-Ryu Karate Academy is a classic success story of a small, entrepreneurial firm. The owner wants to grow, but is uncertain as to how to achieve growth. With this in mind, the case:

- combines entrepreneurial "dreams" with the realities of day-to-day operational concerns,
- allows in-depth analysis of marketplace size with market penetration opportunities,
- addresses the effectiveness of various marketing communication mediums and shows the need for understanding such effectiveness (or lack thereof), and
- forces students to make a decision regarding target markets and how to reach the market.

Discussion Questions

1. What external factors affect the Shorin-Ryu Karate Academy's long-term success?
2. How is the Shorin-Ryu Karate Academy doing relative to its competition?
3. What are the strengths and weaknesses of the internal operation at the Shorin-Ryu Karate Academy?
4. What should (if anything) Sensei Jim do in addressing his firm's internal weaknesses?
5. How is the karate market segmented in general? Specifically at the Shorin-Ryu Karate Academy?
6. Are there any markets more/less appropriate for the Shorin-Ryu Karate Academy?
7. What are Sensei Jim's options for growth?

---

* This teaching note was prepared by Victoria L. Crittenden, Boston College, and William F. Crittenden, Northeastern University, as an aid to instructors using the case, "Shorin-Ryu Karate Academy."

8. What is your recommendation to Sensei James True?

Analysis

1. What external factors affect the Shorin-Ryu Karate Academy's long-term success?

Exhibit TN–1 provides a sample SWOT analysis. The opportunities and threats sections provide an overview of external factors that must be considered when thinking about the organization's long-term success.

2. How is the Shorin-Ryu Karate Academy doing relative to its competition?

Exhibit TN–2 provides a quantitative analysis of SKA and its competition. With respect to both revenue and enrollment, SKA is the most successful of the martial arts organizations in the three-town market area. Interestingly, American Karate Academy is located in the smallest and poorest of the three communities, but charges the highest monthly fee and has a fairly substantial enrollment. Shorin-Ryu's monthly rate is consistent with that of its competition (except for the American Karate Academy).

(Keep in mind that Shorin-Ryu does not offer one-month rates. The $60 monthly rate can be roughly calculated based on the Academy's 12-month, 2 times per week program. Thus, monthly rates will vary based on the program. Exhibit TN–3 provides a more thorough analysis of average price per student per month. Interestingly, if students use income data from Exhibit 8, monthly price varies substantially from the $60 per month. For example, 1995 tuition income was $75,000. This is $6,250 per month in tuition income. With 325 students, the average monthly tuition would only be $20. However, given the concerns with the academy's financial accounting records, it is more reliable to look at each individual program to determine average monthly tuition. In doing this, we see that $60 is fairly standard.)

3. What are the strengths and weaknesses of the internal operation at the Shorin-Ryu Karate Academy?

Strengths and weakness are presented in the SWOT analysis in Exhibit TN–1.

4. What should (if anything) Sensei Jim do in addressing his firm's internal weaknesses?

Three major areas comprise the organization's internal weaknesses: financial record-keeping, marketing communications, and student instructors.

Financial

Not unlike many entrepreneurs, Sensei Jim has complicated his financial records with many personal expenses. Net income for 1995 was ($11,650). However, the organization really saw a positive cash flow if personal expenses are not included in the calculation (for example: $750 in new car expenses, $7,178 new home expenses, $13,400 personal credit card expenses). The adjusted net income would be around $10,000 if such personal expenses were not included in Sensei's business accounts.

Marketing Communications

Exhibit TN–4 looks at student responsiveness relative to the academy's marketing communications expenditures. Referrals are the biggest source of new students at the academy. However, Sensei Jim has no system in place to follow-up with referrals. For example, many organizations will send out "thank-you" letters to the person who referred the new customer/client to the organization. This would be a relatively cost-free method for Sensei Jim to show his appreciation to his current student base. Currently, a referral is left unacknowledged from the viewpoint of the referring student. Sensei Jim's YMCA program brings in a considerable number of students. Since the cost of this program is measured in time (Sensei Jim being at the YMCA to conduct the classes), Sensei might want to offer as many of these programs as possible (as long as they do not conflict with his programs at the academy). The Bring-A-Friend Week program is relatively cost-free (other than the key chain that is given out to class visitors). Again, however, Sensei has no follow-up system. Thus, a youngster visits the class, receives information, and never hears from the academy again. Sensei should send out a follow-up letter to the visiting youngster and invite him/her to come to class again (with his/her parents).

Regarding where Sensei spends his communications money, the cost of direct mail is too high on a per student basis. The best value is the use of the yellow pages, and, interestingly, the yellow pages bring in almost as many students as does newspaper advertising. The quantitative breakdown in the Exhibit TN–4 does not look at any add-on costs that might accompany a newspaper ad. For example, a newspaper ad might include a promotional offer, whereas the yellow pages simply list Shorin-Ryu as a karate school (no add-on costs). So, it might be that the yellow pages are an even less expensive source of new students than these numbers are showing. However, it would be unwise to recommend no newspaper advertising since it does bring in almost 20 percent of the academy's students. Direct mail is too high on a per new student basis. Only five percent of the academy's students are at Shorin-Ryu because of the company's direct mail campaign. Sensei would be wise to allocate this $2,500 to another communications medium.

Student Instructors

Sensei Jim is the backbone of the academy (exemplified in the survey results). There is some concern that students are not receiving the full benefit of their program when Sensei Jim is not instructing the class. Since it is reasonable to assume that Sensei cannot always be there, he needs to implement some fairly simple measures to ensure customer satisfaction. One fairly easy measure would be a formal introduction of instructors to the academy membership. This could be done in the academy's monthly newsletter. The newsletter could outline the student instructors' achievements and why they are qualified to instruct a group of students. Also, the training program for student instructors should be described in detail. Sensei Jim also needs to determine the student load per class, per day. He could attempt to be available at heavy usage times so that a fewer number of students are affected by his absence.

5. How is the karate market segmented in general? Specifically at the Shorin-Ryu Karate Academy?

In general, the two major criteria for segmentation are age and gender. At the Shorin-Ryu Karate Academy, one sees several forms of segmentation: Age, Geography, Usage, Responsiveness, and Income. Interestingly, the SKA does not provide data for gender segmentation, which leads one to believe that gender is not a method of segmentation at the academy (the classes are mixed—males and females in the same class).

Regarding age segmentation, the academy has six major groups: Little Dragons (ages 4-6), Junior Ninjas (ages 7-9), Samurais (ages 10-14), Daimyos or Shoguns (ages 8-14), Teens (ages 13-17), and adults. The youth market comprised 65 percent of the academy's membership base.

Geography is a critical segmentation variable at the Shorin-Ryu Karate Academy. The majority of students are from the Waltham area, with neighboring communities comprising most of the balance. Given competitive martial arts organizations, as well as travel times in the Boston area, it would be highly unlikely that students would travel from non-neighboring towns to attend the SKA. Combining SKA's current enrollment based on survey results with population statistics for its current geographic markets, we see:

	# of potential students (5-17 years)	% enrolled
Waltham	6,119	2.30%
Watertown	3,124	0.93%
Newton	10,887	0.25%

Usage is an interesting segmentation variable as seen in Exhibit 4 of the case. While Sensei Jim (as well as martial arts instructors in general) prefers that a student attend class two times a week, SKA students seem to prefer attending once a week. This may be due to conflicts with other sporting events. Whatever the reason, once a week draws the largest crowd of users.

Exhibit 7 provides an overview of student responsiveness to the academy's marketing communications by geographic location. Combining responsiveness data with location provides valuable insight to Sensei Jim regarding how to target particular groups. For example, newspaper advertising seems to be work better outside of the academy's site location (Waltham), as does direct mail.

Income segmentation is rather vague in the case, but does show up in the youth survey conducted by the consulting group. However, while the majority of youth families have annual incomes greater than $50,000, karate is considered to be less expensive than other sports students are involved in. (Students using the SKA case may need to be reminded that a $50,000 annual income is fairly low in the Boston area. The survey probably needed to include additional income categories at the higher dollar end.)

6. **Are there any markets more/less appropriate for the Shorin-Ryu Karate Academy?**

Any of the markets appear appropriate for SKA. There are, however, a few caveats. One, Sensei Jim will probably want to limit himself geographically. Commitment to the martial arts requires being at the dojo. Distance might inhibit a student's regular attendance, which in turn might prevent student commitment. The adult women market could add value to SKA, but this would, in all likelihood, mean that Sensei Jim would have to expand his hours of operation (e.g., a.m. hours). This could result in 9 a.m. to 10 p.m. days for Sensei Jim. Usage could be a critical segmentation variable to consider. Most martial arts academies want students to attend two times per week. However, enrollment at the SKA suggests that customers prefer one time per week (Exhibit 4). This may be due to other activities children are involved in (i.e., according to survey results, 89 percent of the youth members participate in other sports). Income may not be a differentiating factor. Although 58 percent of responding families reported annual income greater than $50,000, karate cost less than other activities.

7. **What are Sensei Jim's options for growth?**

The product/market grid is a good approach to evaluating growth options. The four options are:

Market Penetration: This would mean increasing the number of students at the current location.

Market Development: This could mean either opening a second location outside of the current market area (towns surrounding Waltham) or attempting to gain students from towns outside of the Waltham area.

Product Development: This would involve developing new product offerings for the Waltham facility. Examples might include cardio-karate, gender-specific classes, or classes for the elderly.

Diversification: Given Sensei Jim's interest in physical fitness, he could expand into new markets with new product offerings. For example, he could open a health club in a new market location.

8. What is your recommendation to Sensei James True?

Many students will probably recommend a combination of market penetration and product development. Others will lean toward market development.

Issues to consider in **market penetration** would include: market potential, instructor training, and marketing communications. Instructor training and marketing communications have been discussed previously in this note. Students should take a hard look at market potential in the current marketplace. For example, the MBA consulting group recommended that Sensei Jim target the youth segment in Waltham, Watertown, and Newton. Market potential analysis for this alternative shows:

Town	Youths	SKA Share	% Taking Self Defense (based on Exhibit 11*)	Unserved Market
Waltham	6,119	2.3%	15%	5,200
Watertown	3,124	0.93%	14%	2,690
Newton	10,887	0.25%	6%	10,233

*Using this percentage results in a gross estimation of the unserved market since it assumes that student participation at each school is solely from the town in which the school is located. As seen with the SKA, we know this is not the case. As well, the percentage could result in an underestimation of the unserved youth market since it is based on all ages in each of the towns. Nor does the calculation take into account inhabitants who live in one of the three towns, but travel to an undisclosed town to participate in the martial arts. Nevertheless, the calculation shows that the unserved market in each town is potentially very large.

As well, capacity at the current location has to be considered. How many students can Sensei Jim teach six days a week?

Ideas for **product development** are endless, but would likely include cardio-karate classes, a greater focus upon weapons classes, gender-specific classes, elderly offerings, and more family-oriented programs. Again, capacity issues are important (e.g., How many classes can Sensei Jim teach? What about instructor training for each of these classes/programs?).

Market development could involve moving into surrounding areas such as Weston, Lincoln, Wellesley, Lexington, Belmont, or Arlington via the current Waltham facility or the opening of a second facility. Demographic information, as well as other market research, would need to be collected from each of these towns. The opening of a second location appears questionable at the present time unless Sensei Jim wants to invest in human resources. Current market data shows that the main instructor is an important component of facility success. Also, this might move Sensei from an entrepreneurial manager with a hands-on approach (i.e., lead instructor) to more of a professional manager. James True has to decide if this is really something he wants personally, as well as professionally.

Critical to all three of these options is the target market Sensei Jim should go after.

While an option, **diversification** is probably not in the active decision set for Sensei Jim at this time.

Teaching the Case

The class discussion of SKA flows fabulously utilizing the traditional situational assessment opening. Opening the class with a SWOT analysis forces students to categorize many of the concerns faced by Sensei James True. The instructor can easily begin the case discussion with a look at the external environment, "What's happening in the martial arts industry?" The natural flow, then, is to the organization's internal strengths and weaknesses.

It is obvious that Sensei Jim has many smaller issues that need to be addressed. A "What do you recommend?" opening leads to students providing one-liners about each issue (e.g., separating personal and business finances, where to advertise/not advertise) rather than addressing these issues in the grander scheme of things regarding the academy's future growth.

A good class flow takes the students through a SWOT analysis and various options available to SKA, including which markets to target within each option.

Epilogue

Sensei James True opted for a strategy consisting of product development and market development. Regarding product development, he began offering a Cardio-Karate Program from 6:00-6:45 p.m. on Tuesday and Thursday evenings and Friday mornings at 10 a.m. He also began offering a family class from 11 a.m. to noon on Saturday. Regarding market development, a new Shorin-Ryu school, "The Family Martial Arts Center," was opened in Billerica, Massachusetts (can be seen at the top of the map in Exhibit 2 of the case) in September of 1997. The school is run by Sempai Mike Kelly. The Shorin-Ryu Karate Academy also began offering classes to 3-year old students. Little Dragons became ages 3-5 (formerly 4-6) and Junior Ninjas became ages 6-9 (formerly ages 7-9).

Exhibit TN-1 SWOT Analysis

Strengths

- Quality of instruction, including dedication of Sensei Jim
- Modern training facility (2500 square foot studio can accommodate 250-375 students according to the benchmark of 100-150 students per 1000 square feet, male/female locker rooms)
- Location (Waltham) is surrounded by several affluent Boston-area suburbs
- Affordable memberships
- Various programs and times (classes, camps, private lessons, birthday parties)
- Criteria met: parental access to lessons, inexpensive introductory lessons, classes taught by head instructor
- Referral business

Weaknesses

- Little emphasis on referral business
- Lack of consistency and quality of help
- May be getting too large for one owner/manager/instructor and location
- Cash basis for accounting
- No use of accounts payable
- No follow-up for renewals
- Only one location, may be losing potential business
- Sensei Jim may be spreading himself too thin, cannot teach all classes
- School reaching maximum capacity

Opportunities

- Commercialized martial arts instruction is large, with high growth rate
- Increased interest in self-defense and safety
- People of all ages taking martial arts classes
- Media depicts martial arts as glamorous, which increases demand
- Increased awareness of physical fitness
- Interest in martial arts by business community
- Increased demand in leisure time activities
- Numbers show untapped local market

Threats

- Martial arts business is highly competitive with thousands of businesses throughout the United States
- Huge chains of martial arts studios could under price SKA
- Competition could include health clubs (e.g., cardio-karate) which have longer hours, in addition to fitness equipment
- Other sports

Exhibit TN-2

Waltham (57,878 residents; 43.9% over $50,000)

	Style	Price	Students	Monthly Revenue
Bushido-Zen	karate	$60	15	$900
Chung Do	taekwondo	$65	65	$4,225
Integrated	mixture	$70	100	$7,000
Masters	mixture	$50	200	$10,000
Savoy	mixture	$70	150	$10,500
Villar's	mixture	$35	65	$2,275
Shorin-Ryu	karate	$60	324	$19,440

Newton (82,585 residents; 58.9% over $50,000)

	Style	Price	Students	Monthly Revenue
Chos	taekwondo	$90	200	$18,000
Chung Moo Doe	Chinese/Am	$90	100	$9,000
Esposito's	karate	$50	120	$6,000
Master's	karate	$57	150	$8,550
Ye-Sheu	mixture	$30	100	$3,000

Watertown (33,284 residents; 24.7% over $50,000)

	Style	Price	Students	Monthly Revenue
American	karate	$120	150	$18,000
DiRico's	karate	$60	55	$3,300
Tokyo Joe's	mixture	$60	65	$3,900
Wah Lum	kung fu	$50	160	$8,000

Exhibit TN–3

Program	Students	Price	Total	Total/month
3 Month	10	$120	$1,200	$400
6 Month 1/week	62	$240	$14,880	$2,480
6 month 2/week	20	$390	$7,800	$1,300
6 month family 1/week	32	$432	$13,824	$2,304
6 month family 2/week	2	$702	$1,404	$234
12 month 1/week	49	$420	$20,580	$1,715
12 month 2/week	32	$720	$23,040	$1,920
12 month family 1/week	16	$750	$12,000	$1,000
12 month family 2/week	17	$1,020	$17,340	$1,445
Junior Black Belt (18 mos)	16	$1,260	$20,160	$1,120
Adult Black Belt (18 mos)	13	$1,260	$16,380	$910
24 Month Black Belt	13	$1,560	$20,280	$845
36 Month Black Belt	3	$1,980	$5,940	$165
Black Belt family (18 mos)	39	$1,800	$70,200	$3,900
Total	324		$245,028	$19,738

Average price/student/month $60.92 (if all active)
$76.15 (if 80% active)

Exhibit TN–4

Medium	Percent	Students	Cost	Cost/Student
Referral	45%	145.8	$0	$0
Newspaper	19%	61.56	$3,811	$61.91
Yellow Pages	15%	48.6	$2,263	$46.56
YMCA	11%	35.64	$0	$0
Direct Mail	5%	16.2	$2,501	$154.38
Bring A Friend	3%	9.72	$0	$0
Other	2%	6.48		
Total		324		

CASE 4-5
LOJACK CORPORATION*

Synopsis:

LoJack Corporation marketed the LoJack System, a method used to track and recover stolen automobiles. Auto theft was growing quickly in the United States, and as a result, sales of anti-theft devices were expected to grow. Anti-theft devices included systems for both theft prevention and automobile tracking and recovery.

Technology was very important in tracking and recovering devices. LoJack's technology, however, was not as precise as the other methods of tracking vehicles and did not support certain applications for additional services. The competition was becoming more intense, but LoJack had actually started generating earnings.

Dan Michaels, Vice President of Sales for the LoJack Corporation, had to evaluate whether present sales, distribution, and pricing strategies were adequate for future growth. The market was growing, so although LoJack was planning on expanding the use of its technology in the U.S. and international markets, Michaels had to decide if LoJack should also diversify, expand within the product category, or find new applications for the product.

Video Summary:

The video to accompany the LoJack case is short, yet very informative. The first couple of minutes of the video discusses car theft in general—statistics, costs, professional thieves. Then the video explains how LoJack works and its recovery rate. The product is described in understandable detail. The video is particularly great to use in geographic areas where students are unfamiliar with the LoJack anti-theft and recovery system.

Teaching/Learning Objectives:

The case is great for illustrating:

- the relationship between current and future marketing strategies,
- the development of new markets both nationally and internationally, and
- operational constraints placed on new product development.

Discussion Questions:

1. What challenges is LoJack facing? Assess LoJack's internal and external environment.
2. Who are LoJack's customers?
3. Outline LoJack's sales strategy.
4. Outline LoJack's distribution strategy.
5. Outline LoJack's pricing strategy.

---

* This teaching note was prepared by Victoria L. Crittenden and Stephanie Hillstrom, Boston College, as an aid to instructors using the case, "LoJack Corporation." Revised 1998.

6. Who is LoJack's competition?

7. Is LoJack ready to extend its product technology to new markets? Which markets should the company consider?

8. What type of product category expansion is available to LoJack? What issues arise with such expansion?

9. Recommend a market strategy for LoJack.

Analysis:

1. What challenges is LoJack facing? Assess LoJack's internal and external environment.

LoJack operates in a growth market, and faces an increasing number of competitors. The fundamental decision faced by the company is how it can continue to grow. Should the company expand into new markets? Should the company begin to develop new products based on its tracking technology? Should the company identify new uses for its current product? Is the present sales, distribution, and pricing strategies appropriate for helping grow the company, or do changes need to be made in the current operations so that growth will be more feasible?

Exhibit TN-1 provides an example SWOT analysis.

2. Who are LoJack's customers?

LoJack had numerous customers: Federal Communications Commission, state police, state insurance commissioners, government and municipal officials, insurance company executives, new car dealers, and end users (i.e., automobile owners).

LoJack government affairs personnel were the sales people to the Federal Communications Commission, state insurance commissioners, government and municipal officials, and insurance company executives. The Federal Communications Commission was a customer in that this group was in charge of granting permission for the company to use various radio frequencies.

Insurance and government officials were important customers in that they had strong influence in decisions made by state and local law enforcement officers. As well, insurance premiums were usually lower for a car owner using an anti-theft device.

New car dealers were a major source of influence on options buyers selected in their new automobiles, and anti-theft devices were optional in new automobiles. Thus, if the dealer sold and installed LoJack, LoJack's chance to be included in a new car increased.

Finally, the automobile owner was a customer. As the "end-user," the owner could ask specifically for a LoJack system. And, this is what LoJack wanted to happen!

3. Outline LoJack's sales strategy.

Part of the sales strategy involved the influencing of insurance and governmental officials. This was handled by LoJack's government affairs personnel.

The actual hardware sale took two major routes. First, LoJack had to convince the state police to use the LoJack system. Then, the company donated tracking systems to the police department. The company then trained the police officers in using the system. Second, LoJack marketed its anti-theft system to car owners in the market area, as well as new car dealers.

Thus, LoJack had to "sell" its concept to the appropriate officials and had to "sell" its product to the end-user. There was no end user, however, without a successful concept sell.

In addition to the use of LoJack people to sell the company's product, LoJack spent 25 cents out of every dollar of revenue on advertising (primarily radio advertising). Publicity was a popular form of communication as well. Regarding selling to the dealer, discounts were used as a motivational tool.

4. Outline LoJack's distribution strategy.

Ninety-five percent of LoJack's anti-theft system sales were through new car dealers. The dealers would typically offer LoJack as one of several anti-theft devices available as dealer options. The dealer would then install the LoJack system. However, LoJack would also sell direct to the end user and would install the system in a location convenient for end user. These company-installed systems, were handled by LoJack installation technicians who drove company vans to the select installation site.

In late 1993, LoJack began retail distribution of its product. The company licensed its system to Clifford Electronics, a major competitor based in California, for distribution in retail outlets aimed at the "Do It Yourself" market.

5. Outline LoJack's pricing strategy.

The basic system, LOJACK RETRIEVE, was priced to the end user at $595. There was no charge for being always "on-line" or for the tracking and recovery service itself. [This is unlike most anti-theft devices found in many homes. Companies operating these systems charge a monthly service fee for the security of being "on-call" in case the home is broken into.] LoJack's PREVENT option was an alarm and starter-disabler priced at $100 that could be added-on to the RETRIEVE system.

While no cost information is provided, one can assume that the hardware itself probably costs very little to produce when other costs are taken into account. Costs include warranty (if a stolen vehicle is not recovered within 24 hours, LoJack refunds the price of the system to the vehicle owner), the tracking unit which is donated to the state police (the unit was valued at $1,750).

6. Who is LoJack's competition?

There are two basic types of anti-theft devices available in the marketplace: (i) preventive devices and (ii) tracking and recovery devices. LoJack competes directly with companies in the tracking and recovery area. Indirect competition comes from companies in the preventive arena.

Competitors who also made **tracking and recovery devices** were:

The Posse by Audiovox at $599. Using satellite technology, the stolen car was disabled once the thief shut off the engine.

Code Alarm's Intercept at $1,495 + $15 monthly. Using the cellular phone in the stolen car, the car could be disabled and located. [The company had developed strong relationships with automobile manufacturers and supplied them with security devices and keyless entry systems.]

International Teletrac at $599 + $15 monthly. The system was similar to LoJack's in that signals were sent via a transmitter to a company-owned (major difference) monitoring station and police were then notified. The company had also expanded its technology into dispatching and routing systems for truck fleets. **[There is close similarity to the Amtech technology here. This discussion can actually build on the Amtech case if was used.]**

Pinpoint Communications was expected to enter the market in 1994.

Preventive devices focused upon keeping the automobile from ever being stolen. In this way, tracking and recovery would not be necessary. Steering wheel locks and immobilizing devices, in addition to alarm systems, were popular.

Steering Wheel Locks:

The Club by Winner International at $59.95.

The Malvy Lock by Malvy Technology at $600—$800.

The Blocker at $85—$125.

Immobilizing devices:

The Blackjack by Clifford Automotive at $160.

The Viper 500 Plus System by Directed Electronics, Inc. at $299.

The anti-theft market was a $500 million market in 1992, with an expected annual growth rate of nine percent. From the data, one can obtain some idea regarding market share:

Steering wheel locks commanded 20 percent ($100 million) of the market (with The Club by Winner International the biggest player). Directed Electronics held almost 9 1/2 percent of the market with sales of $47 million. Code Alarm with revenue of $45.7 million held nine percent of the market. International Teletrac had six percent of the market with revenue of $31 million. LoJack held a slight 3 1/2 percent of the market with 1992 revenues of $17.5 million.

7. Is LoJack ready to extend its product technology to new markets? Which markets should the company consider?

Regarding geographic markets, LoJack had current operations in the United States in Massachusetts, parts of California, Florida, Michigan, Illinois, Georgia, Virginia, and New Jersey. The company expected to enter four new markets in 1994: Rhode Island, Connecticut, New York, and Washington, D.C. The company had also signed licensing agreements in the Czech Republic, Slovakia, Greece, the United Kingdom, Latin America, and Hong Kong. Thus, the company appeared to be focusing upon taking its products into new markets.

In the U.S., alone, around 1.5 million cars were stolen annually. Even if all of LoJack's current sales were to owners whose cars were stolen, the company would still have only around two percent of the stolen car market. However, we know that the LoJack system is found in cars which are not stolen. Thus, LoJack systems are found in very few stolen cars.

Population density, new car sales, and vehicle theft were variables used to determine new market entry.

There were around 13 million new cars sold annually in the U.S. market. Ten percent of new car sales were in California. Rental companies purchased about 20 percent of the new cars sold, with Florida rental agencies commanding five percent of the new car sales. LoJack operated currently in Florida and parts of California (the case states that Los Angeles was one of its market areas).

Exhibits 4, 5, and 7 allow students to analyze population and auto theft statistics simultaneously. Florida comprises 12 of the top 40 MSA growth areas in the United States. California is the second largest area of population growth with 10 MSAs in the top 40 growth areas. Both of these states also represent two of the highly populated states in the U.S. They are also states currently serviced (at least in part in California) by LoJack. California has five of the top 25 cities for motor vehicle theft, with Florida having two of the 25. Another high growth area and highly populated state is Texas. Texas also has three of the top 25 U.S. cities for motor vehicle theft. However, Texas is not in LoJack's current or 1994 market area.

Hungary, Kenya, and the United Kingdom were three international areas which had expressed concern about auto theft. The United Kingdom was also one the United States' top export markets and a market in which LoJack had signed a licensing agreement. However, population increases were not expected in the near future. Kenya, while not one of the top export markets, was expected to see a tripling of its population between 1987 and 2025.

8. What type of product category expansion is available to LoJack? What issues arise with such expansion?

Ideas had arisen regarding possible uses for the LoJack transmitter. These included applications for child safety, furloughed prisoner and parolee tracking, and high valued item protection. These were all applications which could easily fit well with LoJack's piggybacking on the Police Broadcasting Network. However, other applications such as roadside assistance and fleet management (being done by Teletrac) did not allow for such piggybacking. Thus, a major constraint arises with the connection between LoJack and the Police Broadcasting Network. New product applications outside the law enforcement realm would require development of a new, independent tracking system.

9. Recommend a market strategy for LoJack.

Students will have to make decisions regarding LoJack's current sales, distribution, and pricing strategies. Some may question whether LoJack's pricing strategy is appropriate, and may suggest that LoJack should institute a monthly service charge. A problem with this is the linkage with the police radio system. The monitoring actually occurs with the police system, and LoJack would be charging for something that does not take place in-house. Suggestions may also involve the use of a "pull" strategy where LoJack gets end users to start asking for the anti-theft device and, therefore, get law enforcement support by way of consumer demand. However, there might be some problem with gaining consumer support when the major mechanism for making it happen is not yet available. Some students may go so far as to suggest that LoJack open its own monitoring station rather than relying upon the police force.

Questions 7 and 8 assist in the development of a marketing strategy for the long term. The key issue in market development is where new markets should be opened. Once new targets are decided upon, the marketing strategy will entail determining the best way to enter these markets. For example, more use of licensing agreements and/or outside distributors may have to be relied upon. Regarding product development, the current constraint imposed by the police radio frequency will have to be addressed.

Teaching the Case:

The product, an automobile anti-theft device, is interesting to the students. Many will have some sort of system (probably an alarm), and there is a tendency to want to discuss the pros and cons of various methods and/or company products. This is okay and tends to get the class involved/interested in the product itself. For those students who are not as familiar with the various anti-theft devices, the discussion aids in bringing about clarity. Also, some students may be familiar with LoJack, others will not (usually depends upon where the students are from).

The case works well with either a what do you recommend opening or an analysis first opening. This basically depends upon the instructor's preference. The questions are presented in order regarding analysis first.

It is also interesting to draw upon some of the knowledge acquired in the Amtech case (if it was used). There is some overlap as exemplified by the fleet management offered by Teletrac. Students' additional knowledge about the larger AEI market used in this case discussion tends to give them an immediate showing about the possible long term effects of case discussions!

The video is about seven minutes long and should be used at the beginning of class. Many students will not be familiar with the company's anti-theft and recovery system, and the video does a great job of explaining how the somewhat unusual system works.

Epilogue:

For the 1997 fiscal year, LoJack netted US$8.2 million on revenues of US$61.7 million. Its stock doubled in one year, from $9 to $18. The company has approached its future from three directions: market penetration, market development, and diversification. Regarding market penetration, the company has begun to target leased car customers in its current geographic markets. Radio ads explain the responsibility that rests with the lessee of a car—the lessee is responsible in case of theft. LoJack continues to expand geographically in a strategy of market development. Texas became one of its newest markets in 1997. Regarding diversification, the company is working on a device that would be placed in shipping packages. Similar to the LoJack Retrieve, the device would be hidden in the shipping container and would be activated when stolen.

Interesting stories abound regarding LoJack (and students love hearing them!). The company's brand equity is strong as exhibited by the story of a North Carolina man who called LoJack to report that his LoJack alarm kept going off during the middle of the night while the automobile was sitting in the garage. The man provided LoJack with the vehicle identification number. After much searching through its data base (and thinking that it had screwed up and failed to enter a customer's VIN), LoJack contacted the dealer who had installed the man's security system—only to find out that the man did not have a LoJack system! In another instance, a person in Florida was able to locate his LoJack transmitter and transfer it from his old Jaguar to his new one. Although the vehicle identification number did not match the stolen car (the new one), LoJack did go ahead and retrieve the stolen car even though it was not officially covered by the LoJack system. Crossing country boundaries, transmission signals are different as exhibited by a report from a Latin American country. A person in Latin America purchased a used car from a local dealer. The car had a dent when purchased so the new owner took it to a body shop for a repair estimate. Local police picked up an unidentifiable LoJack signal. They forwarded the signal to LoJack headquarters in Dedham, Massachusetts. Headquarters discovered that the car had been stolen in Miami. However by then, the local police were no longer picking up the signal. A week or so later, the signal was again picked up and traced to the body shop where the car had been brought back for its scheduled repair work. The new owner did not live in the area and had returned for the repair work. The car was confiscated and returned, in excellent condition, to the States. The new owner did not know he had bought a stolen car as the paperwork was in order.

Exhibit TN–1   SWOT Analysis

Strengths

- successful product
- money-back guarantee
- backing of the state police and their independent statistics
- a partnership and exclusive contract with law enforcement personnel
- lower total price relative to other retrieval systems (including monthly fees)

Weaknesses

- one-product line (company)
- product use limited to several states, which hurts not only sales but also effectiveness (e.g., if a car is stolen in Boston and taken to Vermont, LoJack will not work)
- product does not prevent the car from being stolen
- aging technology in rapidly innovative industry

Opportunities

- free promotions through news stories
- incorporate a prevention component to the LoJack package
- offer product which uses a land-based cellular system (greater range, accuracy and versatility)
- incorporate other value-added features, e.g., cellular communications, through joint venture with a cellular communications company
- growing market
- gain presence in 40 states and abroad where LoJack is not yet used
- form a strategic alliance with auto maker(s) after use of technology becomes more widespread
- form a strategic alliance with auto dealers to distribute existing technology
- emphasize the price advantage of LoJack vis-a-vis the competition in recovery systems

Threats

- competitors offering value-added features (e.g., roadside assistance and paging)
- competitors developing new technologies (e.g., POSSE working with GPS) which gain greater acceptance by law enforcement personnel for its accuracy and flexibility to incorporate other features

CASE 4-6
ALGONQUIN POWER AND LIGHT COMPANY*

Synopsis

Algonquin Power and Light Company provides gas and electric service to a large metropolitan area. Its maintenance program to keep power lines free of trees, shrubs, and scrub, incurs annual costs of $58,000 for dumping tree cuttings. Donald Orville, the company's forester, has proposed that the utility begin manufacturing compost from these trimmings. Orville believes that his proposal is meritorious because the compost product could produce a profit for Algonquin.

Teaching/Learning Objectives

1. To show the decisions involved with a new product.
2. To provide an opportunity to develop a marketing plan.
3. To demonstrate the use of customer and competitor information in market opportunity analysis.

Situation Audit

Industry Analysis

The yearly demand for compost within the county is conservatively estimated to be 78,641 cubic yards. There are basically six customer types which make up the demand, and their percent of the market is as follows:

Topsoil Companies	47%
Growers (Farms, Orchids, etc.)	24
Retail Nurseries:	
Specialty	15
Chains and Discounts	<u>6</u>
	21
Landscape Contractors and Gardeners	8
Manufacturers and Distributors	NA
Government	NA

Demand among all of the customer groups appears to be price elastic. They seek comparable products that can be purchased at lower prices.

Competitor and Consumer Analysis

1. Wholesale and/or User Market (Table 3)

    This market purchases compost ranging in size from 1 inch to 1/8 inch or smaller. It typically uses redwood compost; however, fir compost and sawdust are also used. The largest volume customer interviewed, Maynard Sand and Material Co., purchases only Douglas fir wood chips and redwood shavings.

---

* Susan Tate, former MBA student at Texas Christian University, assisted in the preparation of this teaching note.

All of the customers use local suppliers with the majority buying from producers rather than from distributors. Two firms also use out-of-county suppliers. Dave Parker Supplies purchases used sawdust locally and compost from a distributor 200 miles away. The county government uses an out-of-county producer for large orders.

The price that wholesalers and users currently pay ranges from $1 per cubic yard for used sawdust to $9 per cubic yard, plus $3 freight per cubic yard for redwood compost 1 inch or less in size. Red wood shavings and compost can be purchased locally for $4.50 per cubic yard. Marlowe's Nursery pays only $3.50 per cubic yard for large volume orders.

Contrary to Orville's opinion, it does not appear that a "virtually unlimited market exists for all locally-produced humus material at a bulk price of $8.50 per cubic yard." Only one bulk customer is paying anywhere near $8.50 per cubic yard.

2. Retail Market (Table 4)

There are generally four customer types in the retail market: specialty nurseries, discount stores, department stores, and chain drug stores. Nine out of the eleven stores only use redwood products. Of the remaining two, one uses redwood in addition to organic compost; the other uses humus bark compost.

Six of the 11 retailers purchase out-of-county from five different fertilizer producers and one fertilizer distributor. Five retailers purchase from one local manufacturer, Producer A. One retailer sells a private label brand, and another sells a national brand.

Retailers purchase the redwood compost already bagged. Four cubic feet bags are most common. The retail price charged for this size ranges from $2.26 to $400 per bag. Redwood compost is also packaged in 60 and 70 pound bags. The 70 pound bags retail from $1.19 to $2.29. Sixty pound bags range from $2.17 to $2.49. Organic compost is packaged in a 65 pound bag and priced at $2.49. Humus bark is packaged in a 3 cubic foot bag and retails for $2.49. In general, the specialty stores charge the higher prices. Specialty Nursery C prices competitively with the other retailers. Only one discount store, A, prices well below the competition for their redwood compost. Chain Drug A uses the same supplier as Discount Store A but prices its product much higher ($2.29 compared to $1.19 per 70 pound bag).

Algonquin Compost Analysis

The Algonquin compost contains waste tree and shrub cuttings. Two products currently on the market (humus bark and organic compost) have similar composition. The main entrants in the market are red wood and then fir composts. Redwood is the favored compost because it has a slower breakdown period than other materials.

The annual cost of producing the compost is estimated to be $47,000. Orville forecasted annual production and sales of 10,000 to 15,000 cubic yards of compost. This would yield a 13-19 percent share of the present market demand of 78,641 cubic yards. To cover all estimated costs, Algonquin would need to charge $4.70 per yard for 10,000 cubic yards of production ($47,000/10,000), or $3.13 per yard for 15,000 cubic yards ($47,000/15,000).

Orville's proposal to charge $8.50 per cubic yard in the wholesale market is way out of line. However, if savings in residue hauling and dumping fees are considered, Algonquin could give the product away and still realize a cost savings of $11,000 ($58,000—$47,000 = $11,000). Thus by pricing the compost competitively, Algonquin might not earn a profit, but the total cost of disposing cuttings will certainly be reduced.

Company Considerations

Producing compost would provide a means to reduce costs while supplying a product to the marketplace that is demanded. However, it leads to diversifying from Algonquin's core business of gas and electric service. Is Algonquin management content with reducing the present costs, or do they want to generate a profit? The answer to this question will influence marketing decisions regarding the product.

Another consideration is the policy of underground power lines. As the mix of power lines moves more and more toward underground lines, the supply of material for compost will be reduced. Thus, Algonquin will need to determine if this is a short-term or long-term strategy which will affect their aggressiveness in the compost market.

Finally, management must assess whether it is appropriate for this public utility to compete with local businesses. Clearly, any local firms that anticipate losing sales will oppose Algonquin entering the compost business. Algonquin, on the other hand, can argue that savings are being passed along to their customers and that the compost program is environmentally beneficial to everyone.

Problem/Decision Statement

Should Algonquin enter the compost market?

Alternatives

A. Enter the compost market.
   1. Sell to the wholesale/user markets.
   2. Sell to the retail market.
   3. Sell to both the wholesale/user and retail markets.
B. Sell the unprocessed trimmings to existing compost producers rather than dumping.
C. Status Quo—keep dumping waste.

Criteria

1. Market Opportunity
2. Target Market Considerations
3. Competition
4. Marketing Mix—product, price, promotion, distribution
5. Profitability or Cost Savings

Analysis

Let's first consider each of the three options associated with entering the compost market: (1) targeting wholesalers and users; (2) targeting the retail market; and (3) targeting both.

1. Target Wholesale/User Markets

   Market Opportunity

   a. The wholesaler/user market accounts for about 80 percent of all local demand.

b. This market includes government and manufacturers/distributors whose demand is not included in the annual demand estimate of 78,641 cubic yards.

c. It does not appear that any one supplier dominates this market.

d. The future supply of redwood is questionable.

e. If demand is stable, it could be unrealistic for Algonquin to expect to sell 10,000-15,000 cubic yards of compost per year. This would require capturing 16-24 percent of the wholesaler/user market.

f. Most customers in this market currently use, and prefer, redwood compost.

Target Market Considerations

a. This market segment includes the two largest customer types in the local market. Topsoil companies represent 47% of all county demand, and growers represent 24%.

b. This segment purchases in large volumes.

c. The market is not brand loyal. Customers are willing to change suppliers for comparable quality at lower prices.

c. This market is more particular than the retail market regarding product reliability.

d. Potential customers expressed concerns about the availability of a continual future supply.

Competition

a. There does not appear to be any dominant competitors in the local market.

b. Some suppliers are located out of the county, and their prices reflect delivery charges.

c. Compost is an important source of revenue to competitors. For Algonquin, it could be considered a means to reduce costs.

d. Supply contracts may inhibit Algonquin's ability to penetrate the market.

Marketing Mix

a. The product would be sold in bulk. No packaging would be necessary.

b. The product characteristics could be tailored to each customer's specifications and quantity requirements.

c. Algonquin has maximum price flexibility. It could give the product away and still save money ($58,000 current expenses—$47,000 projection to go into the compost business $11,000 savings).

d. Distribution could be tailored to each customer's need

e. Promotion would be simple and inexpensive because potential customers are concentrated geographically and are few in number.

Profitability or Cost Reduction

a. As previously noted, if Algonquin produces the compost and gives it away free, the total cost of cutting disposal will decline by $11,000.

b. All costs may not be included in Orville's estimates.

c. In order for the compost operation to be profitable (disregarding the current cost incurred for dumping), Algonquin would have to sell 10,000 cubic yards of compost at $4.70 per cubic yards or 15,000 cubic yards for $3.13 per cubic yards (assuming that Orville's estimates are accurate).

2. Target the Retail Market

   Market Opportunity

   a. Local fertilizer Producer A is the only local competitor.
   b. Nine of 11 local retailers currently carry only redwood compost.
   c. The retail market only accounts for 16,216 cubic yards of annual demand.
   d. Producer A would probably vigorously object and aggressively respond to Algonquin entering the market.

   Target Market Considerations

   a. The market is small (11 stores), easily defined, and easy to contact.
   b. Retailers are less concerned about compost reliability than are wholesalers and users.
   c. Retailers are less concerned about future supply assurances than are wholesalers/users.
   d. Annual demand is only 16,216 cubic yards, approximately 20 percent of the total local market.

   Competition

   a. Over 45 percent of the local retailers purchase compost from out-of-county suppliers. Algonquin offers competitive advantages of local supply to meet spontaneous demand and minimal delivery costs.
   b. Local Producer A will be most unhappy if Algonquin enters the market. Competitive reaction will probably include protests of unfair competition and aggressive marketing.
   c. It is possible that some long-term contracts exist which inhibit customers from switching suppliers.

   Marketing Mix

   a. Retailers are not as concerned about the quality or future supply of the product as are wholesalers/users.
   b. The product would have to be packaged to sell to this market.
   c. The price to retailers only has to be $91 to break-even, assuming 67,500 bags sold (refer to TN Exhibit 1).
   d. The price to retailers can be as low as $.10 per bag to reduce current costs from dumping, given all bags are sold. [(Total cost of bagging—dumping costs)/# bags = ($64,125—$58,000)/ 67,500 = $.0907]
   e. Since the market is small (11 retailers), promotion will be simple and inexpensive.
   g. Algonquin may have to deliver the product to the retail stores, which will lead to more costs, and a higher price will need to be charged.
   h. The price that competitors are charging to retailers is unknown, and Algonquin may not be able to compete effectively to get the market share that is needed to make this business profitable.

3. Target Both Wholesalers/Users and Retailers

   Market Opportunity

   a. The market potential is larger than focusing on only one segment.

    b. This strategy would allow Algonquin to be less dependent on any one type of customer for sales.

    c. The market share needed to sell 10,000 to 15,000 cubic yards would be 13 percent and 19 percent, respectively.

    d. Wholesalers will probably object vigorously to Algonquin selling to the retail market.

Target Market Considerations

    a. Entering both markets will enhance Algonquin's brand awareness.

    b. The larger potential market may require more personnel to adequately service the market.

Competition

    a. Being the only organization marketing to both market segments could be a competitive advantage.

    b. Marketing to both wholesalers and their customers often creates channel conflict.

Marketing Mix

    a. A wider variety of product size options would be needed to meet a wider spectrum of customer needs.

    b. Algonquin could price bagged compost to the retail market substantially higher than bulk compost to the wholesaler/user market. Marketing to both segments provides substantial price flexibility.

Profitability or Cost Savings

    a. The two markets offer greater sales potential than either one alone.

    b. Servicing both markets reduces the likelihood of having to incur dumping charges.

    c. Promoting to two markets will be more expensive than promoting to one segment. Two other alternatives previously identified are: (1) to sell unprocessed trimmings to existing compost producers and (2) maintain the status quo. Following is an analysis of these options.

Sell Unprocessed Trimmings

It is unclear whether this is a viable option or not. If a market exists, it would: (1) reduce the cost associated with dumping, (2) avoid any accusations of unfair competition, (3) avoid any possible image damage associated with poor product quality or other marketing or manufacturing failings, and (4) be a very low risk alternative to the present procedure. Before this alternative could be given serious consideration, more research would be needed to assess the market opportunity.

Status Quo

The question in this case does not appear to be whether to enter the compost market but rather what segment or segments to target and how to implement the strategy.

All available information suggests that going into the compost business will at least reduce the current cost of dumping and may produce a profit. It appears to be a "no-lose" proposition even if Algonquin has to give compost away (which may not be a bad option to consider).

Recommendation

A good case can be made for entering either the wholesaler/user market or the retailer market. Targeting both immediately would be too aggressive and too risky. Either of the main market segments considered will provide sufficient challenge for Algonquin. If all goes well in the short run, a longer term strategy of targeting both markets might be appropriate.

The advantages of the wholesaler/user segment are that it is larger, buys in bulk, and should respond to a new offering that is comparable in quality to existing suppliers at a lower price. Some assurances of long-term availability may be necessary. The limitations of this option are that the Algonquin product may not be able to meet quality requirements, and it offers less profit per volume sold compared to the retail market. In either case, Algonquin can be very aggressive in terms of price, delivery, and service.

Implementation

The implementation plan should include at least the following components:

1. *Target market strategy* (e.g., the 11 retailers in the county that currently sell compost plus other outlets that sell fertilizer, potted plants, garden tools, or other related items. Information about end uses should be gathered. Further competitive analysis may be needed).
2. *Objectives* (e.g., sales of 10,000 cubic yards of compost to retail customers in year one).
3. *Marketing Program Positioning Strategy*

    Product strategy—(e.g., product will be bagged in four cubic foot bags. Brand name will be Producers Pride).

    Price strategy- (e.g., bags will be sold to retailers for $1.65 with a suggested retail price of $2.49. Non-cumulative quantity discounts will be offered based on a schedule to be developed later).

    Distribution strategy- (e.g., inventory will be stored in existing facilities. Orders of 30 bags or more will be delivered free. Smaller orders will require a flat $5.00 delivery charge).

    Promotion strategy—(e.g., personal sales calls on all prospective customers. In store P.O.P. promotional materials. Advertising in local newspapers).
4. Marketing Organization
5. Preliminary Budget (see TN Exhibit 2)

Epilogue

The marketing program manager in the actual situation that took place made a two step marketing strategy recommendation. First, the company decided to stop dumping the waste, and initial research found two users who would let the company dump the waste on their property. This short run move eliminated dumping costs and brought about reduced handling charges as well. Since the product was thought to have a better profit potential than this, the move was only temporary. The second recommendation was to bag the product and go into the retail market. Company marketing executives believed the profit potential was greater in the retail market; and since supply could not meet demand in both markets, this market was the most logical. Specialty and discount nurseries were to be targeted. The company would form a subsidiary to market the compost rather than use the utility's name.

Exhibit TN-1   Costs Involved In Bagging Compost

Fixed Costs	
Cost of Operations (per Orville report)	$47,000
Bagger	1,313
Equipment Operating Expense	598
Additional Labor	3,000
Additional Labor Overhead	990
Additional Insurance	100
Additional Miscellaneous	1,000
Total Fixed Cost	**$54,000**
Variable Costs:	
Coat of Bags	10,125
Total Costs	**$64,125**
Less Dumping Fee Savings	3,000
Net Annual Cost	**$61,125**

*Cost of bags
   10.000 cu. yd.—270.000 cu. ft.; each bag holds 4 cu. ft.
   270.000 divided by 4—67.500 bags required for 10.000 cu. yd.
   Bags cost $150.00 per thousand.
   Total Cost of Bags = ($150.00) X (67.500) = $10,125.00

Exhibit TN–2 Profit/Loss Based on Volume Sold

100% (10,00 cu. yd. sold)

   10,000 cu. yd. x 27 = 270,000 cu. ft.
   270,000 cu. ft./4 = 67,500 cu. ft. bags

Revenues from Sales to Retailers:

($1.65) x (67,500) =	$111,375
Fixed costs	
(accounting for dumping fee savings)	$51,000
Variable costs	10,125
Total Cost	61,125
Total Profit	$50,250

80% (8,000 cu. yd. sold)

   80,000 cu. yd. x 27 = 216,000 cu. ft.
   216,000 cu. ft./4 = 54,500 cu. ft. bags

Revenues from Sales to Retailers:

($1.65) x (54,000) =	$89,100
Fixed costs	
(accounting for dumping fee savings)	$51,000
Variable costs	8,100
Total Cost	59,100
Total Profit	$30,000

60% (6,000 cu. yd. sold)

   60,000 cu. yd. x 27 = 162,000 cu. ft.
   162,000 cu. ft./4 = 40,500 cu. ft. bags

Revenues from Sales to Retailers:

($1.65) x (40,500) =	$66,825
Fixed costs	
(accounting for dumping fee savings)	$51,000
Variable costs	6,075
Total Cost	57,075
Total Profit	$9,750

Exhibit TN-2   Profit/Loss Based on Volume Sold (continued)

40% (4,000 cu. yd. sold)

    40,000 cu. yd. x 27 = 108,000 cu. ft.
    108,000 cu. ft./4 = 27,000 cu. ft. bags

Revenues from Sales to Retailers:

($1.65) x (27,000) =	$44,550
Fixed costs	
(accounting for dumping fee savings)	$51,000
Variable costs	4,050
Total Cost	55,050
Total Profit	($10,500)

Part 5

Marketing Relationships

CASE 5-1
ABB TRACTION INC.*

Synopsis

ABB Traction Inc. designed and manufactured passenger rail transportation systems for North America. Amtrak was looking for a long term relationship with a supplier of equipment in order to: 1) develop a high-speed train to run on diesel engine and 2) enable a train to negotiate curves at high speeds without exceeding standards of passenger comfort. ABB management thought it was the best company for Amtrak.

There were many other competitors that also felt they were the best company for Amtrak, including Siemens Transportation Systems, GEC Alsthom, Morrison Knudsen, and Bombardier. ABB Traction had to distinguish the X2000 from its competitors' products and convince Amtrak that ABB was the best choice for an alliance. This partnership would advance ABB Traction's position in the high-speed train industry.

Video Summary

Beginning with people's reactions to ABB Traction's high-speed train, the video on ABB Traction's X2000 focuses on the technology that ABB Traction hoped would allow them to partner with Amtrak. The research and development of the X2000 is discussed, with a focus on the three technological advances that accomplished the goal of reduced travel time. The video mentions the two major market segments of ABB Traction and the features that the X2000 included to meet the segments' needs. The testing of the X2000 in the United States is shown, including a segment from NBC's Today Show that showed the media's reaction to the demonstration run. Also discussed are the economic benefits the X2000 would bring to the United States if ABB Traction teamed up with Amtrak.

The video runs for almost 14 and a half minutes. It is a good video to use early in the class discussion, after a brief time for general discussion of train travel, as it provides insights and visuals about the X2000. It can be a good way to get the students more involved in a not-so-familiar product.

Teaching/Learning Objectives

The case provides the opportunity to:

- show the type of long-term marketing relationship (supplier—customer) which has become necessary in today's business environment,
- make a decision which will have a big impact on a company's future market opportunities, and
- demonstrate that even competitors can have amicable relationships.

---

* This teaching note was prepared by Victoria L. Crittenden, Stephanie Hillstrom, and David Angus, Boston College, as an aid to instructors using the case, "ABB Traction Inc." Revised 1998.

Discussion Questions

1. What decision is ABB facing?
2. Regarding ABB's philosophy, what does it mean to balance the contradiction of being both local and global?
3. Assess ABB's strengths, weaknesses, opportunities and threats.
4. Does ABB have any internal and external characteristics which make it a good fit with Amtrak? If so, what are they?
5. What marketing alternatives can ABB pursue?
6. How should ABB market itself to Amtrak?
7. What type of marketing relationship is ABB seeking with Amtrak?

Analysis

The Problem/Decision Statement:

A good starting point is to ask students the problem/decision faced by ABB. In addition to identifying the decision early on, this opening tends to clarify who the decision maker is in the case. Some students may attempt to look at the case from the point of view of Amtrak. However, the case is about ABB and how it can do a good job marketing itself and its product to Amtrak.

1. What decision is ABB facing?

ABB is faced with the ominous task of showing Amtrak that it can offer the best product, as well as be the best partner, for its high-speed rail service in the Northeast corridor. The decision is one of how it can best market itself to Amtrak.

The Situation Audit:

It is useful for students to get a good idea of what the company, ABB, is all about. While the bottom line is that ABB wants to sell its trains to Amtrak, doing so requires relationships beyond offering a good product. While ABB thinks it has the best product, its competitors have also demonstrated their product strengths in various product offerings. It appears that what ABB can offer as a company will be very important to Amtrak, in addition to what the company can offer in terms of its product.

Questions 2 and 3 assist the student in understanding ABB better and getting a better feel for where ABB stands in developing a stronger relationship between ABB and Amtrak.

2. Regarding ABB's philosophy, what does it mean to balance the contradiction of being both local and global?

ABB is a giant. It is the epitome of a "global" company. It has a clearly defined mission and a culture that lends strong support to the mission. It operates without regard to national boundaries. As a matter of fact, it is difficult to use a particular country's name alongside ABB. [The official company language is English and the official currency is the dollar.] The company typifies the phrase, "Think globally, act locally."

ABB's culture, as exemplified by its many cost-cutting actions, is focused on making money by being a hands-on, action-oriented company. Divisions in every country in which the company operates know that it must respond to local market conditions. However, the company sources globally (mainly through its Germany procurement center).

The company sought to be global in its culture, economies of scale, coordination across national boundaries, and R&D/technological support. However, it needed to be "local" in its response to particular country issues and marketplace needs.

3. **Assess ABB's strengths, weaknesses, opportunities and threats.**

Exhibit TN-1 provides an example SWOT analysis.

Identification of Alternatives and Analysis:

In addressing the problem faced by ABB, students must focus upon alternative ways available for ABB to market itself to Amtrak. Understanding ABB's internal and external characteristics helps to identify various options. Questions 4 and 5 focus upon the alternatives evaluation process.

4. **Does ABB have any internal and external characteristics which make it a good fit with Amtrak? If so, what are they?**

Internal characteristics:

1. Product features—The X2000 offers product features which allow the train to perform well within the specifications set by Amtrak.

2. Organizational structure—ABB's organizational structure allows the company to take advantage of economies offered by being a global business firm, while at the same time allowing it to meet customer specifications through its culture of acting locally.

3. Company history—ABB has shown that it can develop and produce the type of train sought by Amtrak. The X2000 has gained market share quickly on the Stockholm/Goteborg route in Sweden.

4. Ability to cut costs—Price will ultimately be an important feature to Amtrak. ABB has demonstrated its ability to reduce costs, all the while maintaining high quality products.

External Characteristics:

1. Ability to work with other companies—ABB has aligned with numerous suppliers and competitors in its course of doing business over the past few years. This demonstrates the company's ability to work closely with outside companies even though the company is huge.

2. Futuristic company—Amtrak wants to work with a company which understands the needs of the rail system in the next century. ABB has demonstrated its ability to focus upon future needs of the rail system. When Sweden wanted to make rail travel competitive with air travel, ABB was able to adapt its technology to the needs of the Swedish railroad system. This was unlike the TGV or Shinkansen Bullet which would have required Sweden to invest heavily in its tracks in addition to the train sets. ABB has recognized that increased train travel must occur within the confines of track availability.

5. **What marketing alternatives can ABB pursue?**

Any of the characteristics described in question 3 could be the focus of ABB's marketing efforts. Or, a combination of the characteristics could be selected. Pros and cons of the various alternatives need to be discussed.

ABB could market itself to Amtrak based on its **product offering**. The X2000 has proven to be capable of meeting Amtrak's needs (both in Sweden and in test runs of the train). The X2000 offers some features not available on the competitive products. For example, the flexible steering and tilt seemed unique to the X2000. Unfortunately, competitors products had shown to perform well under various conditions. And, these products offered their own unique product characteristics that tended to compensate for the tilt component. The ICE was a high speed train due in large part to its asynchronous motor and air-pressurized coaches. The TGV's traction mounts allowed for high speed in mountainous terrain.

ABB's **organizational structure** had proven itself to work well. This could be a great match for Amtrak in that ABB has the ability to draw upon the strengths of a global corporation while at the same time adapt to fit the specific needs of Amtrak. However, there might be some concern that the staff of ABB's U.S. operations might be cut so thin that it cannot provide Amtrak the individual attention it wants. And, some Amtrak officials might be hesitant to do business with Percy Barnevik if they were aware of his leadership style.

Company history is working in ABB's favor. The rapid market share gain in Sweden has to be looked upon favorably by Amtrak. As well, ABB was able to develop and build a train that met the needs of the Swedish railway system rather than the railway system having to adapt to the available product. Yet, the competitors have also demonstrated their abilities through the success countries such as Germany and France.

ABB's **cost-cutting measures** demonstrate the company's desire to continually lower costs to its customers. At the same time, the company's products have maintained/improved quality. Since there seems to be a lot of similarities between ABB and its competitors, ABB could use its demonstrated cost cutting capabilities to show Amtrak it can work with Amtrak to reduce costs and ultimately affect price. A con to this would be concerns Amtrak might have that ABB will cut costs through reduced support staff in the U.S.

ABB's ability to **work closely with various companies** has been demonstrated through its alignments with competitors and suppliers. The sale to Amtrak will not be a one-time affair. Rather, the sale will require close relations between Amtrak and its train supplier as Amtrak is following an "incremental" approach to developing various lines. However, all of Amtrak's competitors seem to have worked closely with various company partners so this might not be anything unique to ABB. Amtrak had already experienced partnerships with various ABB competitors.

ABB has demonstrated the ability to think about the **future requirements** of rail systems. The company seems to recognize that there are miles and miles of railroads in place worldwide. Rather than expect countries to adapt to product requirements, the company has adapted its technology to the available railway system. It saw that the future was in meeting the needs for speed, without the additional investment in new tracks as well. However, if ABB positions itself as the train for areas with existing train tracks in this instance, it might lose out in future sales which also involve the building of new track. It could develop an image which could prove detrimental in later sales (e.g., Texas, Florida).

Recommendation:

6. **How should ABB market itself to Amtrak?**

It is likely that students will suggest some combination of the alternatives. But, students need to be leery of positioning Amtrak so broadly that it really has no positioning. Students should be prepared to discuss how they would implement their recommendation. Would it be through advertising? Should ABB reduce its price on the X2000 in expectation of future cost cuts?

7. What type of marketing relationship is ABB seeking with Amtrak?

ABB wants to be seen as more than just the company providing the trainsets to Amtrak. It wants to develop a long-term relationship with Amtrak which means that Amtrak would automatically consider ABB products in future projects. Additionally, ABB would like to develop a relationship which fosters joint product development between ABB and Amtrak. In this way, ABB could develop products which it knows meets Amtrak's needs. ABB appears to be wanting to show Amtrak that it is market oriented and willing to work alongside Amtrak in new product/market endeavors.

Teaching the Case:

Students may be somewhat hesitant to discuss the case due to the nature of the product. If there is concern about this, it might be wise to open the class with a general discussion of high-speed trains. There may be students in the class who have ridden trains such as the ICE or TGV and are willing to share their experiences. Train travel can also be contrasted with air travel. The fact that train stations tend to be located in the heart of the business area compared to airports which are generally outside the city helps highlight the importance train travel can have to business travelers. Also, product features and amenities could be compared between trains and airplanes. This discussion helps students see that the case is about each one of them and their travel behavior. The technical components of the train are there since these components are what make it possible for train manufacturers to provide the type of train needed to get travelers where they want to be when they want to be there. The case is not about the technical components of the X2000.

After the general discussion about train travel, it is interesting to watch the video. The video supports much of the earlier discussion and shows the students that they do know a lot about train travel. Also, the video provides visuals regarding the X2000 itself.

The general discussion of train travel (and the video) tends to make for an easy transition into the case issues. A good opener or follow-on to the general discussion is the identification of the problem/issue faced by ABB.

It is sometimes difficult to get students to think in terms of alternatives with this particular situation. Rather, there is the tendency to talk in general about what Amtrak can do. Questions 4 and 5 help focus students on alternative courses of action. Also, students often want to make a recommendation without recognizing that there has to be an implementation plan. Be sure to spend time on developing a plan of action for ABB.

Epilogue:

Amtrak expected to offer a complete schedule of high-speed train service between Washington, D.C., New York, and Boston by 1997. A contract was scheduled to be awarded in late 1994 or early 1995. However, this did not happen and by the beginning of 1998, the project was still not complete.

Amtrak tested the X2000 for limited passenger service during the first half of 1993. The test train was almost identical to the trains already in use by the Swedish State Railways. Upon completing the test, the test train was shipped back to Sweden. After testing the X2000, Amtrak began testing Germany's ICE in late 1993. Amtrak had negotiated with the TGV to test its train on the route following the ICE test.

X2000 tests and temporary passenger service on the Northeast Corridor were supported by ABB, Amtrak, the Federal Railroad Administration, and the Swedish State Railways. The X2000 performed well in its tests. While testing was going on, Amtrak was still developing its lists of specifications for train makers. This demonstrates the need for a partner with Amtrak which is willing to make changes during the process of manufacturing a product once the product has been ordered. It is doubtful that Amtrak will list its specifications and then sit back and wait for the product to be delivered. Rather, changes in specifications were an ongoing process.

Transportation officials across the U.S. watched Amtrak's testing procedures very closing. Officials in both Illinois and the state of Washington were interested in testing the X2000 on their rail lines after observing the testing by Amtrak. Many government officials felt that the U.S. was far behind Europe and Japan in the development of efficient ground transportation.

Regarding ABB and its management, Barnevik turned ABB into 5,000 profit centers. Corporate staff in the Zurich headquarters of ABB was reduced from 4,000 to 200. ABB began fostering strong relationships with its suppliers in order to reduce costs by working in tandem on new designs. Additionally, many supplies for all 5,000 profit centers are purchased by a single unit in Mannheim, Germany.

By early 1995, Bombardier had rapidly become a major player in the railcar marketplace. Some industry experts had begun placing Bombardier in the same league as Siemens, GEC-Althsom, and ABB. Bombardier and GEC-Althsom joined forces and formed the Bombardier group. **This group was ultimately selected by Amtrack to manufacture the high-speed train route between Boston and Washington, D.C.** In this partnership GEC-Althsom would make the undercarriages and propulsion systems for the trains. Bombardier would be responsible for manufacturing and assembling them. The project is expected to be up and running by the end of 1999.

Exhibit TN–1   SWOT Analysis

Strengths

Vis-à-vis the Competition

- Siemens/STS's train has lower capacity at 285
- Japanese bullet train slower than X2000—operates at ~142 mph
- GEC Alsthom does not have a U.S. partner yet, a sine qua non of doing business with Amtrak; flagship TGV better on straight tracks and mountains, neither of which is a condition of the NE corridor.
- only one of two (Siemens/STS being the other) to have already demonstrated capabilities with Amtrak
- Japan's Shinkansen Bullet train and GEC Alsthom's TGV both would require the laying of dedicated track, which is more costly

Other

- ABB has relationship with Amtrak already—joint venture in the late 1980s
- cost of project using the X2000 less expensive than TGV or Bullet train options
- global reach, yet able to maintain a focus on the local market and customers through decentralized operations and centralized report and control
- world wide coordination provides economies of scale and R&D, technical support for companies under the ABB umbrella
- U.S. Headquarters and production gives advantage on Amtrak project, since U.S. production a requirement
- diversified both geographically and in production
- "lean" operations in a complacent power and transport industry
- "deep pockets" may allow ABB to offer a pricing advantage to cost-conscious Amtrak
- success of the X2000 thus far (in Sweden, captured 14 additional percent of the market)
    * unique technology
    * speed competitive with others
    * comfort better than others
    * amenities
- train sets better suited to the capacity needs of Amtrak

Weaknesses

Vis-à-vis the competition

- GE, which has the most skilled engineers and technicians in the business
- Mitsubishi, which is the most experienced (in terms of years) in high-speed train technology; has not had an accident
- Siemens/STS has faster train which offers greater amenities and comfort; offers energy-saving product; is teamed with two others (GE and Westinghouse); can share risks with partners

- GEC Alsthom, which is known in high-speed rail transport (TGV), and is about to offer Amtrak a train using "tried and true," safe (has not had an accident), TGV technology already used for ten years.

Other

- current technology incompatible with US rails—diesel or d.c. required, X2000 has a.c. power

Opportunities

- Amtrak seeking long-term relationship
- concerns with safety of air travel
- proposed Northeast corridor project assured $1.3 billion in funding, projected cost only $400 million ($1.73 million / mile) before interest
- joint venture to share risks, capitalize on partner-strengths, as is often done in the rail business—the MK–Fiat partnership appears to be a potential opportunity, since Fiat has the diesel, active-tilt technology.
- American traveler highly demanding re: comfort, amenities—ABB offers both
- American partner for GEC Alsthom—ABB could encourage GEC to focus on straight and mountainous routes, the strong point of TGV technology. Thus, ABB could reduce their competition on Northeast corridor project while getting a piece of the action in an area in which they are at a competitive disadvantage.

Threats

- competition strong, time crucial—decision to be made by late 1994, pre-production trains needed by January 1996.
- future viability of Amtrak, government support for Amtrak in near future uncertain following the $1.3 billion for this project
- government funds, support needed to update, electrify (AC) existing routes
- Amtrak purchases only first 26 trains, does not exercise option for 25 additional train sets
- Maglev technology could prove to be far superior to the products currently offered

CASE 5-2
AMBROSIA CORPORATION, SAN AUGUST*

Synopsis:

The Ambrosia Corporation was faced with increasing competition from foreign companies in its Philippine market for frozen desserts and snacks. Ambrosia, with around 77 percent market share in 1991, was the "premier" name in ice cream and frozen confections in the Filipino market. However, the continuing import liberalization program in the Philippines was broadening the competitive arena.

Non-ice cream food items from foreign brands had very high acceptance in the country, and consumers appeared willing to pay a premium for imported products. Ambrosia's domestic competitors had expressed interest in forming partnerships, of some sort, with foreign brands. There was concern among Ambrosia and San August management that Ambrosia's superior position may be threatened by formal relationships between its competitors and foreign companies.

Foreign companies were courting Ambrosia Corporation with the notion of licensing Ambrosia to produce and distribute the foreign company's products in the Philippines. Andrea Bratten, Senior Assistant Vice President and Operations Director of the Frozen Desserts and Snack business, and her management team were trying to determine "how" Ambrosia could maintain its dominant position in the broadening competitive arena. And, if linking with a foreign partner was the best alternative, then Bratten and her team must decide who that foreign partner would be.

Teaching/Learning Objectives:

The case was written to illustrate both product policy and partner selection decisions. The case is an ideal vehicle to:

- introduce the topic of strategic alliances
- help understand the motives and the decision-making process in determining whether to partner or not
- focus on product policy issues beyond the traditional scope of new product development and line extensions
- understand the nature of foreign entry and the first-mover advantages to preempting international companies who might be aligning with competitors

Discussion Questions:

1. What were the key strategic issues in the industry?
2. What was the market potential in the Philippines?

---

* This teaching note was prepared by Victoria L. Crittenden and Erin L. Quinn of Boston College and William F. Crittenden of Northeastern University as an aid to instructors using the case, "Ambrosia Corporation, San August." Assistance was provided by Stephanie Hillstrom and David Angus, Boston College. Revised 1998.

3. Should Andrea Bratten be concerned about whether the Ambrosia brand was "tops" in the Philippines, or should she just make certain that Ambrosia-related products (e.g., licensed foreign brands) were at the top?
4. Could Ambrosia have prevented a market share loss in its ice cream marketplace? How?
5. Did Ambrosia need a foreign brand segment?
6. Should Ambrosia have entered into a joint venture, or some form of partnership, with a foreign company? With whom?

Analysis:

Industry Analysis *(Questions 1 and 2)*

Capacity Planning

The estimated 1992 Philippine population was 62,000,000. [The 1980 census reported a Philippine population of 48,098,460.] With per capita consumption of 0.24 gallons, the current market size for frozen desserts was 14,880,000 gallons. Volume was expected to double by 1998 (29,760,000 gallons). One can assume that this doubling of volume would be the result of an effort to increase per capita consumption as well as an increase in population figures. The volume increase was expected to come from single serves and a better, more refined geographic target market. Companies must evaluate the possibility of this growth in terms of capacity utilization and production, and balance future growth expectations with current productional issues in order to remain competitive. For example, the future expected growth in the single serves market would require investment in new machinery to produce these products. Ambrosia expected to complete a major capacity expansion by 1993. If one assumes that Ambrosia was doubling capacity, this would get the firm's capacity to 23 million gallons (14,880,000 gallons x .77 [market share] = 11.5 million gallons current capacity). This would get industry capacity up to almost 36 million gallons, which was way above volume expectations. Even if Ambrosia was not doubling capacity but rather increasing anywhere less than 100 percent, the industry would experience excess capacity in the next few years.

Entry of Foreign Brands

Naturally, there was a concern regarding "who" would get this doubling of volume. Tables 7-9 show that competitor capacity was expected to total around 12.65 million gallons in 1993. With these competitors seizing only around 3,422,400 gallons of consumption, Ambrosia could expect some major competitive activity in the near future. The entry of foreign brands into the Philippines frozen dessert market was generating considerable competition among local producers. This heightened competition was leading to the introduction of newer products, flavors, and packaging. Because sixty percent of all sales occurred at the retail store level, producers had to fight for shelf space and premier positioning within supermarkets and retail outlets. Individual store owners had a larger number of products to choose from, therefore enabling them to demand discounts and promotional concessions from producers in exchange for shelf space. Ambrosia must leverage their existing relationships with retailers to retain premium positioning.

Product Differentiation

As competition increased, local companies could not have afforded to compete at every level without a defined marketing plan. Companies should focus on the type of products they want to produce. The key elements that a consumer used in choosing an ice cream product were brand and flavor. Companies must concentrate on the development of new improved flavors that would satisfy the consumers' changing tastes, and concentrate on advertising and promotion to attract consumers.

Potential Partnerships/Alliances Between Foreign and Domestic Companies

As consumer preferences lean towards foreign brands, partnerships could prove to be very lucrative for all involved. Ambrosia was being pursued by several companies because it had the necessary manufacturing facilities, supplier resources, and distribution networks to meet the future needs of the market. Domestic companies were faced with increased competition, forcing them to consider alliances with foreign producers. Small producers that historically did not have the resources or power to compete with Ambrosia could have the financial backing of new foreign partners.

A worst case scenario in 1998 might look like this:

Selecta's market share to 15 percent.
[4.5 million gallon capacity in 1993 is equivalent to about 15% of expected 1998 consumption volume]

Purefoods' market share to 16 percent.
[4.75 million gallon capacity in 1993 is equivalent to 16% of expected 1998 consumption volume. Actual market share in 1991 is 5.5% or 818,400 gallons which is about 55 percent of 1991 capacity of 1,500,000 million gallons.]

Presto's market share is 10 percent.
[This is Presto's actual 1991 market share. However, there is not too much in the case to lead one to believe that much will change here.]

This leaves Ambrosia with market share of 59 percent—an unlikely event, but one would expect the competition to have something up its sleeves given the capacity expansion taking place in the industry.

Ambrosia's Overall Situation *(Questions 3, 4, and 5)*

Ambrosia Corporation was accustomed to the top slot in the Filipino frozen dessert market, as exhibited by their 77 percent market share in 1991. As a company within San August, Ambrosia had close ties with the government, as any change in revenue generation could affect the country's GNP and tax revenues. Therefore, a change in market share would be watched closely by corporate (San August) and government. Bratten was not operating in a division which could make decisions unnoticed. A look at the firm's financial statements shows:

Ratio Name	1991	1990	1989	1988
Gross Margin	10.42%	9.82%	10.51%	11.70%
Operating	5.27%	4.10%	6.62%	6.65%
ROI assuming no taxes	6.65%	5.03%	8.23%	8.59%
ROE assuming no taxes	18.85%	14.22%	22.37%	24.43%

However, given the wide spread between Ambrosia and its closest market share competitor (Presto at 10 percent), a local competitor would have to have a strong Filipino strategy to overtake Ambrosia. Market share in 1991 was:

Ambrosia	77%	(11,457,600 gallons)
Presto	10%	(1,488,000 gallons)
Selecta	7%	(1,041,600 gallons)
Purefoods		
Sorbetero	3.1%	(461,280 gallons)
Coney Island	2.4%	(357,120 gallons)

Pursuing the capacity expansion concerns addressed above, there were concerns regarding the maintenance of Ambrosia's market share numbers. One might then begin to question whether Ambrosia could survive in this mature marketplace by continuing its current market strategy of introducing line extensions (e.g., new Flavor of Month, cones, bars). Competitive market growth strategies available to Ambrosia included: new products—new markets, new products—same markets, same products—new markets, same products—same markets. Ansoff portrays these strategies in a two-by-two matrix which might be useful to the students (Exhibit 1). Further, an "Optimal Entry Strategy" matrix developed by Roberts and Berry may provide a useful framework for considering options for Ambrosia, as well as foreign firms seeking Filipino market entry (Exhibit 2).

Ambrosia did need a foreign brand segment. The strategic decision to introduce a foreign brand segment to Ambrosia's product line fit San August's overall corporate strategy. The company claimed to "stand ready at all times to add, modify, or discontinue products in accordance with changes in the market" and to "adopt a flexible and objective attitude towards change and to pursue an active policy of innovation." Ambrosia needed a foreign segment to meet one of the corporation's objectives of strengthening its market dominance. Ambrosia needed to launch itself into the global marketplace and produce and distribute its products in other parts of the world to help it become a world class competitor.`

Product-portfolio analysis might also aid the student in thinking about Ambrosia's situation. The BCG model would have the student position bulk ice cream, single serves, and soft serves along the dimensions of stars, cash cows, dogs, and question marks. Product-portfolio analysis is based on the philosophy that a product's market growth rate and its relative market share are important considerations in determining marketing strategy (Exhibit 3). While the case does not provide adequate information to plot each of the products accurately on the matrix, using the BCG model as a framework for discussing portfolio analysis can aid the student in understanding market characteristics and possible strategies. Clearly, other portfolio techniques could be applied depending upon the objectives of the class session.

Students should also prepare a SWOT analysis for Ambrosia (Exhibit 4).

Strategic Partnerships *(Question 6)*

The case states quite clearly that San August believed in the importance of strategic alliances in order to remain competitive. San August was involved in many such partnerships in Spain, China, and Japan, and thus did not seem to be hesitant to pursue such a course of action. Regarding Ambrosia, however, it appears that any hesitancy came from a concern over losing its strong market position to its own joint venture. Yet, such a preemptive move may be the only way to maintain a competitive advantage in this increasingly competitive marketplace. The ice cream and frozen desserts industry and its consumers were becoming more sophisticated. Ambrosia could no longer afford to live off of its "first and only" reputation that was established back in the 1920s.

Studies had shown that product availability, visibility, and desirability were important factors to Filipino consumers when making an ice cream purchase. By forming a strategic partnership, San August would benefit from the immediate access to manufacturing facilities, raw materials, and distribution channels. This would be particularly important to San August as the Philippines struggled with its contracting economy. Ambrosia should look to form a strategic partnership with a foreign company that held similar corporate interests and long-term objectives. If Ambrosia chose its partnership carefully, the result could be higher sales and therefore higher profits and a higher market share.

The case provides a great opportunity to pursue a discussion of strategic alliances in general, as well as regarding Ambrosia Corporation specifically. Strategic alliances can often obtain greater achievements with less commitment and lower cost than through a merger/acquisition. Exhibit 5 provides a list of eight motives for a strategic alliance. In addition to understanding the motives for forming partnerships, a discussion of the risks associated with strategic alliances should be encouraged. Exhibit 6 lists some possible risks.

Depending upon the students' level of knowledge, it may be necessary to clarify different relevant forms of alliances/partnerships:

- Joint Venture—entails creation of a new entity, distinct from its parents, with equity held by each parent
- Licensing—an agreement to produce, market, & distribute the product (or service) of another for a fee
- R&D Cooperative—joint R&D work on products of mutual interest—each partner is then allowed to incorporate the results of such work into their own business under a previously agreed upon form (e.g., license fee paid to the cooperative)
- Supplier-Buyer Agreements—can take two forms: (i) simply reselling the suppliers' outputs or (ii) using materials supplied in the buyer's final output, with or without the supplier's name associated with the product for sale.

Regarding partnerships between domestic and foreign firms, some specifics may need to be highlighted for the student: (i) the partnership may or may not be split equally, (ii) the partnership provides legitimacy in the eyes of the host country consumer, (iii) the host country firm is often most dissatisfied, and (iv) partners may have been rivals in the same product class.[1]

It is interesting to evaluate possible competitor considerations regarding strategic partnerships. For example, Selecta seemed to be attacking Ambrosia rather persistently. Selecta had increased its capacity to 2.1 million gallons per year which was equivalent to being able to satisfy 14 percent of the current market. The company could then provide 0.8 million gallons of single serve per year with its new machine, which was equivalent to a possible 5.4 percent of the current market. Therefore, the firm had the capacity to fulfill requests equal to about 20 percent of the market in 1992 (which was 5 percent more than its market share during the first half of 1992, but a shocking 13 percent more than its market share in 1993). Given any degree of success with this frontal attack on Ambrosia, Selecta's negotiations with Cadburry IC Bar for single serves might have proven to be a major thorn in Ambrosia's future competitive position.

---

[1] Pride and Ferrell, *Marketing: Concepts and Strategies*, 7th edition, Houghton Mifflin Publishing Co., pp. 802-803.

Assuming students perceive a need for a foreign partnership, the pros and cons of Nestle, Haagen-Dazs, and Mars must be evaluated. Both Nestle and Haagen-Dazs (through its affiliation with Grand Metropolitan PLC) were large companies. This could be both a pro and a con. A large company such as one of these two is likely to have the financial ability to invest heavily in operational needs, as well as spend money on advertising and promotion. Nestle was a current affiliate with San August, which might make any future associations flow easier. On the con side, ice cream was not a major item in Nestles' product portfolio. Ice cream was basically synonymous with Haagen-Dazs, however. And, Haagen-Dazs had stated that it was committed to heavy investment worldwide. Mars seemed to be a horse of a different color when evaluating the three companies. Mars was a small firm relative to Nestle and Haagen-Dazs (which could be advantageous to Ambrosia if it wanted to take a leadership role in the venture), and the company was in the single serve/bars marketplace (which was where growth was expected in the Philippines). Unfortunately, there might be some concern regarding the money Mars had (or was willing) to spend in a joint venture. In addition, structural issues should be addressed regarding all three firms—i.e., Where would the affiliate fit in the Ambrosia organization and/or vice-versa? What would be the value chain impact (e.g., product R&D, Marketing, Purchasing)?

For those students not pursuing the notion of a foreign partner, there must be some recommendation regarding Ambrosia's course of action in this mature marketplace.

Teaching the Case:

The case is easy to teach. Two options for starting the case exist most readily. One, the instructor can go immediately to the question of "What should Ambrosia do regarding a possible foreign partnership?" Doing this allows the class to gain some perspective on strategic alliances early in the class discussion. This seems to work well for graduate and executive programs. The second option is to begin the class with a discussion of the Filipino frozen dessert market. This allows students to delve into the size of the market place and its potential. Both options have been used and no strong preference for one approach over the other has arisen.

Epilogue:

Ambrosia selected Nestle Corporation as its partner. In 1994, the Nestle Crunch and Drumstick brands were introduced. Durian Delight was also introduced in Metro Manila and Luzon. Until recently, this product was only available in the Southern Philippines. In addition to these new product offerings, the company has upgraded technology in production, rehabilitated their trucks and cold storage, and purchased new freezers.

Exhibit 1   Competitive Market Growth Strategies

	Product Present	New
Present Market	Market Penetration	Product Development
New	Market Development	Diversification

Exhibit 2   Optimal Entry Strategies

Market factors

	Base	New familiar	New unfamiliar
New unfamiliar	Joint ventures	Venture capital or educational acquisitions	Venture capital or educational acquisitions
New familiar	Internal market developments or acquisitions (or joint ventures)	Internal ventures or acquisitions or licensing	Venture capital or educational acquisitions
Base	Internal base developments (or acquisitions)	Internal product developments or acquisitions or licensing	Joint ventures

Technologies or services embodied in the product

Source: Adapted from Edward b. Roberts and Charles A. Berry, "Entering New Businesses: Selecting Strategies for Success," *Sloan Management Review*, Spring 1985, pp. 3-17.

Exhibit 3 **Product-Portfolio Analysis**

	High Market Share	Low Market Share
High Product Market Growth	**Stars** Characteristics • Market leaders • Fast growing • Substantial profits • Require large investment to finance growth Strategies • Protect existing share • Reinvest earnings in the form of price reductions, product improvements, providing better market coverage, production efficiency, etc. • Obtain a large share of the new users	**Problem Child** Characteristics • Rapid growth • Poor profit margins • Enormous demand for cash Strategies • Invest heavily to get disproportionate share of new sales • Buy existing market share by acquiring competitors • Divestment (see Dogs) • Harvesting (see Dogs) • Abandonment (see Dogs) • Focus on a definable niche where dominance can be achieved
Low Product Market Growth	**Cash Cows** Characteristics • Profitable products • Generate more cash than needed to maintain market share Strategies • Maintain market dominance • Invest in process improvements and technological leadership • Maintain price leadership • Use excess cash to support research and growth elsewhere in the company	**Dogs** Characteristics • Greatest number of products fall in this category • Operate at a cost disadvantage • Few opportunities for growth at a reasonable cost • Markets are not growing; little new business Strategies • Focus on a specialized segment of the market that an be dominated and protected from competitive inroads • Harvesting-cut back all support costs to a minimum level; supports cash flow over the product's remaining life • Divestment-sale of a growing concern • Abandonment-deletion from the product line

Source: Pride & Ferrel, *Marketing*, Figure 19.7, p. 613

Exhibit 4 SWOT Analysis

Strengths:

- Currently Held a 75% market share of the Philippines Frozen Desserts and Snacks marketplace
- Considered the Philippines "first and only" name in ice cream and frozen confections
- Considered by the suppliers of major raw material for ice cream and manufacturers of dairy equipment as a "world class" user of their products
- Parent company, San August Group, was the Philippines largest publicly held food and beverage company
- Only dairy manufacturer in the Philippines with its own dairy farm (considered to be one of the most modern and advanced in Asia)
- Major capacity expansion to be completed in 1993 will almost double current capacity
- Due to its expansive geographic locations, Ambrosia was able to ship from various locations throughout the Philippines (domestic competitors distribute from Manila only)
- Wide variety of offerings in the frozen dessert and snacks market
- Diversified company—four market segments
- Strong brand identity and loyal customer following

Weaknesses:

- Slightly higher prices than competition
- Slight decrease in market share in first half of 1992. (75%, down from 77.3% in 1991)
- Filipino consumers were willing to pay a premium for imported goods
- Political and economic instability of the country
- Natural disasters depleted raw inputs which interfered with the production process

Opportunities:

- Foreign companies are interested in licensing Ambrosia to produce and distribute their product in the Philippines
- Other forms of strategic alliances can give Ambrosia the potential to obtain substantial benefits from synergies and the sharing of cost of research and development
- Industry volume in the frozen desserts and snacks category in the Philippines is expected to double by 1998
- Large untapped ice cream market in the Philippines (only 0.24 gallon consumption per capita in 1991, well behind other nations)
- Strong program of new product introductions with long-term focus
- Forecasts predicted that the market opportunities were in single snacks (a big Ambrosia line)
- Strengthen brand loyalty and impulse buying
- Exploit existing affiliation with Nestle
- Exploit technological innovations created out of the most modern dairy
- Strategic alliance could increase market penetration in foreign lands

Threats:

- Continuing import liberalization program in the Philippines was broadening the competitive arena
- Non ice-cream food items from foreign brands had a very high acceptance in the Philippines (consumers were willing to pay a premium for imported products)
- Domestic competitors were interested in having "tie-ups" with foreign brands
- Ambrosia could lose its place in the premium segment to its own foreign brand segment if it entered into a licensing agreement with foreign companies
- Weakening of consumer demand due to political, economic, and natural factors had led to reduced investment and industrial activity in the Philippines
- Emergence of a universal lifestyle in the Philippines was enticing foreign investment
- Increase in the capacity of competitors would lead to increased competition and excess capacity in the industry
- Cost pressures
- The Philippines' per capita consumption was .25—extremely low in comparison to the leader (U.S. 5.95)
- Aggressive marketing strategies of the competition

Exhibit 5	Motives for Strategic Alliances

1. Spread financial risk and/or improve cash flow balance; shares risk, investment, and "know-how"
2. Improve operating efficiency (i.e., lower costs) through access to major asset (e.g., raw materials, capital, management, distribution channels, product, technology, manufacturing)
3. Improve operating efficiency through scale economies
4. Obtain access to better information
5. Gain access to market of foreign country (or circumvent other political barriers)
6. Allows diversification to gain entry in new markets and/or to leverage skills for new uses
7. Cross-distribution agreements can help slow market entry to international firms
8. Supplier protection/backward integration
9. Allows chance for first mover advantage

Exhibit 6	Strategic Alliances Risks

- poor coordination and information flows
- de-skilling of your firm
- builds up a competitor
- possible loss of core competence

CASE 5-3
ELECTRO-PRODUCTS LIMITED*

Synopsis

The newly appointed head of a small marketing and marketing analysis group at Electro-Products Limited (EPL), Mr. Novak, is concerned about the relationship between EPL and LIEM. LIEM is a large European-based international electronics manufacturer and marketer. Prior to the November 1989 changes in Czechoslovakia, EPL and LIEM signed an agreement with the assistance of the foreign trading organization ALFA. Under this agreement EPL became a captive supplier of hand-held vacuum cleaners to LIEM. After the November 1989 changes, EPL expected that the relationship with LIEM would change.

Mr. Novak and his group anticipated that LIEM's marketing personnel would offer assistance and training to EPL in a friendly way in order to help EPL develop its marketing capability. This has not happened. In reality, LIEM is becoming an aggressive competitor in EPLs own market, although, under the contract, EPL has exclusive control over the sales and distribution of its products in Czechoslovakia.

A detailed analysis of the case suggests that there are other serious issues to be considered. The small marketing group in EPL is faced not only with potentially strong competition in their domestic market, it also does not have the technical and marketing ability to enter into foreign markets with EPLs own label. Mr. Novak believes that the agreement with LIEM provided EPL with technical understanding of quality requirements in Western markets. He believes that EPL now can engineer a competitive product, but can it market the product?

The marketing group appears to be relatively inexperienced and organizationally ineffective. Before becoming head of the marketing group, Mr. Novak was an engineer responsible for design and development of new products. Now he and his group are confronted with retail sales, promotion, and distribution decisions.

At the same time, the market for their product is becoming more and more competitive. Foreign competitors are moving into the domestic market. LIEM, a partner in a legal agreement, is becoming a competitor. The market is changing on several levels. The products that EPL markets may not be competitive. Changing market demands, privatization, and financial reforms threaten the strategic survival of EPL.

The latest marketing plans prepared by the marketing group call for three objectives: (1) developing an effective and efficient domestic distribution and sales network for EPL products, (2) broadening EPL's cooperation with foreign firms in areas of product development and cross marketing arrangements, and (3) improving the overall image of EPL's brand name ZETA in Western European markets.

Teaching/Learning Objectives

This case can be effectively used in two areas of marketing: (1) in a marketing management course to discuss (a) the need for a market-orientation among top management, (b) corporate reorganization to introduce marketing philosophy and orientation, and (c) the importance of being in touch with customers;

---

*This teaching note is based on material provided by the case authors.

and (2) in international marketing (or a section on international marketing in the basic MBA course) to discuss the use of foreign trading organizations and foreign market entry strategies.

The case works best when discussions of market changes, organizational changes, and dependence on foreign markets for hard currency income are integrated. Students are encouraged to look at the situation from several perspectives, including top management, the marketing group, and the foreign partner.

Basic issues that are presented include the dependency on the foreign trading organization, the agreement with the foreign partner in the light of the changing needs of EPL and its market, and the competitive position. The students are then asked to prepare a comprehensive strategy for EPL to help it achieve an effective market position in its domestic and foreign markets.

At the beginning of the case, the leader can focus on the advantages and disadvantages of using a foreign trading organization. Since the situation in Czechoslovakia (now the Czech Republic) has changed with respect to the use of foreign trading organizations, the case leader can focus on how a firm can develop an international marketing orientation and eliminate the need for using a foreign trading organization.

From a general perspective, students need to develop an understanding of how all these issues interrelate and how they affect the overall strategic management of the firm. The students need to deal with the fact that EPL is a captive supplier of a product that has been designed by the client firm.

Electro-Products—Objectives

- Develop domestic distribution and sales channels to overcome competitive threats (currently 75% of EPL's sales)
- Expand international market position
- Reduce dependence on LIEM unless a more collaborative relationship is feasible (LIEM is currently important to EPL)
- Expand new product development capabilities
- Develop internal marketing capabilities to increase contact with end users and marketing intermediaries.
- Build the brand image of Zeta both domestically and in other European countries
- Become a market-oriented company

Alternatives

- EPL maintains its current strategy of selling the Zeta line domestically while manufacturing products for LIEM (status quo)
- EPL continues its domestic strategy of selling the Zeta products and aggressively expanding its international operations by seeking retailers in Western European markets to sell EPLs products under their private labels. EPL would maintain separate relationship with LIEM while using ALFA for its export operations.
- EPL discontinues its alliance with LIEM and concentrates solely on strengthening its presence as the dominant Czech Republic manufacturer and distributor of small appliances.

- EPL discontinues its alliance with LIEM but establishes a strategic alliance with another manufacturer in order to further penetrate the domestic and Western European markets. ALFNs support would continue to be used in the new negotiations.

Critical Issues

1. Internal Strengths and Weaknesses
    a. Marketing skills
    b. Financial resources
2. Market Opportunity
    a. Size of market
    b. Market growth
3. Strategic Decision Making
    a. Market targeting
    b. Positioning strategy
4. Marketing Mix
    a. Product
        (1) Product development
        (2) Product mix
    b. Distribution
        (1) New channels
        (2) ALFA relationship
        (3) LIEM relationship
    c. Pricing
        (1) Cost advantages
        (2) Competitor intensity
    d. Promotion
        (1) Advertising
        (2) Sales promotion
        (3) Domestic sales force

Analysis

Status Quo

If EPL maintains the status quo, it will remain a captive supplier for LIEM. EPL formed its alliance with LIEM in order to get marketing training and new product development experience in exchange for the low-cost manufacturing of LIEM's products. However, LIEM has neglected to fulfill its end of the agreement, leaving EPL incapable of marketing its own products on a large scale. EPL certainly has some bargaining power in its relationship with LIEM. Although it has not exercised this power thus far, EPL is LIEM's connection for low-cost production. For instance, according to Morgan Stanley Research, 1993 hourly labor costs in Western Germany were $24.87 versus $1.14 in the Czech Republic. Unfortunately, EPL has not used its leverage to better the relationship with LIEM.

LIEM is also considering expanding into EPL's domestic market. This constitutes a major potential threat to EPL. Therefore, EPL must play a more powerful role to protect its market share. However, the LIEM relationship is still important to EPL if it is to expand internationally because of the marketing and technical experience LIEM holds in Western Europe. Without this market knowledge of the international sector, EPL's future plans to expand internationally will be unsuccessful.

In summary, this alternative is not recommended for EPL because LIEM gains more control over EPL and yet LIEM gives up nothing. LIEM would most likely take away market share from EPL's Zeta line, using EPL's low-cost production and its own marketing knowledge to switch EPL's customers. At the same time, it is most likely LIEM would not help EPL expand into foreign markets because it will continue to see EPL as a captive supplier only.

Seeking Retailers

In essence, this strategy would allow EPL to decrease its dependency on LIEM for international distribution by establishing another route to market. While the LIEM relationship will continue to some degree, EPL will seek out other distribution channels such as retailers in Western Europe to carry its products. However, these products will not be marketed under EPL's brand name but the retailers private labels instead. In this manner, EPL would only be responsible for the manufacturing while the retailers would take care of marketing the products.

ALFA's services would still be free of charge. EPL would maintain this relationship for its international business. However, it would be wise for EPL to begin searching for another person or persons that can assume ALFPCs responsibility. If the company desires to expand into foreign markets, it needs to hire people that can help it reach that goal instead of relying on the old state system to sustain it in the future.

Although this strategy is sensible, it is important EPL makes an effort to form alliances that will allow it to gain the valuable marketing skills it has been trying to procure. These marketing skills will be essential in both the international sector and the domestic market, where the level of competition is increasing as well. It is clear that merely convincing retailers to carry its products will not help EPL to accomplish this objective. In fact, EPL may not control any of the marketing strategy behind its products.

Pure Domestic Strategy

This strategy ignores international expansion. ALFA's assistance would not be needed since it only was concerned with EPL's exporting. However, EPL would be foolish not to move into foreign markets. Its cost structure is much lower than Western European manufacturers. EPL's low labor wages give it a distinctive competence over its international competition. While it presently lacks the marketing skills and distribution channels to further penetrate the foreign market, strategic alliances would allow it to do so.

EPL could break its alliance with LIEM since it would only focus on selling its Zeta brand domestically. However, LIEM would eventually form alliances with other lowcost manufacturers and expand into Czechoslovakia. With its marketing expertise and financial strength, LEM would be a fierce competitor for the Zeta brand. If LIEM does acquire low-cost production from other sources, EPL loses its strategic advantage and may have a hard time competing. It would be smart for EPL to retain its relationship with LIEM if only to keep the company from damaging its market share in Czechoslovakia.

EPL must also explore other distribution and sales channels within Czechoslovakia to overcome the LIEM threat. With domestic sales composing 75% of EPL's sales, it is vital that the company locates other ways of selling its products. Direct mail, a more viable sales force, and forward integration (owning the retailers, are a few options to consider.

Form New Strategic Alliances

Although foreign sales account for only 25% of EPLs total sales, it is very important that EPL have a distribution system to get its product into Western Europe. By establishing a strategic alliance with a Western European company, EPL can achieve this market coverage. However, it is important that EPL actually learn more about marketing in the new alliance, something missing from the LIEM partnership. This understanding of marketing is crucial to its future success in a growing global market that gets more competitive daily.

Breaking the LIEM relationship may not be a very smart move now. If this alliance is ceased, LIEM may retaliate in both the international market where it has established extensive routes to market, and in the Czech Republic, where it could form alliances with other local low-cost manufacturers. Therefore, completely severing ties with LIEM may be an option in the future after EPL has established itself in Western Europe, but the relationship is still important to EPL's short-term future.

Recommendations

All of these alternatives are feasible except for the pure domestic strategy (alternative 3). EPL must continue to develop its international expansion. The status quo alternative does nothing to further EPL's marketing capabilities since it is obvious LIEM looks at EPL as a captive supplier only. Alternatives 2 and 4 aim at growing both the domestic and foreign markets. Alternative 2 is particularly attractive since it broadens EPL's distribution to foreign retailers.

EPL needs to explore new routes to market, such as wholesalers, retailers, and direct mail in both the domestic and foreign markets. These new distribution channels will need to materialize over time as EPL~s marketing skills and resources become more viable.

Because domestic sales account for 75% of total sales, EPL must continue to target this segment. New product development is crucial as this market becomes more competitive from the influx of foreign competitors. More importantly, EPL needs to realize that it is not merely a captive supplier for LIEM. EPL should make certain that LIEM does not enter the Czech market. The chances of stopping LIEM's entry is slim, however. Thus, EPL must begin to look for other alliances as well.

EPL should keep the LIEM alliance until it can find a better partner in Western Europe. EPL needs a relationship in which it does more than simply producing a low-cost vacuum in exchange for nothing. The company must get something in return for its manufacturing expertise, such as better marketing and technical experience. The LIEM partnership most likely will not supply EPL with the experience it needs to gain in order to compete in foreign markets.

Finally, EPL needs to begin taking more responsibility for its export operations. While ALFA presently assumes this role, the market is changing and EPL needs to be able to form alliances and communicate without ALFA serving as an intermediary.

Epilogue

Domestically, EPL focused on creating new distribution channels from 1991-1994 because the previous channels disappeared in the process of privatization.

- *Retailing*—Established a network of company stores, a franchising system, and a commission system. The company owns 60 retail outlets that carry full EPL product lines, provides servicing, and monitors the local market for the headquarters.
- *Wholesaling*—Because EPL did not have experienced sales people to organize wholesaling effectively, it switched to independent wholesalers in 1993
- *Direct* mail—Plays a crucial role when new products are introduced and provides a channel for product replacement parts

While the handheld vacuums have not been popular in the domestic market, the product (developed in cooperation with LIEM) was a success in foreign markets. During the introductory phase, export volume of the product was twice as high as expected.

The alliance between LIEM and EPL is now restricted to new product development. LIEM is still responsible for marketing while EPL manufactures the product. The newest product is an upright vacuum cleaner sold under the LIEM brand Zeta in foreign markets and under the EPL brand in the domestic market since mid-1994. Despite this alliance, EPL and LIEM are competitors in the domestic market of home appliances. This relationship is reportedly satisfactory for both partners.

Since EPL's privatization in 1992, its shares have tripled in value. Stock prices are listed below.

1993 ⇒ 1,000 Cz c.
March 1994 ⇒ 3,200 Cz c.

CASE 5-4
SOUTHERN HOME DEVELOPERS*

Synopsis

Southern Home Developers was a manufacturer of modular homes. Located in a rural town in central Arkansas, the company had only recently started operations. The owner. Bill Thompson, was also sales person and plant manager. The firm had six employees—a five-person construction crew and an on-site interior finisher (who was also Bill's wife).

After being in business for only a few short months, Bill had begun accepting orders for customized homes. Bill's strategy for gaining a competitive advantage was to "mass customize" the modular homes. Unfortunately, Bill's small construction crew was not too pleased with Bill's attempt to move away, so quickly, from the company's two standard home designs. Bill Thompson faced the inherent conflict between customer expectations and the operational side of the business.

Teaching/Learning Objectives

This small, entrepreneurial start-up is a great case to show:

- the dilemma many managers (of both large and small companies) confront when attempting to satisfy customer's demands while faced with operational constraints,
- the implementation problems encountered with mass customization, and
- problems that arise when market research data is ignored and/or insufficient and managers rely almost solely on historical success or "gut instinct."

Discussion Questions

1. What are the company's strengths and weaknesses'?
2. Describe the firm's external environment.
3. What type of market research do you think was conducted by Thompson before opening Southern Home Developers? Is this the type of research you would have recommended? If not, what would you recommend'?
4. What does it mean to mass customize in this industry?
5. Why is Bill Thompson starting to have disgruntled employees?
6. Given the current situation, what is the long-term outlook for this company? What needs to be done to make this a positive outlook?

---

* This teaching note was prepared by Victoria L. Crittenden, Boston College, and William F. Crittenden, Northeastern University, as an aid to instructors using the case, "Southern Home Developers."

Analysis

Questions 1-3 comprise the situation audit

1. **What are the company's strengths and weaknesses'?**

Exhibit TN-1 provides an overview of the company's strengths and weaknesses.

Corporate Mission and Objectives: Not unlike many entrepreneurial startups, Southern Home Developers does not have a corporate mission nor does it appear that objectives have been established. The lack of a mission and objectives may contribute to the problems developing at the company—Thompson is trying to be all things to all people without any clarity on what he is trying to accomplish, nor what business he is in.

2. **Describe the firm's external environment.**

Opportunities and threats in the external environment are outlined in Exhibit TN-1.

Buyer analysis/Market target strategy: In general, it appears that there is a market for modular homes. With the geographic segmentation that occurred (due to shipping-related costs), there appeared to be an opportunity for small, regionalized players. Home buying was also strongly related to several economic indicators— unemployment rates, labor force composition, inflation rates, and population growth. Most of these indicators pointed in the direction of a need for more homes in the U.S. However, as discussed in question 3, there is a big question mark regarding the composition of the modular home market. While secondary data suggests that there is a market, Southern Home Developers does not have a clear vision of its target market and how or why someone would purchase a modular home.

Longer-term, there appeared to be many international opportunities for a manufacturer who could successfully address the logistical and financial issues associated with transporting modules to other countries.

Competitors: It was estimated that there were 500 modular housing factories in the U.S. A large percentage of the 500 were small-scale operations with fewer than 100 employees. The small size of the operations was at least partially due to the geographic restrictions upon the company—the 350 mile radius for shipping. However, there were some large competitors: All American Homes, Cardinal Industries, Chadwick International Inc., Ryland Group Inc., and Westchester Modular Homes, Inc. Chadwick had begun to move into international markets such as the Ivory Coast, Benin and Algeria.

Marketing Programs: There did not appear to be any marketing programs in place at Southern Home Developers. Basically, it appears that Bill Thompson went out and sold a home or built on speculation. If built on speculation, the home would probably be placed in the hands of a realtor since Southern Home did not have a real estate group (and we don't get the impression that Bill is a realtor—although he may be a good salesperson). A customer requesting that a home be built would have to first hear about Southern Home Developers and then make the effort to contact the company. Again, there is no evidence of marketing information which would suggest that effort is being expended to get information to potential customers.

3. **What type of market research do you think was conducted by Thompson before opening Southern Home Developers'? Is this the type of research you would have recommended'? If not, what would you recommend?**

It appears that, at best, Thompson used secondary data to establish that there was a market for modular homes. As seen in Exhibit 1 of the case, both existing home and new home starts were on the upswing. Yet, potential buyers were exhibiting some hesitancy as noted by the scaling back that had taken place with some builders. However, forecasts were for an increased interest in prefabricated homes and a simultaneous decrease in the number of on-site construction hours. Given this forecast, and assuming that the housing market was going to continue at a steady state, one could also assume that modular homes would become more popular.

We would hope that students would not be satisfied with this level of research. There appears to be no research to indicate that a 350 mile radius of the manufacturing plant results in a viable market for Southern Home Developers. Basic geography would imply that a 350 mile radius in central Arkansas would indicate that Thompson could probably deliver homes to western Tennessee, northern Texas. northern Louisiana, eastern Oklahoma, and southern Missouri. Arkansas ranked number 11 in mobile homes, Louisiana was number 17, Tennessee was number 21, Oklahoma was number 23, Texas was number 27, and Missouri was number 28. However, no market research was conducted to see if these owners of mobile homes were wanting to trade-up to modular homes or if they even had the buying power to trade up. One also has to wonder if there is a correlation between mobile home and modular home ownership given that the northeast was considered to be a good market for modular homes, yet many of the northeastern states were low in the percentage rankings in Exhibit 3.

Students should be forced to offer some recommendations for useful market research. They might suggest that focus groups would have provided valuable insight into the thinking of potential modular home purchasers. Separate focus groups could have been comprised of mobile home owners, recent new homebuyers, and young professionals. A feasibility study would have helped determine if the central Arkansas location was optimal for this type of manufacturing facility.

Once students start rolling on this, the professor may have to remind them that Bill Thompson probably did not have the financial resources to conduct large-scale market studies. Students need to keep in mind the probable financial constraints faced by Thompson.

Questions 4 and 5 help focus upon the problem faced by Southern Home Developers.

4. **What does it mean to mass customize in this industry?**

Mass customization in the modular home market would mean that a builder could provide quality homes designed to the buyers specifications at a relatively low cost and in relatively short time to market.

However, Thompson did not allow his firm time to get down the learning curve. He seemed to expect to mass customize immediately, rather than mass customizing after he and his crew had honed their skills in modular construction.

5. **Why is Bill Thompson starting to have disgruntled employees?**

This is intimately related to the Thompson's desire to mass customize. Thompson recognized that there was a market for customized modular homes. However, he did not allow his employees to thoroughly learn the trade before he began pushing them to do more. Additionally, he did not seem to understand that a small crew of five could not do everything. Mass customizing in this market would mean a larger crew—

possibly one group of employees working in the factory and another group constructing the modules on site.

As noted previously, mass customization is relative. A buyer would expect costs to be lower than that of a site-built home. However, the buyer would naturally expect to pay more for a customized home than a standardized home. Also, the buyer would know that a customized modular home would take longer to construct than a standardized home.

Question 6 is an all-encompassing question that requires students to think about the company's alternatives and what it should do for long-term success.

6. Given the current situation, what is the long-term outlook for this company? What needs to be done to make this a positive outlook?

Students are generally mixed regarding the long-term outlook for Southern Home Developers. While there is a tendency to think that the product (modular homes) has potential, most students do not think that the company will survive very long with its current mode of operations

Alternatives

Continue current mode of operations

Pros:

the company has been doing well with the current operations, so why *fix* what appears to be working

Cons:

it looks like there might be problems in the near future

would not resolve employee complaints

Conduct market research

Pros:

the company needs to find out more about its current and potential market

Cons:

might be a little late to do much since the company is already in business, a feasibility study might not be too useful right now

may not be able to afford

Begin to put a management structure in place

Pros:

the company would benefit from having more defined positions

a weekly meeting of persons in defined positions would provide an outlet for airing some of the concerns that are arising

Cons:

Bill Thompson would lose some of his autonomy

- crew members may not have the background or desire to take on managerial roles
- the company probably cannot afford, at this time, to hire people with management skills

Hire workers who agree with Thompson's desire to customize and fire workers who only want to produce standardized products

Pros:

- would mean that Thompson could continue along the same path that he is headed, without having crew members question his authority or capabilities
- Thompson may actually know what he is talking about!

Cons:

- may only exacerbate a weak position
- expensive
- no guarantee that new workers will agree with Thompson once they are on the job

Hire additional crews so that the company is not so short-handed when it comes to building the modules and constructing on-site

Pros:

- would allow crews to specialize—one crew in the factory building the modules and the other crew on site
- would speed up the process both in the factory and between the factory and on-site.

Cons:

- more costly, which might have to be reflected in price if the company could not increase sales volume
- locating qualified workers might be difficult
- the larger the crew, the more concern Thompson might have about unionization

Stop operations

Pros:

- could avoid a costly situation in the future
- no identifiable market

Cons:

- this is Bill Thompson's life
- exiting a potentially large market rather than fixing the problem

Students tend to split on whether to shut down or attempt to fix the problem. Continuing as is does not seem to be a feasible option, nor does firing current workers and hiring new ones. Some students honestly think that Thompson jumped into the market without a clear vision and without an understanding of his market target. They feel that he has gone too far to fix the problem and should cut his losses. Other students will combine alternatives into a major company overhaul. The key points of this overhaul are:

- determine the company's mission (what business is it in?)
- decide upon company objectives (where does Thompson want to be in 1, 5, 10 years'?)
- market research (who is in the local area market? how do they buy?)
- resolve current conflict that is festering in Nyman and other crew members by getting their input about the future of the company and how they think it can be successful long-term
- recognize that mass customization is great to think about for the future but not for Southern Home Developers in its initial startup phase
- determine what, if any, marketing needs to be done

Thus, there appear to be two major alternatives: stay in business and correct the problems or dissolve the business. Several of the alternatives actually become part of the implementation plan.

Teaching the Case

The case is fairly straightforward, making it easy to teach. The professor might want to start the class with a general understanding of the manufactured housing market by asking if any of the students are familiar with mobile homes. There are usually many views on mobile homes and the market for mobile homes. Then the same question should be posed for modular homes. While most students are familiar with mobile homes, few are familiar with modular homes. It is good to walk students through the similarities and differences in these manufactured housing units.

After understanding the similarities/differences between mobile and modular home, the class moves easily into a the situation analysis (the professor may have already begun to fill in a SWOT framework when the students were talking about the housing units).

After the situation analysis, the professor should open the discussion about mass customization. Some students may not be familiar with this (isn't it an oxymoron?). A brief discussion of what it means for Southern Home Developers makes the class flow easily into the problem, alternatives, and recommendation for Bill Thompson.

Epilogue

Southern Home Developers was in business just shy of 15 months. While, as seen by the recent success of many modular home companies, the product concept was valid, Bill Thompson was unable to control his urge to be all things to all customers. The company built several homes, with very satisfied buyers of the homes. However, Thompson quickly lost touch with his internal capabilities. Thompson's push to customize homes at about the same speed as standardization resulted in low quality workmanship. Crew size was never increased and Thompson began losing his start-up crew and having to hire inexperienced workers. The reputation of the company was quickly tarnished, and Thompson had begun shutting down the manufacturing facility when it was gutted by fire.

Bill Thompson moved to a small rural town in Missouri and opened a log home manufacturing facility. He kept the modular concept and is attempting to go after a small niche market. Much of the construction of the log homes is done in the factory and then shipped to the site. The major differences between the log home and modular home markets are that log homebuyers are not currently pushing for speed to market and are willing to pay for customization. However, the jury is still out as to Thompson's long term success in this market.

Exhibit TN-1   SWOT Analysis

Strengths

- Thompson's experience in the modular housing market (mobile homes have a similar concept)
- Efficient module construction to enable move-in capability in four weeks
- Workers do both tasks of manufacturing and assembly, potentially improving the product's quality since the same workers were responsible for each product
- Decreased overhead expenses since there was one crew of workers
- Able to offer two different types of houses for potential customers
- Ability to customize
- Low price
- Quick cycle time

Weaknesses

- Workers doing both tasks could lead to slower order completion in times of high demand
- Disgruntled employees
- Complete ownership of properties could be a liability
- Too dependent upon five workers (e.g.. output could be greatly hindered if a worker didn't show up, quit, or was injured)
- Not enough crew members to operationalize the mass customization concept

Opportunities

- Stable unemployment rates
- Low inflation rates
- Increased immigration
- Growth in factory-built homes
- Increase in mobile home residency
- International markets

Threats

- Decrease in 25-34 year old age group from 1994-2005
- Limited target market in relation to factory locations
- Increase in 55+ age group who are less likely to purchase new homes
- Household incomes rising at a slower rate than new home prices
- Population growing at a decreasing rate

CASE 5-5
KONARK TELEVISION INDIA*

Synopsis

Konark Television is a major manufacturer of black and white and color television sets in India. The primary issue in the case concerns Konark's distribution objectives and its distribution strategy to compete in a highly competitive industry that is facing an imminent shakeout. Moreover, the state government of Orissa has just announced that Konark will no longer enjoy a state sales tax exemption, making the retail price of Konark sets the same as retail prices for larger competitors.

To resolve issues in the case, students need to undertake analyses of the company's consumers, competitors, and dealers. They need to analyze the company's internal strengths and weaknesses. They should be asked to make strategic and tactical recommendations. The case is complex and full of learning possibilities.

Teaching/Learning Objectives

The case can be used to meet several objectives. Students have an opportunity to consider the following issues:

1. Typical channel of distribution decisions for a manufacturer include choosing market areas, identifying and selecting wholesalers and dealers, motivating wholesalers and dealers, managing conflict, and controlling wholesalers and dealers.

2. Almost all channels members desire to gain power and achieve some degree of control over channel activities. Some desire to become the channel captain.

3. A multichannel strategy often increases a manufacturer's control over dealers and wholesalers. However, the strategy must be executed carefully or it will increase channel conflict.

4. An important factor in designing channel strategy is understanding how consumers want to buy the product.

5. To develop a distribution strategy requires that the firm first have distribution obJectives.

Teaching Suggestions

Given the complexity of the case, Konark Television India should be assigned in the latter half of the course, particularly after students feel some sense of competence in analyzing cases. The Indian setting has not been troublesome at all, given the description of consumers in the primary segment in the case section headed "Indian Consumers."

The case can be used for discussion or testing purposes. A class or exam period of 75 minutes minimum is needed. Discussion begins well when the instructor reads the following two paragraphs taken from a visitor's letter (written in India in 1989 to friends back in the U.S.):

---

* This teaching note was prepared by Professor James E. Nelson. University of Colorado at Boulder.

I awoke about 9:00 a.m. on Sunday in Dr. Nayak's house, still suffering from what seemed like terminal jet lag. The din outside my bedroom was incredible. On opening the door, I saw a room filled with 16 people! All were focused intently on the TV, which appeared to playing a melodrama set in ancient India. Later that day I learned that the people in the room consisted of the cook and his family, the sweeper and two friends, Dr. Nayak's family, plus Dr. Nayak's next door neighbors. The program was "Ramayana," a religious epic in serial form.

Next Sunday, I went for a walk at about the same time. About a mile from the house I came on a village near a river. Here the same scene was repeated but on a much larger scale. There must have been a hundred people in an open area watching the same program on a TV placed on a shaded stand. No one so much as glanced at me as I went by. 'This program is like the Super Bowl," I thought, "except that its share is twice as high!"

This start begins discussion in an interesting manner and emphasizes a point in the case that there is, indeed, much latent demand for TVs in India. Discussion then can proceed along lines suggested by questions presented in the next section. A typical class session might cover three or four of these questions; the balance could be used as a follow-up written assignment or as an in class exam.

Topics for Discussion/Analysis

A. Describe the buying process from the consumer's perspective.

The buying process for an expensive consumer durable consists of a series of steps: problem recognition, information search, alternative evaluation and decision, purchase, post purchase outcomes. Student discussion might proceed as follows.

According to the case, the target market presently consists of "affluent middle and upper social classes," some 100 to 200 million Indians. (Once this segment begins to mature, Konark might target a much larger segment consisting of middle market consumers.) Almost every household in the target segment is aware of television and desires at least one set. Problem recognition can be stimulated by TV advertising in various media, dealer promotions, group viewing in a neighbor's house, shopping visits to a dealer, etc. The product is likely a status symbol.

Prospective buyers will actively search for information. Marketer dominated sources include advertisements and dealers. Consumer dominated sources consist of opinion leaders via word of mouth. Students should deduce that first time buyers are especially careful shoppers who find it difficult to compare technical merits of this rather complex product (much like first time buyers of home computers in the U.S.). Instead, these buyers will rely greatly on the advice of a trusted friend or salesperson. Most buyers want to bargain with the salesperson to get a good price.

Once purchased, the TV set will be carefully placed in a sitting room. Invited guests as well as domestic help will stare at the device and take pleasure in its performance. Within a few months, a large external antenna or VCR may be added to improve the viewing experience. Later, the household may add a second TV.

To complete the consumer analysis, the instructor might summarize the situation as follows:

'The market is immense and growing. The purchase is important to the buyer in economic and social terms. Buyers often shop around and compare alternatives; they have difficulty evaluating technical aspects of the product and must rely on opinion leaders and dealers for much information. They like to negotiate a fair price."

B. How would you assess the competition?

Level of competition in the industry is intense. The industry is expected to shrink from over 140 manufacturers to just 20 or 30. Statements in the case describe Videocon's strategy; students should conclude that its focus on dealer margins and dealer incentives represents a "push" strategy. Onida, the other leader in color, uses a strategy that students should describe as "pull." Because TVs are the early stages of the product life cycle, competitors are racing to stimulate primary demand and to establish brand awareness. Competitors quickly need to develop a large dealer network-to sell the product and to assure consumers that service is both available and convenient. They need to find dealers before dealers agree to carry a competing line or two.

Competition is probably equally intense in terms of advertising. Only the 'big boys" can afford large budgets with the result that smaller firms will soon disappear. Most advertising budgets are spent in the print media (why advertise TVs to non-owners using the TV medium?). A limited amount of cooperative advertising appears in newspapers with the bulk of these costs paid for by manufacturers. Product features probably are a less intense basis of competition. Most products marketed by major competitors have similar features; differences in quality and performance are "difficult for consumers to recognize." Style and appearance are important for color sets.

Students should spend a few minutes discussing price competition. They should conclude that price is to some degree unimportant for color TVs as long as it is within an acceptable range. Of course, every buyer would like to save Rs. 500 the purchase but Rs. 500 is typically less than 5% of the total price. Besides, the ability of the buyer to obtain, say, a Rs. 300 reduction from list price via bargaining may be more satisfying than to pay a comparable full price. Price is a more important consideration in buying a black and white set.

C. Describe the influence of governmental policy on Konark's marketing strategy.

On the surface, the case seems to represent a company focusing only on its domestic market. Thus, students usually begin their comments by noting the "normal" influences of a national government on business activities inside its borders. They describe such things as the Indian government's attitude toward the industry as a luxury industry and "capable of bearing heavy taxes." They note the high import duties placed on component parts brought into the country and the heavy excise taxes levied on assembled sets. They might guess at a balance of payments problem, a lack of hard currency, and a limited ability of Indian TV sets to compete in world markets as consequences of government policy.

Yet in another sense, the case illustrates a typical international setting. Students should recognize that Konark faces a bewildering set of economic conditions, regulations, restrictions, languages, and governments as it moves from one Indian state to another. An earlier presentation on the political, social, and economic conditions in India would heighten this realization. Alternatively, the Instructor might assign the U.S. State Department's "Background Notes on India" as required reading before students discuss the case. This brief note is sufficient to give students an understanding of conditions in India and costs only $1. Students should conclude that Konark is really "exporting" its TV sets to other Indian states, given these states' great diversity and their sales tax policies favoring the production of sets inside their borders.

D. Who is the channel captain?

Channel captains lead or control their channels of distribution. The captain's identity is limited to manufacturers, retailers, or wholesalers who compete in the channel. In this particular case, students usually conclude that the dealer is the channel captain, at least as far as Konark is concerned. Dealers have a great deal of influence over the consumer's final decision to purchase. Dealer location, image, service, and motivation are crucial to the sale of the product.

Konark's competitors also recognize the power of the dealer in their channels. Videocon's strategy uses high dealer margins and incentives to reward and control its dealers. In contrast, Onida uses consumer advertising as a way to diminish the dealer's importance.

E. How effective are the Konark showrooms?

The effectiveness of Konark's showrooms can be examined in qualitative and quantitative terms. From a qualitative perspective, a good retail outlet should display numerous models that are produced by two or more manufacturers. (However, Konark does not permit its dealers to carry competing products.) Consumers want to compare performance, prices, and styles. Consumers need assurance on operation, service, and warranty because the price of a TV set is high relative to income and because friends and neighbors will be viewing. Consumers want to bargain with the dealer to get a fair price.

Now, Konark showrooms can do only some of these things. Showrooms cannot stock and sell competing TV sets and nor can they bargain on price. However, showrooms can display a full line of Konark products and can provide much better education and "push" than a dealer. They can collect marketing research information about consumers' likes and dislikes. They also can help Konark management understand dealer problems and complaints. Showrooms probably are a sore point with some dealers because they represent lost sales and a threat to the dealer's ability to continue to carry the line. Showrooms shift some channel power back to Konark. (A parallel in the U.S. that most students will recognize are the growing numbers of outlet malls/stores for fashion and other goods.) On balance, students should conclude that Konark showrooms compete with Konark dealers to some degree, particularly when showrooms are located close to dealers.

From a quantitative perspective, students need to analyze financial data for the showrooms. A statement in the case permits an estimate of Konark's sales for 1990 at Rs. 800 million and 333,500 units. Half of these amounts—Rs. 400 million and 167,000 units—come from the home state of Orissa where the 10 showrooms are located. The showrooms account for only 5% of Orissa sales or Rs. 20 million and 8,350 units. The showrooms incur a total cost to Konark of Rs. 1.0 million, an amount that Konark would not pay if these units were sold instead through the state's 250 dealers. The dealers receive an average margin of Rs. 320 per set. Thus, if dealers had sold these units, Konark would have given up a total margin of 8,350 units x Rs. 320 or Rs. 2.6 million. This amount is much more than Konark's cost for the showrooms. However, Konark also ties up its capital in showroom inventory and it may incur hidden costs in the form of additional overhead.

F. Recommend elements of Konark's distribution strategy.

Students usually plunge headlong into a discussion on this topic. They start to describe a selective coverage strategy, complete with Konark owned showrooms and a few branch offices in distant states. They are eager to expand into new market areas because a strategic window is open. All these suggestions are good but poorly timed.

That is, early into this discussion the instructor might call for a time out with a comment like, "While I agree with much of what we've just heard, I'm uneasy because we seem to have the cart before the horse here. That is, we're discussing distribution strategy when we don't even have a good idea on distribution." The missing topic is *objectives*. Students should be pressed to identify several distribution objectives for Konark. Examples include:

- Improve the quality and size of Konark's dealers.
- Reduce the number of Konark's dealers.
- Improve dealer cooperation; reduce channel conflict.
- Expand the dealer network into one new state each year.
- Gain more control over the dealers.

Once Konark knows what it wants to accomplish with its channel of distribution, it can devise a distribution strategy.

Konark's distribution strategy should be based on a smaller number of larger dealers. Videocon, India's largest producer of color TVs, has only 200 dealers in 18 of India's 25 states-compared to Konark's 500 dealers in just 12 states. Obviously, some or many of Konark's dealers are small operations compared to those for Videocon. In general, larger dealers when compared to smaller dealers can carry more inventory from which buyers may choose; they can be reached more efficiently; they can be better trained to sell and service Konark products; they can be more highly and easily motivated because Konark sales are substantial; they have a better image; they are easier for consumers to find; they make cooperative advertising more effective. Most importantly, a smaller number of larger dealers should be easier for Konark to control.

The distribution strategy should include a few Konark showrooms. Showrooms are profitable and help keep dealers in line. However, too many showrooms will make dealers nervous and resentful because of sales perceived to be lost to the showrooms. Probably the best strategy here is to promise dealers that Konark will never: have more than one showroom for every 30 or so dealers; locate showrooms within an existing dealer's sales area; permit showroom salespeople to bargain on price.

Students should undertake an analysis of the branch office vs. independent distributor issue. Disregarding the home state of Orissa, Konark has eight branch offices that will account for about Rs. 240 million in Konark sales revenue in 1990 and three independent distributors that will total about Rs. 160 million. (The single branch office in Orissa accounts for the other Rs. 400 million in Konark revenue and should be considered outside the present analysis.) If the eight branches were replaced by eight distributors, Konark would pay a 3% margin on the Rs. 240 million or Rs. 7.2 million. In contrast, the cost of operating the eight branch offices is given at about Rs. 10 million. Thus, it would seem to be to Konark's advantage to replace branches with distributors. Distributors also would accept risk of loss and may spread some of their overhead over products supplied by other manufacturers.

However, students should also present qualitative arguments in support of the branches. Branches offer much more control than do distributors. Branches probably provide better service and repair; production personnel at the branches should be better trained and should assemble sets having fewer defects. Finally, branches permit Konark to be one step closer to dealers and to better understand conditions in the field. On balance, Konark would be well advised to keep their existing branches but perhaps control their expenses more effectively to bring branch office costs more in line with distributor margins.

The instructor might end this discussion by posing a question raised at the very end of the case, "How does this distribution strategy combat the loss of the sales tax exemption in Orissa? This loss means a 'level playing field' as far as Konark and the larger national competitors are concerned." The answer is that all aspects of the new distribution strategy help combat the loss of the exemption. However, students ought to conclude that the burden of combating the loss should be limited not just to distribution. Instead, Konark's entire marketing and business strategy must be examined in a total effort to compete.

G. What short-term actions would you have Konark take to motivate and control its dealers?

Short-term actions should be consistent with Konark's distribution objectives and strategy and should accomplish one or more of several things: Dealers must be motivated, trained, rewarded, and controlled. Once recognition of this objective is achieved, the instructor might divide students into groups of three or four and give them 15 minutes to come up with a list of specific actions. Actions to motivate dealers can be either positive or negative in terms of reinforcement. The bulk of Konark activities probably should be oriented toward the first category. Reinforcements themselves can be either monetary or nonmonetary. For example, sales contests can be structured so that winners receive money, recognition, and praise. Quotas, when met, can result either in gifts, travel, framed certificates, or mention in a newsletter. Sales meetings can recognize salespeople or dealers that have met quarterly sales objectives set by Konark. A "mystery shopper" program might be started to recognize and reward outstanding performance.

Dealer personnel can be trained by capable Konark field representatives on successful sales techniques, Konark product knowledge, and competitors' products. Personnel can be trained on service procedures and dealers shown how to make money on service activities. Training can be conducted at dealer facilities or at Konark headquarters.

Dealers must be adequately rewarded. Students readily understand that the very nature of a retail margin means that it is "incentive compensation"—the more you sell, the more you earn. However, Konark also should devise one or more short-term programs each year that reward in the form of bonuses or free goods. And, again, not all rewards in short-term programs have to be monetary or economic based. Praise, recognition, and extra support often can be as effective as cash. Students should recognize that some negative or punishment activities also will motivate Konark dealers. If one or two dealers lose the Konark line for failing to live up to the terms and conditions identified in case Exhibit 4, then remaining dealers will take note and perhaps change their own behaviors. Remaining dealers must understand why Konark took such actions and should recognize the behaviors exhibited by the dropped dealers as unacceptable.

Actions to control dealers are perhaps the most difficult to devise and execute. Dealers are, after all independent businesses. To develop some control over dealers, Konark should begin by making its expectations about dealer performance absolutely clear. Expectations can be communicated by the "Terms and Conditions" document, visits to individual dealers, newsletters, sales meetings, objectives and quotas imposed on dealers, and informal conversations. Konark can achieve control most likely through the use of reward power and expert power. It probably cannot achieve control via coercion until sales of Konark products become so important to a dealer that a threat to pull the line away will be seen as substantive.

Summary

As summary, the instructor might present the learning objectives that began this note, to the extent that discussion relevant to the objectives actually took place in the classroom. The instructor might also draw parallels between the case and conditions in the West. Many high tech products (e.g., personal computers, home security systems, home entertainment centers, video camcorders) face similar conditions with respect to first time buyers as Konark. Many manufacturers employ multi channel strategies (e.g., IBM Product Centers vs. IBM sales at Sears; Sony's Gallery of Consumer Electronics in Chicago vs. their normal channels).

Finally, the instructor could use the case as a springboard to discuss the issue of marketing in LDCs. Just how different is it than marketing in developed countries? Should multinational firms in developed countries target selected LDCs or should they instead restrict efforts to the "Triad Markets" (U.S., Europe, and Japan) where cultures, life styles, business practices, and economies are so similar?

Overview of Business in India[*]

After a three-year economic reform beginning in 1991, India is beginning to show the great promise that many analysts have predicted for years. However, some people believe the changes taking place in India are minute and temporary. Nevertheless, between March 1993 and March 1994, about half f the $3.3 billion of foreign proposals approved by the Indian government came from the United States.

India's independence constrained growth of the private sector for many years. Quotas and high tariffs on imports stunted trade while many industries remained under the control of the public sector. The government, however, was able to pay all debts, keep inflation low, and maintain manageable budget deficits.

The business environment changed in the 1980s. In order to spur growth, the government borrowed heavily instead of freeing up the private sector. The budget cuts included subsidies, health, and education. This economic crisis also led to the privatization of many industries. Foreign investment was warmly welcomed and tariffs were slashed from 200% to the 65% in 1994.

India, the second largest potential market, is fast becoming as popular as China for foreign investments. Like China, Indian workers possess good skills, especially in the areas of science and software engineering. However, many companies believe India also has advantages over China. For example, India is relatively stable politically, has many shared values with the Western European and American companies, and primarily speaks English in the business arena. Furthermore, good marketing research, almost non-existent in China, is already in place in India.

Management techniques such as TQM, JIT, and cross-functional teams have also made their way into India's private sector. As salaries continue to rise, private companies will draw more talented managers into their ranks. Moreover, Indian companies are cutting costs and increasing efficiency through restructuring, often reducing layers of management from nine levels to four levels. Quality improvements have also brought about increases in export operations. These well-run companies become great partners for U.S. firms looking for joint ventures.

India's middle-class is growing, bringing millions of additional consumers. Brand loyalty is not a function of social class anymore. Even the poor have been affected by India's shift to consumerism. Moreover, the dramatic increase of households with televisions has provided new propaganda and advertising channels, speeding up the rate of change.

Despite all the changes, however, gross domestic product growth in the early 1990s was still slower than in the 1980s. Indeed, the rate of change in the Indian economy is being hindered by several factors. Distribution is a major problem. Infrastructure is in dire need of repair if it exists at all. Seaports are very slow, and there is a lack of electricity causing problems for many industries.

India's public sector absorbs 50% of the country's capital, yet produces just over 25% of its output. The government remains very bureaucratic in many ways. It has not privatized many government enterprises, restricts a variety of imports, and prohibits the layoffs of workers in most circumstances. Why? A number

---

[*] "Information for this synopsis comes from the following sources:
Lehner, Urban C. (1995), "India is Elbowing Into China's Limelight," *Wall Street Journal*, January 12, pp. A15.
Jacob, Rahul (1994), "India gets moving," *FORTUNE*, September 5, pp. 100-104.
"The state of reform in India," *The Economist*, August 6, 1994, p. 29-30.
"INDIA," *The Economist*, January 21, 1995, pp. 5-30.

of people are surprised to learn that Indians are very diligent in exercising their votes at election times. Unions and public sector employees play a big role in the government's inefficiency.

Many states are bankrupt. Problems with electric power, irrigation, transportation, health, and education are prevalent. If these issues are not addressed, quality and efficiency problems could be the result.

More importantly, some Indians are using the capital generated from increased foreign investment to restructure finances instead of using this cheaper borrowing for investing in real assets.

India's future as a foreign investment gold mine is in its government's hands. The 1991-1994 reforms were a start but more must be done in privatizing industries until quality and efficiency can increase. Mergers and acquisitions requests must be granted in order to encourage more investment. Reforms must continue to occur, but keeping the reformers in office long enough to make great strides is another challenge.

India is indeed ambitious for more foreign investment. India's citizens must demand the continued privatization of industry, cleaner politics, and improved education reforms in order to become a looming economic force. While all of these things take time, a new hope abounds in India that will draw more and more dollars from companies seeking prosperity in this budding marketplace.

CASE 5-6
POWRTRON CORPORATION*

Synopsis

Powrtron Corporation, a privately-held corporation, manufactured and sold electronic analog circuit modules, isolation amplifiers, and power converters. At the beginning of 1998, the company was grappling with constrained capacity that was resulting in late deliveries and customer dissatisfaction. The case is a classic marketing versus manufacturing situation in that each functional manager was blaming the other for the company's problems.

Teaching/Learning Objectives

Cross-functional integration is a much-talked about phenomenon in today's business community. This case focuses upon the interactions between marketing and manufacturing. Specifically, the case:

- Allows students access to the "numbers" that marketing and manufacturing utilize in making their individual department decisions,
- Encourages students to look at the trade-off between product development and existing product management, between customer prioritization and customer service, and among these four variables, and
- Highlights the importance of functional-level decisions on a company's strategic direction.

Discussion Questions

1. What is the problem faced by Powrtron?
2. What are the internal and external environmental factors that affect any decisions made by Powrtron?
3. What is Powrtron's competitive advantage?
4. Why does management view manufacturing as the strongest functional area? Why is marketing viewed as the weakest?
5. What should Allyson Shelton do, internally, to improve her organization's operations?
6. What is the appropriate mix of product development, existing product management, customer prioritization, and customer service at Powrtron?

Analysis

1. What is the problem faced by Powrtron?

This is a difficult question for students in that it is hard to say what came first, "the chicken or the egg." Some students might say that the main problem is the conflict between marketing and manufacturing, and if that problem was cleared up that other issues would readily be resolved. Others might say that the problem

---

* This teaching note was prepared by Victoria L. Crittenden, Boston College, and William F Crittenden, Northeastern University, as an aid to instructors using the case, "Powrtron Corporation."

is one of constrained capacity and that the constrained capacity is leading to the tension between marketing and manufacturing. Customer dissatisfaction is a problem, but seems to be the direct result of the constrained capacity. There might be concern that the company does not know the appropriate mix of products and markets and that they are producing too many products (not understanding the market potential of each). Still others might express concern that the major problem is the company's weak financial condition (i.e., retained earnings are negative $3.5 million, principally capitalized by the note payable to shareholders—the family shareholders also owned the land valued at $9 million so they were willing to continue to fund the organization as long as it was near breakeven due to the separately-owned land value). Basically, this is a multi-dimensional problem that can be construed in many ways.

2. **What are the internal and external environmental factors that affect any decisions made by Powrtron?**

A sample SWOT analysis is presented in Exhibit TN-1.

3. **What is Powrtron's competitive advantage?**

The case states that the company's "perceived" competitive advantage was the ability to provide customized, advanced technology products to quality conscious customers. There will probably be some debate as to whether or not this is really the case at Powrtron or if the company is really fooling itself here. One would think that quality conscious customers would also expect/demand on-time deliveries, which Powrtron is not capable of doing at this time. In reality, for example, the company's competitive advantage may be its small size that enables it to provide customized, small shipments to a few major accounts.

4. **Why does management view manufacturing as the strongest functional area? Why is marketing viewed as the weakest?**

There is probably some history associated with this view. Powrtron appears to have focused, over the years, upon the technological side of the product. This is especially evident when one looks at the company's perception of its competitive strength. As well, the fact that the company produces such a wide product offering leads one to believe that it must have a strong manufacturing presence—otherwise, how could such a small company manufacture so many products? Management's perception of marketing is probably what it is since the company did not seem to have relied upon marketing to get its products in the customers' hands. Basically, marketing's job was that of managing key accounts (who at the time were dissatisfied). Given that most of the "selling" was farmed out to manufacturer's reps, marketing's role was further diminished in the company. As well, initial contacts with Tier One accounts had been made by Bradley Keith (CEO) and were managed by the COO Allyson Shelton.

5. **What should Allyson Shelton do, internally, to improve her organization's operations?**

There is definitely a need to improve interdepartmental communications. The conflict between marketing and manufacturing has reached the point that it is detrimental to the firm's day-to-day operations. Student ideas might include: new organizational structure, weekly meetings, development of common goals and objectives, and a new compensation system that rewards on overall company profitability (not sales revenue or low costs). Powrtron is very functionally-focused. In today's cross-functional, team environment, one has to question whether this structure will be most appropriate in the long-term. Again, this is a classic case of managers looking at the success of their individual functional areas rather than the overall company. Students will even suggest that a move to a larger facility might make the cross-functional conflict worse given that the functions could be physically separated in a larger facility.

6. What is the appropriate mix of product development, existing product management, customer prioritization, and customer service at Powrtron?

Students can take a variety of approaches in answering this question. One approach would be to conduct a product analysis with market potential and firm expectations as the two key variables. Such an analysis might result in the following:

	Met	Unmet
Market Potential: Strong	PIN, DCT	DCZ
Market Potential: Debatable	IAAM, DCD, DCJ	DCX

Firm Sales Expectations

Another approach to looking at the product/customer situation is provided in Exhibit TN–2. This exhibit shows the amount of product capacity allocated to Tier Two accounts/product. Looking at capacity and products within this tier of accounts might help students better understand where the key business is occurring. For example, while there appears to be strong market potential for the PIN, very little of production is devoted to this product within the second tier of customers. However, combining this table with the previous 2 x 2 matrix shows us that dropping the DCX does very little for the company's capacity situation.

Additionally, outsourcing is an alternative to consider. For example, the market for the DCD and DCJ are questionable, with small volume and volatile margins. Combining the outsourcing for these two products, with outsourcing the DCX, frees up at least some production hours for more profitable lines (e.g., the PIN).

If students don't bring it up, the instructor needs to highlight the importance of account and product profitability when looking at the appropriate mix. However, the "how" of doing this is more difficult than the "what." Students should be pressed on how they would accomplish such prioritization, given differing production time and different product margins depending upon order size and/or account relationships. Students adept at computer simulations will probably jump on this and offer some interesting suggestions for "what-if" analysis on products and customers.

Teaching the Case

This is a great case for starting with a "What is the problem here?" opening. As discussed, this question should evoke a myriad of very interesting responses. Interestingly, students have tended to shy away from the discussion of the firm's financial condition. This may be due to the nature of the case in that it tends to lead the student down the cross-functional track. Students may honestly overlook the financial information, but the instructor would be remiss in not bringing it up. By looking at the financials, one has to wonder why the company is even in business. Given that it is in business, one then has to wonder if the owner is really in it for profit. This makes for an interesting twist to the case. The students generally end up attempting to "fix" the short-term issues of products and accounts and ignore the longer-term financial implications since those do seem somewhat irrelevant to the owner. But, this in itself throws some shadows over the company and management's attempt to resolve the short-term problems.

The identification of opportunities and threats has tended to be difficult for users of the case. Basically, there is not an abundance of either (which makes one wonder about why someone would want to conduct business in this industry).

The key in teaching the case is to get the students to think along the lines of products (typically manufacturing's purview) and account management (marketing's purview) and how these two can be meshed in such a way as to provide satisfaction to all parties—Shelton, Thomason, Stewart, and, most importantly, customers.

Epilogue

The initial step taken by Powrtron management was to schedule two management development seminars attended by all Powrtron middle managers. The major focus of the first seminar was "thinking strategically rather than short-term." Topics discussed included: administrative skills and leadership, strategy in a resource-constrained environment, the manager's planning role in a small business, and strategy in a technology environment. The second seminar focused on marketing strategy and business planning. In particular, the marketing strategy component centered on the pricing of new/existing products. The reasoning behind the two seminars was to bring all functional managers together to discuss management topics in general and then relate these topics to Powrtron. Since the seminars were led by an outsider, the expectation *[accurately so]* was that the "in-fighting" would be decreased and good discussion could take place. Additionally, the company began working with an expert in cross-functional decision making to facilitate, via a decision support system, account/product decisions.

The firm moved to a larger, more modern facility south of Boston in June of 1998. Sales for calendar year 1998 were expected to be around $10 million.

Exhibit TN-1 SWOT Analysis

Strengths:

- quality products
- product returns below industry average
- customized, advanced technology products
- manufacturing equipment was kept in good operating condition
- reliable, dedicated workforce
- manufacturing
- Tier 1 accounts (1/3 of sales come from 3 customers)

Weaknesses:

- "vintage" manufacturing equipment
- employees not interested in working additional (overtime) hours
- perceived capacity constraints
- conflict between sales/marketing and manufacturing; management team barely speaking to each other
- late deliveries
- morale problems (resulting from poor internal relations, exacerbated by delayed move announcement)
- marketing
- sales not meeting expectations
- unprofitable products
- issues regarding long-term viability of many of the firm's products
- financial concerns

Opportunities:

- new product development (e.g., DCZ)
- derived demand high (e.g., virtual explosion in CRT devices)
- international marketplace

Threats:

- mature market
- highly competitive market, major players both internationally and in the U.S.

Exhibit TN–2

	Exhibit 5			Exhibit 7				Exhibit 8		
	Unit Volume	Total $ Sale	Average Price	Variable Cost/Unit	Setup Cost Per Run	Production Time/Unit (hours)	Setup Time Per Run (hours)	Yearly Production Hours	Percent
PIN	2701	$1,059,091	$392	$75.00	$5.20	1.00	0.25	2701.00	0.095104562
IAAM	5543	$509,956	$92	$35.00	$4.15	0.60	0.20	3325.80	0.117104314
DCD	398	$66,466	$167	$65.00	$4.15	1.00	0.20	398.00	0.014013927
DCT	1841	$489,706	$266	$75.00	$7.25	1.50	0.35	2761.50	0.09723482
DCJ	917	$80,696	$88	$65.00	$4.15	1.00	0.20	917.00	0.032288369
DCX	80	$9,280	$116	$45.00	$6.25	1.05	0.30	84.00	0.002957713
DCZ	13694	$1,410,482	$103	$55.00	$6.25	1.33	0.30	18213.02	0.641296295
		3,625,677					1.8	28400.32	1

Setup costs appear to run about $20.80 per hour

# CASE 5-7
TAURUS HUNGARIAN RUBBER WORKS[*]

SYNOPSIS

Taurus has recently become a share-holding corporation although it was once Hungary's state-owned rubber monopoly. It is a large firm by Hungarian standards but it ranks thirtieth in sales amongst the world's leading rubber companies. In 1988 its sales were only 3.5% of those obtained by Goodyear, while its profits were 2.7% of those secured by Goodyear. Size, however, does not guarantee success in the rubber business. In recent years the industry has experienced relatively slow growth due to low automobile sales growth, the creation of longer-lasting tires which lowers the amount of replacement demand, a lower use of the automobile for long distance travel, and the entry of certain forms of plastics as substitutes for rubber in many of its original applications. In response to these trends various strategies have been employed. Manufacturers have tried some or all of the following:

1. Merged or have engaged in joint ventures and cooperative arrangements to obtain certain administrative and marketing economies.
2. Created new and extremely efficient and highly automated manufacturing facilities.
3. Sought less competitive niches within the tire industry.
4. Diversified into other related or non-related businesses.

Despite the existence of nearby natural growth markets in Africa and the Middle East, Taurus has basically determined that the tire industry presents a very hostile environment. Michelin et Cie, now the world's largest tire producer lost $1.5 billion between 1980 and 1984. Continental Gummi-Werke AG and Pirelli are additional strong competitors in the European market and they have respectively acquired General Tire and the Armstrong Tire Company. In the face of this competition Taurus has already retreated to the industry's commercial tire segment and has more recently decided that it must pursue a strategy of growth through joint ventures, licensing arrangements, and other forms of cooperation. Because the firm is financially stable although not a stellar performer, top management realizes it can pursue the accomplishment of "strategic alliances" with care and deliberate execution.

Taurus currently operates through four divisions with factories in Budapest, Nyiregyhaza, Szeged, Vac, and Mugi. It also is engaged in a number of joint ventures. Sales have increased annually and international sales have been emphasized more and more over the years. In 1989 the Tire Division generated about 41.4% of the company's total revenues while the Technical Rubber and Trade Divisions produced respective revenue shares of 34.8% and 22.7%.

After reviewing the company's product strengths and weaknesses Taurus's strategic manager is about to suggest to the Technical Rubber Division's Vice President that his division should be restructured into at least three new strategic business units. One unit would serve automobile manufacturers with V-belts, profiles and engine seals, another unit would serve the bus and truck industry with bellows and rubber springs, and a third strategic business unit would target its rubber sheeting for use in the construction industry. The case reproduces many of the materials used by the company's strategic manager to help him

---

[*] This teaching note was developed by the case author.

clarify his thinking about the creation of Taurus's new SBU's. The case also attempts to capture his thought processes as well as the dilemmas he faced as he explored the different options at his disposal.

Teaching/Learning Objectives

Because the Taurus Hungarian Rubber Works has already decided that it must pursue a strategy of diversified growth, the case deals more with issues in the areas of strategy implementation rather than strategic choice. A modest amount of class time can be spent analyzing the nature of world-wide competition in the rubber industry and why Taurus feels it must diversify away from the industry's tire segment. An additional amount of time can be spent debating whether its strategy of accepting "...any type of reasonable alternative or combination that might be offered" will lead to either unprofitable chaos or lucrative growth. The case is most interesting, however, through its presentation of the actual materials used by Taurus' strategic manager as he wrestles with the problems of creating saleable and synergistic strategic business units for his company.

Analysis

A number of fairly standard analyses can be performed on this case. A few analyses should put into relief the strengths and weaknesses possessed by the Taurus Hungarian Rubber Company to establish the basic external and internal conditions from which the firm can launch its strategy of diversified growth. Although the firm appears to be committed to a growth strategy, an analysis should be conducted to determine if a growth strategy ought to be implemented. If such proves to be the case which alternative growth strategy should the firm employ? Should these growth strategies be employed across the board or should they be pursued selectively? It appears from the case that top management is indifferent as to whether the firm's growth comes from either concentric or conglomerate diversifications even though these two strategies differ as to their risks and resource needs.

Financial Analysis

Although some of the company's sales growth has come from inflation the company has generated a respectable profit over the past three years. Table 1 shows that Taurus' costs have been kept under control and bottom line results have improved since 1987, while the ration analysis in Table 2 finds the firm operating at an acceptable level of liquidity. Moreover the company's trends are basically stable which is a condition that is supportive of implementing a growth strategy. A direct examination of Taurus' Balance Sheet in Appendix B reveals that 72.9% of its plant and equipment has been depreciated, which while common for Hungarian firms, indicates that its equipment is quite old and that these assets may be of little value to a potential investor. More importantly for the short term is the fact that the company's long term debt service will be 314.3 million Forints in 1989 and 242.1 million Forints worth of debt is due in 1990.

Divisional Performance Analysis

Data are presented in the case which facilitate a productivity analysis of three of the company's four divisions. The inclusion of an analysis of the Trade Division would produce a major distortion because it operates with unassigned assets therefore creating a false reading of its revenue rate of return.

Table 3 presents each division's revenue rates-of return for 1988 and 1989. This analysis shows that the Tire Division obtained a dramatic improvement in its per employee revenue from 1988 to 1989 while employee productivity remained basically the same in the Technical Rubber and Machines and Molds Divisions. This revenue improvement was obtained through the division's 29.7% between-year increase in sales thus indicating a high break-even point for the division. The Technical Rubber Division obtains its very high rate of revenue productivity per asset due to the lower costs of its assets, while simultaneously producing sales revenues which are about the same as those produced by the Tire Division. In this regard the Technical Rubber Division is more labor intensive than the Tire Division and therefore its costs are more variable but less amenable to economies of scale.

In this analysis the Machine and Molds Division does not appear to be very productive. This may be a false conclusion as the division's output is essential to the productivity of the company's two other manufacturing divisions. In this regard the Machines and Molds Division should be considered a cost center rather than a revenue center.

Industry Attractiveness and Company Business Strengths

The use of the General Electric Nine-Cell Business Portfolio Matrix can be used to summarize the attractiveness of the general rubber industry (as opposed to analyzing the attractiveness of alternative rubber applications) from the perspective of a firm already participating in the industry versus the business strengths Taurus brings to the industry. Looking first at the industry itself several factors make it especially unattractive although this unattractiveness itself will act as a barrier to the entry of additional industry participants.

Although it does not appear that the industry's purchasing behavior is seasonal it is known that its products are investment goods when used as tires for trucks and automobiles as well as for applications in the construction industry. Accordingly, the industry's products are subject to swings in the business cycle. Investment costs are high for plant improvements, plants are constructed or improved in large chunks while economies of scale appear to exist for those already in the industry. Based on the rubber consumption rates displayed in case Table 2, overall demand will increase an average of 2.3% per year from 1990 to 1992, although large demand increases are projected for Latin America, Western Europe, Africa and the Middle East, and the Asian socialist countries. Compared to other industries, as shown in Gyula Bosnyak's analysis in case Table 10, the rubber industry features low growth while case Table 5 demonstrates (weighted) average 1988 profits of 3.2% for the seven listed firms.

Competitive intensity is very strong for all firms in the rubber industry as no markets appear to be protected and true international competitive prevails. While it has been mentioned that the industry's relative unattractiveness acts as an entry barrier, other barriers are in existence. It is unlikely that a radically new tire will be created as was the case for Michelin. Therefore it would be difficult for a new firm to obtain a foothold in the industry with a product which is substantially differentiated from those already available from established manufacturers. These established producers also act as another barrier as they probably possess economies independent of size.

The industry's barriers to exit are also quite high as the production technology is unique and there would be few buyers of unwanted tire-making capacity. Additionally, as was the experience with Bridgestone's purchase of Firestone Tire and Rubber, the purchase of an existing plant is very expensive as those plants are probably very inefficient and substantial reinvestment must be made in them. The case does not give any indication of the nature of the rubber industry's social, environment, legal, and human impacts. However, it could be imagined these impacts are slightly negative as the by-products and wastes of the rubber making process are noxious and used tires are difficult to salvage.

We can assume Taurus's market share is relatively low in overall rubber sales although it dominates the rotary hose market and its PALMA camping gear has a 15.0% world market share. Compared to the industry's 1988 profits of 3.2%, the company's profits for that year of 2.4% are below par in a low par industry. It cannot be deduced from the case whether Taurus can be price competitive but the age of its plant indicates that it is probably operating with equipment that is not as efficient as that being used by the leading rubber companies. The firm's reputation for quality is not known although quality improvements are one of the goals listed in its strategy statement.

It could be assumed that Taurus has superior knowledge of Hungarian and CMEA customers as well as at least an average knowledge of its customers in Western Europe. Overall the firm is probably competitively weak because of the age of its equipment while at least its in-house tire-making expertise is inadequate as the company is currently employing a licensing arrangement with Firestone to produce its new supersingle truck tire. The caliber of Taurus's top management must be judged as being better than average as they have guided the firm through some very turbulent waters and they have been pioneers in the use of strategic management within an economy which had scorned such capitalist practices.

Taurus finds itself in the zone where a Harvest or Divest strategy (or a Rebuild and Reposition strategy in exceptional cases employing some type of turnaround approach) is recommended. Given Taurus has already decided to seek both related and unrelated strategic alliances, it is in the process of implementing a Rebuilding or Reposition strategy within the context of the GE matrix's terminology.

Corporate Strategic Fit

Thompson and Strickland have advanced a schema which employs two dimensions for judging the organization's strategic situational fitness—the industry's attractiveness, as measured by its rate of market growth, versus the firm's relative competitive strength. Five products are in highly attractive markets while possessing weak competitive positions; three products are strongly competitive and reside in highly attractive markets; two products are in weak competitive positions and reside in unattractive markets while one product is a strong competitor in an unattractive market. Overall, however, Taurus' portfolio puts the firm in a weak competitive position in very attractive markets. The sequentially attractive strategies it should pursue are:

1. Reformulation of single-business concentration strategy
2. Merger with another firm in the same business
3. Vertical integration (forward or backward if it strengthens competitive position)
4. Diversification
5. Abandonment.

Based on this analysis Taurus should first ask itself why its current market approach has resulted in a weak competitive position given the relative attractiveness of the industry, and then ask itself what must be done to become an effective competitor. If Taurus determines that it lacks the resources to become a successful competitor it should consider merging or joint venturing with another company which possesses the requisite resources. This should be done, however, only after it has attempted to strengthen its position on its own. It has the time and financial stability to do this and the industry's rapid development presents management with a situation which is generally munificent and charitable.

Strengths, Weaknesses, Opportunities and Threats

A SWOT analysis, presented in Figure 1, summarizes the various elements operating in the Taurus case. In this analysis the Opportunities and Threats have been imported directly from "A Socioeconomic Note on

Hungary in 1990" with additional materials added to reflect further environmental data presented in the case.

Discussion Questions

1. **What are the key success factors or driving forces in the rubber industry? Does Taurus possess those factors? Can the company acquire them through the strategic alliances they are attempting to obtain?**

If a firm wants to compete in the tire segment of the rubber industry it must be able to compete internationally, it must operate at high volumes with highly efficient plants, and it must obtain access to each country's market channels so that its tires can be sold in the more profitable replacement tire market. Even the largest tire firms, however, have found it difficult to be profitable in this industry, so all have diversified to some degree.

Taurus, nonetheless, has already decided it cannot compete head-on in the tire industry. It has chosen to compete in the less competitive commercial tire market while simultaneously searching out alternative applications of its rubber production capabilities. In this regard they have created a number of products positioned in highly attractive markets. Although these products have been placed into potentially lucrative markets many of them are competitively weak and it is these weaknesses which Taurus is attempting to overcome through strategic alliances. Whether these strategic alliances can be obtained is a function of the availability of potential strategic partners, the choices those partners have available to them, and the attractions Taurus has to offer.

2. **What are the growth areas in the rubber industry?**

There are two dimensions to the question of growth in the rubber industry. One dimension deals with the growth in new applications for rubber while the other dimension deals with new and developing geographic markets. While undoubtedly new rubber applications will be found in the future, rubber itself has often been replaced by various forms of plastics. Instead of rubber sponges, many sponges are now made of soft plastic. Many athletic shoe parts are plastic instead of rubber, and the functions performed by the rubber sheeting Taurus wishes to sell in the construction industry can also be performed by vinyl sheeting. Overall, then, rubber is fighting a battle against the substitution effect so overall growth in this area may be quite limited.

The greater growth potential resides in rubber's geographic spread. As other areas of the world become wealthier and automobile consumption increases, the use of tires will correspondingly increase. Additionally, due to the poorer road conditions found in many African, Middle Eastern, and South American countries, the rate of tire replacement should be much higher. These areas, then are the areas for today's tire manufacturers to stake their future claims.

3. **Taurus's Director of Strategic Management is in the process of creating new strategic business units. How should this be accomplished? Is the Director going about this process in the proper fashion?**

A strategic business unit is the grouping together of a number of businesses which share important common strategic elements. These common elements could be an overlapping group of competitors, a closely related strategic mission, a common need to compete globally, an ability to accomplish integrated strategic planning, common success factors, or technologically related growth opportunities. In creating or adopting this structural form, SBU's serve to provide diversified companies with a way to rationalize the organization of many different businesses as well as providing cohesive direction to separate but related areas engaged in by the total enterprise.

It appears the company may be applying "window dressing" to a group of products rather than creating units which can be internally controlled while being aggressively competitive in the market place. Before SBU's are created, a firm should carefully consider the advantages and disadvantages of this organizational form so that the real benefits of the SBU form can be realized. Figure 2 provides a summary of those advantage and disadvantages.

4. **Taurus stated it would enter into alliances "...whether they were related or unrelated to the rubber industry. The only real criteria for accepting an alliance would be its profitability and growth potential." What are the advantages and disadvantages to Taurus of adopting this particular posture or attitude towards its diversification effort?**

The posture of considering any and all types of alliances demonstrates that the company will go to great lengths to improve its profitability and growth. This posture also means that Taurus will not overlook any ventures, industries, or product lines which may ultimately be very successful. Given the number of alternative alliances presented to Taurus, however, this posture could at best lead to a default strategy of diversified growth. This is a more risky strategy to pursue than concentric growth or at worst an agglomeration of products or businesses which lack any degree of synergy in corporate administration, production technology, common customer base, or marketing channels. Based on a Thompson and Strickland Corporate Strategy Fit analysis, most of Taurus products are situated in attractive industries but those products lack competitive strength. At this juncture the company needs to reformulate its product strategy to improve the competitiveness of its products. Should they be unsuccessful at accomplishing this, Taurus should next attempt a merger or joint venture with a company in the same business in which it is currently engaged. A conglomerate diversification strategy should be pursued only after the company has been unable to find backward and forward vertical integrations which strengthen its competitiveness.

5. **The Taurus Hungarian Rubber Company appears to be predisposed towards accomplishing joint ventures. What are the advantages and disadvantages of engaging in joint ventures? Should Taurus employ joint venturing as its first method for increasing its competitiveness in various markets?**

A firm may not have the financial strength, management skills, market access, or product quality needed to take advantage of the situation being faced. In recent years it has become increasingly appealing for domestic firms to join with foreign businesses. In the case for Hungarian firms, many lack either capital, a sophisticated product line, marketing skills, and efficient manufacturing operation, or management know-how to be competitive in international markets. Therefore a joint venture may provide an almost instantaneous injection of the requisite resources for company success. While joint-venturing allows a business to extend its strengths into competitive arenas it might be hesitant to enter alone, or allows it to compensate for serious competitive deficiencies, joint ventures limit the amount of discretion possessed by each venture partner while other problems of strategic and operational control can arise. Moreover, just as the risks are shared in a joint venture, so are the profits derived from the venture.

The company should be selective regarding the businesses which it joint ventures, but more importantly, it should first attempt to improve its competitive position through internal development methods before seeking outside aid and therefore ultimately diminished profits, control, and organizational creativeness.

Additional Readings

Berg, S., and P. Friedman, "Corporate Courtship and Successful Joint Ventures," California Management Review, (Spring 1980), pp.85-91.

Bettis, R.A., and W.K. Hall, "The Business Portfolio Approach—Where It Falls Down in Practice," *Long Range Planning,* Vol. 16, No. 2 (April 1983), pp.95-i 04.

David, F.R., "How Do We Choose Among Alternative Growth Strategies?" *Managerial Planning,* Vol. 33, No. 4 (January-February 1985), pp. 14-17, 22.

Hall, W.K., "SBU's: Hot, New Topic in the Management of Diversification," *Business Horizons,* Vol. 21, No. 1 (February, 1978), pp. 17-25.

Exhibit TN–1   Costs and Profits as a Percent of Sales

	1987	1988	1989
Basic activities	62.9	64.5	72.2
Non-basic activities	7.1	35.5	27.8
Total revenues	100%	100%	100.0%
Direct costs	71.1	69.3	66.9
Indirect costs	25.1	26.3	27.7
Production and operating costs	96.2	95.6	94.5
Before tax profit	3.8	4.4	5.5
Taxes	1.7	2.0	2.4
After tax profit	2.1	2.4	3.1

Interpretation: Basic activities have increased their share of company sales and direct costs have fallen 5.9% since 1987. Although indirect costs have risen 8.0% over the safe time period pretax profits have increased 44.7% as a percent of revenues since 1987 due to lower overall production and operating costs.

Exhibit TN–2   Ratio Analysis

	1987	1988	1989
Current ratio	2.24	1.90	1.78
Quick ratio	1.18	1.10	1.10
Total asset turnover	1.75	1.61	1.60
Fixed assets turnover	2.32	2.09	2.19
Inventory turnover	4.37	4.67	4.78
Rate of return on assets	3.7	3.9	5.0
Working capital	3217.0	3166.0	3330.6
Inventory to working capital	0.85	0.89	0.87

Interpretation: The analysis shows a picture of good overall health. Although the firm's liquidity ratios have fallen slightly since 1987 its inventory turnover has increased slightly and its rate of return on assets has improved 35.1% in the past three years.

Exhibit TN-3 Revenue Return Rates by Fixed Assets and Employees (In Billions of Forints)

	Tires		Technical Rubber		Machines & Molds	
Revenue Returned by:	1988	1989	1988	1989	1988	1989
Gross fixed assets	1.27	1.55	2.35	2.58	0.79	0.83
Net fixed assets	2.25	2.83	5.41	6.41	1.72	1.79
Employee	1.65	2.13	1.66	1.87	0.38	0.44

Interpretations: The revenue generated by each employee within the Tire Division has increased dramatically from 1988 to 1989 while employee productivity has remained basically the same in the Technical Rubber and Machines and Molds Divisions. The Technical Rubber Division obtains a very high rate of revenue productivity per asset due mainly to the lower cost of its assets while it simultaneously produces sales revenues which are roughly comparable to those obtained by the Tire Division.

The Machines and Molds Division does not appear to be very productive based on this analysis but it must be remembered that it is an important in-house supplier to the work performed by the company's two main divisions.

Exhibit TN-4

Long-Term Industry Attractiveness

+ Market size
- Market growth rate
- Historical profit margins
- Projected profit margins
- Competitive intensity
- Cyclicality
+ Economies of scale
- Technological requirements
- Capital requirements
- Social, environmental, legal, and human impacts
+ Barriers to entry
- Barriers to exit

Business Strength/Competitive Position

- Relative market share in tire industry
+ Relative market share in rotary hose market
+ Relative market share in camping gear market
- Profit margins relative to competitors
- Ability to compete on price
o Ability to compete on quality
+ Knowledge of Hungarian customer and market
+ Knowledge of CMEA customer and market
o Knowledge of West European customer and market
- Competitive strengths and weaknesses
- Technological capability
+ Caliber of top management

Exhibit TN–5 SWOT Analysis

Strengths

- Company is financially stable.
- Top management appears to be skilled in strategic management. Company appears to be flexible and Willing to change.
- Firm has been able to keep its costs in line despite high Hungarian inflation.
- Company has been able to increase the revenue productivity of its Tire Division personnel.
- Has been able to increase its international sales.
- Company has experience with joint ventures.
- Company has a number of products in very attractive industries/markets.
- Company has products which are strong competitors in highly attractive industries/markets.
- Company is in a strong bargaining position in rotary hoses, waterproofing sheets, and machines and molds.
- Recently expanded company's all-steel radial truck tire operation.

Weaknesses

- Company operating with antiquated plant in an industry characterised by high capital intensity.
- Two major products, camping equipment and bias tires, operate in unattractive industries.
- Seven of eleven products are in weak competitive positions.
- Company does not seem to be able to create its own new products and processes.
- Indirect costs have increased as a percent of revenues.
- 314.3 million HUFS long term debt due; 242.1 million HUFS due in 1990.
- Company losing market share to new Hungarian, domestic rubber producers.

Opportunities

- New sources of equity and debt capital available.
- Hungarian government is working very hard to help its firms find foreign markets for their products.
- Specialized banks exist to help foreign investment and joint ventures in firms like Taurus.
- Hungarian government extremely cooperative and has gone the furthest of the Soviet block nations to attract foreign investment.
- Hungary and Taurus are natural stepping-stones to the larger markets of Poland, East Germany, and the Soviet Union.
- Positive "word-of-mouth" publicity about the skills and abilities of Hungarian managers could help attract foreign investment to Taurus.
- Western technology now more freely accessible.
- Taurus situated near some of the fastest growing rubber consuming countries.

Threats

- Hungarian political environment in flux.
- Possibility of counter-reform may dampen Taurus management's enthusiasm to implement any necessary changes.
- Strong, foreign rubber companies could enter the Hungarian market.
- Many foreign markets already being supplied by advanced rubber products and technologies.
- Hungarian economy a low growth economy and is experiencing stagflation.
- Hungarian market relatively small and language unique compared to other countries which could be entered into by foreign investors.
- Bank lending capacity may be restricted.
- Only half of foreigners' salaries can be taken out of the country.
- Taurus could be "used" by foreign investors.
- Foreign manufacturers may consider Hungarian operations to be of minor importance and therefore will not implement their best products or most advanced technology in any joint venture operation.
- Firm competes in an industry which is basically unattractive for all but the strongest competitors.
- Plastics serve as reasonable substitutes for rubber in many applications.

Exhibit TN-2 Advantages and Disadvantages of the Strategic Business Unit Organization Structure

Advantages	Disadvantages
• Provides a logical means for decentralizing a diversified organization.	• May raise administrative overhead costs by requiring the duplication of staff functions at the corporate level and within each business unit.
• Places authority closer to each business's unique environment.	• Organization must decide which decisions can be decentralized and which decisions must be retained by top management.
• Allows each business unit to organize around a set of activities and functional requirements necessary for the accomplishment of the unit's purpose.	• Can lead to excessive inter-SBU rivalry for corporate resources or top management's attention.
• Allows the organization's top management to deal with corporate strategy rather than business strategy.	• Autonomous SBU's frustrates the coordination of related activities which are being accomplished within each SBU.
• Places clear profit and loss accountability on units capable of creating profits and losses.	• Top management becomes heavily dependent upon the abilities and results of each SBU's management.
• Allows top management to compare performance of SBU's and their management.	• Corporate management may lose touch with the situations faced by the SBU's.
• Improves coordination among products or businesses facing similar strategic issues.	• It may be difficult to create a number of homogeneous SBU's.
• Facilitates the creation of distinct strategies and in-depth strategic planning.	• Increases the number of organizational levels.
	• SBU's may pursue goals that differ from corporate goals and philosophies.

Note: All material on strategic business units in these case notes has been adapted from A. A. Thompson and A.J. Strickland, *Strategic Management: Concepts and Cases.* Plano TX. Business Publications, 1987, p. 220; and J.G. Thomas, *Strategic Management: Concepts, Practices, and Cases.* NY: Harper & Row, 1988, p. 270.

Epilogue (August 28, 1991)

Economic conditions in Hungary were very turbulent in 1990. No new strategic alliances were formed by Gyula Bosnyak and several of Taurus' largest customers went bankrupt. Tire sales fell but sales to the company's hard currency markets increased 5.0%. The Engineering and Molds Division was spun off and the company established the strategic business units of Tires, Technical Rubber Goods, and Trade with complete autonomy of business authority and accountability, under the support of Hungary's State Property Agency the company will be completely privatized with the pnvatization process beginning in early 1991.

Dr. Ilona Tatai took her scheduled retirement as Taurus' President and Dr. Laszlo Palotas was voted into the offices of President and CEO. A new line of *point* 7 farm tires was introduced at the "Salon

International de la Machine Agricole in Paris, and Taurus also showed its products at trade shows in Brighton, UK, and Moscow.

Balance Sheet (In thousands of HUFs)

Assets

	1990	1989
Current Assets		
Cash and bank deposits	102,600	50,317
Accounts receivable	3,563,395	3,596,106
Other receivables	244,964	116,793
Inventories	3,099,231	2,888,307
Other current assets	831,243	675,284
Investments	724,729	263,266
Total Current Assets	8,566,162	7,590,073
Gross value of fixed assets	11,566,661	9,440,693
Less: Accumulated depreciation	4,942,733	4,687,741
Net value of fixed assets	6,623,928	4,752,952
Capital projects	354,211	541,618
Total Fixed Assets	6,987,139	5,294,570
Total Assets	15,433,301	12,884,643

Liabilities and Equity

	1990	1989
Current Liabilities		
Short term loans	2,050,808	1,443,950
Accounts payable	2,584,062	2,072,757
Accrued expenses	143,338	151,601*
Provisions for taxes	258,813	34,658
Long Term Debt Service	523,987	314,361
Other Near-Term Liabilities	676,465	242,188
Total Current Liabilities	6,237,473	4,259,515
Provisions and non-current liabilities	1,970	363
Long Term loans	2,290,403	1,815,716
Equity and retained earnings	7,135,769	6,351,636
Other funds	173,743	182,406
Profit after tax	52,429	639,819
Total Equity and Funds	7,014,455	6,809,049
Total Liabilities and Equity	15,544,301	12,884,643

Income Statement

	1990	*1989*
Operating Revenue	13,221,652	14,918,563
Non-Operating Revenue	4,968,239	5,747,068
Net Revenue from Sales	18,189,981	20,665,631
Production and Operating Costs		
Direct cost of sales	12,060,638	13,819,638
Depreciation	487,832	457,832
Interest paid	1,055,003	715,003
Cost of R&D	173,667	203,125
Other indirect costs	4,103,952	4,077,852
Net other income/expense	254,986	260,986
Total Production and Opr. Costs	18,135,978	19,534,436
Profit before Taxes	54,003	1,131,195
Repayment of government contribution	1,574	2,641
Profit tax		488,735
Profit after Tax	52,429	639,819

USD = 61.4492 HUFs December 31, 1990

Part 6

Marketing Program Development

CASE 6-1
DUNKIN' DONUTS BAGEL BLITZ[*]

Synopsis

Dunkin' Donuts was attempting to transform its image from a quality donut seller to a bagel expert. However, two weeks before its US$25 million advertising campaign was to begin, the company was experiencing problems in its bagel supply chain. Chris Booras, in charge of purchasing, had to make a recommendation—the results of which, he knew, had long-term ramifications for his and his team's reputation with the parent organization and the franchise community.

Video Summary

Eddie Binder, Vice President of Integrated Marketing at Dunkin' Donuts, provides an overview of why bagels are important to Dunkin' Donuts and describes how the company is supporting the bagel introduction. The video starts with a few statistics about the bagel business (as typical with much marketing research, the numbers vary slightly from the industry figures provided in the case). Mr. Binder then describes the integrated marketing program that Dunkin' Donuts has developed: quality product, store support, and advertising. The video segment ends with a sampling of the ads that introduced the bagel rollout. The video runs about five minutes and is a great opening for the class.

Teaching/Learning Objectives

The case focuses upon a well-known company that is ready to roll out an elaborate, new product marketing program. Unfortunately, due to supply problems, the entire rollout is under question. Specifically, the case allows students the opportunity to:

- see the important connections that are fundamental components of the value chain,
- consider the risks associated with new product entry—particularly when there is such heavy reliance on an external partner,
- address issues of conflict between partners in an alliance, as well as what appears to be some internal conflict that was not allowed to come to surface early in the product development process, and
- make a recommendation in a situation that has strong senior management involvement.

Discussion Questions

1. Assess Dunkin' Donuts' strengths, weaknesses, opportunities, and threats.
2. How important are bagels to the Dunkin' Donuts business?
3. Provide an overview of the bagel market.
4. Evaluate the alternatives available to Booras and his bagel team.
5. What is your recommendation?

---

[*] This teaching note was prepared by Victoria L. Crittenden, Boston College, and William F. Crittenden, Northeastern University, as an aid to instructors using the case, "Dunkin' Donuts Bagel Blitz."

6. Is there anything that Dunkin' Donuts management could have done to avoid the current situation?

Analysis

1. **Assess Dunkin' Donuts' strengths, weaknesses, opportunities, and threats.**

Exhibit TN-1 provides a sample SWOT analysis.

2. **How important are bagels to the Dunkin' Donuts business?**

The bagel business, as a whole, is of substantial importance. With a mid-1990s business amounting to US$2.5 billion, Dunkin' Donuts would be remiss to not see the industry's importance. There was no doubt that bagels were becoming an important food item (with possible expansion beyond the breakfast food segment). As no dominant market player had emerged, a strong player in the market had much to gain in terms of dollars and share. With geographic concentration in only a few states, the 2,700 Dunkin' Donuts North American outlets would give the company immediate access to new bagel consumers.

In examining this importance, students should look at the various players involved in the Dunkin' Donuts bagel business: Chris Booras and the marketing team, Dunkin' Donuts senior management (Kussell, Shafer), franchisees, and Harold's Bakery Products.

Booras and the marketing team: Booras feels that his and his team's reputations are on the line with the bagel rollout. The company had spent $10 million developing the product and has planned a $25 million advertising campaign. Bagels are very important to this group!

Senior management: Naturally, bagels are important to Kussell, Shafer, and senior management at Allied Domecq since the long-term growth of the company is dependent upon new products. The company has expanded geographically and while it could open new stores, the company already had over 3,200 shops. Further penetration of the donut market seems risky as a long-term growth option. Thus, product development (as with the bagels) is of prime importance to senior management. Additionally, bagel shops were beginning to steal market share from the more traditional players in the breakfast food segment (e.g., Dunkin' Donuts).

Franchisees: By August of 1996 Dunkin' Donuts had already begun to introduce bagels into its fast-track stores. Structural changes (at a franchisee cost of $25,000) had taken place at these facilities in order to accommodate the bagel cases. It would be difficult to undo these structural changes within the shops. As well, franchisees were probably feeling the need to battle the bagel shops that were opening across the street from them. Bagels were very important to the franchisees.

Harold's: Initially, it would seem that the Dunkin' Donuts bagel business would be very important to Harold's—particularly since it had begun construction of the production lines. However, there does not appear to be a penalty clause in the contract between Harold's and Dunkin' Donuts (other than a relationship termination agreement). So, while Harold's might lose the Dunkin' contract, it would probably secure another retail outlet for its bagel line given the long-term supplier contracts that were being signed. So, one might question the relative importance to Harold's of this particular piece of business.

3. **Provide an overview of the bagel market.**

- Size/Market Potential: $2.5 billion industry by mid-1990s
- Number of Retail Establishments: 700

- Growth Rate: greater than 30%
- Major Players: Bruegger's, Manhattan Bagel, Einstein Brothers (no dominant player)
- Types of Outlets: retail shops and bakeries = 44%, in-store bakeries = 26%, food service = 20%, wholesale bakeries (selling frozen bagels) = 10%
- Geographic Concentration: 70% of bagel stores were in New York, New Jersey, Florida, & California
- Product Characteristics: quality, flavor variety, augmented product of cream cheese, low-fat, freshness, homemade feel
- Industry Consolidation: Einstein Brothers had acquired Noah's, Manhattan Bagel and Specialty Bakeries had formed an alliance

4. **Evaluate the alternatives available to Booras and his bagel team.**

Exhibit TN–2 provides an overview of the pro/con analysis that the students should undertake in their evaluation of the alternatives. Students might add additional alternatives, such as a lawsuit against Harold's. The pros/cons of additional options need to be carefully evaluated along with the three alternatives presented in the case.

5. **What is your recommendation?**

Students' recommendations will vary. Students need to address the process Booras will go through once he decides what to recommend. Who are the major players in the recommendation? What concerns will these major players have about the recommendation? How will Booras (and others) address the concerns? What are the risks involved with the recommendation?

6. **Is there anything that Dunkin' Donuts management could have done to avoid the current situation?**

A major item that comes up with this issue is Dunkin' Donuts' decision to work solely with one supplier. There needs to be a brief discussion about Dunkin' Donuts placing "all of its eggs in one basket." The pros/cons of such a supplier decision need to be addressed. For example, a positive aspect of working closely with one supplier is the ability to be hands-on with respect to the final product. Since this was of extreme importance to Dunkin' Donuts, working solely with Harold's allows Dunkin' Donuts to exert some control over production and ultimate quality. On the flip side, we see the issue that the case is centered around—lack of supply for Dunkin' Donuts to meet its marketing program obligations. Some students will suggest that Dunkin' Donuts should have worked with a few suppliers—the instructor needs to find out how Dunkin' Donuts would ensure "same" product across the U.S. with different bagel producers. Would the same recipe result in the same standard bagel product—or would there be taste, texture, size, etc. differences?

Purchasing and operations students will probably delve into the fact that purchasing and quality assurance folks had expressed concern about the aggressive rollout schedule. However, these concerns were largely ignored and were overshadowed by senior management's drive to start a new fiscal year with a bang. An interesting discussion can take place around the issue of how functional-level middle managers can adequately present concerns to upper management. Greater involvement of all functional areas could have helped avoid the current supply problem. It appears that purchasing and quality assurance would have moved at a much slower pace on the planned rollout.

Teaching the Case

The video is a great way to start the class. As discussed in the video overview, the short five-minute clip provides a great look at what Dunkin' Donuts has done to make the bagel successful. Since the video addresses the issues asked in Questions 2 & 3, the instructor may not need to address these questions directly. If the video opens the class, the instructor might then ask the students to step back and identify the strengths, weaknesses, opportunities, and threats at Dunkin' Donuts. If the video is not used, the SWOT works well as a lead-in to the issues in Questions 2 & 3. The bulk of the class will be spent on evaluating alternatives and making a recommendation to Booras as to how to proceed. A great wrap-up is to focus on what could have been done to avoid the situation currently faced by Dunkin' Donuts.

Students are enthusiastic about the case. There is no lack of personal knowledge or opinions about the company and its products, and it is good to air some of these experiences/opinions. A small amount of this adds to the natural excitement about discussing a company that the students are intimately familiar with. To add to this natural excitement, the instructor could open the class with, "Who has eaten a bagel in the last five days?" One (or a few) student could then be asked to describe his/her bagel buying process (Why a bagel? What brand of bagel? Why that brand? Price? Service?). If this format is used, the instructor could show the video after this general buying process discussion.

An added treat would be for the professor to bring bagels (Dunkin' Donut bagels, of course) to the class!

Epilogue

Dunkin' Donuts put two major actions in place in order to stick closely to its market plan for the bagel roll out:

1. The company set up a task force to monitor the day-to-day supply of bagels. The task force controlled the pace of the rollout—slowing the rollout for a short time period. The task force realized that Dunkin' Donuts could not have bagels in all stores by the first of August. The result was that some stores that had been redesigned for bagels did not receive their bagel deliveries on time. The delay in getting bagels to all stores, however, was only about a month (which meant all stores who were supposed to have bagels by August 1 did have them by September 1). So, the bagel rollout was slowed on a store-by-store basis for about one month.

2. During this time, Dunkin' Donuts and Harold's operations teams took control of the day-to-day facilities of the supplier from which Harold's was outsourcing the bagel production. The Dunkin' Donuts and Harold's management teams were able to get the bagel quality above expectations as well as increase productivity of the outsourced supplier.

The $25 million advertising campaign planned by Dunkin' Donuts was only delayed about a week. The two major actions outlined above enabled the company to move full steam ahead with only minimal delays. As everyone probably knows, Dunkin' Donuts bagels have been a phenomenal success.

Total 1997 bagel sales in the U.S. were estimated to have topped $2.5 billion. This sales figure was the result of sales in grocery stores, delis, and specialty shops. For 1998, Dunkin' Donuts predicts sales of its bagels to top $200 million. This is six times what the company sold when it ended its fiscal year in August of 1996.

Dunkin' Donuts has not stopped with its bagel introduction. The latest product breakthrough has been its blends of fresh-brewed coffee—served hot or cold. It sold $75 million of its Coffee Coolatta in just short of a six-month period. However, the company has not had this success at the expense of its core product—the doughnut. Doughnut sales rose 10% in 1997.

To facilitate the image change that has taken place with the more sophisticated product offerings, Dunkin' Donuts has also made interior changes to its stores. The traditional pink and orange décor has been replaced with what the company calls an upscale "ripe raisin" color. Also, the company retired Fred the Baker—replacing him with a $50 million marketing communications campaign focusing upon the new Dunkin' Donuts. The theme for the new campaign (stressing the changes at the company) is: *Dunkin' Donuts: Something Fresh is Always Brewin' Here*. No longer is the focus at Dunkin' Donuts on "time to make the donuts." With the menu and décor changes, sales increased around 12% for the year ended August 1997. This compares to a fast-food industry average of 2% growth.

By the beginning of 1998, the focus of attention at Dunkin' Donuts is the move into the luncheon market. In July of 1997, Allied Domecq acquired Togo Eateries. The intent of the acquisition was to buy a lunch partner for Dunkin' Donuts (much the same way as Wendy's acquired Tim Hortons for a breakfast partner).

[Note: Since the case was written, it has become public knowledge that Heinz is the producer of the Dunkin' Donuts bagel. Some students may ask if Harold's is a pseudonym for Heinz, and the answer is "yes."]

Exhibit TN–1   SWOT Analysis

Strengths

- Name recognition
- Strong brand leads people to the stores
- Good reputation
- Distribution infrastructure (easy to add new breakfast product to current product categories)
- History of successful spin-off (e.g., munchkins)
- Store interiors are inviting to customers
- Financially sound
- Top management commitment to new product introductions
- Success of franchise strategy

Weaknesses

- Geographically dispersed franchisees might lead to quality control issues
- Organizational turbulence could lead to breakdown of solid management team
- Reliance on one bagel supplier

Opportunities

- Bagel industry is a US$2.5 billion industry
- Growth rate of bagel industry (30% annually)
- Lack of dominant market leader leaves room for new players in the bagel market
- Concentration of bagel shops in northeast leaves huge segment of U.S. to develop
- Health conscious consumers

Threats

- Competition from large, well-known bagel shops (e.g., Einstein Bros., Manhattan Bagel, Bruegger's)
- Competition from supermarkets
- Infrastructure for making bagels is becoming scarce, leading to supply concerns

Exhibit TN–2   Pro/Con Analysis of Alternatives

Option 1: Continue rollout, current pace, partial product line

Pros:

- Would keep franchisees happy since they have redone their stores to accommodate bagels
- Prevent Dunkin' Donuts from becoming further behind its competitors that have already introduced bagels
- Consistent with senior management's drive to get the new fiscal year off to a great start
- In tune with new budget projections
- Consistent with Dunkin' Donuts history of always moving fast to stay ahead

Cons:

- Dunkin' Donuts prides itself on having the "best" product—continuing at the same pace could result in product quality problems from an already troubled supplier
- Consumers are expecting full product line offering at each store and anything less than this could hurt Dunkin' Donuts image

Option 2: Slow rollout—limit advertising/store expansion

Pros:

- Give bagel supplier time to get production lines up and running
- Projections may have been overstated to start with, and the slower rollout may be more in tune with the marketplace
- Savings in advertising dollars could be plowed back into the bagel production process

Cons:

- Could anger franchisees who do not receive bagels as planned (and who may have already made the $25,000 investment in store remodeling)
- Lost sales that could not be recaptured
- Retrenching could be looked upon unfavorably in financial markets
- Another delay would make outsiders wonder if Dunkin' Donuts could really pull off such a major new product introduction

Option 3: Stop rollout

Pros:

- Prevent Dunkin' Donuts from having more problems since capacity numbers were only theoretical to start with
- Would give Dunkin' Donuts needed time to secure a better bagel supplier
- Allow Dunkin' Donuts the opportunity to "cleanly" terminate the contract with Harold's who does not seem able to hold up its end of the arrangement

Cons:

- Booras would probably lose his job
- Angry franchisees—would feel they had wasted the $25,000 store remodeling money
- Miss out on great opportunity to expand into new product offerings and possibly even new markets (e.g., health conscious consumers, lunch crowd)—speed to market was essential
- Send wrong message to stakeholders
- Might not be able to find new supplier due to the long-term supplier contracts that were being signed

CASE 6-2
ROLLERBLADE, INC.*

Synopsis:

Started as a small business with hockey players as the only customers, Rollerblade, Inc. quickly became extremely successful in the in-line skating market and captured the number one position. Rollerblade's initial marketing strategy was developed on a small budget. Mary Horwath came up with four strategies that required little money: she gave Rollerblade's in-line skates to celebrities and athletes, teamed up with other companies, demonstrated the in-line skates at events where the target market went, and created related projects, like teams, books, and videos, that caught consumers' attention.

Because of the many competitors in the 1990s, Rollerblade could not just sit back on past success. As the leader in the market, the name "Rollerblade" was used as a generic name for in-line skating. This was a concern for the company because of the importance of brand recognition in a growing market. In addition to building brand recognition, Rollerblade had to continue expanding its product offerings and possibly find a new technology which could preempt in-line skating.

Video Summary:

In the video, Mary Horwath discusses the guerrilla marketing strategy the company used to create awareness for in-line skates. Horwath discusses how Rollerblade, Inc. marketed the product in an attempt to create a new sport for everyone. She mentions the challenges that the company faces, including competition and the generic use of its brand name. Also, Horwath talks about the different products that Rollerblade has created to meet the needs of consumers.

This is an exciting video, due largely to the inserts showing in-line skaters in action. The video runs slightly over 12 minutes. The video does show some of the newer products developed by Rollerblade, making it more appropriate for end-of-class viewing.

Teaching/Learning Objectives:

The case allows the class to:

- evaluate the marketing strategy of a successful start-up firm and determine what changes, if any, need to be made to lead the company into the mature stages of market development,
- determine how the product life cycle affects positioning techniques,
- illustrate the importance of differentiation in a mature market, and
- challenge students to develop a complete market plan for a well-established product in a mature market.

---

*This teaching note was prepared by Victoria L. Crittenden, Stephanie Hillstrom, and David Angus, Boston College, as an aid to instructors using the case, "Rollerblade, Inc." Revised 1998.

Discussion Questions:

1. What is in-line skating? What is Rollerblade?
2. What is the expected growth for in-line skating? for Rollerblade?
3. What is "guerrilla marketing" according to Rollerblade?
4. Should Horwath be concerned about market saturation? Why/why not?
5. Are Horwath's concerns about Rollerblade being included in the Webster dictionary well-founded?
6. Should Rollerblade focus more on a "push" strategy? Why?
7. Develop a marketing program for Rollerblade for the second half of the 1990s.

Analysis:

*These first four questions make up the **situation analysis** regarding Rollerblade, Inc. A sample SWOT analysis is included in Exhibit TN–1.*

1. What is in-line skating? What is Rollerblade?

In-line skating can be described in many ways. Students tend to describe it, initially, based on its physical characteristics. It has wheels like roller skates, but the wheels are lined up similar to the blade on an ice skate. Thus, it looks like an ice skate with wheels. [If the instructor has access to a pair of in-line skates, it offers class appeal to bring the skates to the classroom for this case discussion. Naturally, bringing a pair of Rollerblade skates is consistent with the case company. However, students also like to take a look at a competitive product and do their own "side-by-side" product comparison. So, access to more than one brand is great. It is doubtful that there is a student in the class who has not seen a pair of in-line skates, but the focus of attention is different when it is the topic of class discussion.]

In-line skating is a sport. It ranks second, behind family camping, for growth expectations for the first half of 1990. The product is classified as a part of the sports/recreation equipment market. The sport has its own industry association, the International In-Line Skate Association.

Some students may describe in-line skating as a fad. But, it has been around quite a while and has excellent growth projections through 1998. Expect some heated arguments between in-line skating enthusiasts and those who offer the notion of a fad, should the description arise.

In-line skating is "fun." Not only is the skating itself fun, in-line skating can lead to other activities. For example, street hockey has become a prominent form of outdoor activity, with in-line skates as an important piece of street hockey equipment.

Rollerblade is a company which helps make this "fun" possible. The bottom line is that Rollerblade is a manufacturer of in-line skates and the company which holds the largest share of the in-line skate market. However, the mission of the company is fun. Such a mission allows the company to focus upon more than just the fact that it can produce a high quality product. Rather, what the company has done is to position itself as a manufacturer of "fun." This led to users and nonusers of the product seeing in-line skating and fun as "Rollerblading." The successfulness of Rollerblade's initial strategy is a part of the problem (i.e., genericide) the company is experiencing currently.

Some students will even suggest that the Rollerblade, Inc. is the creator of the in-line skate market.

2. **What is the expected growth for in-line skating? for Rollerblade?**

This information is provided for the student in various parts of the case. Looking at the growth between 1990 and 1993, one sees a market expanding from $120 million to $300 million. Expectations are that the worldwide market could reach (and peak at) $1 billion by 1998. In 1993, there were 3.5 million in-line skaters located primarily in the United States.

Rollerblade, Inc. would, naturally, like to capture a huge chunk of this larger market. However, the company knows that its market share dropped from 70 percent in 1990 to 60 percent in 1993. From a dollar basis, however, the company went from $84 million in 1990 ($120 million x .70) to $180 million ($300 million x .60). Because of the growing market, the company saw increased revenue even with its market share dropping. One would expect that even with a decrease in market share that Rollerblade, Inc. would still see phenomenal sales numbers in the future.

3. **What is "guerrilla marketing" according to Rollerblade?**

Guerrilla marketing, according to Mary Horwath, is the use of aggressive, unorthodox, fairly cheap methods to attract positive publicity quickly. The four major points of the strategy center on: (i) samples to the "right" people, (ii) joint promotions, (iii) product demonstrations, and (iv) supplementary material. Thus, it seems that Horwath's guerrilla marketing uses the promotional component of the marketing mix as the major factor in Rollerblade's marketing strategy.

*Questions 4 and 5 comprise the **problem/decision statement** element of the case analysis.*

4. **Should Horwath be concerned about market saturation? Why/why not?**

Yes, market saturation in the in-line skate market means that more and more competitors are entering a market which is expected to reach its growth potential in the next few years. Rollerblade, Inc. essentially developed the in-line skate market. The number of in-line skate users is increasing, and the number of competitors has grown dramatically. With at least 30 competitors around the world, Rollerblade, Inc. will face competition in any market it attempts to enter, whether it be through market expansion or product development.

The market saturation concern also brings with it concern over the longevity of the market. This is brought up at the end of the case with Horwath's thoughts about what could preempt in-line skating. With 5,000 new sports and recreation product introductions annually, one can easily see Horwath's concern that one of these new products may do to in-line skating what in-line skating did to roller skating.

Even with the market becoming saturated, Rollerblade will be receiving a smaller piece of a bigger pie with the bottom line being increased sales for Rollerblade. However, Horwath knows that smart marketing is what will keep Rollerblade ahead of the competition.

5. **Are Horwath's concerns about Rollerblade being included in the Webster dictionary well-founded?**

Rollerblade's success at making Rollerblade and in-line skating synonymous could eventually lead to the dreaded "genericide" referred to in the case. And, there seems to be a good chance that the term will be included in the dictionary. Students may see a mixed blessing here. Some will view the move as positive, while others will see the possibility as negative.

On the positive side, students will say that calling the sport, "rollerblading," will keep the Rollerblade brand at the forefront of consumers minds. There is even a chance that consumers will ask salespeople about rollerblades and will be shown "Rollerblades." Others will say that it really does not matter because most people call the sport rollerblading anyway. So, including the word in the dictionary really will not matter. These students will not see that it will make a difference, positively or negatively, to Rollerblade's sales. Rather, these students suggest that Rollerblade's marketing strategy will make a difference regardless of what the Webster dictionary does. Some may even suggest that if Horwath spends time worrying about this issue then time is taken away from the important matter at hand (market/product development). That is, Horwath's worrying about the matter is what will be detrimental to the company.

On the negative side, students will talk about the loss of the brand name as was experienced by products such as shredded wheat and yo-yo. [Students may even be surprised to learn that these products were brands at one time.] The fear is that a potential user will no longer think of Rollerblade as a company but rather as the sport itself. Thus, Rollerblade's name recognition in the market will become useless. These students may suggest a strategy much like Xerox who has waged war against their name become generic. Xerox focused upon preventing the generic use of its name for photocopying in much of its marketing efforts.

This issue could lead to a short discussion surrounding why some names become generic and others do not.

Questions 6 and 7 helps focus upon the **alternatives** *available to Rollerblade.*

6. Should Rollerblade focus more on a "push" strategy? Why?

An interesting approach here is to outline Rollerblade's marketing strategy thus far.

Target Market:

active adults ages 18—35 years

Product:

Top of the Line

Price:

High

Distribution:

Limited (no mass merchandise stores)

Advertising:

very little/consumer-oriented

Promotion:

extensive/consumer oriented

Sales Results:

$180 million

There should be a brief discussion about why Horwath (apparently) thinks Rollerblade has been following a pull strategy. The central issue supporting a pull approach is promotional events that Rollerblade has been involved in. When outlining some of the important marketing variables, some students may suggest that Rollerblade has used both push and pull in its approach. The very little advertising, top of the line product offering, high prices, and limited distribution would typify more of a push approach currently. [However, the lack of consumer advertising is somewhat misleading in that Horwath's guerrilla marketing is really consumer advertising in forms other than print/television.]

More of a "push" strategy might mean maintaining the limited distribution and top of the line product offering and resulting high prices (unlike First Team Sports who has made their product widely available). A push strategy might also mean that Rollerblade focus upon particular segments of the 18 to 35 year old market.

Student opinions will be mixed on the strategy being followed currently by Rollerblade. The instructor should keep track of the variables on the board since this discussion, while focusing upon the "push" idea, tends to offer the various alternatives available to Rollerblade.

*Question 7 forces students to **develop and recommend** a marketing program to Rollerblade.*

7. Develop a marketing program for Rollerblade for the second half of the 1990s.

The marketing program recommended should focus upon the issues outlined in question 7. The framework used in that question is easily extended to this question.

Students are likely to suggest that Rollerblade pursue, heavily, product line expansion. The general consensus tends to be that lower priced products should be offered. Also, students tend to think that Rollerblade should make its product available in mass merchandise outlets. Looking back over this recommendation, a mass market approach is being taken. And, it appears to be a heavy "pull" strategy when combined with Rollerblade's current promotional approach.

The instructor should question the class to find if anyone thinks that Rollerblade should focus on a push approach. That is, should the company keep its top of the line product offering, high prices, and limited distribution as a way to differentiate itself from the other 29 competitors in the market?

Teaching the Case:

The case is fun to teach, largely because of the familiarity of the product. Many students will be "in-line skaters," with individual views to share. This should be allowed, as long as it is not overdone. The class seems to flow well if the discussion starts out very general, much like questions 1-4. Identifying the problem/issue at the start of class seems to make it difficult to move students back into the nature of the product.

The use of visuals, such as various brands of in-line skates, adds an element of life to the class (especially if one pair belongs to the instructor).

It is unlikely that a SWOT analysis will come out of the class discussion. The example SWOT is a good way to summarize the class discussion and show how the strengths, weaknesses, opportunities, and threats led Rollerblade and its competitors to where they are today. Essentially, these elements are reflected in the marketing program recommended by the class.

The class can end with the Rollerblade video. There is an upbeat tenor which can have students leaving the class with "fun" on their minds. Also, the video shows, modestly, some of the line extensions Rollerblade undertook.

Epilogue:

In addition to educating consumers, Rollerblade wanted to educate their retail accounts and store sales teams about their products. Blade School University was opened, which offered full-day training seminars to retailers at 50 locations across the United States. The program offered selling tips, profiles of Rollerblade programs and technology, and seminars on more ways to attract consumers.

To bring more people into the sport, Rollerblade introduced its ABT braking system. This system made the skates safer for participants. The company hoped that the new brakes would attract beginners and experienced skaters as well.

Another effort to increase sales was an emphasis on rentals. Rollerblade believed that an entry into the rental market would be effective if it coincided with new technology.

Rollerblade Inc will be forced to face these challenges without Mary Horwath. She became COO of Sled Dogs Co., marketing a boot-and-abbreviated ski-in-one snow skate which is usable in both cross-country and downhill conditions. Horwath is attempting to transport her guerrilla marketing strategy into this new marketplace.

Exhibit TN–1 SWOT Analysis

Strengths

- brand strength, recognition
- partnership with Nordica, a global company with established channels of distribution in sporting goods industry, experience in R&D for products which involve physical risk, and a strong reputation as the world's number one ski boot manufacturer and producer of tennis rackets (Prince), mountain boots (Asolo), and skis (Kastle)
- marketing expertise (i.e., "guerrilla marketing") able to overcome initial lack of cash for promotions
- product less susceptible to economic fluctuation—at least during recession of late 1980s/early 1990s, in-line skates grew in popularity while more costly sports declined in value
- product appealing to the same markets targeted by other companies (e.g., Pepsi, MTV)—strategic fit for cross-promotional tie-ins
- media attention
- first mover advantage—better able to go head-to-head with competition when and if shakeout occurs
- number one in marketplace

Weaknesses

- product in its current form not difficult to copy
- relatively frequent and apparently arbitrary pricing changes
- price points higher than competition for similar models
- capacity—having trouble meeting orders
- as market leader, everyone is gunning for Rollerblade, Inc.

Opportunities

- expanding and growing markets (e.g., youth)
- market niches based on demographics to stay ahead of growing competition, e.g., in-line skates for women, children, and other segments
- market niches based on use of product to stay ahead of growing competition, e.g., in-line skates for transportation, racing, and other segments
- use Nordica connection and expertise to develop market-focused, proprietary technology
- new sport/recreational products which fit the in-line skate "lifestyle"
- increasingly health-conscious American public
- join with main competition to promote in-line skating as an Olympic sport, e.g., be official sponsor of U.S. in-line skating team
- with Benetton, develop safety products for specific segments of in-line skating and other populations

Threats

- "genericide"
- product ends up being a fad again, as it was in 1860s
- US federal government deemed in-line skating a health hazard
- increasing competition, decreasing market share—roller and ice skate makers and boot manufacturers all capable of entering in-line skate market
- established companies with deep pockets are trying to gain access to the in-line skate market, e.g., Nike buying Canstar Sports Inc
- cannibalization from new mass merchandiser distributed, low-end in-line skate
- new sport/recreational products displacing in-line skating in popularity (5,000 entering market yearly)
- market saturation, industry "shakeout" as number of competitors increases

CASE 6-3
L'OREÀL NEDERLAND BV*

L'Oreàl is a global cosmetics company. Its strategy is to introduce new products in one country, frequently France, its home market. If the products are successful it then "rolls them out" into other markets. The issue in this case is whether two product lines, skin care and hair color, in a mid-priced family line should be offered to Dutch consumers. One complicating issue is that L'Oreàl already offers brands of these products and these existing lines are facing more competition.

The case provides some market research data. Students can address the questions of how do consumers perceive these new products? How are the products viewed in relation to currently offered products including L'Oreàl's brands? What are the pros and cons of introducing one or both product lines? If the products are introduced what should be the marketing mix for their introduction? Finally, will the retail trade want to stock the product lines?

Students do not need any in-depth knowledge of the Netherlands. Product introduction strategy can be the focus of the case or if time permits market mix development can also be addressed. Perceptive students should discuss retailer interest in adding another family line of products in a mature market.

Synopsis

L'Oreàl Netherlands was considering the introduction of Garnier family brand Synergie facial skin care and Belle Color hair coloring products. Both lines were developed and successfully sold in France.

Synergie Facial Skin Care Line

In the early 1990's, Dutch women used fewer skin care products than the French and Germans. However, the population was aging and the Dutch women's labor force participation rate was increasing. Thus their incomes and desires for these products were on the increase. Synergie emphasized anti-aging and anti-wrinkling formulations. Large chain drug stores and supermarkets were the most important unit volume distributors of skin care products. On a monetary value basis, large and small independent drug stores were more important. Synergie was a mid-price line, directly competitive with ['0r~al's Plenitude line and Procter & Gamble's Oil of Olaz (Olay). Both L'Oreàl and Procter & Gamble spent above average advertising dollars.

Consumers were brand loyal, fearing allergic reactions, and purchased skin care products once or twice a year. However, Dutch consumers were becoming interested in natural ingredient products, the positioning of Synergie. Test market results were mixed. Interest in the anti-aging cream had a sharp decline once the participants learned its price. The moisturizing cream elicited more interest. One troubling finding was that over half of L'Oreàl's Plenitude users said they would switch to the Synergie moisturizer.

---

* This teaching note was prepared by the authors of the case, Frederick W. Langrehr, Valparaiso University, and Lee Dehringer, Butler University. The teaching note is based on information from the graduate thesis of Anne Stöcker, Nijenrode University, the Netherlands.

Belle Color Hair Colorant

As Dutch women grew older they were more likely to use hair color, although less frequently than French women. Competition in this product category was more intense than in the skin care lines.

Consumers were very brand loyal, not wanting any surprises when they changed their hair color. Market research indicated consumers were initially very positive about the Belle Color concept and increased their buying intentions once they learned the price. However after using the product, buying intentions sharply declined. Dissatisfaction with Belle Color centered on the final color. Belle Color was formulated for the French market and Dutch women preferred lighter blonds and brunettes and stronger reds than French users. Cannibalization was a concern since participants who most favorably rated Belle Color were current users of L'Oreàl's higher priced Recital.

Case Questions

You have to make some product strategy and most likely some tactical marketing mix decisions. From the strategic perspective you need to decide if l'Or~al should have introduced Synergie and/or Belle Color?

If you decide to introduce one or both lines you then need to develop the marketing mix(es). Specifically:

1. Should the products nave been changed for the Dutch i.,arket and if yes, what changes were needed? Why might L'Oreàl France not have made any changes for the Dutch market?
2. Which retailers should have carried the lines?
3. What should the advertising positioning statements have been? Should they simply have translated the French ad copy?
4. Tentative prices were set. Should they have been lowered, raised or kept at the suggested levels?
5. When developing the marketing plan how could have L'Oreal reduced the cannibalization effects on the Gamier lines? What marketing activities could L'Oreal have taken with its currently offered products, Plenitude and Recital, to reduce the cannibalization from the Gamier lines?

Analyses

Product Line Introduction Decisions

Synergie

Pros:

- The demographics of the market were favorable. Dutch women were increasingly working outside the home and thus had more income to spend on these types of products. They also had a greater need to use them more frequently.
- The population was getting older and thus had a greater need or felt need for skin care products.
- The natural ingredient appeal was becoming more important. Therefore, if L'Oreàl did not introduce Synergie, a competitor could easily copy this product and introduce it before L'Oreal.
- Dutch consumers wanted value. Thus introducing a mid-price line positioned against higher price, institute lines might be attractive to the women who needed to use the product more frequently.

- The results of the market testing were generally favorable. From one-fifth to one-third of the participants said they would buy the product.

Cons:

- Cannibalization was a serious concern. This was especially true for the moisturizer. The implication was not only would L'Oreàl real need to spend money on introducing Synergie, it would also have to spend guilders defending Plenitude.
- The market introduction would be expensive. Both Procter & Gamble and L'Oreàl were spending over twice the expected guilders on advertising. In a steady state situation the percent of a brand's ad spending of total industry ad spending should be about equal to its market share. (If market share equals 10% then share of voice or ad spending should be 10% of total industry ad expenditures.) But, Procter and Gamble and L'Oreàl were spending 2.6 percent for every 1 percent in market share.
- Dutch consumers were not as sophisticated about skin care and needed to be "educated."

Decision:

The pros probably outweigh the cons. This may be a good time to discuss the concept that trying to avoid cannibalization only gives a competitor the opportunity to attack the company's currently offered products. If the concept is sound, and it appeared the Dutch consumer was receptive, if L'Oreàl did not introduce the product, a competitor would. And, in many cases it is better to lose customers to another SBU than to an external competitor.

Students can make a case to delay the introduction to give L'Oreàl time to develop a competitive strategy for Plenitude. This will be discussed in depth later but the pricing and positioning of Plenitude needed to be examined and possibly changed. But, the delay should not go beyond six to nine months.

Belle Color

Pros:

The demographics were favorable. Dutch women were increasingly working outside the home, had higher incomes and becoming older. As a result they were more likely to have the income and perceived need for hair color products to cover gray. Appeals to these "new customers" may have been a way to relaunch these products from the mature stage of the PLC into a new growth phase.

- The product line had a long history of market leadership in France.
- It filled a void in the industry price lines. It was priced below the high (13 percent lower) and above the low (20 percent higher) prices of other brands and there was no direct price competitor. The next highest priced product was a third more expensive than the cheapest brands.
- Introducing it at the same time as Synergie would provide more ad mentions of the Gamier family brand name. The cost of developing the family brand was thus spread across two product lines.

Cons:

- The product needed to be reformulated for the Dutch market. A large minority of the test participants wanted more lightening and brighter reds. This deficiency may be the strongest case for not introducing the product.

- The product did not appear to offer a unique advantage. Synergie could have made a unique claim of natural ingredients. Belle Color's only advantage was price. The lower priced brands could have easily retaliated to Belle Color's introduction with a theme of "The color <u>Dutch</u> women prefer for a better value."

- Cannibalization of Recital (L'Oreàl's currently offered hair color) was a problem. Recital users were the ones that rated Belle Color the highest. They were more likely to like the resulting color and to think Belle Color met expectations and was better than their currently used brand. Given Belle Color was about 13 percent cheaper (14.95-12.95/14.95 guilders) L'Oreàl could have anticipated a significant shift to the cheaper brand. The ad platforms for both products were also the same—covering gray hair.

- Although the market was still growing at 15 percent per year, it appeared to be entering the maturity phase. Four brands held 80 percent share and the two leaders, Recital (L'Oreàl's brand) and Poly Color, were losing shares. As a result advertising spending jumped 60 percent in one year. Distribution was also changing to intensive from selective with drug chains playing a more important role.

- The product line required a large amount of retail shelf space (about 5 feet). To provide shelf space for a new product retailers wanted evidence of consumer acceptance and a good rationale for a new product's development. Based on the test market results it might have been difficult to sell retailers on either of these points.

Decision:

A strong case can be made not to introduce this product. It had no unique advantage. It required a significant amount of space in retail stores and the poor performance of this line could have negatively impacted retailer and consumer attitudes and behavior towards Synergie and future Gamier lines.

A reformulated product might be a viable alternative. This approach is discussed in the marketing mix, product section.

Marketing Nix Development

Synergie

<u>Product</u>—Based on the use test the participants generally liked the Synergie products. In the concept test they liked the idea of natural ingredients and its French origin was positively received.

<u>Promotion</u>—L'Oreàl would have had to develop both selective demand for the Gamier line and primary demand for some of the new products like anti-wrinkling and aging creams within the line. This would have been a costly proposition. L'Oreàl along with Procter & Gamble were already spending 2.5 times more on advertising than would have been expected for Plenitude and Oil of Olaz. Thus spending on Synergie would have to at least match this level.

Some synergy could come from promoting both the new needs, new users, new products and new brands at the same time. Students need to recognize that one reason why participants in the market test reacted negatively to the price of the anti-wrinkling cream may have been less attributed to the price than to the participants' lack of perceived need and thus a resulting product higher cost and lower benefit ratio. Dutch consumers may have reacted favorably to the natural ingredient positioning. But as part of building primary demand Synergie needed to "educate" consumers in the different types of products and their uses.

Stressing natural ingredients may also be supported when looking at cannibalization effects. With 52 percent of L'Oreàl's Plenitude users stating they would certainly buy Synergie moisturizer, cannibalization was a concern. Cannibalization was less of a problem for the anti-aging cream since only 21 percent of the buyers said they would buy it. Thus a promotional theme of natural ingredients for Synergie may be a way to distance Synergie from Plenitude. Too heavy of an emphasis on anti-aging may have attracted the Plenitude buyer.

Price—The mid point pricing of the product appears viable. As discussed in the promotion section the negative reaction to the price was probably less due to the cost side of the equation and more to the benefit side.

Distribution—Synergie needed to be distributed through chain and large and small independent drug stores. The question to be addressed is, should it be sold through supermarkets also? The negative side to selling in supermarkets was it might have cheapened the image of the brand. However, as more Dutch women worked outside of the home one-stop shopping for mid-priced product lines in food stores might have been appealing. Also on the positive side supermarket operators may have been more receptive to carrying Synergie since they offered fewer cosmetic product lines.

Belle Color

Product—The product probably needed to be reformulated for the Dutch market. Given that Recital's users were the ones most likely to like Belle Color, Recital probably was not reformulated when it was introduced into the Dutch market. It now appears L'Oreàl wanted to offer Belle Color at a lower price point to a broader segment of the Dutch market. The number of younger users of hair color was also growing and they liked the lighter and redder shades of Andrelon and Guhl. This is further supported by the main reason to color hair was to achieve warm/red tones. Finally a reformulated Belle Color could have been positioned away from Recital. The new Belle Color could have been used to emphasize lighter tones and brighter reds while Recital remained as the more traditional, dark shade hair colorant. A major problem here is that L'Oreàl corporate and not the Dutch subsidiary controlled manufacturing. How likely is it that corporate would reformulate a product for your percent of the EU market?

Promotion—L'Oreàl could have promoted the French heritage and popularity of Belle Color since this French tie-in was acceptable for Synergie. But it should also have emphasized that the product was adapted to the tastes of Dutch women. Whatever the message, L'Oreàl had to plan on spending an above average number of guilders on advertising. Hair coloring products were entering the maturity stage of the life cycle. The two leading brands were already losing market shares. Thus, ad spending had gone up and would likely go up some more with any new, heavily promoted brands. This along with a mediocre product was one of the main reasons for seriously reconsidering introducing the original formulation of Belle Color.

Price—If Belle Color was reformulated and was differentiated from L'Oreàl's Recital on the basis of product and promotion differences, staying at the mid-price point of 12.95 can be defended. If the product was NOT changed then establishing a lower price for Belle Color may be proposed.

L'Oreàl could have used Belle Color as a price brand against Andrelon and Poly Color. As a price brand distributed in chain drug stores and possibly supermarkets Belle Color might have blunted the share gains of Andrelon. Recital users might also have been less likely to trade down from 14.95 guilders to 9.95 guilders. They may have perceived fewer quality differences between Recital at 14.95 and Belle Color at 12.95 but if Belle Color drops to 9.95 this may have been too large of a price spread and may have had an impact on the psychological evaluation of quality.

This low price strategy, however, could have had a negative impact on the other Gamier lines like Synergie which were being introduced as mid-price lines. A compromise at 10.95 guilders may be defended. But much depended on whether L'Oreàl could have differentiated Belle Color on a basis other than price.

Distribution—Belle Color to be successful had to be sold through chain and large and small drug stores. As a differentiating tactic, sales in supermarkets can be proposed. Although almost no hair color (3 percent of total) was sold in supermarkets, this may be one way to differentiate Belle Color from the competition. With more women working outside of the home, more of them may have been interested in buying hair color at supermarkets. Supermarkets may also have been more willing to devote shelf space to Belle Color since they were not carrying other brands. Also offering supermarkets both Belle Color and Synergie would have helped supermarkets gain greater customer recognition for selling cosmetics and toiletries.

The Gamier Family of Products

Students need to answer the prior individual product line marketing mix questions in light of the Gamier family. Proposing a different pricing or distribution strategy for the two lines is probably not defensible when looking at the Gamier family brand.

Low prices on the hair coloring line would impact a mid-price approach for Synergie. Also if the Belle Color was available in supermarkets Synergie would also likely have to be sold there since consumers would expect to find products with the same brand name sold at the same stores.

Plenitude and Recital Considerations

Students also need to recognize that by introducing the Gamier line of products the Netherlands division would have less time and money to spend on the currently offered L'Oreàl products. This was especially critical for Recital since it was already losing market share. With Procter and Gamble's aggressive promotion of Oil of Olaz against Plenitude this line also required attention. One question the students need to pose was how much money does L'Oreàl headquarters want to invest in the Dutch market? Was the market large enough to profitably support two L'Oreàl product lines? With only four percent of total EU sales of C&T, this is probably a key issue. This cannot be quantitatively answered, but a qualitative discussion is possible.

Criteria for an Excellent Analysis

An excellent analysis should address most of the following points:

1. Product line management
   - Marketing mix decisions on Synergie or Belle Color have an impact on the other product line since both share a family brand, Gamier.
   - Decisions related to Gamier products will impact current L'Oreàl products in the Dutch market.
   - If the product concept was viable, competitors could offer the product benefits and L'Oreàl could possibly lose even more than if it competed with itself.
2. Investment—L'Oreal France was not going to subsidize any Dutch market introductions.
3. Segmentation—Segmenting in the 60 million population French might be profitable but in the smaller 15 million population Dutch market this might not be profitable.
4. Synergie
   - Dutch consumers were receptive to the product.

- Promotion for developing primary as well as selective demand was required.
5. Belle Color
    - Reformulation was needed.
    - No differential advantage other than an easily countered mid-price position.
    - Distribution into supermarkets may have been a viable differentiating tactic. (Students then need to realize Synergie would also need to be distributed in supermarkets.)
6. The funds that were needed to introduce these two new products may be better spent on defending L'Oreàl's Plenitude from Oil of Olaz. Also, L'Oreàl's Recital was losing share and probably required additional funds.

Teaching Plan

The discussion could flow from general to specific. First address issues of whether segmentation strategies that work in a larger market will work in a smaller one. Also, was it possible to Eurobrand and formulate products or must they be country specific? Then the discussion could move to analyzing the research data and developing specific product line and individual product marketing plans and mixes.

Students could role play the Dutch product managers for the existing L'Oreàl brands (arguing for increased marketing support of established brands) versus the managers for the new brands (arguing that they need funds to enter the market with competitively distinctive products). Role playing on either side of the Eurobranding versus country specific mixes is also possible.

Epilogue

Neither of the products was introduced. The Dutch market was too small to support the targeting of smaller segments in light of the cost of promotion and distribution to these small targets. Synergie required heavy promotion to develop primary demand for the products as well as selective demand for the brand. Belle Color required product reformulation and headquarters thought the Dutch market too small to justify this investment.

CASE 6-4
APACHE POWER, INC*

Synopsis:

Apache Power, Inc., a manufacturer of gasoline engines used in small outdoor power equipment, developed a gasoline engine for use in large outdoor power equipment. In the small engine market, API had an excellent reputation for the quality and dependability of its products. Since it had held a solid position in the market for so long, API never put much effort into promotion.

Recently, API invested much time and money on designing a gasoline engine to be used in large outdoor power equipment, and it had to figure out a way to introduce and price the new engine. The product was of high quality, but API realized that a marketing program or combination of marketing programs was needed to compete in the large engine market.

Teaching/Learning Objectives:

The major emphasis in the case is the development of a marketing program for the large engine. In doing so, several issues are addressed:

- ascertaining the impact of past decisions involving trade discounts, sales expenses, credit expenses, and other expenses involving the development of the new product
- assessing the company's financial capabilities
- discerning API's competitive position, including market share, marketing mix, and the cost and profit position (ratios and breakeven analysis)
- introducing the concept of market entry barriers

Discussion Questions:

1. What are the objectives of API's management team?
2. What are API's strengths and weaknesses?
3. What decisions must be made by Furnas and the API management team?
4. What industry information is pertinent to these decisions?
5. What trends can be identified from a review of API's income statement?
6. What trends can be identified from a review of API's balance sheet?
7. How does Apache currently segment its market? Are there other segmentation approaches which might be useful? What is API's market share?
8. What is the size of the large engine market?
9. Are there any entry barriers for the large engine market? If so, identify them.

---

*This teaching note was prepared by William F. Crittenden, Northeastern University, as an aid to instructors using the case, "Apache Power, Inc."

10. Calculate API's likely breakeven (units and percent of market) for the large engine market.
11. What recommendations for a marketing program for the large engine do you have for API's management team?
12. What response do you expect from Brighams?

Analysis:

1. What are the objectives of API's management team?

The objectives of API's management team are to successfully introduce a large engine line, to offset slow growth and increased competition in the small engine line, and to return to profitability.

2. What are API's strengths and weaknesses?

Strengths:

- established customer base
- own sales force
- new technology for large engine (e.g., safer, quieter, better fuel economy) which hopefully API can translate to small engine line

Weaknesses:

- lack of name recognition
- little promotion, less advertising
- difficulty finding qualified people

While not asked in the discussion question, it is also useful to examine the competitors' strengths.

Hachi Strengths:

Small engines:

- national sales & distribution
- manufacturers own outdoor power equipment (vertically integrated with 98% captive sales)
- 13% of market

Large engines:

- exceptional performance record
- superior technology ("best engine" according to trade journals)
- 8% of market

Brighams strengths:

- strong name recognition among older males
- lots of experience
- established customer base

- excellent reputation for dependability
- best parts & service network
- national sales & distribution
- "former" technological leader
- holds 30% of the small engine market
- created large engine market and holds 42% share

3. What decisions must be made by Furnas and the API management team?

The market related issues for Furnas and the API management team are:

a. the appropriate price

b. trade discounts

c. advertising—trade journals? TV?

d. promotions

e. sales force
   1. dedicated on both product lines?
   2. training needed?
   3. are more sales personnel needed?
   4. commissions vs. salary

Regarding the salesperson commission vs. salary issue, the following calculations are informative per how much API'salespeople make per year:

$$\text{Salary} \quad \frac{\$554,000}{14} = \$39,571$$

$$\text{Commission} \quad \frac{\$226,000}{14} = \$16,143$$

$$\text{Average Salary + Commission} = \$55,714$$

[Note: This assumes all salaries are devoted to selling and are divided among the 14 salespeople and no additional sales support staff are included. This appears to be a reasonable assumption given the size of the firm.]

Is this too much? Enough?

[Note: The case indicates salespeople must be technically knowledgeable and good communicators, and that recently it has been difficult to find qualified salespeople.]

The strategic issues include whether or not API'should continue the same level of R&D expenditures, if they should seek a strategic alliance to assist with new model introduction, if they should diversify their customer base, and if they should convert some or all of their small business to captive status.

4. **What industry information is pertinent to these decisions?**

Industry Economic Issues:

Market Size (1990)

Small engines: $45 * 5,700,000 units = $256,500,000

Large engines: $350 * 1,020,000 units = $357,000,000

Scope of Rivalry

National marketplace for small and large engine

Two "national" competitors, rest are regionally focused

However, some competitors are international firms

Market Growth Rate (derived demand, outside power equipment)

Small engines < 1% with 2 1/2% decrease last year and 3 1/2% decrease expected this year

Large engines = 10% (1988 & 1989) with 2.8% decrease last year

Small engines in maturity/decline with no price increase

Structure of Suppliers/Buyers

Small engines:

27 competitors, most with small market share

Engines appear somewhat standardized (switching may be easy)

But, engine is critical to success of outdoor power equipment manufacturers

Large engines:

Brighams dominate

Probably less than dozen competitors

Product appears more differentiated

Some captive (backward integration?) -> 33%

Industry Profitability

Small engines:

decreasing margins, increasing capital needs, no price increase

Large engines:

Brighams has around 4% operating margin in large engines

5. **What trends can be identified from a review of API's income statement?**

The income statement reflects revenue generating activities of the company over a period of time (usually a year). Other issues include calendar vs. fiscal period, year vs. quarter vs. month, and P & L (profit and loss). [Exhibits TN–1—TN–3 show important manipulations of income statement data.]

For simplicity, one could address the figures from API's income statement directly, although, realistically, they should be adjusted for inflation. Sales (growth and net) and the gross margin had declined in the last two years. There had been no change in the advertising expenditures for five years. Salaries for salespeople had gone up each year, and all other costs had gone up each year:

Administration	.0175	last year
Depreciation	.0319	"depends on other decisions"
R & D	.0394	
Supplies	.0762	
Insurance	.0163	
Interest	.0060	

The profits dropped each year, and API lost money last year.

6. **What trends can be identified from a review of API's balance sheet?**

Trends identified from the balance sheet:

- decrease in cash
- increase in prepaid expenses
- large increase in machinery, especially the last year
- increase each year in total fixed assets and total assets
- decrease each year in current notes payable
- increase each year in long term notes payable
- decrease the last year in retained earnings

Additionally, Exhibit TN–4 provides ratio analyses for API.

7. **How does Apache currently segment its market? Are there other segmentation approaches which might be useful? What is API's market share?**

Current:

Customer

    geographic—regional

    organization type—outdoor power equipment manufacturer

    age—established firms

Product-related

    price sensitivity

Additional approaches to consider might focus on the *product-related* segments by looking at benefits sought such as safety, gas saving, or less noise.

Exhibit TN–5 shows the calculations for API's market share of the small engine market.

8. **What is the size of the large engine market?**

The approximate size of the large engine market in revenue is $357,000,000. Brighams holds the largest market share with 42%. Calculations are shown in Exhibit TN–6.

9. **Are there any entry barriers for the large engine market? If so, identify them.**

- scale economies (purchasing materials, purchasing advertising)
- cost disadvantages independent of scale (experience curve, technology)
- capital requirements
- distribution channels (captive, vertical integration)
- product differentiation
- switching costs facing buyers

10. **Calculate API's likely breakeven (units and percent of market) for the large engine market.**

Since API is not in the large engine market, it must estimate its breakeven in a round-about way. Exhibit TN–7 shows the breakeven for the small engine market. Exhibit TN–8 shows Brighams' estimated breakeven for the large engine market. Exhibit TN–9 shows how to use Brighams' data to estimate a large engine breakeven API.

Expect much surprise from the class with the approach taken for the large engine market. It is interesting to allow the student to criticize the approach taken here. Be sure to have the critical students suggest a better method. Also, some students may not be comfortable with the straight percentage calculation for all items. Several alternative approaches or questions may be raised. The following discussion identifies several issues which might come up.

In projecting a breakeven for API's large engine business, variable costs might be adjusted using the percentage cost comparison derived from Exhibit 1 and the Brighams exhibit in the case. For example, average variable costs might be approximated as:

$350 x 0.73 = $255.50

This is $21.89 cheaper than the $277.39 approximated in Exhibit TN–9. However, this does not take experience curve effects into account. Nor does it include adjustments in commissions (a suggestion that many students are likely to make).

Fixed costs include two of the key decisions identified early on (e.g., advertising and promotional expenditures). These costs must help overcome existing entry barriers, recognizing that API will have to capture sales from existing competitors as the large engine business is not growing fast enough to achieve their implicit objective. [Decisions regarding these two variables may be highly subjective, but students need to be able to explain their logic.]

Fixed cost categories include substantial opportunities for cost sharing (e.g., administrative salaries, supplies, insurance, interest). These costs may not go up appreciably with the addition of the large engine business and would be absorbed by the small engine business if the new business did not exist. However, traditional cost accounting philosophy suggests these costs should be divided among the various businesses. In the very near term, this may be inappropriate. Until the new product or business has "shaken out," it seems appropriate to only allocate additional incremental costs.

Equipment and R&D expenses incurred in staying in the business must be allocated. In addition, some allocation of the pre (sunk) costs is generally made. This is done to acknowledge the earlier "hit" earnings took as a result of these expenditures and to "prepare" for future investments.

Comparing costs of API's small engine business and Brighams' large engine business can be misleading. For example, there may be differences attributable to the manufacture of different product sizes in the normal amount of non-recyclable, wasted raw materials. However, differences may exist due to:

1. Brighams probably gets quantity discounts on purchases of *raw materials*.
2. API may keep *direct labor* down due to better employee relations and/or simpler work rules.
3. Due to smaller sales, API may have difficulty *shipping* in full car (railroad car) or full truck loads, thus modestly increasing transportation costs.
4. Although *salaries* for sales and administrative personnel combined average eight percent for both firms, API is behind in overall compensation due to lower sales commissions paid.

Yet, one must be especially leery of comparing Fixed Costs as there may be substantial cost sharing between Brighams' divisions. However, cost sharing should be anticipated when projecting API's large engine costs.

11. What recommendations for a marketing program do you have for API's management team?

Examples might include:

- seek sales outside of the outdoor power equipment industry
- target 5% of market
- raise price above average
- dedicated sales force
- advertise and promote heavily

Some students may even suggest dropping the large engine product. Whatever the recommendation, students should be pushed for specifics regarding the plan.

12. What response do you expect from Brighams?

(Assuming the decision is to continue with the introduction of the large engine)

Short term:

- price war
- promotional blitz

Long term:

- accelerate pace of R&D
- attack API's small engine market

Teaching the Case:

To achieve the objectives of the case, it is necessary to spend much time looking at the company's financial statements and at the other exhibits in the case. It is useful to have transparencies ready to use regarding much of the financial analysis and especially for the breakeven calculations. There are a lot of numbers and varying ways to use the numbers, which is often confusing to the students. The case is great for showing the importance of understanding the numbers when developing a marketing program.

A typical approach to teaching the case is to follow the six steps outlined in the Cravens, Lamb, Crittenden text. The 12 questions suggested in this note fit nicely within the framework and help students get at the necessary detail to conduct a thorough analysis of the case.

Epilogue:

API introduced the large engine and captured 4.5 percent of the market. Components of the marketing program were:

Price: The company followed a premium pricing strategy, pricing the product higher than current products in the market. This was done to avoid direct price competition with Brighams. Variable costs were higher initially for the large engine when compared to the small engine. Variable costs averaged around 76 percent.

Communications: The initial budget was $2 million. (Naturally there was some cost sharing here.) API spent $500,000 of this on advertising.

Distribution: The company kept the same sales force for both small and large engines. Commissions were increased an additional one percent.

Exhibit TN-1 Income Statement

	1990	Percentages	
Gross Sales	$12,556		1.0000
Sales Discounts	1,249		.0995
Net Sales	$11,307		1.0000
Cost of Goods Sold			
Raw Materials	4,862	.4300	
Direct Labor	2,256	.1995	
Variable Overhead	678	.0600	
Shipping	192	.0170	<.7065>
	3,319		.2935
Gross Margin			
Selling Costs			
Advertising	9	.0008	
Salaries	554	.0490	
Commissions	226	.0200	
Promotional Materials	226	.0200	
Other Costs			
Administrative	348	.0308	
Depreciation	97	.0086	
Research & Development	1,583	.1400	
Supplies	113	.0100	
Insurance	187	.0165	
Interest	167	.0148	<.3105>
Operating Income	($192)		<.0170>
Taxes	(80)		
Income After Taxes	($111)		<.0098>

Exhibit TN-2 Income Statement (in percentage terms)

	1990	1989	1988	1987	1986
Net Sales	1.000	1.000	1.000	1.000	1.000
Cost of Goods Sold					
Raw Materials	.4300	.4300	.4280	.4280	.4280
Direct Labor	.1995	.1990	.1980	.1960	.1960
Variable Overhead	.0600	.0580	.0580	.0590	.0580
Shipping	.0170	.0170	.0169	.0169	.0170
	.7065	.7040	.7009	.6999	.6990
Gross Margin	.2935	.2960	.2991	.3001	.3010
Selling Costs					
Advertising	.00080	.00079	.00079	.00078	.00078
Salaries	.0490	.0460	.0450	.0440	.0430
Commissions	.0200	.0200	.0200	.0200	.0200
Promotional Materials	.0200	.0200	.0190	.0191	.0210
Other Costs					
Administrative	.0308	.0292	.0281	.0281	.0280
Depreciation	.0086	.0080	.0078	.0078	.0075
Research & Development	.1400	.1300	.0925	.0300	.0300
Supplies	.0100	.0090	.0085	.0080	.0070
Insurance	.0165	.0158	.0153	.0153	.0150
Interest	.0148	.0142	.0140	.0140	.0140
	.3105	.2930	.2510	.1871	.1863
Operating Income	<.0170>	.0030	.0481	.1130	.1147
Income After Taxes	<.0098>	.0018	.0279	.0656	.0666

Exhibit TN–3   Income Statement (percent change from previous year)

	1990	1989	1988	1987
Gross Sales	-0.0330	-0.0085	0.0061	0.0060
Sales Discounts	-0.0181	-0.0290	0.0061	0.0062
Net Sales	-0.0346	-0.0063	0.0061	0.0060
Cost of Goods Sold				
Raw Materials	-0.0346	-0.0016	0.0060	0.0060
Direct Labor	-0.0322	-0.0013	0.0166	0.0061
Variable Overhead	-0.0015	-0.0073	-0.0010	0.0237
Shipping	-0.0352	0	0.0051	0
Gross Margin	-0.0427	-0.0165	0.0028	0.0029
Selling Costs				
Advertising	0	0	0	0
Salaries	0.0278	0.017	0.0291	0.0279
Commissions	-0.0342	-0.0085	0.0085	0.0043
Promotional Materials	-0.0342	0.0446	0	-0.0041
Other Costs				
Administrative	0.0175	0.0301	0.0061	0.0123
Depreciation	0.0319	0.0217	0.0110	0.0460
Research & Development	0.0394	0.3972	2.1054	0.0057
Supplies	0.0762	0.0500	0.0638	0.1463
Insurance	0.0163	0.0222	0.0056	0.0229
Interest	0.0060	0.0061	0.0061	0.0061
Operating Income	-6.3333	-0.9365	-0.5718	-0.0090
Taxes	-6.3333	-0.9370	-0.5719	-00089
Income After Taxes	-6.2857	-0.9362	-0.5716	0.0090

Exhibit TN–4   Ratio Analysis

I. Liquidity

			1990	1989	1988	1987	1986
Current	$\dfrac{11{,}752}{7{,}673}$	=	1.53	1.46	1.25		
Quick	$\dfrac{8{,}423}{7{,}673}$	=	1.10	1.05	.85		
Cash	$\dfrac{628}{7{,}673}$	=	.08	.11	.10		
Inventory to net working cap	$\dfrac{3{,}329}{4{,}079}$	=	.82	.90	1.59		

II. Profitability Ratios

			1990	1989	1988	1987	1986
Net profit margin	$\dfrac{-111}{11{,}307}$	=	−.0098	.0018	.0279	.0656	.0666
Gross profit margin	$\dfrac{3{,}319}{11{,}307}$	=	.2935	.2960	.2991	.3001	.3010
ROI	$\dfrac{-111}{68{,}018}$	=	−.0016	.0003	.0054		

ROE (Average equity info. not readily available)

EPS (Number of shares info. not readily available)

Productivity of Assets	$\dfrac{-111}{45{,}711}$	=	−.0024	.0005	.0072		

Exhibit TN–4 Ratio Analysis (continued)

III. Activity Ratios

		1990	1989	1988
Inventory turnover	$\frac{11{,}307}{3{,}329} =$	3.40	3.72	3.17
Net working capital t/o	$\frac{11{,}307}{4{,}079} =$	2.77	3.35	5.03
Asset turnover	$\frac{11{,}307}{68{,}018} =$	.17	.19	.19
Fixed asset t/o	$\frac{11{,}307}{56{,}266} =$	.20	.23	.24
Average collection period	$\frac{6{,}455}{30.98} =$	208	184	189
Accounts receivable t/o	$\frac{11{,}307}{6{,}455} =$	1.75	1.99	1.93
Accounts payable period	$\frac{2{,}488}{13.63} =$	183	151	177
Cash turnover	$\frac{628}{30.98} =$	20.3	26.6	28.6
Days of inventory	$\frac{3329}{21.88} =$	152	139	164

IV. Leverage Ratios

		1990	1989	1988	1987	1986
Debt to asset	$\frac{22{,}307}{68{,}018} =$	.33	.27	.25		
Debt to equity	$\frac{22{,}307}{45{,}711} =$	.49	.36	.34		
Current debt to equity	$\frac{7{,}673}{45{,}711} =$	.17	.165	.21		
Long-term debt to equity	$\frac{14{,}364}{45{,}711} =$	.32	.20	.14		
Times interest earned	$\frac{-25}{167} =$	-.15	1.22	4.44	9.07	9.2

Coverage of fixed charges (Lease info. not readily available)

Exhibit TN–5   Market Share Small Engine Market

Year	OPE Using Small Engines	Percent Change Prior Year
1986	5750	N/A
1987	5785	.0061
1988	5820	.0061
1989	5850	.0052
1990	5700	-.0256
1991	5500	-.0351
1992	5700	.0364
1993	5900	.0351

Approximate Small Engine Market in Revenue (no price increase last two years)

1990   5,700,000 x $45 = $256,500,000
1989   5,850,000 x $45 = $263,250,000

Market Share Small Engines

Brighams	30.00%
Hachi	13.00%
Apache	3.75%
24 others average	2.22%

Calculating Apache's Market Share

85% Apache sales are in Small Engines

1990

$11,307,000 x .85 = $9,610,950
$9,610,950 / $256,500,000 = .0375

1989

$11,712,000 x .85 = $9,955,200
$9,955,200 / $263,250,000 = .0378

Exhibit TN–6   Market Size Large Engine Market

Actual and forecasted unit sales of large outdoor power equipment (in thousands of units)

Year	OPE Using Large Engines	Percent Change Prior Year
1986	565	N/A
1987	875	.55
1988	950	.09
1989	1050	.11
1990	1020	-.0286
1991	1025	.0049
1992	1070	.044
1993	1100	.028

Approximate Large Engine Market in Revenue

1,020,000 x $350 = $357,000,000

Market Share Large Engines

Brighams	42.00%
Hachi	8.00%
Other Captive	25.00%
Unidentitied U.S. Mfr.	7.00%
Unidentified U.S. Mfr.	6.00%
Remaining Market	12.00%

Exhibit TN–7   Breakeven Analysis Small Engine Market API

How many engines did Apache sell in 1990?

$11,307,000 x .85 = $9,610,950
$9,610,950 / $45 = 213,577

Variable Costs

Raw Materials	4,862,000	x	.85	=	$4,132,700
Direct Labor	2,256,000	x	.85	=	1,917,600
Variable Overhead	678,000	x	.85	=	576,300
Shipping	192,000	x	.85	=	163,200
Commissions	226,000	x	.85	=	192,100
					$6,981,900

$6,981,900 / 213,577 = $32.69 average variable cost per unit

Fixed Costs

Advertising	9,000	x	.85	=	7,650
Salaries	554,000	x	.85	=	470,900
Promotional Materials	226,000	x	.85	=	192,100
Administrative	348,000	x	.85	=	295,800
Depreciation	97,000	x	.85	=	82,450
Research and Development	1,583,000	x	.85	=	1,345,550
Supplies	113,000	x	.85	=	96,050
Insurance	187,000	x	.85	=	158,950
Interest	167,000	x	.85	=	141,950
					$2,791,400

Breakeven = Fixed Costs / (Unit Price—Unit Variable Cost)

$$\frac{\$2,791,400}{\$45 - \$32.69} = 226,759 \text{ units}$$

Note: This BEP will slightly underestimate Apache's needs because of the fifteen percent unaccounted for in this calculation.

Exhibit TN–8 Breakeven Analysis Large Engine Market Brighams

How many large engines did Brighams sell?

Brighams Large Engine Division Sales = $149,940,000
Average Market Price for Large Engines = $350

$$\$149,940 / \$350 = 428,400 \text{ units}$$

Variable Costs
Raw Materials	$60,576,000
Direct Labor	33,437,000
Variable Overhead	8,397,000
Shipping	1,799,000
Commissions	6,747,000
	$110,956,000

$110,956,000 / 428,400 = $259.00 average variable cost per unit

Fixed Costs
Advertising	$1,649,000
Promotion	3,374,000
Depreciation	2,999,000
Interest	3,749,000
R & D	5,623,000
Supplies	1,005,000
Insurance	2,249,000
Salaries	12,295,000
	$32,943,000

Breakeven = Fixed Costs / (Unit Price—Unit Variable Cost)

Brighams estimated breakeven

$$\frac{\$32,943,000}{(350 - \$259)} = 362,011 \text{ units}$$

Exhibit TN-9 Breakeven Analysis Large Engine Market API (Scenario One)

Apache's large engine capacity is 50,000 units per year
This is approximately five percent of the industry's projected unit sales for 1991 (i.e., 50,000 / 1,025,000 = .0488)
It is slightly less than $1/8^{th}$ (53,550) of Brighmams' 1990 sales
Let's begin our estimation of Apache's large engine costs by using 1/8 of Brighams' Large Engine Division costs. (Note: this will likely over-estimate Apache's probable costs, but it is a starting point for the students to begin discussing appropriate values).

Variable Costs

Raw Materials	$60,576,000	x	.125	=	$7,572,000
Direct Labor	33,437,000	x	.125	=	$4,179,625
Variable Overhead	8,397,000	x	.125	=	$1,049,625
Shipping	1,799,000	x	.125	=	$224,875
Commissions	6,747,000	x	.125	=	$843,375
	$110,956,000	x	.125	=	$13,869,500

$13,869,500 / 50,000 = $277.39 average variable cost per unit

Fixed Costs

Advertising	$1,649,000	x	.125	=	$206,125
Promotion	3,374,000	x	.125	=	$421,750
Depreciation	2,999,000	x	.125	=	$374,875
Interest	3,749,000	x	.125	=	$468,625
R & D	5,623,000	x	.125	=	$702,875
Supplies	1,005,000	x	.125	=	$125,625
Insurance	2,249,000	x	.125	=	$281,125
Salaries	12,295,000	x	.125	=	$1,536,875
	$32,943,000	x	.125	=	$4,117,875

Breakeven = Fixed Costs / (Unit Price—Unit Variable Cost)

Apache's estimated break-even

$$\frac{\$4,117,875}{(\$350 - \$277)} = 56,409 \text{ units}$$

CASE 6-5
CAPITAL (A) MAGAZINE*

Synopsis

Prisma Presse, the French subsidiary of the German publishing company Gruner+Jahr, itself a subsidiary of the giant multi-media Bertelsmann Group, is considering the launch of a new business magazine called Capital. Prisma Presse has a remarkable track record. Started only 13 years ago, it has become the second-largest magazine publisher in France, thanks to a pervasive marketing culture.

The case describes the various steps Prisma Presse went through in the development of the new magazine. Although focus group results suggest that readers like the product, there are good reasons for not launching it: the market is declining, most existing business magazines are losing money, and Prisma Presse has no experience in the business magazine market, having produced mainly women's magazines until now. Last but not least, the financial risk is high (F60 million, i.e., about $10 million), and Prisma Presse has not done any quantitative market research which could be used to forecast sales.

Capital was actually launched very successfully, becoming not only the new industry leader from the start but also the business magazine with the largest circulation in Europe. Capital's success combined with a 40% drop in the advertising market caused great problems for the incumbent magazines, most of which either folded or changed owners in spite of numerous repositioning attempts.

Teaching/Learning Objectives

To discuss

- the concept and implementation of a marketing culture in a non-traditional industry,
- the role of innovation for competing in a mature/declining industry,
- the product development process, especially the role of customer and competitive research,
- marketing mix decisions and financial analysis for new products, and
- the sustainability of competitive advantage in an industry where imitation appears to be easy.

The case has been used successfully both with MBA and executive audiences. The teaching contexts have usually been basic marketing courses or new product/innovation courses.

---

*This teaching note was prepared by Reinhard Angelmar, Professor of Marketing at INSEAD, France as aid to instructors in the classroom use of the case *Capital (A)*. Copyright © 1994 INSEAD, Fontinebleau France.

Discussion Questions

The following questions cover both basic marketing and new product innovation issues. Depending on the teaching context, instructors may select a subset of the questions:

1. How market oriented is Prisma Presse? What factors (organizational structure, incentive systems, etc.) influence its market orientation?
2. How attractive is the French business magazine market, and what are Prisma Presse's strengths and weaknesses in this market? Would you have recommended that Prisma Presse develop a magazine for this market?
3. What are the key elements of the process through which Prisma Presse has developed Capital? What are the strong and weak points of this process and what changes do you recommend?
4. Assess the likelihood that Capital will be successful. Would you launch Capital? If so, when and how?
5. Assume that Capital were launched successfully: how easy is it to imitate Capital? What would you do to sustain Capital's competitive advantage?

Prisma Presse's Market Orientation

How to define market orientation? TN–Exhibit 1 uses the definitions proposed by Kohli and Jaworski (1990; see also Kohli et al., 1993) and Narver and Slata (1990). The discussion can be structured on the blackboard through a drawing as shown in TN–Figure 1.

Figure 1   **Prisma Presse's Market Orientation**

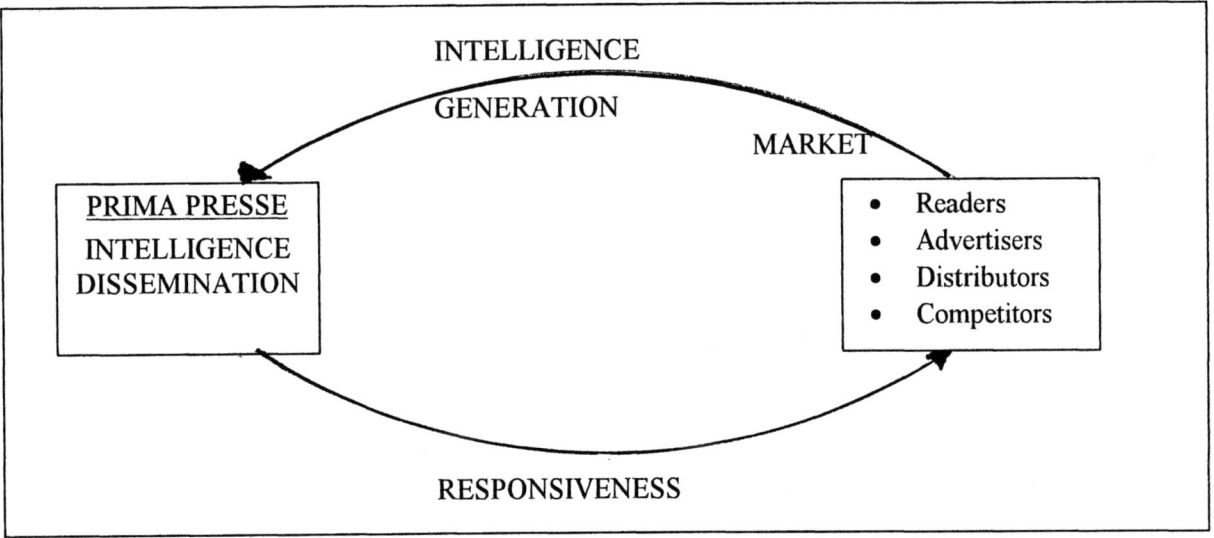

Prisma Presse appears to be quite market oriented. Issues arise in regard to how they deal with the distribution system and advertisers:

Distribution. Prisma Presse's main distribution channel are the newsstands (p. 3). Although the case does not describe PP's policies toward this channel, the success of their titles suggests that their channel relations must be at least comparable to those of their competitors.

Advertisers. To be profitable, magazine publishers must satisfy both readers and advertisers. But there is potential for conflict: readers may love to learn about business blunders, whereas companies dislike negative reporting and may threaten to withdraw their advertising business. Figure 2 shows 3 of the possible orientations.

TN–Figure 2   Possible Stakeholder Orientations for Magazines

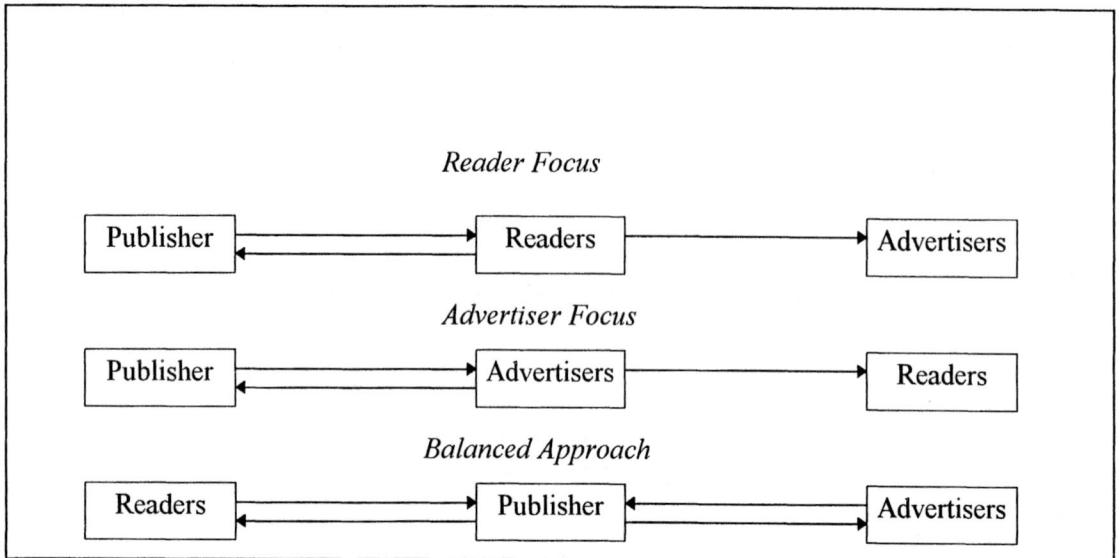

If market orientation is interpreted to mean that PP's offering should always satisfy both the readers and the advertisers, then PP is deficient: "PP has a policy of not letting advertisers interfere in editorial content" (p. 3).

Opportunity Analysis

How attractive is the French business magazine market?

Market size:

- circulation: compared to PP's existing magazines (Exhibit 2), neither the total circulation nor the circulation of individual magazines are impressive
- total industry revenue: F640 million (F240 million circulation revenue, Exh. 6, plus 60% of FF660 million ad revenue, Exh. 7) = 32% of PP's total 1990/91 revenue (Exhibit 3)

Growth:

- circulation is stagnating (Exh 6)
- advertising is declining (Exh 7)

Competition:

- *concentration:* the three strongest competitors (top three) have a 73% share of the circulation and 64% of the advertising market (Exh. 6 & 7). A PIMS study on corporate venture success (in industrial markets) (Tsai et. al., 1991) found that a high top three share, contrary to what was expected, actually increased the new entrant's market share and ROI two years after entry. They speculated that markets dominated by a few large players might be characterized by competitive complacency

- *Competitors' dependency:* the higher the competitors' dependency on the target market, the stronger they can be expected to react (Tsai et at., 1991). 44% of the L'Expansion group's sates are estimated to derive from their two business magazines (L'Expansion: 35%; L'Entreprise: 9%; Exh 8). Other magazines accounting for a high share of their group's sates are Dynasteurs (15% of Pearson France) and Challenges (10% of the Nouvel Observateur Group).

Industry Profitability:

Information from Case Exhibits 6, 7, 8 and 15 can be used to estimate the profitability of the existing business magazines (see Table 1).

TN–Table 1   Profit Estimates for Business Magazines in France

	L'Expans	Le Nouvel Econ	S&V Eco	Dynas-teurs	L'Enter-prise	A Pour Affaires	Chall-enges
1990 Profit Estimates (million F)*							
Total Net Revenue	*202F*	*137F*	*26F*	*49F*	*51F*	*32F*	*27F*
Net Circulation Revenue	44F	46F	18F	20F	13F	9F	16F
Net Advertising Revenue	159F	90F	8F	29F	38F	24F	12F
Cost of Goods Sold	*64F*	*58F*	*17F*	*19F*	*21F*	*18F*	*15F*
Mechanical Costs	38F	31F	8F	8F	10F	5F	6F
Editorial Costs	26F	27F	8F	10F	11F	13F	9F
Departmental Costs	6F	6F	6F	6F	6F	6F	6F
Subscriptions Costs	61F	32F	20F	27F	12F	7F	19F
Media Adv, Adv Promo, Mkt Res	17F	14F	5F	3F	7F	9F	4F
Operating Profit	*54F*	*26F*	*-20F*	*-6F*	*6F*	*-8F*	*-17F*
Operating Profit (% of Net Rev.)	27%	19%	-78%	-11%	11%	-24%	-64%
1991 Profit Estimates (million F)**							
Total Net Revenue	*171F*	*119F*	*25F*	*43F*	*43F*	*28F*	*25F*
Net Circulation Revenue	44	46	18	20	13	9	16
Net Advertising Revenue	127F	72F	7F	23F	31F	19F	9F
Cost of Goods Sold	*60F*	*56F*	*16F*	*18F*	*20F*	*18F*	*15F*
Mechanical Costs	34F	29F	8F	8F	9F	5F	6F
Editorial Costs	26F	27F	8F	10F	11F	13F	9F
Departmental Costs	6F	6F	6F	6F	6F	6F	6F
Subscriptions Costs	61F	32F	20F	27F	12F	7F	19F
Media Adv, Adv Promo, Mkt Res	16F	13F	4F	3F	6F	8F	4F
Operating Profit	*28F*	*12F*	*-22F*	*-10F*	*-0.3F*	*-11F*	*-19F*
Operating Profit (% of Net Rev.)	16%	10%	-87%	-24%	-1%	-42%	-77%

*Assumptions: as in Exh 6, 7, 8 and 15, except for editorial costs (adjusted for differences in output/staff) and self promotion yield per issue (0,3% for L'Expansion, a bi-weekly, 0.2% for Le Nouvel Econ, a weekly)
**Same assumptions as for 1990, except far a 20% decline in advertising market (6080 instead of 7600 pages)

Of the seven magazines, only three are estimated to have made profits in 1990, and only two in 1991: L'Expansion and le Nouvel Economiste. To make money in this market, you must have both high circulation (90,000 or more) and a strong advertising business: the circulation share:adv share is 29:31 for L'Expansion and 34:30 for Le Nouvel Economiste (see Exhibits 6 and 7).

In view of the above figures, it is no surprise that A pour Affaires folded and that Science & Vie Economie stopped its relaunch campaign (p. 10). Unless the advertising market grows significantly above the 1990 level in the future, or unless the money-losing magazines make significant changes, they are likely to disappear.

The case indicates that the L'Expansion group is rumored to be in the red (p. 10). Because of the good profitability of the business magazine L'Expansion, this magazine must be the group's cash cow, and the losses must be due to some other publication(s). In fact, the financials problems were caused by the business newspaper La Tribune, which the group sold in July 1992.

Conclusion on Market Attractiveness:

Overall, the market does not appear attractive: its size is not impressive, it stagnates (circulation) or declines (advertising), some competitors are highly dependent on the market and likely to fight, and only two magazines are making money.

What are Prisma Presse's strengths and weaknesses in this market?

Strengths:

- Gruner+Jahr, PP's parent organization, has the leading business magazine in Germany. But is the experience in the German market applicable to France? How much international versus national coverage do French managers want? Given Fortune France's small number of French journalists (8, p. 4; compare with Avg. Nr of Staff Members of the other Business Magazines, Exh. 8), they probably had a high share of international coverage and failed.
- PP's editorial principles (pp. 2-3) may bring something new to the French business magazine market

Weaknesses:

- PP has no experience in the business/economic press
- PP's reader/circulation focus is reflected in its revenue structure: circulation:ad revenue is about 4:1 (Exhibit 3). In the business magazine market, the relation is about 1:2 (from Case Exhibits 6 and 7 and TN–Table 1). Can PP afford to ignore advertisers' desire to influence editorial content in this market?
- the companies which advertise in business magazines are probably not the same as the ones which advertise in women's magazines; among PP's magazines, only GEO (upper middle class readers, Exhibit 2) may have significant reader and advertiser overlap with Capital;
- only a minority of readers of business magazines buy them at newsstands (see Exhibit 8), PP's main distribution channel

Would you have recommended that Prisma Presse develop a magazine for this market?

The market is not especially attractive, and PP has significant weaknesses. A recommendation against targeting the business magazine market is quite defensible.

Recommendations in favor of targeting the French business magazine market are usually based on the perception that significant opportunities for innovation exist:

- the existing magazines do not completely satisfy reader needs (Exhibit 11)
- only 59% of all senior and middle managers in business firms read business magazines (p. 6)
- personal finance magazines have experienced 8% annual growth over the last 10 years (p. 5); yet many of the existing French business magazines do not provide good coverage of personal finance topics (Exhibit 9); more generally, "personal service" topics receive less coverage than in other countries (p; 6; Exhibit 9);
- the French business magazines under-invest in editorial content (p. 6)
- there is an opportunity to expand newsstand sales of business magazines

An additional argument in favor of targeting the business magazine market is that PP may already be present in all of the big-circulation segments. For further expansion in the magazine market, they may be obliged to target segments with a lower circulation potential.

The Development of Capital

What are the key elements of the development process?

TN–Exhibit 2 provides a summary of the product development process. The dominant characteristics of this process are:

- systematic progression from idea to pilot product (zero issue)
- market input at every phase
- strong personal involvement of top management, i.e., Axel Ganz, both in the substance and the process of development
- Axel Ganz hand picks the core team which, in turn, coopts other members as the need arises
- the mixed staffing (insiders + newcomers), combined with careful selection and socialization of the newcomers allows Prisma Presse to grow, while maintaining and transmitting its culture (see Figure 3)
- the team is working full time on this project only
- the milestones are highly demanding (some around-the-clock work)

Important characteristics of the context in which the development process took place are:

- the company is resource-rich and willing to take risks (F60 million investment, p. 9)
- Capital was the only development project at that time; focus on one development project at a time is general PP policy (see Figure 4)
- more generally, the development of Capital is constrained by a general set of new product policy guidelines ("Product Innovation Charter,. see Crawford, 1987, 1991), as shown in Table 2.

TN–Figure 3   "Cell Division" at Prisma Presse

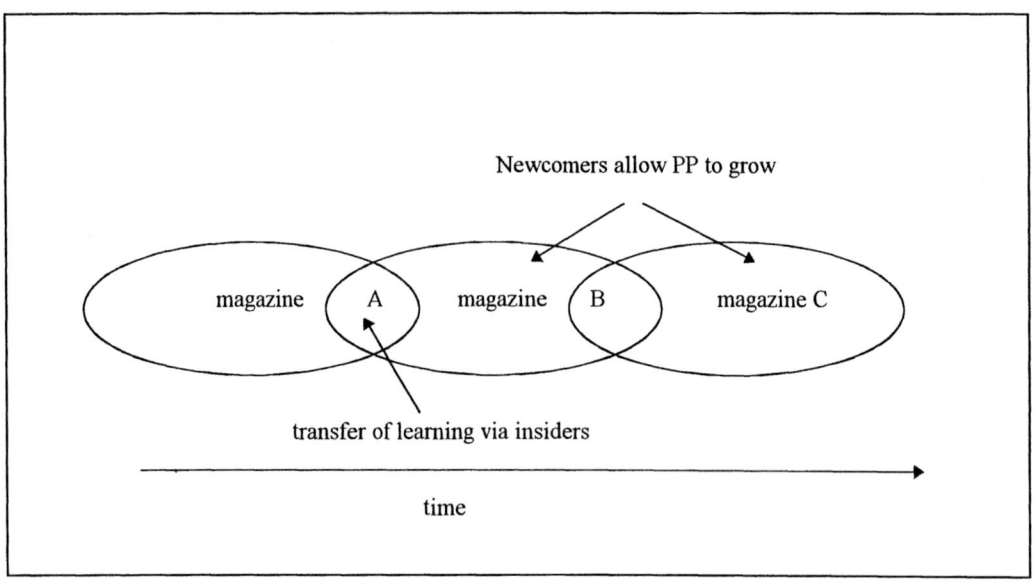

TN–Figure 4   New Product Ideas, Concepts, and Development Projects at Prisma Presse

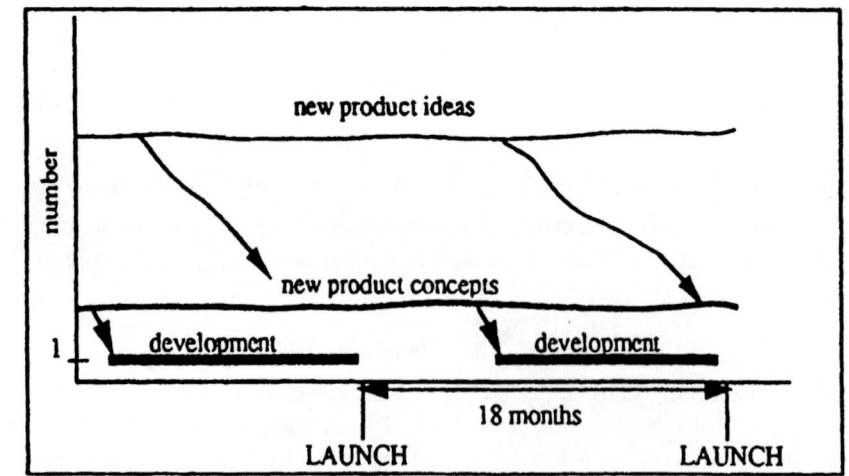

TN–Table 2   Product Innovation Charter of Prisma Presse

1. Strategic arena (p. 3):
   - no newspapers and news magazines ("Voice of Germany" perception)
   - distribution primarily through the newsstand channel

2. Goals of the new product activity
   - one new magazine every 18 months
   - target high circulation potential markets
   - financial criteria: breakeven 34 years; payback 5-8 years; long-term ROI 15%; (p. 10)

3. Program to achieve goals:

   Sources of key innovative element
   - competitors' products and features, worldwide
   - Gruner+Jahr's successful concepts in other countries
   - PP's editorial principles
   - user studies, unmet needs

   Degree of innovativeness used:
   - create products which are new to the target segment
   - newness is achieved mainly through combining features which already exist somewhere m new ways

   Timing: markets in all life cycle stages can be attractive
   - e.g., GEO created the travel magazine market in France
   - e.g., Prima and Femme Actuelle were launched into a declining market

What are the strong and weak points of the product development process at Prisma Presse?

	Strong Points	*Weak Points*
Opportunity Identification	• global scanning • goes beyond aggregate trends to detect unsatisfied customer needs (Ganz perceives opportunities which others don't see)	• Axel Ganz = idea source and idea judge: posible overdependence on Axel Ganz
Concept Development	• no a priori constraints • broad range of market intelligence: consumer *and* competitor analysis; aggregate market analysis *and* focus groups • target market defined • positioning versus competition defined by 6 key points • concept goes beyond what consumers say they want (e.g., "entertainment" is not mentioned in Exh 11) • check for consistency between the concept and the feature (content areas, allocation of pages, specific articles, presentation, etc.)	• no quantitative consumer research: how widespread is dissatisfaction? Are there differences in dissatisfaction and needs across segments? • No "core benefit proposition" • no concept tests • links between concept and features assumed, not systematically tested • no research on price, communication and distribution
Product Development	iterative process ("periodic prototyping"): 1st prototype ↓ consumer research 2nd prototype ↓ consumer research 3rd prototype (zero issue) ↓ consumer research (market launch)	• no alternatives tested • exclusive reliance on focus groups • no consumer research on other mix elements (name, price, communication, distribution)

Prisma Presse's exclusive reliance on focus groups and lack of use of quantitative market research is similar to what has been observed for US companies (Mahajan and Wind, 1992).

What changes in Prisma Presse's development process do you recommend?

Students often recommend the following changes:

- large sample testing of several product concepts
- large sample testing of several prototypes
- a large sample product (and marketing mix) test to forecast expected sales

To bring out the assumptions underlying the choice of different market research methods during new product development, the instructor may ask: What reasons could explain why PP proceeded the way they did, and why they did not do the kind of research which you are recommending? The answers will reveal implicit assumptions about the validity (error) of different types of research and their associated costs. TN–Figure 5 (see Urban and Hauser, 1993, p. 477) can be used to structure the discussion. TN–Exhibit 3 provides cost estimates by development stage.

TN–Figure 5   Cost /Error Tradeoffs for Consumer Research Methods

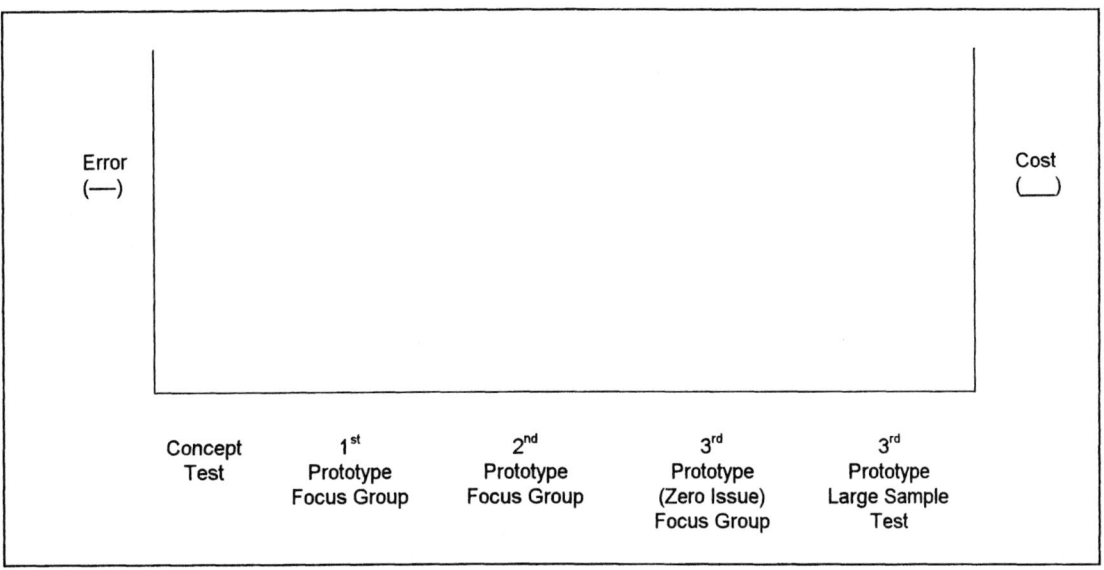

Why was no concept testing done?

PP must believe that concept tests have poor validity. But this depends on how the concept is described: verbal statements (e.g., "broad scope, entertaining, etc.") are indeed questionable, because different respondents will interpret the attributes differently. But more realistic concept descriptions such as mock-up cover pages and tables of contents are less costly than actual prototypes and may still provide valid information.

Why did PP not propose several concepts or prototypes for reader testing?

PP could have created many different concepts, e.g., by varying the amount of space dedicated to the different content areas (people, business, international service topics, etc. see Exh 13) and by designing concept / product tests to obtain reader response to the different concepts / products. One possible research design would have combined sequential and multiple testing, as shown in TN–Figure 6. The circled alternative at each stage refers to the one selected for progression to the next stage.

TN–Figure 6   Sequential and Multiple Concept / Product Testing

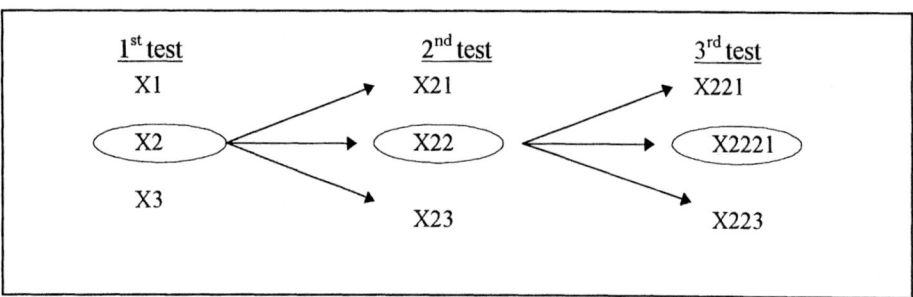

PP tested only one alternative at each stage, modifying the prototype for the next stage as a function of reader response (see Exh 12 and 13). Basically, they used their judgment to cut down on consumer testing at each phase. This reduced the cost and increased the speed of product development, against a higher risk of missing the optimal concept. On the whole, they must have judged that Axel Ganz's market knowledge plus the sequential testing approach would lead them to a pretty good concept, and that the costs and delays of a more systematic approach would not pay off.

Why was the first prototype (January 1991) not representative of the magazine, and what did PP learn from the focus groups?

The first prototype was not representative of the magazine concept as defined in October 1990 (p. 7), as it contained mainly sensational articles. PP was exploring the boundaries of the concept of a business magazine: would a significant increase along the entertainment dimension eject the magazine from the business magazine category?

Since they decided to keep the articles from the first prototype in the second prototype which comprised other, serious articles in addition, they must have concluded that high entertainment would be acceptable in combination with other, more traditional features (=interaction between product features).

Why was the 2nd prototype not already a "pilot product" (i.e., printed like the regular magazine)?

The predictive validity of consumer response would have been higher, for only marginally higher costs: the main costs (department and editorial) are identical and mechanical costs (i.e., paper, printing, shipping from Gütersloh in Germany) are small (several hundred copies). The main reason why PP did not go for a pilot product at this stage is probably that pilot products are always disruptive for the plant. Usually, only one pilot product (zero issue) is produced, and they wanted to keep this option for the 3rd prototype. Why did they produce a 3rd prototype (zero issue) instead of moving directly to market after the positive focus group response to the 2nd prototype? Possible reasons are:

1. increased predictive validity of consumer response to a "real" magazine;
2. to bring the staff up to speed and to create a backlog of articles, to ensure that the first issues would be of high editorial quality;
3. to bring the printing plant up to speed;

4. timing: with everybody in France being on holidays in July and August, there is no point in rushing to the market;
5. the "real magazine" may give PP a better chance to attract advertising for the launch; advertisers may be used to seeing a zero issue before committing themselves;

Why did PP not carry out large sample research as a basis for sales forecasts?

Here, the question to ask is: what is the cost of making a wrong sales forecast in this industry (as compared to other industries)?

a. if the sales forecast is too high: cost-6.88F per magazine (see TN–Table 3), i.e., 688,000F for 100K copies too many. For the next month, this error can be corrected in two ways: first, by reducing production; second, by changing the product (and other mix elements). In the past, PP has achieved spectacular sales increases in a fairly short time: Cuisine Actuelle and Guide Cuisine were acquired in 1989, and by 1991 their circulation had increased by a factor of 3 (Case p. 1). Voici went from 240K to 600K over a three year period (Case p. 2). In other industries (e.g., book publishing, automobiles), where the product cannot be changed every month, getting the sales forecast right is much more important than in magazine publishing.

b. if the sales forecast is too low: cost = lost contribution=11.71F per magazine (see TN–Table 3). Again, this error can be corrected quickly

c. is it better to forecast too low or too high? The lost contribution per copy is almost twice as high as the cost of producing one copy too much. This is the reason for the high unsold rate (i.e., % of copies delivered to newsstands which are not sold)—50% according to Exhibit 15. The unsold rate is generally high in France. This is due to state regulations, which keep the distribution system for newspapers and magazines in an archaic situation.

Some students also criticize the fact that the journalist team had no contact with staff from other PP and Gruner+Jahr magazines, including Capital in Germany (case p. 8). Two points can be made to counter this criticism:

- Communication / exchange of experience is particularly important during the concept development phase. At that stage, there was a great deal of exchange of experience through Axel Ganz, Andreas Wiele (coming from Germany), the art director, and the market researcher (the latter being both old PP hands). By the time the journalists were hired, the contents ("flat plan") were well defined, and it was merely a matter of actually doing the research and writing the articles. i.e., concept implementation. Sealing the team off during that phase probably helped to speed up development.
- The sealing off minimizes the likelihood that competitors learn about the specific approach and contents of Capital. Although competitors heard about the concept (p. 5), they did not take it seriously. It's good to keep it that way by not exposing them to details about the implementation.

TN–Table 3   Contribution Analysis

Assumptions:				
Circulation Market				
nr. Editorial pages/issue		110		
editorial / total nr. pages		80%		
total nr. Pages		138		
nr. Ad pages / issue		28		
retail price		15F		
Distribution margin		55%		
Advertising Market				
price of 4 color ad page/1000 circulation (CPM)		755.00F		
avg net adv revenue/4C ad page		57%		
Mechanical cost/page		0.05F	Contrib. Per Copy	
(i.e., paper, printing, shipping, etc.)				
Circulation Revenue	Gross Revenue	15.00F		
	Net Revenue	45%	6.75F	36%
Advertising Revenue	Gross Revenue			
	(nr. Ad pages x CPM/1000)	20.76F		
	Net Ad Revenue	57%	11.83F	64%
Total net Revenue			18.58F	100%
Mechanical Costs			6.88F	58%
Gross Contribution per Copy			11.71F	63%

Assess the likelihood that Capital will be successful. Would you launch Capital? If so, when and how?

Assess the likelihood that Capital will be successful

What factors should be used to assess the likelihood that Capital will succeed? TN–Exhibit 4 uses Urban and Hauser's (1993, Ch. 3, Ch. 22) summary of the correlates of new product success.

The picture is mixed. There are many positive aspects. The main negative aspects are the unfavorable competitive environment, and the high risk due to the lack of a quantitative basis for sales forecasts.

Would you launch Capital? If so, when and how?

The above discussion supplies good arguments both for and against a launch. At some point during the discussion I usually ask for students' sales estimate:

"Who thinks that, if launched, Capital will during its first year sell

(Nr. of Students)
less than 50,000 copies?
between 50 and 100,000 copies?
between 100 and 150,000 copies?
between 150 and 200,000 copies?
more than 200,000 copies?"

Usually, the majority of estimates are far below Capital's actual results.

When should Capital be launched?

In Fall 1991

- the product is ready and all the staff is in place; what to do with the staff in case of a delay?
- the bad economic situation may actually increase interest in a magazine like Capital, which combines information with service topics
- unlike Fortune France, which had high goodwill from the start, the advertisers are likely to hesitate for Capital until circulation is good; by that time, the ad market hopefully has recovered

Later

- everybody else is in trouble right now; better to wait until the economy recovers

How should Capital be launched?

An Excel spreadsheet which allows to make a 8-year financial projections is available. TN Exhibits 5 and 6 show examples of results for both the "subscription" and the "newsstand" strategy. The assumptions and results in TN–Exhibit 5 are similar to those actually used by Prisma Presse.

Arguments in favor of the "Subscription strategy":

- fits with present readers' purchasing habits for business magazines
- better targeting possible through direct mail

Arguments in favor of the "Newsstand strategy":

- more attractive from a financial point of view (see TN Exhibits 5 and 6)
- the attractive cover design is most effective in a newsstand display
- many target group members already go to the newsstands to pick up a news magazine (p. 10)
- PP believes it has a good product; therefore, the key is to get high trial; this is probably easier and cheaper to obtain through a massive newsstand launch:

```
strong distribution
+ strong advertising
+ attractive cover
+ low price                                          = high trial
                                                          ↓
good product (high customer satisfaction)            = high repeat
                                                     (maybe in the form
                                                     of subscriptions)
```

Assume that Capital were launched successfully: how easy is it to imitate Capital? What would you do to sustain Capital's competitive advantage?

How easy is it to imitate Capital?

The two key questions are: 1) what are the potential sources of Capital's competitive advantage; and 2) how easy are they to imitate? Instructors who wish to have an in depth discussion of the imitation issue might assign the article by Bharadwaj et al. (1993).

Students often feel that, if successful, Capital could be quite easily imitated. This is true at the level of specific product features. But the real question is the extent to which Capital will evolve, and how easy it will be for competitors to imitate the corporate culture (editorial principles) that will drive this evolution.

Potential sources of competitive advantage of Capital	*Potential barriers to imitation*
scale: magazine publishing has high fixed costs (the journalist / art team necessary to create each issue) and low variable costs	• can all competitors obtain high awareness and distribution levels? • availability of capital to make up-front investment in large team • risk-taking ability
brand equity	however, high purchase frequency, great ease of search (flipping through at the newsstand), and low trial risk reduce the importance of brand equity
corporate culture: because magazine publishing is highly "people" intensive, this is an important factor	causal ambiguity: • tacit nature of corporate culture • complexity: interrelationships are important; hiring one or a few PP staff members is probably not sufficient • uncertain imitability • competitors are likely to imitate specific features of Capital, instead of the underlying principles
organizational expertise / experience effects	same comments as for corporate culture

What would you do to sustain Capital's competitive advantage?

Apply PP's editorial principles (pp. 2-3) consistently:

- market intelligence to find out about reader needs and competitor behavior
- evolution of the magazine in response

Epilogue

Capital's Launch

Capital was introduced in October 1991 with the following marketing mix:

- price: 15 F
- subscription discount: 20%
- distribution: newsstands
- communication: about F24 million were spent during the first fiscal year (10 issues: October 91—July 92), F9 million of which were spent on the first issue

Circulation, Advertising and profits

Circulation (see also TN–Exhibit 7)

- first issue: 200,000 copies
- first year (91/92): 205,000 copies per issue
- second year (92/93): 217,000 copies per issue
- third year (93/94): 320,000 copies per issue; of those, about 20% come from subscriptions. The subscriptions have resulted mainly from newsstand readers (self-promotion), i.e., Capital has done almost no direct mail.

Prisma Presse claims that Capital has become the business magazine with the largest circulation in Europe!

Advertising

The total market dropped to about 5000 pages about 75 pages in 1991 and 700 in 1992. Capital sold about 75 pages in 1991 and 700 in 1992.

Profits

- break-even: during the second year (92/93) compared to fourth year (94/95) as expected
- pay-back: end of third year (93/94) compared to eighth year (98/99) as expected

Competitive Response

All competing magazines have changed their price and their product (cover, layout, content coverage, etc.), following Capital's success. L'Expansion went through big internal turmoil, changing editors-in-chief and other key staff members several times since. Some magazines have hired staff away from Capital (art team, journalists). Still, the only magazine which has succeeded a turn-around is Challenges. All the others have run into big trouble:

- Science & Vie Economie folded in mid-1992
- Le Nouvel Economiste and L'Expansion ran into big financial problems and changed owners in December 1992 (Le Nouvel Economiste) and January 1994 (L'Expansion) respectively

Initially, the established magazines tried to stop Capital's penetration in the advertising market by arguing that Capital was too popular to be read by senior and middle managers in business firms. In fact, Capital's 1993 penetration with this group was practically identical to that of L'Expansion (15.3% versus 15.7%). Capital's penetration among "executives" (a target group definition which is also important for advertisers) was 11.7% vs. 12.7% for L'Expansion.

Capital has been evolving incrementally through small changes in layout (e.g., the color and presentation of the central macro-economic section) and content (e.g., in response to rising unemployment among managers, Capital has increased job-market-related topics). Regarding potential editorial synergies with Capital Germany, less than a handful of stories have been exchanged (i.e., sold to the sister publication) since the launch Capital Germany which, at the time of the launch of Capital France was rather austere looking (traditional cover, little color inside) has adopted some of Capital France's aspects, e.g., its colorful cover page.

New Products at Prisma Presse

Gala a glossy celebrities' magazine, was launched in early 1983 first as a monthly and, when its success became apparent, it became a weekly. 1993 circulation: 326,464.

Cuisine Gourmande was launched in March 1994. Circulation: 250,000.

Prisma Presse are preparing the launch of a *new business magazine* in addition to Capital. As of May 1994, its concept and launch date are not known.

Key Points

1. **Market orientation:**

   - market oriented organizations gather market intelligence through a wide variety of mechanisms (formal and informal), broad in scope (local and global market; all stakeholders), to get both an aggregate view (overall market trends) and a bottom-up view (customer needs, perceptions, and behaviors)
   - they distribute that intelligence internally so as to create a shared picture of the market across different functions
   - they take quick action in response to perceived threats and opportunities

2. **Opportunity identification:**

   - *market attractiveness:* markets which, on the surface, do not look attractive (size, growth, profitability, competitive structure), may offer significant opportunities through across-the-board innovation. Capital represented an innovation in terms of product (integration of text and visuals; information and entertainment; managers' professional and personal needs are addressed), price (lower than competitors), distribution (newsstands versus subscription) and communication (attractive cover, push and pull; powerful launch campaign), as well as in the production process (completely integrated PC-based publishing system)
   - *business strength:* poor initial fit can be overcome in two ways: 1) by acquiring the lacking competences (e.g., PP hired journalists with content knowledge); and 2) by "changing the rules of the game" such that they fit the company's strengths. PP's "core competencies" are: integrated production of text and visuals resulting in magazines which are easy and pleasurable to read; an

orientation in favor of readers in cases of conflicts between reader and advertiser needs (easier for an international publisher with deep pockets and who is less dependent on local advertising revenue); the ability to obtain strong newsstand distribution (high penetration and good displays); managing a magazine like a brand, with a clear concept and a consistent implementation.

3. **New product development:**

    - new product market research must be adapted to each situation. Key aspects to consider are: the validity (error) of each method in the specific setting; its cost; the impact of the market research on development speed (time to market); the quality of the managers' market knowledge (intuition); the cost of being wrong, as well as the speed and cost of correcting errors.
    - when the cost of making a mistake in the market is relatively low, when actual market feedback is significantly more valid than pre-launch research, and when errors can be corrected fast and inexpensively, market-based trial and error is a sensible decision strategy
    - new product decisions which are based on a combination of market research and managerial intuition are probably superior to decisions that are based primarily on either one or the other (see also Blattberg and Hoch, 1990)
    - organizations with a sustained track record of successful innovation often have the following features: a well-defined blueprint for innovation (new product policy); senior management commitment to and involvement in the innovation process; multifunctional, dedicated teams; individual learning which is transformed into organizational learning through "apprenticeship" and people transfer

4. **Aggressiveness of market entry:**

    - the more aggressive the market entry, the greater the probability of success (see also Tsai et al., 1991)

5. **Sustainability of the competitive advantage of a new entrant against reactions by incumbents: incumbents suffer the following disadvantages**

    - repositioning is slow because of inertia in consumer perceptions (incumbents may overcome this obstacle by launching new brands, but this is costly)
    - repositioning is slow because of organizational inertia: incumbents may find it difficult to adopt the new attitudes, behaviors and processes that are necessary to compete successfully against the new entrant

REFERENCES

Bharadwaj, Sundar G., P. Rajan Varadarajan, and John Fahy (1993), "Sustainable Competitive Advantage in Service Industries: A Conceptual Model and Research Propositions," *Journal of Marketing*. 57 (October), 83-99

Blattberg, Robert C. and Stephen J. Hoch (1990), "Database Models and Managerial Intuition: 50% Model + 50% Manager," *Management Science*. 36 (August), 887-899

Crawford, C. Merle (1987, 1991), *New Products Management* 2nd, 3rd ea., Homewood, Ill: Irwin.

Kohli, Ajay K., and Jaworski, Bernard (1990), "Market Orientation: The Construct, Research Propositions, and Management Implications," *Journal of Marketing*. 54 (April), 1-18

Kohli, Ajay K., Jaworski, Bernard, and Ajith Kumar (1993), "MARKOR: A Measure of Market Orientation," *Journal of Marketing Research*. 30 (November), 467-477

Mahajan, Vijay and Jerry Wind (1992), "New Product Models: Practice, Shortcomings and Desired Improvements," *Journal of Product Innovation Management*. 9:128-139

Narver, John and Stanley Slater (1990), "The Effect of Market Orientation on Business Profitability," *Journal of Marketing* 54 (October), 20-35

Tsai, William Ming-Hone, MacMillan, Ian, and Murray B. Low (1991), "Effects of Strategy and Environment on Corporate Venture Success in Industrial Markets," *Journal of Business Venturing*, 6 (January), 9-28

Urban, Glen L., and John R Hauser (1993), *Design and Marketing of New Products*. 2nd ea., Prentice Hall

TN–Exhibit 1 How Market Oriented is Prisma Presse?

Elements of Market Orientation		Prisma Presse's (PP) Market Orientation	Factors Influencing PP's Market Orientation
Kohli & Jaworski (1990)	Narver & Slater (1990)		
Intelligence generation	Customer orientation	• reader circulation focus (pp. 2-3) • constant stream of market research (p. 3) • but what is PP doing about advertisers and distributors/newsstands as customers? • Market entry based on competitors' weaknesses, e.g., Prima and Femme Actuelle (p. 4)	• dominance of newsstand sales (vs. subscriptions) provides for rapid market feedback (p. 2) • focus groups are institutionalized (p. 3) • top management behavior: "Axel Ganz monitors market trends in all segments and different countries" (p. 4)
	Competitor orientation	• competitive analysis, e.g., Exhibits 8 and 9	
Intelligence dissemination	Interfunctional coordination	• Axel Ganz watches focus groups (p. 9) • team members watch focus groups (p. 3) • integration of text and visuals (pp. 3-4)	• top management behavior: Axel Ganz participates in discussions (p. 10) • circulation figures are highly visible; celebration of outstanding results (p. 2) • organization structure: managing duo with complementary perspectives; multifunctional teams (journalists + art team + advertising) focused on one product only • teams composed of insiders + newcomers: newcomers are socialized by the Insiders—shared PP culture • physical closeness: open plan offices facilitates communication • multifunctional attendance at focus groups is institutionalized
Responsiveness		• disappointing circulation triggers quick response, e.g., Voici's repositioning (pp. 2-3) • evolution of Capital in response to focus group reactions	• top management behavior: "obsession with circulation" (p. 2) • market (i.e., circulation) based incentives for managing duo and regular staff members: between 16% and 60% of annual salary; lack of responsiveness gets you fired (p.2) • staffing policy: PP hires people who are willing to adapt to PP principles and culture; those who cannot adapt are asked to leave (p. 6) • information technology: PC-based publishing increases flexibility (p.10) • outsourcing of many functions (p. 1) increases flexibility

TN–Exhibit 2   The Development of Capital

Nature of Phase	Opportunity Identification	Concept Development	Product Development 1st Prototype	2nd Prototype	3rd prototype/ Zero Issue
Main results of phase:	*market identification:* • business magazines *idea generation:* • "a magazine with a more attractive presentation and higher editorial quality than existing magazines"	*product concept:* 6 points • broader scope and more…. • entertaining • useful • informative • international • visual than existing magazines *product architecture:* share of content areas *article content*	*partial prototype:* 50 pages: not representative of total content (people, service, and life style over-represented) in color, but mediocre print quality no ad pages no cover no name no price	*complete prototype:* 100 pages: content of 1st prototype plus other articles in color, but mediocre print quality no ad pages no cover no name no price	*pilot product:* 110 pages printed like regular magazine some ad pages real cover name: "Capital" no price
Market intelligence	informal monitoring	reader analysis: circulation (Exh 6) reader profile (Exh 10) attitudes/needs (Exh 11) advertiser analysis: adv market (Exh7) competitor analysis: products (Exh 9) mktg mix/financials (Exh 8)	reader analysis: 2 focus groups market monitoring	reader analysis: 2 focus groups market monitoring	reader analysis: 2 focus groups market monitoring
Role of Axel Ganz	opportunity identification champions (sponsors): development budget approval by G+J (Gruner+Jahr)	concept development hand picks the core team defines milestones	monitors progress and product integrity	monitors progress and product integrity champions (sponsors) G+J launch approval	monitors progress and product integrity ultimate decision to launch (risk taking)
Full time (dedicated) staff (at end of phase)		3; hand picked by Ganz (1 insider; 1 from G+J Germany; 1 outsider)	8 (5 new outsiders)	8	32 (new recruits mostly outsiders)
Role of full time staff		market intelligence concept development	market intelligence product development	market intelligence product development marketing mix design investment analysis	market intelligence product development marketing mix design investment analysis
Ends of Phase:	Fall 1989	October 1990	January 1991	April 1991	July 1991
Duration of phase:	several years	12 months	2 months	3 months	3 months
Months since first full time staff (July 1991)		4 months	6 months	9 months	12 months
Cost of phase (TN–Exh 3)	F 0	F 1.1 million	F 2 million	F 2.5 million	F 3.8 million
Cumulative investment	F 0	F 1.1 million	F 3.1 million	F 5.6 million	F 9.4 million

TN–Exhibit 3 Estimated Development Costs of Capital

	Opportunity Identification	Concept Development	Product Development			First Issue (5)
			1st Prototype	2nd Prototype	3rd Prototype	
Duration Nr ot months with full time staff	Several Years 2 (1)	Fall 89-Oct 90 2 (1)	Nov-Dec 90 2	Jan-Mar 91 3	April-June 91 3	July-Sept 91 3
Department Cost F500 000 x Nr of months(2)		1,000,000 F	1,000,000 F	1,500,000 F	1,500,000 F	1,500,000 F
Editorial Cost Nr of pages F20,000 x Nr of pages (3)			50 1,000,000 F	50 (4) 1,000,000 F	110 2,200,000 F	110 2,200,000 F
Mechanical costs/page (6)			N.A.	N.A.	N.A.	1,300,000 F
Market Research Nr of focus groups F25 000 (7) x Nr of focus groups		2 50,000	2 50,000	2 50,000	2 50,000	N.A
Total Cost per Phase	0 F	1,050,000 F	2,050,000 F	2,550,000 F	3,750,000 F	5,000,000 F
Cumulative Cost	0 F	1,050,000 F	3,100,000 F	5,650,000 F	9,400,000 F	14,400,000 F

(1) Wiele arrived in July 1990, Dessarts in September, and the Art Director Thierry Rouxel also around September.
(2) Case Exhibit 15: department costs: F6million per year; i.e., F0.5 million per month
(3) Case Exhibit 1 5: editorial costs/editorial page: F20 000
(4) The second prototype included the 50 pages from the first, partial prototype
(5) Assumptions: launch end of September; total Nr of pages: 130 (110 edit.+20 ad pages); 200000 copies printed.
(6) Case Exhibit 15: mechanical printing costs / page: F0.05
(7) Assumption: Cost per focus group: F25 000

TN–Exhibit 4 How Likely is it that Capital will be Successful?

Correlates of New Product Success	Capital Rating (5-point scale: 5=highest)	Comments
match to customer needs	4	Exhibit 14
high value to the customer	4	Exhibit 14
innovative	4	Exhibit 14: • consumers perceive it as new • Capital redefines the concept of a business magazine "business or news or 'people' magazine?" Exhibit 13: combination of contents is new to French market Case Cover and Exh. 5: style of cover is new to French market
technical superiority	5	• presentation competence: this is PP's core competence • content competence: acquired through hirings; no stars, attractive presentations;
screening, analysis, and decision support systems	3	see discussion on strong/weak points in development
favorable competitive environment	2-3	• stagnating/declining market • key competing magazines face financial difficulties
fit with internal company strengths	3-4	• see TN discussion on PP strengths/weaknesses in the "opportunity analysis" section • to remedy its lack of experience in business/economic publishing, PP has hired some experienced journalists • to remedy its lack of experience in the advertising market for business magazines, PP has just hired L'Expansion's head of advertising
communication among functions	5	see discussion on development process
top-management support	5	same
enthusiastic champion	5	same
new-product organization	5	same
use new-product process	3-4	disciplined process, but market input debatable
avoid unnecessary risk	3	focus groups not projectable; but see discussion on the cost or sales forecast errors
short time to market	5	
worldwide strategy	4	knowledge of other markets used in opportunity identification and concept development
quality and customer satisfaction	4	iterative product development with customer input

TN–Exhibit 5 Capital: Financial Analysis of Newsstand Strategy

CAPITAL	91/92	92/93	93/94	94/95	95/96	96/97	97/98	98/99
Market Evolution								
Circulation/Month (1,000)	1,050	1,050	1,050	1,050	1,050	1,050	1,050	1,050
Advertising Pages/Year	7,500	7,500	7,500	7,500	7,500	7,500	7,500	7,500
Capital: Market Share								
Circulation Share (in %)	8	10	12	14	14	15	15	16
Adv Pages Share (in %)	5	7	11	14	14	14	14	14
Circulation Mktg Mix								
Nr of Editorial Pages/Issue	110	112	114	116	118	119	120	120
Subscription Sales (% of Circulation)	9	17	24	30	34	36	37	38
Price per Copy	15 F	18 F	20 F	22 F	22 F	25 F	25 F	28 F
Subscription Discount (%)	17.50	17.50	17.50	17.50	17.50	17.50	17.50	17.50
Newsstand Distrib Margin (%)	55	55	55	55	55	55	55	55
Adv and Newsstd Promotion/Copy	21.00 F	10.00 F	5.00 F	5.00 F	5.00 F	5.00 F	5.00 F	5.00 F
Advertising Mktg Mix								
4 Colour Ad Page Cost/1000	755 F	785 F	817 F	849 F	883 F	919 F	955 F	994 F
Adv Business Promotion /Ad Page	3,200 F	2,000 F	1,600 F	1,664 F	1,731 F	1,800 F	1,872 F	1,947 F
CALCULATIONS								
Circulation								
Paid Circulation/month (1,000)	84	105	126	147	147	158	158	168
Total Nr of Subscribers(1,000)	8	18	30	44	50	57	58	64
Selfpromotion Yield (%)	1%	1%	1%	1%	1%	1%	1%	1%
Nr Subscript. From Selfprom. (1,000)	8	13	15	18	18	19	19	20
Subscription Renewal Rate (%)	0%	59%	57%	55%	54%	54%	53%	53%
Nr Subscription Renewals (1,000)	0	4	10	17	24	27	30	31
Nr Subscript. fm Direct Mail (1,000)	0	0	5	10	9	11	9	13
Subscription Costs								
Cost/New Subscriber (Dir Mail)	300 F	300 F	456 F	518 F	504 F	533 F	514 F	551 F
Cost/New Subscriber (Selfpromo)	20 F	21 F	21 F	22 F	23 F	23 F	24 F	25 F
Cost/Subscription Renewal	20 F	23 F	30 F	37 F	46 F	49 F	53 F	54 F
Subscript. Service Cost/copy	4 F	4 F	4 F	4 F	5 F	5 F	5 F	5 F
Advertising Market								
Nr Adv Pages/month	31	44	69	88	88	88	88	88
NrAdv Pages/Year	313	525	825	1,050	1,050	1,050	1,050	1,050
Adv Pages/Total Pages (%)	22%	28%	38%	43%	43%	42%	42%	42%
Price 4Color Adv Page	63,420 F	82,446 F	102,893 F	124,843 F	129,837 F	144,675 F	150,462 F	166,913 F
Production and Overhead								
Editorial Cost/Page	20,000 F	20.600 F	21,218 F	21,855 F	22,510 F	23,185 F	23,881 F	24,597 F
Mechanical Cost/Page	0.05 F	0.05 F	0.05 F	0.05 F	0.06 F	0.06 F	0.06 F	0.06 F
Total Nr Page/Issue	141	156	183	204	206	207	208	208
Unsold Rate (%)	50	45	40	35	30	30	30	30
Prprinted Circulation/Issue (1,000)	160	176	190	202	189	201	200	213
Nr of Isues/Year	10	12	12	12	12	12	12	12
Income Statement (1,000F)								
Net Circulation Revenue	6,095 F	11,662 F	16,330 F	21,830 F	22,412 F	27,641 F	27,818 F	33,445 F
Net Advertising Revenue	11,297 F	24,672 F	48,385 F	74,719 F	77,707 F	86,588 F	90,052 F	99,897 F
Total Net Revenue	17,392 F	36,324 F	64,715 F	96,548 F	100,119 F	114,229 F	117,870 F	133,343 F
Mechanical Costs	11,331 F	16,970 F	22,084 F	27,006F	26,170 F	28,827 F	29,736 F	32,559 F
Editorial Costs	22,000 F	27,686 F	29,026 F	30,422 F	31,874 F	33,109 F	34,389 F	35,420 F
Departmental Costs	6,000 F	6,300 F	6,615 F	6,946 F	7,293 F	7,658 F	8,041 F	8,443 F
Total Production Costs	39,331 F	50,956 F	57,725 F	64,373 F	65,338 F	69,594 F	72,165 F	76,422 F
Direct Mail—New Subscriptions	0 F	0 F	2,260 F	5,029 F	4,292 F	5,888 F	4,803 F	7,105 F
Cost of Self-Promotion	168 F	206 F	321 F	386 F	397 F	438 F	451 F	496 F
Direct Mail—Subscription Renewals	0 F	102 F	302 F	627 F	1,089 F	1,314 F	1,592 F	1,660 F
Cost of Servicing Subscriptions	302 F	883 F	1,540 F	2,313 F	2,700 F	3,155 F	3,340 F	3,769 F
Total Subscription Cost	470 F	1,244 F	4,423 F	8,355F	8,479 F	10,796 F	10,186 F	13,029 F
Adv and Newsstand Promotion	17,640 F	12,600 F	7,560 F	8,820 F	8,820 F	9,450 F	9,450 F	10,080 F
Adv Business Promotion	1,000 F	1,050 F	1,320 F	1,747 F	1,817 F	1,890 F	1,965 F	2,044 F
Marketing Research	3,000 F	1,500 F	1,560 F	1,622 F	1,687 F	1,755 F	1,825 F	1,898 F
Total Marketing Costs	22,110 F	16,394 F	14,863 F	20,545 F	20,803 F	23,890 F	23,426 F	27,051 F
Operating Profit	-44,050 F	-31,026 F	-7,873 F	11,631 F	13,978 F	20,745 F	22,279 F	29,869F
Cumulative Operating Profit	-44,050 F	-75,076 F	-82,949 F	-71,318 F	-57,340 F	-36,595 F	-14,316 F	15,553 F
Operating Profit (% of Net Revenue)	-253%	-85%	-12%	12%	14%	18%	19%	22%

TN–Exhibit 6 Capital: Financial Analysis of Subscription Strategy

CAPITAL	91/92	92/93	93/94	94/95	95/96	96/97	97/98	98/99
Market Evolution								
Circulation/Month (1,000)	1,050	1,050	1,050	1,050	1,050	1,050	1,050	1,050
Advertising Pages/Year	7,500	7,500	7,500	7,500	7,500	7,500	7,500	7,500
Capital: Market Share								
Circulation Share (in %)	8	10	12	14	14	15	15	16
Adv Pages Share (in %)	5	7	11	14	14	14	14	14
Circulation Mktg Mix								
Nr of Editorial Pages/Issue	110	112	114	116	118	119	120	120
Subscription Sales (% of Circulation)	70	70	70	70	70	70	70	70
Price per Copy	25 F	28 F	30 F	33 F	35 F	38 F	40 F	43 F
Subscription Discount (%)	30.00	30.00	30.00	30.00	30.00	30.00	30.00	30.00
Newsstand Distrib Margin (%)	55	55	55	55	55	55	55	55
Adv and Newsstd Promotion/Copy	11.00 F	5.00 F	3.00 F	3.00 F	3.00 F	3.00 F	3.00 F	3.00 F
Advertising Mktg Mix								
4 Colour Ad Page Cost/1000	755 F	785 F	817 F	849 F	883 F	919 F	955 F	994 F
Adv Business Promotion /Ad Page	3,200 F	2,000 F	1,600 F	1,664 F	1,731 F	1,800 F	1,872 F	1,947 F
				CALCULATIONS				
Circulation								
Paid Circulation/month (1,000)	84	105	126	147	147	158	158	168
Total Nr of Subscribers (1,000)	59	74	88	103	103	110	110	118
Selfpromotion Yield (%)	1%	1%	1%	1%	1%	1%	1%	1%
Nr Subscript. From Selfprom. (1,000)	8	13	15	18	18	19	19	20
Subscription Renewal Rate (%)	0%	53%	52%	51%	50%	50%	49%	49%
Nr Subscription Renewals (1,000)	0	31	38	45	51	51	54	54
Nr Subscript. fm Direct Mail (1,000)	50	30	35	41	34	40	37	43
Subscription Costs								
Cost/New Subscriber (Dir Mail)	797 F	682 F	715 F	746 F	708 F	743 F	725 F	759 F
Cost/New Subscriber (Selfpromo)	20 F	21 F	21 F	22 F	23 F	23 F	24 F	25 F
Cost/Subscription Renewal	20 F	54 F	62 F	71 F	79 F	79 F	83 F	83 F
Subscript. Service Cost/copy	4 F	4 F	4 F	4 F	5 F	5 F	5 F	5 F
Advertising Market								
Nr Adv Pages/month	31	44	69	88	88	88	88	88
Nr Adv Pages/Year	313	525	825	1,050	1,050	1,050	1,050	1,050
Adv Pages/Total Pages (%)	22%	28%	38%	43%	43%	42%	42%	42%
Price 4 Color Adv Page	63,420 F	82,446 F	102,893 F	124,843 F	129,837 F	144,675 F	150.462 F	166,913 F
Production and Overhead								
Editorial Cost/Page	20,000 F	20,600 F	21,218 F	21,855 F	22,510 F	23,185 F	23,881 F	24,597 F
Mechanical Costs/Page	0.05 F	0.05 F	0.05 F	0.05 F	0.06 F	0.06 F	0.06 F	0.06 F
Total Nr Pages/Issue	141	156	183	204	206	207	208	208
Unsold Rate (%)	50	45	40	35	30	30	30	30
Printed Circulation/Issue (1,000)	109	131	151	171	166	178	178	190
Nr of Isues/Year	10	12	12	12	12	12	12	12
Income Statement (1,000F)								
Net Circulation Revenue	13,125 F	22,050 F	28,350 F	36,383 F	38,588 F	44,888 F	47,250 F	54,180 F
Net Advertising Revenue	11,297 F	24,672 F	48,385 F	74,719 F	77,707 F	86,588 F	90,052 F	99,897 F
Total Net Revenue	24,422 F	46,722 F	76,735 F	111,101 F	116,295 F	131,476 F	137,302 F	154,077 F
Mechanical Costs	7,712 F	12,587 F	17,589 F	22,781 F	23,023 F	25,531 F	26,424 F	29,031 F
Editorial Costs	22,000 F	27,686 F	29,026 F	30,422 F	31,874 F	33,109 F	34,389 F	35,420 F
Departmental Costs	6,000 F	6,300 F	6,615 F	6,946 F	7,293 F	7,658 F	8,041 F	8,443 F
Total Production Costs	35,712 F	46,574 F	53,230 F	60,149 F	62,190 F	66,298 F	68,854 F	72,894 F
Direct Mail—New Subscriptions	40,166 F	20,375 F	25,060 F	30,207 F	24,067 F	29,784 F	26,748 F	32,615 F
Cost of Self-Promotion	168 F	260 F	321 F	386 F	397 F	438 F	451 F	496 F
Direct Mail—Subscription Renewals	0 F	1,683 F	2,375 F	3,158 F	4,028 F	4,028 F	4,494 F	4,494 F
Cost of Servicing Subscriptions	2,352 F	3,634 F	4,491 F	5,397 F	5,559 F	6,135 F	6,319 F	6,942 F
Total Subscription Cost	42,686 F	25,951 F	32,247 F	39,148 F	34,051 F	40,385 F	38,012 F	44,547 F
Adv and Newsstand Promotion	9,240 F	6,300 F	4,536 F	5,292 F	5,292 F	5,670 F	5,670 F	6,048 F
Adv Business Promotion	1,000 F	1,050 F	1,320 F	1,747 F	1,817 F	1,890 F	1,965 F	2,044 F
Marketing Research	3,000 F	1,500 F	1,560 F	1,622 F	1,687 F	1,755 F	1,825 F	1,898 F
Total Marketing Costs	55,926 F	34,801 F	39,663 F	47,810 F	42,847 F	49,700 F	47,472 F	54,537 F
Operating Profit	-67,217 F	-34,653 F	-16,158 F	3,142 F	11,257 F	15,479 F	20,976 F	26,646 F
Cumulative Operating Profit	-67,217 F	-101,470 F	-118,028 F	-114,885 F	-103,628 F	-88,150 F	-67,174 F	-40,527 F
Operating Profit (% of Net Revenue)	-275%	-74%	-21%	3%	10%	12%	15%	17%

TN–Exhibit 7   Circulation of Main Business Magazines in France

	Launch Year	Frequency	Paid Domestic Circ per Issue (in thousand copies)					Share of Monthly Paid Circulation	
			1989	1990	1991	1992	1993		
CAPITAL*	1991	monthly			205	217	320		26%
L'Expansion	1967	bi-weekly	159	150	139	141	141	29%	23%
Le Nouvel Economiste	1975	weekly	84	90	83	81	80	34%	26%
Science& Vie Economie**	1984	monthly	117	107	99			10%	
Dynasteurs / Enjeux les Echos***	1985	monthly	100	95	90	93	97	9%	8%
L'Entreprise	1985	monthly	65	65	66	66	66	6%	5%
Tertiel / A pour Affaires****	1985	monthly	35	47				4%	
Challenges*****	1986	monthly	73	74	74	95	143	7%	12%
Total Monthly Paid Domestic Circulation (1,000)			1044	1048	1210	1077	1228	100%	100%
AnnualGrowth (%)				3%	0%	15%	-11%	14%	
Gross Annual Circulation Revenue (million F)******			240	239	235	N A	N A		
Annual Growth (%)				3%	0%	-2%			

*Capital: launched in October 1991
**S&V Economie: folded in June 1992
***Dynasteurs: relaunched as Enjeux les Echos in April 1992
****A pour Affaires merged into L'Entreprise in June 1991
*****Challenge: relaunched in June 1992
******Gross Circulation Revenue = Average price per copy (Retail price—Subscription Discount) x Total Paid Circulation (Domestic and Export)

CASE 6-6
NATIONAL BREWERIES*

Synopsis:

National Breweries had been the sole manufacturer of clear beer in Zimbabwe. As a result of economic difficulties in Zimbabwe, price increases were expected to place stress on the price-sensitive brewing industry. Additionally, two competitor breweries were expected to enter the Zimbabwe market in the near future. One of the breweries was going to enter through a South African subsidiary funded primarily by an American company, and the other brewery was going to enter through a joint venture with a German brewery. In addition to these problems, NatBrew was also perceived negatively by consumers. Herb Maridadi had to come up with a plan to protect the company from these potentially devastating issues.

Teaching/Learning Objectives:

The National Breweries case focuses upon an African company that is about to face competition for the first time. In addition, government activity has led to economic changes that are having a profound impact on the company. The case shows:

- the role of government in creating various market situations,
- the problems a company faces when moving from a monopolistic form of competition, and
- the important role marketing must play when a firm is no longer operating as a monopoly.

Discussion Questions:

1. What is Maridadi concerned about?
2. What role does the government of Zimbabwe play in NatBrew's market situation?
3. Compare NatBrew to its neighboring counterparts.
4. Assess the situation at NatBrew.
5. What elements of NatBrew's marketing strategy will be affected by competition?
6. What can Maridadi do to overcome the company's "fat cat" image?
7. Where should Maridadi begin upon his return to Zimbabwe?

---

* This teaching note was prepared by Victoria L. Crittenden and Stephanie Hillstrom, Boston College, and William F. Crittenden, Northeastern University, as an aid to instructors using the case, "National Breweries."

Analysis:

The case is very straightforward regarding the issues facing National Breweries and concerns Maridadi has

*Question 1 centers upon the **problem/ decision statement** facing Maridadi and NatBrew.*

1. **What is Maridadi concerned about?**

This question gets to the heart of the problem at National Breweries. Students should be questioned about the problem Maridadi and National Breweries are facing. Students may divide the overall problem into short-term and long-term issues. In the short term, Maridadi must determine the best possible market strategy to overcome negative consumer perception of NatBrew while tackling the problems associated with decreased consumer spending on clear beer. In the longer-term (yet not too far off it appears) is the competitive arena that is opening up in Zimbabwe. National Breweries, until now, has been the sole producer of clear beer in Zimbabwe. National Breweries needs a new marketing strategy which will help them compete in a new competitive environment.

*Questions 2 through 4 focuses upon elements of the **situation audit**.*

2. **What role does the government of Zimbabwe play in NatBrew's market situation?**

The government plays a key role, economically, in NatBrew's market situation. An I.M.F./World Bank package was adopted by the Zimbabwe government in 1990. With this package came price and labor decontrols and reduced government spending, which resulted in price increases and decreased consumer disposable income. The reduced spending by Zimbabwean consumers was felt, primarily, in non-essential products such as beer.

3. **Compare NatBrew to its neighboring counterparts.**

Exhibit TN–1 provides a comparative summary of NatBrew and its neighboring beer producers, based on information provided in the case. Unfortunately, all information is not available for all companies. However, there are not a lot of differences amongst the companies.

This type of comparison helps students see similarities among the neighboring country beer producers. It shows students that NatBrew will face stiff competition should border impediments be removed (which appears to be happening).

4. **Assess the situation at NatBrew.**

Exhibit TN–2 provides a sample SWOT analysis.

*Questions 5 through 6 get the student thinking about various **alternatives, the criterion for analysis**, and the **analysis of these alternatives** which lead to the recommendation.*

5. **What elements of NatBrew's marketing strategy will be affected by competition?**

Students will likely say that all elements of NatBrew's marketing strategy will be affected by competitive activity. Examples might include:

<u>Product</u>: In looking at the comparison completed in question 2, one sees that many of the brands distributed by South African companies are the same ones distributed by NatBrew. Various product options will have to be considered by NatBrew: (i) focus more marketing effort on its Zambezi Lager, (ii) new product

development might become more important, or (iii) importing of popular international brands may need to take place.

Price: This element of the marketing program will be hit hard by competitive pressures. Government issues have driven beer prices very high. However, competitive pressures will tend to work counter to the high prices. NatBrew may find itself in a real quandary here.

Communication: NatBrew already has a sizable communications budget. This is interesting given that it has not faced competition in its home market. The way this money is spent, as well as the focus of the advertising, may need changing with competition in the picture.

Distribution: It is unlikely that NatBrew will stop its service via NatBrew trucks. And, the company has good retail penetration since it has been "the" beer producer in Zimbabwe. The impact may be felt in the need for more/better account nurturing. Some students may question the pay schedule for sales people. With more competitive activity, some students may suggest a different salary/commission ratio. Also, there may be the need for more sales people since building account relationships takes a considerable amount of one-on-one salesperson time.

It is interesting to have students rank the level of competitive impact on each of the elements of the marketing mix. For example, product may see the greatest impact, pricing next, communications next, and then distribution. Some students may not be comfortable in ranking the marketing issues, as they may feel that all elements will be affected to pretty much the same degree. However, the question leads to a good class discussion since there tends to be quite a bit of variation across the rankings, including those who don't see any variation.

As a whole, it is unlikely that NatBrew has ever really considered such issues as how it can maintain and grow its account base (e.g., market penetration issues). Nor, has it probably spent much time thinking about product development and market development concerns. NatBrew's marketing strategy will not be affected just in the tactical way things are done (e.g., the 4 P's), but in the whole area of marketing strategic planning.

6. What can Maridadi do to overcome the company's "fat cat" image?

It is doubtful that students will see an easy way out of this problem. NatBrew created this image (inadvertently, but not surprisingly given that it had not concerned itself with competitive issues) over a long period of time and changing the image will not happen over night. Students tend to focus upon various ways NatBrew can work at changing the image. These might include: social responsibility, advertising, market research, and/or product development.

Students may think that NatBrew could begin to give something back to its community (i.e., issues surrounding social responsibility). NatBrew could link itself to a particular cause (much like Ryka shoes in the Battered Women Fighting Back! case if it was used in the class).

Advertising could begin to focus upon, possibly, NatBrew as a part of the Zimbabwean culture. It could even welcome the competition for the "good of the country."

Market research could begin to focus upon finding out concerns of Zimbabwe consumers and how the company can help address these concerns. The nature of the market research could be that of broader societal issues rather than only on increasing NatBrew's sales. Focus groups might even allow consumers to feel as though they are actually talking personally with NatBrew.

New product development which focused on developing good, cheap beer could serve to show Zimbabwe consumers that the company is concerned about developing products to meet the consumers' needs. This is probably unlike the way NatBrew has done business in the past.

*Question 7 focuses upon the **recommendation** component of the case analysis process.*

7. Where should Maridadi begin upon his return to Zimbabwe?

This is a very difficult question for students. There is a sense of urgency given the negative image of the company and decline in beer consumption. As such, some students will focus upon making changes immediately as identified in questions 5 and 6. However, some students may suggest that now is the time for Maridadi to begin formal, structured marketing planning. They will suggest that making any immediate changes will only be "putting out fires" without knowing how all of the pieces should fit together. Students should be pushed hard on what they would tell Maridadi that he should do upon landing in Zimbabwe. Also, students should provide detail to Maridadi. Should he hire more market researchers (budget?)? Should he meet with the company president and begin the process of marketing strategic planning? The instructor should ask the student what Maridadi should do first upon his return to work on Monday.

Teaching the Case:

The case is somewhat difficult to teach. Students say that this is largely due to the lack of information in the case. Unfortunately, Maridadi was having to make decisions with the same limited information. It helps to forewarn students (either on the syllabus or a few days before the class discussion) that decisions have to be made with very little to go on and that this is very similar to what was happening to the Marketing and Public Affairs Director for the company. Also, the development of a marketing program will not likely be the outcome of the class. Rather, issues surrounding the development of the marketing program—where the focus needs to be, what information needs to be obtained—needs to receive considerable attention in the class. Specific recommendations for elements of the marketing mix would only be made haphazardly at this point in time. Yet, students need to understand that Maridadi wants to get off of the airplane with his own "plan of action" in hand.

Epilogue:

Zimbabwe experienced a drought in 1991/1992, and the inflation rate went from 25 percent in 1990 to 47.6 percent in 1992. The prices of beer had more than doubled, and carbon dioxide, a key ingredient in beer, was in short supply because of the drought.

National Breweries' earnings fell 11 percent from 1991 to 1992. This figure, however, was not as large as the company had expected. The export sales of National Breweries were improving during this time, which helped make up for the drop in the domestic market.

In 1993, the major breweries in Zimbabwe were National Breweries, Chibuku Breweries, African Distillers, and Cairns Wineries.

Exhibit TN–1

Company	Location	Annual Capacity	Brands	Exports
NatBrew	Southerton & Harare, Zimbabwe		Castle Lager Lion Lager Carling Black Label Castle Pilsener Zambezi Lager	yes
Fabrica de Cerveja da Beera	Beira, Mozambique	240,000 hectolitres	Manica Clara Monica Preta Impala	no
Cia. de Cerbesjas Erefrigerantes Mac-Mahon	Maputo, Mozambique	100,000 hectolitres		
Fabricas de Cervesia Reunidas de Mocambique	Maputo, Mozambique	230,000 hectolitres		
Zambia Breweries	Lusaka, Zambia	400,000 hectolitres	Castle Lager Lion Lager	
Alrode Brewery	Alrode, Rep. of South Africa	4,300,000 hectolitres	Castle Lager Lion Lager Castle Milk Stout Hansa Pilsener Amstel Lager Ohlsson's Lager	
Ohlsson's Brewery	Claremont, Rep. of South Africa	2,200,000 hectolitres	Castle Lager Lion Lager Black Label Hansa Pilsener Castle Milk Stout Ohlsson's	yes
South African Breweries	Port Elizabeth Rep. of South Africa	950,000 hectolitres	Castle Lager Lion Lager Black Label Hansa Pilsener Castle Milk Stout Ohlsson's Amstel	

Exhibit TN–2   SWOT Analysis

Strengths

- large supply of labor
- currently only producer of clear beer in Zimbabwe, only one of two beer producers in Zimbabwe—they have the necessary equipment and work force in place
- partial employee ownership (10%) a motivation to the work force

Weaknesses

- increasing prices
- declining volume sales
- declining image among consumers
- product difficult to differentiate
- limited product line (mostly lagers and pilseners)
- export limited to one brand—lack of a global presence/initiative
- lack of presence in a large export market, e.g., U.S.

Opportunities

- joint venture with one of the potential competitors—NatBrew would get access to financial capital, new entrant would have access to already constructed brewery and intact work force
- opaque beer market
- export opportunities with decreasing trade barriers, improved communications and transportation technology
- import raw materials to combat effects of price decontrols
- look into forming/joining buying consortium of southern African breweries to import raw materials at lower cost
- export opportunity—more than one brand, as is currently the case
- find niche market to be able to survive in a concentrated industry
- concentrate on global markets

Threats

- political instability
- inflation
- climatic difficulties, i.e., drought $\Rightarrow$ shortage of raw materials (CO_2)
- two new potential competitors trying to enter market, both of which have substantial financial capital and skills
- worldwide beer production increasing yearly
- established international companies becoming more sophisticated in their operations and marketing
- difficulty surviving in concentrated industry, especially with prices increasing
- cuts in international aid, e.g., via the World Bank and IMF

CASE 6-7
CHEMICAL ADDITIVES CORPORATION
SPECIALTY PRODUCTS GROUP*

Synopsis

Specialty Products Group (SPG), a division of Chemical Additives Corp., was struggling to meet changing competitive conditions. Chemical Additives Corporation (CAC) was a medium-sized company ($294 million in sales,) faced with maturing and declining primary markets, severe price competition, a changing set of competitors, and a need and desire to develop new products and markets. CAC's Specialty Products Group had several strategic problems in 1990 that management needed to resolve quickly:

1. Its position as a high-cost supplier of commodity products to mature and declining industries.
2. How to compete against emerging global competitors in its largest single market—the U.S.
3. How to price, position, and in general, market specialty products to segments or niche.
4. How to prevent a foreign supplier (Corblok) from capturing a major share of SPG's home market.
5. Relying on price as a first-choice competitive weapon.

In addition, there was an immediate decision needed on how to price one of SPG's products, given the market inroads of products made by competitors. The company/division has to make some tough strategic choices and the answers are far from obvious.

There's ample data for student analysis and the challenge for students to dig into the numbers, get a solid grip on the issues, and come to some pragmatic conclusions about what to do.

Teaching/Learning Objectives

Though the case is short (14 pages), it is tough—partly because the product and industry are unfamiliar and partly because there are no easy answers. The case requires that students assess the competitive environment, evaluate SPG's core competencies, consider market segmentation alternatives, develop a pricing strategy, and make strategic recommendations for rolling out new products. The roll-out of SPG's newest additive involves some thorny market segmentation issues and figuring out how to achieve a competitive advantage in key segments. The case is first and foremost an exercise in crafting a marketing strategy that meshes with the rest of the company's strengths, competitive positioning, and strategic capabilities. There are significant functional and operating-level strategic issues in this case, as compared to broad business strategy issues. Yet, the pricing of SPG's new additive goes to the heart of SPG's competitive strategy.

Additionally, the instructor may want to emphasize: (1) how difficult it is to change from a manufacturing/sales mentality (prevalent in the U.S. chemical industry) to a market-driven strategy of developing products and business plans in response to environmental changes; (2) that reorienting sales people from a commodity to a specialty approach can be a difficult process; and (3) that there may also be

---

*This teaching note is from Instructor's Manual for Thompson and Strickland, *Strategic Management*, and is based on the work and analysis of the case authors, Lester A. Neidell and Charles Hoffheiser, University of Tulsa.

an "ego" problem, "We are the worldwide leaders in oil field corrosion control, there's no reason we can't blow the competition away in the fertilizer industry."

This case is especially good for written case assignments and group presentations because of its challenging nature and emphasis on action recommendations (the issue of "what-to-do" is paramount in this case and can't be dodged). Suggested written assignment questions are as follows:

1. Please prepare a 3-5 page report to Nick Williamson, general manager of CAC's Specialty Products Group, providing your recommendations on the pricing and positioning of R&D 601, 602, and 603 and on any other strategic issues that he needs to address. Be sure to fully support your recommendations with appropriate analysis and persuasive arguments.

2. Please prepare a 3-5 page report to Nick Williamson, general manager of CAC's Specialty Products Group, detailing what strategic issues confront his division and what actions he should take to address each one. Support your position with appropriate analysis and reasoned judgment.

Answers to Discussion Questions

1. Does SPG have the core competence/competitive advantage potential to dominate the UAN corrosion inhibitor? Why or why not?

SPG has a strong position in corrosion control technology, chemical process development, and application know-how. However, it is doubtful these translate into a dominate competitive edge. SPG's competitors are reasonably formidable and have enjoyed some market success. SPO has yet to develop a sales and marketing strategy, much less prove that it will work in the marketplace. SPG's management team has not yet settled upon a consensus strategy; opinions seem divided. Thus, one cannot realistically conclude the SPG can dominate the UAN corrosion inhibitor market, even though SPG's new products seem to have substantial promise—SPG must pass its test in the marketplace before it can claim to have competitive edge.

One of SPG's biggest marks is the strategy-making skills of its senior management team. Walker and Brown may have the skills and talent to come up with a good game plan, but they may have to spend lots of hours "educating" White and Williamson on how to proceed. White especially may prove to be a problem. One option would be to appoint either Brown or Walker as the business manager for agricultural markets, including the anti-dust and anti-caking additives for solid fertilizers. Give either one full profit-and-loss responsibility for this business, and management authority over R&D, technical service, selling, etc. In fact, either one could wear both hats of business manager and corrosion inhibitor sales representative. Outfitting this business unit with a larger management bureaucracy doesn't make a lot of sense, given the financial condition of the fertilizer industry at this time.

Of course, White would not like this arrangement, so Williamson may have to show some fortitude and leadership in handling White. If he expects to move SPG toward the premier specialty supplier objectives, he will have to build strategic consensus and push White hard for results in the sales area. The friendship between the two certainly could delay and possibly derail this essential decision; it's not an easy one.

2. Who is the biggest competitive threat to SPG's corrosion inhibitor business currently? In the future? Why?

Concurrently, Corblok is the product SPG has to beat out. Over the long haul, Consolidated and Western likely are the biggest threats to SPG's inhibitor business because of their profitability, numbers of sales/technical service people, knowledge of corrosion control, and existing sales activities at the UAN plants, albeit in water management. Their incremental cost of a sales call on the UAN side is virtually zero, because the people running the steam and cooling systems are the same ones producing UAN. These two companies are already well-versed in specialty, consultative selling concepts; SPG, except for Brown and Walker, is not. SPG has yet to prove it can successfully and profitably market specialty chemicals (as opposed to standard commodity chemicals) to customers whose end-uses and needs vary.

3. Evaluate the pros and cons of using Brown or the existing sales force to sell the new products.

Brown seems to possess the necessary skills; he understands how to sell value-added products (i.e., both tangible and intangible value) and, from his trip with the Fertex sales representative, he understands the needs of the various stages of the UAN distribution channels. A case can be made that using the existing sales force would be a mistake. Even though the cost of this option would be less than having Brown function as a one-person sales force, this doesn't consider training costs, habits such as negotiating price before performance, and an overall commodity mentality that just doesn't fit in specialty segments. The existing sales force is unlikely to develop the skills needed to convince customers to pay a price premium for chemicals (e.g., to point out the impact on capital budgets of a well designed corrosion-control program).

A logical way to segment potential customers is in terms of desired product performance. A performance-based segmentation approach yields four segments:

   a. Premium performance segment-pipeline users and Corblok users who can't tolerate foam and are willing to pay a premium to receive the value of corrosion control that minimizes repair and replacement of plant equipment.

   b. Premium performance segment without foaming problems.

   c. Moderate performance segment—DAP, OA-5, borax and users without foaming problems.

   d. Indifferent about corrosion—ammonia users.

   e. The 601 and 602 products would be positioned as premium materials in a frontal assault on Corblok, since this product's technical service is supplied from 5,000 miles away. To undermine Corblok's market dominance and take market share away form Corblok, SPG will probably have to sell at a price nearly equal to that of Corblok.

Table 1 of this note rearranges the data in case Exhibit 6 to illustrate the size and character of the four performance segments listed above. Students should note from case Exhibit 6 that SPG's Stealth 3662 achieved significant shares by mid-1988 before performance problems became evident. This is a strong signal that premium performance can really be used in industrial markets to capture share. Customers *DO* evaluate product offerings on a price/performance basis—the key success factor is to recognize and meet specialized needs that different end-users have. A differentiation-based focus strategy is called for in positioning SPG's new products in the market.

Table 1   **Van Corrosion Inhibitor Customers, Segmented by Customer Needs**

Company	Potential SPG Volume 000 Lbs.	Mid 1988 Inhib.	Mid 1989 Inhib.	Needs Easy Mix Product	SPG Advantage	Segment Code:	Best Product Offering
Georgia Chemical	170	Ammonia	Ammonia	No	Perform.	I	603/3662
Illini Fertilizer	82	Ammonia	Ammonia	No	Perform.	I	603/3662
Jackson Chemical	'25	Ammonia	Ammonia	No	Perform.	I	603/3662
Nitro Products	16	Ammonia	Ammonia	No	Perform.	I	603/3662
RJS Inc.	58	Ammonia	Ammonia	No	Perform,	I	603/3662
Cherokee Nitrogen	68	Dap	Dap	No	SVC/PITS	M	603
Farm Products	63	Dap	Dap	No	SVC/PITS	M	603
Ferticon	20	Dap	Dap	No	SVC/PITS	M	603
Illini Fertilizer	25	Dap	Dap	Yes	SVC/PITS	M	603
Illini Fertilizer	75	Dap	Dap	No	SVC/PITS	M	603
Illini Fertilizer	38	Dap	Dap	No	SVC/PITS	M	603
NC Fertilizer	58	Borax	Borax	No	SVC/PITS	M	603
Nitrogen Inds..	40	Dap	Dap	Yes	SVC/PITS	M	603
Nitrotech	6	Dap	Dap	Yes	SVC/PITS	M	603
Nitricorp	250	Dap	Dap	No	SVC/PITS	M	603
Nutricorp	125	Dap	Dap	No	SVC/PITS	M	603
US Industries	16	Dap	Dap	No	SVC/PITS	M	603
CAN-AM	20	3662	3662	Yes	–	P	603/3662
Farm Products	63	3662	3662	No	–	P	603/3662
CAN-AM Corp.	4	3662	3662	Yes	–	P	603/3662
Agriproducts	60	3662	3662	No	–	P	603/3662
Nitron Indus..	3	3662	3662	Yes	–	P	603/3662
Iowa Fertilizer	3	3662	Corblok	Yes	–	P&F	603
Iowa Fertilizer	58	3662	Corblok	No	SVC/Cost	P&F	601/602
Marathon	45	3662	Corblok	No	SVC/Cost	P&F	601/602
Ferticon	138	3662	Corblok	No	SVC/Cost	P&F	601/602
Nitrogen Inds.	40	3662	Corblok	No	SVC/Cost	P&F	601/602
Fertex	350	3662	Corblok	No	SVC/Cost	P&F	601/602
Iowa Fertilizer	13	3662	RG-2064	Yes	?	P&F	603
RJS Inc.	32	Chromate	chromate	No	Cost/Safe	P&F	601/602
Edsel Chemical	50	Corblok	Corblok	No	Cost/Safe SVC/Cost	P&F	601/602
RJS Inc.	53	Corblok	Corblok	No	Cost/Safe SVC/Cost	P&F	601/602
Novatec	44	Corblok	Corblok	No	Cost/Safe SVC/Cost	PAF	601602
Eagle Industries	44	Corblok	Corblok	No	Cost/Safe SVC/Cost	P&F	601/602
Edsel Chemical	14	Corblok	Corblok	Yes	Cost/Safe SVC/Cost	P	603
Comanche Powder	5	Corblok	Corblok	No	Cost/Safe SVC/Cost	P&F	601/602
Edsel Chemical	23	Corblok	Corblok	No	Cost/Safe SVC/Cost	P& F	601/602
Edsel Chemical	50	OA-5	OA-5	No	SVC/Foam	P	603
Fertilex	25	OA-5	OA-5	No	SYC/Foam	P	603
Fertilex	50	OA-5	OA-5	No	SVC/Foam	P	603
Canadian Nitrogen	30	OA-5	OA-5	No	SVC/Foam	P	603
Total (000 pounds)	2,442						

Segment Code*	Segment Pounds (000)	Segment Customer Needs	SAG Pro
P&F	888	Premium, foam a problem	601
P	319	Premium, foam not a problem.	603/3662
M	784	Moderate performance, foam not a problem.	603 or Ret
I	451	Ammonia users, seemingly Indifferent about corrosion.	603 or Ret

5. **Evaluate SPG's decision to develop the new products. What is the likelihood that they could meet corporate ROI guidelines given the market environment?**

While this is a candidate question for opening the class discussion, a penetrating answer requires an understanding of the markets and the potential for market segmentation.

The data in Table 2 of this note illustrates that it is reasonably certain that corporate revenues, profits, and ROI goals can be met from sales of the new products, provided sufficient market share can be gained. The profit goal can be met with only a 45% share and a price of $1 .30/lb. Table 3 develops break-even volumes at several different price levels. Analysis of this table indicates that the introduction of a new product, priced as low as $1.30, need only achieve 92% of Stealth 3662's mid-1988 volume in order to break even. Thus, by simply regaining its past position versus Corblok, SPG could realize a healthy return on investment from its new products. A 20% share of the moderate performance segment would give SPG the $800K gross profit required within three years. Likewise, a moderate share of the ammonia segment should also be possible with the inhibitor cost-versus-capital-expense argument offered by Walker and Brown. They're probably capable of convincing potential buyers that the value of SPG~s new products exceeds its added cost. With the proper pricing and selling strategies, SPG might eliminate Corblok from the North American market, and block entry by Consolidated and Western. Admittedly, it is a delicate balance to price high enough to generate substantial profits but not so high as to make entry attractive for other competitors.

6. **What strategy would you recommend for the initial roll-out of the new products? What are the new products' (601,602, 603) strengths and weaknesses as compared to Corblok? Where is Corblok vulnerable? What selling points would you use with customers to get them to switch away from Corblok to SPG's new products?**

The major question is whether SPG can develop a strategy to effectively market its new products. With any "reasonable" set of assumptions about price and obtainable market share, there appears to be a potentially lucrative marketing opportunity for the new products. Tables 2 and 3 indicate that SPG could be a strong and profitable competitor in the premium segments, even at lower pricing levels. Table 4 illustrates one possible pricing scenario for SPG products in each market segment. Data from this table indicate that SPG could optimistically achieve an annual total volume of 1,681,600 pounds and annual revenues of $1 ,632,730 with $1,015,781 in profits. Even from a pessimistic perspective, annual volume would be 786,700 pounds with annual revenues of $1,313,250 and profits of $654,881. With some effort and a change in SPG's managerial philosophy, SPG is clearly capable of meeting its $800,000 per year gross profit objective. For the "premium but foam not a problem segment," the 603 product could be used to deliberately cannibalize 3662 by positioning 603 as a premium inhibitor that doesn't foam nearly as much. Using the information that UAN trading is widespread, and that there is no clear pattern to foaming problems, SPG could deliberately position 603 as an "insurance policy" against processing problems. Product 603 could be priced at $1 .30/lb or higher to generate the same or greater gross profit as 3662, without substantially increasing the treating cost($0.325 versus $0.24 per ton). Such a strategy also limits further advances by Corblok, the target of the frontal assault in the premium/no-foam segment. 603 probably should not have the same brand as or similar numbering to 601 or 602, because the objective is to segment and differentiate at the same time, and to avoid cannibalizing 601 and 602 sales with a lower-priced product.

Either 3662 or 603 could be positioned for the moderate performance segment. It can be argued that SPG made a strategic pricing error when it introduced 3662 at $0.80/lb. and now must figure out how to solve the problem. One way would be to increase the price of 3662 on a gradual but regular basis, citing "raw material cost increases," "environmental compliance cost increases," and so on until 3662, with its much greater risk of foaming, is priced out of the market. Under this approach, it would be essential to convince the market of the 'benefit of the new technology" and that's where Brown's selling expertise is a key. Even at $1.50/lb, the treating cost ($0.375/ton of UAN) of 603 is not significantly higher than other inhibitors, given the capital cost of corrosion repairs, but the regular sales force may not be able to sell that concept.

Table 2   Comparative Profit Projections for SPG's New UAN Corrosion Inhibitors Assuming Market Share Penetration Rates of 45%, 65%, and 73% and Selling Prices of $1.30, $1.50, and $1.80 per Pound

Premium Segment Size[a]	pounds	1,202.000		
	revenues	$2,163,600 at $1.80/lb		
		1,803,000 at $1.50/lb		
		1,562,600 at $1.30/lb		

Investment	In 1989	In 1990	Total
Labor	$200,000	$200,000	$400,000
Marketing	40,000	40,000	80,000
Total	$240,000	$240,000	$480,000

Estimates at 45% Share

Price:	$1.80/lb.	$1.50/lb	$1.30/lb.
Pounds to produce	540,900	540,900	540,900
Revenues	$973,620	$811,350	$703,170
Costs per lbs. Produced[b]	346,176	346,176	346,176
Gross profit	627,444	465,174	356,994
Fixed costs[c]	95,000	95,000	95,000
T&E Expense[d]	19,472	16,227	14,083
Earnings before interest and taxes[e]	512,972	353,947	247,931
Taxes	169,281	116,803	81,817
Net Income	$343,691	$237,144	1$66,114
First year ROI	143%	99%	69%

Estimates at 65% Share

Price:	$1.80/lb.	$1.50/lb.	$1.30/lb.
Pounds to produce	781,300	781,300	781,300
Revenues	$1,406,340	$1,171,950	$1,015,690
Costs per lbs. Produced	500,032	500,032	500,032
Gross profit	906,308	671,918	515,658
Fixed costs	95,000	95,000	95,000
T&E Expensed	28,127	23,439	20,314
Earnings before interest and taxes	783,181	553,479	400,344
Taxes	258,450	182,648	132,114
Net Income	$524,731	$370,831	$268,230
First year ROI	219%	155%	112%

Estimates at 73% Share

Price:	$1.80/lb.	$1.50/lb.	$1.30 lb.
Pounds to produce	877,480	877,460	877,460
Revenues	$1,579,428	$1,316,190	$1,140,698
Costs per lbs. Produced	561,574	561,574	561,574
Gross profit	1,017,854	754,616	579,124
Fixed costs	95,000	95,000	95,000
T&E Expensed	31,589	26,324	22,814
Earnings before interest and taxes	891,265	633,292	461,310
Taxes	294,117	208,986	152,232
Net Income	$597,148	$424,306	$309,078
First year ROI	249%	177%	129%

[a] P and P+F segments from Table 1
[b] Var (.48) + Fixed (.16) = Total (.64)
[c] Fixed Costs = $80,000 (Brown's selling expense) + 10,000 (tech. service) +5,000 (ANPSG) = $95,000
[d] T&E =2% of revenues
[e] Corporate rate of 33%

Table 3: Breakeven Volumes At Various Prices For New Products

Selling Price	$1.80	$1.50	$1.30
Premium Segment Revenue (Where foam is a problem)	$1,598,400	$1,332,000	$1,154,400
Premium Segment Volume	888,000 lbs.	888,000 lbs.	888,000 lbs.
Investment costs	$480,000	$480,000	$480,000
Variable Cost Per Pound	$0.48	$0.48	$0.48
Contribution Margin	$1.32	$1.02	$0.82
'Breakeven" Volume Needed to Recover $480,000 Investment	363,636 lbs.	470,588 lbs.	585,366 lbs.
Required Share of Premium Segment Volume for Investment Breakeven"	41%	53%	67%
Stealth 3662 Volume (Mid-1988)	637,000 lbs.	637,000 lbs.	637,000 lbs.
Stealth 3662 Share (Mid-1988) of Premium Segment Volume	72%	72%	72%
New Product Volume as a Percentage of Stealth 3662 Volume	57%	74%	92%

Total investment over 2 years from Table 1.

Table 4: New Product Positioning Strategies

Segment:	Premium No Foam		Premium Foam OK		Moderate Performance	Ammonia Users
Product(s)	601/601	601/602	3662	603	603 or 'New	603 or New
Price	$1.80	$1.80	$1.00	$1.50	$1.50	$1.50
COGS $/lb.	$0.64	$0.64	$0.40	$0.64	$0.64	$0.64
GP $/lb.	$1.16	$1.16	$0.60	$0.86	$0.86	$0.86
Segment Volume	888,000 lbs	888,000 lbs.	319,000 lbs.	319,000 lbs.	784,000 lbs.	451,000 lbs.
Share	70%	50%	30%	30%	20%	20%
Annual Volume	621,600 lbs.	444,000 lbs.	95,700 lbs.	95,700 lbs.	156,500 lbs.	90,200 lbs.
Annual Revenue	$1,118,880	$799,200	$95,700	$143,550	$235,200	$135,300
Annual Gross Profit	$721,056	$515,040	$57,420	$82.302	$134,848	$77,572
Reasoning	Frontal assault on Corblok		Selectively raise 3662 price to cannibalize with 603's higher profit margin.		May need a second rebrand of 603 to appeal to cost conscious; does not pit like DAP/Borax.	May need a second rebrand of 603 to appeal to cost conscious; does not pit like ammonia.

Finally, at the risk of allowing a foothold for both Consolidated and Western, the ammonia users could be ignored. However, ammonia allows pitting and either a second re-brand of 603 or a completely new product could be introduced to this segment. The key is to protect the premium segment from being cannibalized by this lower priced entry. Value-based selling skills are germane.

Regarding the dosage question, the new products perform equally as well as Corblok at any dosage. The market needs to be convinced of this, and a targeted direct mail campaign of side-by-side corrosion test results could be very effective, as long as follow-up occurred. This would be difficult for Corblok to copy or refute. The point that needs to be made with customers is high doses of all products are required under drastic conditions, and then allow the customer to decide if the dosage is increased. With this approach, the excessive cost issue is handled, and any product liability claims would be alleviated.

Epilogue

Walker prevailed in the pricing decision, and initial offerings of 601 and 602 were at $1.64; 603 was not released because of a fear that its low foam rate still might cause further damage to SPG's reputation (even though R&D's test said this would not happen). Initial positioning was as a Corblok replacement, with value-added corrosion monitoring services and with a new brand name. The products were also positioned as alternatives to those plants still using 3662. This was a defensive strategy to mitigate further losses to Corblok.

Brown and the R&D director developed a presentation notebook containing side-by-side test results and explanations of the complexities of UAN corrosion control. This was used to train the existing sales force and regional managers so that they could become expert enough to contact customers alone.

Initially each member of the sales force was asked to identify a primary target customer. Then a team of Brown, the research director and the appropriate sales representative made two presentations to each. The first covered proper testing techniques (including demonstrations) and arrangement for samples of uninhibited and inhibited UAN to be sent to SPG in Fort Smith, so that customers and SPG were working from the same knowledge base. The second contained dosage and service program recommendations. Then the sales representative followed up in attempts to gain business.

Evaluations on the use of the presentation material were discouraging. Few of the sales force actively used it as intended during the calls. It often was simply given to prospects with a "here, read this" approach, common to the commodity selling style already in use. White apparently made little effort to motivate his people to sell differently.

The first presentation was at Fertex and resulted in a problem with cost/dosage. Fertex claimed to use Corblok at 0.25lb/ton, while SPG's tests showed it to be 0.3, and resulted in a recommendation to use 601 at 0.3. Fertex thus perceived 601 to cost $0.025/ton more to use than Corblok—another example of SPG's lack of customer awareness and their technology-based approach to sales. Perhaps even worse was that SPG's western regional manager concluded that the new products were "not as good as Corblok." His background was 20 years in commodity wax sales; he simply didn't comprehend the side-by-side test results.

Fertex continued this stance for over a year. This prompted Williamson to cancel any further funding for the program because "Fertex was not negotiating in good faith."

Williamson became company (CAC) president in mid-1991. Before this occurred, Walker moved to director of marketing for the Refinery Chemicals Group. Rumor was that Williamson pressured the GMNP of this group to select Walker to end the conflict between Walker and White.

SPG offered a 10% discount early in 1991 on the first order placed by all Corblok users. No one bought.

Part 7

Organizing, Implementing, and Assessing Performance

CASE 7-1
CUTCO*

Synopsis

CUTCO International is a wholly-owned subsidiary of ALCAS Corporation that manages the marketing and distribution of CUTCO cutlery. While the company was seeing record sales and profits for the first six months of 1997, senior management was not satisfied with these record levels. The goal was 20-25 percent over 1996 sales, not 11 percent. The international unit was especially responsible for the under performance relative to goal. Management viewed international expansion as a critical element of growth for its cutlery products and for the Direct Selling marketplace as a whole. The senior management team is very actively involved in this growth opportunity.

Video Summary

The video, Direct Selling in a Global Frontier, was produced by the Direct Selling Education Foundation. Approximately 15 Direct Selling companies are identified in the video (e.g., Amway, Avon, Mary Kay, Tupperware). The video begins with an overview of the issues Direct Selling companies are addressing as they attempt to move internationally. Then, the video moves into an extensive discussion with executives from Alcas Corporation (CUTCO Cutlery Corporation and Vector Marketing Corporation). The question and answer format of the discussion makes it easy for students to understand. After the lengthy discussion with CUTCO executives, the video wraps up with comments from two other Direct Selling companies (Nature's Sunshine Products and Amway Corporation).

[Included as an appendix to this note is the video teaching note prepared by Larry Chonko. This teaching note focuses specifically on the three major parts of the video.]

Teaching/Learning Objectives

The Direct Selling industry is very large—with vast opportunity for growth. The case allows students to:

- better understand the nature of Direct Selling,
- observe the level of market analysis engaged in by a firm considering international expansion,
- look at management styles in a privately-held, large U.S. company, and
- illustrates that success is relative to company objectives.

Discussion Questions

Students should be asked to address the following four questions that are posed at the end of the case. Since these questions focus upon the final recommendation that will be made to CUTCO, students will necessarily have to work their way through the analysis process.

---

* This teaching note was prepared by William F. Crittenden, Northeastern University, and Victoria L. Crittenden, Boston College, as an aid to instructors using the case, "CUTCO International." Some of the analysis was derived from a case presentation by Kimberly Boyle, Kellie Cullity, Lisa Glass, Ernest Grasso, and Cynthia Fuguet Mare of the Northeastern University MBA program.

1. What criteria should CUTCO use to select countries for market entry?
2. Which countries offer the best market opportunities for CUTCO products?
3. What should be the composition of the new country's management team?
4. Should CUTCO continue to develop countries using both the "Party Plan/Hostess Program" approach and the "College Program" approach?

Analysis

Situation Audit

Environmental factors that affect this market include:

Market

- Decrease in number of firms
- Firm consolidation
- Increase in cutlery sales
- Increase in Internet sales

Sales

- Direct/retail sales
- Seasonal sales
- $80 billion annual worldwide direct sales (with the U.S. firms responsible for slightly less than 25% of this)

Customer

- $60,000+ income
- bachelor degree or higher
- married with older children
- 40—54 years of age
- homeowner

Primary Competitors

Henckels

- 266 year old German manufacturer
- upscale cutlery presence in 100+ countries
- retail as primary distribution channel
- sales expansion strategy focuses upon new customers and further penetration of existing customers
- company expansion strategy focuses upon moderately priced products and non-German sources

Fiskars

- 348 year old company based in Finland
- diversified product offerings: steel, iron, architectural, industrial, agricultural, housewares
- cutlery represents 13% of sales
- innovative
- expansion strategy includes acquisitions and greenfield start-ups

A sample SWOT analysis is provided in Exhibit TN-1.

Problem/ Decision Statement

What is the best growth alternative for CUTCO Cutlery? Internationally, what is the sequence of countries for market entry?

Identification of Alternatives and Criteria for Evaluation

Regarding the best growth alternative for CUTCO, the product/market expansion grid provides four major alternatives:

1. *Old Products/Old Markets*—this means that CUTCO could penetrate the U.S. market via, for example, changes in its marketing program. Alternatives within this option would include retail sales and Internet sales. As well, the company is continually improving the quality of its product via such measures as ergonomically designed handles and material upgrades.

2. *Old Products/New Markets*—this means that CUTCO begin marketing and distributing its current product mix in new international markets.

3. *New Products/Old Markets*—this means that CUTCO develop new products for its current U.S. market and for the international markets it is in. As can be seen in the case, CUTCO continually introduces new products into its existing markets. For example, it acquired KA-BAR Knives in 1996 in order to offer sporting knives to its existing customer base.

4. *New Products/New Markets*—this would entail developing products specific to local customs/cultures in new international markets.

Criteria for evaluating these options could include:

Does the option leverage the company's strengths?

Does the option minimize the company's weaknesses?

What is the expected competitor reaction?

Does the option support the organization's goal of 75 percent?

Countries under consideration for market entry are Argentina, Austria, Brazil, Ireland, Italy, Japan, Mexico, Poland, Taiwan, and the U.K. Criteria *(question 1)* for evaluating each of these countries include:

What is the extent of college education?

What is the popularity of Direct Selling?

What are the direct sales per salesperson?

What is the mode of transportation?

What percent of the population is a part of the workforce?

What percent of the population is urban?

What percent of the population resides in major cities?

What is the population density?

Analysis

A sample schematic for looking at growth options relative to criteria is:

Option	Leverage Strengths	Minimize Weaknesses	Competitor Reaction	Support Goals
International Expansion	yes (direct sales)	yes (increase sales)	none	yes
Retail Sales	yes (quality & name recog.)	no (retail exp.) yes (smooth seasonality)	retaliatory	no
Internet Sales	yes (low overhead, maintain image)	yes (smooth seasonality, low overhead)	minimal	yes

A sample framework for evaluation of the country options relative to the criteria is included in Exhibit TN-2.

Recommendation

The tendency is for students to go with the international expansion (old products/new markets) alternative. In following through on this option, the question of country sequence has to be addressed *(question 2)*. A likely country entry sequence (using the country options framework as a guide) is:

1998: Japan and Taiwan
2000: U. K. and Italy
2002: Argentina and Ireland
2004: Austria and Poland
2006: Brazil and Mexico

Implementation of the country recommendations would include decisions regarding:

- Direct Selling or distributor
- "one-on-one" or "party plan" *(question 4)*
- management structure in each country *(question 3)*
- service organization in each country

Teaching the Case

The case is fun and interesting to teach. The class will probably be split more in favor of those who have never heard of the company. However, there is a strong chance that those students who have heard of the company have either worked in direct sales at CUTCO or have a relative/friend who has. The stories that may be told about working at the company will be mixed. Some students did not have good experiences in that they did not sell much. However, on the flip side, many students have worked in direct sales at CUTCO and have done extremely well. Most of the firm's local area managers started in sales as a college student. If there are students who have stories to tell about working for the company, it is probably good to let these get out in the open as soon as class starts. Such comments may fit easily into a SWOT analysis that makes this line of discussion reasonable. However, the professor has to be careful not to let this go too far. Many times, students who work in a company part-time are not privy to the strategic analysis process that goes on a company. Therefore, it is important to move into the actual facts, data of the case without becoming bogged down in personal war stories.

The video adds an extra level of excitement to the class. It is 13 minutes long and works well during the early stages of the case discussion. The video has been used successfully immediately after the class has conducted a situation analysis and identified the problem(s) faced by the company. Switching to the video does away with many assumptions that students would have to make since the question and answer format allows CUTCO executives to respond to many questions that students in the classroom might have. After watching the video, the class is ready to make recommendations regarding growth options and country entry sequencing.

Epilogue

Although some new product lines were under investigation, CUTCO executives felt strongly that international expansion was the best possible growth option. The case was completed and to press before country-specific decisions were made. Updates on the company's Web page might be a good source of current information.

Exhibit TN-1   SWOT Analysis

Strengths

- High quality products
- Variety of such products
- Management structure
- Management commitment
- Excellent customer service domestically
- Backward integration
- Sales growth
- Profits and sales at all-time high

Weaknesses

- Seasonal sales force
- Seasonal sales
- Demand forecast
- Questionable customer service internationally
- High turnover amongst sales staff
- Reliance on college students

Opportunities

- U.S. consumers buying not only more cutlery, but more name brand cutlery
- Growth in direct sales industry both in U.S. and internationally

Threats

- Two major competitors with diverse product lines and global presence
- Unstable economic conditions could lead to lower expenditures on non-necessity items such as high end cutlery
- Better economic conditions might make it less likely that students would support themselves via Direct Selling

Exhibit TN-2

	College Education	Direct Sales	Direct Sales/Sales Person	Trans. System	Workforce % Pop.	% of Pop. Urban	% of Pop. Major Cities	Population Density
Argentina				Medium	Low	Medium	Medium	Low
Austria	N/A	Medium	Medium	Medium	N/A	Low	Medium	Medium
Brazil	Medium	Low	Medium	Medium	Medium	Low	N/A	Low
Ireland	Medium	Low	Medium	Medium	Medium	Medium	Medium	Medium
Italy		Medium	Medium	Medium	Medium	Medium	Medium	Medium
Japan	Low	Medium		Low	Medium	Medium	Medium	Low
Mexico	N/A	Low	Low	Low	Low	Low	Medium	
Poland	Medium	Medium	Low		Low	N/A	Medium	Medium
Taiwan	N/A	Medium	Medium	N/A	Medium	Medium	Low	Medium
U.K.	N/A				Medium			

Key:

Low
Medium
High

APPENDIX TO CUTCO CASE
(Notes to accompany the video
"Direct Selling on the Global Frontier")[*]

Introductory Comments

These notes are designed to accompany the video "Direct Selling on the Global Frontier" sponsored by the Direct Selling Education Foundation and the Direct Selling Association. As you play the video in you class you will notice that there are several distinct aspects of the video.

1. Direct Selling, as a collection of world class companies. is truly globally minded.
2. Direct Selling, like any other business strategy, has advantages and disadvantages that must be accounted for in each unique global marketplace.
3. The Direct Selling strategy is illustrated through the presentation of a short case scenario involving the CUTCO/Vector Corporation and its experiences in several international ventures.
4. Some concluding comments on what it will take for Direct Selling companies to be successful in the ever-expanding global marketplace.

Teaching Note Approach

Throughout this set of notes I will attempt to follow the video as closely as possible. However, there are many questions, points of discussion. etc. that are provided that are not directly answerable by viewing the video. However, the video serves as a catalyst for these discussion points by providing actual examples and a case concerning the global activity of Direct Selling companies.

Classes in Which Video is Applicable

The video is also applicable in several marketing classes. Instead of trying to pigeon-hole specific video materials with specific classes, the notes presented follow the video script, since there are, I'm sure, many different ways in which these classes are taught. All the materials in the video have at least one linkage global marketing. I believe that every aspect of the video can be discussed in the context of any of the classes designated above. As the script is followed questions are posed which are appropriate for discussion in several marketing classes including the following:

1. Principles of Marketing
2. Professional Selling
3. International Marketing
4. Marketing Research
5. Channels of Distribution
6. Consumer Behavior

---

[*] This teaching note was prepared by Dr. Larry Chonko, Holloway Professor of Marketing, Center for Professional Selling, Baylor University.

Scope of Direct Selling

Learning Opportunities for Students.

Direct Selling companies generate huge revenues around the globe. Direct Selling companies are a force in the global marketplace. Direct Selling represents exciting opportunities for some students. Direct Selling is a legitimate form of distribution and students must be aware of the scope of Direct Selling. More products are sold Direct than through the Internet, yet we tend o ignore the Direct Selling approach to distribution, but do not hesitate to discuss the "sexy" technological side of marketing. One is not more important than the other. Students, as future decision makers. must be aware of all the business alternatives available to them if they are going to make intelligent marketplace decisions.

As students watch the video, they will experience the presentation of many Direct Selling companies. They will also see that these Direct Selling companies have successfully ventured into the global marketplace.

Employment Opportunities for Students

One item can be brought up here. Direct Selling represents a real entrepreneurial opportunity. As large companies downsize, reduce hiring, etc. we've seen more and more individuals (older and graduating students) enter into their own business. Direct Selling provides one of those business opportunities.

Below is a listing of the Direct Selling companies identified in the video.

- Amway
- Avon
- Tupperware
- Mary Kay Cosmetics
- Nature's Sunshine
- World Book International
- Party Lite
- Kirby
- Regal
- Shaklee
- Herbalife
- Creative Memories
- Alcas Corp. (CUTCO)
- The Pampered Chef
- Jafra

Direct Selling Factoid: There are 149 companies that are members of the Direct Selling Association.

Here is a listing of the countries mentioned in the video in which Direct Selling organizations are actively developing markets:

- Brazil
- Japan
- Germany
- United States
- Canada
- Australia
- Korea
- Costa Rica
- Mexico
- Argentina
- The Philippines
- England
- China
- Venezuela
- India
- Russia
- Puerto Rico
- Hong Kong
- Columbia
- South Africa

Direct Selling Factoid: Direct Selling companies operate in 100 countries around the world.

Direct Selling Factoid: In 1995, Direct Selling sales volume in Japan was 530,32 billion.

A useful starting question might be to see how many students were aware that the companies mentioned in the video are direct sellers. It might also be interesting to determine if any of your students can describe Direct Selling.

Direct Selling Factoid: There are 17.6 million individuals around the world employed as independent contractors for various Direct Selling organizations. In the United States, 6.3 ,billion people are employed with Direct Selling companies.

Direct Selling Factoid: About 2 million people were employed by Direct Selling companies in 1995 both Japan and Taiwan.

Direct Selling Factoid. In 1995, Direct Selling Companies had collective revenues of $16.55 billion in the U.S. Worldwide Direct Selling sales were $67.3 billion in 1995.

The Video:

Part One: The Global Marketplace and Direct Selling

The early portion of thy video stresses the movement of Direct Selling companies into the global marketplace. It provides a brief overview of some exciting things that are happening with Direct Selling companies in the global marketplace.

The narrator opens with a reference to the founder of Coca cola, John Pemberton. The video refers to Coca Cola starting in Atlanta, Georgia, and Pemberton's thoughts about expanding distribution to the state of Georgia. Obviously, everyone knows that Coca-Cola is (and has been) one of the great domestic and global marketing success stories in history.

The video builds on this expansion concept with a few comments about expending distribution, focusing on the notion of satisfied customers. domestically and around the globe. Direct Selling companies, like all other companies, have found that the key to market growth lies in the global marketplace, gaining new customers and offering exciting and excellent potential to many entrepreneurs around the world.

In the video, Mr. Rick Goings of Tupperware states, very simply, that global business is "very important" to Tupperware. He notes that 85 percent of their sales are generated outside the U.S. Mr. Dick Bartlett of Mary Kay Cosmetics adds that his company has used their teaching oriented marketing approach in 25 countries around the world. The result has been rapidly increasing market share in almost every country in which Mary Kay Cosmetics has a presence.

At this point, you might consider discussing the expansion into the international marketplace in terms of the growth/strategy matrix:

- **old products/old markets**—for direct sellers, this is the U.S.
- **old products/mew markets**—for direct sellers, this means expansion into other countries
- **new products/old** markets—for direct sellers this means the U.S. and countries in which operations are well established (e.g. Amway in Japan)
- **new products/new markets**—for direct sellers, this strategy can be useful domestically and globally

Key Issues

- How is the competition for Direct Selling companies defined?
- How can a company penetrate a saturated market? (e.g. direct sellers in the U.S.)
- How can a company enter a foreign market?
- Can a channel of distribution be a company's distinctive competency?
- Can a channel of distribution strategy be used to define a marketplace?
- Is the Direct Selling channel of distribution a reflection of the corporate culture of the Direct Selling company? What is the relationship between a company's corporate culture and its marketing strategy?

What is Direct Selling?

In the video, the narrator suggests that students may **not** be familiar with Direct Selling. They probably know some of the companies by name and probably purchase some products from Direct Selling companies. But do they really understand the unique nature of Direct Selling?

You might ask students some questions like these:

1. Is Direct Selling a selling strategy?
2. What are some of the unique elements of Direct Selling?
3. What are some of the advantages and disadvantages of Direct Selling?

In the video, several aspects of Direct Selling are presented in an effort to provide students with some understanding of the nature of Direct Selling. You and your students may have some differing perspectives on these various aspects of Direct Selling. Obviously, any of the points mentioned below are subject to discussion and disagreement. As a suggestion, my personal feeling is that the uniqueness of Direct Selling lies in its positioning as a channel of distribution.

1. **Direct Selling is not an industry**, as defined by traditional standards of companies that are in the business of marketing similar products and services, as the myriad of Direct Selling companies provide an incredibly broad range of products and services.
2. **Direct Selling is not just selling.** Direct Selling companies engage in all business functions in order to successfully market products around the world.
3. **Direct Selling is a channel of distribution.** It is a method of delivering products and services to customers directly in their homes and in their workplaces.

Selected Features of Direct Sellers

- direct sellers do not market their products and services through traditional retail channels
- direct sellers market their products and services directly to the final customer
- direct sellers do not employ salespeople
- Direct Selling "salespeople" are independent business people
- direct sellers have long developed a reputation for excellent products and service
- direct sellers view the globally marketplace as an opportunity to serve customers worldwide
- direct sellers go directly to their customers
- The customers home or place of business is where direct sellers serve their customers
- direct sellers, as independent business people, incur very low start-up expenses
- direct sellers do not have to penetrate existing distribution channels
- direct sellers create their own channel of distribution by recruiting others
- direct sellers have the opportunity to present products and services without interference from competitors
- direct sellers have excellent earning opportunities
- Direct Selling is based on building long-term relationships with customers
- direct sellers build markets by relying on personal relationships, not brand names

- Direct Selling companies do little advertising

You and your students may be able to identify some other features of direct sellers. Direct Selling does come with some disadvantages. A few of these are mentioned in the video.

Disadvantages of Direct Selling

- direct sellers are independent and not as easily managed as traditional sales forces
- Direct Selling turnover is very high
- Some customers do not like the idea of in-home shopping

You and your students may be able to come up with some other disadvantages. One interesting point of discussion might revolve around the notion that Direct Selling has an advantage of convenience of shopping because of its emphasis on in-home sales. Historically, this has been an advantage for many consumers, but not all. Today, with technological changes marketing efforts in areas like catalogues, television home shopping shows and the Internet have greatly improved and expanded, making it convenient for consumers to shop at home. Students might find it interesting to discuss the relative merits of these alternative channels of distribution from the standpoint of convenience and other factors that might have an impact on their purchase decisions.

This section of the video concludes with three questions that you might consider asking your class.

1. How do changes in demographics, culture, political climate, and the socio-economic environment affect companies that sell directly to the consumers?

This question is relatively basic from the standpoint that these factors are discussed in many classes as having an impact on marketing activities, whether domestic or international. In the video. Mr. Jim Preston of Avon notes that there is no difference in how Avon evaluates markets today versus they way they did it 20 or 30 or 40 years ago. Intuitively, this may not make sense to students who are most likely told, consistently, of massive changes in the way marketing is done. However. Mr. Preston's comments certainly lead to some interesting questions:

- How do you evaluate markets today?
- What factors might have been considered in evaluating markets 20 years ago? years ago? 40 years ago?
- Are the questions raised and the factors used to evaluate markets really different, or do we just get different answers to those questions and different insights about those factors?
- Going back to the first part of the video, what are the commonalties that exist across global markets? What are the differences?

2. What affect will the laws and customs of each new market have on how companies gain access to their customers?

Once again, this material is discussed in many marketing classes and can be used to generate some discussion about global marketing activities of Direct Selling companies.

3. What impact will the computer and the Worldwide Web have on the way products are bought and sold around the globe?

This question poses an interesting challenging to direct sellers. One of the hallmarks of Direct Selling has been the convenience with which customers can purchase products in the home. Indeed, for many customers, in-home purchasing is a key reason for purchase. For direct sellers, it has also been a source of competitive advantage. As technology improves, and security problems are overcome, and the marketplace becomes comfortable with purchasing via computes, will the in-home shopping advantage enjoyed by direct sellers cease to exist?

This issue ties in very nicely with a discussion of the temporary nature of *competitive advantage*. Direct Selling companies must strive to build and maintain advantage as technologically based competitors react to marketplace phenomenon (e.g. desire for quality products. lower prices, and purchase convenience) and **seek** to develop ways to meet one or more of these marketplace needs.

After these questions arc asked in the video. Mr. James Preston of Avon addresses some of the criteria for entering foreign markets. Avon, as noted in the video, has entered into 1220 countries around the globe.

Part Two: The CUTCO/Vector Case

The second portion of the video presents a global based ease prepared by representatives of the CUTCO/Vector (Alcas Corporation), headquarters in Olean New York.

Company Background

Alcas Corporation, founded in 1949, manufactures and markets CUTCO cutlery, a very high quality kitchen cutlery. Alcas is a holding company with two major subsidiaries CUTCO Cutlery Corporation, the manufacturer of CUTCO cutlery, and Vector Marketing Corporation, the direct sales marketer for CUTCO throughout all of North America. The company established CUTCO international in 1994 as a subsidiary to handle the marketing of CUTCO cutlery on a global basis. Since 1985. the company has experienced an annual sales growth of about 22 percent. with sales in 195 exceeding S80 million.

The Product

The CUTCO cutlery product line consists of a broad range of food preparation knives, table knives and hunting, fishing and utility pocket knives (approximately 53 individual items and 110 SKUs counting gift packs and set combinations). The product line is identified as "CUTCO . the world's finest cutlery," and testing against competitors' product offerings worldwide consistently supports that claim. Product is sold as individual open stock or in a variety of gift boxed sets and a variety of wood block sets for the countertop.

Pricing

Product retail pricing is consistent with the identification of CUTCO as "the world's finest cutlery. CUTCO products are priced at the high end of the spectrum. The pricing is comparable to Henckels and Wustof knives, both of which are at the high end of the price range for cutlery products available in conventional retail stores.

The Case on Video

CUTCO sales through Vector Marketing have shown consistent sales growth, but the rate of growth has stabilized in the last two or three years. In the 1980s and early 1990s. high growth rates occurred because of the wide open opportunity for "geographic growth." Company representatives feel that the primary way in which growth of the 1980s can be reestablished is through international markets.

The CUTCO/Vector case is presented in a question and answer format, with Mr. Erick Laine, President and Chief Executive Officer and several other CUTCO executives responding to questions about their company and some recent global marketing efforts. As a guide for discussion, the following questions are asked in the video:

1. What is CUTCO/ Vector?
2. How successful is CUTCO in the U.S.?
3. What does the future hold for CUTCO in the U.S.?
4. Has CUTCO made any entries into the global marketplace to date?
5. Has Canada been a satisfactory experience?
6. Have all your international entries worked well?
7. What happened in Korea? Why?
8. What did CUTCO/Vector determine it needed to do differently in order to grow in the Korean Market?
9. Any lessons for the future?
10. What countries do you plan to enter next?

Answers to these questions, provided in the video, should provide students with the opportunity to learn about marketing on a global level. CUTCO/Vector is a very successful U.S. company. They have excellent products and a program that encourages college students to learn sales skills while earning money to pay for college.

CUTCO/Vector began its international ventures by attempting to take existing products and an existing distribution technology and transplant it into other countries. As you saw from the video, this approach worked with varying degrees of success. What is also evident from die video is that CUTCO/Vector did not quit. They evaluated their global efforts and, after thorough analysis, were willing to make departures from their U.S. based strategy in order to better serve the needs of customers from other countries.

Sales and Marketing Approach in the U.S. and Canada

CUTCO is sold by Vector Marketing Corporation through a "one-to-one" in-home demonstration technique using a sales force made up primarily of college students. In 1995, 35,000 salespeople were recruited, approximately 85–90 percent being college students. Most of the salespeople are recruited during the summer months. Some of the students continue to sell throughout the year and the business definitely exists as a year-around business. Volume in September-April is considerably less than volume generated in the summer Recruiting and training and ongoing counseling of salespeople are all decentralized with about 165 district sales managers located in communities throughout the U.S. and Canada. During the summer months, the company opens up about 200 additional "branch offices" which are temporary summer offices occupied by college students with prior selling and management experience with CUTCO/Vector.

CUTCO in Korea

In the video. CUTCO executives discuss what they learned from their experiences in Korea, including the following:

1. The market in Korea is different than the market in Canada.
2. Student salespeople worked well in Canada but not in Korea?
3. Korean born, but "Americanized" sales representatives had difficulty in managing aspects of the Korean culture.
4. Korean customers are more receptive to Korean women as sales representatives.

With these experiences, an interesting discussion might be generated around technology transfer. Can marketing technologies simply be transferred from one marketplace to the next? What factors might have to be considered as a company expands it marketing from one country to another?

Another interesting point is that CUTCO did not sit idly by and watch their initial efforts in Korea without reacting. Students should take note in the video that CUTCO executives were on top of the situation and began thinking of adjustments to their marketing program long before it became to late to salvage their efforts. The key point here is that companies can recover from mistakes it, like CUTCO, they do their homework and monitor the results of their marketing efforts very carefully.

CUTCO in Other Countries

The discussion of CUTCO concludes with some brief comments about other countries in which CUT~CO has entered or is planning to enter. Students should take note that CUTCO's strategies in entering these markets are somewhat different, based on their experiences in Canada and Korea. At this point it may be interesting to ask students to identify aspects of CUTCO's marketing strategy that are (or may have to) changed in order to increase the odds of successful marketplace entry. It may also he interesting to ask students to identify aspects of CUTCO's strategy that have not changed (e.g. product line, product quality), If you have a class that has several international students it may be interesting to here their comments on the CUTCO strategies and how effective they might be in their respective countries.

Questions Related to the CUTCO/Vector Case

1. CUTCO/Vector began their global initiative in Korea with Korean born students who had become "Americanized. These students were than asked to go back to Korea and initiate CUTCO operations. What are the possible advantages and disadvantages of this approach?
2. For what reasons do you think CUTCO/Vector chose to enter the Korean market using the Direct Selling approach?
3. The life expectancy of a CUTCO product is "for a lifetime." CUTCO provides a lifetime guarantee on all of its cutlery. Comment on this as a marketing tactic.
4. What is the relationship between a sales representative and culture in which he/she sells?
5. What is the relationship of the sales representative and the product he/she sells?
6. What impact do culture and the nature of the product being sold have on the transferability of a marketing and sales approach?

7. In 1992 through 1994. CUTCO/Vector sales in the U.S. were flat. Speculate on what might have led to this type of sales situation. Other than going international, what other strategies might CUTCO/Vector use to improve its sales picture?
8. If you were the president of CUTCO/Vector, considering entry into the Korean market, what market research information would you like to have to guide your decision making?
9. In general, what are the advantages and disadvantages of the Direct Selling channels approach in comparison to other channel options?
10. Of what value is having a uniform distribution system to the company? Are there disadvantages to employing a uniform distribution strategy?
11. CUTCO/Vector prices are high relative to most competitors? What value does (could) CUTCO/Vector provide in order to justify its higher prices?
12. CUTCO/Vector does not employ an installment payment policy in its pricing strategy. What are the advantages and disadvantages of this pricing approach?
13. How does exchange rate information affect the decision to enter into the global market place?
14. One of CUTCO/Vector major competitors is located in Germany. This company alto produces cutlery that is priced at the high end of the marketplace. Comment on the strategy of distributing products to a country in which a direct competitor is located.
15. CUTCO/Vector, as do Direct Selling companies in general, follows a channel driven marketing strategy. That is. these companies attempt to enter new markets using the Direct Selling strategies of in- home sales. What are the advantages of such an approach? What are the disadvantages?
16. How easy is it to transplant a marketing technology from one country to the next?
17. Should a company wishing to enter global markets focus on transplanting its technology? Or should that company focus on identifying needs and wants and then determine if those needs and wants can be satisfied using the current marketing technology?
18. How much adaptation of a company's marketing technology can take place before that company's identity and experiences are "lost?
19. At what point does a company issue a "NO GO!" on markets being considered?
20. What criteria would you use to select countries as targets for entry?
21. How would you prioritize target countries if you chose to enter several countries?
22. Based on the U.S., Canada, and Korean experiences of CUTCO/Vector what recommendations would you make to companies considering entry into global markets?

Part Three: Concluding Video Segment

The video concludes with a brief comment from two Direct Selling executives—Alan Kennedy of Nature's Sunshine and Richard DeVos of Amway. They address the following questions respectively:

1. What are the upsides and downsides of the dramatic international growth you've experienced with Nature's Sunshine?

Comments from Mr. Alan Kennedy. Mr. Kennedy's comments center on opportunity in two ways. One is the opportunity provided by Direct Selling companies to potential entrepreneurs around the globe. Second. is the opportunity afforded to countries like Nature's Sunshine through expansion into the global marketplace. Among his comments is one that champions entering into medium-sized markets rather than the largest markets. Here might be a place to get students to discuss such a strategy in light of the seemingly endless "bigger is better" philosophy and stories to which they are exposed. It might be interesting to here the students comments on entering smaller markets versus larger markets.

2. China is the biggest "new market" in the world. Which of your assumptions about China were correct? What was the biggest surprise?

Comments from Mr. DeVos. Mr. DcVos discusses Amway's entry into China, making particular reference to market potential and the receptivity of the Chinese government. Today. Amway is very successful in China, but their entry into China was a bit more challenging than Mr. DeVos' comments may imply. There is much work that needs to be done when entering a foreign country, particularly from the standpoint of all of the government red tape, learning Chinese regulations and business customs.

The executives' responses to these questions will provide additional insight into the problems and opportunities associated with taking Direct Selling global. Using information from the CUTCO/Vector case concerning Canada and Korea, you may find it more advantageous to lead a discussion focuses on the statement made early in the video and near the conclusion of the video - that "People are pretty much the same everywhere." You may be able to identify some of those similarities, using a discussion of needs versus wants as a basis. Simple questions like "Do people around the globe have similar needs?" and "Do people around the globe satisfy their needs in similar ways?" can provide a starting point for a discussion on market analysis and a discussion of elements common across countries and unique to each country that impact marketing efforts of Direct Selling companies. The discussion of common and unique elements can be framed in terms of concepts like market analysis, segmentation. and niche marketing.

CASE 7-2
YOPLAIT USA*

Synopsis:

Sales of yogurt had increased in the 1980s because of the health food trend, but growth slowed in 1990 due, largely, to the many alternatives to yogurt. Yoplait USA, a subsidiary of the Consumer Foods Group of General Mills, had gained the number two market position in the yogurt industry, but it was not at the level hoped for by management. Although Yoplait was number two, its share of the market and profitability were declining.

Yoplait's current strategy was the same as it had been in the product's first days of introduction. Chap Colucci conducted a situation analysis to help in determining a new marketing strategy to challenge Yoplait's competitors. Yoplait's pricing strategy, communication strategy, product strategy, geographic marketing strategy, and costs all had to be changed.

Video Summary:

The video focuses upon Yoplait's different marketing techniques, including its advertising strategy. Many different Yoplait commercials are shown. The video deals with the packaging of the company's products, the personalities in its campaigns, and the product attributes. Yoplait executives discuss why Yoplait failed initially and then went on to survive and then why the business share later declined and what the company did to take action. The video runs for slightly over 15 minutes and should be shown at the end of the case discussion.

Teaching/Learning Objectives:

The case focuses upon the number two player in the yogurt market. The problems that the company have show that a high marketplace ranking does not mean that the product is doing great. The case shows that:

- internal measures of performance are critical for keeping a product successful--external market measures may be misleading, and
- a product's marketing program has to evolve/change continuously.

The case allows students to:

- develop a comprehensive marketing program for a product which is already in the market place, and
- determine the appropriate marketing organization that will aid in reversing alarming trends that the current organization has helped cause.

---

*This teaching note was prepared by Victoria L. Crittenden, Stephanie Hillstrom, and David Angus, Boston College, as an aid to instructors using the case "Yoplait USA." Revised 1998.

Discussion Questions:

1. The outcomes from a situational analysis are presented in the case. Try to reconstruct the specifics of this analysis.
2. Profile the yogurt consumer. How does Yoplait's target market compare?
3. Compare Yoplait to its leading competitors.
4. What is wrong with Yoplait's marketing organization?
5. What measures of performance are used at General Mills? What measures would you recommend for future assessment of Yoplait's performance?
6. Recommend a marketing program for Yoplait:
7. What additional information would you like to have? How would you go about obtaining this information?

Analysis:

1. The outcomes from a situational analysis are presented in the case. Try to reconstruct the specifics of this analysis.

Exhibit TN1 provides a sample of what Colucci may have seen in a SWOT analysis.

2. Profile the yogurt consumer. How does Yoplait's target market compare?

The yogurt market could be segmented based on both consumer characteristics and buying situations. Regarding consumer characteristics, demographic variables such as family size, income, education, and age were part of the consumer profile. Geographically, the early yogurt market experienced regional differences. From a psychographic perspective, lifestyle was an important segmentation variable. When examining yogurt buying situations, one can identify segments of consumers looking for particular product features (e.g., fruit on bottom, swiss, etc.), usage status (e.g., user, nonuser, regular user), buying condition (e.g., convenience, specialty product), and intentions/awareness (e.g., brand preference, informed buyer). An exact profile of the yogurt consumer would likely contain information in each of these areas.

From the case information, we know that the yogurt consumer was likely to be a health conscious person (psychographic variables). The yogurt consumer wanted the nourishment of dairy products, without the associated cholesterol, calories, fat, and sodium. This consumer sought convenience, variety, and premium choices (buying situation variables).

At a broader level, research had shown the following factors (largely demographic variables) concerning the dairy consumer:

- household consuming unit—size and composition
- age
- geographic—degree of urbanization and regionality
- employment status
- lifestyle/nutrition

Most students feel safe in assuming that Yoplait profiled their yogurt consumer in much the same way as the larger marketplace. However, the emphasis had been upon the geographic component.

3. Compare Yoplait to its leading competitors.

There were around 45 brands of cup yogurt produced by 30 manufacturers in 1986. The top three producers were BSN-Gervais Danone with Dannon (#1 with 33% market share), General Mills with Yoplait (#2 with 16% market share), and Kraft with Breyers and Light n' Lively (#3 with 14% market share). This left 27 manufacturers sharing the remaining 37 percent of the yogurt market. [It is interesting to allow students to identify some of these other competitors in the market just to get a feel for some of the smaller players. Examples might include TCBY, Whitney's by Kellogg Co., Weight Watchers, Columbo.]

In comparing Yoplait with Dannon and Kraft's products, students tend to focus on marketing mix related issues.

Marketing Variables	Yoplait	Dannon	Kraft
Positioning	nutritional	nutritional/value	nutritional/taste
Target	broad appeal	non-traditional yogurt eater	light/non users
Distribution	warehouses	store-door	warehouses
Media	#3 (in spending)	#1	#2
Product	6 oz. cups no line extensions	8 oz. cups line ext.	8 oz. cups line ext.
Price	high	average	average
Promotion	trade/no coupons	consumer/coupons	consumer/coupons

In looking over the matrix, it is evident that there are some real differences between Yoplait and its competitors.

4. What is wrong with Yoplait's marketing organization?

The marketing group was organized on a geographic basis. This was the result of the early geographic differences in yogurt consumption. However, as the marketplace changed, Yoplait's marketing organization did not change. This caused Yoplait sales and marketing people to focus on geographic issues such as increased sales to a particular customer in a certain region rather than focusing upon increased sales as a whole.

5. What measures of performance are used at General Mills? What measures would you recommend for future assessment of Yoplait's performance?

It appears that Yoplait is measured by market share and profitability set by General Mills. While Yoplait is number two in the market, its share has been declining and its profitability, measured against standard gross margins, were low (production and overhead costs were escalating). These two measures are not unusual measures of performance.

Students may suggest some options to consider regarding market share. Since market share is an important measure, students may suggest that more detail regarding market share will provide a better measure. For example, there is probably interest in looking at the **size of the market**. If Yoplait's market share percentage is decreasing, yet the market is growing and many competitors are entering, the brand may not be doing so poorly. Also, who (e.g., Dannon, Breyers, Light n' Lively, store brand, etc.) Yoplait is **losing**

share to is important to know. It is unclear how Yoplait compared to **market share goals** established by General Mills. Performance would need to be assessed relative to these goals.

Sales revenue and unit sales are performance measures which students may offer as additions/alternatives. Students may also suggest looking at individual marketing mix performance. This might include evaluating price, distribution, and promotion results relative to the competition. For example, if Yoplait spent three times as much money on advertising as a competitor but the competitor's advertising got better results, then there is something wrong with Yoplait's approach.

Behavioral variables are often mentioned by students. These might include managerial expectation, effort expended, environmental conditions, and competitive reactions.

6. **Recommend a marketing program for Yoplait:**

Issues which should be addressed in a marketing program for Yoplait include:

- target market
- product
- price
- distribution
- communication
- marketing organization

Student responses here generally cover a broad array of options. An interesting approach is to divide students into groups and ask them to determine a marketing program for Yoplait. [Allow about 20 minutes for this. If the case has been a group assignment, then this in-class exercise is not necessary.] Then, randomly select one of the groups to present the group's program (make sure all of the above items are addressed) to the class. Ask the groups if they had any differences relative to the presenting group. There is always something different, so ask one of the responding groups what their marketing program would be. This allows for a broad array of programs. Be sure to have the groups tell why they put their marketing program together the way they did.

6. **What additional information would you like to have? How would you go about obtaining this information?**

Students tend to always want to have additional information. In this particular case, as with many consumer goods, additional information would always be helpful. Issues will probably come up throughout the case discussion where a student will comment on "if I only had more information about..." On a side board, keep track of these additional information requests. Then, at the end of class ask students what they wish they knew and how they could go about obtaining the information. This is a great way to link market research tools and techniques to specific information requests.

Teaching the Case:

The case is easy for students to relate to since they are all familiar with yogurt, and most likely are all familiar with Yoplait. It may come as a surprise to many to find that Yoplait's performance was not what the company would have liked. Students tend to see Yoplait as one of the top brands and do not expect to see such problems (especially since Yoplait was number two in the market).

A good way to start the class is with the identification of Yoplait's problem/issue. Students will immediately focus upon Yoplait's performance assessment and there is likely to ensue a discussion about these measures (question 5). Whether or not students agree with General Mills' measures, the instructor must keep the class on track with the fact that General Mills has a problem with Yoplait's performance and therefore something must be done.

Students are probably used to doing their own SWOT analysis by this stage of the class. After identifying the problem, it is interesting to have students reconstruct Colucci's situational analysis. What must he have found as strengths, weaknesses, opportunities, and threats?

The class is usually anxious to develop a new marketing program for Yoplait. If using the in-class group project, be sure to allow time to complete the group work and allow time for at least one group presentation. Classroom timing is critical here. The vast majority of the time is spent on developing a new program for Yoplait. Yet, since the development is driven by the fact that the company's performance assessment has found something wrong with the current program, the new program has to be driven strongly by a thorough analysis of what has been happening.

The video can be shown in the last 20 minutes of class to show what Yoplait did.

Epilogue:

In 1993, Yoplait USA's pricing strategy consisted of many coupons, accounting for half of the coupons offered in the yogurt category in the first six months of the year. This was twice the number of coupons used by Dannon, the market share leader. The coupon promotions were to not only discount the price but also add value. Yoplait's typical coupon offered $0.50 off six cartons of yogurt, including new products. This coupon strategy was to encourage consumers to stock up on yogurt. Yoplait used this to move away from trade promotion and strengthen brand equity. Yoplait had many promotional ads in 1992 that highlighted the new tastes, new formulas, and new sizes, but there were fewer of these in 1993.

Yoplait also increased advertising in the first quarter of 1993. The company spent $2.1 million on media, compared to $830,000 for the same quarter in 1992 and $6.9 million for the whole year.

As part of the product strategy, Yoplait introduced Crunch 'n Yogurt, a yogurt that included crunchy mix-in ingredients. The company also introduced Trix yogurt, which was borrowed from another product of General Mills, and Light Custard Style. In addition to these new products, Yoplait improved its Yoplait Light and Fat Free Fruit on the Bottom offerings.

Yoplait introduced three new products in the UK's chilled desserts sector. The packaging was a French look that accented the indulgence of eating the desserts. The products were targeted at professional couples, and women were expected to buy them. Yoplait continued to launch new products into UK's dairy desserts market through a joint venture with the Milk Marketing Board's Dairy Crest. Products included the Chocolate Yop drink, Yoplait Light, and Fruit On the Bottom.

These new strategies helped Yoplait's unit volume, market share, and profits grow. Unit volume was up 23 percent, and after a market share gain in 1992, Yoplait's market share grew again in 1993 to 20 percent of the $1.4 billion retail yogurt market.

Yoplait continues to grow and add new products. In 1994, unit volume was up again by 21% over the previous year. New products such as the Fruit Roll-Ups Lowfat Yogurt with flavors such as Strawberry in

Strawberry, Cherry in Banana, Grape in Watermelon, and Strawberry in Tropic (the yogurt flavor is listed first, the Fruit Roll-Up flavor is the second flavor listed) are hoped to continue this trend of growth by targeting children. Positioned toward kids, this product brings the taste of a fruit roll-up to yogurt. The actual product is a cup of Yoplait yogurt, with the center of the yogurt being a "gel" which features a Fruit Roll-Up flavor. In addition, Yoplait now offers products such as Crunch Light , Light, and Custard. Each of these categories has a variety of flavors.

Exhibit TN1   SWOT Analysis

Strengths

- number two in market share (16%)
- parent company experienced in R&D, new product development
- entrepreneurial management team
- premium product is in line with trends in consumer tastes

Weaknesses

- product priced 20% higher despite providing 25% less product/serving
- declining profitability
- increasing costs leading to margin problems
- lack of a focused, current strategy for Yoplait vis-à-vis its competitors
- old strategy still in use does not look at Yoplait USA as a whole, i.e., regionally focused to reflect initial regionality of product
- not as experienced in refrigerated products with more limited shelf life
- limited product line
- virtually no new product development
- decision to use smaller packaging appears to be more a "sense" than known fact, should be investigated
- unresponsive to moves of the competition, i.e., couponing
- few promotional efforts directed toward end consumer
- target of mass media communications efforts not clear

Opportunities

- new markets in southwest and midwest
- new products for niche markets, like its competitors (e.g., children, as a competitor has done)
- new flavors of yogurt
- new styles, especially frozen yogurt
- increasingly health conscious dietary habits in U.S.
- additional distribution through General Mills restaurant chain, e.g., as a substitute topping for potatoes or as a dessert
- dairy products the fastest growing part of the supermarket

Threats

- proliferation of new yogurt (e.g., low and no-fat yogurts, yogurt drinks, and yogurt for kids) and non-yogurt (e.g., refrigerated pastas and sauces) products into the market
- declining industry-wide yogurt sales (-4.5% between 1989 and 1990)
- competition has segmented market not by geography but by lifestyle
- competition has tailored product offerings to the needs of the customer

Competitors' Strengths

Dannon

- clearly positioned product as "nutritional" and "good value"
- attempted to expand the market by transforming yogurt's image to a healthy snack for everyone, not just health food junkies
- #1 in media expenditures, #1 in market share (33%)
- distribution via store-door delivery $\Rightarrow$ image of freshness

Kraft, Inc.

- coherent strategy, focusing on:
    * good value
    * high quality
    * visibility
    * efficient manufacturing
    * focused marketing
- has achieved consumer loyalty across different categories and markets
- product line which appeals to different market segments, i.e. Breyers (superior taste and "natural" ingredients) and Light and Lively (targeted toward light users and non-users and emphasis on superior natural taste)

CASE 7-3
CIMA MOUNTAINEERING, INC.*

Introduction

Cima Mountaineering is a strategic marketing case on selecting a marketing strategy for expansion in the recreation footwear market. Students will have the opportunity to evaluate a strategy for expanding the sales of a product they are quite familiar with, hiking boots. Additionally, the case is designed to allow the instructor to use student teams to conduct marketing research, make a presentation, and apply the concepts of financial analysis, product design and advertising, sales forecasting, discounting to present value and payback to evaluate a marketing proposal. The Internet can also be used to gather some of the information.

The case is nicely suited to a course project near the cud of a marketing management course. The issue centers on the evaluation of two marketing opportunities competing for the resources of the firm. The instructor can form project teams of 3 to 5 students and assign each team to research and evaluate onc of the two marketing proposals. (See case Exhibits 1, 2 and 3) Following the research, student teams prepare a written report on the assigned proposal and present it to the class. Following the presentations, class discussion centers around selecting the most reasonable alternative for the company.

Teaching/Learning Objectives

1. To introduce students to an important strategic issue in marketing management; selecting a marketing strategy for future growth.

2. To teach students teamwork and enable them to gain experience using marketing research to guide the development of marketing strategy.

3. To reinforce the interrelationship of marketing, accounting, and finance in the marketing management process.

4. To develop financial analysis skill in evaluating the profit implications of a marketing proposal.

Decision Situation

Cima Mountaineering, Inc. (Cima) is at a crossroads in 1996. After several years of success, Cima's management faces the challenge of increasing foreign competition and slowing growth in its primary product lines; addressing these threats is necessary in order to realize continued revenue and income growth. However, it is at odds on the best strategy to employ in order to combat the threats and refocus the Company

There are several issues that Cima must address:

- Identify which (if any) new products are essential to the Company's growth
- Identify which market segments the Company should target
- Development of an effective approach to the distribution of its products

---

* This teaching note was prepared by Michael Glass, Matthew Head, Kristie Kimminau, and Michael Pavell, MBA students at Texas Christian University. Used by permission.

In short, Cima needs to design an appropriate marketing strategy that specifies its targeting, posItioning, and new product strategies and then create the marketing mix to implement the strategy.

Cima's situation analysis will be critical in guiding these decisions. Specifically, the market segmentation analysis and competitor evaluation will strongly influence the marketing strategy design. A brief synopsis of the results of these steps will be helpful in evaluating the alternatives.

The following product market graph shows how the market is segmented:

Figure 1: **Product Market Segmentation**

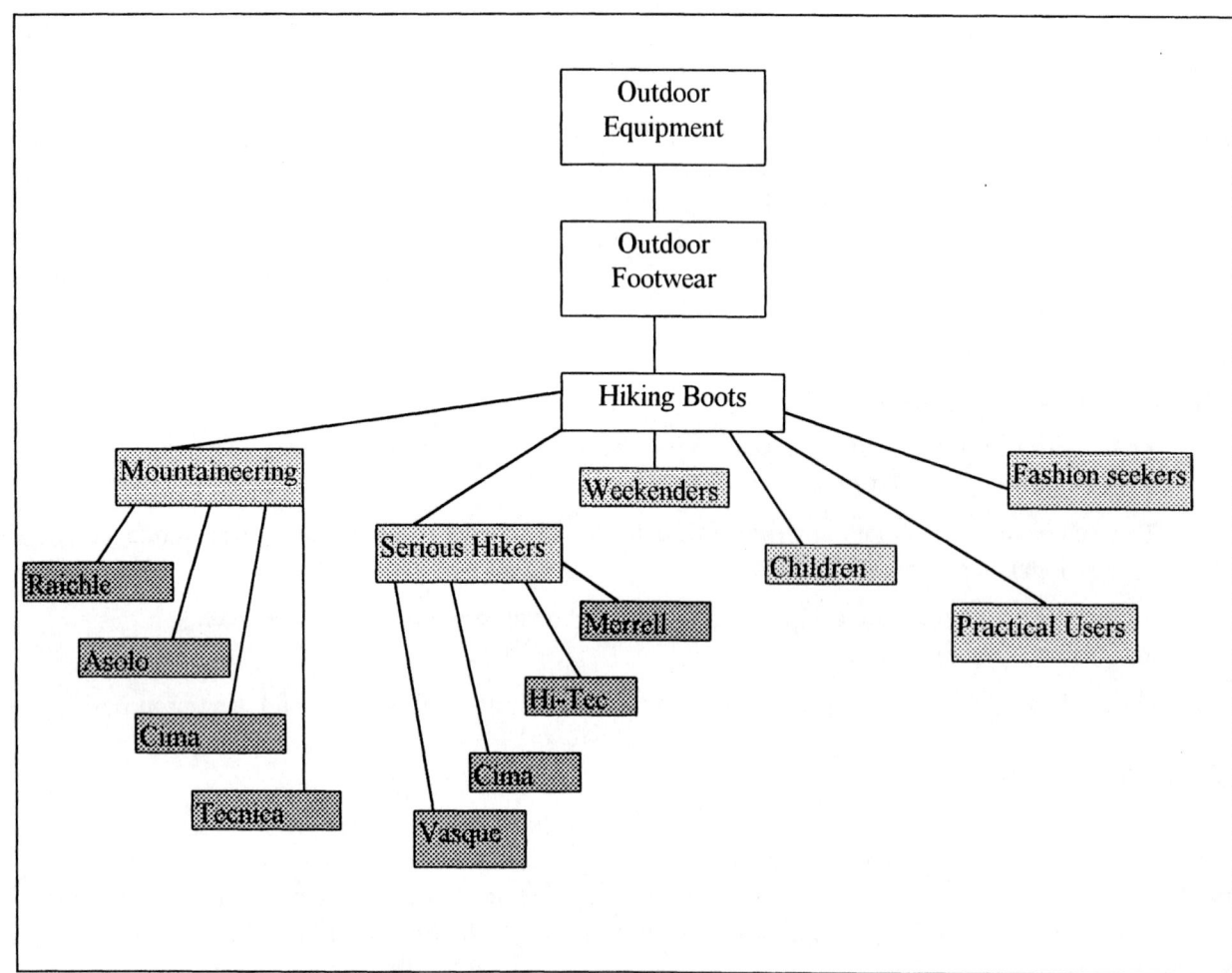

As the above product-market tree shows, the basis for segmentation in the hiking boot market is use situation. Cima currently targets the Mountaineer and Serious Hiker segments. The following chart describes the responsiveness of different segments and identifies the end-users and key competitors in each segment.

Table 1: Market Segmentation Analysis

	Mountaineers	Serious Hikers	Weekenders	Practical Users	Children	Fashion Seekers
Attributes	durability, support, warmth, traction	durability, stability, traction, comfort, protection	lightweight, comfort, durability, versatility	lightweight, durability, good value, versatility	durability, protection, lightweight, traction	stylish, lightweight, inexpensive
Demographics	young, mostly male	young to middle aged men/women	young to middle aged men/women	young to middle aged men	young married couples	young men & women
	shops in specialty stores, catalogs	shop in specialty stores, outdoor catalogs	shop in shoe retailers, sporting stores good stores, mail order	shop in shoe retailers, department	shop in department stores, outdoor catalogs	shop in show retailers, department stores, catalogs
Lifestyle	adventuresome independent risk taker	nature lover sportsman backpacker	recreational hiker enjoys outdoors	practical sociable work recreation	enjoys family, outdoors value conscious	trendy materialistic price conscious
Competitors	Asolo, Raichle, Salomon	Raichle, Vasque, Tecnica, Hi-Tec	Reebok, Timberland, Merrell, Nike, Vasque	Merrell, Nike, Tecnica	Vasque, Nike, Merrell	Nike, Reebok, Hi-Tec
Market Share	5%, slow growth	17%, moderate growth	25%, high growth	20% stable growth	5%, slow growth	28%, peak of rapid growth
Price range	$210-$450	$120-$215	$70-$125	$40-$80	<$40	$65-$100

This case study picks up in the middle of Cima's new product planning process. Management has already analyzed customers' needs, identified potential satisfaction gaps, and initiated idea generation to meet those needs in an effort to foster new growth. This paper proceeds with the screening and evaluation of those strategies, including concept testing and business analysis, and then recommends a strategy to guide the new product design and commercial launch. Included in the recommendation are implementation requirements along with a suggested timeline.

Alternatives

1 Maintain the current product strategy

In this alternative, Cima would not expand its product line in any segments nor change its marketing mix.

2. Enter the Weekender segment with 2 new boot designs

Cima would introduce two new boots targeted at the weekend hiker. These boots would be more versatile and stylish than the current product offerings, incorporating leather and nylon uppers and priced at $69 and $89.

3. Continue focus on Mountaineer and Serious Hiker segments, but expand product line.

This scenario maintains Cima's focus on the high-end segments, but expands Cima's offering in these segments by three new boot designs, a woman's Glacier boot, and two low-end Summit boots, priced at $89 and $119, with leather and nylon uppers.

4. **Expand current product line and enter the Weekender segment**

This combines alternatives 2 and 3 with Cima introducing three new boots targeted at the Mountaineers and Serious Hikers and two new boots for the Weekender segment (or some combination thereof).

5. **Sell the business**

Cima could sell its operations to a competitor looking to enter the high-end segments or to an outerwear company looking to expand into hiking boots.

In concert with the analysis of the above alternatives, Cima's management will need to decide the best branding and distribution strategies for each of the plans and determine if those strategies are feasible for Cima.

Criteria

The alternatives will be evaluated based on the following criteria:

- Mission implications: How well does the plan fit Cima's mission statements and strategic focus?
- Market potential: What is the market size and growth rate?
- Market segments: Are there identifiable and actionable segments? What are the differences in responsiveness?
- Competitor assessment: How strong is the competition, and do they have any weaknesses?
- Distinctive competencies: Does Cima have any unique capabilities that give it a competitive advantage?
- Product advantages: In what ways are Cima's product the best in the market?
- Targeting strategy: Does the alternative target the correct market segments?
- Positioning strategy: Does Cima's market perception fit the strategy?
- Branding strategy: Does the alternative leverage, protect, or create brand equity?
- Marketing mix: Does this support the positioning strategy and reach the targeted segments?
- Production capabilities: Do these provide any advantages or limitations?
- Organizational changes: Does the current company structure work with the new strategy?
- Financial implications: What are the associated costs and revenues?

Alternatives Analysis

Maintain Current Product Strategy (Alternative 1)

An important part of the Cima business strategy for the past fifteen years has been the boot company's *strategic intent*. The Cima brand, stamped on the side of each boot, has grown to represent a high quality pair of mountaineering and hiking boots, priced at the high-end and designed to meet the performance needs of the serious outdoor customers. This intent, matched with the company mission to continue to grow each year in sales and profits, has proven to be a successful formula. Even though sales revenues and net income have steadily increased over the past five years, Cima is experiencing slower growth and rising competition in their boot segments. If it maintains the current business strategy, the competition will continue to erode its market share; due to the slow growth in their boot segments, Cima's goals will be difficult to achieve.

The outdoor boot *market* has grown in size over the past five years due in part to the increasing popularity of the hiking boot. The consumer application of the hiking boot has migrated from the serious hiker to being fashionable as everyday casual footwear. This change uncovered new segments of potential customers in the boot market, expanding current demand throughout the children to weekend user market. By maintaining the status quo in regard to its current product strategy, Cima's current product strategy will not adequately capitalize on developing the new customers available in the expanding outdoor boot market.

Cima has developed boots in only two *segments* of the market, the mountaineer and the serious hiker segments with a 15.4% and 15.2% market share, respectively. In these segments, buyers are looking for rugged, high quality boots that can stand up to the requirements of the serious climber and hiker. The purchasing profile of this type of customer indicates that this is usually a seasonal purchase in the summer months of the sport. This has a major financial impact on Cima due to the cyclical nature of the segment.

Cima currently faces stiff *competition* in both the mountaineering and hiking boot segments as seen in figure I in Appendix A. In the slow growing mountaineering boot market, Cima faces relatively few competitors. However, in the hiking boot market, Cima has become a smaller player with the influx of strong foreign boot companies with numerous styles to offer the customer. The domestic side of the hiking market is being challenged by new, high volume manufacturers such as Reebok and Nike who offer products that appeal to younger buyers. By following Alternative 1, Cima will continue to lose market share as it is squeezed out of the high-end segment.

Through the years, Cima has earned brand recognition from outdoor enthusiasts by designing durable, comfortable boots with exceptional performance. These *product advantages* allowed Cima to create a *distinctive competency* in superior high-end boots. If Cima maintains its current business strategy, its brand equity development will stagnate, and the Company would be susceptible to losing a key competitive advantage. Cima is losing brand leverage over the competition with a *branding strategy* that is not taking advantage of potential options such as co-branding, multiple branding and brand extension.

The market segments that Cima targets account for 22% of the hiking boot market as seen in Figure 1 (Product Market Segmentation). With a pricing strategy as the high-end boot maker, Cima has targeted only a small piece of their segments The selective targeting strategy adopted by Cima focuses on a slow-growth segment and ignores the high-growth segment that comprise over half of the hiking boot market. Although they are targeting a small segment, Cima remains as a strong producer in the serious hiker segment. Cima's functional *positioning strategy* is appealing because of the performance characteristics of their hiking boots. This strategy is threatened by the introduction of foreign competition such as Asolo, Hi-Tec, Salomon and Raichle, whose lines are also positioned with a reputation as a high performance boot with expanded product lines, while offering a much greater variety of boots than Cima.

The current marketing strategy includes the *high-end pricing strategy* mixed with limited distribution channels reaching only regional-based customers. Cima sells only to specialty outdoor equipment retailers in the western half of the United States and Canada. This arrangement ignores half a continent.

One of the most attractive aspects of this alternative is that it requires no *organizational changes* nor financial outlays. Assuming that the recent trends experienced by Cima continue (slower sales growth, increasing competition), a cash flow projection was created. The key assumptions are as follows:

- Declining sales growth from 7.0% growth for 1996, to 3.0% growth in 2000 and thereafter
- Cost of goods sold as a percentage of revenues equaling *71.5%*, based on 1995 levels

- Selling, General and Administrative Costs growth of 7.0% in 1996, and 6.0% thereafter
- Perpetual cash flow growth of 2.0% going forward after the 2000 period
- 15% discount rate, as stated in the management's assumptions

Using the above assumptions, Cima would generate approximately $25 1MM in revenues by fiscal

2000, with a net cash flow of $1 5MM. This level of cash flow produces a net present value of $ 10.9MM for the Company.

Enter the Weekender segment with 2 new boot designs (Alternative 2)

Although somewhat in conflict with Cima's reputation and strategy of making the best high-end boot available, this alternative fits the company's *mission* of providing high quality hiking boots to the outdoor enthusiast. Entering the Weekender segment has many attractive aspects. This alternative allows Cima to respond to a shift in the hiking boot market towards a more casual, stylish hiking boot used for a variety of activities. It definitely offers *growth opportunity*. The Weekender segment accounts for 25% of the $600 million/year hiking boot market and is in a high growth phase. Just a 5% market share represents $3,500,000 in additional sales revenue for Cima, assuming retailers take a 50% mark-up on Cima's prices. However, this market share will be hard to achieve with only two styles in such a heavily populated segment. While addressing Cima's growth goals, it does not consider the erosion of Cima's market share in the high-end market. The biggest obstacle Cima will face in entering the Weekender segment is the *competition*. Cima will have to compete with marketing gurus such as Nike and Reebok and well known boot makers such as Merrell, Timberland, and Vasque. Even though Cima is lacking a *distinctive competency* in this segment, the company should be able to leverage its reputation and experience in the Serious Hiker segment, especially in the cross-over consumers between the two segments, where Cinia boots' comfort and exceptional performance will be an advantage. Cima could look at *targeting* a specific niche in the Weekender segment to help buffer itself from the competition. In changing its targeting strategy, Cima will have to change many other aspects of its marketing strategy design and marketing mix to effectively serve this segment. A revised *positioning strategy* is needed since consumers in this segment are more concerned with comfort and versatility than with traction and stability. Also, Weekenders are more price conscious and style conscious, so Cima would have to break away from its premium price position and classic, conservative styling. Cima should carefully consider its *branding strategy*. It does not want to damage its reputation in the high-end segments by offering an inexpensive, casual boot, nor does it want to waste brand equity that could help establish the company in this segment.

The recreational hiking boots employ different design and construction techniques than the mountaineering and backpacking boots. Not only does Cima have to develop a *new product* for a *lower price*, but it will also have to change the *promotion* tactics to reach a broader audience. This alternative will require a significant change in Cima's *marketing mix*, such as utilizing alternative *distribution channels* like large sporting good stores and shoe retailers. Establishing these distribution relationships will be critical, and difficult given the competition. Looking at Cima's *production capabilities*, Cima does not have experience in assembling the lightweight nylon and leather uppers popular in the Weekender segment. The company will have to develop this expertise. Furthermore, the company is currently operating at *85% of capacity*, a manufacturing ideal. The projections show production quantities on the new boot designs around 10,000 in 1997-1998 and increasing to 41,000 by 2001. Assuming Cima's average sale price in 1995 was $87, based on the weighted average of average mountaineering boot prices and average hiking boot prices, Cima's production for the year can be estimated at sales revenue divided by average wholesale boot price, which results in 231,000 boots sold. Assuming also that Cima sells all the boots it makes, 231,000 boots represents 85% of the company's manufacturing capacity, which computes to approximately 272,000. If

Cima's projections for the Weekender segment materialize, its factory will be operating at capacity by 2001, which is not the most cost-effective situation. Additionally, this allows no headroom if actual sales exceed Cima's projections. Production capabilities could not only limit Cima's growth, but also prevent the company from filling orders, which in turn leads to lost customers. The bottom line is that Cima needs to add production capacity. Cima will need to add manufacturing personnel to handle the additional production. Marketing and sales representatives will also need to be added to develop the new marketing mix and handle the new distribution channels. Other than this added staff, the *organizational changes* should be minimal.

The *financial impact* of the proposal is demonstrated in the table below:

Table 2: Weekender Segment Financial Projections

($000s)	1997	1998	1999	2000	2001
Incremental Sales	392.7	561.2	875.6	1,525.4	1,847.3
Incremental Cash Flow	56.9	86.8	143.6	265.9	336.6
Additional Costs	350.0				
Additional Equipment	150.0				
Net Present Value					26.7
Payback period					3.8 years

The core set of assumptions are essentially the same with all of the projection cases, as follows:

- Sales volume as presented by Cima management
- Variable cost of 85% of wholesale cost, as stated by management
- Debt financing equal to 80% of Equipment cost, at a 10% interest rate

This proposal would generate incremental sales of $392.7M in the first year; the related cash flow after debt service for this proposal would be $56.9M in the first year, increasing to $336.6M in fiscal 2001. Taking into consideration the additional development costs and equipment needs for this proposal, the cash flow yields a positive net present value of $26.7M, demonstrating that this alternative provides incremental value to the Company.

Expand existing lines with three new boots (Alternative 3)

Alternative 3 mirrors Anthony's recommendation for addressing the current concerns within the firm. This alternative consists of adding two new hiking boot styles and one new mountaineering boot. The new hiking boot styles will focus on the lower end of the Summit hiking boot line. The new mountaineering boot will be intended for women, a market not presently served by Cima's Glacier line.

In terms of the *strategic fit* for Cima, this alternative is very attractive. Expanding the existing product line in the specialty markets served falls directly within the current mission and scope of Cima. Little or no adjustment to the overall focus of the firm would be needed to successfully implement and manage this alternative.

The *market potential* provided by this alternative is moderate. The two market segments served by the Summit and Glacier lines are the mountaineers and serious hikers. While these two segments make up 22% of all hiking/outdoor boots sold, the growth rates of these segments are not as attractive as some of the others. The mountaineering segment represents 5% of the market ($30,000,000 in total annual sales in

1994) and is characterized by having slow growth. The serious hiker segment is larger, comprising 17% of the market ($102,000,000 in total annual sales in 1994) and has shown moderate growth. In each of these markets, Cima has shown slightly more than a *15%* market share. Cima offers fewer boots in each of its product lines than just about every competitor (as shown in figure 1, Appendix A) and by offering additional styles, they should be able face the rapidly increasing competition more effectively. In addition, the extension of the Summit line to lower price points should help attract the younger purchasers, a concern evidenced by a retailer dropping Cima's lines because they did not offer a boot which younger buyers (typically college-aged buyers) find affordable. In terms of *market segmentation,* the extension of the two established product lines should help the company obtain a greater market share in the targeted market segments. If the combination of the two segments targeted represent approximately $140,000,000 in total market sales, then a 1% increase in overall market share would mean a $1,400,000 increase in Cima's sales.

For this alternative, *competition* will be the same as that discussed in Alternative 1. Cima will continue to combat the same group of competitors, but do so with an expanded product base. This alternative is a natural outgrowth of the increased competition felt by the company.

Broadening the product line allows the company to leverage off of its *distinctive competencies* which have been discussed earlier.

In addition, the *product advantages* are consistent with the advantages of the other products offered by Cima.

The *targeting* and *positioning* strategies for the line extensions are consistent with those for the existing product line. It will be important to position the boots offered at the lower end as having the same quality and durability as all Cima products, except that they offer a few less features. Otherwise, the new product offering may affect the positioning strategy of the company s other products.

This alternative allows the company to leverage its existing *brand equity* with little danger of harming it or extending it too much. The products are a natural extension of the existing product lines. The company would still offer significantly fewer boots in its lines than many of the competitors. As discussed before, the company has positioned its corporate brand as having the highest quality outdoor footwear in the market. This alternative continues that brand positioning strategy.

There is little adjustment needed to the *marketing mix* with this alternative. The company can continue to use its existing distribution channels and promote the new lines in a similar fashion. Cima will need to reach the price-centered shopper to inform them that they now have a Cima boot which they can afford. In addition, reaching the women mountaineers to inform them of the new product offering will be a key. In terms of pricing, Cima's least expensive Summit hiking boot is the HX150 which is priced at $129.00. The HX100 will be priced at $119.00 and offers a similar number of features. It is possible that some cannibalization will take place and the pricing strategy could be altered to create a larger price difference between the HX100 and HX150. The product strategy here is solid. The company does not serve the lower end of the serious hiker segment and presently does not have a mountaineering boot designed for women.

The *production capabilities* required for the manufacturing of a women's mountaineering boot is identical to the company's existing product lines. However, the low end Summit boots will require the company to gain expertise in the sewing of nylon and leather for the uppers, a process which has not been done by the company in the past. This design could create challenges to the water resistance and waterproofing of the new boots and will require the company to obtain some expertise in this area, whether through extensive research and development, or by hiring plant personnel experienced with this new design area. The construction of the sole and base for the new boot will be consistent with existing processes.

No significant *organizational changes* will be required given that the product line extensions are similar to existing products. The following table projects cash flows for this alternative.

Table 3: Expanded Product Line Financial Projections

($000s)	1997	1998	1999	2000	2001
Incremental Sales Growth	455.3	888.4	1,196.1	1,695.5	2,882.8
Incremental Cash Flow	66.3	98.2	196.9	293.5	368.4
Additional Costs	400.0				
Additional Equipment	150.0				
Net Present Value					*62.4*
Payback period					*3.6 years*

The *financial implications* of this alternative are positive. The company could expect to add $455M to sales in the first year, with incremental revenues reaching $2.9MM by fiscal 2001. In terms of profitability of this alternative, the cash flow after debt service would be $66.3M in the first year. The net present value of this alternative is $62.4M, which indicates that it is a viable alternative, with a payback period of 3.6 years.

Expand high-end focus and enter Weekender segment (Alternative #4)

This alternative seeks to leverage the merits of addressing both the Weekender segment and expansion of Cima's presence in the high-end boot market. Although the evaluation of the criteria against each proposal has already been addressed in this analysis, some general observations are necessary. The *mission implications* and strategic fit of this alternative is less focused on the current strategy of the company, as this proposal seeks to generate growth through two different markets. There is some concern with this alternative that the development of a lower-end boot for the Weekender segment would dilute the quality image of Cima's existing lines. In addition, such an ambitious project could create *financial constraints* on the company. The challenge facing management is to manage the impact on Cima's *positioning strategy* through the changes in pricing, promotion, and distribution that would be required with this alternative.

The cash flow analysis below assumes that Cima initiates both proposals (Weekender and expansion of existing product line). The sales volume for the five proposed new lines generates the following incremental sales and cash flow:

Table 4: Financial Projections for Combined Alternatives

($000s)	1997	1998	1999	2000	2001
Incremental Sales Growth	848.7	1,194.6	2,071.7	3,220.9	3,880.1
Incremental Cash Flow	123.3	185.0	340.5	557.4	703.1
Additional Costs	750.0				
Additional Equipment	300.0				
Net Present Value					*89.1*
Payback period					*3.7 years*

As noted previously, attempting to implement both plans results in $1.05MM in incremental costs/equipment in the first year of the program, and results in a positive net present value of $89.1M.

Through analysis of the sales volume and expected contribution margin of each proposed new line, it became apparent that the proposed women's Glacier boot (MX 350) contributed the least to the cash flow of the Company. For this portion of the analysis, the proposal was analyzed without the inclusion of the MX 350, and a portion of the related costs.

Table 5: Combined Strategy excluding MX350

($000s)	1997	1998	1999	2000	2001
Incremental Sales Growth	803.3	1,133.3	1,965.5	3,001.9	3,592.0
Incremental Cash Flow	116.9	175.7	323.2	519.6	650.9
Additional Costs	650.0				
Additional Equipment	270.0				
Net Present Value					*147.8*
Payback period					*3.6 years*

Even though the cash flow generated in each year of this scenario is slightly lower than in the case with the full benefit of all five new lines, the net present value of the revised proposal is significantly higher. This is a result of the higher contribution margin for the remaining four lines, and a result of an adjustment to the cost structure of the proposal. By eliminating the MX 350 line from the proposal, it was assumed that Cima could cut $100M in incremental costs and $30M in equipment needs. This does not reflect a pro-rata decrease in the cost structure (based on the elimination of one of the five boots), as there is invariably some crossover costs between all of the lines that would not be avoidable with the elimination of a given product.

Sell Cima (Alternative 5)

This analysis would be remiss if it did not take into consideration a direct sale of the Company to a third party. This scenario would be appropriate should management fail to find a viable strategy to turn around the negative trends Cima has experienced. A minimum acceptable value that Cima ownership would accept in a buyout scenario was established by discounting expected cash flows assuming no major changes in product mix or strategy. The significant assumptions used in projecting the cash flows are outlined below:

Assumptions:
- 7.0% annual revenue growth, based on 7.2% historical growth from 1994 to 1995. This assumes that a new buyer would add some incremental value that would be reflected in sales growth.
- Cost of goods sold as a percentage of revenues, based on 1995 levels

- Selling, General and Administrative Costs growth of 7.9% from the base level in 1995, based on historical growth rate
- Perpetual cash flow growth of 4.8% going forward after the 2001 period
- 15% discount rate, as stated in the management's assumptions

Based on the above, a bid that management would be willing to accept would have to exceed $ 15.9MM. Note that this value exceeds the net present value of Alternative 1 ("do nothing") by approximately $5.0MM.

Recommendation and Implementation

As discussed in the Decision Situation, Cima is at a critical point in determining its course in the changing landscape of the industry. The second generation of ownership is now faced with a crucial decision to strategically guide the company into the future. The proposals presented by Margaret and Anthony, represented by Alternatives 2 and 3, respectively, each have a great deal of potential. However, it should be noted that these two proposals are somewhat diametrically opposed. On one hand, Margaret's proposal is to enter the weekender segment, which is representative of the company appealing to the masses. On the other hand, Anthony's proposal is to strengthen its position in the niche markets the company presently serves. This decision is simply not one of which products to offer, but encompasses a broader decision concerning the operating focus of the company. These decisions are difficult for any firm to face, but can be magnified when it involves family members and the business started by the principal's parents. Concurrence on the strategic focus of the firm is needed to allow for future success.

Given the analysis presented above, a strong case could be made in support of each of the alternatives Alternative 1 (Maintain the status quo) was not selected because it essentially ignores current market trends in the face of changing customer needs and wants. It does not address many of the issues presently facing Cima. Alternative 2 (Enter the weekender segment) is an attractive alternative but Cima's name would not likely be recognized by the masses. This lack of brand equity accompanied with significant competition in the weekender segment makes a growth strategy solely focused on this segment somewhat suspect. Alternative 3 (Add three boots to existing lines) further entrenches the company in its well-established markets, but lacks the powerful growth that the company desires. Alternative 5 (Sell the business) is also attractive, given the market price which this company may demand. However, the value of the firm to outside investors could be maximized with the implementation of a successful growth strategy.

At the present time, the best strategy for Cima would be to adopt a combination of Alternatives 2 and 3, which was presented in the analysis as Alternative 4. The benefit of this alternative is that it offers very strong growth opportunities by involving the company in the highest growth segments while strengthening the position of Cima in the segments in which the company has traditionally excelled. With two managers supporting their prospective recommendations, Cima could very well achieve historic results. There are a number of challenges surrounding this alternative, the largest of which may be a lack of apparent focus for the company and spreading valuable management resources too thin. These concerns can be mitigated by Anthony and Margaret's level of experience in this product market and their willingness to hire knowledgeable staff when necessary. as evidenced by their addition of Harris Fleming years ago. The other significant concern with adopting this alternative is the apparent cost involved in a combination strategy. However, there will be some common expenses in the research and development of the new boot styles. In addition, the company appears able to borrow sufficient funds to develop and market additional designs. Given this recommendation, questions remain regarding which products to offer, preparation of the company to take on such a challenge, and implementation of the new strategy.

This recommendation does not support the full adoption of both Alternatives 2 and 3. Specifically, Cima should proceed with the development of the two lower end boots in the Summit line and the creation of two new lines of boots for the weekender segment. The less expensive boots for the Summit line address the problem of retailers dropping Cima's products because they are priced too high for their clientele. The boots for the weekender segment have tremendous revenue potential and gives the company access to a whole new base of customers. The production of these four boots generate significant returns for the company and fit very well in the mission and scope of the company. There are a number of specific strategies which need to be adopted for the successful implementation of a combination product strategy such as this.

As part of this combination strategy, a women's Glacier mountaineering boot should not be produced by Cima. The projected unit sales of this boot are lackluster and returns are insufficient to cover the fixed expenses associated with the development and production of the boot. The cash flows associated with the development of this women's boot have a negative net present value and lower the results of every combination in which the women's boot is included. This is a difficult decision to make for a number of reasons, the least of which is that the company's president is a woman. In terms of fit in the company's mission, product, distribution, and branding strategies, a women's mountaineering boot makes tremendous sense. However, at this time, the market does not seem large enough to support the production of this boot. This decision is guided more by the poor projected financial results of the product offering than by its overall fit in the product line of the company. In the future, it may make sense for the company to address the need to produce a women's mountaineering boot.

Specific recommendations regarding the implementation of the combination strategy are as follows:

Alter the branding strategy to effectively penetrate the weekender segment. One of the primary concerns of Cima's management regarding the production of a line of boots to reach the weekender segment is that the lower priced boots would compromise the positioning strategy of the company as the premier, high quality provider. If Cima were to create a new brand name for the two boots serving this segment, it could alleviate some of the concern regarding the corporate position. In order for a new brand to be effective, it would be necessary to tie the brand to the company while positioning the new brand as an affordable yet quality alternative provided by the industry leader in high-end boots. This is similar to the branding strategy embraced by Genesco in creating the J. Murphy line as an affordable alternative to its Johnston & Murphy shoe and by Bausch & Lomb m creating the I's line of sunglasses, a less expensive alternative to its Ray Ban line. The key to success in both of these is tying the corporate name to the new product. However, working against this new brand for the weekender is that Cima's name may not be widely known by the large number of people in this segment, therefore limiting Cima's ability to leverage its brand equity. For this reason, Cima would be better off finding a partner with which it could co-brand its less expensive line. For example, partnering with a company such as North Face, Columbia, or Eddie Bauer could link an established well-known brand name to its new offering, providing instant name recognition. For the partner firm, Cima would be providing a high-quality product to extend the partner's product line. For Cima, the partner firm would provide the established brand equity as well as access to the appropriate distribution channels to reach the mass market represented by the weekender segment. Cima's present distribution channels do not include the larger sporting good stores and department stores required to reach the weekender. The Company must remain cognizant of potential loss of control that is possible in a co-branding scenario; this can be handled contractually at the consummation of the relationship. Co-branding the boots for the weekender segment is highly recommended for Cima.

Think about a niche, not the masses. While co-branding will help Cima compete with some very large companies in the weekender segment, it would be most advantageous to avoid head-to-head competition.

There are a number of outdoor footwear products which are used by this high growth segment. Finding a niche in this broad segment will help Cima to establish itself as a producer of high quality yet affordable footwear. Opportunities exist for the manufacture of mountain biking shoes, trail running shoes, and approach boots, which could help the company avoid direct competition in the early stages of entering the broad market.

Change the pricing strategy to minimize cannibalization. In terms of a pricing strategy, there are two prevalent issues which need to be addressed. The first issue is that the Summit line of hiking boots contains two boots whose prices do not serve two different price points. The HX100 recommended for manufacture by Anthony has a suggested retail price of $119, while the HX150, an existing boot, is priced at $129. Both boots offer similar features such as a waterproof inner lining, with the only difference being that the HX1SO has a leather upper and the HXIOO has a leather/nylon upper. If possible, the HX 100's price should be dropped to $110–$115, to clearly distinguish this new nylon upper boot from the more traditional full leather HX15O. The same pricing concern exists between the HX15O and the HX2SO, two other models with only $10 difference in their retail prices. The other pricing strategy issue is that the HXSO boot in the Summit line will have a retail price of $89, the same price as the WX550, the upper end boot for the weekender segment. The co-branding strategy above alleviates this pricing concern in that the boots should be positioned entirely differently and sold through vastly different channels.

There is still over half of the country left. One area for increased sales growth for Cima would be to expand the geographic region in which its products are sold. The company sells its products in a handful of states in the western half of the United States. Marketing its products on more of a national scope could generate sales rather rapidly for the company. The most significant expense in establishing these territories would be the hiring and training of additional sales representatives.

Catalogs can move more product and can reach the hard to reach enthusiast . Another key for quality long term growth for Cima comes from the use of catalogs for the distribution of its products. Catalogs put the company's products in front of a large number of potential buyers, many times in rural areas that do not have access to outdoor specialty stores. In addition, the company would be able to gauge the success of expanding its geographic territory by monitoring shipments from catalog sales to the Eastern U.S. There are a number of outdoor enthusiast catalogs that would be highly desirable distribution outlets for Cima's products.

Look for the "crossover boot". The recommendation so far has focused on providing a less expensive boot to the serious hikers and a new line of boots to the weekender. It would appear possible to develop a boot that could serve both of these markets at the same time. Searching for this "crossover boot" which may serve the lower end of the serious hiker market and the upper end of the weekender market has the potential to streamline the manufacturing and development process. This benefit would make the development of the "crossover boot" a very attractive goal. A co-branding strategy as presented above would help to overcome any image issues arising out of manufacturing the same boot for two different segments. Minor cosmetic alteration could help disguise the underlying similarities.

Capacity issues are present. As mentioned earlier, the company needs to be proactive in addressing the capacity issues present. Rapid sales growth in any one of these new product offerings could put the plant beyond full capacity and possibly create supply problems. A supply glitch to a new product line could prove disastrous to the overall success of the venture. A possible solution would be the use of outsourcing for some degree of the manufacturing process without losing the breadth of control currently maintained by Cima.

Having fully discussed the recommended alternative and the underlying business strategy concerns, it is now appropriate to return to the new product process to complete the recommendations for Cima. In terms of marketing strategy and testing, these products are not necessarily prone to test marketing. Cima's reputation and conservative styling are indicative of success for the line extension for the Summit line. Retailers are highly desirous of a more affordable product to complete the Cima's product line. For the WX450 and WX550, some sort of market study may be more appropriate. While customer needs and wants have been assessed by the company in the preliminary product alternatives presented by Margaret and Anthony, it would be beneficial to get a market reaction prior to the full scale release of the product. The co-branding strategy strengthens the argument for obtaining a market reaction. A limited product release to select markets would serve as a test market for this product. The company can make adjustments as necessary given the results of the test marketing.

Successful implementation will take place over the course of a year. Most likely the Summit line extension can be produced a little more rapidly. perhaps within the year time frame. Cima will need to take more time to develop and produce the weekender line and to seek and choose a partner for co-branding this line. Cima must proceed cautiously, not to release its idea to too many prospects for the fear of a competitive response. It must adequately assess the current capabilities of any partner prior to approaching the company. With this in mind, Cima could expect to roll out the weekender line in 18-24 months. Cima will need to begin its search for a partner immediately, in order to incorporate any special design considerations which the partner may have.

Cima's work is not yet done. As Cima launches these new projects, it will need to carefully monitor the hiking boot market for changes in customer demands and anticipate competitors' actions. The company needs to recognize that this is not a one-time step but an ongoing process. Therefore, Cima will need to revisit their new product planning process on a regular basis in order to identify satisfaction gaps and new value opportunities.

TN-Figure 1   Price Range

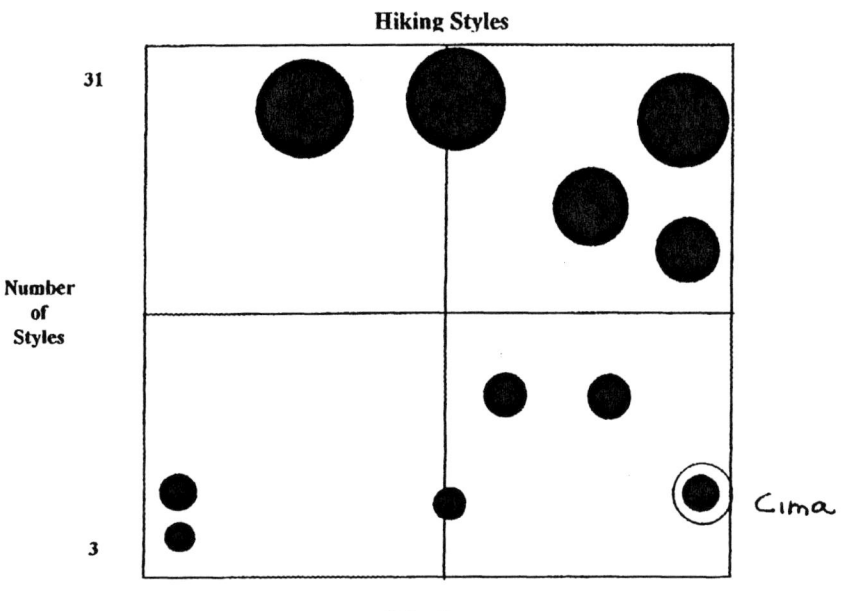

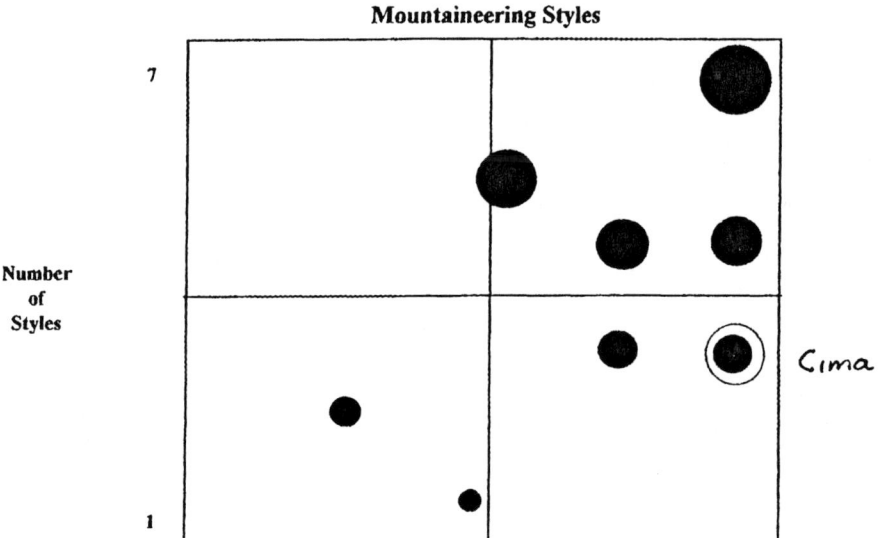

TN-Figure 2   Sales Mix and Net Profits

Sales Mix

Unit Sales	1990	1991	1992	1993	1994	1995
Mountaineering (Units)	19.70%	18.80%	18.00%	17.20%	15.90%	15.00%
Hiking (Units)	80.30%	81.20%	82.00%	82.80%	84.10%	85.00%
Mountaineering (Sales)	27.86%	26.71%	25.68%	24.64%	22.93%	21.74%
Hiking (Sales)	72.14%	73.29%	74.32%	75.36%	77.07%	78.26%

Net Profits

Year	1990	1991	1992	1993	1994	1995
Sales	13,034,562	14,221,132	15,614,803	17,281,683	18,738,529	20,091,450
Net Profit	522,606	602,976	776,056	838,162	809,505	857,134
Profit Margin	4.01%	4.24%	4.97%	4.85%	4.32%	4.27%

CASE 7-4
LONGEVITY HEALTHCARE SYSTEMS, INC.*

Synopsis

Longevity Healthcare Systems is a case on marketing strategy in the long-term health care industry. The case study presents an opportunity to formulate marketing strategy for health care products and services and evaluate marketing opportunities to assure future growth. Students will learn about marketing in a growth industry and how to strategically position a diversified business that is facing health care reform and increasing competition.

Longevity is a comprehensive case emphasizing marketing strategy for consumers and institutions. The issues center on marketing health care to older adults, marketing the products and services of an institutional pharmacy, and marketing subacute care to managed care organizations, such as HMO's. Student's are also required to consider the options of vertical integration and geographic expansion as they develop a corporate marketing strategy in the context of limited resources.

Teaching Objectives

1. To introduce students to a rapidly growing industry that will offer challenging opportunities for the practice of marketing.

2. To illustrate and teach marketing strategy formulation for health care products and services marketed to consumers and organizations.

3. To provide an opportunity for students to integrate marketing strategies for different products and services into an overall corporate marketing strategy.

Discussion Questions

1. What is your assessment of Longevity's financial condition?

Students should analyze the financial statements in Table 1 and Table 2. The analysis is helpful in identifying any financial constraints on the firm's marketing strategy.

The analysis is summarized in the Teaching Note, Exhibit 1. Students should conclude that Longevity is in strong financial condition and able to diversify and expand its business if it desires.

Instructors should review the historical growth in sales and earnings as shown in Table 3. From 1989 to 1993, the compound annual growth rates of sales and net income was 27 percent and 47 percent respectively Cash flow from operations was about $6,000,000 in 1993.

The current ratio is low, but the profitability ratios are strong and the business is not highly leveraged. Longevity seems to be in a favorable position to continue its growth in sales and profitability.

---

* Prepared by Lawrence M. Lamont, Professor of Management, and Elizabeth W. Storey, Class of 1994, Washington and Lee University, 1994. Copyright ©1994, Lawrence M. Lamont.

2. What marketing strategy is appropriate for Longevity to attract private pay residents? What role should advertising play in a health care marketing strategy?

The nursing home decision is highly emotional for older adults and family members. For the prospective nursing home resident, it represents change and a loss of independence. For family members, the decision to commit a loved one to a nursing home is usually accompanied by feelings of abandonment and guilt. A successful marketing strategy must address these issues.

Family members (often sons and daughters over 50) play the major role in the selection of a nursing home for an older adult. They are usually the first to recognize the need, especially if they are caring for a parent or relative in a home setting. However, they know very little about nursing facilities, so the marketing strategy must address the emotional issues and provide consumer information.

Unless the decision is made during an emergency or crisis, selecting a nursing home is an example of complex decision making. Research shows that a high priority is placed on selecting a location that is convenient for the family and nearby medical facilities such as hospitals and physicians' offices.

A successful marketing strategy targets family members with carefully designed promotion that provides information on the services, quality of care, recreation and activities, and the atmosphere of the residential setting. In the case of private pay patients, pricing can be an important competitive factors and it plays a role in the marketing strategy. There is limited, if any, price competition with respect to Medicare and Medicaid patients, since rates are controlled and based on cost reimbursement principles established by HCFA and individual states.

Prospective residents and family members should be encouraged to visit the facility on different occasions to get acquainted with the residents and staff, sample the food, observe the activities and examine the accommodations. During these visits, the administrator and admissions officer play key roles in providing information, answering questions, conducting tours and making whatever arrangements are necessary to help the family make an intelligent choice.

The nursing staff should also be involved in a successful marketing strategy. Prospective residents and family members look for employees that are friendly, conscientious, and capable of caring for their loved ones. The atmosphere created by the staff communicates what it would be like to live there. Staff training on how the facility is being marketed and what is important to the customer is essential.

Attractive promotional literature is an important part of the strategy because it helps to position the facility and is used in the decision making process. Literature should be available during a visit and as a response to an inquiry. Instructor's can illustrate this aspect of the strategy by having students contact local nursing facilities and request literature for review during classroom discussions.

Instructors should emphasize that marketing is a continuous process. Once a person is admitted, retention of the customer becomes important. Successful strategies focus on customer satisfaction, services for family members such as education, support and counseling, participation in social events and activities, and involvement in planning the resident's program of care.

Nursing home administrators complement the marketing strategy by contact with local physicians, home health care organizations, the retirement community, and hospital administrators. In this way they reinforce the image of the facility, learn of prospective residents and obtain referrals.

Advertising for all locations in a market will provide consistent positioning and economies of scale. Yellow Page advertising for continuous exposure is essential. Longevity also should use print advertising to position its facilities as attractive to private pay residents and to generate inquiries for literature and personal selling. Corporate advertising that uses a blend of emotional and rational appeals is appropriate. The advertisements should identify the nursing home locations in the Grand Rapids or Toledo markets and offer promotional literature for a telephone inquiry or a coupon from an advertisement. The inquiries resulting from the advertising would then be converted into facility visits.

Longevity should commit the resources to hire a marketing specialist to work with the Grand Rapids and Toledo facilities. The person would direct the development of marketing strategy and a corporate advertising campaign that would benefit all Longevity nursing homes and at the same time preserve local identity. Nursing home administrators generally welcome marketing research on market demographics, information on how to target a geographic market, assistance with a marketing plan, and regular newsletters with suggestions to improve local marketing efforts. The Toledo facilities should be given immediate attention. Nursing homes become quite profitable as occupancy levels exceed 90 percent.

3. **What marketing strategy is appropriate for subacute care? Should Longevity convert part of a Toledo nursing facility to subacute care?**

Subacute care is marketed to organizations so the marketing strategy will be different for these services. The buyers are case managers for HMO's, insurance companies and hospital administrators (called discharge planners). The purchase of Longevity's services will be negotiated on the basis of patient services needed, quality of care and price.

Personal selling is the key strategy element here. A marketing manager should be hired at the corporate level to work directly with the buyers mentioned above. In addition, the manager should have the responsibility for developing the promotional materials and sales literature. Improving the marketing strategy for these services is a high priority since subacute care is profitable and the growth is strongly supported by market trends discussed in the case. Some firms are using trained nurses in this position.

Since an 80-bed Toledo nursing home is operating at 60 percent capacity, Longevity should convert the 32 vacant beds to subacute care. Even though conversion costs are high ($25,000 per bed as stated in the case), it would strengthen Longevity's competitive position in Toledo and be consistent with the desire to integrate health care services and increase occupancy. The most compelling reason is enhanced profitability. Patient revenues per bed and the profit margins for subacute services are higher. Using the data in the case, students should be able to make an estimate of the profit and capital implications of converting 32 vacant beds in a nursing home to subacute care. Exhibit 2 in this Teaching Note provides some sample computations using data provided in the text and the tables of the case study.

In general, profitability is enhanced by converting nursing beds to subacute care even when the nursing bed can be occupied by a long-term care patient. Using the data in Table 6 of the case, an annual comparison suggests that the profit per bed increases substantially for each conversion that takes place. The additional computations for the comparison are shown in Teaching Note, Exhibit 3.

However, the conversion process cannot be carried to extremes. The instructor should note that the average length of stay for subacute care patients is less than that for nursing residents. This fact along with market demand, the availability of skilled nurses and the patients use of other services such as rehabilitation therapy must be considered when arriving at the proper balance for a facility.

4. What should Longevity do to measure customer satisfaction with its health care services?

Longevity needs to design and administer a customer satisfaction survey in each nursing home on a regular basis. Family members and able residents would be asked to rate various aspects of service, the quality of care, the staff's responsiveness to customers and the atmosphere and appearance of the facility. The surveys would be conducted independently of individual facilities by a corporate marketing manager and the results summarized and provided to the nursing home administrator as information to insure quality care and the need for staff training.

Customer satisfaction is a vital element in a successful marketing strategy. Word of mouth where satisfied residents and family members recommend the facility to relatives and friends is a very important factor in the process of selecting a nursing facility.

5. Should Longevity purchase the Toledo pharmacy?

Yes, Longevity should purchase the pharmacy to expand its health care business in the Toledo market. Although the profit margin for the proposed pharmacy is lower than the subacute care and nursing care businesses, the incremental earnings are attractive and the acquisition would strengthen Longevity's competitive position in Toledo. Exhibit 4 in the Teaching Note summarizes the financial analysis using the information provided in the text and Table 4 of the case study. The acquisition of the pharmacy along with the conversion of nursing beds to subacute care (discussed in question 3) moves Longevity closer to marketing a full-range of health care products and services in Toledo.

A trained pharmacist with selling and customer service skills should be used to provide regular personal contact with the existing customer base. If one is not on the staff of the pharmacy at the time of the acquisition, then a person possessing the appropriate skills should be hired.

6. Should Longevity enter the Alzheimer's treatment market in Grand Rapids?

Yes, the market provides an attractive opportunity. The case study indicates that a need exists in the Grand Rapids area and that the market is growing because of changing population demographics. Additionally, little evidence exists that a cure or prevention will be developed in the near future. For many, long-term nursing care is the only alternative. This opportunity represents a low risk diversification because of low facility conversion costs and the absence of a need for highly specialized equipment and personnel to provide the care.

In most cases, the same nursing facility (with some upscale amenities) can be used to care for Alzheimer's patients. Nursing homes find that Alzheimer's patients are more profitable than nursing home residents because of the lower intensity of care and the lower costs to provide it.

Additionally, most are private pay and have an average length of stay considerably longer than nursing home residents. Recent estimates indicate an average life expectancy of 8 to 10 years for those afflicted at a current cost of approximately $250,000 to $400,000 for care and treatment.

The same marketing staff used to market the long-term care services can also market the Alzheimer's facility. Referral sources and community support groups are important so regular contact with these organizations is helpful.

Separate advertising and promotional literature is probably advisable for an Alzheimer's unit to avoid customer confusion. Some firms even use a different name for their Alzheimer's treatment facilities to position them as distinct from the nursing home operations.

7. Should Longevity purchase the South Bend nursing homes?

Students are intrigued with this marketing opportunity. Table 7 and Figure 2 in the case suggest an attractive market and the firm probably has the financial resources to make the acquisition. South Bend provides geographic diversification, proximity to other Longevity facilities, an attractive price, and the possibility that a single institutional pharmacy could eventually be constructed in Michigan to serve all three locations.

However, the purchase is probably not advisable at this time. Since Longevity has not completely integrated its health care business in any single location, its marketing strategy is not fully tested. In addition, Toledo is still only a break-even operation and the ability of the firm to earn profits in this market is yet to be proven.

Finally, the marketing capabilities of the company need substantial improvement before it undertakes more geographic expansion. Additional staff are needed and a comprehensive strategy needs to be formulated and tested. To spread limited resources into a new market at this time would seem to be an unnecessary risk; at least until Longevity has strengthened its competitive position in Grand Rapids and Toledo.

8. Prepare a short statement describing your corporate marketing strategy for Longevity.

This is an important part of the case analysis because it asks students to conceptualize marketing strategy for a corporation as opposed to a strategy for a product or service.

Statements of corporate marketing strategy should contain many of the following elements:

- High occupancy in Longevity health care facilities.
- An increasing percentage of "private pay" customers.
- The development of a vertically integrated health care system.
- Geographic diversification with emphasis on facilities conveniently located to customers and medical services.
- Emphasis on products and services with high profit margins.
- Quality care and customer satisfaction as cornerstones for positioning and a successful marketing strategy.
- Promotional emphasis on information and education.
- The ability to compete as a leader in the markets where health care facilities are located.

Student's statements will vary depending on their interpretation of the case and the opportunities they find attractive for Longevity.

9. Summarize your recommendations for staff additions and capital expenditures.

Personnel

- A marketing manager for the Grand Rapids and Toledo nursing facilities.
- A marketing manager for the subacute care facilities.
- A registered pharmacist to provide personal selling and customer service for the Toledo institutional pharmacy. (If needed)

Capital Expenditures

- Conversion of Grand Rapids facilities to Alzheimer's units.
  60 units converted x $2,500 each = $150,000.
- Conversion of Toledo nursing beds to subacute care.
  32 units converted x $25,000 each = $800,000.
- Acquisition of a Toledo institutional pharmacy, $1,050,000.

TN-Exhibit 1 Longevity Healthcare Systems, Inc. Analysis of Financial Statements

Cash Flow from Operations

Net income, 1993	$6,209,334
Less: Changes in Accounts Receivable	(563,032)
Changes in Inventories	(638,417)
Plus: Depreciation and Amortization, 1993	575,000
Plus: Changes in Current Liabilities	
Accounts Payable	206,553
Accrued Expenses	122,146
Accrued Compensation	71,851
Accrued Interest	(7,260)
Operating Cash Flow	$5,976,175

Financial Ratios

Current Ratio	$6,370,170 / $4,614,071 = 1.38
Profit Margin	$10,348,889 / $57,500,000 = .18 (18%)
Return on Total Assets	$10,348,889 / $45,175,693 = .23 (23%)
Debt to Equity Ratio	$10,506,622 / $33,055,000 = .32 (32%)

TN-Exhibit 2 Longevity Healthcare Systems, Inc. Revenue and Profit Analysis for Conversion of Vacant Nursing Beds to Subacute Care

Revenues, $500/ day x 365 days/ year*	$182,500
Profit Margin, 17.94 % x 1.25**	22.43%
Profits before taxes	$40,935
Capital Requirements, $25,000/bed x 32 beds	$800,000

*Average revenues / day ($750 + $250) / 2 = $500 / day.

**Computed from case Tables 1 and 4. Eliminates pharmacy revenues and operating profits from the profit margin computation.

$57,500,000 - $3,000,000 = $54,500,000
$10,348,889 - $570,000 = $9,778,889

Profit margin = $9,778,889 / $54,500,000 = .1794 or 17.94 %

17.94 % x 1.25 (subacute profit margins 25.0 % higher) = 22.43 %

TN-Exhibit 3   **Longevity Healthcare Systems, Inc. Revenue and Profit Analysis for an Occupied Nursing Bed**

Revenues, $105.00/ day x 365 days / year	$38,325
Profit Margin	17.94%
Profits before taxes	$6,876

TN-Exhibit 4   **Longevity Healthcare Systems, Inc.**
                    Revenue and Profit Analysis for Acquisition of a Toledo Pharmacy

Revenue, existing business	
$1,450/ bed x 700 beds x 60 % retention	$609,000
Revenue, Longevity nursing homes	
$1,450/ bed x 280 beds x 81 % occupancy	$328,860
Total Revenue	$937,860
Profit Margin (provided in case)	12.5%
Profits before taxes, $937,000 x 12.5 %	$117,233
Capital Requirements	$1,050,000

CASE 7-5
THE LA-Z-BOY CHAIR COMPANY*

Synopsis

The La-Z-Boy Chair Company (LZB) is a Michigan-based furniture conglomerate which has enjoyed one of the most widely recognized trademarks in the United States. Since its founding in 1927, LZB has built a reputation of producing a unique, high-quality recliner chair. Its first manufacturing expansion outside of Michigan was made in 1961 and has continued to the present 16 facilities in the U.S. and Canada.

During the last ten years, LZB's sales grew by 216 percent while the industry was growing by 52 percent. LZB moved from eighth to the third largest company in the upholstered furniture industry. This expansion was accomplished by internal growth and by acquiring four furniture companies which accounted for 27 percent of LZB's 1988 sales. Sales are made through two divisions, residential and contract. The residential division sells through 100 independent manufacturers representatives using Galleries and Showcase Shoppes extensively. Extensive national advertising and cooperative local advertising is used by LZB. Promotional material is supplied to retailers.

The case is about the efforts of the growth-oriented managers who want to build a diversified business in the midst of ever increasing competitive pressures.

By 1989, LZB was faced with developing a strategy for integrating its recent acquisitions into its organization, including manufacturing and marketing so as to take advantage of potential synergism while competing in a market which is becoming more and more consolidated.

Teaching/Learning Objectives

This case deals with analyzing the current situation in order to develop future strategies. It was written to accomplish the following teaching/learning objectives:

1. To characterize the strategies of a company whose mission is to be the best in the industry, while being a complete source of furniture for the home and office environment.

2. To illustrate the workings of an overall corporate philosophy that is intent on manufacturing a wide array of upholstered furniture with high standards of quality and service.

3. To expose students to some of the rigors of managing a more diversified product line portfolio.

4. To put students in the role of top management who must develop and implement a strategy to integrate recent acquisitions as well as to compete in an industry that is experiencing consolidation and increasing competition from larger companies with more extensive financial resources.

The case adapts well to role playing. The best way to use this learning technique is to divide the class into three groups. The first group represents stockholders, the second assumes the role of senior managers, while the third group could assume positions of junior or entry-level managers.

---

* This teaching note was based upon a teaching note prepared by the author of the case Professor Robert Crowner, Eastern Michigan University. Used with permission.

Whatever technique you choose, you can begin the discussion by asking whether LZB should continue to acquire or whether they should refocus on improving current operations. Expect the different groups to give lively contrasts to these analytical perspectives.

The Case Issues

The case focuses on a number of major and minor issues over the 1983 to 1988 period. The major issues of the case involve:

Major Issues

1. How can LZB continue to grow beyond industry growth rates? Should they expand by merger of acquisitions with smaller companies, or should they expand through product line changes and international marketing?

2. Has LZB adequately integrated its recent acquisitions to take full advantage of potential synergies between marketing and manufacturing?

Minor Issues

3. One of the short-term strategic issues facing LZB is that there seems to be a softening in demand for major purchases such as upholstered furniture. Can LZB continue its growth patterns uninterrupted, or will it need to make adjustments in the near future?

4. LZB's marketing strategy has been characterized by a narrow distribution and customer base. With a potential erosion to its gross margin, how can manufacturing costs be reduced further while maintaining quality standards?

Answers to Discussion Questions

The case includes much data on the company, its close competition and general industry happenings. Looking into the future that LZB will soon enter, one can see similarities between the furniture industry and the automobile industry. There may soon be only the big American three fighting for market position in the furniture industry too.

1. Give a general profile of LZB's senior management.

Charles Knabusch: 48-year-old Chairman of the Board and President, son of one of the founders of LZB. He has been director of the company since 1970. He literally grew up with the company and has been a part of the growth and maturing of the company. His philosophy is to "treat people like people," and his family owns about 13.4 percent of the common stock.

Edwin J. Shoemaker: Executive Vice President of Engineering, founded the company then known as Kna-Shoe Manufacturing Company in Monroe, Michigan in 1927 with Edward M. Knabusch. Shoemaker currently owns 6.6 percent of the common stock.

Patrick H. Norton: Senior Vice President. Norton is 66 years of age, joined LZB in September, 1981, following a successful career with Ethan Allen, Inc. The sales and marketing departments are under Norton's direction. He is mainly responsible for LZB's rapid expansion.

John J. Case: Vice President of Advertising and Sales Communications, joined LZB in 1977 as assistant national accounts manager and progressed through several positions to his present one in 1985. He is responsible for all of LZB's national corporate advertising and public relations for the residential, office products, and Burris divisions, as well as the sales training program for dealers and sales representatives.

Charles W. Nocella: Vice President of Manufacturing is responsible for the extensive manufacturing organization and all manufacturing plants except Waterloo, Canada; Rose/Johnson, Kincaid, and Hammary. In addition, Mr. Nocella is also responsible for Purchasing, Safety and Traffic.

Marvin J. Baumann: Vice President of Product Planning and Development is responsible for product development, product engineering and the mechanical engineering and other test laboratories. All product designs are developed internally. Frederick H. Jackson: Vice President of Finance, who is 60 years old, has been a director of LZB since 1971 and was the treasurer prior to election to vice president in 1983. LZB has a very conservative financial philosophy.

2. How well has LZB performed in its economic development?

During the 1980's, the economy experienced one of the best periods of low inflation and unemployment when compared to the decades of the 1970's and 1960's. This positive growth in the economy enabled companies to have an easier time obtaining financing for capital expansion projects, etc. Listed below are the average inflation rates and unemployment rates for the decades of the 60's and 70's, and 80's.

	Average Inflation %	Average Unemployment %
1960-69	4.2%	5.1%
1970-79	7.1%	6.7%
1980-89	5.5%*	7.7%

*Denotes very high stat for 1980 & 1981

In the following table one can see that La-Z-Boy in fact had real growth in its sales when adjusted for periods of inflation.

Year	Sales in ('000)	% Change	Nominal CPI	Sales in Constant $	Real Change %
1983	196,973		99.6	197,764	—
1984	254,865	29.3	103.9	245,298	24.03
1985	282,741	10.9	107.6	262,770	7.12
1986	341,656	20.8	109.6	311,730	18.60
1987	419,991	22.9	113.6	369,710	18.60
1988	486,793	15.9	118.2	411,490	11.30

The average customer for La-Z-Boy is middle class. Typical chair customers are 35 and older as contrasted with sleeper customers who tend to be younger, newly married couples or renters. With the aging baby boomers and more dual income/career-oriented families, an increase in discretionary spending is likely, which will help with the growth in sales for LZB.

3. What is LZB's position in its industrial environment?

In the last few years, many smaller furniture companies have been swallowed up by larger manufacturing firms. The trend for the future will be to have a few large firms competing in the market. However, there will still be some small furniture companies servicing the remote areas of the country. With the expansion of European markets, the international divisions of the furniture industry should see remarkable growth. Listed below are the top 10 U.S. furniture manufacturers.

Rank	Company	1987 Revenue in millions	Percent of market share	1996 Revenue in millions	Percent of market share
1.	Interco	$ 1,100	7.4	$ 635	4.6
2.	Masco	600	4.0	335	2.4
3.	La-Z-Boy	538	3.6	418	3.0
4.	Mohasco	507	3.4	400	3.3
5.	Bassett	475	3.2	423	3.1
6.	UnIversal	399	2.7	191	1.4
7.	Ladd	387	2.6	379	2.7
8.	Armstrong	361	2.4	314	2.3
9.	Chicago Pacific	245	1.7	111	0.8
10.	Saunder Woodworking	225	1.5	203	1.5
Top 10 total		$4,837	32.6	$3,469	25.1
U. S. industry Total		$14,830	100.0	$13,820	100.0

In looking at the overall industry, there is tremendous growth potential for LZB in that the top ten furniture companies only represent 32.6% of the entire furniture industry.

4. How healthy is LZB's financial posture? What concerns should management address?

EXHIBIT TN-1   LA-Z-BOY Comparison of Key Financial Ratios to Competition 1984-1967

		1984	1985	1988	1987
Financial Liquidity Ratios:					
Quick ratio:	LZB	2.5	2.4	2.0	2.1
	Ind	1.0	1.0	1.1	.9
Current ratio:	LZB	3.1	2.1	2.6	3.0
Activity Ratios:					
Inventory turnover	LZB	10.1	9.7	9.2	7.3
	Ind	9.6	10.1	10.3	10.5
Average collection period (days)	LZB	115.8	110.9	98.9	97.9
	Ind	27.7	30.3	29.0	27.2
Leverage Ratios:					
Debt-to-equity ratio	LZB	49.4	58.5	63.2	97.4
	Ind	75.8	84.1	74.6	86.5
Current debt to Inventory ratio	LZB	162.8	146.6	157.4	108.3
	Ind	104.4	110.9	99.8	96.5
Profitability Ratios:					
Net Return on Sales:	LZB	7.6	6.7	5.9	5.4
	Ind	2.8	2.4	3.1	3.0
Return on total assets	LZB	11.0	9.9	9.1	7.9
	Ind	7.7	6.3	7.9	7.1
Return on stockholders equity	LZB	16.5	15.7	14.9	17.4
	Ind	14.3	13.3	16.1	14.3

*LZB = La-Z-Boy
*Ind = Industry

Exhibit TN-2   Selected Comparisons and Projections of EPS to the Industry

	Last 5 Years Actual (%)	90/87 (%)	91/90 (%)	Next 5 Years (%)
LZB	6.5	6.2	16.5	11.0
Industry:	2.7	2.0	14.3	14.1
(Furniture) S&P 500	9.6	2.4	12.4	7.7
Company/Industry	2.4	3.1	1.1	0.8
Company/S&P	0.7	2.6	1.3	1.4

Key financial ratios and EPS are listed in TN Exhibit 1 and 2 to indicate the financial strengths and weaknesses of La-Z-Boy. Industry averages are also listed to compare La-Z-Boy to the industry.

Exhibit TN-3   La-Z-Boy Common Size Income Statements

	1983	1984	1985	1986	1987	1988
Net Sales	100.0	100.0	100.0	100.0	100.0	100.0
Cost of Sales	69.5	65.6	67.7	68.9	69.0	72.3
S.G.&A. Expense	19.6	18.0	19.4	19.2	20.4	18.8
Interest Expense	.5	.3	.3	.5	.4	.8
Operating Income	10.4	15.9	12.6	11.4	10.2	8.1
Other Income	1.0	1.2	1.1	.8	.5	.5
EBT	11.4	17.1	13.7	12.2	10.7	8.6
Current Taxes Fed	.1	5.8	3.3	4.3	4.7	3.7
Deferred Taxes Fed	4.4	1.6	2.3	.8	(-.3)	(-1.0)
State Taxes	.4	.6	.6	.3	.5	.5
Total Taxes	4.9	8.0	6.2	5.4	4.9	3.2
Net Income (%)	6.5	9.1	7.55	6.8	5.8	5.4
Net income per C/S	$.69	$1.16	$1.17	$1.26	$1.34	$1.45

The key areas for concern are the liquidity ratios. LZB is a very liquid company. A company with a strong cash flow of 38 million and low debt, and a rock solid name along with low earnings and share values poses a problem in the future of a possible takeover attempt. Although it has a strong cash flow, it needs to work on its average collection period in days to bring it closer to industry norms. There are no real major weaknesses for LZB in its financial ratios and it seems to be a solid company with a strong growth potential due its acquisitions.

As is apparent from the figures in TN Exhibit 3, cost of sales, selling, general and administrative expenses and interest expense are all on the increase. This, in turn, is causing downward pressure on gross and net income. TN Exhibit 4 indicates that cash levels are below normal, and most working capital is tied up in inventory of receivables.

Exhibit TN-4   LA-Z-BOY Comparative Balance Sheet to the Industry 1987

	La-Z-Boy	Industry
Cash	6.3%	14.7%
Accounts Receivable	43.5	19.2
Inventory	22.2	31.8
Current Assets	72.0	65.7
Fixed Assets	28.0	22.7
Other Assets		11.6
Total Assets	100	100
Current Liabilities	24.0	31.3
Long-Term Debt	25.3	15.1
Total Debt	49.3	40.4
Equity	50.7	53.6
Total Liabilities & Equity	100.0	100.0

5. **Evaluate LZB's Planning System.**

In 1985 La-Z-Boy went on an $80 million spending spree and acquired several upscale furniture manufacturers to extend its product lines. Since then, La-Z-Boy has nearly doubled its sales to $486 million. Despite an overall softening in the market, LZB sales have continued to advance for the eighth successive year of record sales. Part of this growth was due to the acquisition of Kincaid Furniture Company, an important move in developing La-Z-Boy as a complete source of residential furniture. La-Z-Boy is slowly converting each company acquired to meet the high standards and philosophies of La-Z-Boy.

The management team at LZB believes in treating each employee as an important person. The fact that LZB has labor unions at only two of its eleven plants attests that the policy works and is appreciated by employees. Efficiencies will result as LZB integrates activities such as research, computer-assisted product design, tooling, factory engineering, plus centralized purchasing, transportation, and administrative support. In April, LZB announced it will no longer use furniture foam containing chlorofluorocarbons, the compounds blamed for eroding the earth's protective ozone layer. In the years ahead, distributors and retail dealers will have to produce and sell with heightened effectiveness. With sound management strategies, technologically advanced facilities, employee dedication and commitment, and one of the best training programs in the industry, it is no wonder that American furniture buyers are comfortable with "La-Z-Boy." Because of its image, LZB should expect sales growth to exceed the industry average as it has done in the past.

6. **Should the stockholders be satisfied with the way LZB is progressing?**

   Note: The stock is tightly held by the Monitor Bank and the Rounding family (30%), the Knabusch family (13.4%), and the other officers and directors (20.7%).

The strengths of LZB: Why the stockholders can be pleased.

1. LZB has a highly regarded, quality recliner chair product.
2. The trademark, La-Z-Boy. has very high recognition among consumers, and the product names of the acquired companies are also well respected.
3. LZB has a strong product development activity.
4. LZB has a strong group of independent manufacturer's representatives selling its product line.

5. The advertising and promotional support given to its retailers is strong and well conceived.
6. LZB is using the gallery and showcase concepts in its marketing effort.
7. The centralized fabric warehouse provides quick delivery along with a broad selection at a favorable price.
8. Employee relations are strong because of the piece rate method of payment which provides above average wages in a non-union setting and generates a high level of productivity. Other benefits are provided along with treating its employees with respect.
9. Computers are utilized in planning, scheduling, and pattern layout to minimize material usage.
10. LZB has strong balance sheet and financial controls (See TN Exhibit 1-4).
11. LZB is quite closely held by the original founders' families and is less vulnerable to takeover attempts than many companies.

The shortcomings of LZB: Why the stockholders and managers may show concern.

1. The recent acquisitions have not been integrated into the organization as yet.
2. Marketing and manufacturing strategies have not been developed as yet to take advantage of potential synergism from the acquisitions.
3. The gross margin is eroding as price competition has become more intense. This has not been counteracted by further improvements in manufacturing i.e., the punch presses are old and outdated (See question 4).
4. Considerable capacity has been added through construction and acquisition but has not been integrated, creating some duplication and inefficiencies.
5. The distribution system and product line tend to be narrow.
6. The company name and trademark, while strong in recognition, has the image of a chair producer, which is not reflective of the current broad product line of LZB.

7. How is the competitive arena for LZB and the furniture industry changing?

Key opportunities

1. The 'baby boomers" have now reached their forties, when furniture purchases are typically high so the market for LZB's upscale products for the next several years should be expanding.
2. The industry consolidation taking place offers further acquisition possibilities, as well as accentuating LZB's size advantage compared to competition.
3. Exchange rates currently favor U.S. production and provide a disadvantage to importers.
4. There is an increasing trend toward the use of galleries and showcase shoppes.

Key Threats

1. The growth rate in furniture sales is slowing because of a slow growth in the total population (low birth rate) and the slowing in new house building.
2. Housing starts, which are a major influence on furniture sales, are very heavily influenced by the state of the economy and more specifically by interest rates. Interest rates are currently rising.

3. Discounters are becoming an important factor in furniture sales, which will bring about changes in traditional methods of distribution.

4. Larger competitors resulting from the industry consolidation will be stronger, more aggressive competitors with more marketing, manufacturing, and financial resources than LZB's smaller competitors in the past.

5. The pricing point for the typical recliner chair has continued to be $299, which limits LZB's ability to raise prices and, therefore, limits the potential gross margin.

6. A hostile takeover could be undertaken.

Exhibit TN-5 LA-Z-BOY SWOT Analysis Profile

Internal strengths	*Internal weaknesses*
• Adequate financial resources • Well known name brand recognition • Increase in age population • Very competitive due to quality of product and advertising campaigns • Quality product due to good engineering • Strong in-house development and planning departments	• Too narrow a product line • Sub Par profitability because of recent acquisition • Expansion of gallery programs and showcase • Stock distribution
External opportunities	*External threats*
• Untapped foreign markets • Acquiring new firms • Expanding product lines to meet more of the customers' needs • Potential market growth	• Growing competitive pressures • Possibilities of takeover attempts • Low return on shareholder earnings

8. What long-range strategies could be recommended to LZB's senior managers? What are the implications?

a. With limited market potential in only recliners and sleeper sofas, LZB will want to expand its product line to include a complete offering for residential and commercial use.

   Pros:

   1. Will give the consumer more of a selection and could conceivably become a one-stop shop.

   2. Will expand product line and allow for more sales growth.

   3. Will expand them to stay abreast of the competition.

Cons:

1. Consumer demand may not be there, which may result in a loss to the industry.
2. By expanding to other areas, may cause a heavy debt burden to La-Z-Boy.
3. Acquiring other companies to expand the current furniture line may result in these companies not being profitable.

b. LZB should attempt to appeal to the 'baby boomers" by stressing the upscale products of the recent acquisitions presented as an integrated line through the gallery and shoppes programs. Department stores should be reconsidered to unite the various names in use. A further diversification into bedroom furniture, carpeting and cabinetry for kitchens, by acquisition or internal expansion, should be considered. A change in the advertising spokesperson of Alex Karras should be considered.

At the same time, LZB should make every effort to reduce manufacturing costs by modernizing equipment such as punch presses. Specialization by plant for various products should be considered within the confines of geographical needs, thus integrating the recent acquisitions into the manufacturing system of LZB. The use of computers to control manufacturing efficiency should be extended.

Finally, the acquired companies should not report directly to top management as a unit but rather be separated into their components and report at the function level. This would promote integration. Divisions may be appropriate under Senior Vice President Norton, which would also allow grooming for someone to replace him when he retires.

c. With only having a small market share in the United States, LZB may want to consider expanding into international markets.

Pros:

1. New potential markets, some of which are untapped
2. Fewer furniture industries competing in immediate areas
3. Have some international divisions that have proven to be successful

Cons:

1. High costs—especially in labor and initial capital investments
2. Risky—may not provide for a profitable return to the company
3. Consumer buying habits and needs may be different than what is generally the trend in the United States.

d. With La-Z-Boy for the most part being an effectively run organization, should it set up some safety measures to avoid a hostile takeover?

Pros:

1. By initiating poison pills, etc. LZB can turn off or reduce the chance for a takeover attempt
2. Allows the company to continue to run as it has done in the past without having to worry about someone coming in and liquidating the company's assets.

Cons:
1. Sets up golden parachutes, etc., which will only benefit those receiving the benefits in the event the company is taken over
2. Not fair to the shareholders of the company if a better return on their investment can be earned

LZB needs to look at international markets if it wants to remain profitable and continue to grow since this is one of the goals of the company. As stated by CEO Charles Knabusch, the goal for LZB is to continue growing while remaining profitable. The other alternatives should also be considered. LZB does fit the picture of a takeover attempt. It has high cash reserves, low debt, low P/E ratio, and a strong cash flow from the income statement. LZB has in the past acquired several furniture companies and has been slow to turn them around; however, these are proving to be successful. LZB should continue in this direction with future companies to help in building sales and expanding the product lines of LZB. By doing this, not only will it help with profits, but will help in reducing cash flow, which will help to reduce chances for a takeover.

Implementation

La-Z-Boy has made several attempts to reduce a takeover attempt, such as staggering the terms for directors and requiring a 67 percent stockholder vote for approval of any merger. Because of the stock distribution, LZB may want to consider increasing the dividend payouts to stockholders to satisfy them and help reduce some of the profitability. As seen in the past, LZB is successful at acquiring other firms, and it needs to move toward a more fully integrated operation. With newly acquired firms, it needs to go step by step in integrating these firms with LZB, and it needs to follow a strategy that is solid and look for a long-term strategy above instant results. International markets will take some initiative and will require research. A thorough market study should be done to see if LZB has the potential to meet consumers' needs in specific countries and if it would be profitable for it to set up operations overseas or if it should set up a distribution network. A thorough market study should provide LZB with the data that it needs to evaluate entering foreign markets.

In looking at La-Z-Boy Company as a whole, it is a pretty well run company that is planning for the future. In examining its income statement, there are not real trouble spots except for the decline in net income, but this is due to the large acquisitions of other furniture companies. The other area that LZB could improve on is the yield of its wood products. It is currently attaining 65-70 percent yield, and 80 percent is what it is striving for.

As one source put it, "La-Z-Boy is a company that is attracting investors who base their decisions on ethical and social considerations as well as on business factors. These investors buy stock in companies that have safe, clean environments, support affirmative action, assist cultural and charitable groups, and respect the environment." La-Z-Boy fits this need!

Epilogue

LZB is planning to expand into more stationary chairs and sofas. The need to integrate has been recognized but has not progressed very far as of 1989. An additional 300,000 square feet of manufacturing space is being added, and new equipment is being purchased, such as 200 ton punch presses for the recliner mechanism, in order to upgrade and improve efficiency. It takes a 500 ton press to do the sleeper mechanisms, so LZB is continuing to buy these for the present. Burris and Hammary are being combined under the LZB name and are being sold in the Showcase Shoppes. Acquisition of vendors is being examined.

CASE 7-6
BEAR CREEK GOLF RANGE*

Synopsis:

Dan Shay is a professional golfer who has retired from tournament play because of a wrist injury. His interest and skill in the game has motivated him to start a golfing range business where, hopefully, he still will be able to earn a good living in the sport he loves while teaching others how to improve their golfing skills. With his partner and fellow PGA professional, George Patton, he developed a plan for a first class golf range in the Dallas/ Fort Worth area which would cater primarily to serious golfers interested in improving their golfing games via practice and instruction. Plans for the Bear Creek Golfing Range called for a first class driving area, 35 individual hitting areas (tees), an awning, a putting green, a "clubhouse" building, video equipment, night time lighting, paved parking, lighted signs and other attractive amenities. Equipped with a nice set of plans for the facility and the necessary pro forma financial projections, Dan was able to secure a bank loan to supplement his and George's investments. They acquired an excellent location on the Dallas - Fort Worth highway where they set out to construct the Golfing Range.

Dan's plans called for construction of the facility during the Fall and Winter months of 1992-93, with a targeted opening date of March 1,1993. Problems with the local planning board, the EPA, bad weather, and water seepage caused the construction costs to significantly exceed their estimates. The higher costs and the delays made it necessary for them to cut back on many of the desirable features that they had included in their original plan. They were finally able to open on May 1st, two months late. The first abbreviated year of operation was both disappointing and unprofitable. Customers did not flock to their new golfing range and they were forced to recognize that their local competitors offered better facilities, more aggressive promotions and /or lower prices resulting in significantly higher usage rates. By September, the partners were facing the reality that they needed a more effective marketing strategy if they were to succeed and prosper in the years ahead. They hired a college student, Martha Rawls, on a part time basis to prepare a marketing study as the basis for taking appropriate marketing action in preparation for year #2.

The marketing study explored the situation in the golfing industry as a whole and in the local marketing area. It identified the relevant golfing segments and discussed the needs and behavior of the customers in the various segments. The four local competitors were evaluated in terms of their target markets, facilities, pricing and advertising practices. Comparative usage rates were developed and compared with those at Bear Creek. Finally, the study concluded that the market was healthy but that Bear Creek was not exploiting the opportunities that were there. It called for the owners to develop a sound marketing strategy, including a full description of the strategy, its objectives, necessary changes and specific action steps for carrying it out. Armed with this study and with the pro forma and actual financial results for the first year, the two partners are meeting in January, 1994, to formulate their marketing strategy for the coming year and for the years ahead.

Teaching/Learning Objectives:

The case was written to provide students with a realistic understanding of the start-up problems and challenges that confront owners of new businesses, especially in the area of marketing strategy formulation. Specific case objectives:

---

* This teaching note was prepared by Raymond Keyes, Boston College, as an aid to instructors using the case, "Bear Creek Gold Range."

- To illustrate the problems often faced by start-up businesses when they concentrate primarily on product oriented versus market oriented issues in the formulation of their plans.
- To show the danger of excessive optimism in a typical new business undertaking where the owners over estimate sales and under estimate costs, and fail to make provisions for unforeseen circumstances.
- To give students experience in performing a situation analysis, with particular emphasis on evaluating market segments and in considering and weighing the different strategies for the various segments.
- To give students experience in analyzing financial data and, more specifically, in weighing their marketing alternatives against the financial realities of a situation.
- To provide an opportunity for students to (re-)formulate a marketing strategy for a new business venture.

Discussion Questions:

1. What is your analysis of the situation confronting Dan Shay and George Patton?
2. What conclusions do you reach concerning the target market(s) that Bear Creek should go after and how they should adapt their facilities, services and marketing programs to attract customers in the targeted segment(s)?
3. If the partners decide to complete the facilities and carry on a more aggressive marketing program, can they realistically afford to do so with their existing financial resources? If not, what options do they have?
4. What strategy do you recommend? What market(s) should they target? What objectives should they establish for their strategy? What changes or improvements should they make in their marketing mix elements? What specific steps should they take, short term and long term, to implement the strategy?

Situation Audit: (Question #1)

The case lends itself to relevant analysis in several areas: The external environment would include consideration of such uncontrollable variables as market behavior, extent of demand, the competitive situation, and the environmental climate. The internal analysis would cover the company's marketing mix strategy, its skills and experience, its financial position, its cost structure and its ethical practices.

External Factors

Market Behavior: *(Question #2)*

The case is written to incorporate various market segments - the serious golfer at one end of the spectrum and the entertainment golfer at the other end. The case contains individual descriptions of the Serious Golfer, Frequent Golfer, and Occasional Golfer segments. There is less information about other possible markets: the women's, learners' and Wanabee (entertainment) segments. The trick is to get the students to consider the various markets in relation to the Bear Creek situation:

- Which markets best fit the existing configuration of facilities, capabilities and owner interests?

    It is important to acknowledge the importance of existing facilities. They have been designed and built with the serious golfer in mind. The range is clearly an instructional, practice, skills development design. Dan Shay, as a former professional golfer, wants to build on his own background, reputation and skill as a golfing instructor. He has designed the range with this in mind.

- Why do they have a problem developing this market?

Very simply, it is a new business which is not completed according to plan and which lacks customer awareness. The higher than planned construction costs caused the owners to cut back on some important features. While the range does have the basic essentials (tees, fairway, target greens, distance flags, sand traps, night lighting, a customer service area, equipment repair and advice and, most importantly, PGA quality instruction), it does not include amenities that are consistent with its target market expectations. It has no putting green, awnings, "clubhouse", snack bar, landscaping, or other esthetic features (indoor plumbing). In the minds of the owners, it has the necessary facilities and services but lacks some of the "cosmetic" features. Nevertheless, it is incomplete. Had it been completed and had they developed customer awareness via advertising and promotion, then it is quite likely that the range would have accomplished its planned business objectives.

- What market segments should they go after?

In its current state, the business requires significant corrective action to turn things around. With this in mind, the students may speculate that the owners should expand into other markets. Clearly, there are some interesting possibilities (women's market, learners' market, entertainment market) but the fact remains that they have to complete the facilities and do some basic marketing for their primary target market before they can consider costly expansion into new market segments. It is significant to note that the most successful part of their business in year #1 was the lessons area which performed 16 % better than planned. This suggests that they might do well, short term, to concentrate on the market segment that seeks skills improvement via practice and lessons. Such a marketing focus would position them to target the learning- oriented portions of several markets including the serious golfers, frequent golfers, women golfers and learners markets. Such an approach would also provide the focus for their marketing programs and advertising/ promotional campaigns. Some students may feel that the entertainment market provides attractive opportunities for future growth. While this may be true, they should be reminded that it will cost money to acquire the additional property for miniature golf, pitch and put and for the video games and other amusement type facilities. While the profit potential of such entertainment forms is tempting, the up front investment is simply not practical under the current financial constraints. (Exhibit TN1 summarizes the main golf segments.)

Conclusion: We can conclude that Bear Creek has been designed primarily to meet the needs of the Serious Golfer segment. The owners are knowledgeable about this segment and most interested in responding to its needs. However, it is the smallest segment at 9% of the market and it is the segment whose members will most likely have affiliations with private golf clubs with their practice and instructional services. Most students will conclude that the owners should expand their target market focus to cover the frequent golfers and perhaps some of the other segments (women, learners, youth, retired persons, school golf teams). A reasonable strategy would be to address these various segments in terms of the common denominator of skills development. In short, they could define a "skills development" market segment which attracts interested parties from the more traditional market segments. Towards this end, they should complete the planned facilities, expand their instructional services, and design advertising and promotional programs designed to develop a skills development image for the business. Little or no effort would be directed toward the less serious and/or the entertainment oriented segments of the market.

Extent of Demand:

In this section of the analysis, students should be encouraged to use available facts to calculate estimated market size, growth and market shares.

Industry Size: The information in the case sets the total industry size at $42 billion. There are 24.8 million golfers and the market is growing at 3% per year. Women comprise 22% of the total market and 37 % of beginner golfers.

Area Market Size: Of more immediate concern is the market size in the Bear Creek service area. The population in the ten mile radius comprising the Bear Creek market area is 777,082, 70% of whom are adults and 25% of these adults are golfers. This gives us an area market size of 135,989. (777,082 X .70 X .25 = 135,989)

Segment Size: The case also tells us that the Serious Golfer segment is 9% of the market, the Frequent Golfer 29%, and the Occasional Golfer 62%. Applying these percentages to the area market size, we come up with the segment sizes as follows:

Serious Golfer Segment	135,989 x .09	= 12,239
Frequent Golfer Segment	135,989 x .29	= 39,437
Occasional Golfer Segment	135,989 x .62	= 84,313
		135,919

Female/Male Markets: Women comprise 22% of the total market (5.4/24.8) and spend $1,789 per year on the sport Men comprise 88% and spend $1,689 per year. The Area market size is 135,989. Therefore, we can calculate the numbers of male and female golfers in the area market and their golfing expenditures:

Women	135,989 x .22	=	29,918	x $1,789	=	53,523,000
Men	135,989 x .78	=	106,071	x $1,689	=	179,155,000
			135,889			232,678,000

Market Growth: Applying the 3% national growth rate to the area figures, we can anticipate the following increases in segment populations:

Serious Golfer Segment	12,239	x	.03	=	367
Frequent Golfer Segment	39,437	x	.03	=	1,183
Occasional Golfer Segment	84,313	x	.03	=	2,529
					4,079

37% of new golfers are women. 4,079 X .37 = 1,139 women golfers are added each year.

Market Share: Case facts on competitive tees and usage rates positions us to calculate capacity and market share data:

	Total Tees		%	Usage Rate	Avg. # Tees in use /hr		Mkt Share
Greenbrier	40	(40/149)	27%	35%	14	(14/42)	33%
Golfarama	30	(30/149)	20%	30%	10	(10/42)	24%
Bear Creek	35	(35/149)	24%	20%	7	(7/42)	17%
Hit 'Em Out	24	(24/149)	16%	25%	6	(6/42)	14%
Discount	20	(20/149)	13%	25%	5	(5/42)	12%
	149		100%		42		100%

- Greenbrier, with 27% of the tees captures 33% market share
- Bear Creek with 24% of the tees captures 17% market share

Conclusion: Clearly, the market potential is there for success in this business. Not only is current demand quite healthy but future growth, particularly in the women's segment, is good as well. The women's segment offers significant opportunities, particularly insofar as more and more women are coming into the sport and many of them are candidates for skills development--lessons and practice. Expansion into the Women's market and the Frequent Golfer market suggests opportunities to expand the lessons business by offering a lower cost option for individual and group lessons. Not all new golfers are willing to pay the premium price for PGA level instruction.

Competition:

The case describes four direct competitors: *(Also, see Exhibit 4)*

1. Greenbrier competes directly for the same market segment, provides all necessary facilities, charges a little more and is the market leader. (33% market share)

2. Golfarama is also successful going after the entertainment market, with miniature golf, pitch and putt, and other entertainment facilities. (24% market share)

3. The other two competitors, Hit 'Em Out Range and Discount Driving Range, were both low price, minimum services operations. (14% and 12% market shares)

4. It should also be noted that Bear Creek has competition from the driving areas and lessons available at the local golf clubs.

Students should recognize Greenbrier as its main competitor. Bear Creek is not really matching them, because of their incomplete facilities and their limited market awareness. One positive note is the golfing instruction portion of Bear Creek's business which is running ahead of projections and is significantly higher at $60 per 3/4 hour than the Greenbrier rate of $25. However, Greenbrier has two instructors which suggests that there is a significant demand for instruction at a lower rate. (Frequent golfers?)

It is significant for the students to note that all of the competitors advertise and promote their ranges while Bear Creek does almost nothing because of its financial limitations. Students should be quick to recognize that, as a new product/service, it is critical for Bear Creek to advertise effectively and to provide some promotional incentives to attract customers.

Students may be tempted to say that Bear Creek should expand its services to attract more of the entertainment type business. Golfarama appears to be doing well and Bear Creek might consider adding miniature golf, pitch and putt, or other games or amusements to attract more of the entertainment segment. Here, it is appropriate to ask the students if Bear Creek has the resources to finance such an expansion.

This raises the question of their financial situation which will be addressed in a subsequent section of the analysis.

Conclusion: It is clear that Bear Creek is not matching its main competition in either facilities or marketing. In view of its commitment to date and its financial constraints, Bear Creek is not well advised to explore either the entertainment or the low price segments of the business. Rather, they must set their short term goal at matching and outperforming the Greenbrier Range. They must have comparable or superior facilities, they must develop a differential; advantage (skills development?), and they must market themselves (advertising and promotion) to build awareness and attract customers to their range.

External Environment:

Most of the external trends are positive. The growth of golfing and golfing related business is strong, particularly in the women's segment. Local economic and weather conditions are favorable. Although economic conditions might be generally down, this might be a positive rather than a negative factor for this low cost golfing substitute.

Conclusion: Generally speaking, the conditions in the external environment are favorable. Most of the demographic, economic social trends are positive.

Marketing Mix:

The previous analysis of the external conditions provides the background for the evaluation of the internal factors (controllable variables). It is particularly important for the students to see the connection between their findings in the Market Behavior Section (Target market selection, needs and buying behavior) and the company response in terms of its marketing mix strategy. Students are encouraged to review and evaluate the individual marketing mix elements as they relate to the target market needs and behavior.

a. *Product:* Discussion of the product should quickly determine that Bear Creek is not meeting the needs of its Serious Golfer target market. Although basic services are provided, the "professional" atmosphere is lacking due to the incomplete facilities. The original concept is good as is evidenced by Greenbrier's success. Students should be encouraged to identify the specific facilities that are lacking and to price them out referring to the individual cost estimates in the Financial Development Plan (Exhibit 5). *(Question 3)*

	Original Est.	Revised Est.*
Building	$165,000	$100,000
Parking Lot	18,750	13,350
Toilet	9,500	7,500
Signs	12,850	8,550
Awning	3,000	3,000
Landscaping	13,500	11,500
Practice Putting Green	10,000	10,000
	$232,000	$153,900

* Revised estimates reflect adjustments for costs already incurred.

As the students identify the necessary facilities and other improvements that that they might feel are desired, they should be reminded that the business is financially strapped. Do they have the necessary funds? If not, can they get them? This should lead them into some meaningful analysis in the Financial Resources section ahead.

Students may also be encouraged to focus on the lessons area of the business. They are doing quite well here and, with some creative marketing, they may be able to build on this success. For example, they might focus on the women's market and offer special group and individual lessons for women, possibly offered by a successful woman golfer. The beauty of expanding the lessons business is that it can be done with almost no increase in fixed costs.

b. *Price:* Students are prone to compare apples and oranges (various sized buckets) when they compare the prices of the competitors on page 5. They can make a valid comparison if they calculate a price per ball for a full bucket:

Greenbrier	$7.50 for 100	7.5 cents per ball
Bear Creek	$6.50 for 90	7.2
Golfarama	$6.00 for 100	6.0
Hit 'Em Out	$4.00 for 100	4.0
Discount Dr.	$4.00 for 100	4.0

It is significant to note that Greenbrier can charge almost twice as much as the discount ranges because it offers quality facilities and services. Bear Creek charges almost as much as Greenbrier but it does not have comparable facilities or services. Why go to Bear Creek?

Bear Creek also charges $60 per lesson versus Greenbrier's $25. This substantial price differential is justified by the professional qualifications of the Bear Creek instructors. However, one wonders whether there are other potential customers for lessons who could be attracted by lower prices and less qualified instructors. Greenbrier's experience tends to bear this out.

Bear Creek does not offer any pricing incentives to attract customers as do their competitors. There is significant room to do some creative pricing in both the range business and the instruction business.

c. *Location:* The location of the range is already an established reality and there is little to be gained from questioning it. In fact, the location appears to be quite good. They are located on a major highway, between two large cities, close to the airport and visible from the highway. The question here is not whether the location is good but rather whether they are taking advantage of this excellent location. Students might well question whether they are drawing attention to themselves with visible signs, local mailings, advertisements in local media and sports publications and other marketing initiatives designed to create awareness and trial.

d. *Promotion:* The major finding here is that they are not doing any promotion to speak of (Yellow Pages). As has been mentioned previously, the competition advertises and uses special promotional offerings. As a new business, Bear Creek needs to build awareness and initiate trial. It has to spend money to advertise, to offer pricing and other promotional tools, to do some personal selling, etc. Here is where the students can generate some good ideas as to ways that the business can apply marketing logic. How can they get their message to their target markets? What promotional vehicles and tools will be effective? If the students understand the significance of their findings in the Market Behavior section, they will be able to develop good ideas for advertising and promotional programs directed at the target markets, focused on the needs of these markets, and positioned in appropriate media for these markets.

Conclusions: In terms of its Marketing Mix strategy, it is important that Bear Creek decide which market or markets it is targeting and that it provide the facilities, services, prices, promotional programs, and advertising messages that focus on the needs and preferences of the potential customers in these markets. Moreover, Bear Creek must not only seek to match the facilities and services of its main competitor, it must identify ways to differentiate itself in order to attract customers who are largely satisfied with the services currently being offered.

Skills of the Firm:

In assessing the skills of the Bear Creek management, students should recognize that the management possesses excellent golfing expertise and reputations. They have a sound concept for their business. However, like so many start-up businesses, they are confronted with problems that result from their unrealistic optimism. Simply stated, they overestimated the income and underestimated the costs of their first year of business. Their financial skills are suspect and their marketing skills are nil. Are these weaknesses crucial? Not necessarily. Students should recognize their deficiencies and consider ways that they may strengthen themselves in these areas. All too often, however, when confronted with such weaknesses, students recommend that they hire a "Vice President of Marketing" or a "Marketing Consultant." In response to these suggestions, students should be asked to estimate the additional costs of these positions and to determine the additional business required to cover these costs. (Here a breakeven can be helpful in showing the impact.)

Conclusion: Bear Creek has some obvious management and marketing weaknesses but these are not necessarily fatal. If the owners can acknowledge their weaknesses and take necessary steps to strengthen themselves via study, counsel, and possibly some management development programs, they should be able to acquire the necessary skills for this fairly simple business operation.

Financial Resources: *(Question #3)*

Many of the problems uncovered in the previous analyses are the direct result of the financial limitations of the company. A comparison of their pro forma figures versus their actual results (see exhibits 7 and 8) indicates that the unexpected increases in expenses led to curtailment of facilities and services and this, in turn, led to a significant shortfall in revenues and income. Students should be encouraged to examine the financial statements to determine these relationships. Faced with a $25,000 loss rather than a $50,000 profit in year number one, the owners are confronted with a serious financial crisis coming into year number two. The Financial Development Plan (Exhibit 5) shows that they were counting on the $50,000 income to contribute to the necessary development costs. The unexpected costs of the drainage system ($40,000) and the resulting delay in opening the range contributed to their financial crisis. At the end of year #1, they do not have the funds to complete the facilities or to launch the necessary marketing programs. Therefore, the question that the students must face is whether they can raise the necessary funds to carry out the recommended facilities improvements and marketing programs that they deemed necessary in the previous sections of their analyses.

As indicated previously, the students should determine how much money they will need for facilities improvements and for marketing expenses. These estimates will most likely range in the order of $150,000 - $200,000 depending on the extent of their plans. Now the students should evaluate the current financial condition of the company to determine how the company can raise the necessary funds. They may consider additional borrowing (considering the debt to equity ratio) or equity financing (considering the dilution of ownership) or increasing their own investment in the business (can they afford to do this?). The students may not be able to come up with clean answers to the financial problem but they can benefit from the experience of considering the financial implications of their various proposals. All too often, students shoot off a barrage of recommended actions with little or no regard for a company's financial capabilities.

Moreover, when additional capital is required, it is useful for students to gain some insights concerning the sources of funds and the pros and cons of the various alternatives.

Conclusion: Analysis of the financial statements shows that the company was seriously under capitalized at the outset—with no provisions for cost overruns and with heavy reliance on net income to finance first year expenses. Future success is dependent on facilities improvements and marketing programs. The relatively high costs of these actions must be provided via additional financing, most likely involving further investment in the business by the two partners.

Cost Structure:

There are some interesting things that can be done with the Balance Sheet data (Exhibit 7) in terms of Breakeven analysis. Some examples are discussed below:

a. Breakeven Analysis: Using the Pro Forma and Actual figures from the Income Statement, students can calculate the breakeven for the whole company. Subtracting income from other operations, the breakeven can be adjusted to show the breakeven for range business only and, this, in turn, can be manipulated to show the daily or weekly usage rate required to breakeven. The daily usage rate can be a valuable figure for management to use in monitoring their actual business on a day-to-day basis. The running total of actual users versus these target numbers will give management an early, ongoing reading of their performance.

b. Breakeven Formula:

$$\frac{\text{Gross Profit}}{\text{Sales}} = \text{Gross Profit \%} \quad \frac{\text{Fixed Cost} + \text{Mkt. Cost}}{\text{Gross Profit \%}} = \text{B/E in \$}$$

c. From the Pro Forma figures:

We get Gross Profit by subtracting the Variable Costs (Cost of Sales and Taxes from Total Sales) or 301,470 - 29,250 - 3,000 = $269,220 Gross Profit

We get Fixed Cost by subtracting Variable Costs from Total Expense or $ 250,700 - 29,250 - 3,000 = $218,450 Fixed Cost

$$\frac{269,220}{301,470} = 89.3\% \text{ Gross Profit \%} \quad \frac{218,450}{89.3\%} = \$244,625 \text{ Breakeven}$$

d. From the Actual figures:

$$\frac{182,684}{206,274} = 88.6\% \text{ Gross Profit \%} \quad \frac{207,627}{88.6\%} = \$234,342 \text{ Breakeven}$$

e. Usage Rates:

Using the Pro Forma Breakeven, we can subtract the income from the other operations ($111,280) from the Breakeven to determine how much we will have to earn from Range Income to break even. This range income figure can be divided by the average income per customer (the typical customer hits ninety balls or one bucket at $6.50). The resulting figure tells us how many buckets must be hit per year for the range income to make its necessary contribution. The yearly total can be broken out into monthly, weekly or daily usage rates.

Pro Forma B/E $244,625
Subtract Other Income 111,280
Necessary income from Range 133,345

$$\frac{133,345}{6.50} = 20,361 \text{ total customers}$$

$$\frac{20,361}{240 \text{ days}} = 85 \text{ per day} \quad \frac{85}{11 \text{ hr} / \text{day}} = 8 \text{ per hour}$$

The targeted usage figure by day or by hour provides a useful guideline for assessing daily performance. The figures can be adjusted to account for differences in hours or differences in weekday versus weekend traffic. In any event, students should be encouraged to push the pencil to develop useful measurements from their breakeven calculations. As mentioned previously, it is often quite helpful to use the breakeven to add a sense of reality to student recommendations (e.g. "add a vice president of marketing"). When the estimated costs of such measures are included in the fixed costs in the breakeven, the students can see the impact in terms of the necessary business required to offset the additional expenses.

Conclusion: The breakeven analysis provides students with valuable experience in weighing the impact of costs on performance. There are a number of things that can be done with the various applications of the breakeven. Once the breakeven is set up, it is a relatively simple matter to add or substitute different numbers to see what would happen. In this case, it is also worthwhile to point out that the high fixed cost or high leverage situation creates a formidable barrier but also a high profit potential for the company when it exceeds its breakeven.

Ethical Considerations:

There is a specific situation in the case that raises an ethical question. Difficulties arose for the Bear Creek partners at the outset in getting building clearances from the local planning board. A potential two month delay was reduced to three weeks with a timely $500 contribution to the political campaign fund of one of the planning board members. Students may be asked whether they believe that such a payment was unethical? Some will see this as being clearly unethical while others will feel that it is a necessary cost of doing business. Although a discussion of the issue is unlikely to bring consensus one way or the other, it can be valuable insofar as it raises awareness and causes students think about a difficult area of ethical action.

Evaluation of Alternatives and Recommendation

Against the background of the preceding situation analysis , students should identify and evaluate the strategies that Bear Creek should consider and select the one that they deem to be most appropriate. These alternatives will most likely include some or all of the following:

- Continue as is, focusing on the Serious Golfer Segment and depending on word of mouth to improve business in year #2. Refrain from significant increase in debt or equity funding. Look for year #2 to produce increased business as more people learn about the range. Use reinvested earnings to finance future improvements and modest advertising.
- Expand target market to include the Frequent Golfer Segment. Complete facility as originally planned. Launch aggressive marketing effort. Raise additional capital from loans, equity or partner investment to fund facilities improvements and marketing expenses.

- Shift market focus from Serious Golfer Segment to the larger Occasional Golfer Segment. Add attractions for entertainment oriented users - miniature golf, pitch and put, video games, etc. Raise additional capital to finance expanded operations.
- Curtail immediate improvements, reduce operation expenses, lower prices and compete directly against the discount ranges. Advertise aggressively and offer coupons and promotions to attract customers.
- Redefine the market to focus on Skills Development. Target those serious golfers, frequent golfers, women golfers and learners who are committed to improving their golfing skills and performances via practice and lessons. Complete range facilities and launch a marketing program that emphasizes skills development. Develop additional skills development services. Raise additional funds for facilities completion and for marketing programs.

Students should discuss these alternatives and others that they may develop and, considering the pros and cons of each one, reach a decision concerning the strategy that they would recommend. Upon reaching a decision, the students should be asked to lay out the main elements of their recommendation. Especially, in a written case assignment, the students should be asked to provide a more detailed description of their recommended strategy, including the objectives of the strategy and the specific changes to be undertaken. Finally, students should be asked to lay out the action program that they would envision to implement the recommended strategy. *(Question #4)*

Teaching the Case:

This case tends to be challenging for both the students and the instructor. The case was written to give students experience in performing a full situation analysis with emphasis on "pushing the numbers". Marketing students are not always comfortable or curious about the quantitative aspects of marketing problems. The case includes relevant numbers relating total market size, segment size, market growth, and market share. It includes financial statements for students to interpret in terms of the company's plans (pro forma statements) and actual results. It is possible for students to prepare breakeven analyses as the basis for weighing the implications of proposed actions. Information on various market segments allows students to weigh the potential of the segments against the practical realities of the company position.

The case is particularly effective in pointing out the problems of a new business where, as is so often the case, the principals over estimate first year income and under estimate start-up costs. This perspective allows students to see the importance of adequate financing for a new business and it causes them to consider the various options for raising additional funds for necessary improvements and marketing efforts.

Epilogue:

Nothing dramatic has been done at Bear Creek. The owner has been a little more aggressive in his advertising and promotion efforts, but no major changes have been made.

Exhibit TN–1   Main Segments

There are three main segments in the golfing market: Serious Golfers, Frequent Golfers and Occasional/Recreational Golfers.

Serious Golfers are generally defined as those who play 25 or more times per year, belong to private clubs, have low handicaps, and practice a great deal to improve their games. They comprise approximately 9% of the total golfing population. The golf range needs of the serious golfer segment would include a first class driving area with quality grass, several target greens, distance flags, non-Astro-turf mats, sand traps, awnings, practice putting green, lighting for night use, a snack bar, a customer service counter, a Pro shop, quality PGA instruction (individual lessons), custom club fitting and repair, advice in ordering golfing equipment, and a well manicured facility (for esthetic value). This is the market that Bear Creek has targeted and incorporated in its plans for the golf range facilities and services. Due to shortage of capital, however, the range has not been finished and it fails to meet the needs of this market segment - i.e. it has no putting green, awnings, "clubhouse", snack bar, or other esthetic features (indoor plumbing). It does have the range, the hitting areas, distance flags, target greens, sand traps, night lighting, a customer service area, equipment repair and advice and, most importantly, PGA quality instruction. In the minds of the owners, it has the necessary facilities and services but lacks some of the "cosmetic" features.

Frequent Golfers enjoy the game, play between 7 and 24 times a year, have respectable handicaps and play at private and public courses. They would like to play more if it weren't for business and personal obligations They are also eager to improve their games and often take lessons. They comprise approximately 29% of the total golfing population. The needs of the frequent golfer are basically the same as the serious golfer with a few important differences. Although they want high quality instruction, P.G.A. instruction is less of a concern. They would be receptive to both individual and group lessons. Highly important to the frequent golfer is an awning for practicing in inclement weather (for their time for practicing is limited), lighting for night practice, and a snack bar (to grab a bite after work). They also desire a first class facility, with target greens, distance flags, sand traps, a putting green, advice and assistance in ordering equipment and some esthetic features. As with the Serious Segment, Bear Creek is meeting the basic needs but falls short when it comes to the "cosmetic" features.

Occasional/Recreational Golfers enjoy the game but are not highly skilled. They usually play between 1 and 6 times per year on public courses. Although they would like to play more skillfully, they are less apt to take lessons. They comprise 62% of the golfing population. The needs of this segment include lighting for night use, a snack bar, awnings for inclement weather, target greens and distance flags (generally for amusement purposes, clubs provided by the range, and other forms of recreation on the premises such as miniature golf, pitch and put, video games, batting cages, etc. Occasional/recreational golfers are less concerned with quality grass, a Pro Shop, PGA instructions, club repair and advice in ordering equipment. Bear Creek does not wish to go after this market segment and has purposely avoided providing the services that would attract these entertainment seekers.

Other Segments: There are other ways to segment the markets, i.e. the Women's Golf Segment, the Learners' Segment, and the Wanabee Golfers Segment. There is no evidence that the Bear Creek owners have designed their products or services or marketing programs to appeal to these market segments.

CASE 7-7
WENTWORTH INDUSTRIAL CLEANING SUPPLIES*

Overview

Wentworth Industrial Cleaning Supplies (WICS), located in Lincoln, Nebraska, is currently experiencing a slowdown in growth; sales of all WICS's products are below the projected volume. Total sales for the industry have increased but WICS's share of this growth has not kept pace. Griffith, Vice-President of Marketing, has been directed to determine what factors are responsible and to develop a program that will lead to improved performance.

In response, Griffith asked for suggestions from a variety of managers on what WICS should do to turn the performance around. The proposals covered several marketing activities including introduction of new products, lower prices, adding more distributors, using incentives, redesigning the job descriptions of the sales force, pressuring the distributors to sell more, and trying to add more new end users. In addition, a consulting firm had been retained to study distributor and sales force attitudes and opinions.

Griffith realizes that the problem facing WICS is not simple and that the entire marketing mix needs evaluation. He knows that merely pushing the sales force to sell more is not the answer.

Teaching Objectives

1. To teach students to recognize the potential impact of changing specific company policies on potential market share;
2. To consider both short-run and long-run implications of alternative strategies; and
3. To recognize that sales is part of marketing and that the entire marketing effort must be considered.

Teaching Suggestions

The Wentworth case can be used early in the course to illustrate the relationship between sales and the rest of the marketing activities. Too often the sales function is viewed as not being part of marketing. If used early, students should be able to discuss the problems and make recommendations for most. Sales force problems may be recognized but recommendations will not be as well developed. We assume that most students have taken a basic marketing course which will facilitate their ability to discuss and recommend solutions for the problems.

Students should be encouraged to look for the less obvious solutions to the problems in WICS. Certain issues have been highlighted which are not intended to be the focus of this case. The recommendations are marketing oriented, not just sales management oriented. An integrated program is needed to help WICS reverse a stagnate and declining market share situation.

---

* This teaching note was developed by the case authors.

Discussion Questions

1. **What problems and issues does Griffith face?**

The first issue that needs to be clarified is WICS's market share.

Calculating Market Share

In order to determine whether the present distribution system could be more efficient, i.e., whether WICS's sales force and distributors could be more effective, we must first calculate potential and real market shares.

The two necessary components are product coverage and distribution reach; the combined effect of these two factors ascertains what percent of the total market is, in fact, addressed by WICS.

WICS's product line fulfills 75% of the users' needs. Due to the premium pricing of the product offerings, 40% of the market is addressed by WICS. Thus, 30% (.75 x .40) of the total market is actually served by WICS's products.

The present distribution system further limits market potential. Approximately 65% of the market buys through distributors. Of the total distributor dollars, SSDs "see" only-65% of the market. Therefore, 42% (.65 x .65) of the total market is actually seen through the current distributor network.

The combined effect is that 12.6% (.30 x .42) of the served market is addressed by WICS. Assuming that survey results are accurate, and consequently that WICS holds a market share of 75% of the addressed market, the firm's actual market share is 9.5% (.126 x .75).

With a potential market share of 12.6% and actual share of 9.5%, it appears that SSDs are doing a reasonable job of marketing WICS's products through present channels. The issue, then, concerns the necessity of determining the optimal strategy for increasing market potential. Presumably, WICS will be able to retain or exceed its current share of 75% and experience an increase in actual sales dollars as a result. Although we are currently interested in providing salespersons and distributors with sufficient incentives for maximizing the efficiency of the distribution system, it is not the focus of this study. Our major concern is to find a means of facilitating growth, making it easier for sales representatives and distributors to fulfill their roles and responsibilities in an efficient manner.

WICS, because of its strength in consumer markets from products sold by another division, is assumed to have a market share much larger than 9.5%. It is unlikely that WICS will be able to increase its market share by further "greasing" the channels of distribution. WICS's situation can be compared to the problem of trying to pour more water through a funnel. WICS's past strategies were just that, trying to get a given number of distributors to handle more volume. As it stands, the case indicates that the SSDs resent WICS's efforts to pressure them to sell more to existing end users and to call on new end users. SSDs see WICS as being manipulative and unreasonable. In addition to the problem of negative distributor attributes, WICS faces similar problems with the sales force. The area managers are frustrated by a sales role that they see as ineffective. Area managers view themselves as "lackeys" who are denied the opportunity to use their own creative skills. Job descriptions do not reflect reality and need revising.

WICS's product line does not reflect end user needs. Existing products only cover part of the market. Prices are too high which serves to limit the market further.

WICS marketing program assumes that their products are in the growth stage of the life cycle. Focus has been on market development using high distributor margins to encourage SSDs to emphasize selling benefits, demonstrations, and cold calls on new end users. Exhibit 1 illustrates WICS's position.

Exhibit 1   The Market has Moved Beyond SSD's Marketing Thrust

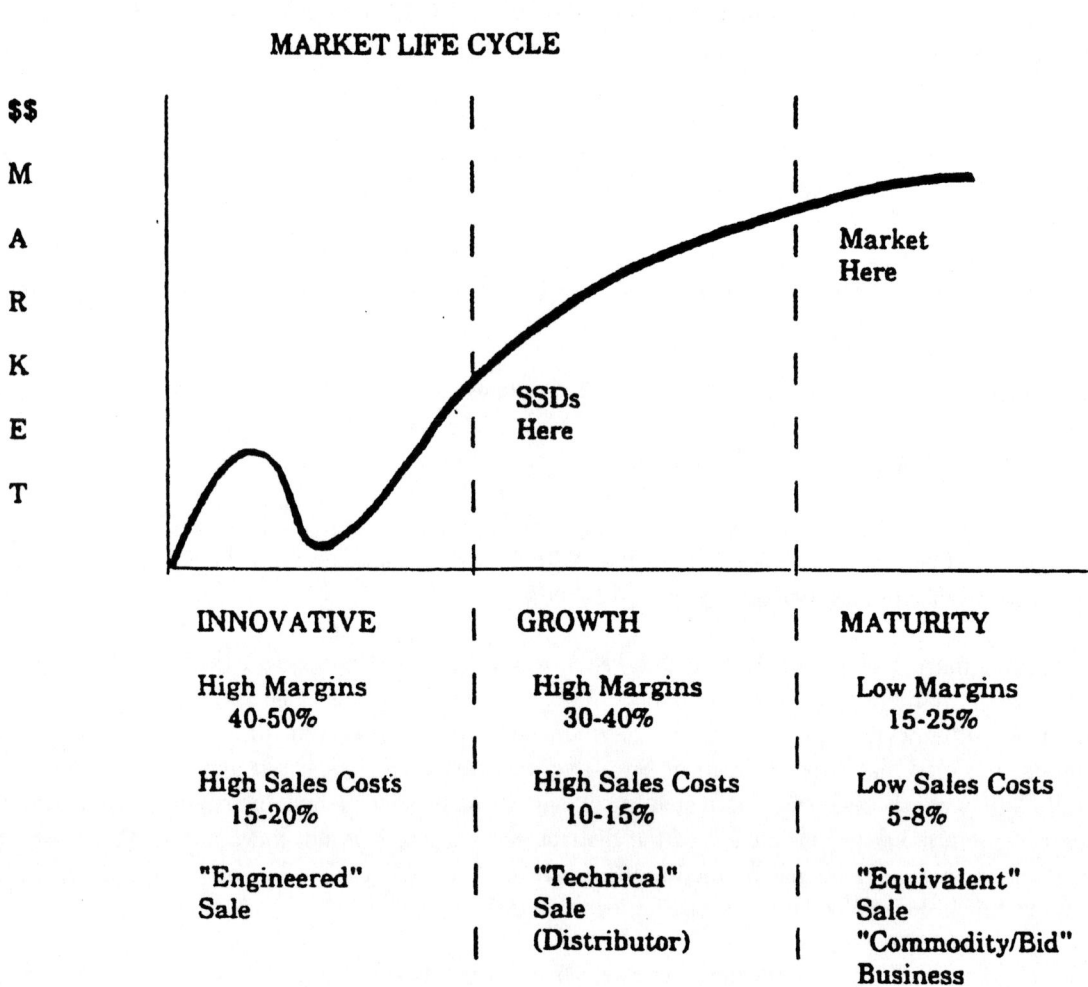

2. What alternatives are open to Griffith? What are the advantages and disadvantages of the suggestions made by his staff?

One alternative is to do nothing. Obviously this has dire consequences, including Griffith looking for a different job. It is unlikely that the problem will go away or be self-correcting. Marketing mix problems exist that must be resolved if WICS's position is to improve.

Toner's Proposal

Toner's suggestions lead to more area managers and to more SSDs.

Advantages:

- More AMs and SSDs should lead to an increase in sales.
- Will lead to greater market exposure since new SSDs will call on new end users for WICS.

Disadvantages:

- SSDS who are doing a good job will resent the addition of more SSDs.
- Ignores the fact that current job descriptions are inappropriate.
- More AMs doing the wrong activities.
- More AMs will mean more territory managers and maybe another regional manager, adding to overhead costs.

Summary:

More SSDs in selected markets should be considered in greater depth. Other changes in the marketing mix may be needed first. More SSDs would produce more sales. Attitudes of present SSDs need to be considered.

Hart's Proposals

Hart wants to use incentives to motivate the AMs and SSDs to sell more. She also favors establishing quotas for the SSDs and dropping those who fail to meet quota. Hart favors bonuses for securing new end user accounts, to be awarded to both AMs and SSDs.

Advantages:

- Hart's proposals will probably generate an increase in sales both to existing and new users.
- SSDs will be given objectives to meet which might cause them to do a more effective job with WICS's products.
- Bonuses will call attention to the importance of new accounts.

Disadvantages:

- Hart's proposal is a "bandaid" solution to a major problem.
- More incentives will not be readily accepted by both the AMs and the SSDs.
- SSDs will perceive this as more pressure.
- Short-term benefits only.
- AMs are already doing the wrong activities; this will encourage a continuation.

Summary:

Incentives and quotas and bonuses may play a role in helping WICS resolve some of its problems. They may be used in connection with other recommendations.

Michael's Proposal

Michael is critical of how the AMs spend their time. He favors a job analysis of the AM's position. He wants to determine what rewards AMs value, feeling that more contests are not the answer.

Advantages:

- Could lead to a better definition of the AM's job.
- Eventually could lead to an increase in sales especially to new end users.
- AMs will be better able to determine how they should spend their time. They will be more satisfied with their jobs.
- Could lead to an improved reward package or system.

Disadvantages:

- Ignores other problems, such as margins that are too high and distributors that are not happy. Will take time to implement.

Summary:

- Revised job descriptions are necessary to be sure.
- WICS has other problems that need attention.

Webber's Proposal

Webber wants to expand the product line to include economy products. She also favors the addition of more SSDs, primarily in the $500,000 to $1,000,000 range.

Advantages:

- Will overcome WICS's lack of product coverage in the economy class.
- Should lead to an increase in sales and market share.
- Present SSDs will be pleased since they will have a full line of WICS's products to sell.

Disadvantages:

- Will increase R&D costs.
- Could lead to negative image problems.
- Expansion of product line may lead to more pressure being applied to the AMs and the SSDs.
- Additional sales training will be required.

Summary:

Expanding the product line to include the economy class is reasonable if incorporated with other changes.

Smith's Proposal

Smith advocates reducing prices to increase sales volume. She also feels that margins are too high and should be cut, due to her perceptions of where the product is in the life cycle.

Advantages:

- If her assumptions are correct, price cuts could lead to an increase in market share.
- Gutting prices is easy to implement.
- SSDs would find the WICS's line easier to sell.
- Lower prices may attract other SSDs who have "windows" composed of customers who are price conscious.

Disadvantages:

- If it does not work, WICS loses profit margin.
- May have a negative effect on WICS's image.

Summary:

If product is in a later stage of the life cycle, then cutting prices is reasonable. However, other marketing actions are needed.

3. What should WICS do to correct its market share problem?

Throughout this analysis, two basic strategies aimed at obtaining WICS's growth objectives emerge.

a. WICS needs to increase its market coverage by increasing the number of SSDs. The addition of distributors with different "windows" will improve sales to new end users

   More aggressive selling efforts are required which means that the AMs will have to spend less time with existing distributors. Job descriptions will need to be revamped and sales training programs will have to change to reflect new activities.

   Incentive programs will be needed to encourage AMs to secure new SSDs and new end users.

b. WICS needs to broaden its product coverage to include the economy class. Presently, WICS is excluded from the low end of the market because of its limited product line.

   WICS has to lower prices on its premium products but avoid going too low and competing against "schlock" products. Selling costs need to be lowered. Eliminating market developments costs for new products is one example. SSD's selling costs can be reduced by teaching their salespeople low cost sales techniques. In other words, since the products are in the mature stage of the life sales efforts are not necessary. The products do not need demonstration. Reallocating the AM's efforts reduces selling costs for mature products.

Epilogue

Prior to instituting the proposed program at a national level, WICS test marketed in Cincinnati. Four major changes were introduced in the Cincinnati test market:

1. Progressive discounts were offered in relation to total order size.
2. New products were introduced, targeted at the economy-priced, medium-performance category.
3. Distributors were added selectively to fill voids in the distributor network.
4. The daily routine of the AM was reoriented to increase productivity. (Directives limited distributor calls to 20%..

If present trends continue, real volume can be expected to increase by 53% during the first year of the new program.

SECTION VI

TRANSPARENCY MASTERS

STRATEGIC MARKETING MANAGEMENT CASES

PowerPoint Presentation

DAVID W. CRAVENS
CHARLES W. LAMB, JR.
VICTORIA L. CRITTENDEN

©The McGraw-Hill Companies, Inc., 1999

Market-Driven Strategy

©*The McGraw-Hill Companies, Inc., 1999*

The Hierarchy of Strategy

Corporate Strategy  Business Strategy Functional Strategy

©*The McGraw-Hill Companies, Inc., 1999*

Types of Organizations

- Consumer Product Firms
- Industrial Product Firms
- Service Organizations
- Not-For-Profit Organizations

©*The McGraw-Hill Companies, Inc., 1999*

Strategies

- Overall Cost Leadership
- Differentiation
- Focus

©*The McGraw-Hill Companies, Inc., 1999*

Strategic Vision

- When to compete
- How to compete
- Where to compete
- Whether to compete

Provide unique benefits that more than offset a higher price

Create Superior Customer Value

Offer lower prices than competition for equivalent benefits

©*The McGraw-Hill Companies, Inc., 1999*

Low Cost Leadership

Objective:

- Open up a sustainable cost advantage over competitors -- use the lower-cost edge as a basis for:
  - Underpricing competitors and reaping market share gains

  OR

  - Earning a higher profit margin selling at the going market price

- *Note: A cost advantage generates superior profitability only when it is not entirely eaten away by efforts to underprice competitors and grab away their business!*

Source: Michael E. Porter, <u>Competitive Strategy</u>, The Free Press, 1980.

Low Cost Leadership

Keys to Success

- Make the achievement of low-cost relative to competitors the theme of the company's entire business strategy.

- Low-cost leadership means low OVERALL costs not just low manufacturing and production costs.

- The game plan must be to manage across-the-board costs down, year after year after year.

Source: Michael E. Porter, <u>Competitive Strategy</u>, The Free Press, 1980.

Differentiation Strategies

A. Objective

- Incorporate differentiating features into product/service offering which will cause buyers to prefer the company's product/service over the brands of rivals

B. Keys to Success

- Finding ways to differentiate that CREATE VALUE for buyers and that are not easily copied or matched by rivals
- Having a distinctive competence (being able to do something BETTER than rivals)
- Not spending more to differentiate than the price premium that differentiation will command

Source: Michael E. Porter, Competitive Strategy, The Free Press, 1980.

Differentiation Strategies

■ Successful differentiation allows a firm to:
- Command a premium price for its product and or service
- Sell more units and service
- Gain greater buyer loyalty to its brand

Source: Michael E. Porter, Competitive Strategy, The Free Press, 1980.

Focus and Niche Strategies

Objective:

- Do a much better job of serving niche members than rival competitors

Keys to Success:

- Choosing a market niche where buyers have distinctive preferences or requirements
- Developing a unique ability (as compared to rivals) to serve the needs of the target buyer segment

Source: Michael E. Porter, Competitive Strategy, The Free Press, 1980.

New Product Strategy

"twice as good, twice as fast, with half the resources"

©*The McGraw-Hill Companies, Inc., 1999*

The New Marketing Mix: 4 P's an S and C

- Product
- Price
- Place
- Promotion
- Service
- Customer Sensitivity

©The McGraw-Hill Companies, Inc., 1999

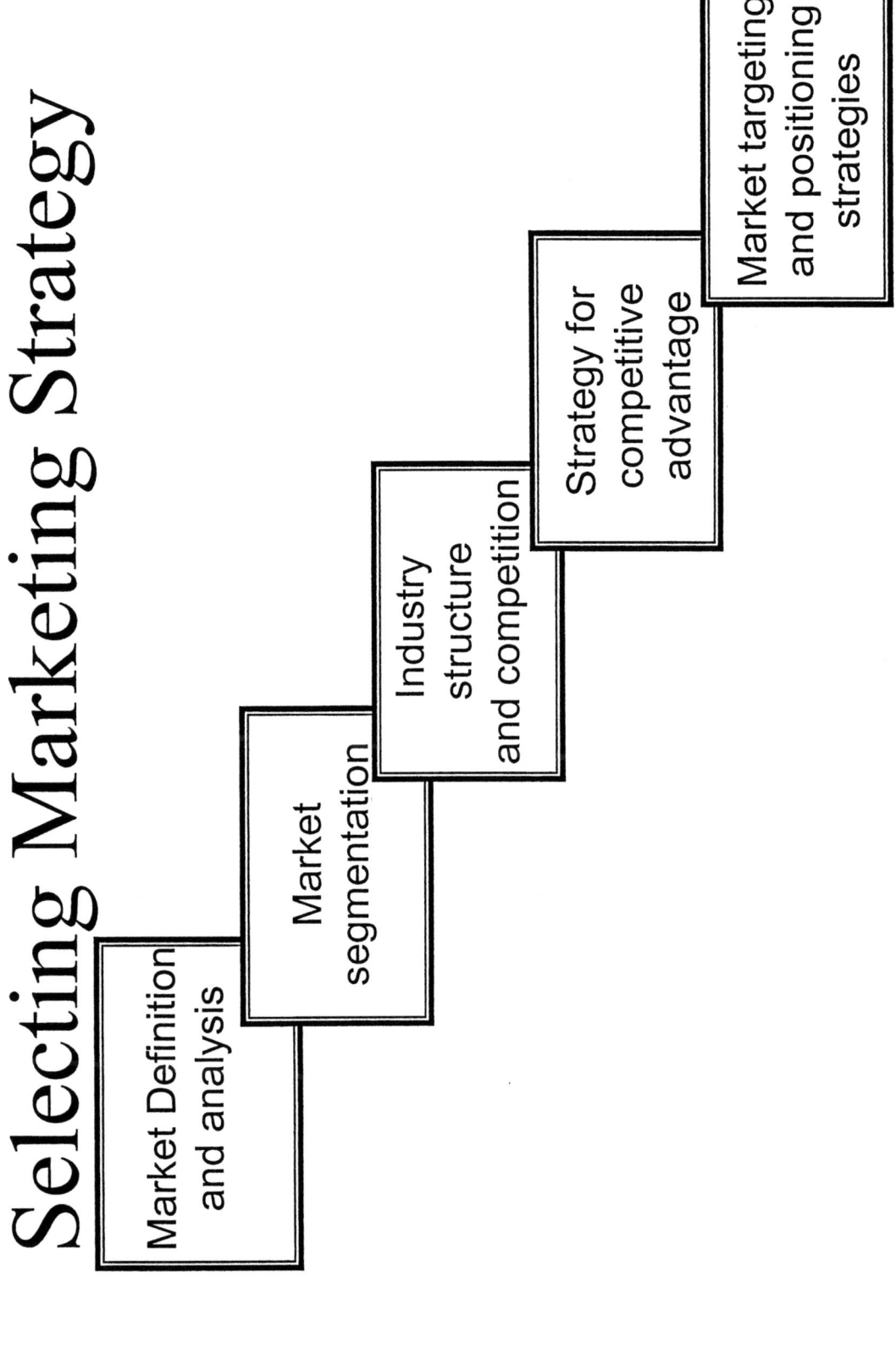

Market Definition and Analysis

- What are the buyers' needs?
- What products will meet their needs?

Market Segmentation

Similarities/Differences

Industry Structure and Competition

- How many companies are attempting to satisfy a customer's particular wants and needs?

- Are new competitors entering the market?

©*The McGraw-Hill Companies, Inc., 1999*

Competitive Advantage

- **Superior value through:**
  - Lower prices than competition for equivalent benefits

  and/or

  - Unique benefits that more than offset a higher price

Building a Distinctive Competence

- A distinctive competence is something a company does well in comparison to its competitors
- A distinctive competence is important to strategy formation because of:
  - The unique capability it gives an organization in capitalizing on a particular opportunity
  - The competitive edge it may give a firm in the marketplace
  - The potential for using a distinctive competence as the cornerstone of strategy

Types of Distinctive Competencies

- Manufacturing excellence
- Better service capability
- Low-cost manufacturing know-how
- Superior design capability
- Ability to choose good retail locations
- More innovativeness in new product development
- Better mastery of an important technology
- Better feel for customer needs and tastes
- More effective sales force

©*The McGraw-Hill Companies, Inc., 1999*

ILLUSTRATIVE COMPARISON OF BUSINESS AND MARKETING STRATEGIES

- Perspective
- Decisions
- Strategic Focus
- Informational Needs

©*The McGraw-Hill Companies, Inc., 1999*

Perspective

Corporation/Business Units

- Organizational and/or competitive focus, often with a heavy industry orientation

Marketing

- Customer and/or product focus, often with a heavy end-user orientation

©The McGraw-Hill Companies, Inc., 1999

Decisions

Corporation/Business Units

- Mission determination
- Allocation of business resources to business units
- Acquisition/diversification
- Elimination of business units
- Product development and management
- Selection and importance of SBU strategies

Marketing

- Identification of market opportunities
- Choice of target market(s)
- Marketing program positioning strategy
- Product, distribution, price, and promotion strategies

©*The McGraw-Hill Companies, Inc., 1999*

Strategic Focus

Corporation/Business Units

- How to gain and keep strategic advantage
- How to determine business strategies
- How to organize the business for planning/control

Marketing

- How to divide product/markets into segments
- What segment(s) to serve
- How to position for each segment

©*The McGraw-Hill Companies, Inc., 1999*

Information Needs

Corporation/Business Units

- Financial performance
- Business opportunity assessment
- Market performance and forecasts
- Competitors' strategies and performance

Marketing

- Financial performance by market target
- Customer/prospect description and requirements
- Market position and forecasts
- Competitors' marketing strategies

Elements of Competitive Advantage

SOURCES OF ADVANTAGE
1. superior skills
2. superior resources

POSITION
1. superior customer value
2. lower relative costs

PERFORMANCE OUTCOMES
1. satisfaction
2. loyalty
3. market share
4. profitability

Investment of profits to sustain advantage

Source: George S. Day and Robin Wensley, "Assessing Advantage: A Framework for Diagnosing Competitive Superiority," <u>Journal of Marketing</u>, April 1988, 30.

Market Targeting and Positioning

- Which buyers to target
- Determining marketing program

7 Choice Criteria For Determining Which Marketing Strategy

- Sustainable competitive advantage
- Realistic assumption
- Skills, Resources, and Management Commitment
- Cohesiveness
- Risks and Contingencies
- Flexibility/Adaptability
- Value added

Source: Geroge S. Day,"Tough Questions for Developing Strategies," *Journal of Business Strategy*, Winter 1986, pp. 60-68.

The Strategic Marketing Plan -- Steps in Preparing & Implementing

1. Marketing situation analysis ⇧
2. Market-target strategy ⇧
3. Objectives for each target market ⇧
4. Marketing program positioning strategy ⇧
5. Evaluate the marketing organization ⇧
6. Prepare the plan and budget ⇧
7. Implement the plan ⇧
8. Evaluate results and manage the plan ⇧

(Strategic Marketing Plan)

©*The McGraw-Hill Companies, Inc., 1999*

Is Marketing Everything??

©The McGraw-Hill Companies, Inc., 1999

Market Orientation and Organizational Learning

©The McGraw-Hill Companies, Inc., 1999

The Wrong Message

Unhappy customers tell twice as many people about bad experiences as good ones.

©The McGraw-Hill Companies, Inc., 1999

What is it?

- Customer focus
- Competitor intelligence
- Interfunctional coordination

How?

- Information acquisition
- Interfunctional assessment
- Shared diagnosis and action

Market-oriented Action

- Market and customer feedback
- Focus on target market
- Customer satisfaction orientation
- Quality obsession
- Innovation
- Interfunctional teamwork
- Trade partnership
- Strong communications program
- Green consciousness
- Globalization

©The McGraw-Hill Companies, Inc., 1999

Components of Market Orientation

Information Acquisition → Interfunctional Assessment → Shared Diagnosis and Coordinated Action → Superior Customer Value

Customer Information
Competitor Information
Other Market Information

Source: Stanley F. Slater and John C. Narver, "Market Orientation, Customer Value, and Superior Performance," Business Horizons, March / April 1994, 22-27 at page 23.

Growth Strategies

	Product	
	Present	**New**
Market Present	Market penetration	Product development
Market New	Market development	Diversification

Source: Adapted from *Corporate Strategy* by H.I. Ansoff, p. 109, McGraw-Hill, 1965.

©*The McGraw-Hill Companies, Inc., 1999*

Product-Portfolio Analysis

	High Market Share	Low
High Product Market Growth	Stars	Problem Child
Low	Cash Cows	Dogs

©The McGraw-Hill Companies, Inc., 1999

Stars

Characteristics

- Market leaders
- Fast growing
- Substantial Profits
- Require large investment to finance growth

Strategies

- Protect existing share
- Reinvest earnings in the form of price reductions, product improvements, providing better market coverage, production efficiency, etc..
- Obtain a large share of the new users

Source: William Pride & O.C. Ferrell. Marketing. Boston: Houghton-Mifflin Co., 1991.

©*The McGraw-Hill Companies, Inc., 1999*

Problem Child

<u>Characteristics</u>
- **Rapid growth**
- **Poor profit margins**
- **Enormous demand for cash**

<u>Strategies</u>
- invest heavily to get disproportionate share of new sales
- Buy existing market share by acquiring competitors
- Divestment (see Dogs)
- Harvesting (see Dogs)
- Abandonment (see Dogs)
- Focus on a definable niche where dominance can be achieved

Source: William Pride & O.C. Ferrell . Marketing. Boston: Houghton-Mifflin Co., 1991
©*The McGraw-Hill Companies, Inc., 1999*

Cash Cows

Characteristics

- Profitable products
- Generate more cash than needed to maintain market share

Strategies

- Maintain market dominance
- Invest in process improvements and technological leadership
- Maintain price leadership
- Use excess cash to support research and growth elsewhere in the company

Source: William Pride & O.C. Ferrell. Marketing. Boston: Houghton-Mifflin Co., 1991.

©*The McGraw-Hill Companies, Inc., 1999*

Dogs

Characteristics

- Greatest number of products fall in this category
- Operate at a cost disadvantage
- Few opportunities for growth at a reasonable cost
- Markets are not growing; little new business

Strategies

- Focus on a specialized segment of the market that can be dominated and protected from competitive inroads
- Harvesting- cut back all support costs to a minimum level; supports cash flow over the product's remaining life
- Divestment- sale of a growing concern
- Abandonment – deletion from the product line

Source: William Pride & O.C. Ferrell. Marketing. Boston: Houghton-Mifflin Co., 1991.

©*The McGraw-Hill Companies, Inc., 1999*

Options

- Build
- Hold
- Harvest
- Divest

Market Share Gains

- Increase in New Product Activity
- Increase in Relative Product Quality
- Increase in Expenditures for Sales Force, Advertising, and Sales Promotion (*relative to the growth rate of the served market*)
- Successful share-building strategies usually involve a combination of several competitive factors
- Most successful share-building strategies are based on giving primary emphasis on one of more segments within the served market

Source: Buzzell, R. D. and Frederik D. Wiersema (1980). "Successful Share-Building Strategies," Harvard Business Review, Jan.-Feb., 135-144.

©*The McGraw-Hill Companies, Inc., 1999*

Elements of Strategy
(low market share businesses)

- Segmentation
- Use R&D efficiently
- Think small
- Ubiquitous chief executive

Source: Hammermesh, R.G., M.J. Anderson, and J.E. Harris (1978). "Strategies for Low Market Share Businesses," Harvard Business Review, May-June, pp. 95-102.

Five Creative Strategies
(mid-sized firms)

- Dominance
- Product Emphasis
- Distinctiveness/Uniqueness
- Focus/Coherence
- High-Profile Chief Executive

Source: Kuhn, Robert L. (1989). <u>Creativity and Strategy in Mid-Sized Firms</u>. Englewood Cliffs, NJ: Prentice-Hall, pp. 10-13.

Five more Creative Strategies
(mid-sized firms)

- Employee Opportunity
- Efficient Innovation
- External Perception
- Growth-Profits Trade-Off
- Flexibility/Opportunism

Source: Kuhn, Robert L. (1989). <u>Creativity and Strategy in Mid-Sized Firms.</u> Englewood Cliffs, NJ: Prentice-Hall, pp. 10-13.

The Industry Attractiveness - Business Position Matrix

Industry Attractiveness

	High	Medium	Low
High	1	1	2
Medium	1	2	3
Low	2	3	3

Industry Attractiveness

1 Invest/Grow 2 Maintain Position 3 Harvest/Divest

©The McGraw-Hill Companies, Inc., 1999

Illustrative Positioning Strategies in Growth Markets

	Narrow Market Scope	*Broad Market Scope*
Product	Product designed for segment target or focused on a specific product or component in non-segmented market.	Broad product line designed to meet multiple needs of a wide range of buyers.
Channel	Typically a single channel using intermediary or direct contact with end users.	Multiple channels likely to be used unless a single channel network provides extensive market coverage.
Price	Price determined by value provided by product. Margins should be relatively high.	Pricing strategies likely to vary between market targets. Intensity of competition may impose price pressures.
Promotion	Advertising targeted for cost effectiveness. Personal selling may target middlemen or end users.	Advertising may be broad or focused depending on targets. Personal selling varies according to targets and role in marketing program

Source: David W. Cravens, Strategic Marketing, 4th ed. (Homewood, Ill: Richard D. Irwin, Inc., 1994), p. 336

The Industry Attractiveness-Business Position Matrix

Competitive Position
- Size
- Growth
- Relative Share
- Customer loyalty
- Margins
- Distribution
- Technology
- Marketing skills

Industry attractiveness
- Size
- Growth
- Competitive Intensity
- Price Levels
- Profitability
- Technological Sophistication
- Gov't Regulations

Segmentation Bases and Descriptors

	Consumer Markets	Industry / Organizational Markets
Characteristics of people / organizations	Age, gender, race Income Family size Life-Cycle state, life style Geographic location	Type of Industry Size Geographic location Corporate Culture Stage of Development Producer / Intermediary
Use situation	Occasion Importance of Purchase Prior experience with product. User status	Application Purchasing procedure New task, modified rebuy, straight rebuy
Buyers' needs / preferences	Brand loyalty, Brand pref. Benefits sought Quality Proneness to make a deal	Performance requirements Brand preferences Desired features
Purchase behavior	Size of purchase Frequency of purchase	Volume Frequency of purchase

Source: David W. Cravens, <u>Strategic Marketing</u>, Irwin 1997, p. 133.

©*The McGraw-Hill Companies, Inc., 1999*

"Hot" Industries

- Paper products
- Chemicals
- Instruments
- Rubber/Plastics
- Electronics
- Banking
- Insurance carriers
- Food products
- Primary metals
- Nondurable

Source: "Fast Track, Most Fast-Growing Firms Found in Older Industries," The Boston Globe, July 13, 1994, p. 44.

Target Market Strategy

©The McGraw-Hill Companies, Inc., 1999

The Targeting Process

- Deciding how to form segments in the product-market
- Describing the people/organizations in each segment
- Evaluating target market alternatives
- Selecting a target market strategy

©*The McGraw-Hill Companies, Inc., 1999*

Criteria for Segmentation

- Responsiveness
- Identification
- Ability
- Profitability
- Stability

©*The McGraw-Hill Companies, Inc, 1999*

Market Segmentation

- Mass Market
- Segmented Markets
- Micromarkets
- Individual Customer Markets

Market Segment Options

- Single Coverage
- Selective Coverage
- Extensive Coverage

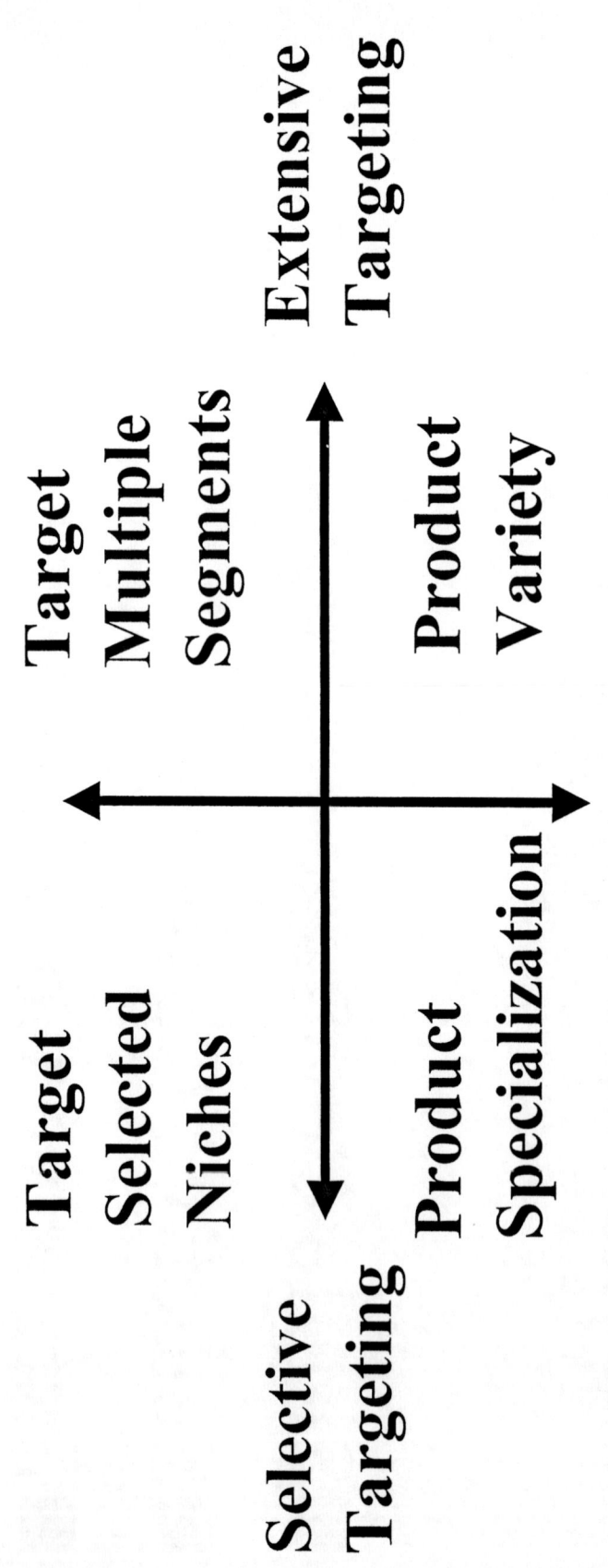

SEGMENTATION STRATEGY

- Identify segments within the product-market
- Decide which segment(s) to target
- Decide and implement a positioning strategy for each targeted segment

©*The McGraw-Hill Companies, Inc., 1999*

Advantages and Limitations of Selective Market Targeting

Advantages
- Requires fewer resources than extensive targeting
- Builds competitive advantage through specialization
- Opportunity to target the most promising buyers

Limitations
- Potentially vulnerable to competition from large firms
- Affected by major change in segment market demand

©*The McGraw-Hill Companies, Inc., 1999*

Advantages and Limitations of Extensive Market Targeting

Advantages
- Opportunity to develop strong market position
- Major opportunity for expanding sales
- Market knowledge extensive due to breadth of market scope

Limitations
- Major resource and marketing expertise requirements
- Complexity in selecting favorable segment portfolio strategies
- Possibility of diluting competitive advantage

©*The McGraw-Hill Companies, Inc., 1999*

Summary of Factors Influencing Market Targeting Decision

	Single Target	*Selective Targeting*	*Extensive Targeting*
Life Cycle Stage	Introductory	←——————→	Mature
Buyer Diversity	Low	←——————→	High
Market Position	Low	←——————→	High
Intensity of Competition	Low	←——————→	High
Availability of Resources/Skills	Low	←——————→	High
Scale Economies	No	←——————→	Yes

Source: David W. Cravens, Strategic Marketing, Fourth Edition, Irwin, 1994.

Marketing Relationships

©The McGraw-Hill Companies, Inc., 1999

Objective

- High levels of customer satisfaction through collaboration of the parties involved

©*The McGraw-Hill Companies, Inc., 1999*

Relationship Partners

- Customers
- Suppliers
- Distributors
- Competitors
- Other internal functional groups

©The McGraw-Hill Companies, Inc., 1999

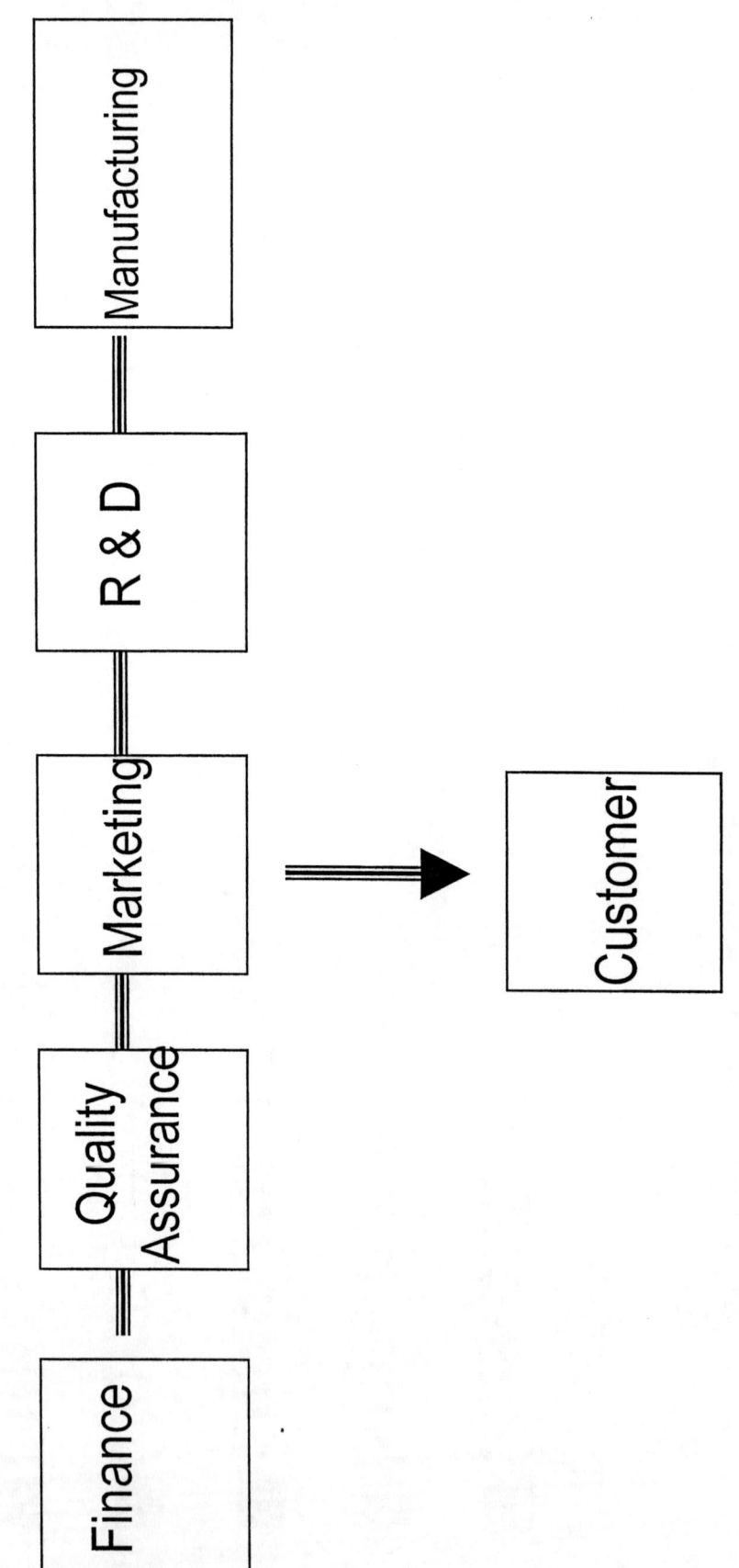

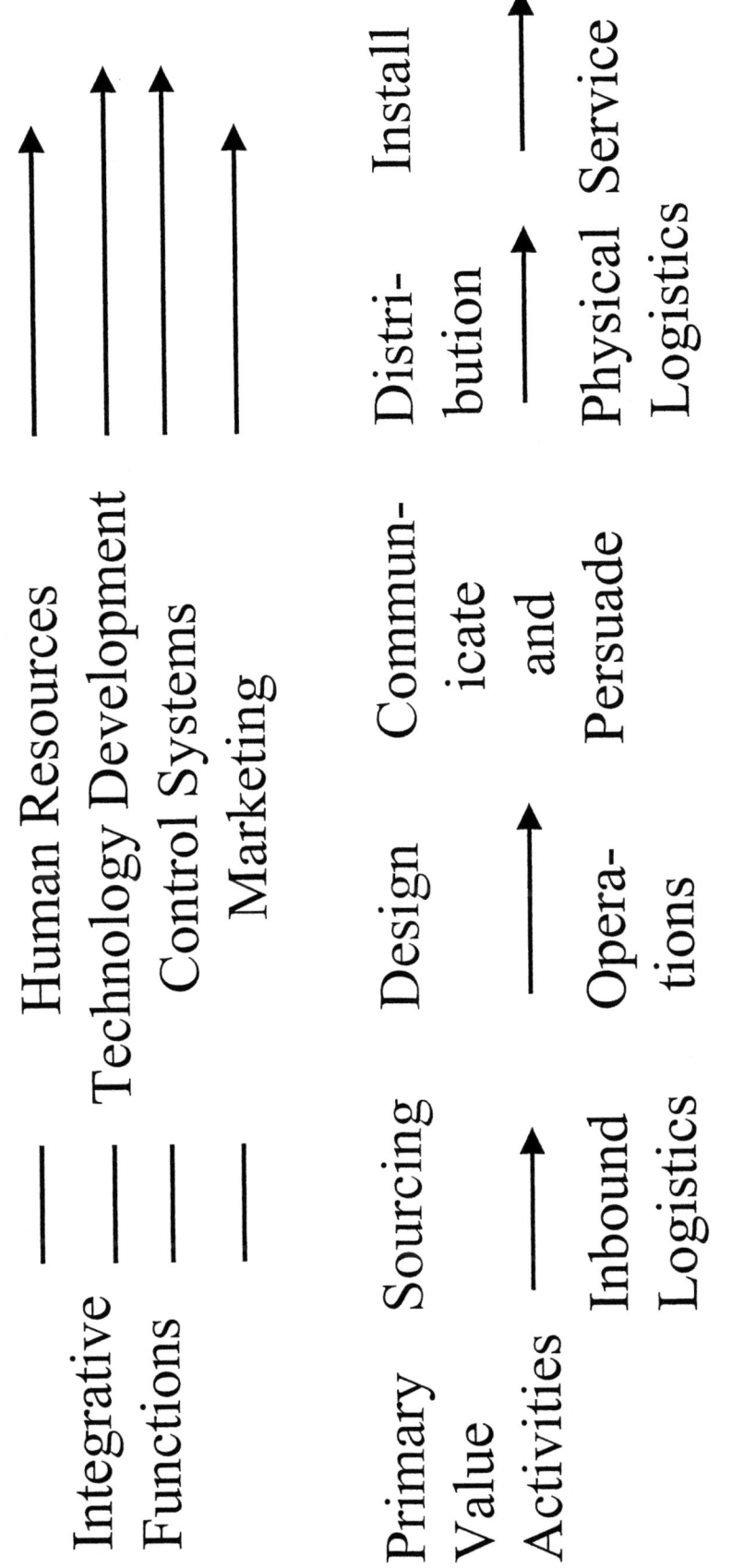

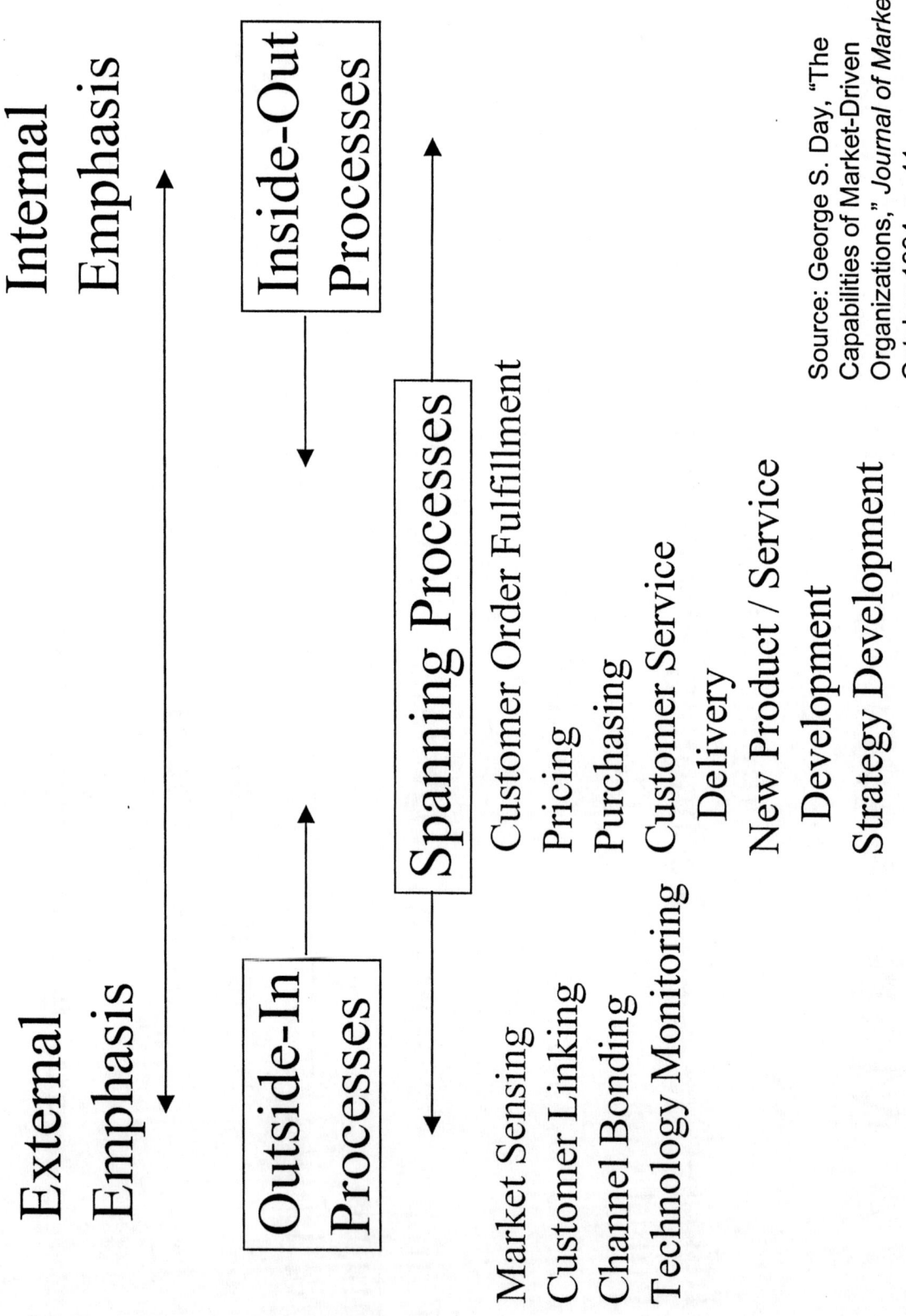

Source: George S. Day, "The Capabilities of Market-Driven Organizations," *Journal of Marketing*, October 1994, p. 41.

©*The McGraw-Hill Companies, Inc., 1999*

Cornerstones of Competitiveness

Source: David W. Cravens, Strategic Marketing, Irwin, 1997, p. 55.

©The McGraw-Hill Companies, Inc., 1999

Collaborate to Win
The Wisdom of Relationships

©*The McGraw-Hill Companies, Inc., 1999*

Relationship Strategies

- Why Consider Relationships
- Types of Relationships
- Developing Effective Relationships
- Supplier/Customer Relationships
- Alliances and Joint Ventures
- Critical Role of Trust and Commitment
- Network Organizations

What's Relationship Marketing All About?

- Create an obsession for quality internally and in external relationships.
- Respond to customer needs and requirements quickly and courteously.
- Build the competence and professionalism of people serving customers directly or indirectly.
- Apply mass customization concepts and methods to customize standard products/services.
- Improve the price value to customers by reducing the cost of doing business.
- Develop new products/services by anticipating future customer expectations.

- *Continued....*

What's Relationship Marketing All About? *(cont.)*

- Deploy front-line information systems.
- Organize business teams and functions around customer and/or markets.
- Encourage active involvement of customer in product/service design and process improvement.
- Build a customer retention culture by centering reward and recognition systems on retention and loyalty.

Source: Dr. Jagdish N. Sheth, Center for Relationship Marketing, Goizueta Business School, Emory University, June 1994.

The rush to collaborate often masks the important issue of deciding whether teaming up with another firm is the best option, and whether a particular candidate will prove to be a promising partner.

Various Forms of Organizational Relationships

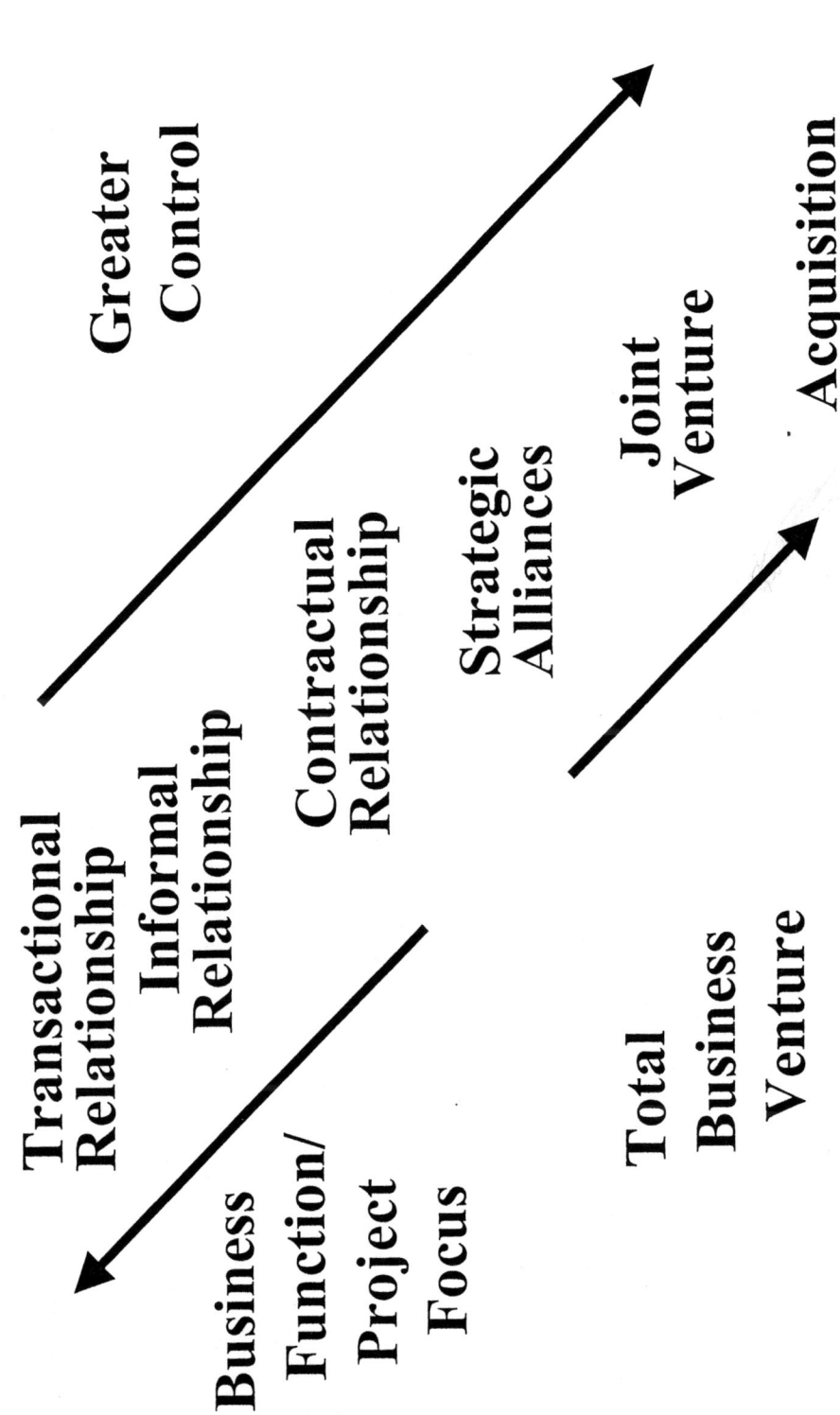

©The McGraw-Hill Companies, Inc., 1999

Rationale for Hybrid Organizational Arrangements

Skill/ Resource Gaps *High*	ACQUISITION/ MERGER	ALLIANCE
Low	IN-HOUSE STRATEGY	JOINT VENTURE
	Low	*High*

Environmental Complexity/Risk

WHY COMPANIES COOPERATE

SKILL/RESOURCE GAPS

ENVIRONMENTAL COMPLEXITY/RISK

©*The McGraw-Hill Companies, Inc., 1999*

SUCCESS GUIDELINES FOR STRATEGIC PARTNERSHIP MANAGEMENT

- The Critical Importance of Planning
- Balance Trust with Self Interest
- Anticipate Conflicts
- Establish Strategic Leadership
- Provide Flexibility
- Accommodate Cultural Differences
- Orchestrate Technology Transfer
- Learn from Partner's Strengths

Source: David W. Cravens, Strategic Marketing, Irwin, 1997, p. 233.

©*The McGraw-Hill Companies, Inc., 1999*

Why Strategic Alliances Fail

Logic Failures

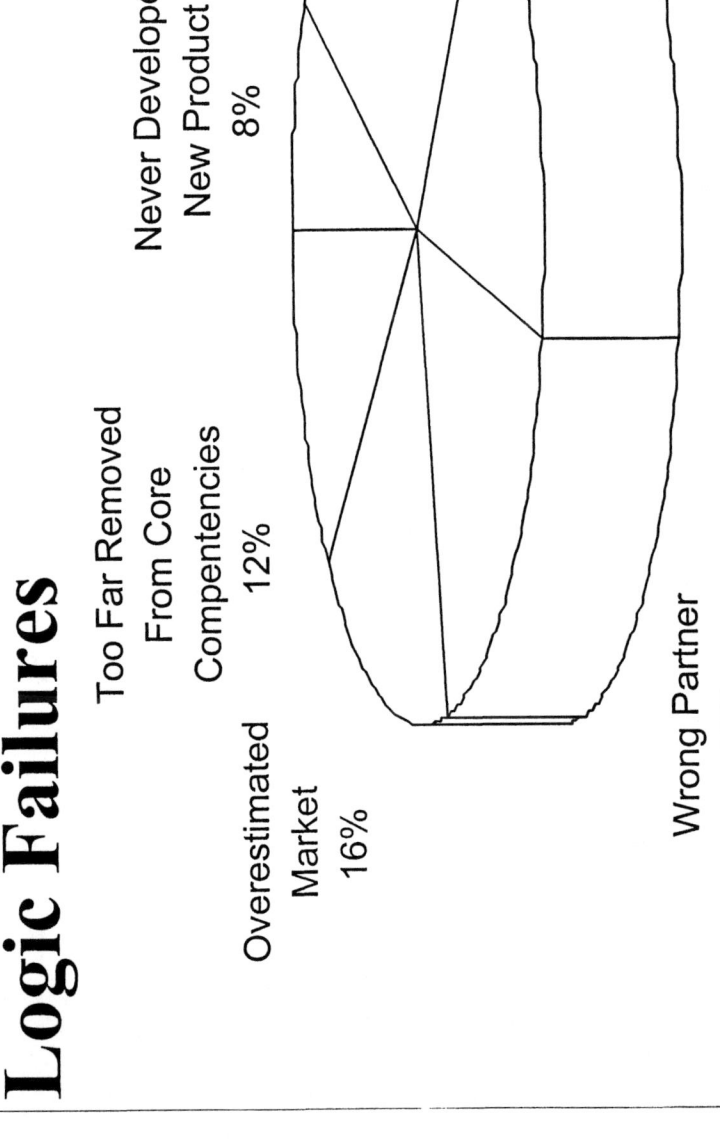

- Too Far Removed From Core Compentencies 12%
- Never Developed New Product 8%
- Environment Changed Drastically 28%
- Insufficient Information About Partner 18%
- Wrong Partner 18%
- Overestimated Market 16%

Source: Margaret Hart and Stephen J. Garone, *Making International Strategic Alliance Work*, R-1086 (New York: The Conference Board Inc., 1994) p.19.

Why Strategic Alliances Fail *(cont.)*

Process Failures

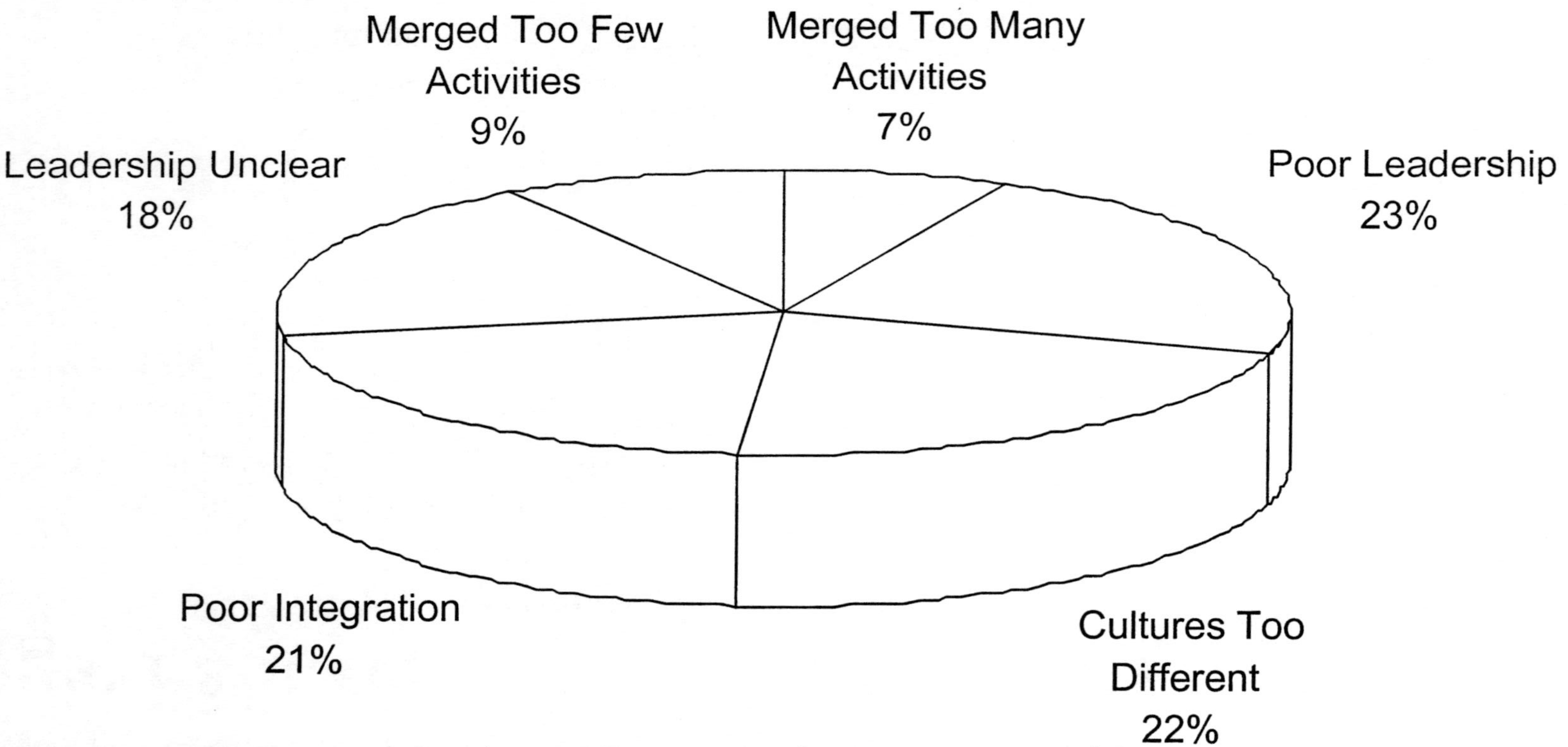

- Merged Too Few Activities 9%
- Merged Too Many Activities 7%
- Poor Leadership 23%
- Cultures Too Different 22%
- Poor Integration 21%
- Leadership Unclear 18%

Source: Margaret Hart and Stephen J. Garone, *Making International Strategic Alliance Work*, R-1086 (New York: The Conference Board Inc., 1994) p.19.

Marketing Program Development

Objective Setting

■ **Positioning**
- product/service strategy
- distribution strategy
- price strategy
- promotion strategy

©*The McGraw-Hill Companies, Inc., 1999*

Positioning Strategy Development

- Product strategy
- Distribution strategy
- Price strategy
- Promotion strategy

Positioning strategy / Market target

©*The McGraw-Hill Companies, Inc., 1999*

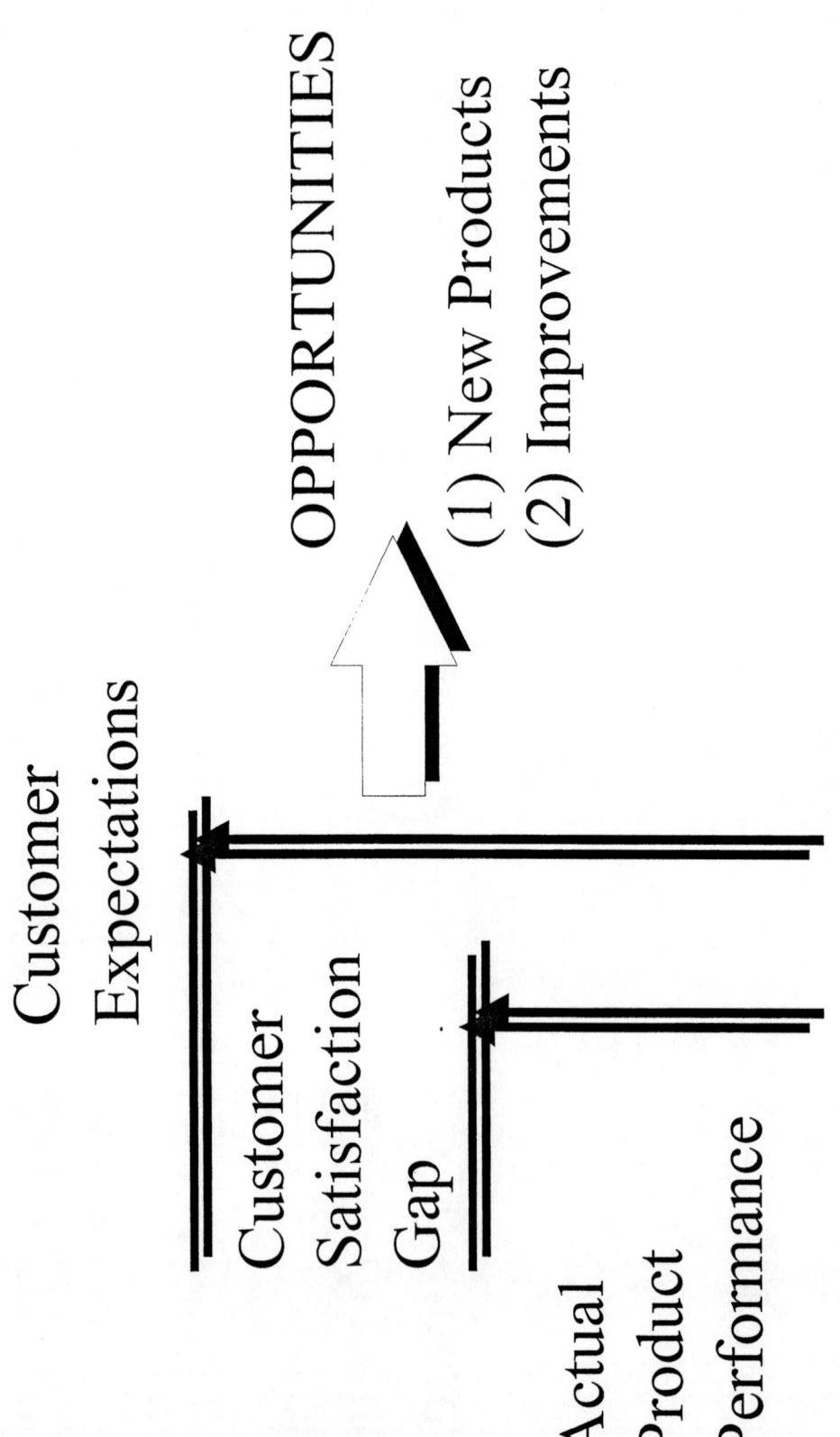

Product Scope Illustration

SBU's	Heating and air conditioning equipment	Household appliances	Vending and dispensing equipment

Product mix	Freezers + refrigerators	Ranges + ovens	Washers + dryers

Product lines	Countertop ranges	Conventional ovens	Microwave ovens	Ranges and oven combinations

Specific product: Microwave ovens

Attributes	Durability	Reliability	Appearance	Controls

©*The McGraw-Hill Companies, Inc., 1999*

MANAGING THE PRODUCT PORTFOLIO

Market-Driven Product Planning
- Market Orientation
- Customer Value and Satisfaction
- Continuous Learning About Markets

NEW PRODUCT PLANNING

Organization for Product Management
- Team approaches
- Relationship Strategies
- Inter-organizational Relationships

Source: David W. Cravens, *Strategic Marketing*, Irwin, 1997.

©*The McGraw-Hill Companies, Inc., 1999*

Product improvement →
Cost reduction →
Add new product(s) ⇈
→ **Product line strategy** ← **Alter marketing strategy** ⇆
← **Eliminate specific product(s)**

Product line strategy ⇓ → Product mix strategy

Product mix strategy → **Add new product line(s)**
⇓ **Change product line priorities**
⇐ **Delete product line(s)**

Source: David W. Cravens, <u>Strategic Marketing</u>, Irwin, 1997, p. 302.

©*The McGraw-Hill Companies, Inc., 1999*

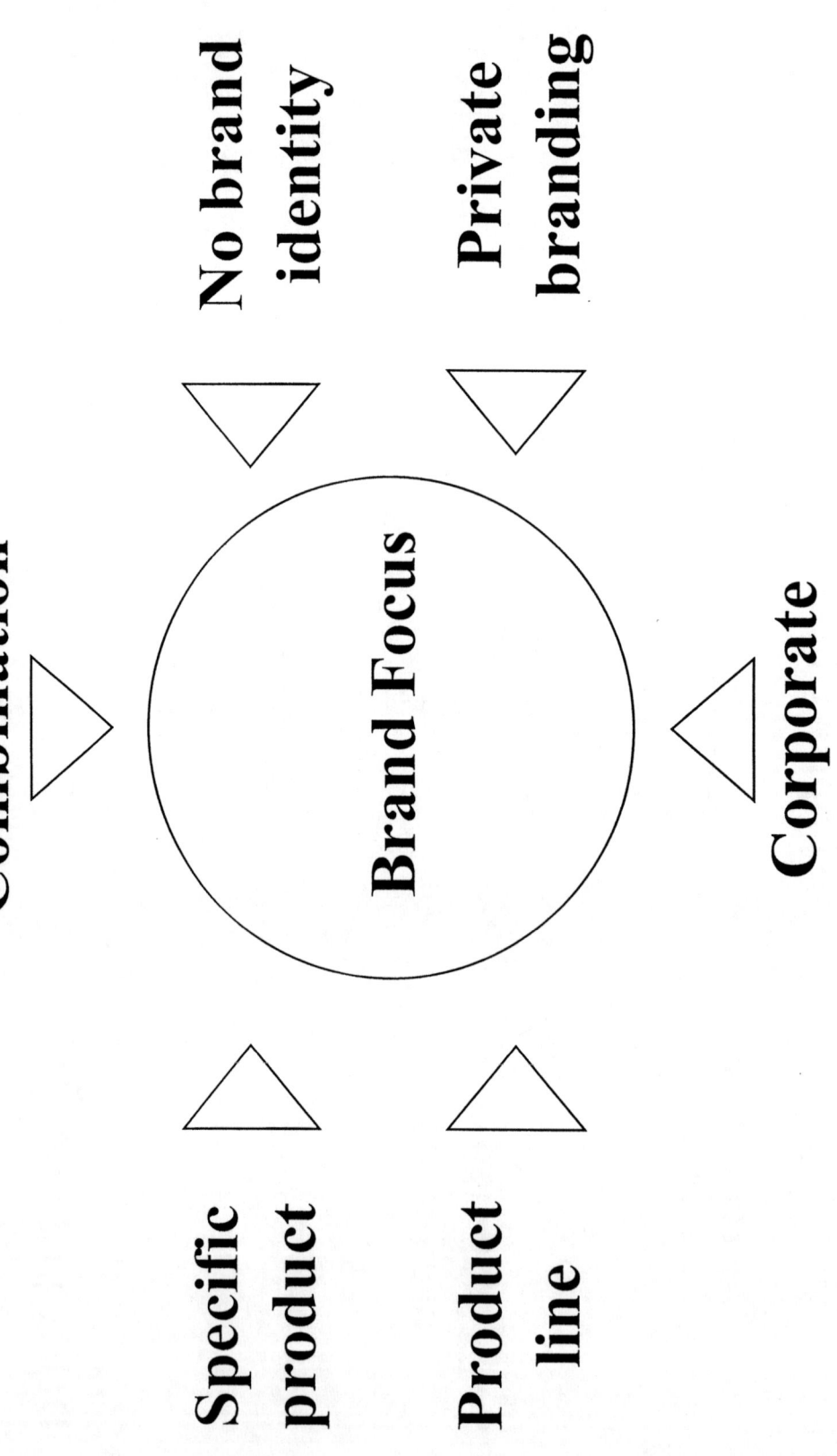

Types of New Product Introductions

Size of the circle denotes number of introductions relative to total.

New product lines 20%		New-to-world products 10%
Improvements/ revisions to existing products 26%	Additions to existing product lines 26%	
Cost reductions 11%		Repositionings 7%

Newness to company (vertical axis)

Newness to market (horizontal axis)

Source: *New Products Management for the 1980s*, Booz, Allen, & Hamilton, Inc., 1982, 9.

©*The McGraw-Hill Companies, Inc., 1999*

IDEA POOL

- Search
- Marketing research
- Internal development
- External development
- Incentives
- Acquisition

©*The McGraw-Hill Companies, Inc., 1999*

Customer needs analysis → Idea Generation → Screening and evaluation → Marketing strategy development → Business analysis → Product development → Testing → Commercialization

Source: David W. Cravens, Strategic Marketing, Irwin, 1997, p. 248.

New Product Success Factors

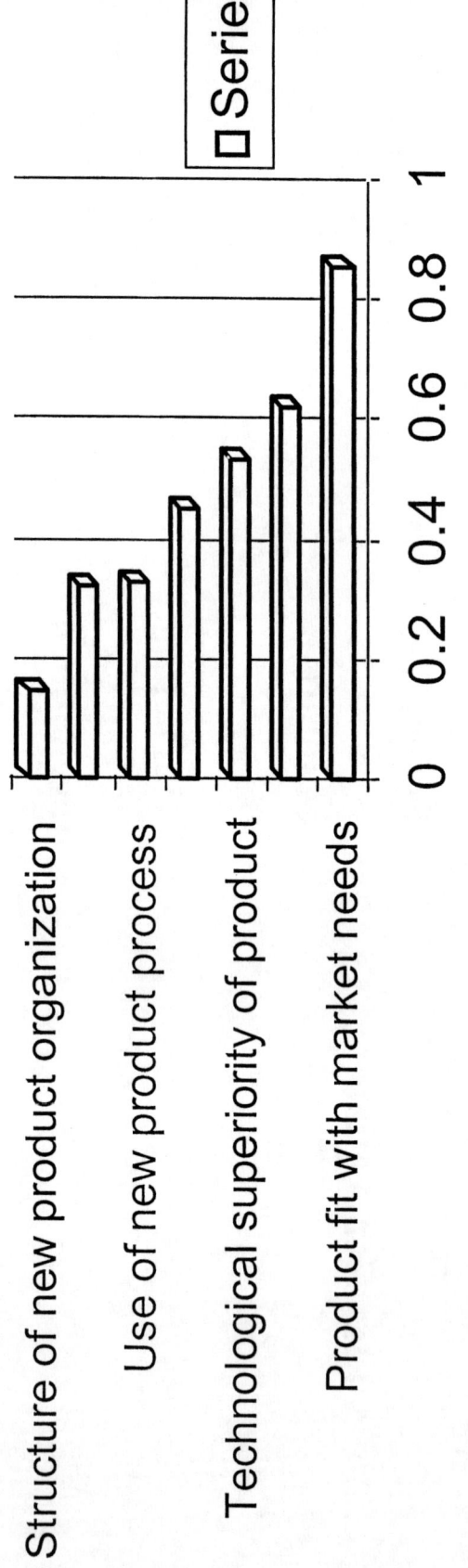

Source: *New Products Management for the 1980s* (New York: Booz Allen & Hamilton, 1982), p. 16.

©*The McGraw-Hill Companies, Inc., 1999*

Illustrative Channel Strategy Evaluation

Evaluation Criteria	Manufacturer's Representatives	Company Salesforce
Market access	Rapid	1 to 3 year development
Sales forecast (2 years)	$10 million	$20 million
Forecast	High	Medium to low
Estimated costs	$1 million*	$2.4 million**
Selling Expense (cost/sales)	10%	12%
Flexibility	Good	Fair
Control	Limited	Good

* Includes 8% commission plus management time for recruiting and training representatives.

** Includes $100,000 for 10 salespeople, plus management time.

Source: David W. Cravens, Strategic Marketing, Irwin, 1997, p. 331.

©The McGraw-Hill Companies, Inc., 1999

Design Stages & Decision criteria

Design Stages → **Decision criteria**

Identification of channel alternatives
- Intensity of distribution
- Access to end users
- Prevailing distribution practices
- Necessary activities and functions

Evaluation and selection of channel(s) to be used
- Revenue-cost analysis
- Time horizon for development
- Control consideration
- Legal constraints
- Channel availability
- Select the channel

Selection channel participants
- Market coverage
- Capabilities
- Intermediary's needs
- Functions provided
- Availability

©*The McGraw-Hill Companies, Inc., 1999*

Marketing Channels

```
Manufacturers/Producers
    │         │         │              │
    │         │         │              ▼
    │         │         └──► Agents/Brokers ──┐
    │         │                    │          │
    │         │                    │          └──────────────┐
    │         │                    ▼                         │
    │         │              Retailers ──┐                   │
    │         │                          │                   │
    │         ▼                          │                   │
    │   Wholesalers/Distributors ────────┼───────┐           │
    │         │                          │       │           │
    │         ▼                          │       │           │
    │     Retailers ──┐                  │       │           │
    │                 │                  │       │           │
    ▼                 ▼                  ▼       ▼           ▼
Consumer and Organizational End Users
```

©*The McGraw-Hill Companies, Inc., 1999*

The Marketing System

Manufacturers and processors

Facilitating organizations
- Financial
- Transportation
- Advertising
- Other

Marketing intermediaries
- Retailers
- Agents-brokers
- Wholesalers-distributors

End users
- Consumer
- Industrial-institutional

Agriculture and raw materials suppliers

©*The McGraw-Hill Companies, Inc., 1999*

6-15

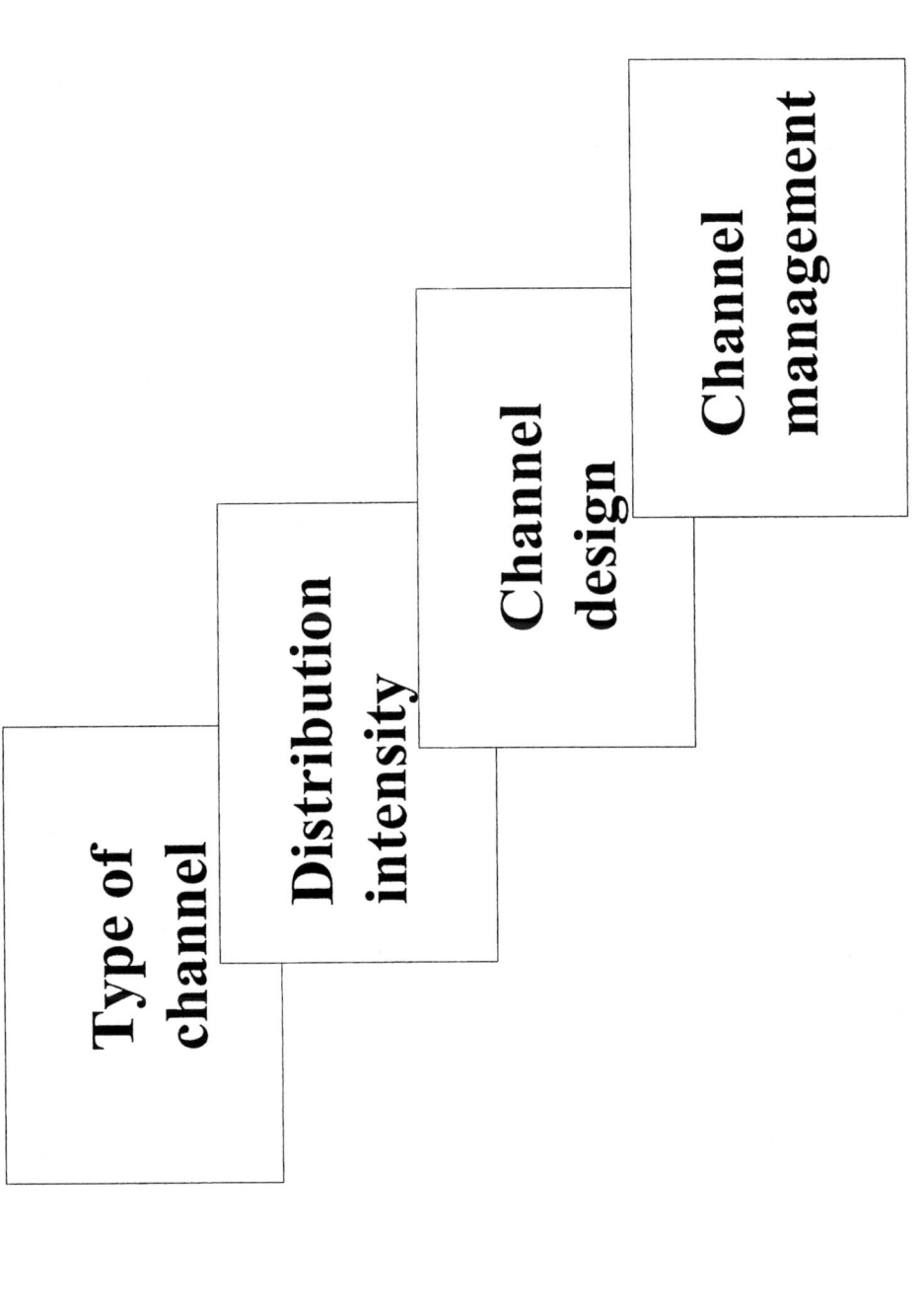

Distribution Intensity

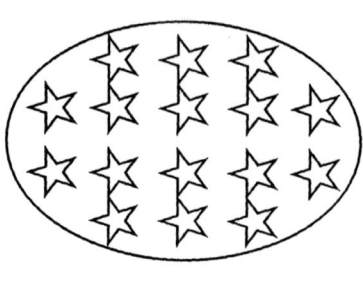

A — Exclusive distribution

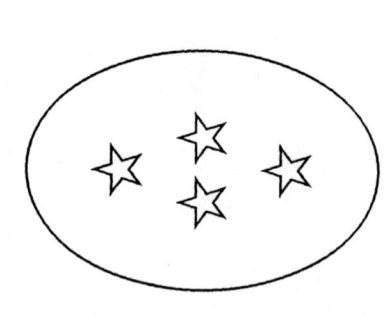

B — Selective distribution

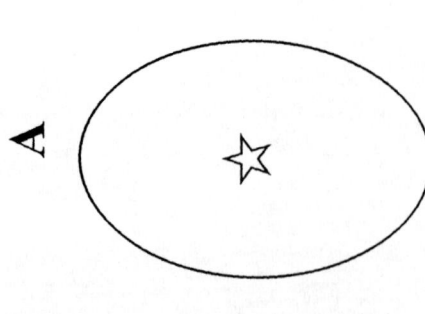

C — Intensive distribution

Illustrations

Cadillac automobiles
Caterpillar equipment

Ethan Allen furniture
Estee Lauder cosmetics

Revlon Cosmetics
Timex watches

©*The McGraw-Hill Companies, Inc, 1999*

Approaches to Promotion Budget Determination

Method	Features	Limitations
Percent of sales	• Budget is determined by using fixed percent of sales, often based on past expenditure patterns	• The method is very arbitrary and may yield a budget that is too high when sales are high and too low when sales are low.
Comparative Parity	• Budget is largely based upon what competition is doing.	• There may be other differences in marketing strategy that require different budget levels.
Objective and Task	• Set objectives and then determine tasks (and costs) necessary to meet the objectives	• The major issue in using this method is deciding the right objectives so measurement of results is important.
Budgeting Models	• Budget is determined by a computational model, often developed from analysis of historical data.	• Are the relationships found in the model correct, and if so, will they apply in the future?

©*The McGraw-Hill Companies, Inc., 1999*

Developing a Promotion Strategy

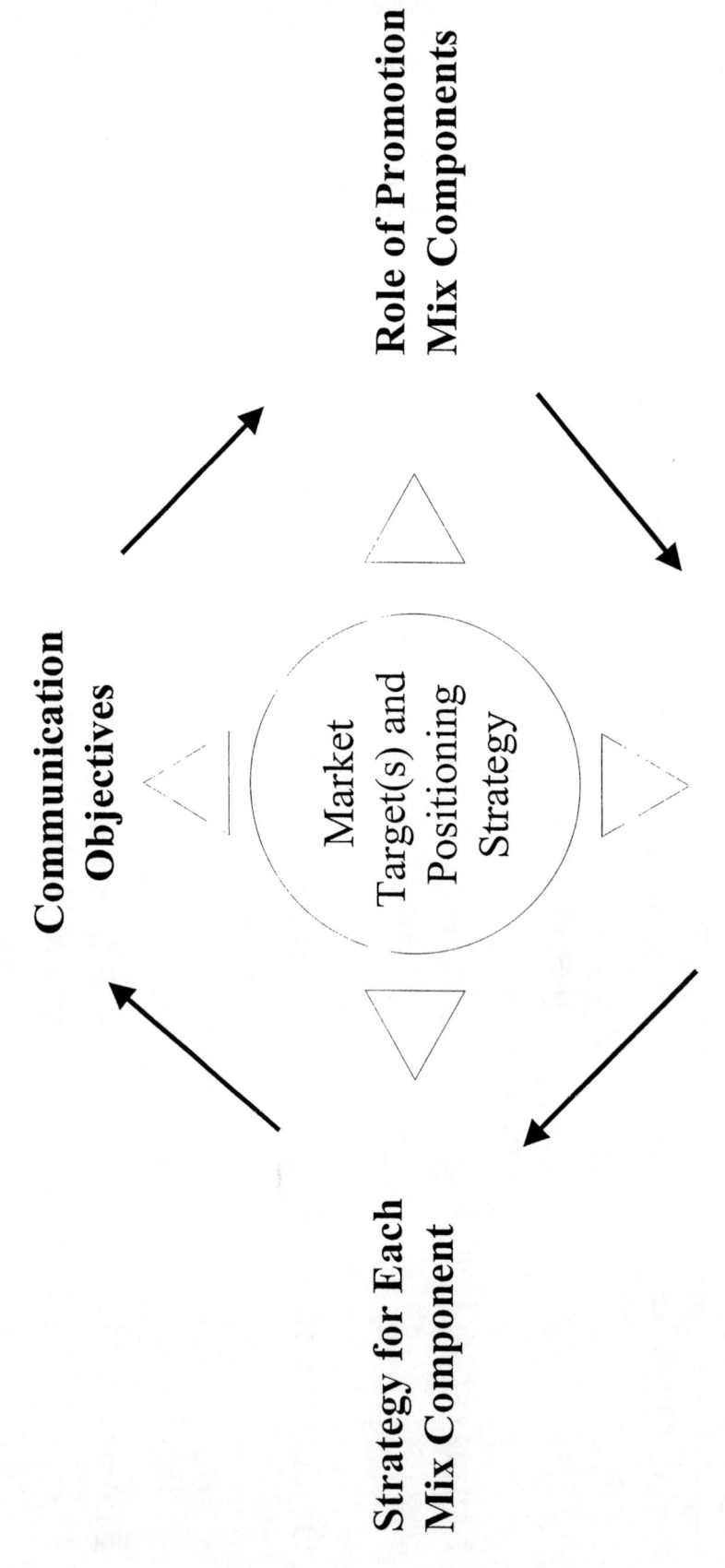

©The McGraw-Hill Companies, Inc., 1999

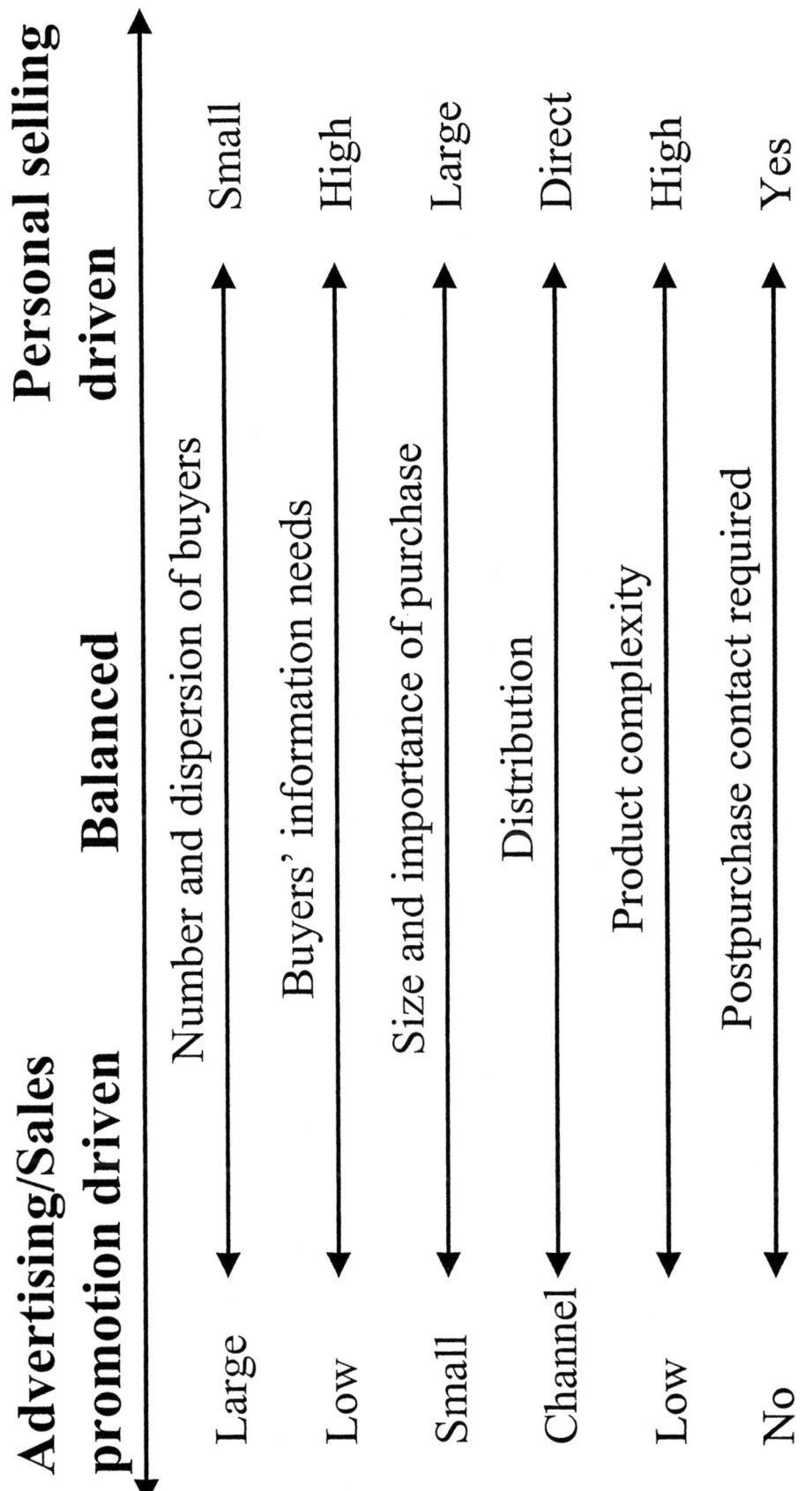

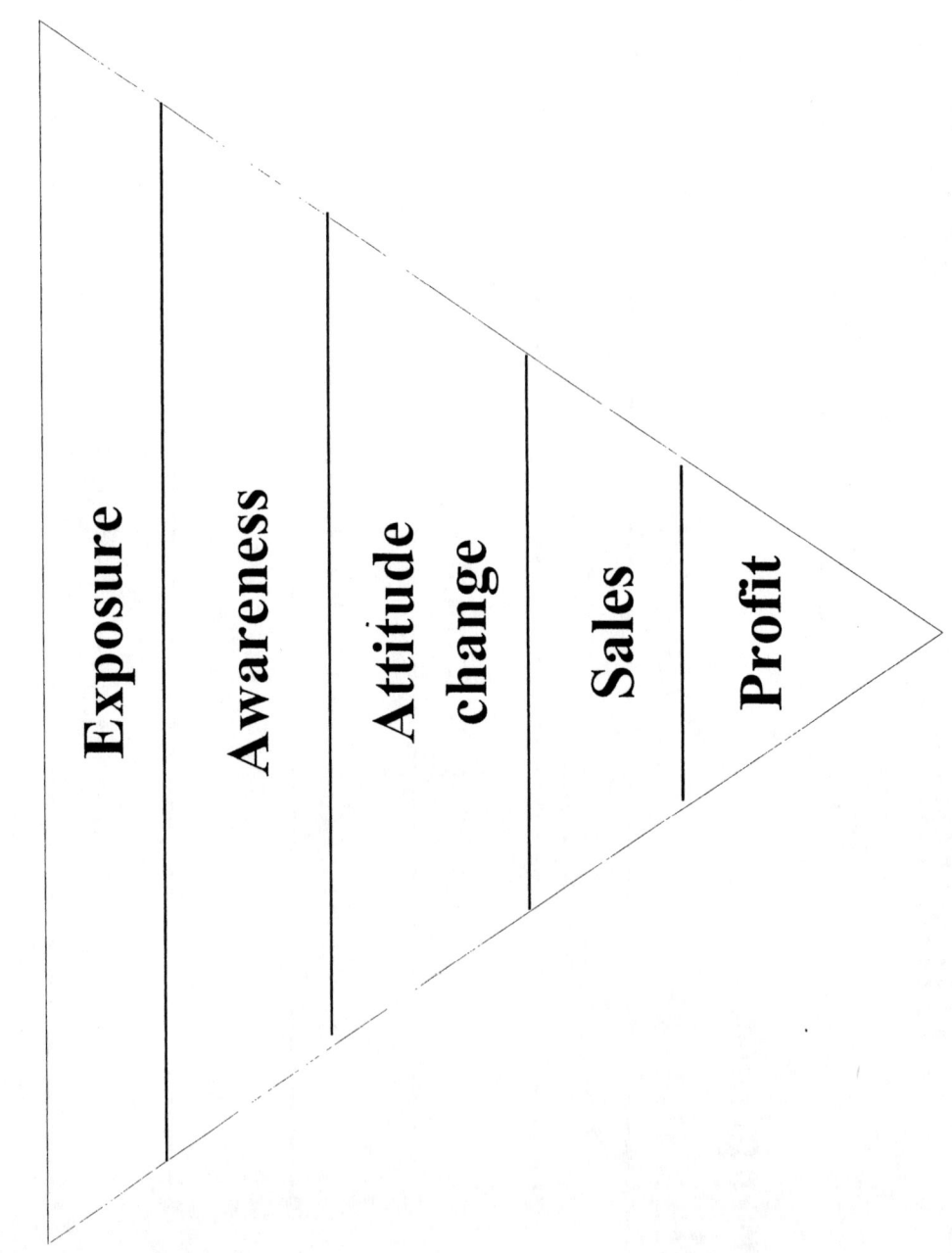

Sales Promotion Target

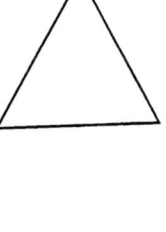

Consumer Buyers

Business Buyers

Middlemen

Salespeople

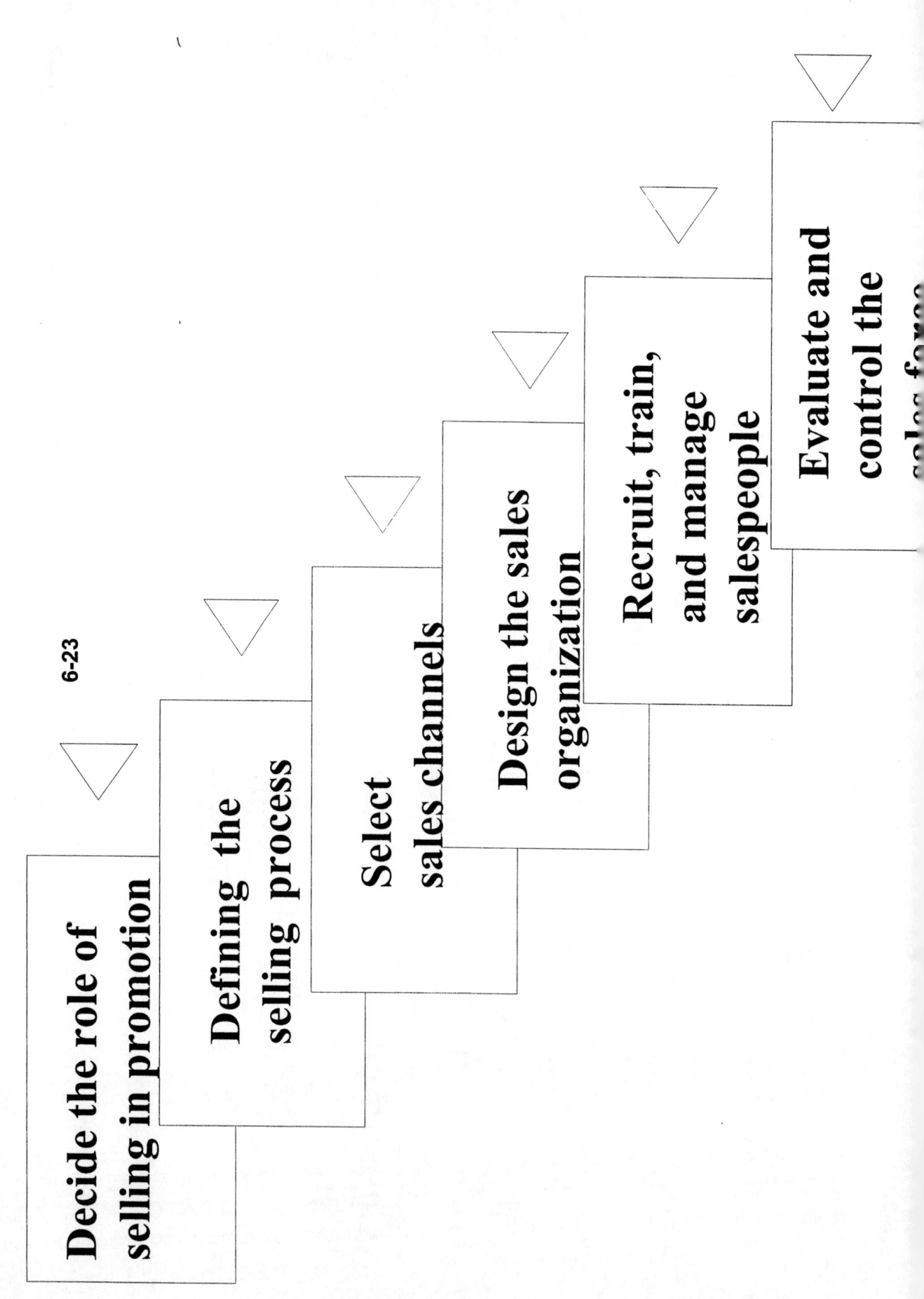

Examples of Distribution Channel Selling Activities

Wal-Mart
Channel

Suppliers →   Suppliers sell goods and services to producers

Manufacturers →   4000 manufacturers' major account teams sell and provide supporting service to Wal-Mart

Wal-Mart →   Greeters at Wal-Mart stores welcome customers as they enter stores

Consumers

©*The McGraw-Hill Companies, Inc., 1999*

Examples of Distribution Channel Selling Activities

Deere & Co. Channel

Suppliers
→

Materials and parts suppliers sell to Deere using field salesforces, major account teams, and manufacturers' representatives

Deere & Co.
→

Deere salespeople provide product information and sales support to independent dealers

Dealers
→

Dealer salespeople sell equipment to farmers and agricultural companies

Farmers and Other End Users

Dealer also provides service to equipment users

©*The McGraw-Hill Companies, Inc., 1999*

6-26

Sales Channel	Knowledge of Customer Needs/ Requirements	Direct Access to Customers	Time/ Customer	Cost/Contact
Major Account Manager (MAM) Coordinate sales and support activities to one or a few customers representing high volume annual purchases.	Very high level of understanding of needs/requirements.	Access typically concentrated at headquarters location.	Calls are typically frequent and lengthy.	Very high due to length of contact and relatively high compensation of MAM.
Field Salesperson Field salesperson responsible for several customer/prospects assigned on the basis of geographical area, product scope, or market scope.	High to medium level of understanding of needs/requirements (highest when needs are similar across customer base).	Face-to-face contact with assigned accounts. May include team selling activities.	Call patterns vary but are typically shorter than MAM calls.	High due to medium depending on call duration.
Telemarketing Assignment of a large number of customers/prospects to a salesperson who contacts accounts by phone.	Medium to low level of understanding of needs/requirements.	Access by telephone and electronic support	Calls are relatively short.	Low relative to face-to-face contact.
Electronic/Mail Contact Customer/prospects contacted by computer, FAX, or mail	Low level of understanding of needs/requirements unless purchasing is routine repurchase of standard items.	Contacts indirect.	Direct contact is not involved.	Very low indirect contact costs.

Source: Raymond LaForge, et al., *Journal of Business Research*, Fall 1991.

©*The McGraw-Hill Companies, Inc., 1999*

Sales Organization Designs

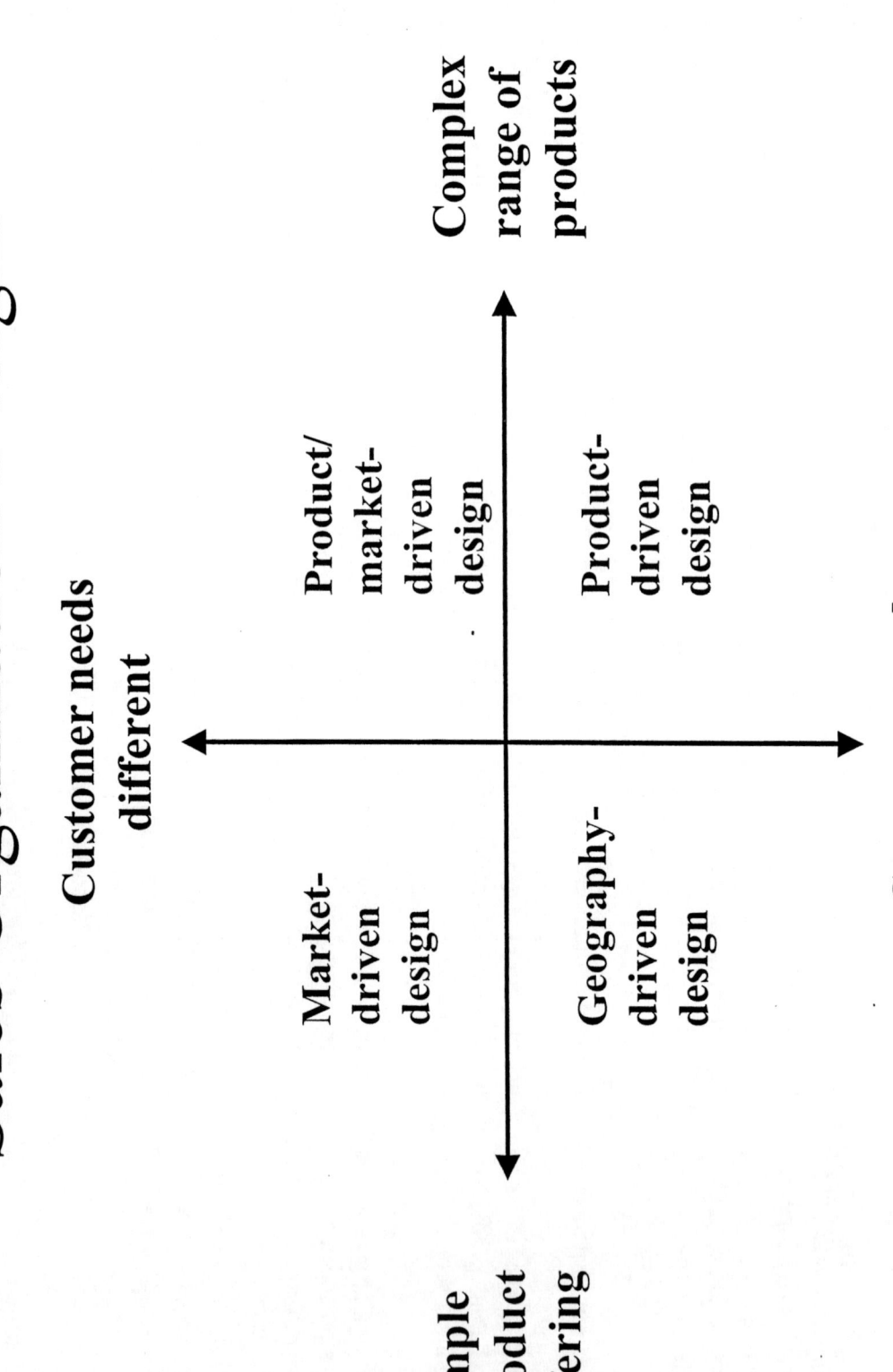

Source: David W. Cravens, Strategic Marketing, Irwin, 1997, p. 401.

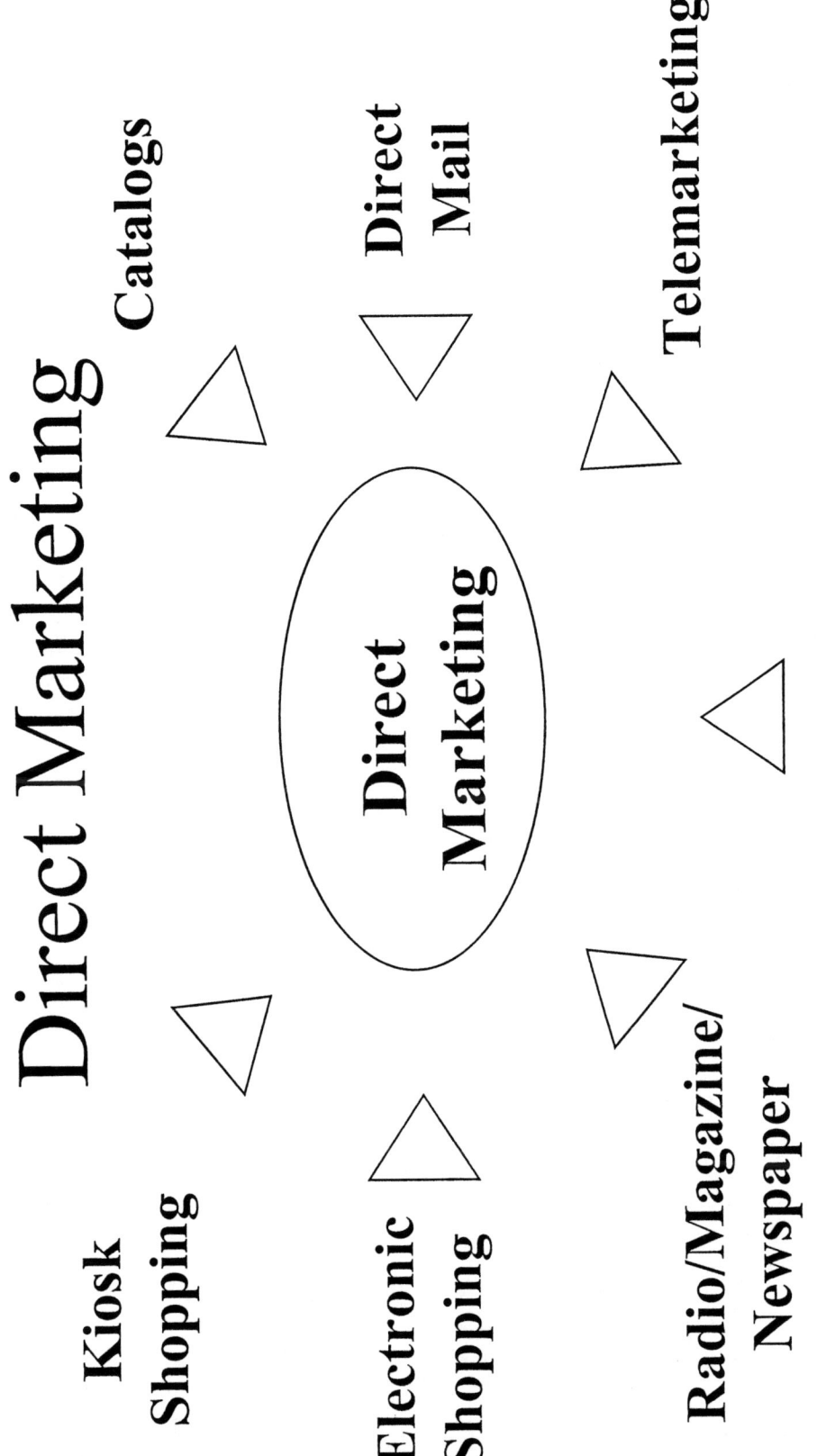

Organizational Design Options

Functional Design

Product Design

Organizational Design Options

Market Design

Matrix Design

©*The McGraw-Hill Companies, Inc., 1999*

6-30 Marketing strategy considerations

Types of brand strategies

Type	Brand development	Brand reinforcement	Brand repositioning	Brand modification
Objectives	Establish market position	Expand target market	Seek new market segments	Modify features
Product strategy	Assure high quality	Identify weaknesses	Adjust size, color, package	Modify features
Advertising objectives	Build brand awareness	Provide information	Use imagery to differentiate from competitors	Educate on changes
Distribution	Build distribution network	Solidify distribution relationships	Maintain distribution	Reestablish and deliver new version
Price	Skimming or penetration	Meet competition	Use price deals	Maintain price
Phase in life cycle	Introduction	Growth	Maturity	Decline

Source: Adapted from Ben M. Enis, Raymond La Grace, and Arthur E. Press, "Extending the Product Life Cycle," *Business Horizons 20* (June 1977), p. 53. Copyright 1977 by the Foundation for the School of Business at Indiana University.

Organizing, Implementing, and Assessing Performance

The Strategic Marketing Plan -- Steps in Preparing & Implementing

1. Marketing situation analysis
2. Market-target strategy
3. Objectives for each target market
4. Marketing program positioning strategy
5. Evaluate the marketing organization
6. Prepare the plan and budget
7. Implement the plan
8. Evaluate results and manage the plan

Strategic Marketing Plan

©*The McGraw-Hill Companies, Inc., 1999*

Strategic Marketing Plan

- Logical process
- Decisions
- On-going process
- Coordination

What organization will be facilitating success?

Organizational Approaches for Managing New and Existing Products

Full-time personnel

Upper-left quadrant (Temporary organization, Full-time personnel):
- Venture team
- Task force
- Individual

Upper-right quadrant (Permanent organization, Full-time personnel):
- Product manager
- Brand manager
- New products department / group

Temporary organization ← → **Permanent organization**

Lower-left quadrant (Temporary organization, Part-time personnel):
- New product team
- Steering committee
- Individual

Lower-right quadrant (Permanent organization, Part-time personnel):
- New product screening committee
- Product review committee
- Product planning committee

Part-time personnel

Source: David W. Cravens, *Strategic Marketing*, Fourth Edition, Irwin, 1994.

Marketing Organization Based on a Combination of Functions and Products

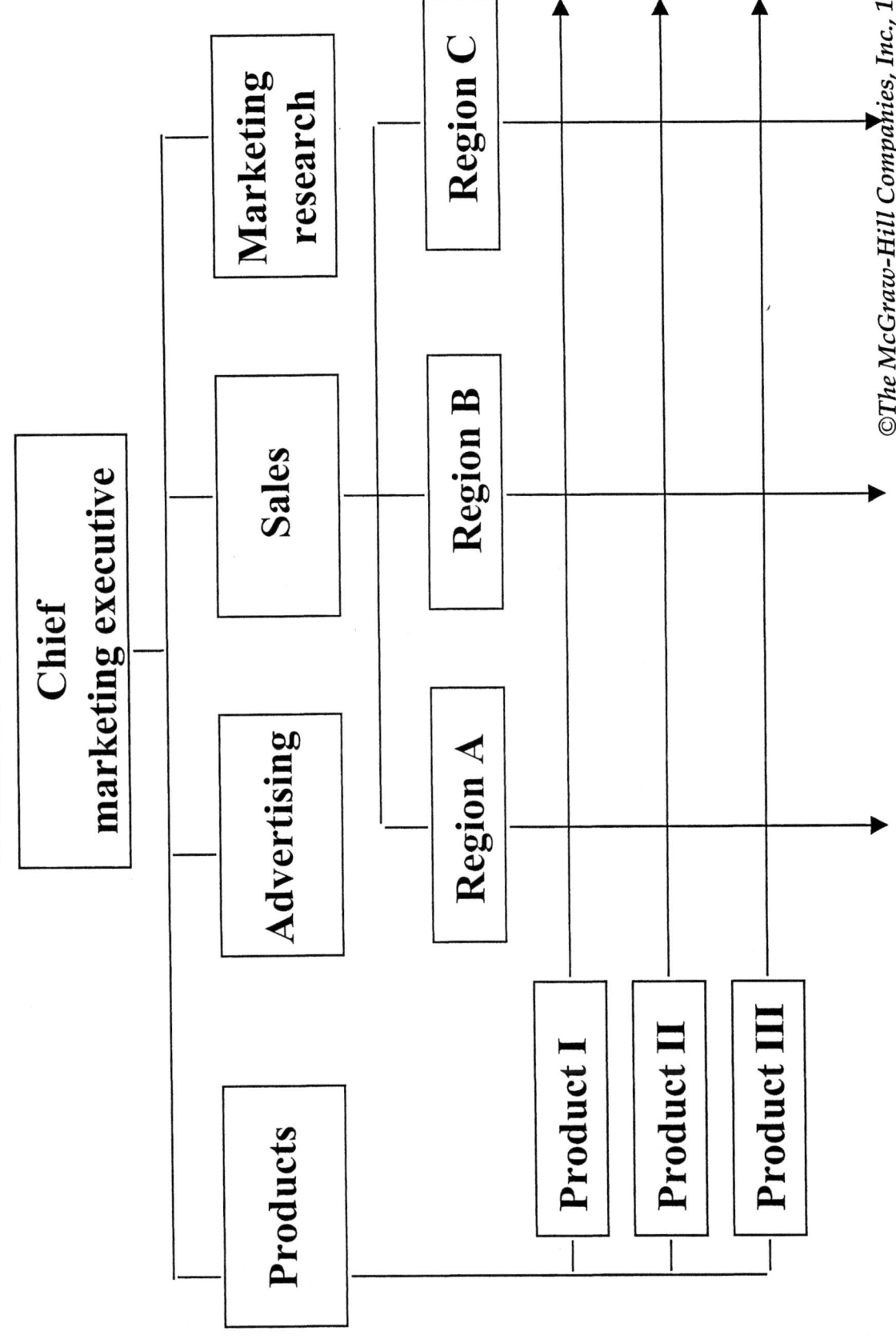

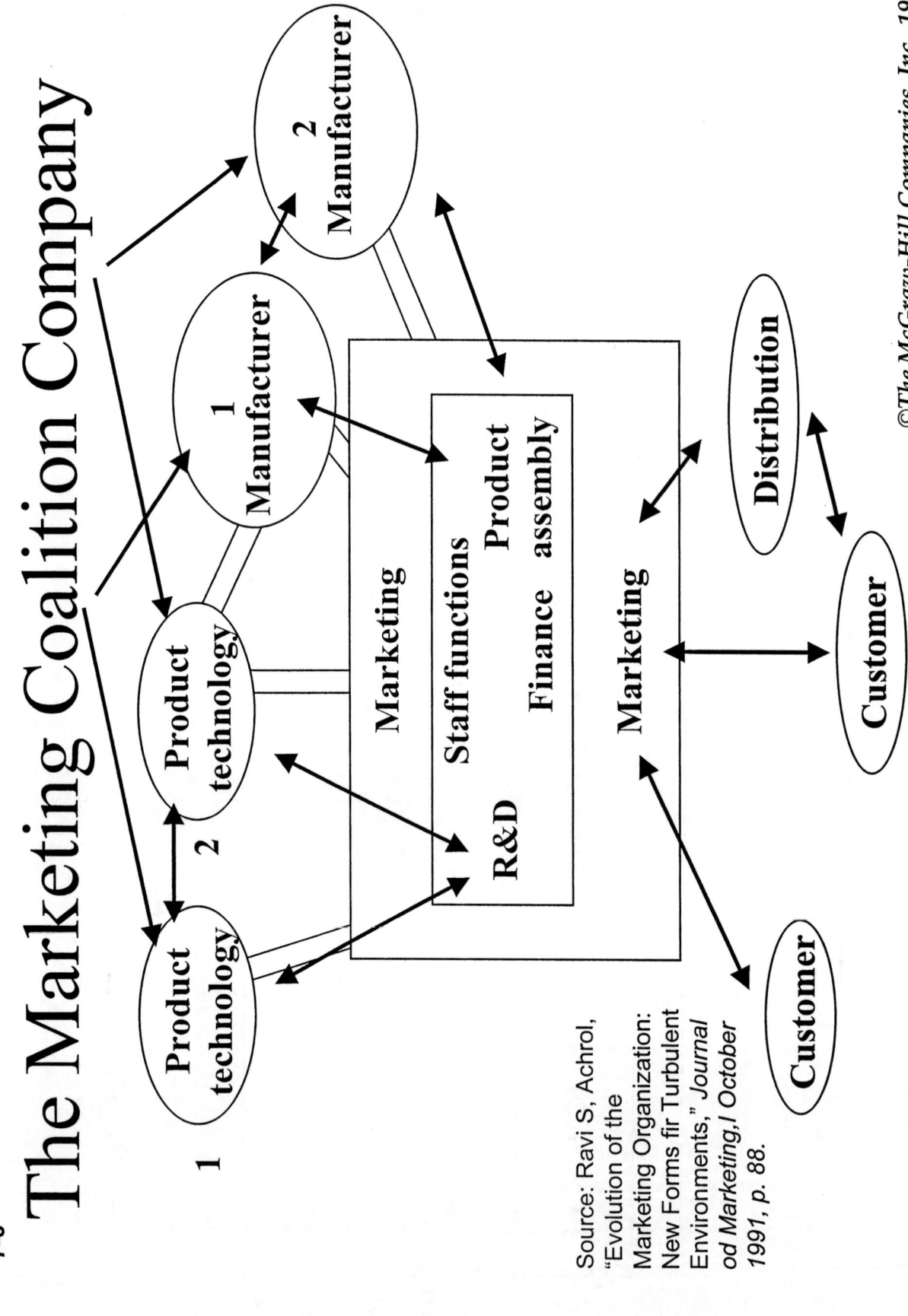

Structure-Environment Match of the Marketing Organization

7-7

High	**I** *Decentralized organization* ← Conventional integration methods	**II** *Matrix organization* Unconventional integration methods →
Complexity of environment	High differentiation	
	III *Functional organization* ← Conventional integration methods	**IV** *Brand management* Unconventional integration methods →
Low	Low differentiation	
	Low	**High**

Unpredictability, interconnectedness of environment

Source: Barton Weitz and Erin Anderson, "Organizing the Market Function," *Review of Marketing 1981*, ed. Ben M. Enis and Kenneth J. Roering (Chicago: American Marketing Association, 1981), 137.

How will the marketing strategy be implemented?

The Implementation Process

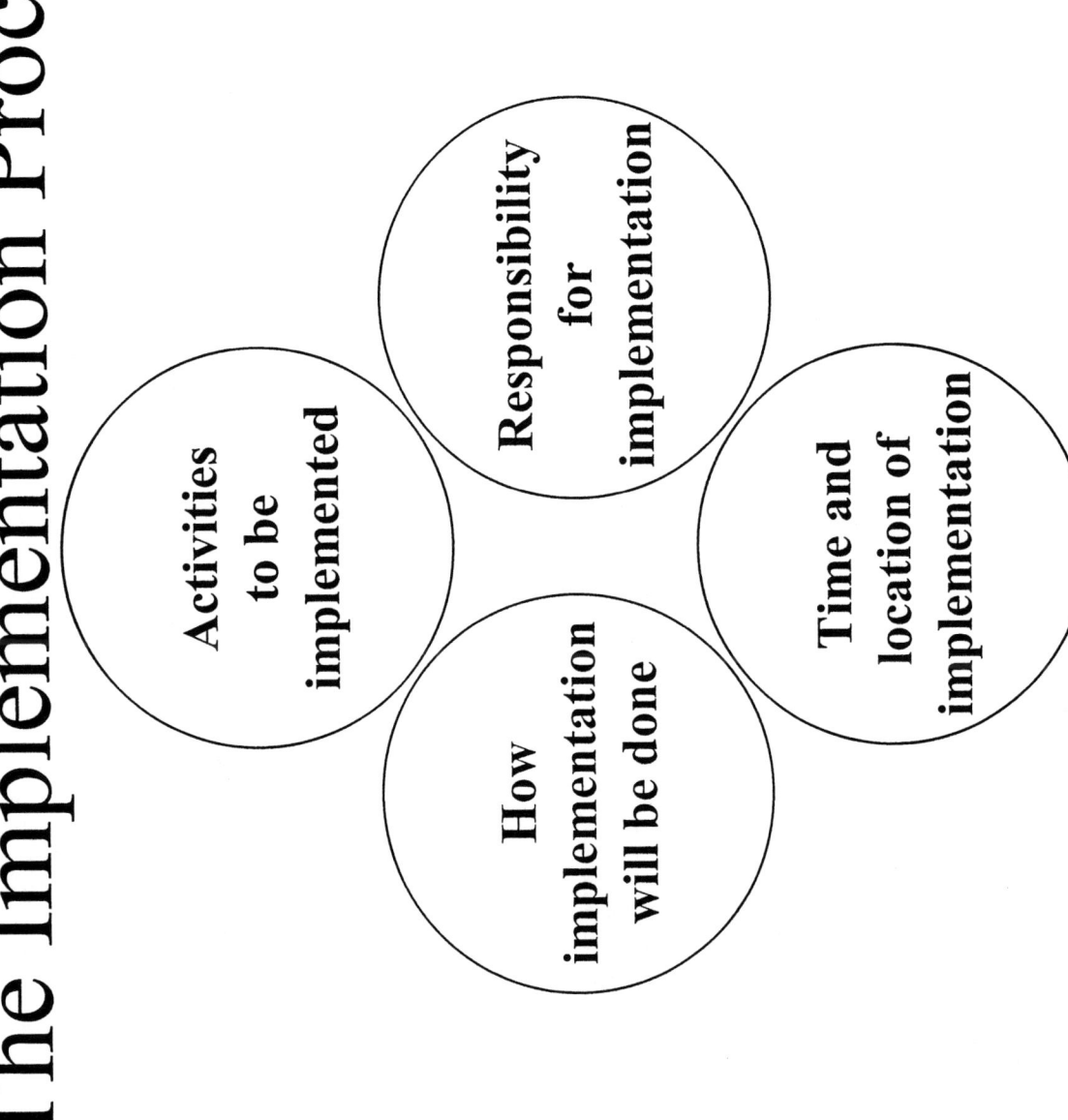

What should be the performance measures?

Strategic Planning and Performance Assessment

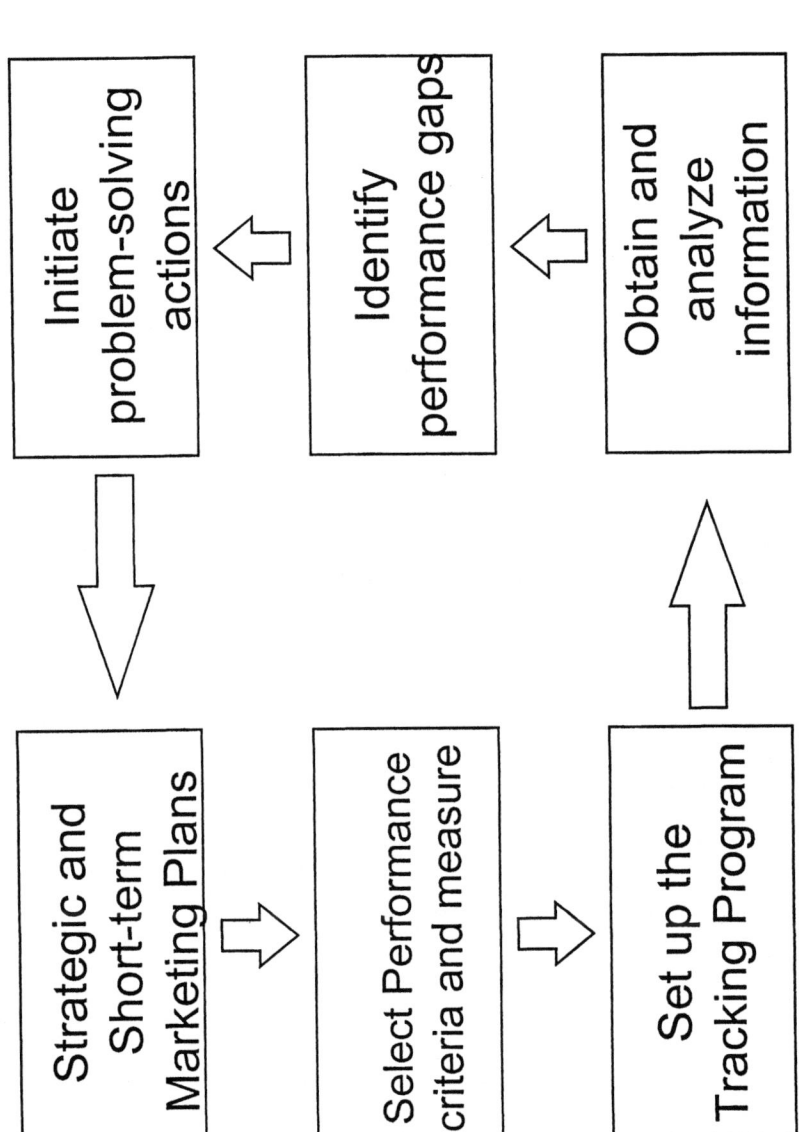

Case Analysis Process

©The McGraw-Hill Companies, Inc., 1999

Tell me, I'll forget;
Show me, I may remember;
Involve me, I'll understand.

An Old Proverb, Source Unknown

©*The McGraw-Hill Companies, Inc., 1999*

Case Process

With case discussion we develop the:

- ability to see interrelationships of facts
- capacity to make sound decisions
- skill to effectively communicate those decisions
- art of listening to the ideas of others
- recognition that there may be numerous effective ways to dealing with issues
- understanding that there are many perspectives to an issue

Analysis & Preparation

No "one best way to approach a case"

- Read the case quickly to see what is going on
- Review the exhibits
- Read preparation questions to help focus intent of the case
- Thoroughly re-read case and analyze available information

Analysis & Preparation

- Succinctly state the problem(s)
- Identify key players and decision maker(s)
- Denote relevant facts, data, and rationale
- Determine feasible alternative actions or programs
- Evaluate the alternatives
- Make a decision

©*The McGraw-Hill Companies, Inc., 1999*

Making a Decision

- Specific and fully elaborated
- Clearly indicate key actions
- Take a stand (*avoid generalities*)
- Be clear on decision criteria
- Be prepared to state position and how to implement (*develop a timetable*)
- Be sure action recommendations are thoroughly compatible

©*The McGraw-Hill Companies, Inc., 1999*

Nothing is so hard to come by as a new and interesting fact.

Nothing is so easy on the feet as generalization.

John Kenneth Galbraith

Classroom Discussion

- **Student Roles**
  - *Provide comprehensive analysis*
  - *Identify the problem(s)*
  - *Take historical perspective*
  - *Assume a personality*
  - *Bail out a colleague*
  - *Question a colleague*
  - *Summarize the discussion*
- **Listen and Keep an Open Mind**
- **Recognize Discussion Flow**

©*The McGraw-Hill Companies, Inc., 1999*

Effective Participation

- Depth of analysis
- Breadth of coverage
- Persuasiveness
- Facility at speaking
- Don't assume that just because a colleague communicates his/her alternative well that the alternative is the "right" one or that your colleague has his/her facts straight

Class Format
Wide Variety

- Dialogue between individual students and professor
- Dialogue among students
  - ɞconfrontation
  - ɞcooperation
  - ɞrole playing
- Informal small group discussion
- Group presentation
- Lecturettes

©*The McGraw-Hill Companies, Inc, 1999*

Keys to Success
Start with....

- **C**ommunication
- **A**dding Value Through Diversity
- **S**pirited Cooperation
- **H**onesty

©*The McGraw-Hill Companies, Inc., 1999*

A teacher opens the door...

You enter by yourself.

©*The McGraw-Hill Companies, Inc., 1999*

ALPHABETICAL INDEX OF CASES

ABB Traction, Inc. [Video]
Algonquin Power and Light Company
Ambrosia Corporation-San August
Amtech Corporation [Video]
Angostura Bitters, Inc.
Apache Power, Inc.
Bacova Guild Ltd.
Banco Nacional de Comercio Exterior, S.N.C.
Battered Women Fighting Back! [Video]
Bear Creek Golf Range
Blockbuster Entertainment Corporation
California Valley Wine Company
Capital
Chemical Additives Corporation-Specialty Products Group
Cima Mountaineering Inc.
Coca-Cola (Japan) Company [Video]
Cutco [Video]
The Dunkin' Donuts/Bagel Blitz [Video]
Düring AG (Fottle)
Enterprise Rental Co. [Video]
Electro-Products Limited
The Faith Mountain Company
Floral Farms
Food Lion, Inc.
Golden Valley Microwave Foods, Inc. [Video]
Konark Television India
La-Z-Boy Chair Company
LoJack Corporation [Video]
Longevity Healthcare Systems, Inc.
L'Oreal Nederland B.V.
The Metropolitan Museum of Art
Murphy's Brewery Ireland, Ltd.
National Breweries
Navistar International Transportation Corporation [Video]
Optical Fiber Corp.
Powrtron Corporation
Quality Plastics International S.A. de C.V.
Rollerblade, Inc. [Video]
Shorin-Ryu Karate Academy
Southern Home Developers
SystemSoft
Taurus Hungarian Rubber Works
Wentworth Industrial Cleaning
Wind Technology
Yoplait USA [Video]

First edition
Copyright © 2016 JP Amlin. All rights reserved.
JP Amlin, Sales Training and Executive Business Coach
Villa 61, Jalan Raya Tanah Lot, Kediri
Tabanan, Indonesia 82171
www.b2bprofessionalsales.com
jpamlin@gmail.com, jpamlin@outlook.com

Design and layout by Laura Brown.
Editing by Nanette Day.

ISBN 978-988-14088-2-2 (hard cover version)
ISBN 978-988-14088-4-6 (b/w paperback version w/ color cover)
ISBN 978-169-10056-2-8 (color paperback version)
ISBN 978-169-74153-8-4 (b/w paperback version)
ISBN 978-988-14088-3-9 (Kindle version)
ISBN 979-878-20136-2-2 (hard cover case laminate color Volume 1)
ISBN 979-879-08523-6-7 (hard cover case laminate color Volume 2)

This book is copyrighted. No part may be stored or transmitted in any form or by any means, electronic or mechanical, including recording or storage in any information retrieval system, without permission in writing from the author. No reproduction may be made, whether by photocopying or by any other means, unless a license has been obtained from the publisher or its agent.